IMAGE AND BELIEF

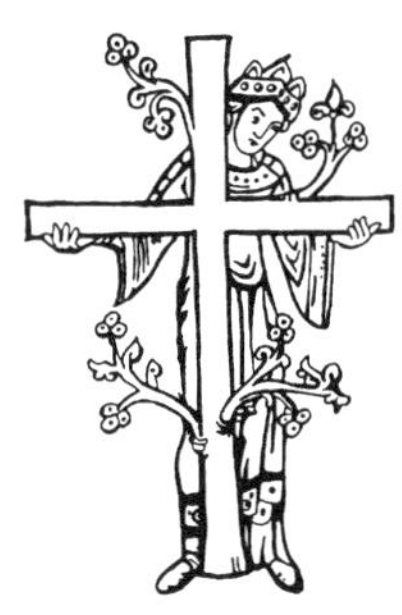

Image and Belief

STUDIES IN CELEBRATION OF
THE EIGHTIETH ANNIVERSARY OF
THE INDEX OF CHRISTIAN ART

·

EDITED BY
Colum Hourihane

INDEX OF CHRISTIAN ART
DEPARTMENT OF ART AND ARCHAEOLOGY
PRINCETON UNIVERSITY
IN ASSOCIATION WITH
PRINCETON UNIVERSITY PRESS

Library of Congress Cataloging-in-Publication Data

Image and belief : studies in celebration of the eightieth anniversary
of the Index of Christian Art / edited by Colum Hourihane.
p.   cm.—(Occasional papers / Index of Christian Art ; 3)
Includes bibliographical references and index.
ISBN 0-691-01002-1 (cloth : alk. paper).—ISBN 0-691-01003-X (paper : alk. paper)
1. Christian art and symbolism—Medieval, 500–1500—Themes,
motives.   2. Christian art and symbolism—Medieval, 500–1500—
Methodology.   3. Art—Historiography—Data processing.   4. Art—
Historiography—Databases.   I. Hourihane, Colum, 1955–   .
II. Princeton University. Dept. of Art and Archaeology. Index of
Christian Art.   III. Series: Occasional papers (Princeton
University. Dept. of Art and Archaeology. Index of Christian Art) ; 3.
N7850.I42   1999   99-11356
704.9′482—dc21

Printed in the United States of America by
Parker Communications Group, Lawrenceville, New Jersey 08648

Designed and produced by Laury A. Egan

1 3 5 7 9 10 8 6 4 2

TO THE MEMORY OF

CHARLES RUFUS MOREY

FOUNDER OF THE INDEX OF CHRISTIAN ART

Contents

·

PART 2. METHODOLOGY

Preface

·

TO CELEBRATE the eightieth anniversary of the founding of the Index of Christian Art, a conference entitled "Iconography at the Index" was held in Princeton in the fall of 1997, and the papers given there form the core of this volume. Apart from wishing to mark the occasion of the Index's anniversary, the purpose of this conference was to highlight two of the many features for which it has been justly renowned since its inception in 1917. These are the twin strengths of iconographical scholarship and methodology.

It would have been unfair to select a particular iconographical concept or theme on such an occasion, since this would not have adequately reflected the scope of the archive. It is for precisely that reason that the papers deal with a range of subjects, styles, periods, and media dating from the sixth to the seventeenth century and ranging from the Near East to Britain, and that they investigate such varied subjects as the theme of rejection, the device of conflation, and the meaning of colouration, to name but a few. The second day of the conference was devoted to the concept of subject classification of works of art and how this should be best accomplished. In this respect ICONCLASS, which is now the most widely used subject system in the world, received particular attention. Accompanying the conference papers in this publication are several studies which were written especially in honour of the Index but which were not presented at the conference.

My thanks go to all the speakers at the conference, firstly for contributing their fine papers, and secondly for their cooperation in meeting the rather stringent deadlines which have allowed this volume to appear so promptly. There were many others who contributed to the success of the conference and this publication. Within the Index of Christian Art, particular thanks must go to Marie Holzmann and John Blazejewski for their willing and practical assistance in the organization and planning of both the conference and this volume. Marie Holzmann, in her able and efficient manner, was always willing to undertake whatever organizational challenge arose, and John Blazejewski was equally considerate and diligent in completing the many photographic tasks that accompanied the conference and its publication.

I offer thanks to the moderators for their good work during the two days of the conference: James Marrow, Anne-Marie Bouché, Joseph Busch, and Kirk Alexander. The organization of the conference was generously supported by many colleagues at Princeton University, and it is my pleasure to acknowledge the contributions of the Princeton Council of the Humanities, the Program in Medieval Studies, the Department of Art and Archaeology, and the Department of Romance Languages and Literatures. The publication of this volume was encouraged and supported financially by the Publications Committee of the Department of Art and Archaeology under the chairmanship of John Pinto. James Marrow in particular was a constant source of encouragement and enthusiasm. I also benefited enormously from the practical advice and assistance of Susan Lehre,

Manager of the Department of Art and Archaeology. Sincere thanks must also go to Irving Lavin, of the Institute for Advanced Study in Princeton, and to Marilyn Lavin for their support and involvement.

The second day of the conference was financed entirely by the Getty Information Institute, which has a long-standing history and interest in developing electronic resources for art-historical application. The support and encouragement of Eleanor Fink, Director of the Getty Information Institute, is gratefully acknowledged, and particular mention must also be made of my debt to Murtha Baca, Joseph Busch, Kathleen McDonnell, and Marilyn Schmitt, who assisted in many ways.

My greatest acknowledgment must go to Christopher Moss, Editor of Publications for the Department of Art and Archaeology at Princeton University. His diligent work as managing editor has made this publication possible. His copy-editing skills and his willingness to search out that elusive image, check that Latin inscription, or sort out that missing reference has made it better. All of this was done with much enthusiasm and good humour, and even the hassled contributors acknowledged that it was a work of perfection. It has been a pleasure to work alongside such a professional and to learn from him.

This publication has to be dedicated to Charles Rufus Morey, without whose initiative the Index of Christian Art would not have been founded. It is his experience, foresight, and scholarship that is rightfully remembered and celebrated on this occasion. It would take a considerable volume to name all the contributors who have given of their skills over the years to develop what is now the most important source of medieval iconography in existence, and for that reason I hope that nobody will be take offense if I offer here a general but very heartfelt acknowledgement of thanks to everyone who has contributed to the success of the Index throughout its first eighty years.

COLUM HOURIHANE, DIRECTOR
INDEX OF CHRISTIAN ART

THE GETTY INFORMATION INSTITUTE, which has a long-standing interest in and commitment to the development of standards to enhance access to visual arts and humanities information, was honored to sponsor the second day of the 1997 conference "Iconography at the Index" commemorating the eightieth anniversary of the Index of Christian Art.

The papers presented at the conference on iconographic indexing and access point to a missing link in the development of the World Wide Web: easy, abundant subject access. Networking evokes interoperability and interconnecting information across time and space. This interworkability, facilitated by the World Wide Web, can ultimately bring us universal access to digitized information through a single interface, no matter where the data resides.

This concept of a rapidly growing digital library of text and image information still lacks several important research tools or finding aids. Unlike conventional libraries, the Web has yet to become a curated resource benefiting from professionally developed subject headings and indexing terms that let users evaluate material and carry out accurate searches.

The participants in the conference have already begun to address the lack of subject headings and finding aids through their ongoing commitment to the development of knowledge bases: The Index of Christian Art, ICONCLASS, the *Art and Architecture Thesaurus,* the *Union List of Artist Names,* and the Getty Thesaurus of Geographic Names, to name a few. These resources have enormous potential as enhanced search engines that could function as "subject gateways" to images and art information on the Web.

But if these resources are to serve as primary modes of access on the Web that help people navigate the on-line obstacle course of names, places, and subjects, we need to become more flexible in how they are curated and expanded. All of us who work with subject access should focus not only on what is or has been, but also on what can be. We should use the networking and interworkability potential of the Web to form international consortia to help sustain and develop our knowledge bases. Working together, we can engage electronic technology to its fullest. We need only the courage to make it serve our vision.

ELEANOR E. FINK, DIRECTOR
GETTY INFORMATION INSTITUTE

Notes on the Contributors

HANS BRANDHORST is an art historian who has been attached to the Universiteit Utrecht since 1990. Prior to that he worked for Leiden University and the Royal Library in the Hague. He holds a Ph.D. in art history and has done extensive research in the field of English manuscript illumination. He is presently compiling an electronic catalogue of such illuminations.

JAMES D'EMILIO received his Ph.D. from the Courtauld Institute of Art, University of London, in 1989, writing his dissertation on the Romanesque architectural sculpture in the diocese of Lugo, Spain. He is presently associate professor at the University of South Florida, and has also taught at Tulane University and Reed College. His particular interest is in Spanish Romanesque architectural sculpture, and he has published extensively on Iberian medieval art, most recently "Working Practices and the Language of Architectural Decoration in Romanesque Galicia: Santa María de Camporramiro and Its Sources" (*Arte medievale*, 1996).

JOHN V. FLEMING is the Louis W. Fairchild '24 Professor of English and Professor of Comparative Literature at Princeton University. He received his Ph.D. from the same university in 1963, and has also taught at the University of Wisconsin. Throughout his career he has been actively involved in most medieval associations and has also written extensively on literature, including *The Roman de La Rose: A Study in Allegory and Iconography* (1969), *Classical Imitation and Interpretation in Chaucer's "Troilus"* (1990), and *1492: An Ongoing Voyage* (with Altman and Hébert) (1992). He is presently working on studies of Christopher Columbus and the Franciscan spiritual milieu.

JAROSLAV FOLDA began his study of medieval art history under Kurt Weitzmann while majoring in history at Princeton, graduating in 1962. He continued his studies at Johns Hopkins University under Adolph Katzenellenbogen and also worked as a research assistant for Dorothy Miner at the Walters Art Gallery. His dissertation, "The Illustrations in Manuscripts of The History of Outremer by William of Tyre," was supervised by Hugo Buchthal. Appointed as an instructor at the University of North Carolina at Chapel Hill in 1968, he has risen through the ranks to his current appointment as N. Ferebee Taylor Professor of the History of Art. His recent book, *The Art of the Crusaders in the Holy Land, 1098–1187* was published by Cambridge University Press in 1995. He is currently working on a second volume of this study, dealing with the years 1187–1291.

GIOVANNI FRENI graduated from the Università di Messina in *Lettere Moderne*, and was subsequently awarded a research fellowship by the Fondazione Bonino-Pulejo to study medieval painting in Umbria at the Università degli Studi di Perugia. He obtained his Masters' degree at the Courtauld Institute in 1995, where he is currently finishing his Ph.D. thesis, "Art and Patronage in the Political Context of Fourteenth-Century Italian Communes." He was also an editor of the CD-ROM publication of Garrison's *Italian Romanesque Painting: An Illustrated Index.*

ADELAIDE BENNETT is a research scholar in the Index of Christian Art and received her Ph.D. from Columbia University, where her work was supervised by Robert Branner. She has published extensively in the area of manuscript illumination and is presently compiling a catalogue of French books of hours from 1200 to 1320.

CYNTHIA HAHN received her Ph.D. from Johns Hopkins University in 1982 and is presently teaching at Florida State University. She has also taught at the Universities of Michigan and Delaware, as well as at Goucher College in Maryland. She has published in the area of saintly iconography, and her forthcoming book, *Engraved on the Heart: Narrative and Genre in Illustrated Lives of Saints of the Central Middle Ages,* is currently in press.

DEBRA HASSIG holds an M.A. in anthropology and a Ph.D. in medieval art history (1993), both from Columbia University. Her book *Medieval Bestiaries: Text, Image, Ideology* was published in 1995 by Cambridge University Press, and a collection of essays, *The Mark of the Beast: Medieval Bestiaries in Art, Life, and Literature,* is currently at the press. She has taught at the Universities of Oregon, Toronto, and Oklahoma, and is currently a Research Fellow at the Institute for Advanced Studies in the Humanities at the University of Edinburgh, where she is beginning a new study of Pictish symbol stones.

AVRIL HENRY has a National Diploma in Design and an Art Teachers certificate, as well as a D.Phil. (Oxford). She has taught at Queen Mary College, London, St. Catherine's, Trinity and Homerton Colleges, Cambridge, and has been Professor of English Medieval Culture at the University of Exeter since 1970. Her particular interests focus on the relationships between text or performance and image. She has published extensively in the area of manuscript illustration and is presently compiling, with Anna Hulbert, the *Catalogue Raisonné of the Medieval Interior Sculptures and Their Polychromy* for Exeter Cathedral.

LUTZ HEUSINGER undertook his art-historical studies in Munich in 1967 with a study of Jacobello and Pierpaolo dalle Masegne. He was appointed Director of the Bildarchiv Foto Marburg in 1975 and in 1992 was made Professor of Computer Science in Art History in Phillips University in Marburg. His publications range from studies in art history such as *Michelangelo, Alle Werke* (1976) and *Die Sixtinische Kapelle* (1976) to being responsible for the DISKUS Series of

CD-ROM publications. He has a particular interest in cataloguing standards and the application of modern technology to art history.

ANDREAS PETZOLD was educated at Manchester University and the Courtauld Institute of Art where he was awarded his Ph.D. in art history for a study on color in Romanesque manuscripts. For the last ten years he has worked at the Victoria and Albert Museum and is currently in the records department. He is the author of numerous publications, including a recent book, *Romanesque Art* (1995). He is also an associate lecturer for the Open University in medieval and Renaissance art.

HELENE E. ROBERTS is currently attached to Dartmouth College and is editor of *Visual Resources: An International Journal of Documentation* and of the series Documenting the Image. She has compiled two iconographic indexes on Old and New Testament Subjects in works of art represented in the Visual Collections, Fine Arts Library, Harvard University. She has also published extensively on visual imagery and nineteenth-century art and criticism. She is the editor of the recently published *Encyclopedia of Comparative Iconography* (1997).

ALISON STONES holds a Ph.D. in medieval art history from the University of London (1970). She is currently teaching at the University of Pittsburgh and is also a Research Associate at the Center for Medieval and Renaissance Studies at the University of California, Los Angeles. She has published widely on medieval illustration; her most recent study is *Le Livre d'images de Madame Marie.*

PETER VAN HUISSTEDE received his Ph.D. from Leiden University, where he undertook a study of Aby Warburg's role and work. He is an art historian who has been attached to the Universiteit Utrecht since 1990. At present, he is working on a publication entitled *Image and Word,* which discusses the relationship between Dutch printers' devices and the associated texts. This project involved the compilation of an electronic catalogue raisonné of Dutch printers' devices from the sixteenth and seventeenth centuries, as well as illustrated poetry of the same period.

Carol Togneri has been attached to the Getty Provenance Index of Inventories since its inception in 1983. Prior to this she was Assistant Curator of paintings at the J. Paul Getty Museum from 1978 onwards. She holds a Masters' degree in art history, with a specialization in Italian sixteenth- and seventeenth-century painting, from the California State University, Los Angeles (1977). She is the editor of the *Diaries of Otto Mundler* (1985) and *Collections of Paintings in Naples, 1600–1780* (1992).

Jörgen van den Berg studied geology and geophysics at the Universiteit Utrecht, where he received his Ph.D. From 1974 to 1985 he was employed at the Faculty of Earth Sciences of the Universiteit Utrecht, where he published extensively on paleomagnetism and continental drift reconstruction. In 1985 he joined the Utrecht University Computer Center, where he was responsible for the development of computing in the humanities. He is presently Professor of Information Science at the Universiteit Utrecht and is involved in a number of projects including ICONCLASS and Image and Word.

Gerda G. J. Duijfjes-Vellekoop is attached to the Universiteit Utrecht. Since 1972 she has worked on the electronic publication of ICONCLASS at the Universities of Leiden and Utrecht, and has been involved in the publication of the DISKUS series of CD-ROMs, the Marburger Index, and the Garrison electronic database.

Dorothy Hoogland Verkerk holds a Ph.D. from Rutgers University (1992) and is currently assistant professor of art history at the University of North Carolina, Chapel Hill. She has published on topics ranging from Roman manuscript illumination to Early Christian funerary art. Her most recent publication is *The Ashburnham Pentateuch: A Painted Primer.*

List of Illustrations

•

ALISON STONES
*"Nipples, Entrails, Severed Heads, and Skin:
Devotional Images for Madame Marie"*
(following p. 64)

DOROTHY HOOGLAND VERKERK
"Moral Structure in the Ashburnham Pentateuch"
(following p. 81)

ADELAIDE BENNETT
*"A Woman's Power of Prayer versus the Devil in a
Book of Hours of ca. 1300"*
(following p. 102)

8. Cambrai, Bibliothèque Municipale, Ms. 87, f. 50v. Hours of the Virgin, None (photo: author)
9. Cambrai, Bibliothèque Municipale, Ms. 87, f. 53v. Hours of the Virgin, Vespers (photo: author)
10. Cambrai, Bibliothèque Municipale, Ms. 87, f. 60r. Hours of the Virgin, Compline (photo: author)
11. Cambrai, Bibliothèque Municipale, Ms. 87, f. 73r. Psalm 6 of the Seven Penitential Psalms (photo: author)

CYNTHIA HAHN
"Interpictoriality in the Limoges Chasses of Stephen, Martial, and Valerie"
(following p. 120)

1. Church of Saint-Pardoux, Gimel (Corrèze). Reliquary of St. Stephen (photo: Stohlmann Archive, Department of Art and Archaeology, Princeton University)
2. Paris, Musée du Louvre, OA 8101. Reliquary of St. Martial, front (photo: Louvre, ©Photo RMN-Arnaudet)
3. Reliquary of St. Martial, back (photo: Stohlmann Archive, Department of Art and Archaeology, Princeton University)
4. St. Petersburg, State Hermitage Museum, Φ 175. Reliquary of St. Valerie (photo: Stohlmann Archive, Department of Art and Archaeology, Princeton University)

ANDREAS PETZOLD
" 'Of the Significance of Colours': The Iconography of Colour in Romanesque and Early Gothic Book Illumination"
(following p. 134)

1. Stuttgart, Württembergische Landesbibliothek, Ms. HB. II 24, f. 73v. Crucifixion (photo: Württembergische Landesbibliothek)
2. London, British Library, Ms. Royal 1.D.X, f. 8v. Christ in Majesty (photo: British Library)
3. London, Victoria and Albert Museum, Ms. 661, recto. Mocking of Christ (photo: Victoria and Albert Museum)
4. Copenhagen, Royal Library, Ms. Thott 13 2º, f. 14. Betrayal (photo: Royal Library, Copenhagen)

JAMES D'EMILIO
"Looking Eastward: The Story of Noe at Monreale Cathedral"
(following p. 144)

1. Palermo, Palatine Chapel, south wall of nave, east end (photo: Artini, Florence)
2. Palermo, Palatine Chapel, south wall of nave, central section (photo: Artini, Florence)
3. Palermo, Palatine Chapel, south wall of nave, west end (photo: Artini, Florence)
4. Palermo, Palatine Chapel, north wall of nave, west end (photo: Artini, Florence)
5. Palermo, Palatine Chapel, north wall of nave, central section (photo: Artini, Florence)
6. Monreale, Cathedral, south wall of nave, eastern section (photo: Artini, Florence)
7. Monreale, Cathedral, south wall of nave, central section (photo: Artini, Florence)
8. Monreale, Cathedral, south wall of nave, west end (photo: Artini, Florence)
9. Monreale, Cathedral, west wall of nave (photo: Artini, Florence)
10. Monreale, Cathedral, north wall of nave, west end (photo: Artini, Florence)
11. Monreale, Cathedral, north wall of nave, central section (photo: Artini, Florence)

GIOVANNI FRENI
"The Architecture and Sculpture of the Portal of the South Side of Arezzo Cathedral"
(following p. 161)

1. Arezzo, Cathedral, south side, portal (photo: Conway Library, Courtauld Institute of Art, London)
2. Arezzo, Cathedral, south side, portal, detail of the lower section of the left pilaster (photo: Conway Library, Courtauld Institute of Art, London)
3. Arezzo, Cathedral, south side, portal, detail of the lower section of the right pilaster (photo: Conway Library, Courtauld Institute of Art, London)
4. Arezzo, Cathedral, south side, portal, detail of the Madonna *lactans* group (photo: Conway Library, Courtauld Institute of Art, London)
5. Arezzo, Cathedral, south side, portal, before restoration (photo: Conway Library, Courtauld Institute of Art, London)
6. Arezzo, Cathedral, south side, portal, interior decoration (photo: Conway Library, Courtauld Institute of Art, London)
7. Arezzo, Cathedral, south side, portal, interior, angel of the Annunciation (photo: Conway Library, Courtauld Institute of Art, London)
8. Arezzo, Cathedral, south side, portal, interior, Virgin of the Annunciation (photo: Conway Library, Courtauld Institute of Art, London)
9. Florence, Santa Croce, Baroncelli monument, detail (photo: Conway Library, Courtauld Institute of Art, London)
10. Arezzo, Cathedral, south side, portal, detail of the decoration of the embrasure (photo: Conway Library, Courtauld Institute of Art, London)

by Eduard Šafařík in *Collezione dei dipinti Colonna, inventari 1611–1795* (Munich, 1996)

1. After Guido Reni, *The Christ Child Asleep on the Cross*, National Museums and Galleries on Merseyside, Walker Art Gallery, Liverpool (photo: after *Foreign Catalogue, Walker Art Gallery, Liverpool* [Liverpool, 1977], 233, no. 2801)
2. Guido Reni (studio?), *The Christ Child Asleep on the Cross*, The Art Museum, Princeton University, gift of J. Lionberger Davis, Class of 1900 (photo: The Art Museum, Princeton University)
3. Entry for Antonio de Pereda's *Vanitas* from the inventory of the Almirante de Castilla, 1691 (photo: Getty Research Institute)
4. Antonio de Pereda, *Vanitas*, Kunsthistorisches Museum, Vienna (photo: after W. B. Jordan and P. Cherry, *Spanish Still Life from Velázquez to Goya* [London, 1995], 81, no. 26)
5. Attributed to Pieter Claesz. Soutman, *Judith with the Head of Holofernes*, Philadelphia Museum of Art, Philadelphia, Pennsylvania, gift of Mrs. George H. Frazier (photo: Philadelphia Museum of Art)
6. Guido Cagnacci, *A Dead Martyr (Saint Mustiola?)*, Musée Fabre, Montpellier (photo: after R. Morselli, *Guido Cagnacci* [Milan, 1993], 93)

HANS BRANDHORST
"Ululas Athenas: Owls to Athens"
(following p. 279)

1. Six examples of the Baptism of Christ (screen shot: author)
2. Six additional examples of the Baptism of Christ (screen shot: author)
3. Baptism scene in Copenhagen, Royal Library, Ms. Thott 142 2°, f. 13r (screen shot: author)
4. Baptism scene in Oxford, Bodleian Library, Ms. Gough lit. 2, f. 21r (screen shot: author)
5. Models of the Flight: Jacob and his family on their way to Joseph in Egypt and the Flight into Egypt in Cambridge, Trinity College Library, Ms. B.11.4, ff. 1v and 8r (screen shot: author)
6. Models of the Flight: Jacob and his family on their way to Joseph in Egypt and the Flight into Egypt in Munich, Bayerische Staatsbibliothek, Ms. Clm. 835, ff. 16v and 23v (screen shot: author)
7. "Startled shepherds" in the Winchester Psalter (London, British Library, Ms. Cotton Nero C. IV, f. 11r), and the Sacramentary of Robert of Jumièges (Rouen, Bibiothèque Municipale, Ms. Y 6, f. 33r) (screen shot: author)
8. Results of a query in the database on the ICONCLASS concept 31A2531(+9161), "hand bent toward the head, protecting," but filtered for the Annunciation to the Shepherds (screen shot: author)

9. The rest of the search result for 31A2531(+9161), "hand bent toward the head, protecting" (screen shot: author)
10. The Annunciation to the shepherds in the Winchester Psalter, f. 11r, and the Codex Egberti (Trier, Stadtbibliothek, Ms. 24, f. 13v) (screen shot: author)
11. Shepherds from the Winchester Psalter, f. 11r, the Codex Egberti, f. 13v, and Cambridge, Emmanuel College Library, Ms. 252, f. 7v; and Jesse from the Winchester Psalter's Anointment of David, f. 7r (screen shot: author)
12. Jesse from the Winchester Psalter (mirror image of the last detail in Fig. 11), Pierpont Morgan Library, Ms. M 619, and the Harding Bible, f. 13r (screen shot: author)
13. Results of browsing by "Subject," with a list of broad ICONCLASS categories (screen shot: author)
14. Results of selecting a broad ICONCLASS category (screen shot: author)
15. Digital reproduction of a miniature with the accompanying iconographic description of its subject matter (screen shot: author)
16. Results of browsing for the concept 31AA25161 (arm or hand held in front of the chest)–AA–both arms or hands (screen shot: author)
17. Intermediate step in browsing for tituli and inscriptions (screen shot: author)

JÖRGEN VAN DEN BERG AND
GERDA G. J. DUIJFJES-VELLEKOOP
"Translating ICONCLASS and the Connectivity Concept of the Iconclass2000 Browser"
(following p. 299)

1. DIAL (Decimal Index of the Art of the Low Countries) photocard with ICONCLASS notation. (photo: authors)
2. Record in a HIDA (Marburg Classification Standard) database (photo: authors)
3. Document showing the evolution of "the circle of death / I" (Rudi H. Fuchs) (photo: authors)
4. "See also" references from "death" (photo: authors)
5. Biblical iconography displayed in French on an existing CD-ROM, *Wallraf-Richartz-Museum Cologne: Collection of Paintings and Sculptures* (DISKUS series 007; Munich, 1996) (photo: authors)
6. "See also" references from "morte" (photo: authors)
7. Multilingual ICONCLASS: three browsers running simultaneously, each accessing a different data file (photo: authors)
8. Option in "File Preferences" (photo: authors)

Abbreviations

·

ArtB	*The Art Bulletin*
ARV ²	Beazley, J. D. *Attic Red-Figure Vase-Painters,* second edition. Oxford, 1963.
ASCII	American Standard Code for Information Interchange
Berlin, Staatsbibl.	Berlin, Deutsche Staatsbibliothek
B.M.	Bibliothèque Municipale
Brussels, B.R.	Brussels, Bibliothèque Royale
BSS	*Bibliotheca Sanctorum.* 13 vols. Rome, 1961–70.
CahArch	*Cahiers archéologiques*
Cant.	Song of Solomon
CSEL	Corpus Scriptorum Ecclesiasticorum Latinorum
Dan.	Daniel
DIAL	Decimal Index of the Art of the Low Countries
DISKUS	Digitales Informationssytem für Kunst- und Sozialgeschichte
DOP	*Dumbarton Oaks Papers*
EETS, ES	Early English Text Society, Extra Series. 12 vols. London, 1867– .
Ex.	Exodus
GCS	Die griechischen christlichen Schriftsteller der ersten [drei] Jahrhunderte. Berlin and Leipzig, 1897– .
The Hague, K.B.	The Hague, Koninklijke Bibliotheek
Heb.	Hebrews
HIDA	Hierarchischer Dokument-Administrator
Hos.	Hosea
ICCD	Istituto Centrale per il Catalogo e la Documentazione, Rome
IRDG	ICONCLASS Research and Development Group
Is.	Isaiah
Jer.	Jeremiah
JWalt	*Journal of the Walters Art Gallery*
JWarb	*Journal of the Warburg and Courtauld Institutes*
LCI	*Lexikon der christlichen Ikonographie.* Ed. E. Kirschbaum et al. 8 vols. Rome, Freiburg, Basel, and Vienna, 1968–76.
LIMC	*Lexicon Iconographicum Mythologiae Classicae.* 8 vols. Zurich, 1981– .
Lk.	Luke
London, B.L.	London, British Library
MGH, *Scriptores*	Monumenta Germaniae Historica, *Scriptores Rerum Germanicarum*

MIDAS	Marburger Informations-, Dokumentations- und Administrations-System
Mk.	Mark
Mt.	Matthew
Munich, Bayer. Staatsbibl.	Munich, Bayerische Staatsbibliothek
NEB	New English Bible
New York, Morgan Lib.	New York City, Pierpont Morgan Library
OLE	Object Linking and Embedding
Oxford, Bodl.	Oxford, Bodleian Library
Paris, Arsenal	Paris, Bibliothèque de l'Arsenal
Paris, B.N.F.	Paris, Bibliothèque Nationale de France
PG	Patrologiae Cursus Completus, Series Graeca. Ed. Jacques-Paul Migne. 161 vols. Paris, 1857–66.
PL	Patrologiae Cursus Completus, Series Latina. Ed. Jacques-Paul Migne. 221 vols. Paris, 1844–55.
Ps.	Psalms
Rev.	Revelation
Rome, Bibl. Vat.	Rome, Biblioteca Apostolica Vaticana
SGML	Standard Generalized Markup Language
Vienna, Ö.N.B.	Vienna, Österreichische Nationalbibliothek
Zeph.	Zephaniah

1

ICONOGRAPHY

.

Introduction

·

COLUM HOURIHANE

IT IS difficult to follow as pivotal a publication as *Iconography at the Crossroads*[1] with a conventional collection of essays without being accused of going backwards on one of the many iconographical paths outlined in that volume. This collection of diverse papers does not attempt to deal with the concept or theories of iconography, but rather with its practice. The essays published here are also intended to present a balance between some of the most eminent scholars in their respective fields and some younger and developing art historians, all of whom have applied their inventive approaches to reassessing the old and creating the new. It is reassuring that many of the papers in this publication, without any conscious effort on the part of the authors, tend to expand on and develop further some of the general iconographical and iconological trends and approaches treated in *Iconography at the Crossroads.*

No collection of this kind could be published without repeated homage to such iconographers and art historians as Emile Mâle, Erwin Panofsky, Kurt Weitzmann, and Ernst Kitzinger, whose work is naturally referred to in many of the essays; but underlying all those studies, and often unstated, is the debt which is owed to Charles Rufus Morey (Fig. 1) and his colleagues in the Index of Christian Art. Morey's legacy lies not so much in direct theoretical advancement of the discipline but in the practical approaches used and even more in the subjects and themes that have been analysed and examined during the last eighty years. If Panofsky can be seen as the great theoretician, Morey should be viewed as the complementary practician whose archaeological background and interest in the material data underpinned his approach to iconography and the foundation of the Index. While Morey's interest was not primarily in iconology, many of the papers in this collection focus on precisely that, and the wish to delve into the mentality of the medieval audience and viewer is the guiding force behind a significant number of them. Whereas in the past such responses have been largely dictated, sometimes at great cost, by textual references to medieval art appreciation, this approach is no longer satisfactory. The responses are now very much guided by an effort to abandon modern perceptions of appreciation and adopt a more holistic approach to iconography in all its complexity. Essays such as those by James D'Emilio, Cynthia Hahn, Avril Henry, Dorothy Verkerk, and Alison Stones attempt to recreate the medieval reception of their respective studies.

The first paper in this collection is, significantly, written by a graduate of Princeton University who began his studies under Kurt Weitzmann. Jaroslav Folda traces the interpretative history and

---

[1] *Iconography at the Crossroads: Papers from the Colloquium Sponsored by the Index of Christian Art, Princeton University,* *23–24 March 1990,* ed. B. Cassidy (Princeton, 1993).

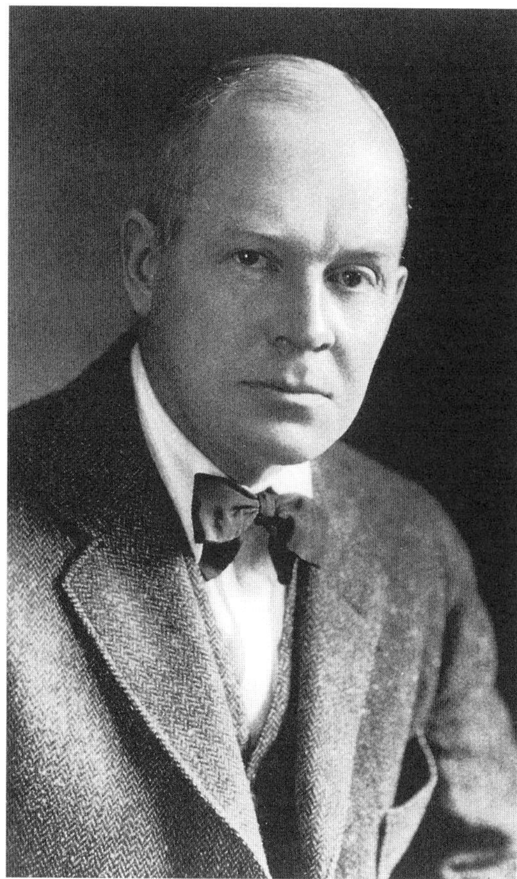

1. Charles Rufus Morey, founder of the Index of Christian Art

cultural milieu in which art historians have viewed Crusader art since the modern concept was first proposed at the start of the twentieth century with the British and French mandates in the Near East. Problems such as those highlighted by Folda present convincing evidence, if any is needed, for a separate classification and handling of Crusader iconography, which has been very much viewed as an eastern extension of the Western world without a full understanding of the local contributions and influences. Within his study he takes a subset of this art even further with an analysis of nonfigural works in a variety of interrelated media, demonstrating a unity in purpose whose meaning lies not only within the work itself but in the society which created the work. Folda's work underlines the fact that it is only recently that the case has been made for extending iconographical evaluation to encompass that which is not based on textual sources. Considerable reevaluation of general descriptors such as "animal" or "foliate ornament," which were used in early iconographical analyses as a means of classifying what were then viewed as secondary or possibly decorative elements, will yield significant results in the future. Anthropomorphic interlace and animal motifs on Irish high crosses and Pictish slabs, or the animals which are liberally found in Anglo-Saxon art, are case studies that would add significantly to our understanding.

Of the eighteen media represented in the Index, manuscripts constitute the largest and possibly the most significant grouping. Prior to founding the Index, Morey is recorded as paying particular attention to their study due to the fact that "the Latinity of the past was preserved there with more continuity than in the other arts."[2] It seems natural, therefore, that a significant number of papers in this celebratory volume should be devoted to manuscript studies in one form or another. In the first of these, Debra Hassig examines the concept of the ostracised and rejected in medieval society, especially the Jew. Her thematic study extends Ruth Mellinkoff's study[3] by looking in particular at deformed and monstrous beings. The concept of physical deformity was equated with moral turpitude, evil, and sin in the later Middle Ages, and social groups were similarly described in those terms. The animal characteristics that were used initially later developed into features of monstrous creatures, with interesting use of colouration and iconographical stereotyping of racial characteristics.

Several other scholars combine thematic approaches to particular manuscripts into wider analyses of particular themes. One such paper is that written by Alison Stones on a number of related scenes from a devotional picture book written in the late thirteenth century for an unidentified lady called Madame Marie. Stones focuses on the unusually dominant number of severed heads and breasts, disembowelments, and mutilations found throughout this manuscript, which was, unusually, written for a female reader. The investment of such care by the medieval illustrator in depicting these themes in intricate detail and in prominent positions is not unusual. Such subjects usually show the disbeliever directly involved in meting out punishment to the suffering believer, who will eventually profit: painful suffering and death was a guarantee of salvation in the afterlife and must have been viewed as welcome. Christ's crucifixion on the Cross was the ultimate suffering, and as depictions of his passion and ordeal changed over time, increasingly emphasising the corporeality of the scene, more realism can also be seen in such saintly sacrifices. What distinguishes Madame Marie's manuscript is the frequency and detail of such iconographical scenes for a female reader. Stones establishes the history of such subjects in a variety of media spanning the later Middle Ages and contextualises these depictions in relation to the manuscript which she examines.

Female patronage is also an important element in another manuscript which is described by Adelaide Bennett of the Index of Christian Art. Her paper examines an unusual book of hours (Cambrai, Bibliothèque Municipale, Ms. 87) written somewhere on the Franco-German border in the late thirteenth or early fourteenth century. She describes the themes and subject of the book's various pictorial programmes against a more extensive study of thirteenth-century French books of hours which she is presently compiling. Although less gruesome than the illustrations in Madame Marie's picture book, the general themes of temptation and penitence in relation to a female reader provide some revealing insights into how manuscripts were written for particular audiences and users.

Iconographical interpretation varies significantly from one viewer to another even where the subject can be firmly established. The subjective element in our mental analysis of motifs and sym-

<hr>

[2] C. H. Smyth, "Concerning Charles Rufus Morey (1877–1955)," in *The Early Years of Art History in the United States,* ed. C. H. Smyth and P. M. Lukehart (Princeton, 1993), 115.

[3] R. Mellinkoff, *Outcasts: Signs of Otherness in Northern European Art of the Late Middle Ages,* 2 vols. (Berkeley, 1993).

bols makes objective, noninterventionalist interpretation difficult. Iconographical significance and meaning are made even more difficult when elements are compounded, unified, or conflated, as is frequently the case. Avril Henry provides a compelling example of this with her examination of a particular scene in the Eton Roundels (Eton College, Ms. 177, f. 2r) which she proposes is a purposeful conflation of several ideas. Its central position in the narrative sequence offers hints as to what it could represent, but it is only through an analysis of its compositional elements in parallel depictions that the possible multiple meanings can be fully appreciated. Her study, like that of Hans Brandhorst later in this volume, relies heavily on the important and detailed classification of gestures and their significance in elucidating a full iconographical analysis. Henry's paper, like a number of other studies in this publication, must contribute to a deeper understanding of the sophisticated and highly developed nature of the medieval reader's visual literacy. The role of structure and its impact on meaning, specifically of context used to extend the meaning of a particular symbol, is also dealt with in James D'Emilio's paper on the Monreale mosaic cycle.

Kurt Weitzmann, like so many other art historians whose studies of the fragmentary remains of the Ashburnham Pentateuch (Paris, B.N.F. Nouv. acq. lat. 2334) preceded and followed his, found the manuscript to be intriguingly enigmatic.[4] The immediate focus is on the unusual and apparently random placement of scenes on the folios and their striking colouration, which is not found elsewhere. In a new evaluation of this manuscript, Dorothy Verkerk takes up the mantle of interpretation and shows that the swathes of colour on these highly detailed pages, together with the arrangement of the scenes, are governed by didactic conventions which would have made perfect sense to the Late Antique reader but demand a breakdown in approach by the modern viewer, since the narrative sequence is sublimated to exegetical principles. She proposes that these idiosyncracies were intentional and related to the use of the codex, and supports this contention by examining the cathechical works of Augustine and John Chrysostom. Her paper convincingly reenforces yet again the sophisticated appreciation and understanding of the medieval viewer.

The significance of colouration in iconographical interpretation is a field which has received significant attention within the last decade. The lack of good-quality colour images prior to the 1970s, especially in the area of illuminated manuscripts, prevented serious investigation of how medieval illuminators used colours to impart particular meaning. Jonathon Alexander has shown how important and meaningful colouration is in Anglo-Saxon manuscripts which precede the period dealt with here by Andreas Petzold.[5] Obvious and well-known colour associations include Christ's red mantle and the Virgin's blue one, the red faces associated with the angel at the tomb, and the general tendency for evildoers to be dressed in black. In his paper in this volume, Petzold examines some of the principles and difficulties involved in colour symbolism in medieval art as well as focusing on the particular examples of Judas and Synagogue depicted in yellow. His study makes good use of the manuscript evidence, and it would be interesting to see if colour symbolism in other media, which is treated in instructional manuals such as that of Theophilus, follows the same pattern.

The Index of Christian Art lists over 3,000 saints in its subject files, one of the largest collections of such figures in existence. It is therefore entirely appropriate that Cynthia Hahn's study ex-

---

[4] K. Weitzmann, *Late Antique and Early Christian Book Illumination* (New York, 1977), 118–25.

[5] J. J. G. Alexander, "Some Aesthetic Principles in the Use of Colour in Anglo-Saxon Art," *Anglo-Saxon England* 4 (1975), 145–54.

amines three of these saintly figures and their reliquaries. Although the Limoges chasses of Saints Valerie, Martial, and Stephen were, like so many other examples of this type of metalwork, replicated and distributed widely throughout Europe, Hahn has focused on the special significance of this triple grouping for the medieval viewer in Limoges, where these three saints were especially venerated. Although the narratives on the three shrines differ and do not share overlapping elements, she uses historical and liturgical evidence to examine the visual dynamics of these chasses in a particular context. Her handling of the theme is cautiously developed in relation not to a modern audience, but to the twelfth-century audience in Limoges. This innovative approach to the iconography of the chasses based on their "interpictoriality" provides a methodological framework for the study of localised saintly cults and their interaction with the viewer.

A similar examination of the medieval audience's appreciation of a work underlies James D'Emilio's reinterpretation of the narrative and stylistic features of the twelfth-century mosaic cycle at Monreale cathedral, which he compares with the similar but slightly earlier cycle in the Palatine Chapel in Palermo. His approach is influenced by similar spatial studies undertaken by Marilyn Lavin on Italian frescoes.[6] The emphasis on arrangement, disposition, and interpretation at Monreale are, according to D'Emilio, a conscious attempt at emphasising or minimising movement within the narrative cycle of Noah, depending on whether the viewer was moving away from or toward the sanctuary. His interpretation of the scenes against their architectural setting offers an insight into why the artists altered the narrative and, significantly, used the architecture to extend and develop the meaning of the cycle of images. The subtle unity of meaning and structure are thus highlighted in a revealing and insightful manner.

Giovanni Freni has adopted a more traditional approach in his stylistic analysis of the southern portal of the Cathedral of Arezzo. This is the only surviving fourteenth-century portal of the cathedral still *in situ*, and it was originally decorated with a series of reliefs depicting the Virtues and Vices along with other allegorical figures, all of which are now unfortunately weathered beyond recognition. Nevertheless, Freni uses the available architectural, sculptural, and iconographic evidence successfully to date this work and place it within the broader context of the artistic culture of fourteenth-century Tuscany.

John Fleming, a contributor to previous conferences and publications devoted to the Index of Christian Art, presents here a paper in which he develops even further his studies on the iconography and significance of the personal signature. His essay highlights the possible reasons underlying the appropriation of universal forms for individual and personal purposes. It also subtly links the iconographic form of the tau sign, used by St. Francis as his personal signature, with his belief in its multiple meanings. Francis structured his life after a number of pictorial ideas, and his use of the tau was based on the scriptural history of its meaning, which he personally chose to represent his role in life. Fleming also shows that a similar yet more adventurous role in the history of the world's salvation may underlie the choice of visual motifs in Christopher Columbus's signature. Both of these case studies examine the close relationship between form and text, the universal and the individual.

Up to the introduction of computers in the Index of Christian Art in 1991, the 26,000 subject terms, beginning with Alpha and Omega and ending with St. Zwentibold of Lorraine, provided

---

[6] M. Lavin, *The Place of Narrative: Mural Decoration in Italian Churches, 431–1600* (Chicago, 1990).

the main access point to the text files. They were developed in a thesaurus type structure with underlying and supporting data elements such as scope notes, related terms, bibliographic references, and so forth, a format that lent itself ideally to computerization. The focus of these terms was collection-generated and largely reflected the interests of the Index, which was Christian art. The subject terms in themselves were always high-level descriptors to concepts or themes and in many ways did not reflect the particular and individual details of the works of art. Concepts such as "Annunciation" or "Nativity," for example, may differ in their representation from one work to the next. The unique yet controlled free-text description which was developed by the Index from the beginning is where such details and relational aspects of the individual work of art are described. Concepts such as colour and position, either within the individual work or between different elements in the work, are detailed in this description. No other subject-term listing offers such a wealth of iconographical analysis.

Despite these strengths, the system does not cater to some of the demands made by modern research and scholarship, for example, in the area of gestural language. One of the strengths of a subject classification system like ICONCLASS is that it does offer the possibility of recording such details using an existing fully configured structure which complements and strengthens the Index's own. The complementary nature, interests, and approaches of the founders of these two projects have already been noted by Irving Lavin at an earlier conference organised by the Index.[7] To celebrate the introduction of ICONCLASS into the Index of Christian Art, a number of papers on the concept of subject classification in art history, and ICONCLASS in particular, are included here. ICONCLASS will never replace the existing approaches within the Index, but its use will certainly complement and open up even further the wealth of data available within the archive.

Despite the fact that the history of subject classification goes back as far as the seventeenth century, with studies such as those of Ripa and Molinus, the art-historical world was still unprepared for the demands that computerization have placed on this field of classification within the last twenty years. Studies such as those by Enser[8] and Gordon[9] have shown that subject access is the most widely used field in art-historical archives. It is an area which is still undergoing development, and a classification standard in which the Index can share its experience with the outside world.

The possibilities of improving art-historical standards through computerization and the Internet is proposed by Lutz Heusinger in the first of the methodology papers in this volume. The concept of making in-house classification standards available to the world was pioneered by the Index of Christian Art as early as 1942, with the publication by Helen Woodruff of its subject terms. This was a practice which was sadly not followed by other archives in the ensuing years and which could have prevented the unnecessary replication of subject classification systems. This sharing of the Index's structure was later followed by a sharing of its data, with the distribution of four copies of the file holdings throughout the world. The current availability of the Index database on the Internet is in keeping not only with the established practice of the archive, but also with the wish ad-

---

[7] I. Lavin, "Iconography as a Humanistic Discipline (Iconography at the Crossroads)," in *Iconography at the Crossroads* (as in note 1), 33–43.

[8] P. Enser, "Query Analysis in a Visual Information Retrieval Context," *Journal of Document and Text Management* 1, no. 1 (1993), 25–52; and "Pictorial Image Retrieval," *Journal of Documentation* 51, no. 2 (1995), 126–70.

[9] C. Gordon "Patterns and Benefits of Subject Enquiry in an ICONCLASS Database," *Visual Resources Bulletin* 23, no. 2 (1996), 2.

vocated here by Heusinger that the sharing of data is the way of the future. This sharing, he believes, will be further facilitated by a sharing of classification standards such as ICONCLASS.

Helene Roberts discusses in a wide-ranging paper the general concept of transfer and mutation of iconographical forms and how they are classified. Signs or symbols, as John Fleming has already shown in his paper, are not static entities but can be adopted to various needs and ends, in which they may assume different meanings and existences. In her general introduction to the concept of iconographic change, Roberts isolates several themes such as Orpheus, charting its pagan origin, its adoption by the Christian community, and its mutation in different media such as music, cinematography, and theatre over the ensuing centuries.

Three of the methodological papers deal with individual applications of the ICONCLASS system by scholars to different projects ranging from personal manuscript studies to large-scale provenance indexing. All of the articles highlight the need for the art historian to have in-depth and detailed classification of even the most minute features in a work of art, and the advantages offered by such classification. No longer is it satisfactory to apply only high-level descriptors such as "shepherd" or "musical instrument" when large databases are being searched. In his study, Hans Brandhorst shows that such detailed classification can lead not only to the discovery of a wealth of new comparative material, but also to a re-evaluation of what was previously believed to be similar or related material. The database which he has compiled, although limited to prefatory miniatures in English psalters from the mid-eleventh through the early twelfth century, clearly shows the potential for larger application.

A similar plea for detailed iconographical description is made by Carol Togneri, who shows its significance by tracing the provenance of works of art now in Princeton and Liverpool to seventeenth-century Italy. The unusual application of ICONCLASS to titles of works of art which have no visual record shows yet another approach to subject classification. As Togneri revealingly demonstrates, the mutation of iconographic descriptions and confusion of works which have been erroneously and inaccurately described over time is a problem which the standardization of ICONCLASS is helping to overcome.

Peter van Huisstede's article also contributes to this theme, showing the value of detailed classification and the advantages of computerizing large bodies of material, in this case Dutch printers' devices of the fifteenth to seventeenth century. These devices document an unrivalled wealth of popular culture and iconography which extended far beyond the boundaries of their origins on the printed page. The motifs and legends used in printers' devices were transferred into different media, and their meanings were widely understood, as Van Huisstede shows by ingeniously tracing the associations and history of several such devices which appear in Rubens's painting *The Ship of State*, now in the Musée du Louvre in Paris. Central to Van Huisstede's new evaluation of this painting was the development of a comprehensive database of printers' devices classified iconographically using ICONCLASS. Rubens's choice of four motifs with widely understood meanings is convincingly placed by Van Huisstede against the historical background of the early seventeenth century, when Louis XIII rivalled his mother, Maria de Medici, for political control.

In their joint article, Ger Duijfjes-Vellekoop and Jörgen van den Berg present some of the most recent developments in ICONCLASS. Since its publication over a period of twelve years from 1973 to 1985, new developments and enhancements have been undertaken and controlled on a continuous basis by the ICONCLASS Research and Development Group (IRDG). Now in its twenty-fifth year, the English-language system has developed into the most widely distributed subject classification structure in the world, and ICONCLASS continues to expand into countries as linguistically as diverse as Brazil and Poland. Recent multilingual translations of the system assisted by the IRDG are described by Ger Duijfjes-Vellekoop, who maintains that controlled projects such as these are the best solution for even wider application and enhancements of the existing structure. Whatever doubts may have existed about the early applications of computers to art history, it is clear that their value is now widely appreciated. Their use in art history has paralleled their more widespread applications in other fields, but without a comparable investment of finances or creativity; yet users of art-historical databases do not make allowances for this fact, expecting the computer to provide immediate solutions to all their queries in a multi-media format with little difficulty. Ease of use and coordination with non-art-historical applications was the guiding purpose and aim of the recent developments in the newly published Iconclass2000 Browser which Jörgen van den Berg describes. This is the second electronic release of the system, and Van den Berg highlights its modifications, which range from new search abilities to updates in indexing terms, and which should provide a stable platform for the system well into the twenty-first century.

Despite the fact that much criticism has been levelled against iconography in the last twenty years and numerous questions have been posed as to its relevance in modern art history, it continues not only to survive but, as can be seen in the papers collected here, to flourish. The changes that have occurred have been driven by a logical progression within the discipline, not as a response to its imminent demise. Its role is destined to increase even further with greater availability of material and improved access to archival holdings such as that of the Index of Christian Art. The Index has been successful in its aims over its first eighty years and looks with optimism towards the next.

Problems in the Iconography of the Art
of the Crusaders in the Holy Land:
1098–1291/1917–1997

·

JAROSLAV FOLDA

THIS STUDY proposes that there is a corpus of art that can be defined as "Crusader," and that it is, generally speaking, those works produced for Crusader patrons between 1098 and 1291 in the Holy Land, and mainly in the Latin Kingdom of Jerusalem. Furthermore, it is argued that this art has distinctive iconographic aspects. Certain characteristics of these works, together with their iconography, are explored in this paper, firstly, by considering how the idea of iconography in Crusader art has developed over the years and, secondly, by looking at some current problems in this area.

INTRODUCTION

The notion of Crusader art probably never crossed the mind of Charles Morey. The fact is that the modern study of Crusader figural art essentially dates from the period after 1917, with the British and French Mandates in the Near East,[1] and its evolution parallels the period in which the Index of Christian Art has come to be a major tool for art-historical research. The subject of Crusader iconography as such only came to be investigated intensively in the 1950s and 1960s.

Before examining the nature and development of Crusader iconography, it is necessary to define more fully the art that is being discussed here. Crusader art and architecture in the Holy Land were produced for Crusader or Frankish patrons by Crusader, Frankish, Byzantine, or other local Christian artists in the territories of the mainland Crusader States in Syria-Palestine between 1098 and 1291. Its function can be identified as that of pilgrimage art; ecclesiastical art; royal art; art for the military orders, especially the Hospitallers and the Templars; and religious and secular art for knights, men and women of the aristocracy, bourgeois, and merchants. It was an art made for Crusaders who took the cross, as well as for settlers and merchants who remained in the Crusader East during and after the great expeditions.

---

[1] The fundamental publication of the art historian Camille Enlart, *Les Monuments des Croisés dans le Royaume de Jérusalem: Architecture religieuse et civile* (Paris, 1925–28), grew out of the work of archaeologists like P. Viaud, H. Vincent, and F.-M. Abel carried out between 1909 and 1926.

In approaching the idea of iconography in Crusader art, some important formulations by major scholars in the field provide an interesting introduction. T. S. R. Boase was the first to address the figural arts (and architecture) in the Crusader East as meeting and effecting exchanges in Palestine.[2] Although his well-known 1939 article tended to emphasize archaeology, style, and classical survivals—part of the agenda of the Warburg Institute—in the study of the Crusader material, he also took an art-historical interest in iconographic aspects. In his discussion of the Nazareth capitals, for example, he sought to identify their subject matter, the mission of the apostles, by locating appropriate medieval texts to explain their unusual iconography.[3] This was the classic approach to iconography pioneered by Emile Mâle, Erwin Panofsky, and others: finding the important texts that would enable the art historian to explicate the meaning and content of visual material. Not only did Boase articulate the interpretative components of each capital, he also proposed linking the ensemble together in terms of a program, and concluded by observing, "the fact that . . . the apostolic missions were given such prominence [instead of the expected scenes of the life of the Virgin] is all the more striking testimony to the careful thought behind the choice of subject. The Nazareth capitals foreshadow the missionary journeys of the following century, and the new teaching of Francis and Ramon Lull."[4] Although Boase did not refer to this phenomenon as "Crusader" iconography as such, he did specify that it is unusual, that it is rooted in the local context of the Holy Land, that some of the imagery has no known Western iconographic models, and, finally, that the program shows special interest in the Christian East more broadly defined.

When Boase refers to the "local interest" in the iconography at Nazareth, Bethlehem, and in the Melisende Psalter, it is a forerunner of one aspect of the study of Crusader iconography. Hugo Buchthal, in his landmark study *Miniature Painting of the Latin Kingdom of Jerusalem*, published in 1957, used much more intensive methods of iconographic analysis, and on occasion he referred explicitly to "Crusader's manuscripts," but he shared with Boase the identification of "local" features as distinctive of Crusader iconography. In his discussion of the major manuscripts, for example, Buchthal gives detailed examinations of the iconographic and stylistic sources from Byzantium, the Latin West, and even the Islamic East. His approach, like that of Boase, is also rooted in the Warburg tradition, which he, unlike Boase, had learned directly from Erwin Panofsky, his mentor in Hamburg. Buchthal carefully evaluates the miniature cycles in terms of biblical and liturgical imagery from Byzantine and other sources, bringing important texts to bear when relevant. But he also discovers special characteristics of the iconography that unmistakably refer to their Crusader context, for example, the imagery of the Anastasis image in the Melisende Psalter, which reflects the apse mosaic of the church of the Holy Sepulchre;[5] the architectural imagery of Crusader Jerusalem that appears as visual markers in the miniatures of the Riccardiana Psalter;[6] and the Near Eastern costumes and poses of the figures in the Arsenal Bible.[7]

In sum, Buchthal argues that the manuscripts ascribed to the scriptorium of the Holy Sepulchre in three groups were distinctive. "Certain characteristics of style and iconography recur in all three groups; they show that something like a common workshop tradition existed throughout the

---

[2] T. S. R. Boase, "The Arts in the Latin Kingdom of Jerusalem," *JWarb* 2 (1938–39), 20.

[3] Ibid., 9–10. He refers to Gervase of Tilbury, *Otia imperialia*.

[4] Boase, "Arts in the Latin Kingdom" (as in note 2), 10.

[5] H. Buchthal, *Miniature Painting in the Latin Kingdom of Jerusalem* (Oxford, 1957), 4, 23.

[6] Ibid., 45.

[7] Ibid., 65.

whole period." Moreover, he says, "miniature painting in the Crusading Kingdom . . . had a distinctive style of its own, which was not derived from any single source, but emerged as the result of copying illuminations from a variety of Byzantine and western manuscripts, and of developing certain features of these models in a highly original and individual manner." Finally, "the surprising thing is . . . that . . . something like a local style and a local tradition of unmistakable identity should have emerged at all."[8] For Buchthal, the local tradition and the bringing together of Byzantine, French, Italian, and even Muslim components were essential to the identification of the distinctive iconography of the miniature painting of the Latin Kingdom.

In the wake of Buchthal's book, Kurt Weitzmann published in 1963 an exciting article entitled "Thirteenth-Century Crusader Icons on Mount Sinai."[9] It was exciting because it introduced a wholly new and, to some extent, unexpected body of material into the discussion of painting associated with the Crusaders: ten icons at the monastery of St. Catherine at Mount Sinai.[10] Weitzmann compared one of the Mount Sinai icons, an image of the Crucifixion on an iconostasis beam, to the Crucifixion miniature in the Perugia Missal discussed by Buchthal (Perugia, Cathedral Library, Ms. 6). He furthermore identified certain iconographic traits the two images have in common, such as the gestures and poses of the figures of Mary and John. Another aspect these works have in common is the distinctive bevelled cross on which Christ appears.

Weitzmann's discussion of these images is important for the historiography of the art of the Crusaders. After commenting on the stylistic and iconographic features these works have in common, he tentatively proposes that the artist of the Crucifixion on the iconostasis beam was Italian in origin, but he concludes with the following statement: "attempts to distinguish the nationalities of the icon painters may not always be successful, simply because Italian and French artists, working side by side and apparently having models from both countries available, gradually developed a style and iconography which, when fused with Byzantine elements, resulted in what one might simply call Crusader art."[11] Weitzmann's examination of these icons, like Buchthal's of the manuscripts, was intensive and balanced style and iconography, but it was rooted in an investigation of iconographic model and copy, a methodology that Weitzmann had written about explicitly in his famous book *Illustrations in Roll and Codex.*[12] His method is partly adapted from the techniques of biblical text criticism. The results of applying this method to the icons provided scholars with a newly sharpened focus on the iconography of Crusader figural painting. Weitzmann, in this 1963 article, was also the first scholar to refer explicitly to the phenomenon of "Crusader art."

In the evolution of the study of Crusader art the basis was laid in the 1960s for investigating the distinctive features of its iconography, without explicitly identifying it as "Crusader iconography." In looking at some recent findings and problems I am bypassing various challenges to the notion of "Crusader art" that have been forthcoming since the 1970s in the work of Demus, Bulst, Belting, Mouriki, Cormack, and others, and to which I am attempting to respond in a separate study.[13] This paper proposes the notion that not only is there a Crusader iconography, but that it

---

[8] Ibid., xxxii–xxxiii.

[9] K. Weitzmann, "Thirteenth-Century Crusader Icons on Mount Sinai," *ArtB* 45 (1963), 179–203.

[10] Some of the icons Weitzmann discussed as comparanda had appeared in the publication by G. and M. Soteriou, Εἰκόνες τῆς Μονῆς Σινᾶ, 2 vols. (Athens, 1956 and

1958), but none of the ten icons newly associated with the Crusaders had been previously published.

[11] Weitzmann, "Crusader Icons" (as in note 9), 182.

[12] K. Weitzmann, *Illustrations in Roll and Codex* (Princeton, 1947).

[13] I am currently preparing an essay entitled, "What Is

goes beyond the examples analyzed by the "founding fathers" referred to above. Furthermore, this iconography in some instances seems to require new methods to resolve the problems of analysis and interpretation it presents.

Besides the pioneering work Kurt Weitzmann did on the icons, he also explored the notion of *loca sancta* iconography in Early Christian and Byzantine art,[14] a type of iconographic analysis which has proven to be extremely fruitful when applied to the art of the Crusaders. Indeed, it is possible to find an iconography of both *loca sancta* and *loca profana* in Crusader art as seen in coins, miniatures, and pilgrims' souvenirs.[15] Crusader coinage is unusual in the twelfth century because of the architectural iconography found on certain of its major royal issues.[16] The billon deniers of King Baldwin III with the "Tower of David," issued about 1152–53, and of King Amaury I with the Anastasis rotunda of the church of the Holy Sepulchre, which appeared about 1163, focus on the iconography of secular or religious structures that was politically important in their reigns.[17]

The church of the Holy Sepulchre was a pivotal Crusader building, of importance to many different groups in the Latin Kingdom. Pilgrims also sought its image on souvenirs, such as an ampulla now in Berlin, to be dated in the 1150s.[18] The representation of the church of the Holy Sepulchre on this ampulla is iconographically unique and up-to-date among extant Crusader imagery because it represents the Crusader building as very recently rebuilt, with its campanile in place.

The interest in the iconography of place shown by the Crusaders is remarkable and was clearly stimulated by the importance associated with the sites under their control. Furthermore, it extends beyond the confines of the Latin Kingdom and includes other areas, such as Antioch. In the 1260s, the illustrations for a *History of Outremer* manuscript clearly focused attention on the events of the First Crusade in Antioch by rendering a topographical "portrait" of the actual site.[19]

These examples document a special interest in the iconography of *loca sancta* and *loca profana* which is found throughout Crusader art. By themselves they do not define a unique "Crusader iconography," but as one component taken together with other iconographic developments they collectively represent a distinctive phenomenon that justifies this identification. It is possible to identify some of the other components.

Along with the iconography of sites and buildings, there are other examples of "imagery" that are not based on textual sources, but may, for example, be rooted in a culture of orality, and for which other modes of iconographic research and interpretation must be developed.[20] The south

---

Crusader Art?" in which I endeavor to discuss important aspects of the nature and development of the art of the Crusaders in light of recent attempts to redefine the phenomenon.

[14] K. Weitzmann, "*Loca Sancta* and the Representational Arts of Palestine," *DOP* 28 (1974), 31–55.

[15] I explored this topic in a preliminary paper given at the Byzantine Studies Conference at the University of Michigan, Ann Arbor, in 1994: *Abstracts*, 50.

[16] The iconography of imagery on medieval coins is a topic that has been largely ignored by numismatists and would benefit from study by art historians.

[17] J. Folda, *The Art of the Crusaders in the Holy Land, 1098–1187* (Cambridge, 1995), 289–90, 334–36.

[18] Ibid., 294. This ampulla was first published by L. Kötzsche, "Zwei Jerusalemer Pilgerampullen aus der Kreuzfahrerzeit," *Zeitschrift für Kunstgeschichte* 51 (1988), 13–32.

[19] J. Folda, "A Crusader Manuscript from Antioch," *Atti della Pontificia accademia romana di archeologia, Rendiconti* 42 (1969–70), 283–98.

[20] The Princeton symposium *Iconography at the Crossroads*, edited by Brendan Cassidy and published in 1993, included papers that commented on non-text based iconography such as we see here. See, e.g., the introduction by Brendan Cassidy, 3–15, and the article "Mouths and Meanings: Towards an Anti-Iconography of Medieval Art," by Michael Camille, 43–57, among others.

transept facade of the church of the Holy Sepulchre in Jerusalem constitutes one major example (Fig. 1). This facade, with its nonfigural sculpture, was designed by the Crusaders in the 1140s to be the main entrance to the newly rebuilt complex containing the prison of Christ, the hill of Calvary, and the aedicule of the Holy Sepulchre. The church was dedicated on 15 July 1149, and the facade, including the campanile, was finished in the 1150s.[21] This main entrance facade shows a program remarkable for its multicultural Christian diversity and content.

Several prominent features of its nonfigural decoration deserve to be examined: first, the Roman *spolia* which were reused and imitated by Crusader masons for the cornices of the first and second storeys (Fig. 2); second, the hood moldings over the arches of the paired main portals, which are derived from sculpture found on Syrian tomb monuments of the Early Christian period (Fig. 3); third, the capitals decorating the two portals and paired windows, based on Byzantine models (Fig. 4); fourth, the voussoirs of the broad Levantine pointed arches, presented as cushion-shaped godroons (Fig. 3), an arab architectural feature widespread in the Near East; and lastly, various abstract moldings with vegetal or foliate designs related to Romanesque architectural sculpture in the West (Fig. 5). Originally these elements formed a coherent secondary iconographic program of nonfigural architectural sculpture, along with the narrative figural decoration in the tympana, lintels, and spandrels that is no longer extant on the facade.[22] This program proclaimed certain important characteristics about the church of the Holy Sepulchre as a work of architecture at this holy site. It alluded, firstly, to the Roman origins of the church of the Holy Sepulchre at the time of Constantine in the early fourth century. As a second feature it used designs and types of sculptural decoration from Early Christian tomb monuments in the region to refer to the purpose of the building, to shelter the tomb of Christ. It also focused attention on the Byzantine Orthodox heritage of this church, which had been rebuilt by the emperor Constantine IX Monomachus in the 1040s, one hundred years prior to the Crusader renovations. Fourthly, it reflected the important Arab constituency among Christians in the Crusader States by including the striking godroons to emphasize the arches of the portals. And finally, it contained important examples of architectural sculptural designs inspired by contemporary work in Romanesque Europe, the ancestral home of many Crusaders. Furthermore, this ensemble, when taken together, appears to have a powerful message to announce to the Christian approaching this most holy site: to paraphrase the prophet Isaiah (Is. 56:7), this is a house of prayer for all Christian people!

The idea of an iconography of architecture, advocated by Richard Krautheimer in a famous article,[23] is hardly new, but an iconography of nonfigural architectural sculpture appears to be a different aspect of the problem. An iconographic analysis in this medium poses interesting difficulties; the "reading" of this kind of visual "text" also presents problems. The "language" of *spolia* needs to be understood; and the implications of the choice of certain types of voussoirs, capi-

---

[21] Folda, *Art of the Crusaders* (as in note 17), 177–245. The nonfigural program of the south transept facade is the subject of my article "The South Transept Facade of the Church of the Holy Sepulchre in Jerusalem: An Aspect of 'Rebuilding Jerusalem,'" in *The Crusades and Their Sources: Essays Presented to Bernard Hamilton*, ed. J. France and W. Zajac (Aldershot, 1998), 239–57.

[22] Of the figural decoration, only the lintels, currently in the Rockefeller Museum in Jerusalem, survive. The other figural components, mostly mosaics, are known only by mention in certain accounts of pilgrims to Jerusalem. See Folda, *Art of the Crusaders* (as in note 17), 240.

[23] R. Krautheimer, "Introduction to an 'Iconography of Mediaeval Architecture,'" *JWarb* 5 (1942), 1–33.

tals, and moldings for their meaning and content, without being able to interview the patrons or the masons who were responsible for devising and executing them, also need to be evaluated.

If this were an isolated example of nonfigural programmatic decoration, it would be tempting to remain skeptical about the existence of meaningful interpretative strategies at such a cultural and chronological distance. There is, however, another conspicuous ensemble found on the psalter of Queen Melisende (London, B.L., Ms. Egerton 1139), one of the most important twelfth-century manuscripts to have been executed in the scriptorium of the church of the Holy Sepulchre. The exterior of this codex was lavishly decorated on the front and back with ivory carvings that were inlaid with semiprecious stones, gilded, and richly painted in red, blue, green, and black.[24] The front cover (Fig. 6) contains figural and nonfigural decoration including medallions with scenes of the life of David in the Holy Land surrounded by images of the Psychomachia, appropriately represented as the battle between the Virtues and Vices. The back cover (Fig. 7) contains imagery of the six corporal works of mercy found in Matthew 25:35–36, represented by Crusader kings in regalia of mostly Byzantine type, with fighting animals and birds surrounding the medallions. The two covers are joined by a handsome silk spine (Fig. 8) embroidered with a complex cross pattern in silver threads, with tiny equal-armed crosses added in red, green, and blue silk.

Interpreting this decorative ensemble is challenging, but it can be pointed out that it unifies figural and nonfigural, that is, figurative imagery and purely symbolic cross elements. These three components symbolically represent a program enveloping the psalter and relating the Old Testament, the New Testament, and Crusader experience in a continuum relevant to Crusader royalty. The Crusader royal figures who are shown carrying out the works of mercy on the back cover are actively continuing the tradition of Christian kingship in the Holy Land established by Christ. He is symbolized by the "True Cross" imagery on the spine; he is descended from the royal house of David, author of the Psalms and ancestor of Jesus, who appears on the front cover.[25] This amalgamation of figural and nonfigural iconography in a programmatic relationship is a provocative example of complex meaning that may also be relevant for the architectural program discussed above. This is an approach to iconography in the Crusader East that is worth further investigation, both within the Holy Land and elsewhere.

The final example of Crusader art to be discussed here is a major altarpiece executed for the Carmelites on Cyprus sometime after 1287, probably about 1290 (Fig. 9).[26] The altarpiece with the golden Virgin was found in the church of St. Kassianos in Nicosia in modern times and is now in the Icon Museum of the Archbishop Makarios III Foundation in Nicosia. It is a work which qualifies as Crusader for several reasons. There is, firstly, a conjunction of styles, such as Byzantine for the enthroned Virgin, and Frankish for the miracle scenes and the Carmelites under the Virgin's cloak. It can also be described as Crusader because of the remarkable iconography of miracle scenes of the Virgin, which have Latin captions. It is a work "which would appeal to the tastes of a heterogeneous clientele including both Eastern and Western patrons and consumers."[27]

[24] Folda, *Art of the Crusaders* (as in note 17), 152–58 (with extensive bibliography); and B. Kuehnel, *Crusader Art of the Twelfth Century* (Berlin, 1994), 67–125.

[25] Folda, *Art of the Crusaders* (as in note 17), 158.

[26] D. T. Rice, *The Icons of Cyprus* (London, 1937), 48–51, 69, 187–89; D. Mouriki, "Thirteenth-Century Icon Painting in Cyprus," *The Griffon*, n.s., 1–2 (1985–86),

38–48; A. Papageorghiou, *Icons of Cyprus* (Nicosia, 1992), 46, 47, 51, pl. 31; J. Folda, "Crusader Art in the Kingdom of Cyprus, c. 1275–1291: Reflections on the State of the Question," in *Cyprus and the Crusades*, ed. N. Coureas and J. Riley-Smith (Nicosia, 1995), 216–22.

[27] Mouriki, "Thirteenth-Century Icon Painting" (as in note 26), 76–77.

The iconographic problems that this altarpiece presents are complex and in need of further investigation; it is also worth noting some of the questions it poses. It is clear that the large cult image of the golden Virgin in the center is related to the appearance of the golden Virgin in the scenes of the miracles along the sides. It seems that the central scene of the Virgin and Child appearing to and sheltering a group of Carmelites is actually the most important of the ensemble of miracle scenes. Furthermore, the diminutive inscription recently discovered at the lower right side of the large throne, although as yet undeciphered, appears to give the central scene an inscription paralleling the Latin captions to the sixteen miracle scenes on the sides. Although these miracle scenes have not yet been identified precisely, and no extant text of the miracles of the Virgin corresponds to this ensemble of images or their captions, the fact is that the content of the scenes parallels the fully developed tradition of miracles by the Virgin that we find, for example, in the *Cantigas* of Alfonso X El Sabio.[28] Indeed, with the exception of one small miracle scene in which the Carmelites appear—the third scene at the upper left—most of the scenes have generic parallels in the huge collection that forms the content of the *Cantigas*.[29] The argument is not that there is some direct relationship between the miracle scenes depicted on the Nicosia Carmelite altarpiece of ca. 1290 and in the *Cantigas* of ca. 1280, but that they share in a substantial tradition already well established by the late thirteenth century. It is significant to observe, moreover, that whereas the iconography of the miracles of the Virgin has traditionally been thought to have originated in Western medieval art, there is no iconographic tradition of the miracles of the Virgin in Byzantine art. One question posed by the Nicosia Virgin altarpiece has to do with the role of the art of the Crusaders in the development and enrichment of this tradition. The origin of the Carmelites in the Crusader East, the development of the order in the thirteenth century, their intense devotion to the Virgin, and their patronage of holy images of the Virgin and Child in the Latin Kingdom and on Cyprus are relevant and important to the investigation of this question.[30] This is another example of the parallel structure existing between Crusader works in the East and iconography in the Latin West, and where identification of local specifics, as yet not fully comprehended on the Nicosia altarpiece, will yield an understanding of what is distinctively Crusader about the Levantine examples.

CONCLUSIONS

The study of Crusader iconography has adopted many strategies of analysis and interpretation from other fields of Medieval art, especially Byzantine, Romanesque, and Gothic, because the

---

[28] J. G. Lovillo, *Las Cantigas: Estudio arqueológico de sus miniaturas* (Madrid, 1949). The date of the Escorial manuscript of the *Cantigas*, Ms. T-I-1, reproduced in Lovillo is ca. 1280, that is, shortly before the death of Alfonso in 1284.

[29] Consider the recognizable types of scenes such as the Virgin saving pilgrims in their ship at sea; the Virgin healing an infant, the blind or the lame; the Virgin resuscitating the dead; and the Virgin exorcising demons. These events are paralleled in general subject matter, but by no means in terms of the specific stories, iconographic detail, or style, in the *Cantigas*. See, e.g., Lovillo, *Cantigas*

(as in note 28), pl. 12 (Rescue at Sea), pls. 17 or 24 (Resuscitation of the Dead), pl. 25 (Infant Healed).

[30] It is interesting that one of the folios in the *Cantigas* with a narrative mini-cycle deals with the special holiness of images of the Virgin and Child that come from Jerusalem. See Lovillo, *Cantigas* (as in note 28), pl. 12. This work is discussed by M. Camille, *Gothic Art: Glorious Visions* (New York, 1996), 114–15, 118. The source of the Nicosia Virgin is thought to be Crusader Cyprus, but its exact origin and its important relationship to the Carmelites depicted on it are as yet not fully understood.

scholars who studied it were trained in those fields. These approaches have also changed and developed over time as iconographic research in the fields of Western Medieval and Byzantine art has evolved, to a large extent paralleling them, but in some aspects independent of them. The elemental components of Crusader iconography were largely derived from sources in Western and Byzantine medieval art, characteristics depending on the training of the various "Crusader" artists, but the content is frequently unique to the Crusader East. Not all aspects of iconography, and certainly not much in the way of iconology, such as Panofsky's "disguised symbolism," have been adopted for the study of Crusader art, either because of their lack of applicability or because the state of the question of the nature of Crusader art has not yet made certain iconographic/iconological perspectives very attractive. Because of the unique character of Crusader art, however, certain special cases of iconography have emerged. These examples challenge scholars to find new methods of iconographic research and new formulations of iconographic interpretation. Finally, in this study I have endeavored to compare the origins of the study of Crusader iconography with more recent problems that challenge scholars in the 1990s. This is only a selection of issues from a large agenda, which includes, among other perspectives, those of women's studies, the iconography of style, and the problem of iconography in an artistic "lingua franca."

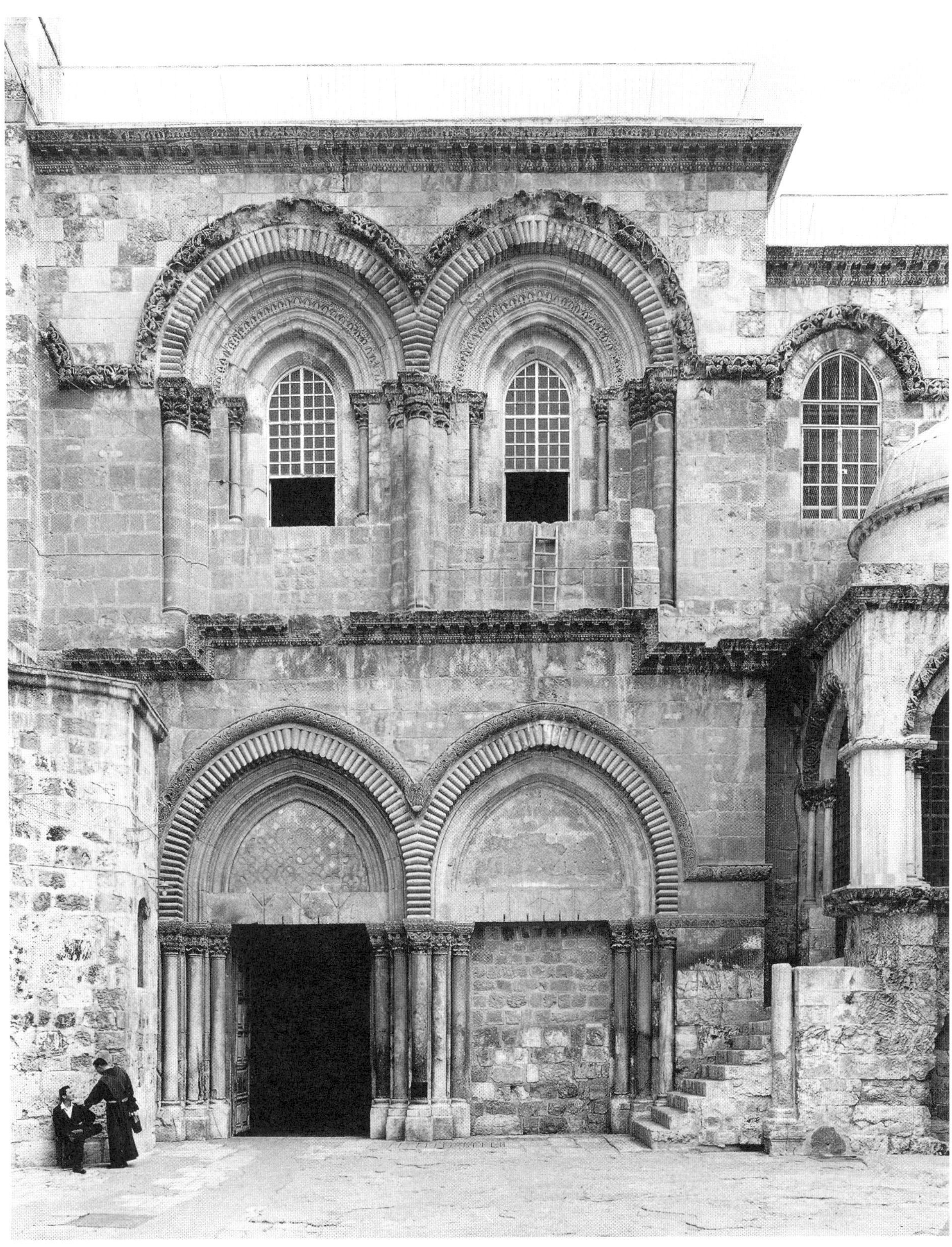

1. Jerusalem, Church of the Holy Sepulchre, south transept facade

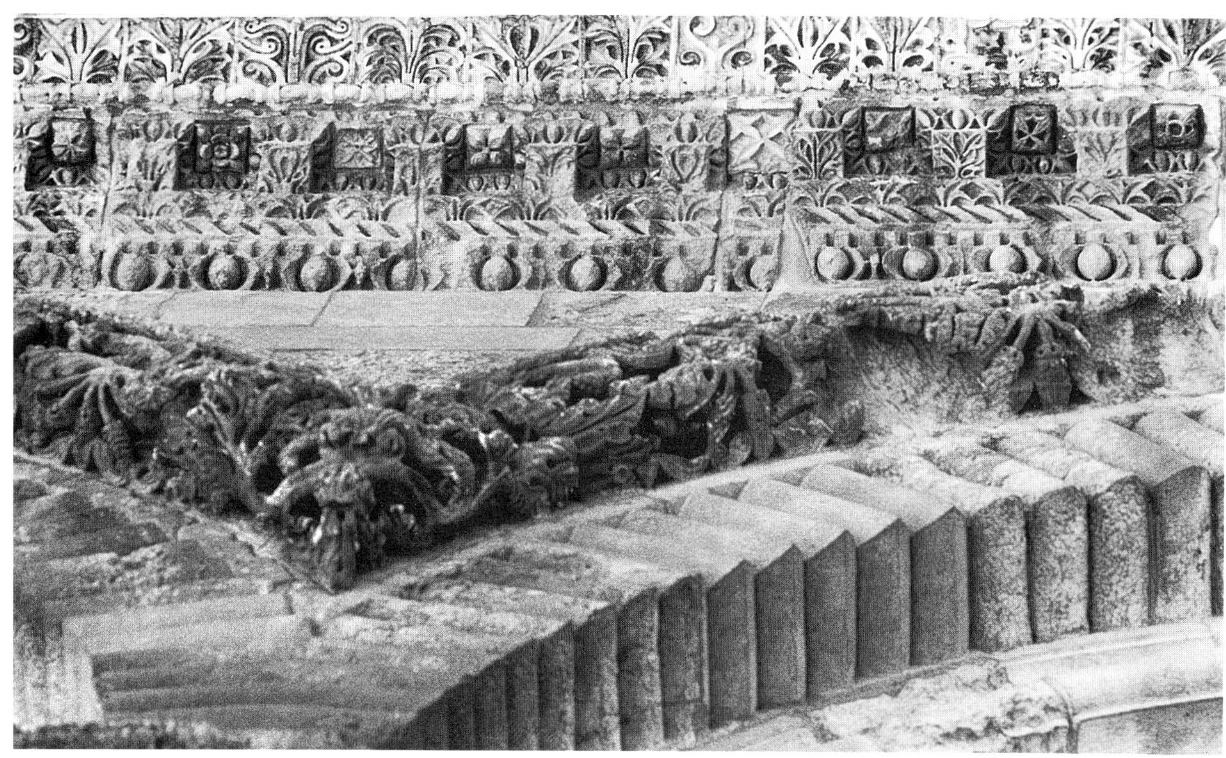

2. Jerusalem, Church of the Holy Sepulchre, upper cornice

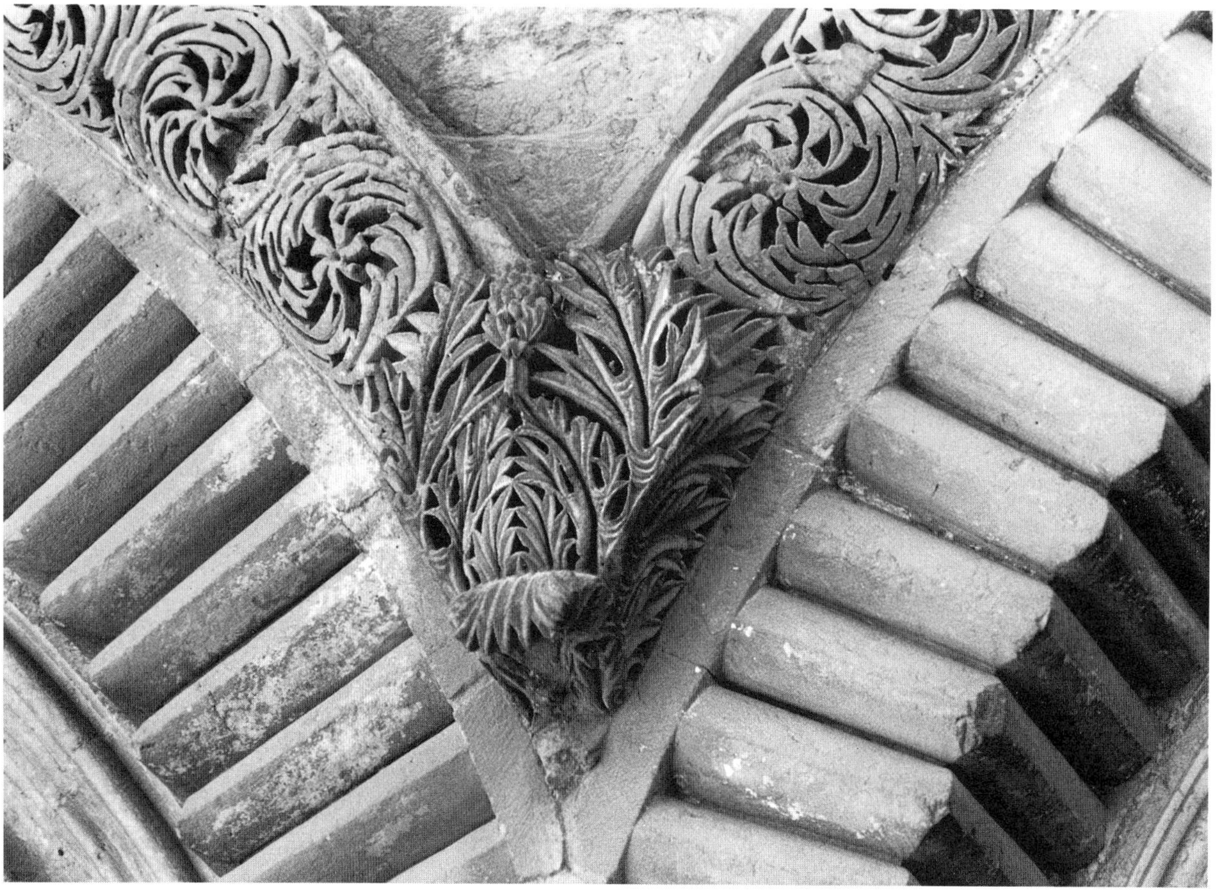

3. Jerusalem, Church of the Holy Sepulchre, hood molding and godroons over the lower portals

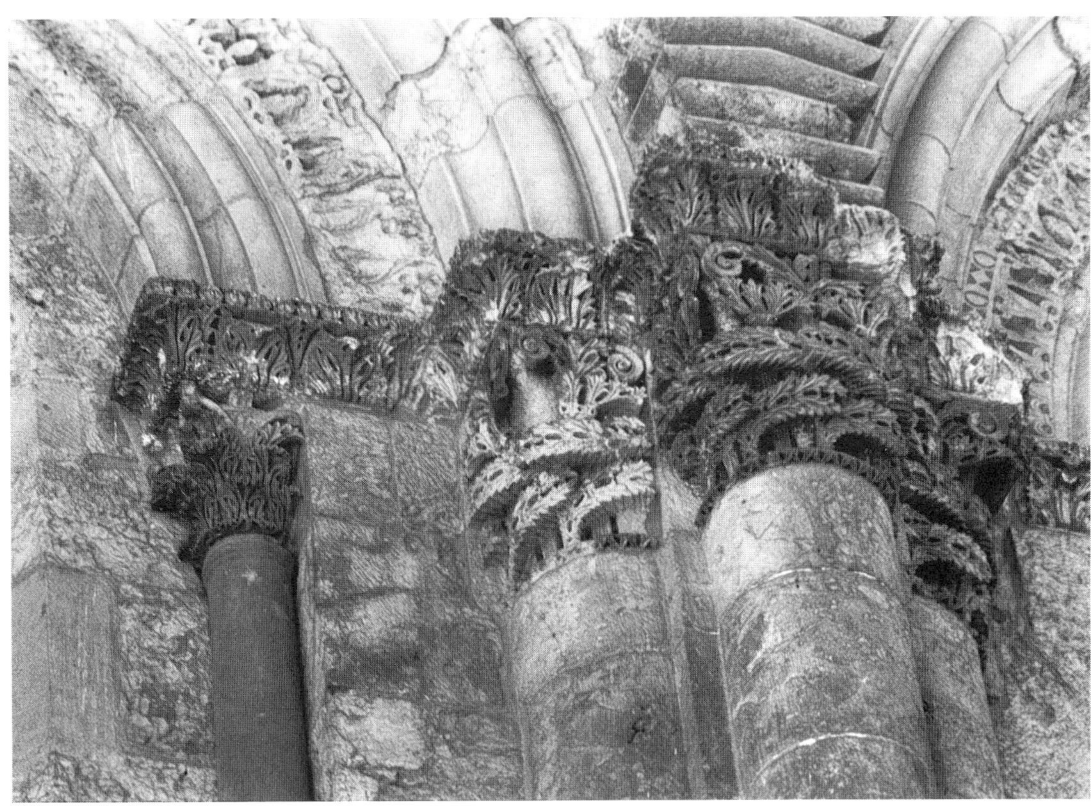

4. Jerusalem, Church of the Holy Sepulchre, capitals between the paired windows, second storey

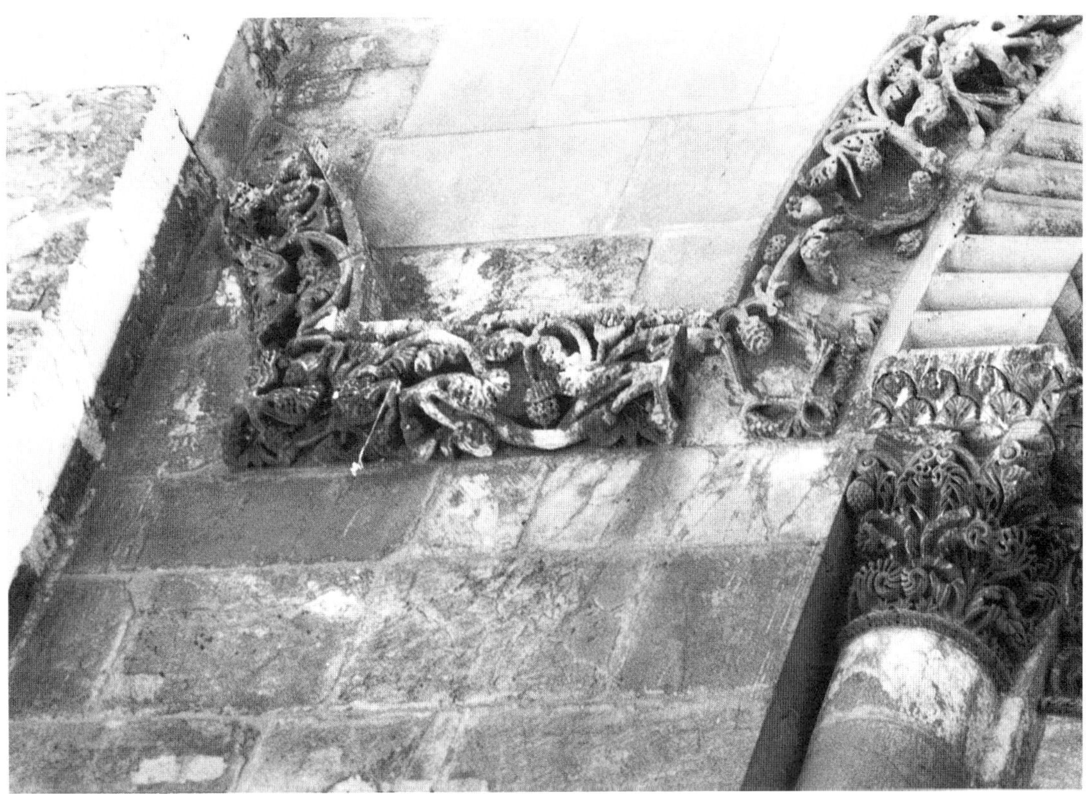

5. Jerusalem, Church of the Holy Sepulchre, frieze molding on the second storey

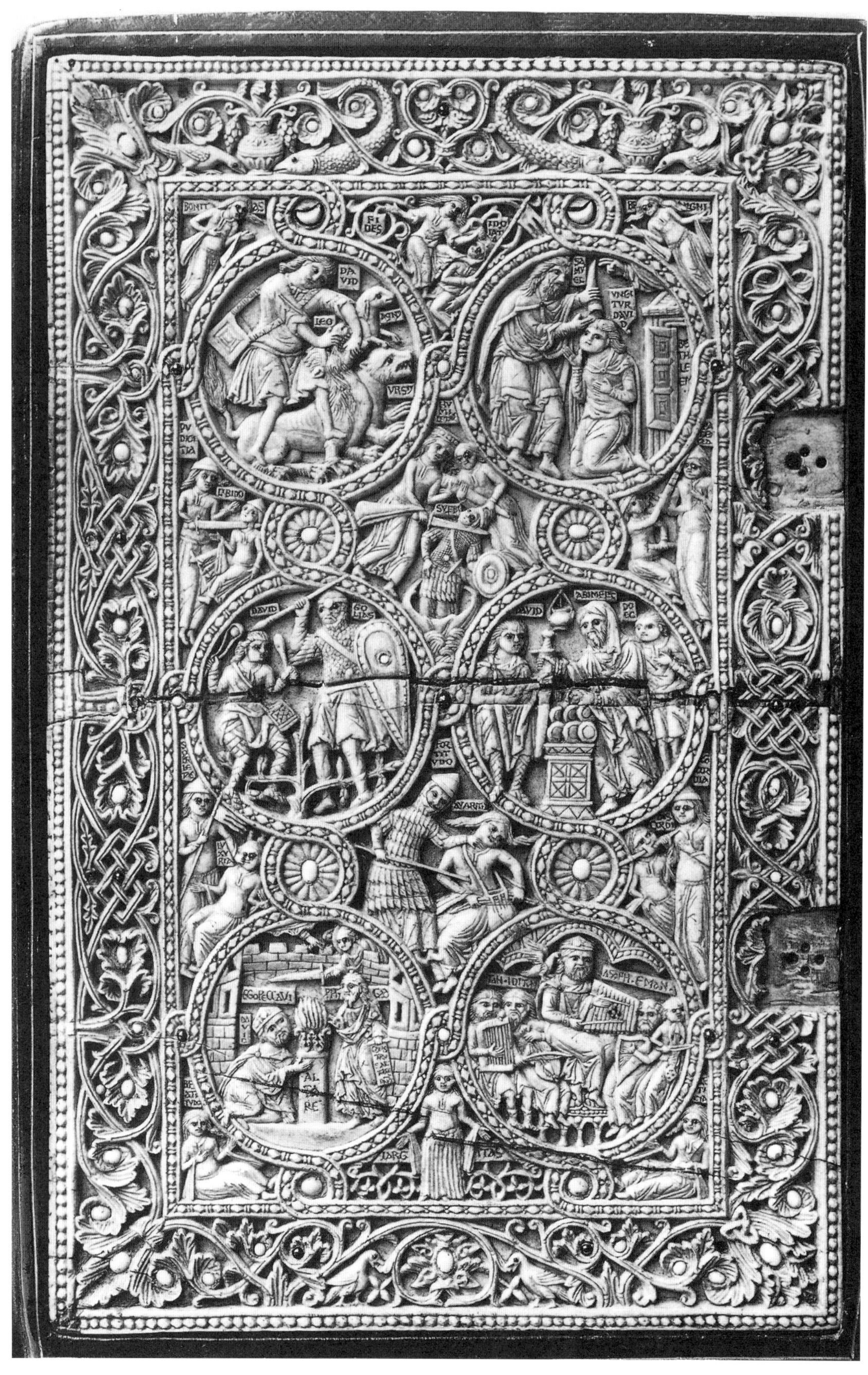

6. Psalter of Queen Melisende (London, British Library, Ms. Egerton 1139), front cover. Ivory carving with scenes of the life of David

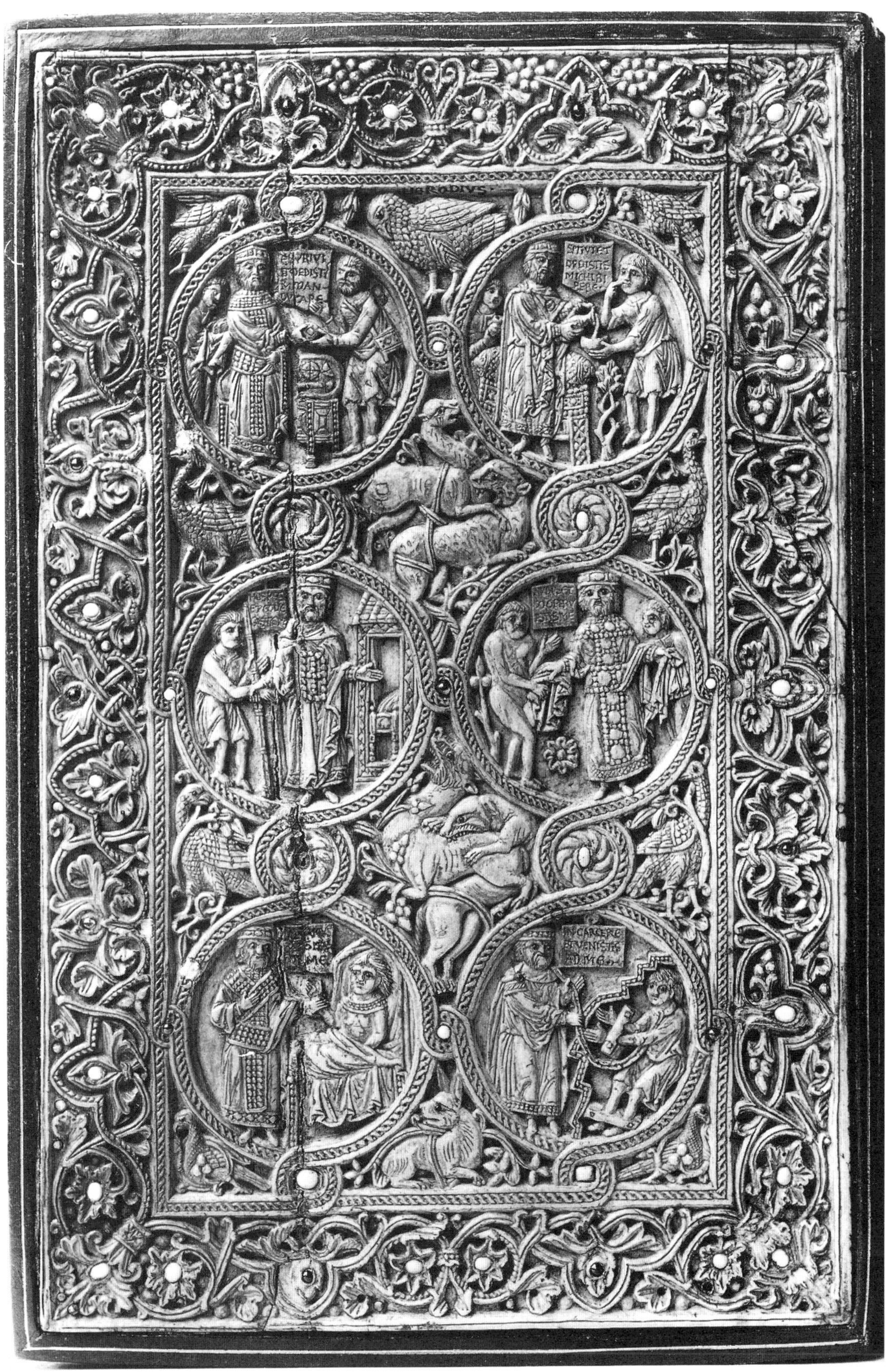

7. Psalter of Queen Melisende, back cover. Ivory carving with scenes of the corporal works of mercy

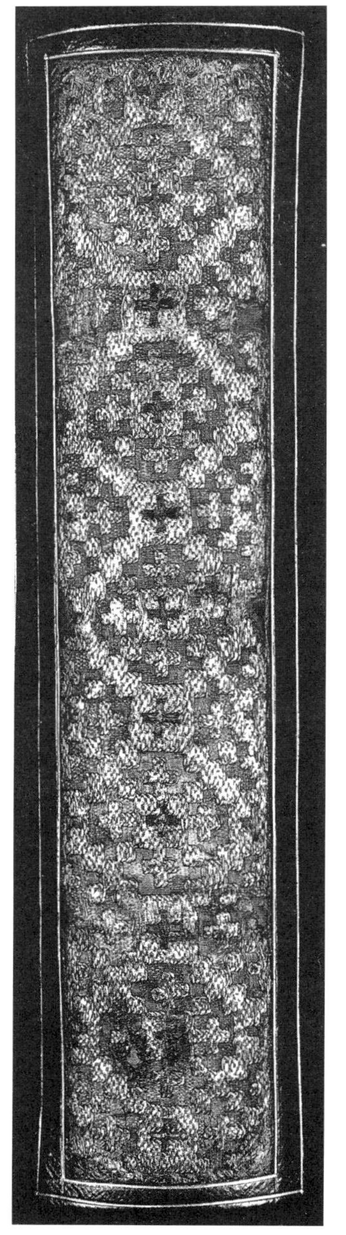

8. Psalter of Queen Melisende, spine. Embroidered silk with silk crosses in red, green, and blue

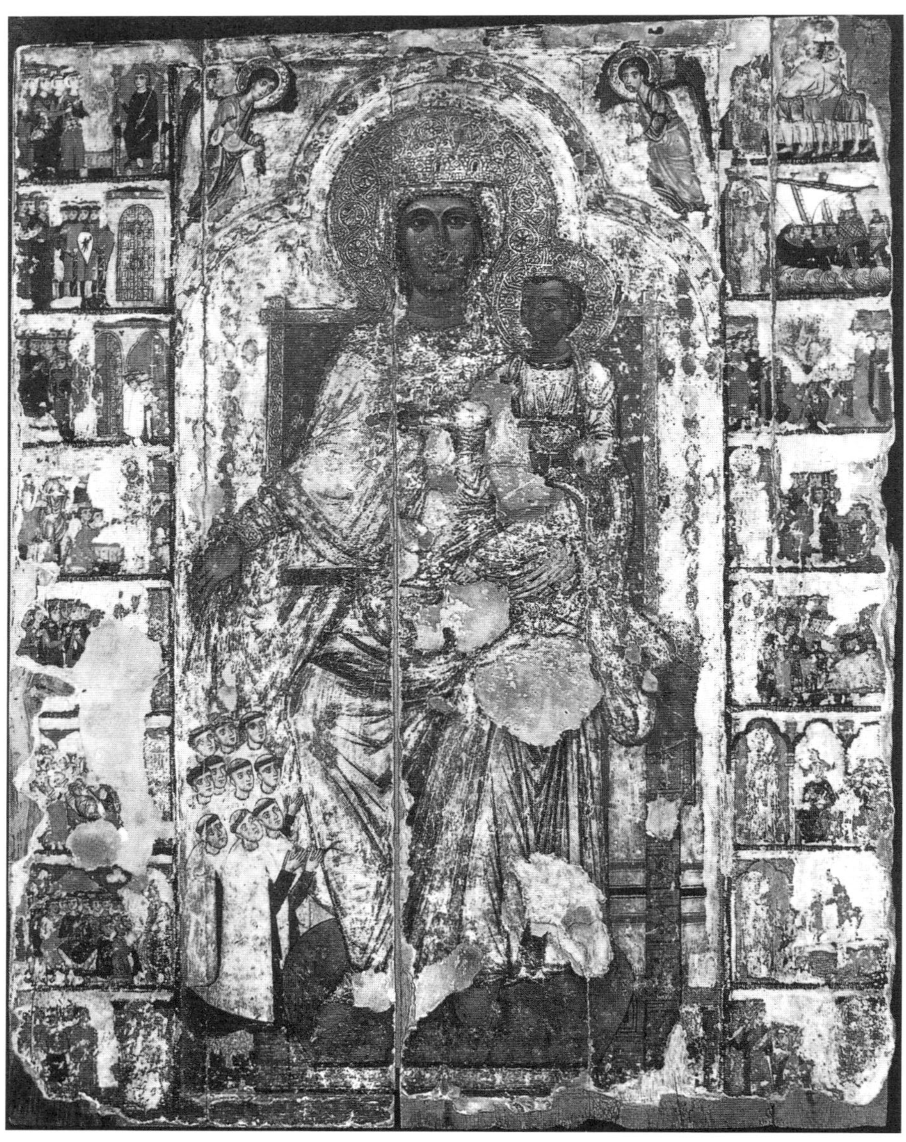

9. Nicosia, Archbishop Makarios III Foundation. Altarpiece of the Virgin and Child Enthroned with Carmelites and sixteen scenes of the miracles of the Virgin

The Iconography of Rejection:
Jews and Other Monstrous Races

·

D E B R A   H A S S I G

T HE MAJOR FOCUS of Ruth Mellinkoff's recent and important study, *Outcasts*, is devoted to the identification and discussion of a specific pictorial code common to later medieval representations of Jews.[1] In this study, Mellinkoff has assembled a rich vocabulary of visual signs that were consistently employed in works of art, especially in northern European painting of the twelfth through the fifteenth century. Besides the familiar pointed hats, these signs include physical distortions or deformities, red hair and ruddy skin, blemishes, badges, and the color yellow. In works of art that juxtapose Jews with other types of people, these signs effectively set the Jews apart from more acceptable social and religious types in a manner at once pejorative and theologically mandated. The imagery is pejorative because it depicts Jews as physically repellent, evil, and subnormal; the medieval theological characterization of Jews as the rejecters and murderers of God encouraged such representations. This was a visual system employed relentlessly in representations of Jews in all artistic media, both private and public, and formed part of a much larger propaganda campaign that helped fuel anti-Semitism all over Europe. The image of a bishop and king physically assaulting a grotesquely grimacing, deformed, dark-colored Jew in the Abingdon Apocalypse is indicative of the level of hostility that this visual expression was capable of reaching, as well as the intense social conflict between medieval Christians and Jews (Fig. 1).[2]

But in addition to the specific signs, such as pointed hats, that lent a decidedly pejorative cast to medieval images of Jews in certain contexts, might there be a more general pictorial code that underlies not only representations of Jews, but also other members of the medieval underclass as well as their ideological parallels? I propose that a general visual code expressive of sin, evil, barbarity, and subhumanity does exist, and that it is firmly grounded in ideas and traditions inherited from antiquity. I would further suggest that ancient principles related to both the universe and the human body informed medieval personifications of sin and evil, ultimately providing a kind of blueprint for images of Jews and other rejected social groups. I am defining the term "rejected so-

---

[1] R. Mellinkoff, *Outcasts: Signs of Otherness in Northern European Art of the Late Middle Ages,* 2 vols. (Berkeley, 1993).

[2] See S. Lewis, "Giles de Bridport and the Abingdon Apocalypse," in *England in the Thirteenth Century,* ed. W. M. Ormrod (Woodbridge, 1986), 116–17; and N. Roth, "Bishops and Jews in the Middle Ages," *The Catholic Historical Review* 80, no. 1 (1994), 1–17. The literature on medieval Christian-Jew social relations is vast: see especially J. Cohen, *The Friars and the Jews: The Evolution of Medieval Anti-Judaism* (Ithaca, 1982); K. R. Stow, *Alienated Minority: The Jews of Medieval Latin Europe* (Cambridge, Mass., 1993); and A. C. Gow, *The Red Jews: Anti-Semitism in an Apocalyptic Age, 1200–1600* (Leiden, 1995).

cial groups" rather broadly, in order to encompass constituencies both real and imaginary. Therefore, consideration will extend to images of not only Jews and other living outcasts, but also to demons and the enigmatic Monstrous Races.

By connecting medieval pictorial representations to classical ideological principles, I also hope to show how the latter were reworked, updated, and harnessed in order to conceptually isolate and denigrate selected social groups. In other words, the dichotomy of "us" versus "them" developed in classical literature and medieval theological tracts was emphatically reinforced and further developed in medieval works of art by means of a recognizable pictorial code. This code is a largely semiotic one, and is not limited to specific attributes, such as exotic headgear and badges, but also involves careful manipulation of line, color, directionality, relative positioning, opposition, and repetition. This essay is a preliminary attempt to draw attention to this code in selected examples of later medieval painting in England, where Jewish-Christian relations were especially tense.[3]

Important ideological principles informing medieval representations of social subordinates were derived from classical astrological and physiological beliefs. According to ancient thought, climate, time of birth, balance of bodily fluids, and physical appearance were related to each other, and, if properly interpreted, could be used to gauge a person's moral character. The effects of climate were analyzed according to the doctrine of influence of the environment, which states that the location of the environment determines the celestial influences to which the body occupying it is exposed and therefore the constitution of that body.[4] This relationship between the macrocosm of the universe and the microcosm of the human body is economically depicted in later medieval images of the zodiac man, such as the famous example in the early fifteenth-century *Très Riches Heures*, which visually coordinates gender, the various parts of the body, and the four bodily humors to astrological influences, climatic conditions, the four cardinal directions, and the four elements.[5]

During the Middle Ages, climatic theory took on social as well as physical significance. According to Galen, one's physical constitution determined moral aptitudes, and moral aptitudes determined behavior.[6] Therefore, amount of sunshine, wind and storms, proximity to mountains (altitude), air quality, and soil quality were all crucial in determining a person's moral character. In the thirteenth century, these considerations informed Thomas Aquinas's discussion of a suitable site for a city. For example, Aquinas maintained that a temperate climate is very advantageous to war and beneficial to political life, and that the quality of air has a direct effect on civil harmony

---

[3] For an excellent summary of scholarly views on the social and economic position of English Jews during this period, see P. R. Hyams, "The Jews in Medieval England, 1066–1290," in *England and Germany in the High Middle Ages*, ed. A. Haverkamp and H. Vollrath (Oxford, 1996), 173–92. I would like to thank Matt Strickland for bringing this article to my attention. See also H. G. Richardson, *The English Jewry under Angevin Kings* (London, 1960).

[4] M. J. Tooley, "Bodin and the Medieval Theory of Climate," *Speculum* 28 (1953), 68.

[5] Chantilly, Musée Condé, Ms. 65, f. 14v (reproduced in M. Meiss, *The Très Riches Heures of Jean, Duke of Berry* [New York, 1969], pl. 14). See also H. Bober, "The Zodiacal Miniature of the *Très Riches Heures* of the Duke of Berry," *JWarb* 11 (1948), 1–34. On the relationship between astrology and medicine, see T. S. Barton, *Power and Knowledge: Astrology, Physiognomics, and Medicine* (Ann Arbor, 1994); and C. Rawcliffe, *Medicine and Society in Later Medieval England* (Stroud, 1995), 82–104.

[6] Tooley, "Medieval Theory of Climate" (as in note 4), 68; Barton, *Power and Knowledge* (as in note 5), 97. Hippocrates was the first to discuss the physiological and moral effects of the physical environment, in *Airs, Waters, Places* (in *Hippocrates*, vol. 1, trans. W. H. S. Jones [London, 1923]), on which Galen wrote a commentary. See A. Wasserstein, *Galen on Airs, Waters, Places in the Hebrew Translation of Solomon Ha-Me'atti* (Jerusalem, 1982).

and the individual health and robustness of the citizens. Conversely, a city built in a climate too hot or too cold will be necessarily inhabited by citizens who are weak, ill-formed, and morally deficient.[7] Earlier, in the twelfth century, Gerald of Wales in his *Topographia Hibernica* and *Descriptio Kambriae* had used both climatic and sociological considerations to explain the different characters of the Germans, English, and Welsh;[8] and in the fourteenth century, the author of the *Travels* of Sir John Mandeville attributed the wanderlust of the English and the sedentary nature of the Indians to contrasting climatic and planetary influences.[9]

Climatic theory worked hand-in-hand with physiological beliefs concerning the makeup of the human body, codified in the humoral system, also of ancient Greek origin and the foundation of medieval medicine.[10] Humoral theory states that the body is composed of four humors: blood, black bile, yellow bile, and phlegm, and that these are associated with conditions of hot, dry, cold, and moist. The balance of humors is controlled in part by a person's astrological connections, which are also coordinated with the different parts of the body, as illustrated in the zodiac man images. Imbalances of the humors result in certain types of character—sanguine, phlegmatic, choleric, or melancholic—and balance can be restored by ingesting certain foods and herbs. This is why instructions in medieval herbals and *tacuina sanitatis* inevitably describe a given plant in humoral terms and coordinate it with the four seasons in order to determine the time of ingestion that will maximize its health benefits.[11]

The results of combining the implications of climatic, humoral, and astrological theories were certain generalizations concerning what people were like, depending on what part of the world they lived in.[12] For example, it was asserted that in the north the air is cold and dry, yielding people who are physically vigorous: tall, strong, broad, and long-lived; in reaction to the cold, they produce a lot of internal heat, which means they have big appetites and rapid digestion. Their coloring is fair, the texture of their skin and hair is fine, and their voices are soft and deep in tone owing to the effect of dampness on the throat. As a result of their hot blood, they have energy, confidence, assertiveness, impatience, and magnanimity, but are greedy for honor and power. They are great fighters and brave; because of their overabundance of blood they do not fear wounds. By contrast, in the south, people are small and feeble, of weak digestion and small appetite because the sun dissipates their vital forces. The sun draws the blood to the surface and darkens the skin, and in the far south, the extreme heat blackens and coarsens the skin and dries and frizzles the hair. These thin-blooded southerners are timid, vengeful, and cruel, but because their spirits are unimpeded they are characterized by fine impressions and speculative acuteness, so they excel in the sciences, especially the occult, religion, and liberal arts.

---

[7] *De regimine principum* I–II (*On the Government of Rulers: De Regimine Principum*, trans. J. M. Blythe [Philadelphia, 1997], 104–8).

[8] R. Bartlett, *Gerald of Wales, 1146–1223* (Oxford, 1982), 201–4. See especially *Topographia Hibernica* 71 and *Descriptio Kambriae* 165 and 192–93 (Giraldus Cambrensis, *Opera*, 8 vols., ed. J. F. Dimock, Rolls Series, vols. 5 (London, 1867 [*Top. hib.*]) and 6 (London, 1868 [*Desc. Kamb.*]).

[9] *The Travels of Sir John Mandeville*, trans. C. W. R. D. Moseley (New York, 1983), 120.

[10] Galen, *Quod animi mores corporis temperiem sequuntur*, ed. K. G. Kühn (Leipzig, 1822). On the humoral system, see R. Klibansky, E. Panofsky, and F. Saxl, *Saturn and Melancholy* (New York, 1964), 1–14; and Rawcliffe, *Medicine and Society* (as in note 5), 29–57.

[11] See F. J. Anderson, *An Illustrated History of the Herbals* (New York, 1977); W. Blunt and S. Raphael, *The Illustrated Herbal* (New York, 1979); and L. Cogliati Arano, *The Medieval Health Handbook: Tacuinum Sanitatis* (New York, 1976).

[12] This paragraph is summarized from Tooley, "Medieval Theory of Climate" (as in note 4), 73–75.

In the temperate (middle) regions, one finds the better-balanced choleric and sanguine types because the temperature conserves the heat of the body without preventing the evaporation of surplus moisture. According to Aristotle, the northern races are naturally independent but undisciplined; the southern races are intelligent but slothful, and thus the predestined subjects of tyrants; while those in the middle zones have enough energy and intelligence to rule not only themselves but others.[13] It is no coincidence that Aristotle, along with other Greeks, lived in the temperate zone. In fact, medieval ethnocentricity was grounded in such ancient Greek thought, which provided a set of criteria against which to measure all other cultures, with the virtual guarantee that outsiders would come up short.[14] During the later Middle Ages, however, the desirable regions had been extended from around the Mediterranean to somewhat farther north.

The next step in understanding the relationship between the body and character, after climatic, humoral, and astrological considerations, has to do with viewing the outward form of the body as a "map" of inner character according to the ancient pseudo-science of physiognomy, credited to Hippocrates.[15] Basic physiognomical principles and their applications are known from several surviving treatises, the earliest being pseudo-Aristotle's *Physiognomonica* (Φυσιογνωμονικά), composed during the third century B.C.[16] Other writers, most notably Polemo, further expanded this system, which found both medical and political applications.[17]

Physiognomical theory rests on the acceptance of two basic principles. The first of these asserts that mental disposition follows bodily characteristics, and the second, that the body suffers with affectations of the soul. Hence, a person's character may be determined by observing the following physical signs: movements and gestures; color of skin, hair, and eyes; characteristic facial expressions; growth of hair, skin texture, and voice; condition of the flesh, proportions of parts of the body, and the build of the body as a whole. In other words, the system is a semiotic one, in that parts of the body are read as signs of inner character, including courage, cowardice, good disposition, dullness of sense, shamelessness, well-ordered behavior, high spirits, low spirits, effeminate nature, harshness, hot temper, gentle disposition, meanness of spirit, gambling instincts, abusiveness, compassion, gluttony, lasciviousness, and good memory.[18]

For example, according to pseudo-Aristotle, signs of courage include coarse hair; upright carriage of the body; size and strength in bones, sides, and extremities; a broad and flat stomach; sturdy (but not overly fleshy) neck; a gleaming eye; dry skin; and sharp forehead.[19] Conversely, small bodies are a sign of small-mindedness;[20] swarthiness or dark skin indicates a coward, as does extremely wooly hair, as in the case of Egyptians and Ethiopians.[21] That this last principle has ob-

[13] *Politics* VII.vii; in *Aristotle*, 23 vols., ed. H. Rackham, rev. ed. (Cambridge, Mass., 1990), vol. 21.

[14] On Greek ethnocentricity, see E. Hall, *Inventing the Barbarian: Greek Self-Definition through Tragedy* (Oxford, 1989); and R. Garland, *The Eye of the Beholder: Deformity and Disability in the Graeco-Roman World* (Ithaca, 1995).

[15] See E. C. Evans, "Physiognomics in the Roman Empire," *Classical Journal* 45 (1949), 277–82; and *Physiognomics in the Ancient World* (Transactions of the American Philosophical Society, n.s., vol. 59, pt. 5) (Philadelphia, 1969); Barton, *Power and Knowledge* (as in note 5), 95–101.

[16] Pseudo-Aristotle, *Physiognomonica*, in *Scriptores Physiognomonici Graeci et Latini*, 2 vols., ed. R. Foerster (Leipzig, 1893), vol. 1, 1–91.

[17] On Polemo's political use of physiognomical theory, see E. C. Evans, "The Study of Physiognomy in the Second Century A.D.," *Transactions of the American Philological Association* 42 (1941), 96–108; and Barton, *Power and Knowledge* (as in note 5), 113–30, 174.

[18] Evans, *Physiognomics in the Ancient World* (as in note 15), 8.

[19] *Physiognomonica* 807a–b (ed. Foerster [as in note 16], vol. 1, 26–27).

[20] *Physiognomonica* 808a (ed. Foerster [as in note 16], vol. 1, 36–37).

[21] *Physiognomonica* 812a–b (ed. Foerster [as in note 16], vol. 1, 72–81).

viously negative implications for the intelligence and character of black Africans, among others, is no accident: according to climatic and astrological theories, ideal human types are found in western Europe—not in Africa, India, the Near East, or the far north.

In medieval art, two related applications of physiognomical theory are observable, one theological, the other social. The theological application is the better known and more easily recognizable. Holy persons, such as Christ, the Virgin, and the saints, are consistently depicted in medieval art with the physiognomical attributes of the virtuous: well-proportioned (if slightly elongated) bodies, serene expressions, elegant gestures, fair skin, smooth hair, and smooth complexions. As Mellinkoff has systematically discussed, theologically evil figures, namely Christ's tormentors, display the physiognomical signs of vice. These normally include ill-proportioned bodies, contorted postures, and ugly facial features which might include bulging or crossed eyes; large, pointy, or bulbous noses; mouths with fleshy lips; pointy or missing teeth; grotesque expressions; ruddy or dark skin; and facial blemishes. The contrast between the two theological types may be easily observed in numerous Passion cycle images, in which the physical form of Christ exemplifies that of the virtuous, while that of his tormentors are pictures of evil and vice (Figs. 2, 3).

In this type of image, a figure's degree of virtue or vice can actually be read from his external physical form, in keeping with basic physiognomical principles. In an image from the Salvin Hours (Fig. 2), Christ stands before Caiaphas as a beautifully serene, pale, dignified, and well-proportioned figure, whose physical form contrasts sharply with that of both Caiaphas and the arresting soldier, whose dark skins and grotesque physiognomy reveal their moral degeneracy. In the scene of the betrayal and arrest of Christ from the Chichester Missal (Fig. 3), virtuous types include not only Christ but also St. Peter, shown striking off Malchus's ear. Judas is an interesting case: physiognomically, he must be categorized as the virtuous type, doubtless owing to his status as an apostle. Mellinkoff has pointed to his red hair—a trait shared by some of the tormentors in this same image, including Malchus—as the only physical indicator of his evil character.[22] In other words, in the Chichester image the artist has effectively characterized Judas as a borderline case from the moral point of view by rendering the figure using the semiotic elements of both good and evil.

The same physiognomical principles are also applicable to images of angels and demons. Although these are imaginary beings, they exhibit the same basic oppositional types of human physiognomy that signify virtue and vice. For example, to the left of Christ in the famous Last Judgment tympanum of St. Lazarus at Autun, the stooped angel's elongated, elegant body is accentuated by his flowing robe, serene facial features, smooth hair, and dainty hands.[23] The angel's overall physical type stands in direct opposition to that of the demon grasping the scales, with his sinewy, skeletal body, contorted facial features, fierce expression, open mouth, bared teeth, and deformed limbs. As in images of Christ and his tormentors, the angel's physical form is expressive of virtue while the demon's form is evocative of sin.

Representations of angels and demons pose an interesting conceptual problem, especially given that, according to medieval theological belief, angels were incorporeal.[24] The devil, on the other hand, was believed to take on different physical manifestations as required to better deceive

<hr>

[22] Mellinkoff, *Outcasts* (as in note 1), vol. 1, 151.

[23] Reproduced in D. Grivot and G. Zarnecki, *Gislebertus: Sculptor of Autun* (New York, 1961), pls. A and J.

[24] That angels were incorporeal, and that their visual representations should be interpreted allegorically is emphasized in the *Celestial Hierarchy* 137A–140B, 328A–336C (*Pseudo-Dionysius: The Complete Works*, trans. C. Luibheid [New York, 1987], 147–49, 182–88).

humans.[25] To aid popular understanding of these often difficult theological concepts, medieval artists assigned angels and demons characteristic forms in representations that functioned as visual metaphors for their respective spiritual roles. Certain pictorial oppositions were consistently applied, such as dark demonic versus light angelic coloring,[26] and emphatic demonic physicality, with carefully rendered bones and musculature (Figs. 4, 8, 10), versus the sylphic elongation that suggests angelic incorporeality.

Another striking physiognomical contrast may be observed between representations of Christ and the devil, especially in temptation imagery. The image of the third temptation from a mid-eleventh-century Anglo-Saxon psalter juxtaposes a well-formed, tall Christ with dignified, calm expression, delicately expressive hands, and clad in long robes, with the squat, clawed, hook-nosed demon with disproportionately large head and pointed knees, wearing only a loincloth.[27] An equally striking physiognomical contrast may be observed in a twelfth-century stained glass panel from Troyes Cathedral, today in the Victoria and Albert Museum (Fig. 4). In this image, in addition to his bestial distortion, nudity, and mostly green coloration,[28] the devil's pronounced musculature and disturbing head-dragons serve to further emphasize Christ's serene, well-coifed, well-proportioned, light-skinned, ethereal beauty. Like the angels, the devil also sports wings, but they are in the wrong places, as if a parody, sprouting from his wrists, ankles, and backside. The image fulfills its purpose well, which is to contrast not just the external appearance of Christ and the devil, but also Christ's holy virtue with the devil's monstrous vice.

Physiognomical theory also had its social applications. The belief that sin manifested itself in the form of deformity and disease helped justify the ostracization of diseased, lame, and misshapen people.[29] Leprosy was a particular focus for this type of moral interpretation.[30] That is, according to medieval thought, the diseased and deformed on the one hand were to be pitied, but on the other, their fate was deserved: God had stricken them to make some sort of cosmic point. This belief is manifest most clearly in the stories of Christ's healing miracles, as well as those of the saints, in which the lame and diseased are cured and made visually "whole" as the result of their spiritual excellence. A pair of images in the early fifteenth-century Rohan Hours shows Moses "cursing" the lame and deformed, those with noses too big or too small or too crooked, the blind, those with dropsy, those with bleary or filmy eyes, the eunuchs, and the lunatics (f. 223v).[31] The reason for their ostracization is explained in the image and moralization on the facing folio (Fig. 5).

---

[25] On the physical manifestations of demons, see J. B. Russell, *Lucifer: The Devil in the Middle Ages* (Ithaca, 1984), 67, 132–33.

[26] On popular colors for the devil in medieval art, see Russell, *Lucifer* (as in note 25), 133, n. 12. See also note 28 below.

[27] London, B.L., Ms. Cot. Tib. C.VI, f. 10v. See F. Wormald, "An English Eleventh-Century Psalter with Pictures, British Library, Cotton Ms. Tiberius C.VI," *Walpole Society* 38 (1962), 1–13; reprinted in *Collected Writings*, 2 vols., ed. J. J. G. Alexander et al. (London, 1984), vol. 1, 123–37.

[28] See D. W. Robertson, Jr., "Why the Devil Wears Green," *Modern Language Notes* 69 (1954), 470–72.

[29] Rawcliffe, *Medicine and Society* (as in note 5), 1–28; Garland, *Eye of the Beholder* (as in note 14), 60–70. From antiquity and continuing well beyond the Renaissance, there were proponents of the belief that "monstrous births" were the result of the imagination—and sins—of the parents, especially the mother. See M.-H. Huet, *Monstrous Imagination* (Cambridge, Mass., 1993), 16–31.

[30] M. Barber, "Lepers, Jews and Moslems: The Plot to Overthrow Christendom in 1321," *History* 66 (1981), 14–15. Leprosy is interpreted as a sign of wickedness, and the Fall is described as the point at which "man was spiritually made a leper" in the *Gesta romanorum*, chap. 151 (ed. H. Oesterley [Hildesheim, 1963], 507–9). See also P. Richards, *The Medieval Leper and His Northern Heirs* (London, 1977).

[31] Reproduced in M. Meiss, *The Rohan Master: A Book of Hours* (New York, 1973), pl. 106.

Here it is stated that of these physical ailments, imperfections, or deformities are actually moral blemishes which mark those afflicted as the devil's prey. The cripple, upon whose shoulders a devil has fastened himself, represents the person who has become rich by dishonest means; the blind man is someone who doesn't understand divine teaching; the deaf man is one who refuses to listen to the Gospel. The man with a skin disease is likened to a usurer; the man with dropsy signifies a glutton; the rheumy-eyed man is a lecher.[32] Thus, it is implied that the lame and diseased were socially outcast with justification, owing to their own moral shortcomings.

In another very prominent social or sociological application of physiognomical theory, certain physical characteristics ascribed to holy persons were also transferred to portraits of the nobility, in order to flatter wealthy patrons but also to visually differentiate the upper and lower classes. For example, representations of Geoffrey Luttrell, patron of the well-known Luttrell Psalter, may be contrasted with those of his indentured servants.[33] Geoffrey and members of his family have the elongated, elegant, well-proportioned bodies of the virtuous, with smooth hair and dressed in their finery, while his servants, shown performing various agricultural activities and domestic chores, are short, squat, with bent bodies, dark skin, grotesque expressions, and frizzled hair. At some point, the idea of virtue and social status merged, as if part of the definition of nobility involved virtuous character. In all likelihood, this idea was developed in order to defend the status quo, by implying that those with wealth deserved it owing to their superior moral fiber.

Physiognomical theory carried to its logical extreme explained the physical forms of the Monstrous Races, fabulous peoples believed to inhabit the fringes of the known world.[34] These Races were described and cataloged by classical writers such as Pliny and later by medieval authors, including Isidore of Seville and the authors of the eighth-century *Liber monstrorum* and Anglo-Saxon *Marvels of the East*.[35] Texts and images pertaining to the Monstrous Races show very clearly the confluence of physiognomical and climatic/humoral/astrological theories, through their combination of physical deformity and inhospitable locations. That is, the Monstrous Races were believed to dwell in those geographical locations considered otherwise uninhabitable, such as mountains, the torrid equatorial zone, the far north, and the mysterious Antipodes.[36] Given the relationship between climate and physiology, it follows that the inhabitants of such inclement regions would be physically abnormal, even grossly deformed.

The tiny *mappa mundi* included in a thirteenth-century English psalter situates various Monstrous Races along the dangerous and climatically disadvantageous periphery (Fig. 6), often char-

<hr>

[32] For the text, see Meiss, *Rohan Master* (as in note 31), commentary on pl. 107.

[33] London, B.L., Add. Ms. 42130. Geoffrey Luttrell is depicted on ff. 202v and 208r. There are numerous depictions of his servants in both domestic and agricultural activities; see especially ff. 172v and 173r. For color reproductions, see J. Backhouse, *The Luttrell Psalter* (London, 1989), pls. 1, 25, 26, 48.

[34] The seminal study on the medieval Monstrous Races is J. B. Friedman, *The Monstrous Races in Medieval Art and Thought* (Cambridge, Mass., 1981).

[35] For a thorough summary of the medieval sources, see S. Zajadacz-Hastenrath, "Fabelwesen," in *Reallexikon*

zur deutschen Kunstgeschichte, vol. 6 (1973), 742–48. See also Isidore of Seville, *Etymologiae* XI.3 (PL 82:419B–24B); *Liber Monstrorum*, ed. F. Porsia (Bari, 1976); M. R. James, *Marvels of the East* (Oxford, 1929); and *An Eleventh-Century Miscellany*, ed. P. McGurk, et al. (Baltimore, 1985) (facsimile of London, B.L., Ms. Cot. Tib. B.V). For the text and English translation of both the *Marvels of the East* and the *Liber monstrorum*, see also A. Orchard, *Pride and Prodigies: Studies in the Monsters of the Beowulf-Manuscript* (Woodbridge, 1995).

[36] On the controversy surrounding the Antipodes, see V. Flint, "Monsters and the Antipodes in the Early Middle Ages and Enlightenment," *Viator* 15 (1984), 65–80.

acterized as a torrid or uninhabitable southern region on climatic zone maps.[37] The Races themselves, some representative members of which are depicted on a folio from the thirteenth-century
Douce 88 bestiary, exhibit all manner of physical deformities (Fig. 7). Descriptions of the various
Races and their habits reveal consistently fearsome, aggressive, murderous, and sometimes canni-
balistic tendencies, although a few were noted for their chronic shyness or cowardice. While I have
not attempted a one-to-one match-up between particular physical deformities and ancient Greek
physiognomical readings thereof, the general principal linking deformity to moral shortcoming in
the form of various sins clearly emerges in medieval commentary on the Monstrous Races, such as
that found in the *Gesta romanorum* and in the commentary on Thomas de Cantimpré's book of
monsters, *De monstruosis hominibus.*[38] Just a few examples will demonstrate the pattern. The Blemmyae, who lacks a head and whose face is therefore on his chest, was interpreted by medieval
moralists as the embodiment of greed or gluttony.[39] The centaur is an adulterer, and the dog-
headed Cynocephalus is a slanderer. The one-legged Sciopod is compared to the recluse who for-
gets his earlier vows and relies on his carelessness, with which he covers himself.[40] According to the
text that accompanies the images in Douce 88, the Panotii use their giant ears to hear evil, the
barking Cynocephalus is a nay-sayer, the Giant is a figure of pride, and the Amyctyrae—with his ab-
normally large lower lip—is a mischievous person.[41]

From a social and ethnic point of view, the Monstrous Races were an important vehicle for
clarifying definitions of civilization and humanity, again, largely through the application of principles inherited from classical thought. That is, characteristics common to many of the Monstrous
Races, such as living outside cities, going about naked, eating strange diets (including human flesh
and each other), and speaking incomprehensively or not at all, corresponded with ancient Greek
notions of the barbarian—defined basically as all non-Greeks—who were also considered uncivi-
lized and often inhuman.[42] It is probably no coincidence, therefore, that from the medieval Christian point of view, Jews shared many traits in common with the Monstrous Races: living outside of
cities (in ghettos), strange dress and dietary restrictions, incomprehensible speech (Hebrew),
even physical deformity, according to the prevailing belief that Jews concealed tails, horns, and
other physical abnormalities.[43]

Like images of the Monstrous Races, the salient feature of demons is physical deformity and
bestiality expressed in visually similar ways, through the use of open forms, hybrid structure, su-

[37] See, for example, Los Angeles, J. Paul Getty Museum, Ms. Ludwig XV 4, f. 177v (reproduced in A. von
Euw and J. M. Plotzek, *Die Handschriften der Sammlung
Ludwig*, vol. 4 [Cologne, 1985], unnumbered plate [mis-
foliated as 177r]).

[38] *Gesta romanorum*, chap. 175 (ed. Oesterley [as in
note 30], 575); *Eine altfranzösische moralisierend Bearbeit-
ung des Liber de monstruosis hominibus orientis aus Thomas
von Cantimpré, De naturis rerum*, ed. A. Hilka (Berlin,
1933).

[39] Much later, the Blemmyae was interpreted as a
"stomach servant" (*Bauchdiener*) by Johannes Praetorius
(*Anthropodemus plutonicus, das ist eine neue Weltbeschreibung*
[Magdeburg, 1667], 381). According to the *Gesta romanorum*, the headless Blemmyae is a figure of humility (as
above, note 38).

[40] See *Liber de monstruosis*, ed. Hilka (as in note 38), 25,
lines 31–46 (centaur); 36, lines 485–92 (Cynocephalus);
43, lines 777–86 (Sciopod). See also E. J. Beer, *Die Rose der
Kathedrale von Lausanne und der kosmologische Bilderkreis des
Mittelalters* (Bern, 1952), 25–26.

[41] Oxford, Bodl., Ms. Douce 88, f. 69v.

[42] See W. R. Jones, "The Image of the Barbarian in Medieval Europe," *Comparative Studies in Society and History* 13
(1971), 376–407; B. Laurot, "Idéaux grecs et barbarie
chez Hérodote," *Ktema* 6 (1981), 39–48; F. Hartog, *The
Mirror of Herodotus: The Representation of the Other in the
Writing of History*, trans. J. Lloyd (Berkeley, 1988), 212–59;
and Hall, *Inventing the Barbarian* (as in note 14), 1–17.

[43] See J. Trachtenberg, *The Devil and the Jews* (New York,
1961), 44–53; and R. Mellinkoff, *The Horned Moses in Medieval Art and Thought* (Berkeley and Los Angeles, 1970).

pernumerary body parts, and grotesque physiognomy. Hence, demons in the extensive pictorial series included in a fifteenth-century French manuscript copy of a treatise on hell, Antichrist, and the end of the world, consistently sport multiple heads, scaly bodies, claws, tails, fangs, and additional faces on their bellies, elbows, and knees (Fig. 8). They are dark-colored and monstrous in overall aspect. The Monstrous Races are also characterized as bestial hybrids of various types, and although generally not as threatening as demons, are fully monstrous by means of grotesque distortions and excessive openness of form, mainly through an emphasis on or displacement of their various orifices.[44] The Blemmyai from a fifteenth-century manuscript copy of the *Travels* of Sir John Mandeville are especially monstrous primarily because they lack heads, one of the proposed locations of the human soul and a primary sign of humanity (Fig. 9).[45] It is also true that devils are sometimes depicted with their heads on their chests as an especially emphatic form of demonic monstrosity (Fig. 8).

From a medieval Christian point of view, darkness, openness, physical distortion, and grotesque physiognomy are visual signs of distance from God. These principles are well demonstrated in images of the Fall of the Rebel Angels, such as that depicted on a leaf of the Psalter of William de Brailes (Fig. 10). In this image, the angels' fall from grace is expressed in physiognomical terms, whereby the farther from heaven the figures are located, the darker and more distorted their faces and bodies become. In the famous image of the Fall of Lucifer in the Caedmon manuscript, Lucifer transforms from the image of a bright angel in the top register to the dark Satan as he tumbles into hell in the lower register.[46] The change in Lucifer's external form from brightness to the dark grotesqueness that identifies him as Satan is referred to repeatedly in the text of the accompanying Anglo-Saxon poem, *Christ and Satan*, which is a detailed chronicle of Lucifer's fall from heaven and its consequences for humanity.[47] The angels falling from heaven in the De Brailes Psalter leaf also take on the distorted and darkened physical forms of the damned as they move away from the closed, perfect circle of heaven toward the open maw of hell (Fig. 10).

According to medieval Christian belief, demons and Jews shared a conceptual distance from God. The demons suffered their distance owing to their excessive pride,[48] while the Jews achieved theirs following their refusal to accept Christ. Concomitantly, Jews were "demonized" in medieval society, and were accused of kidnaping and murdering Christian children, poisoning wells, and desecrating the Eucharist and holy images.[49] Pictorial representations of Jews and demons in ca-

[44] For analysis of monstrous forms, see D. Williams, *Deformed Discourse: The Function of the Monster in Mediaeval Thought and Literature* (Montreal, 1996), 107–76.

[45] On varying opinion concerning the location of the soul, see Evans, *Physiognomics in the Ancient World* (as in note 15), 25; and M.-C. Pouchelle, *The Body and Surgery in the Middle Ages*, trans. R. Morris (New Brunswick, 1990). In addition, a creature without a head lacks one of the four chief organs by which to identify a human being, namely a brain. The other three humanity-defining organs are the heart, liver, and testicles, at least according to Alfred of England or of Sareshal in *De motu cordis* 16.1 (ed. C. Baeumker, *Beiträge zur Geschichte der Philosophie des Mittelalters* 23 [1923], 85–86).

[46] Oxford, Bodl., Ms. Junius 11, p. 3 (reproduced in A. G. Hassall and W. O. Hassall, *Treasures from the Bodleian Library* [London, 1976], pl. 4).

[47] *Christ and Satan*, in *The Caedmon Poems*, trans. C. W. Kennedy (Gloucester, Mass., 1965), 151, 152, 159, 169.

[48] In *Christ and Satan*, the fallen angels are said to have lost the radiant light of God owing to their intense pride (trans. Kennedy [as in note 47], 151). The inscriptions accompanying the image of the Fall of Lucifer in the mid-twelfth-century *Hortus deliciarum* (f. 3v) identify pride as the cause of his fall, and the image features physiognomical distortion similar to that found in the Caedmon manuscript (R. Green et al., *Hortus deliciarum*, 2 vols. [London, 1979], vol. 1, 90; vol. 2, pl. 2). See also Russell, *Lucifer* (as in note 25), 173–76.

[49] Trachtenberg, *Devil and the Jews* (as in note 43), 97–155.

hoots suggest common moral corruption, and such ideas and imagery helped justify the social reality of discrimination against Jews, even in areas where Jews were considered a necessary evil as
financiers and as conversion targets. That is, the conversion of the Jews was a prerequisite for the
Second Coming of Christ, and so the Jews were converted, sometimes forcibly.[50] In the meanwhile,
medieval Christians saw unconverted or apostate Jews as Christ-killers, heretics, usurers, and idol-
worshipers.[51] Jews sometimes lived in separate sections of town or in ghettos, and by law wore stig-
matizing signifiers, such as pointed hats and badges, that often made their way into medieval imagery.[52]

In a well-known English drawing from a thirteenth-century Jewish Receipt Roll, Isaac of Norwich is pictured as the triple-faced Antichrist in league with demons (Fig. 11).[53] In this image, the
Jews and the demons share not only similar activities, but also similar physiognomical appearance.
In this same vein, it may also be noted that the facial features of the Troyes devil discussed above
include the familiar hooked nose of the Jews (Fig. 4). In the Norwich image, through relative
placement, it is implied that both demons and Jews delight in sin, corruption, and in harming others, and their family resemblance further suggests they are cut from the same cloth. It is also true
that in many other contexts Jews wearing pointed hats and exhibiting stereotypically distorted
physiognomy feature as charter citizens in medieval representations of hell.[54]

Most importantly, like demons, the Jews were rejected by God. This last belief probably lies behind the sentiment expressed by St. John Chrysostom, who indicated that because God hates the
Jews, it is the duty of Christians to hate them, too.[55] According to Christian belief, just as demons
were cast out of heaven, the Jews were barred from entering it, as graphically depicted in the commentary image from the Abingdon Apocalypse (Fig. 1).

Not surprisingly, there are also visual parallels between renderings of Jews and the Monstrous
Races. Both are associated with sin and evil expressed visually as physical deformity. The Jews were
guilty of the sin of rejecting and murdering God, while the Monstrous Races were viewed during
the Middle Ages as signs and embodiments of sin, and had specific negative theological associa-

[50] R. C. Stacey, "The Conversion of Jews to Christianity in Thirteenth-Century England," *Speculum* 67 (1992), 263–83.

[51] L. F. Donald, "Thirteen London Jews and Conversion to Christianity: Problems of Apostasy in the 1280s," *Bulletin of the Institute of Historical Research* 45, no. 112 (1972), 214–29; J. Cohen, "The Jews as the Killers of Christ in the Latin Tradition, From Augustine to the Friars," *Traditio* 39 (1983), 1–27.

[52] A. Cutler, "Innocent III and the Distinctive Clothing of Jews and Muslims," in *Studies in Medieval Culture III*, ed. J. R. Sommerfeldt (Kalamazoo, 1970), 92–116. For a summary of the relationship between the social position of Jews and pejorative medieval imagery, see H. Kraus, *The Living Theatre of Medieval Art* (London, 1967), 139–62.

[53] For a comprehensive analysis of this image, see F. Felsenstein, *Anti-Semitic Stereotypes: A Paradigm of Otherness in English Popular Culture, 1660–1830* (Baltimore, 1995), 27–29.

[54] Three examples will have to represent a much larger group: (1) the cauldron inscribed *Judei* full of bearded Jews wearing tall, funnel caps in the four-register depiction of hell in the *Hortus deliciarum* (f. 254v; Green et al., *Hortus Deliciarum* [as in note 48], vol. 1, 220; vol. 2, pl. 146, 438); (2) in a two-register psalter depiction of heaven and hell, a hellmouth engulfing a cauldron containing at front and center a Jew wearing the *pileum cornutum* and a large moneybag around his neck (N. France, late thirteenth century; London, B.L., Add. Ms. 17868, f. 31r); and (3) in a late thirteenth-century English copy of Guillaume le Clerc's *Bestiaire* (Paris, B.N.F., Ms. fr. 14969, f. 9r, reproduced in Mellinkoff, *Outcasts* [as in note 1], vol. 2, III.121), a hellmouth filled with bearded Jews wearing pointed caps, engulfed in flames and administered by a demon.

[55] See John Chrysostom, *Homilia adversus Judaeos*, Homily 1 (PG 48:843–856; trans. in W. A. Meeks and R. L. Wilken, *Jews and Christians in Antioch in the First Four Centuries of the Common Era* [Missoula, 1978], 83–104); and J. W. Parkes, *The Conflict of the Church and the Synagogue: A Study in the Origins of Anti-Semitism* (New York, 1985), 163–66.

tions, as outlined above. In a multivalent image of Christ's suffering in the Khludov Psalter, Christ is surrounded by dogheads, thus imputing to a Monstrous Race the historical sin of the Jews, while simultaneously defining the Jews as monstrous (Fig. 12).[56] The group portrait of a Giant, a tiny Pygmy, a one-legged Sciopod, and a caveful of Bragmanni from the Westminster Abbey Bestiary is a particularly interesting confluence of physical deformity and sinfulness, given that both the Giant and Sciopod are wearing the pointed *Judenhut* (Fig. 13). In addition, the Giant, belonging to a race interpreted as wholly evil,[57] has the three faces that often characterize images of the Antichrist (Fig. 11),[58] which adds another layer of meaning and functions as still another visual signifier of inhumanity and godlessness. Such an image also likely alludes to the prophesied alliance of the Jews with the Antichrist at the end of time.[59]

Medieval artists were able to marshal classical ideas about physiognomy and morality to form precise visual representations of Christian evil in the form of devils, who represent evil incarnate, and the Monstrous Races, who signify various sins as well as aspects of the foreign, the unknown, and the inhuman. The same visual principles also served the Christian effort to condemn actual living social groups, most notably the Jews, in a very powerful and public propaganda campaign that ran parallel to the *adversus Judaeos* literary tradition popular at this same time.[60] The campaign was successful in that the negative imagery reinforced theological condemnation, fueled social hatred, and helped perpetuate accusations leveled against Jews of desecration of Christian churches and images, ritual murder, and demonic alliances.

Physiognomical theory and its concomitant negative theological associations ultimately helped justify Christian oppression and hatred of not only the Jews, but also of other non-Christian groups, such as the Muslims or "Saracens," and added to the fervor of war waged in the Holy Land against the heathen. Like the Jews, the Muslims were "demonized"; for example, Eulogius of Córdoba referred to Mohammed as an "angel of Satan and precursor of the Antichrist," the same type of language used to describe Jews.[61] Like the Jews, and in spite of their monotheism, Muslims were considered heretics, idolaters, and "equally detestable" enemies of God.[62]

[56] The dog aspect of the iconography also has a scriptural basis (Ps. 21:17). See J. H. Marrow, "'Circumdederunt Me Canes Multi': Christ's Tormentors in Northern European Art of the Late Middle Ages and Early Renaissance," *ArtB* 59 (1977), 167–81; and G. Dagron, "Image de bête ou image de Dieu: La physiognomie animale dans la tradition grecque et ses avatars byzantins," in *Poikilia: Études offertes à Jean-Pierre Vernant* (Paris, 1987), 76–77. In addition to denigrating the Jews, the Khludov Psalter image expresses anti-Iconoclast sentiment and is also a visual reference to Byzantine mime performances. See K. Corrigan, *Visual Polemics in the Ninth-Century Byzantine Psalters* (Cambridge, 1992), 49; and "The 'Jewish Satyr' in the Ninth-Century Byzantine Psalters," in *Proceedings of the Delphi Conference on Hellenic and Jewish Arts* (Tel Aviv, 1997), 351–68. I would like to thank Kathleen Corrigan for allowing me to see the latter article prior to its publication.

[57] The Giants are described as evil in Genesis 6:1–7. See W. E. Stephens, "'De Historia Gigantum': Theological Anthropology before Rabelais," *Traditio* 40 (1984), 47–57; and *Giants in Those Days: Folklore, Ancient History, and Nationalism* (Lincoln, 1989), 66–76.

[58] On the triple-faced Antichrist, see R. M. Wright, *Art and Antichrist in Medieval Europe* (New York, 1995), 95–97.

[59] On the alleged alliance of the Jews and Antichrist, see R. Emmerson, *Antichrist in the Middle Ages* (Seattle, 1981), 46, 79–83, 217; and Gow, *Red Jews* (as in note 2), chap. 5, "The Medieval Antichrist and His Jewish Henchmen," 93–130.

[60] W. A. Lukyn, *Adversus Judaeos: A Bird's-Eye View of Christian Apologiae until the Renaissance* (Cambridge, 1935).

[61] "... angelum Satanae et praevium Antichristi" (*Memorialis sanctorum* I.6; PL 115:744C). On the demonization of the Muslims, see H. Backes, "Teufel, Götter, und Heiden in gestlicher Ritterdichtung," in *Die Mächte des Guten und Bösen*, ed. A. Zimmermann (Berlin, 1977), 417–41; and Russell, *Lucifer* (as in note 25), 83–84.

[62] *The Ecclesiastical History of Oderic Vitalis*, ed. and trans. M. Chibnall (Oxford, 1975), 44. Peter the Venerable labeled the Muslims heretics, pagans, and demons (*Liber contra sectam sive hæresim saracenorum* D180rs; see also *Summa totius hæresis saracenorum*, both trans. J. Kritzeck, in *Peter the Venerable and Islam* (Princeton, 1964), 227,

The image that likely represents Saladin fighting against Richard Lionheart in the Luttrell Psalter depicts Saladin as dark-colored, with grotesque physiognomical features (Fig. 14). Interestingly, these same visual principles have been applied to the heraldic profile image of the Ethiopian shown on Saladin's shield. The darkness and physiognomical features of the Ethiopian on the shield might be interpreted as naturalistic features of a black African, until one remembers that during the Middle Ages, "Ethiopia" was more of an idea than a place.[63] In medieval thought, "Ethiopia" basically signified Elsewhere, and Elsewhere was inevitably an exotic and fearful place inhabited by inhuman barbarians, whether the Monstrous Races or some living constituency. With this in mind, Saladin's shield emblem functions as an additional reference to his own barbarity. In addition, the dark coloration of both Saladin and the heraldic face on his shield is in keeping with the medieval association of darkness—especially the color black—with evil, and with the devil in particular.[64]

On a broader level, similar visual renderings of different types of social outcasts support the theological tendency to categorize them all as one great group of heretics or collectively as the enemies of Christianity, as demonstrated recently by Elizabeth Pastan in her analysis of stained glass imagery of Jews at Troyes Cathedral.[65] That is, demons, monsters, Jews, Muslims, Ethiopians, and other rejected groups, by virtue of physical signs well-understood by contemporary observers, shared the common qualities of sinfulness and godlessness. Because all of them rejected God, they were themselves rightfully rejected by all faithful Christians.

Resulting from this common conception of non-Christian groups are combinations of their individual pictorial features. For example, a marginal image from the thirteenth-century Rutland Psalter depicts a white Sciopod and a dark blue Blemmyae.[66] The latter combines Blemmyae features—no head, with face on the chest—with the physiognomy of the medieval Ethiopian, thus neatly denigrating two outcast groups for the price of one.

The Rutland Psalter also includes an especially effective visual confluence of notions of Jewishness, heresy, monstrosity, and the demonic (Fig. 15). At the top of the folio containing the text of Psalms 19 and 20, a demon with a delighted grimace sits holding a filigree scepter. Below, a monstrous hybrid with dragon body and human head, as well as the grotesque physiognomy, long beard, and pointed cap of a Jew, is shown spewing what must be filigree blasphemy. The pious

---

204–11. On Muslim and Jewish idolatry, see M. Camille, *The Gothic Idol: Ideology and Image-Making in Medieval Art* (Cambridge, 1989), 129–94; and N. Daniel, *Islam and the West: The Making of an Image* (Edinburgh, 1962), 309–13. On medieval Christian attempts to discredit both Mohammed and Islam, see Daniel, 47–78.

[63] On the medieval idea of Ethiopia, see J. K. Wright, *The Geographical Lore of the Time of the Crusades: A Study in the History of Medieval Science and Tradition in Western Europe* (New York, 1965), 302–4; and J. M. Courtès, "The Theme of 'Ethiopia' and 'Ethiopians' in Patristic Literature," in J. Devisse, *The Image of the Black in Western Art*, vol. 2, *From the Early Christian Era to the "Age of Discovery,"* pt. 1, *From the Demonic Threat to the Incarnation of Sainthood*, trans. W. G. Ryan (New York, 1979), 9–32.

[64] Owing to associations between the color black and evil, the black Ethiopians receive negative treatment in the writings of the Fathers, who often identify them with sinners or demons. See, for example, Ambrose, *De Noe* (PL 14:436D–438A); Tertullian, *De spectaculis* III (PL 1:709A–B); and Hincmar, *De praedestinatione* (PL 125:278C). See also Devisse, *Image of the Black* (as in note 63), 13–21. On the colors of the devil, see note 26 above.

[65] E. C. Pastan, "Tam Haereticus quam Judaeos: Shifting Symbols in the Glazing of Troyes Cathedral," *Word and Image* 10/1 (1994), 66–83.

[66] London, B.L., Add. Ms. 62925, f. 87v (reproduced in E. Millar, *The Rutland Psalter* [Oxford, 1937] [facsimile]; and M. Camille, *Image on the Edge* [London, 1992], fig. 6).

figure in the initial shows the conceptual position of the good Christian, threatened by the devil on one side, and the enemies of the Church on the other. This interpretation of the imagery is reinforced by the Psalms text on the facing folio: "Let thy hand be found by all thy enemies: let thy right hand find out all them that hate thee. Thou shalt make them as an oven of fire, in the time of thy anger: the Lord shall trouble them in his wrath, and fire shall devour them" (Ps. 20:9–10).

This system of pejorative representation was such a powerful one that it continued to do service well beyond the medieval period, as Ruth Mellinkoff has so compellingly demonstrated in her recent study. Northern painting of the Renaissance period is an especially good witness to the tradition, as observable in *Christ Mocked* by Hieronymus Bosch (Fig. 16). In Bosch's painting, the serene, white, smooth, well-proportioned, beautiful yet sad countenance of Christ contrasts with the livid, grotesque and grimacing faces of his tormentors. The figure closest to Christ, squinting menacingly, wears a dog collar; the figure in the left foreground, with straggly beard and prominent hooked nose, wears a star and Islamic crescent on the end of his headdress.[67] By now, Bosch was inheritor of an effective visual code, developed and perfected by medieval artists and used for centuries to express notions of evil and social rejection. As long as the Jews and other heretics remained the enemies of Christianity, that code would retain its power.

[67] For description and excellent color reproduction, see J. Dunkerton et al., *Giotto to Dürer: Early Renaissance Painting in The National Gallery* (London, 1991), 348–49. On the dog-collared tormentor, see Marrow, "Circumdederunt Me Canes" (as in note 56), 178.

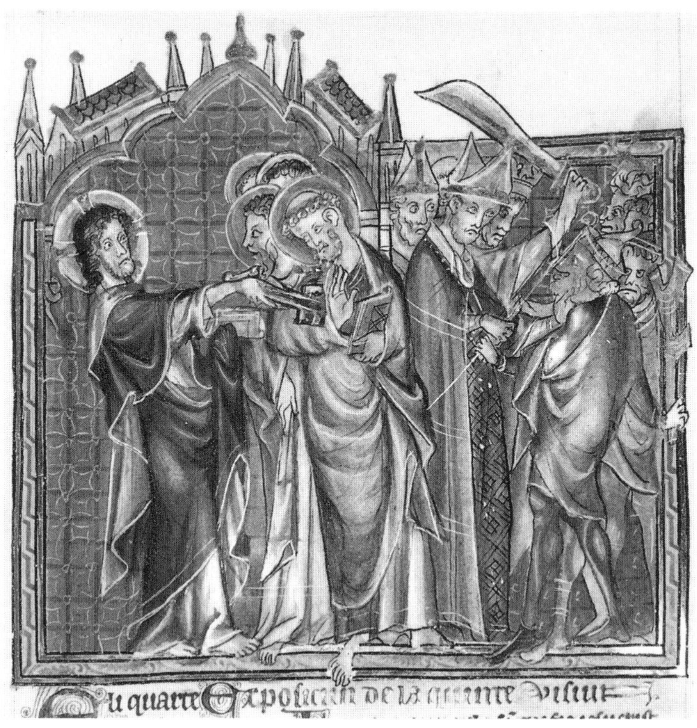

1. London, British Library, Add. Ms. 42555, Abingdon Apocalypse,
f. 59r. Jews barred from heaven

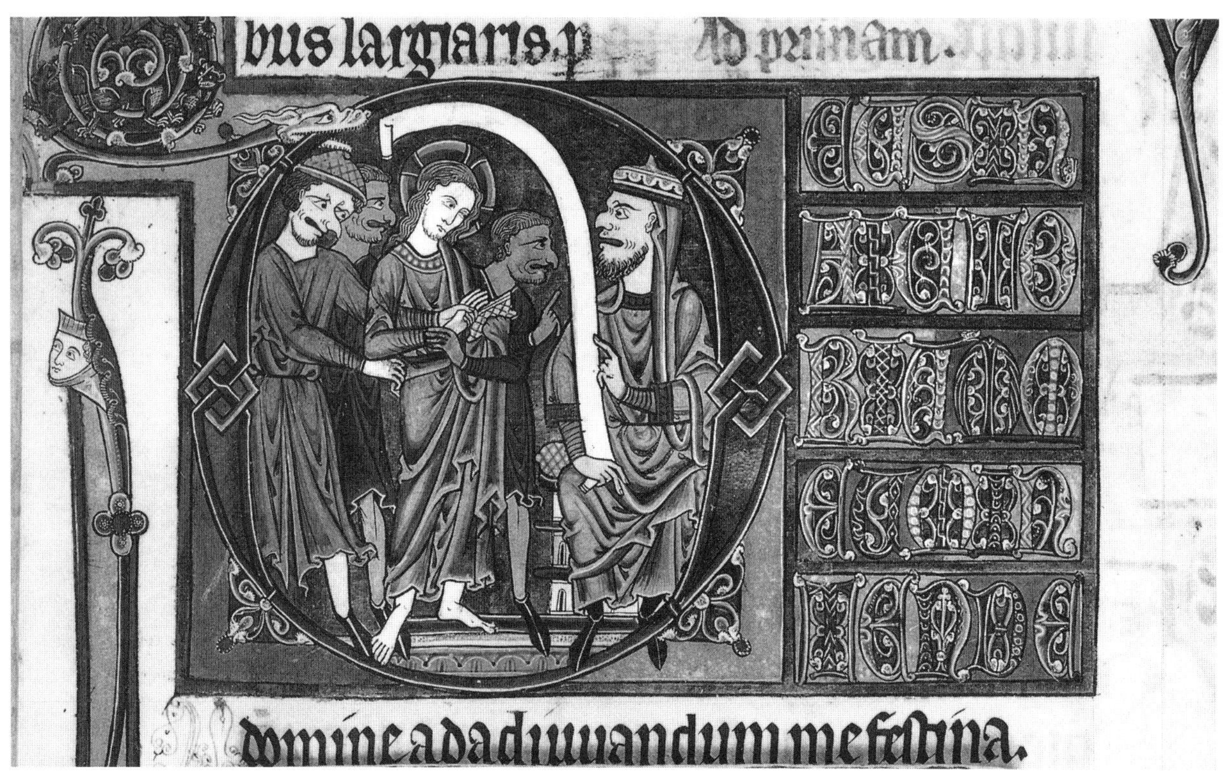

2. London, British Library, Add. Ms. 48985, Salvin Hours, f. 29r. Christ Brought to Caiaphas

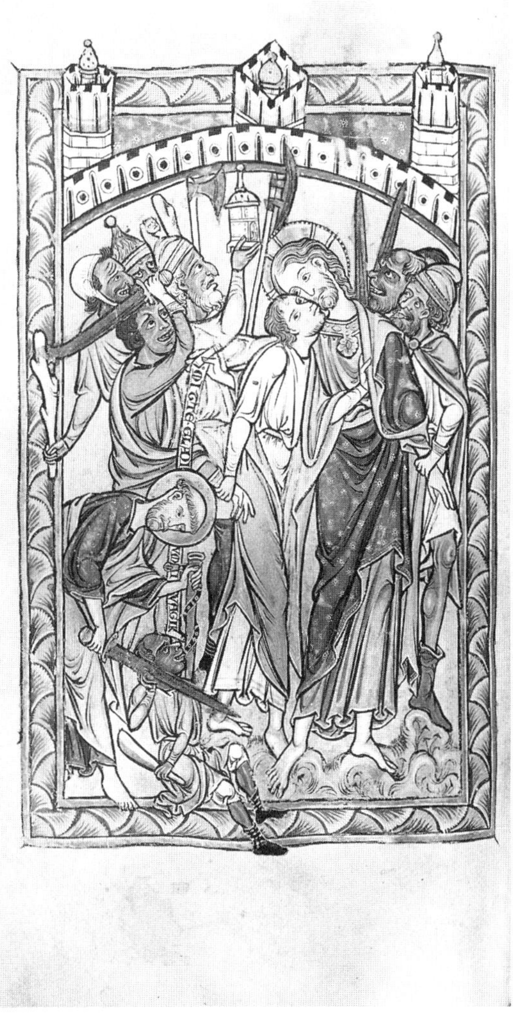

3. Manchester, John Rylands Library, Ms. lat. 24, Chichester Missal, f. 150v. Betrayal and arrest of Christ

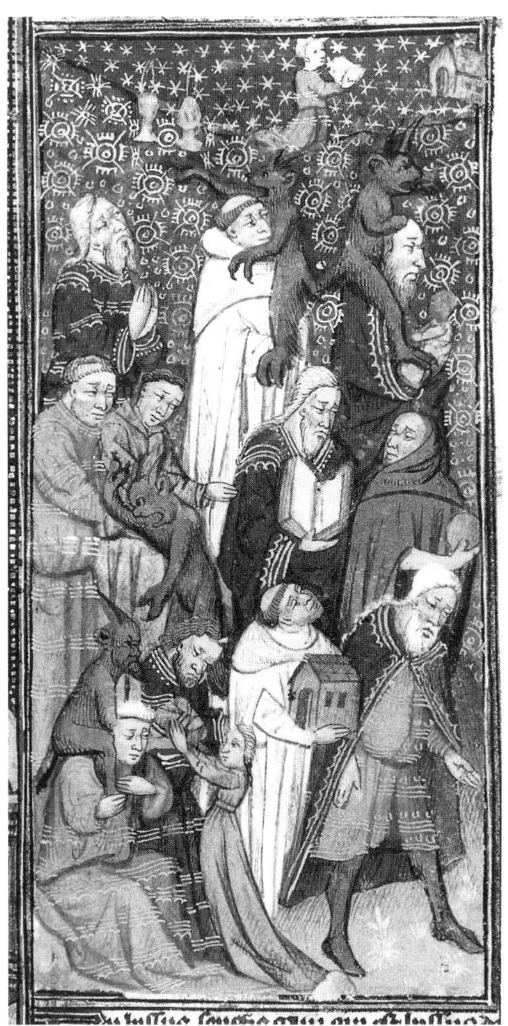

5. Paris, Bibliothèque Nationale de France, Ms. lat. 9471, Rohan Hours, f. 224r. Misshapen and deformed persons

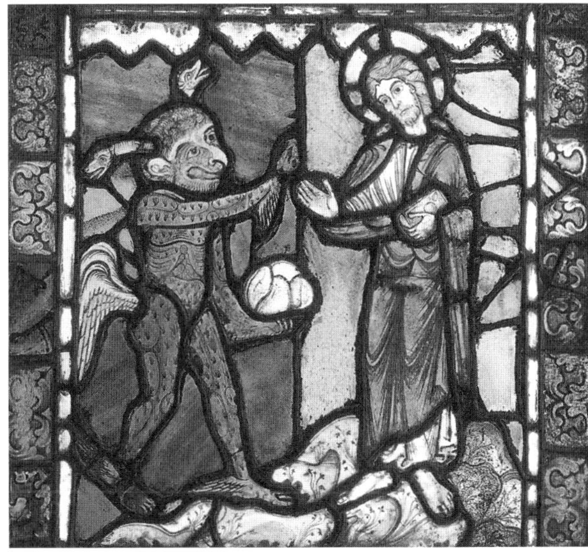

4. London, Victoria and Albert Museum. Temptation of Christ, stained glass panel from Troyes Cathedral

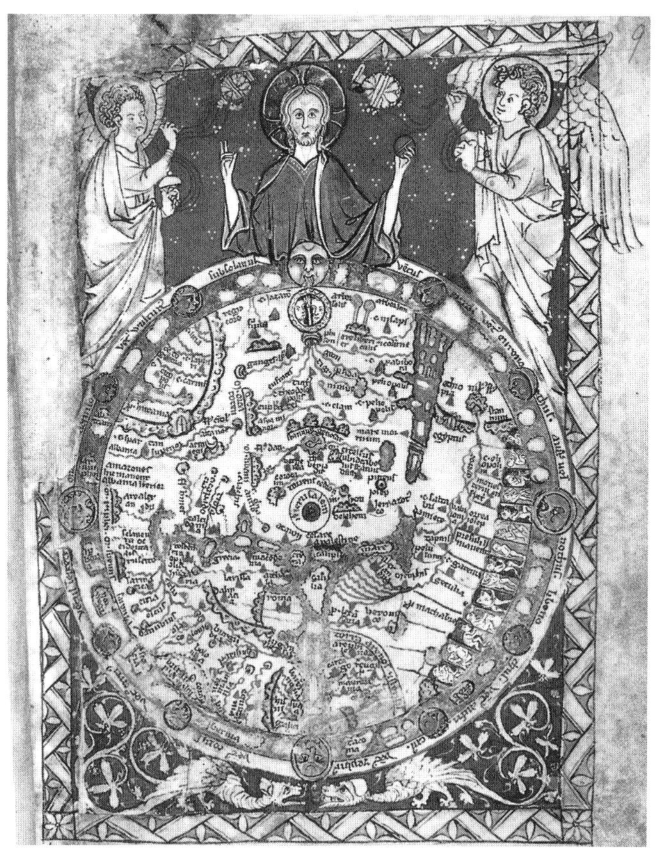

6. London, British Library, Add. Ms. 28681, psalter, f. 9r. *Mappa mundi*

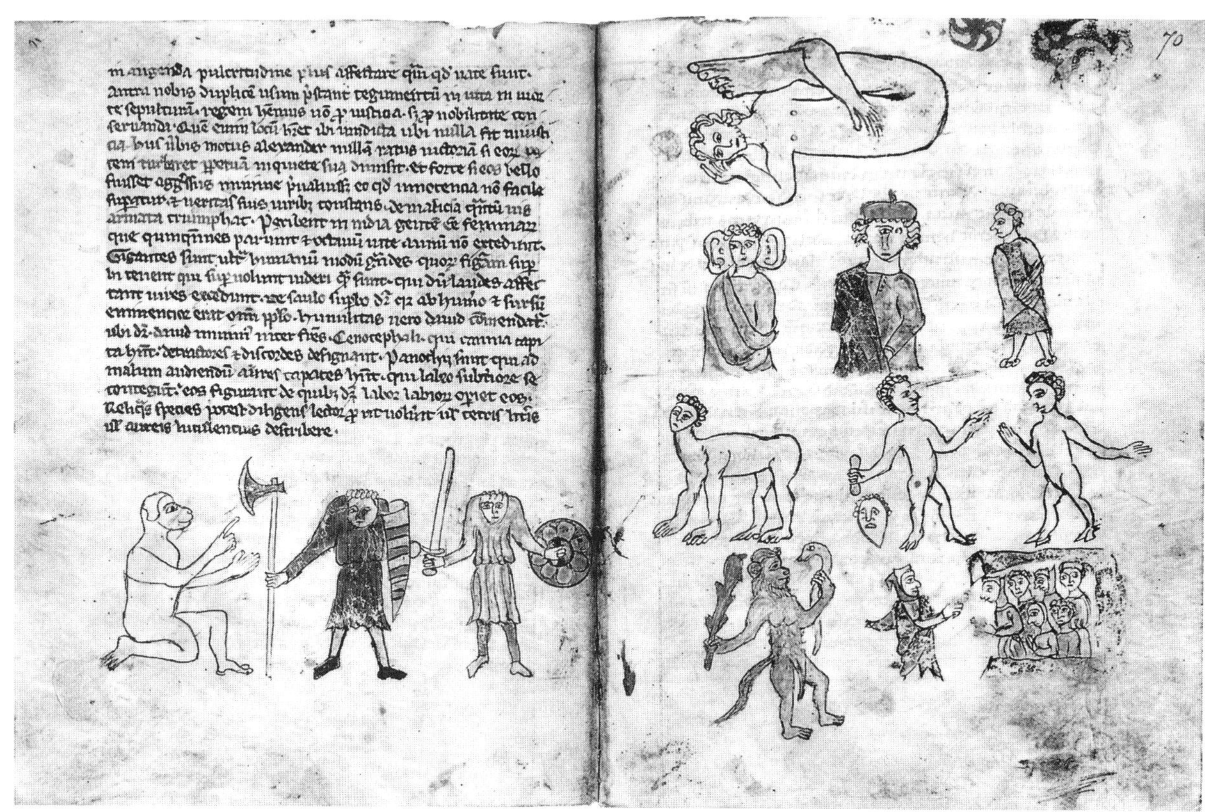

7. Oxford, Bodleian Library, Ms. Douce 88, bestiary, ff. 69v–70r. Monstrous Races

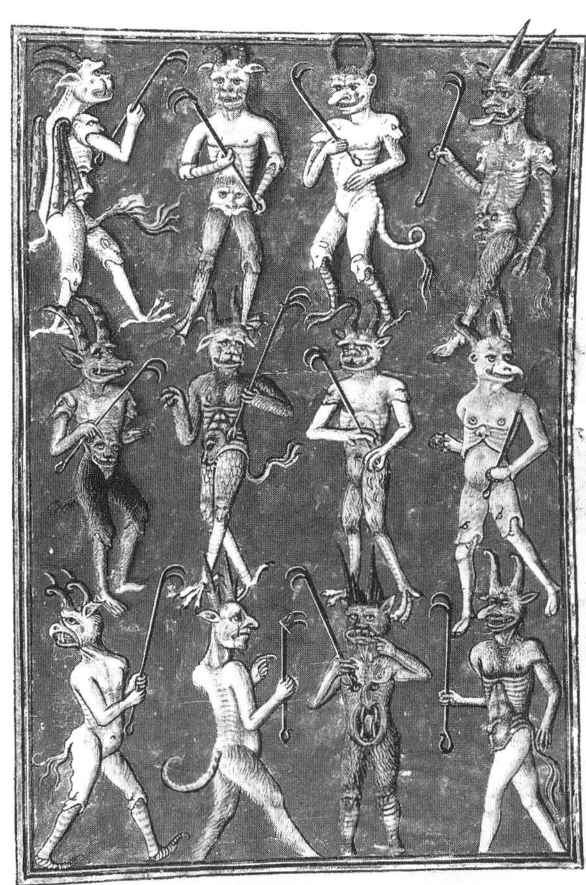

8. Oxford, Bodleian Library,
Ms. Douce 134, *Livre de la
vigne de nostre seigneur*, f. 99r.
Demons

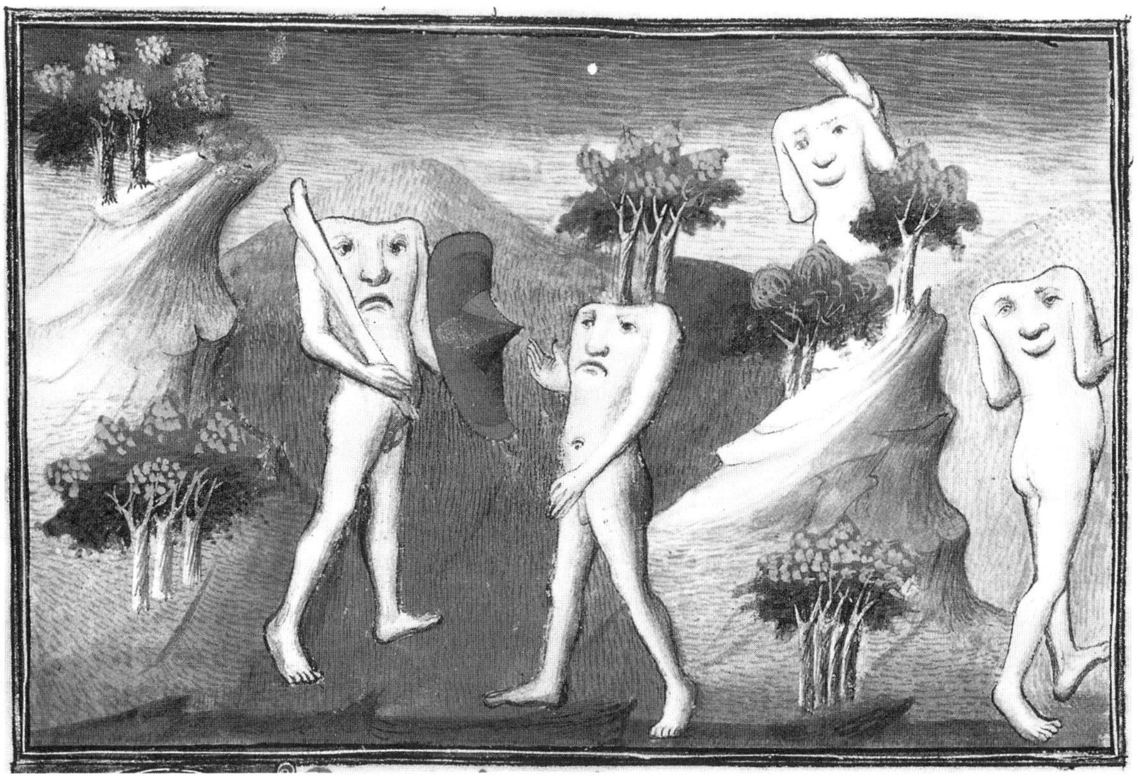

9. Paris, Bibliothèque Nationale de France, Ms. fr. 2810, *Livre des Merveilles du Monde*, f. 194v. Blemmyai

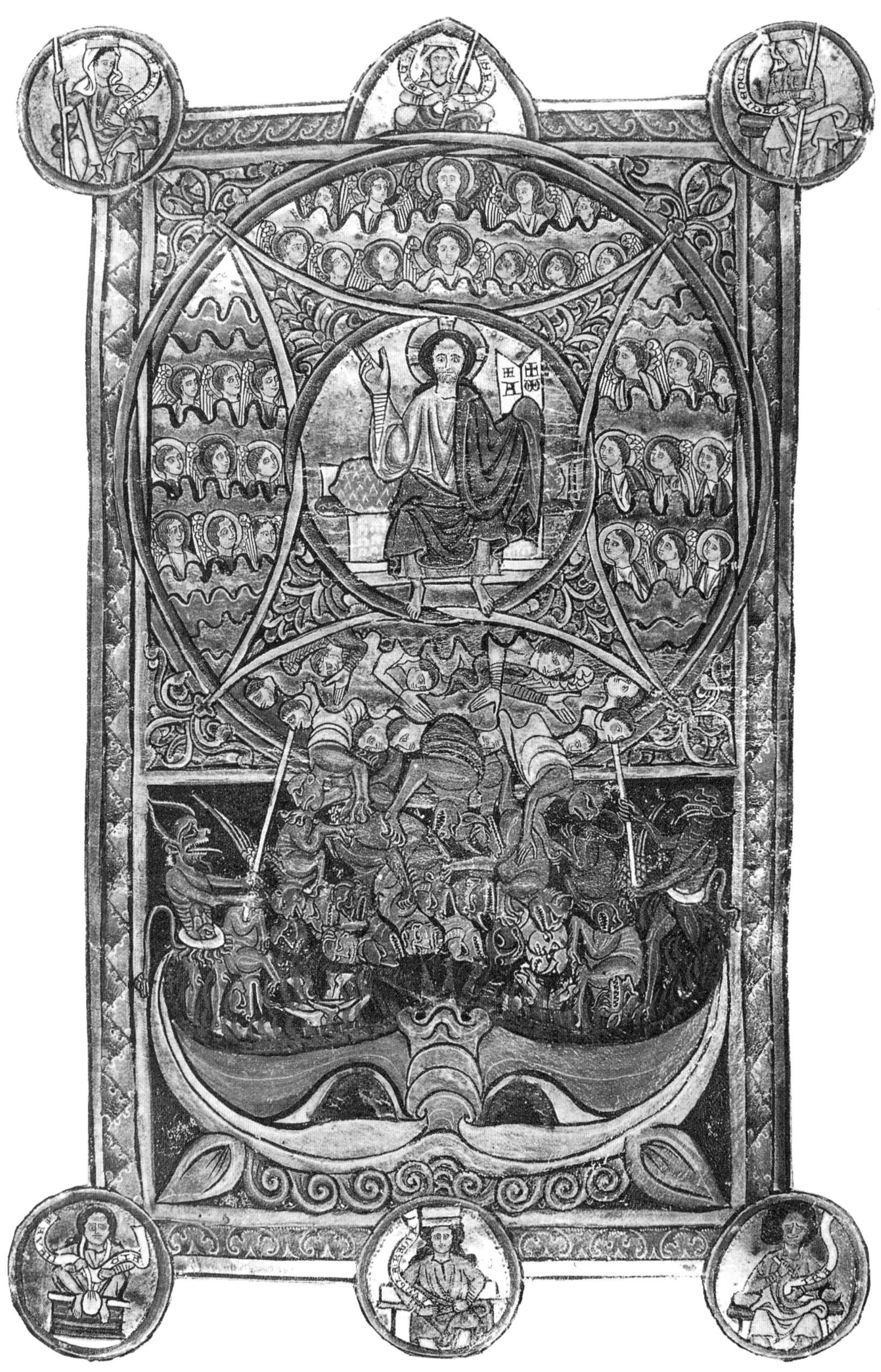

10. Cambridge, Fitzwilliam Museum, Ms. 330, Psalter of William de Brailes, leaf 1. Fall of the Rebel Angels

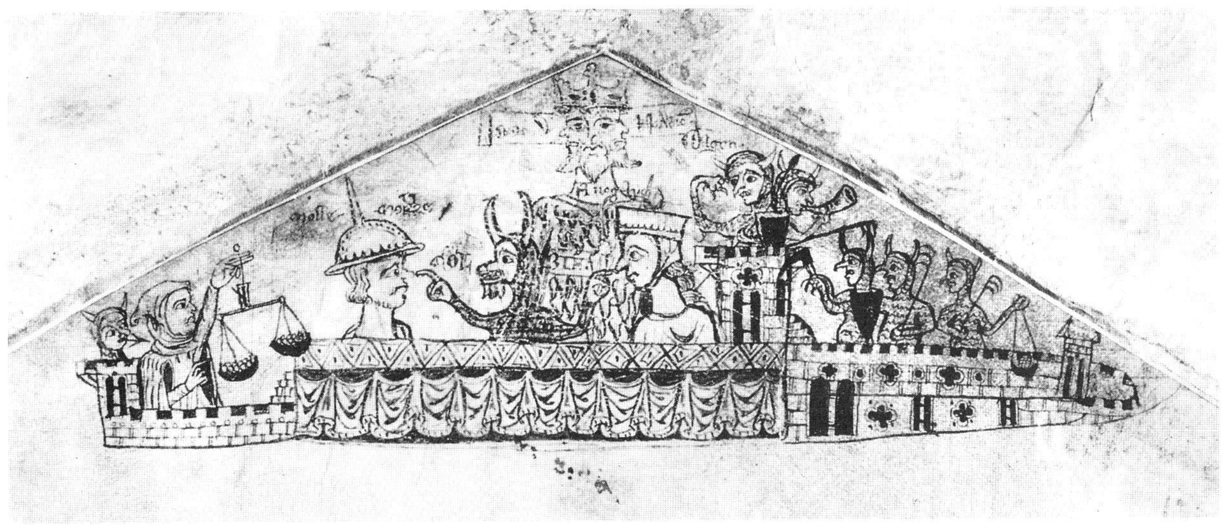

11. London, Public Record Office, Jewish Receipt Roll of 1233, E401, 1565, 17 Hen III. Isaac of Norwich, other Jews, and demons

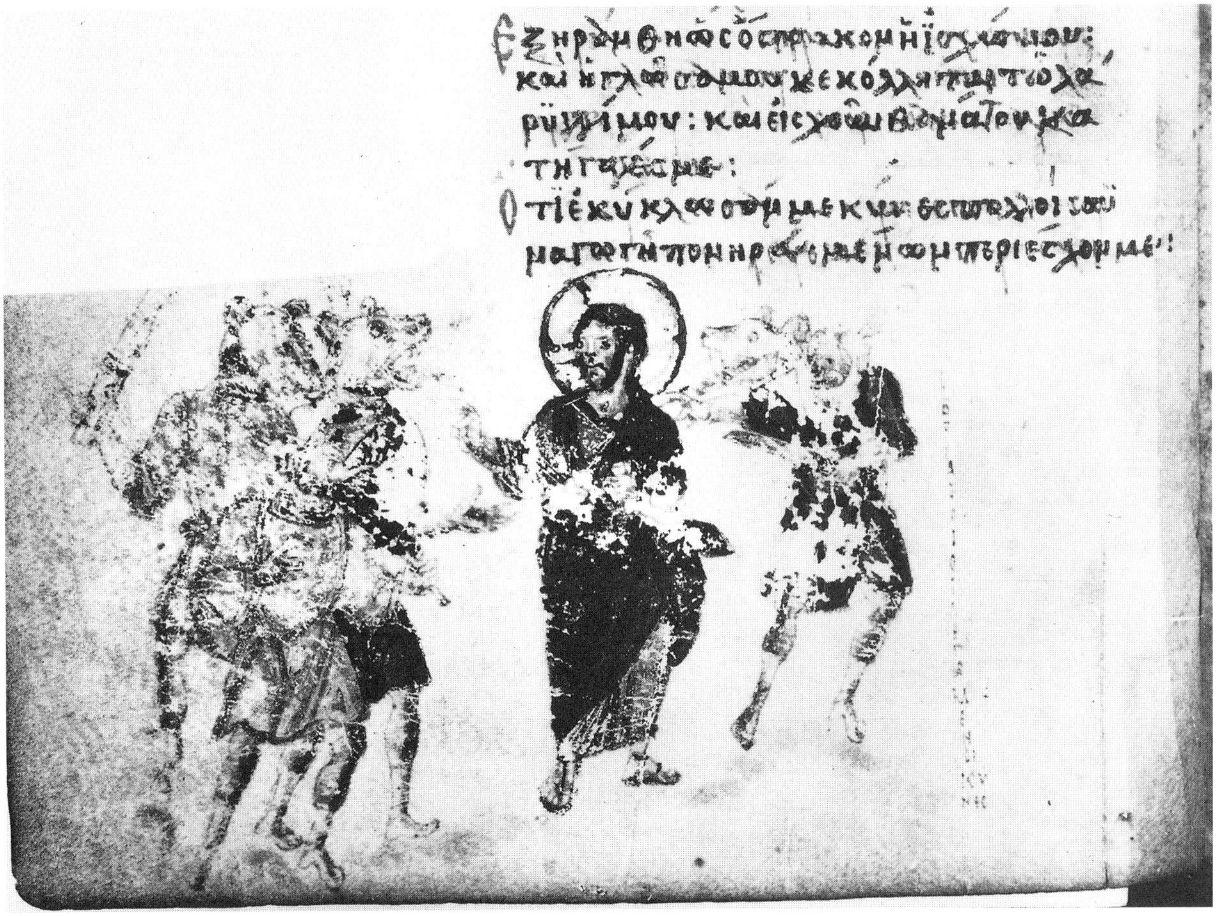

12. Moscow, State Historical Museum, Cod. 129, Khludov Psalter, f. 19v. Christ surrounded by dogheads

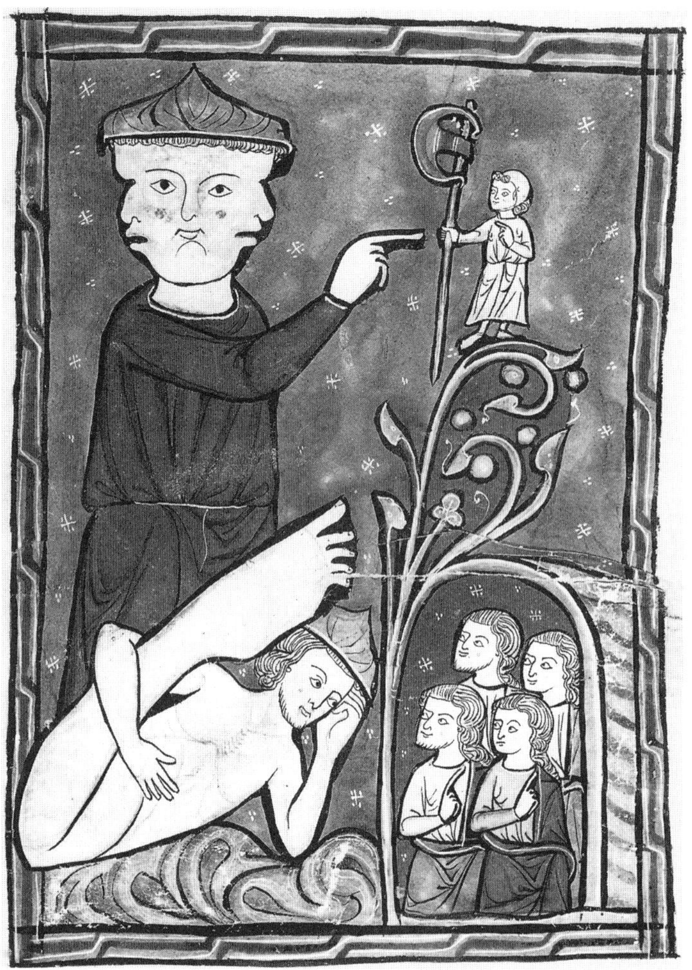

13. London, Westminster Abbey, Ms. 22, Westminster Abbey
Bestiary, f. 3r. Monstrous Races

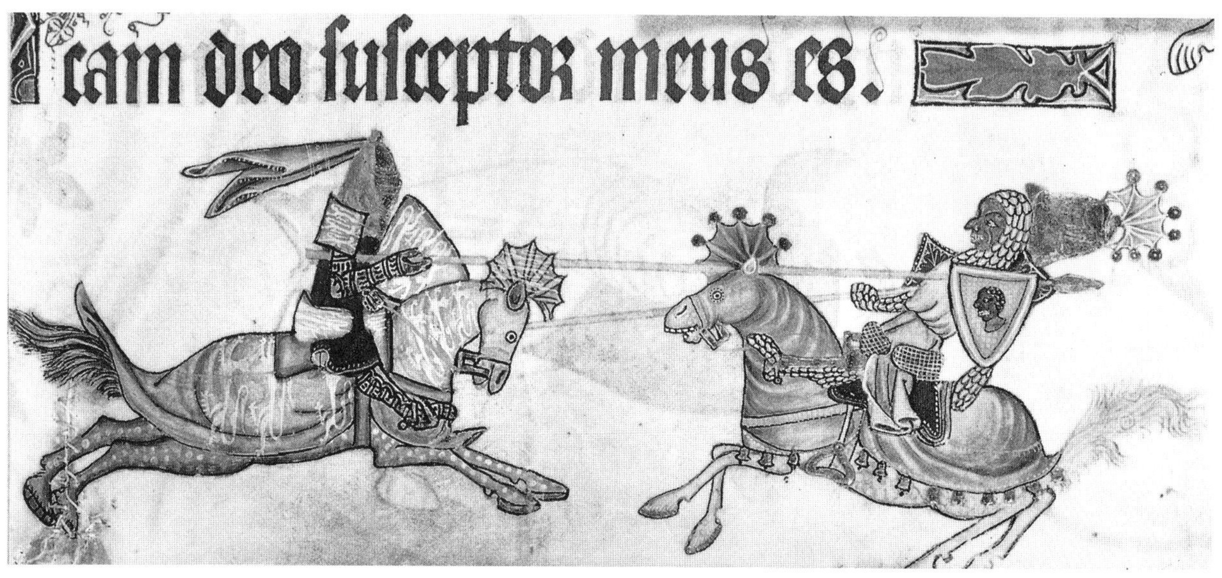

14. London, British Library, Add. Ms. 42130, Luttrell Psalter, f. 82r. Saladin vs. Richard I

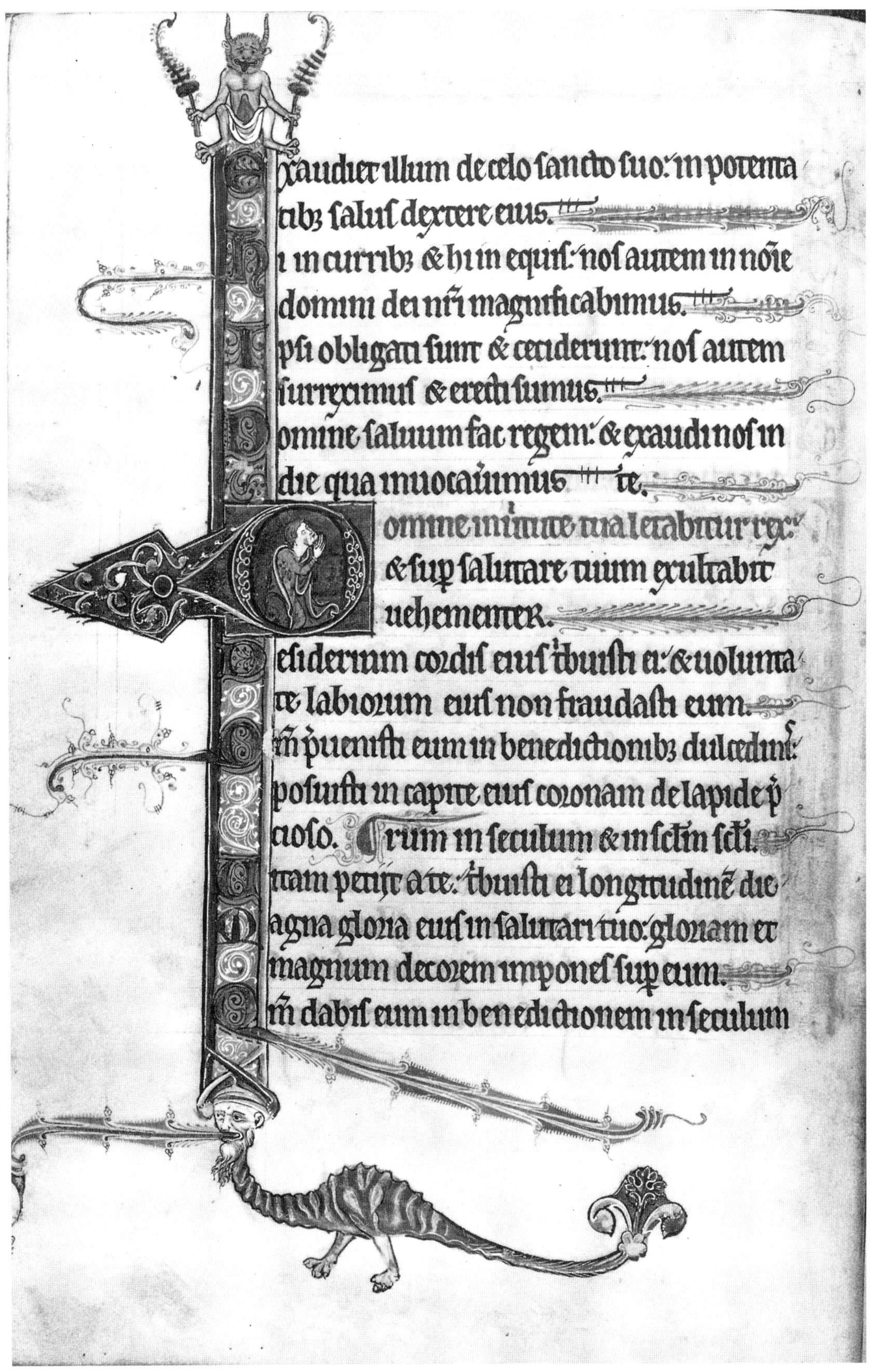

15. London, British Library, Add. Ms. 62925, Rutland Psalter, f. 23r. Hybrid Jew spewing blasphemy

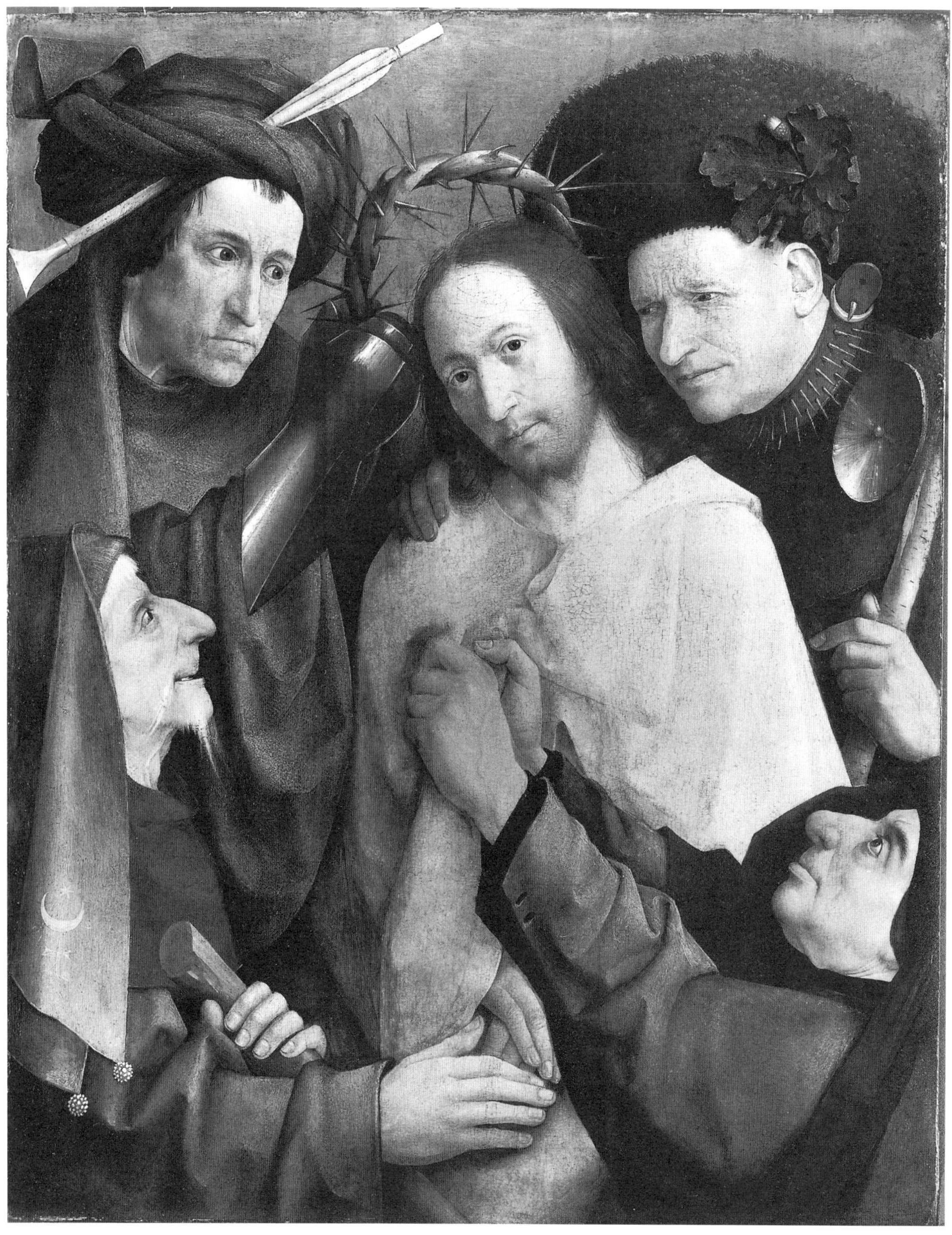

16. Hieronymus Bosch, *Christ Mocked (The Crowning with Thorns)*, oil on panel, ca. 1490–1500, London, National Gallery

Nipples, Entrails, Severed Heads, and Skin:
Devotional Images for Madame Marie

·

ALISON STONES

SEVERAL STRIKING—even sensational—pictures of various tortures visited upon the bodies of saints form a curious sub-group in a late thirteenth-century devotional picture book made for a lady cryptically identified in the list of subjects at the beginning of the book as "Madame Marie."[1] Among the eighty-seven full-page illustrations that form the core of this book, thirty-three show the Life of Christ, and fifty-four contain miniatures depicting the saints in the order of the litany. Of the latter, those at the beginning—Michael, John the Baptist, Peter, Paul, and John the Evangelist—are depicted in two facing-page images, one of which is a portrait and the other a narrative scene. The other saints are accorded a single miniature each and follow one of these pictorial modes or the other.

The patroness was included kneeling in prayer before no fewer than ten of her favourite saints, and there is reason to suppose that the iconographic program in general, its components, structure, and treatment, were specially designed to reflect and project her social status as an aristocratic wife and mother. Particularly striking among the images of the saints are those where the bodies of the martyrs, both female and male, are subjected to extreme forms of torture. In general, the pictures in Madame Marie's book are unusually realistic, to the point that they can be seen as anticipating in some measure the styles and subjects of the Renaissance in northern Europe.[2] Naturalistic elements are particularly exploited in these scenes of torture. This paper proposes an interpretation of these gruesome images, attempts to gauge Madame Marie's reactions to them, and suggests an historical and artistic context for them. Before looking at these issues, the reasons for locating the book itself on the Franco-Germanic border in the last years of the thirteenth century, and for identifying Madame Marie more precisely, may be given.

---

[1] The book is composed of a Cistercian calendar, not an intrinsic component but approximately contemporary; a list of tituli giving the subjects of the miniatures, with some inaccuracies, and naming Madame Marie in the ten images in which her portrait was included; and the eighty-seven full-page miniatures that remain of an original sequence of ninety. For a full description and complete reproduction, see A. Stones, *Le Livre d'images de Madame Marie: Reproduction intégrale du manuscrit Nouvelles acquisitions françaises 16251 de la Bibliothèque Nationale de France* (Paris, 1997). I have not had access to the rival study by Andreas Braem (advertised in the Fall 1997 catalogue of Reichert Verlag, Wiesbaden), whose interpretation of the book and its patron is apparently quite different from mine.

[2] A. Stones, "Madame Marie's Picture-Book: A Precursor of Flemish Painting around 1400," in *Flanders in a European Perspective: Manuscript Illumination around 1400 in Flanders and Abroad* (Proceedings of the International Colloquium, Leuven, 1993), ed. M. Smeyers (Leuven, 1995), 429–43.

The secondary artist of the book, I have proposed elsewhere, may be identified as Maître Henri, an artist named in a colophon of 1285 in another illustrated saints' lives, Paris, B.N.F. fr. 412.[3] Another manuscript that may also have been illuminated by Henri is a Breviary of Anchin, which can be dated after 1299. These, then, allow Henri's career, and probably that of his master, to extend from 1285 to 1300 at the least; it may also have spanned the preceding and following years, encompassing at least five other manuscripts.[4] I have also suggested that Henri's considerably more talented master may have enjoyed a greater career as a monumental painter in glass or wall painting, with manuscript painting as a secondary pursuit, since his hand has not been identified in any other manuscript. The mostly lost monumental painted programs throughout the Province of Reims, surviving details of which at first sight seem compellingly close, should perhaps be considered comparisons of a general, rather than a specific nature.[5]

Further pertinent stylistic and iconographical comparisons can be made with wall painting, embroidery, large-scale and small-scale sculpture, and metalwork from France, Germany, England, and even Italy, suggesting that the artistic experience of these painters was very broad.[6] A comparison of the incised cenotaph slab of St. Piat at Seclin, where the saint is shown frontally and holding the severed crown of his head so that its tonsure is wholly shown, with the painted portrait labelled St. Denis in Madame Marie's book (where he is also accompanied by an image of St. Piat in a different pose) shows that this artist certainly drew upon models in monumental media. Documentary evidence which survives for the city of Tournai demonstrates that artists in this period customarily worked in more than one medium.[7] It is therefore not irrelevant to note, although no connection can be proven, that a sculptor named Henri made the funerary monuments of Roger de Mortagne, seigneur d'Espierres (d. 1275 or 1276), son of the châtelain de Tournai, at St.-Martin's, Tournai, and at Flines.[8]

The saints in Madame Marie's book are presented in litany order. They include, as others have noted, a regional selection in which Nicaise, Quentin, Eloi, and especially Waudru, are significant since their cults point to the Province of Reims in general and the town of Mons in par-

---

[3] I first published this attribution in "Arthurian Art Since Loomis," in *Arturus Rex, II* (Acta Conventus Lovaniensis 1987), ed. W. van Hoecke, G. Tournoy, and W. Verbecke (Leuven, 1992), 21–78, at 21. See also A. Stones, "The Illustrated Chrétien Manuscripts and Their Artistic Context," in *Les Manuscrits de Chrétien de Troyes/The Manuscripts of Chrétien de Troyes*, ed. K. Busby, T. Nixon, A. Stones, and L. Walters, 2 vols. (Amsterdam, 1993), vol. 1, 227–322, at 249.

[4] Those I have so far attributed to Henri are Brussels, B.R., 582–9, 1787, 2512; The Hague, K.B., 74 G 31; and Vienna, Ö.N.B., s.n. 12771, a list I first published in Stones, "Arthurian Art" (as in note 3), 1. To these I add Douai, B.M., 12 (Stones, *Livre d'images* [as in note 1], 18–19), and François Avril has suggested (private communication) that the Carthusian lectionary, Paris, B.N.F. lat. 11520-21, may be a late work by Henri.

[5] See Stones, *Livre d'images* (as in note 1), 24–25.

[6] Ibid., 24–30.

[7] A. de la Grange and L. Cloquet, "Études sur l'art à

Tournai et sur les anciens artistes de cette ville," in *Mémoires de la Société historique et littéraire de Tournai* 1 (1887) and 2 (1888) (two entire volumes).

[8] Ibid., 1 (1887), 89, 109 (placing Roger's death in 1277; according to E. Warlop, *The Flemish Nobility*, 2 vols. [Courtrai, 1975], vol. 1, pt. 1, 916, he died in 1275 or 1276). A. Hocquet, "Le Rayonnement de l'art tournaisien aux XIIIe et XIVe siècles," *Annales de la Société historique et archéologique de Tournai*, n.s., 17 (1921), 246–82, suggests (250–51) that Henri was also responsible for the effigy of Blanche of Castille, mother of St. Louis, made in 1255 for her tomb at Maubuisson, now at Saint-Denis. The name Henri was not uncommon in artistic circles in the region; one Henri de Douai is listed among the goldsmiths active at Tournai in the thirteenth century. See M.-E. Soil de Moriamé, "Les Anciennes industries d'art tournaisiennes à l'exposition de 1911," *Annales de la Société historique et archéologique de Tournai*, n.s., 15 (1912) (entire volume), at 261. I thank Dominique Vanderwijnberghe for discussion of this question.

ticular.[9] Mons is in the Diocese of Cambrai (Province of Reims) and in the county of Hainaut, which was at this time politically a fief of Empire, although in a French-speaking region. I have proposed that "Madame Marie" may well be Marie de Rethel, who in 1266 became the third wife of Wautier d'Enghien (d. 1271), whose brother Jean d'Enghien was bishop of Tournai in 1267–73/4 and later bishop of Liège until his death in 1281.[10] A cousin of the family, Sohier d'Enghien, was châtelain of Mons from 1290–1311.[11]

Marie herself is known for commissioning the French translation of Thomas de Cantimpré's *Liber de monstruosis hominibus* that has survived as an illustrated unicum in Paris, B.N.F. fr. 15106,[12] and for founding hospitals in the region of Mons.[13] After a long widowhood, she died in 1315 and was buried at the nearby Cistercian abbey of Cambron.[14] Her picture book was most likely adapted there, by the addition of the Cistercian calendar and the suppression of all but one of the portraits, before finding its way back to the family and into the records of history.[15] It is recorded in the inventories of Marguerite de Flandre (1350–1405), wife of Philippe le Hardi, Duke of Burgundy (1364–1404) in 1405, and in those of Philippe le Bon in 1420 and 1467.[16] Two marriages in the same generation link the Enghien and Rethel families with the children of Robert III de Béthune, count of Flanders (r. 1305–22).[17] His daughter Yolande married Marie's son Wautier in 1289, but

[9] Amédée Boinet, the first scholar to publish the book, in "Extrait des procès-verbaux du 3ᵉ trimestre de 1923," *Bulletin de la Société nationale des antiquaires de France*, 1923, 247–57, noted the importance of Nicaise and Waudru for the localisation of the book (247).

[10] R. Goffin, *Généalogies enghiennoises*, 7 vols. (Herne, 1965), vol. 1, 34–35; see also Stones, *Livre d'images* (as in note 1), 39, citing further sources. There was another Rethel/Enghien marriage in which Marie's brother, Hugues IV, comte de Rethel, married Marie d'Enghien, widow of Jean comte de Brienne et de Jaffa, in 1270 (Goffin, 31–32). See also *Europäische Stammtafeln*, n.s., ed. D. Schwennicke, 17 vols. (Marburg, 1978–), vol. 7, pt. 2, pl. 79, to which Jeffrey Hamburger kindly drew my attention. The literary and philanthropic activities of Marie de Rethel make her the more likely patron of this book, although its subsequent history, outlined below, suggests that it was for a time in the hands of the descendants of her brother and passed from them into the possession of the counts of Flanders.

[11] Goffin, *Généalogies* (as in note 10), 99. Like Marie and her husband Wautier, he was buried at Cambron; see below.

[12] A. Stones, "Stylistic Associations, Evolution and Collaboration: Charting the Bute Painter's Career," *The J. Paul Getty Museum Journal* 23 (1995), 11–29.

[13] E. Matthieu, "Les Libéralités de Marie de Rethel, dame d'Enghien," *Annales du cercle archéologique d'Enghien* 4 (1891–2), 454–61.

[14] For her possible tomb there, see C. Monnier, "Les Monuments funèbres de la famille d'Enghien existant encore dans les ruines de l'église de l'abbaye de Cambron," *Annales du cercle archéologique d'Enghien* 4 (1891–2), 369–99, at 396–99; A. de Valkeneer, "Inventaire des tombeaux et

dalles à gisants en relief en Belgique," *Bulletin de la Commission royale des monuments et des sites* 114 (1963), 91–308, at 130–31, is skeptical about identifying more closely the owners of the Cambron tombs, only one of which, with an effigy of a knight bearing the family arms (gironny), can be identified as belonging to a member of the Enghien family.

[15] Stones, *Livre d'images* (as in note 1), 40. That the book was at Cambron is suggested by the circumstantial evidence offered by the Enghien family's patronage of that abbey. Cambron's dedication was on 19 October ("postridie S. Lucae, 1240," *Gallia Christiana in Provincias Ecclesiasticas Distributa*, ed. P. Paris, 17 vols [Paris, 1870–], vol. 3, col. 171), not 21 May, the dedication date recorded in the calendar of the book. This suggests the calendar was acquired from elsewhere—perhaps from its dependency, Beaupré, or another Cistercian house. I note that there is much uncertainty concerning Cistercian dedications: of the forty or so Cistercian abbeys in the medieval dioceses of Arras, Tournai, Thérouanne, Cambrai, and Liège, only two, Flines (28 May) and Cambron (19 October), are mentioned in *Gallia Christiana*, vol. 3. Also common in calendars in general is a dedication date of May 13, the consecration of Santa Maria in Martires in Rome (the Pantheon), consecrated in the early seventh century by Pope Boniface IV. See R.-J. Hesbert, *Antiphonale Missarum Sextuplex* (Rome, 1967), xciii, feast no. 100. I thank Elizabeth Teviotdale for this reference.

[16] François Avril was responsible for this important discovery, which he kindly allowed me to publish in Stones, "Picture-Book" (as in note 2), 443; see also ead., *Livre d'images* (as in note 1), 40.

[17] L. de Mas Latrie, *Trésor de chronologie* (Paris, 1889), col. 1601; Père Anselme de Sainte-Marie, *Histoire généa-*

died in 1313,[18] and his son Louis (ca. 1273–1322) married Jeanne, daughter of Hugues IV de Rethel, who was Marie's niece, in 1290.[19] Louis, who predeceased his father, was the great-grandfather of Marguerite. His line provides the more likely channel through which the book came into her possession, although how and when it was retrieved from the Cistercians remains unclear.

Furthermore, I have suggested that the selection of scenes in the book was made to emphasize the themes of motherhood and family which would have presented models appropriate to a woman whose state this was. An example is the two opening diptychs of Anna and Joachim's meeting at the Golden Gate and the birth of the Virgin (ff. 18v–19r), which are presented as parallels to the following diptych of the Annunciation to the Virgin and the Nativity of Christ (ff. 20v–21r). The latter image is particularly notable for the extraordinary poses of the Child and the Virgin: the Child stands up on his mother's knee while she holds out both hands without touching him. This gesture of reverence and encouragement to him to stand up all by himself, with hands held to catch him in case he should fall, appears to be a unique motif.

The inclusion of both the Circumcision (f. 23r) as well as the Presentation (f. 26r) is unusual for this period; Mary and Joseph are also present at both of these events. The selection of two images of St. Margaret (f. 100r), patron of childbirth, also emphasises the patroness's interest in themes of motherhood that must have reflected her own state and concerns. The second Margaret image is missing, but the opening titulus says that Madame Marie was shown kneeling in prayer before the saint in that picture.

Francis (f. 94v) was also among Madame Marie's ten favourite saints, and it is significant that she is shown in prayer before him. The realistic treatment of the subjects in the book in general was probably determined not only by the extraordinarily observant eyes of the painters, but also in some measure by the didactic principles on which Franciscan sermons were based. The inclusion and meticulous depiction of objects of daily life, people, and their costumes and clothes correspond in visual terms to the use of everyday words in Franciscan sermons, a deliberate preaching strategy whereby the spiritual ideal is conveyed and understood through the tangible world.[20] It is worth noting that extra-biblical and allegorical subjects were entirely excluded from Madame Marie's book, as were mystical images like those executed for the unknown nun for whom the so-called Rothschild Canticles manuscript was made.[21] These exclusions appear to have been delib-

---

logique et chronologique de la maison royale de France, 9 vols. (Paris, 1726; repr. New York and London, 1967), vol. 2, 736E; T. Luykx, *Het Grafelijk Geslacht Dampierre en zijn Strijd tegen Filips de Schone* (Leuven, 1952), 113–14.

[18] Goffin, *Généalogies enghiennoises* (as in note 10), vol. 1, 38, gives 1289; *Europäische Stammtafeln* (as in note 10), vol. 7, pl. 79, gives 1287.

[19] Anselme, *Histoire généalogique* (as in note 17), vol. 2, 737C–E.

[20] The Franciscans were of course not the only religious thinkers to exploit this idea, but this focus, taken in conjunction with their ministry to the wealthy laity, does seem to me to offer an important parallel to the visual effect created by the artists of the book. I have gone so far as to suggest that Madame Marie could well have called

upon her Franciscan confessor to act as "program director" for the selection of the scenes and their iconographic treatment; see Stones, *Livre d'images* (as in note 1), 36–38. I also recognize that Franciscan influence is not the only determinant here, since numerous other Franciscan books of the period, such as the psalter-hours supposedly made for Yolande of Soissons, or the Nürnberg Hours, adopted very different illustrative strategies that resulted in very different sorts of miniatures: see K. K. Gould, *The Psalter and Hours of Yolande of Soissons* (Speculum Anniversary Monographs 4) (Cambridge, Mass., 1978); and E. Simmons, *Les Heures de Nurembourg* (Paris, 1994).

[21] J. Hamburger, *The Rothschild Canticles* (New Haven and London, 1990).

erate. This is not to say that there are no images suitable as foci for mediation. Indeed, the purpose of the entire corpus of images must surely have been to stimulate private devotion and prayer. A striking example of an image whose structure and treatment particularly emphasize a contemplative function is the Deposition (f. 40r). Christ is held up from the back by Joseph of Arimathea, and the Virgin Mary presses her face to his in an attitude of tenderness and emotion (*compassio*), similar to what is shown in the Infancy cycle,[22] while the Holy Women also hold his hands to their faces, much like the image that Ailred exhorted his sister to contemplate in her private devotions with weeping and sighs.[23] Yet even here, the realism of the wooden bucket into which Nicodemus has placed two of the nails is a striking detail unusual in the West.[24]

Severed Heads

Scenes of the torture and martyrdom of the saints were primarily intended, like the sufferings of Christ, as an aid to contemplation and emotive reaction by Madame Marie. An exceptional degree of realism characterizes the treatment of these scenes and reveals a mentality that did not shrink from blood and gore. Both were depicted in explicit terms. The calm and beautiful faces of the saints show that they feel no pain and contrast with the contorted grimaces expressed by their wicked, and therefore swarthy-skinned and ugly-featured torturers. Yet none of the torture scenes was witnessed by the patroness in the picture itself. In the scenes where she is shown kneeling before her ten patrons, all of the saints are presented as portrait types (with the exception of Katherine, f. 95r, who is shown disputing with the doctors). Madame Marie's viewpoint is the same as ours—beyond the frame, outside the page, holding the book at an objective distance as she contemplated the fates of the saints.

There are twelve scenes of decapitation among the fifty-four depictions of saints; in these, heads are severed or are about to be. In the Life of Christ sequence, the Massacre of the Innocents (f. 24v, Fig. 1) provides a parallel. The striking emotive details include a mother's hand being cut as she stays the executioner's sword,[25] and another mother caressing the severed head of her child, deliberately underlining again the loving mother-child relationship so prominent elsewhere in this book. The treatment of this Innocents scene can be contrasted with the exploitation of the severed head in a somewhat earlier psalter of Arras use, now in Aix-en-Provence (Bibliothèque Méjanes, 15, f. XI; Fig. 2),[26] where the skewering of the innocents' heads on a lance perhaps reflects the

[22] See especially the Nativity of Christ, the Presentation, and the Massacre of the Innocents, ff. 21r, 26r, 24v.

[23] H. Mayr-Harting, "Functions of a Twelfth-Century Recluse," *History* 60 (1975), 337–52; Stones, *Livre d'images* (as in note 1), 59–60.

[24] The models are probably ultimately Italo-Byzantine rather than English or German; see Y. Nagatsuka, *Descente de croix* (Tokyo, 1979), nos. VIII, XI–402, XIIB. The bucket motif (in different forms) is found at Nerezi and the Cathedral of Aquileia, and probably originally at St. Mark's, Venice: Stones, *Livre d'images* (as in note 1), 59, with further references. For Aquileia, see T. E. A. Dale,

Relics, Prayer, and Politics in Medieval Venetia: Romanesque Painting in the Crypt of Aquileia Cathedral (Princeton, 1997).

[25] The north transept portal at Notre-Dame, Paris, provides an interesting parallel for this gesture; see Stones, *Livre d'images* (as in note 1), 48, citing L. Réau, *Iconographie de l'art chrétien*, 4 vols. (Paris, 1955–59), vol. 3, pl. 20.

[26] V. Leroquais, *Les Psautiers manuscrits des bibliothèques publiques de France*, 2 vols. (Mâcon, 1940–41), vol. 1, 3–4; photographs in the Boîte Porcher in the Bibliothèque Nationale de France.

gruesome use of the severed head motif in Crusader imagery. Crusader manuscripts occasionally show severed heads being used by the Christian warriors as ammunition.[27] Another context in which the Arras psalter model reappears is as the Epitomy of Tyranny in the copy of Papias's *Vocabularium* in Valenciennes, B.M., 397 (Fig. 3), where the Massacre of the Innocents illustrates the initial T in the alphabetical sequence. This is an unsual example of a subject invented for a biblical or hagiographical context used to illustrate a general topos. Common examples of the same principle are St. Paul falling from his horse as an allegory of pride, or St. Martin dividing his cloak to illustrate the concept of "largitas." What is striking in the Papias manuscript is that the other illustrations all show scholars engaged in disputing, observing phenomena, or teaching students, as is typical of the illustration of didactic texts.

The pattern of decapitation as the most common form of Christian martyrdom is continued with the execution of St. John the Baptist (f. 57v). This was requested by Salome at the instigation of her mother Herodias,[28] whom the artist has included in the composition. The meaningful glance exchanged by the two women adds a new dimension to this common scene and distinguishes this example from, among others, the similar configuration in the Breviary of Philippe le Bel, Paris, B.N.F. lat. 1023.[29] The execution of James the Great, the first of the apostles to die for his faith, beheaded in 44 A.D. by Herod Agrippa, reinforced the notion of execution as the principal means of death in the persecution of the Early Christians. This became increasingly common from the time of Nero, beginning in 64 A.D., and gave rise to an enormous corpus of hagiographical illustration in the early martyrologies and menologia in both the East and West. St. James is shown in this book in portrait mode, with Madame Marie and a group of pilgrims before him (f. 66r).[30] Single or multiple heads that have been severed by the sword are features of the martyrdom of eleven saints or groups of saints in addition to St. John the Baptist. Nicaise (f. 79r); John, companion of Paul (f. 80v); two of Maurice's companions (f. 86v); two companions of Ursula (f. 101v); and Denis and Piat (f. 84v) are shown as semi-cephalophores, each holding the tonsured crown of his head.[31] An executioner raises his sword to decapitate the saints John the Baptist (f. 57v); Jude (f. 70r); Mathias (f. 72r, showing him being stoned at the same time); Paul, companion of John (f. 80v); Thomas of Canterbury (f. 81r);[32] Maurice (f. 86v); and Lucy (f. 99v). A falchion is raised to execute Peter Martyr (f. 93r), who already has a bleeding wound on his head. Thomas the Apostle (f. 71v) and Christine (f. 102r) are pierced in the breast by a sword, rather than being decapitated, while Ursula (f. 101v) is shot with an arrow. Many of these depictions can be shown to derive from existing hagiographical compositions,[33] but analogies can also be drawn

[27] See, for instance, Paris, B.N.F. fr. 2630, f. 22v, reproduced in J. Folda, *Crusader Manuscript Illumination at Saint-Jean d'Acre, 1275–1291* (Princeton, 1976), as pl. 175; 33 n. 36, 85 n. 48, 157.

[28] Mt. 14:8–11; Mk. 6:25–28.

[29] V. Leroquais, *Les Bréviaires manuscrits des bibliothèques publiques de France*, 6 vols. (Paris, 1934), vol. 2, 465–75; see also the forthcoming exhibition of art in the time of Philippe le Bel, Paris, Grand Palais, 1998, with catalogue entries on manuscripts by F. Avril.

[30] This is the only miniature in which her portrait, with an added black veil, is preserved. See the discussion in Stones, *Livre d'images* (as in note 1), 75. Reproduced in

Boinet, "Extrait" (as in note 9); *Art and the Courts* (Ottawa, 1971), 12, colour pl. III; F. Avril, *La Passion des manuscrits enluminés* (Paris, 1991), no. 1.

[31] See above for the incised slab of St. Piat at Seclin used as the model for the Denis portrait here.

[32] The artist was clearly unaware of the established iconography for the martyrdom of St. Thomas à Becket, which included the four knights responsible, and an attack on the crown of Becket's head. See Stones, *Livre d'images* (as in note 1).

[33] See Stones, *Livre d'images* (as in note 1), 74, n. 1; 76, n. 2; 78, n. 1; 82, n. 2; 83, n. 2; 84, n. 1; 87, n. 1.

with other artistic, literary, and historical contexts which would have lent added resonance to these depictions from the perspective of the thirteenth-century viewer.

Veneration of the saints in the thirteenth century was concerned with separating their heads from their bodies and creating special reliquaries for them. The head was believed to be the principal part of the body.[34] St. Waudru had her head separated from her body by Bishop Nicolas de Fontaines of Cambrai in 1250;[35] most of the head of St. Louis was removed from Saint-Denis to the Sainte-Chapelle, where on 7 May 1306 it was encased in a splendid reliquary commissioned from the court goldsmith Guillaume Julien in 1299.[36]

The severed head motif enjoyed a considerable vogue in medieval literary circles, associated as it was with notions of wholeness and identity. In the French prose *Lancelot*, for example, the episode where Lancelot finds the severed head of his ancestor of the same name and reattaches it to its body was one that enjoyed something of an illustrative tradition on the Artesian and Flemish borders.[37] There are also notable parallels in the illustration of classical mythology and history, such as the severed head of Pompey being brought before Caesar, and Caesar holding it; episodes illustrated in the French translation of Roman history known as *Fait des romains*, notably in the copies made in the orbit of the Latin Kingdom of Jerusalem[38] and in Italy;[39] or Tonyris holding the head of Cyrus over a dish of blood in the *Fleur des histoires* manuscript of the fourteenth century in Besançon, B.M., Ms. 677.[40] In the *Inferno*, written just a little after Madame Marie's book was made, Dante sees Bertrand de Born (d. 1202) holding his severed head as punishment for inciting the

[34] E. A. R. Brown, "Philippe le Bel and the Remains of Saint Louis," *Gazette des beaux-arts*, VIe période, 115 (1980), 176, and n. 13, with reference to Guillaume Durand; reprinted in ead., *The Monarchy of Capetian France and Royal Ceremonial* (Aldershot, 1991), no. III.

[35] L. Devillers, *Chartes du chapitre de Sainte-Waudru de Mons*, 4 vols. (Brussels, 1899–1913), vol. 4, pt. 1, 250–51. Parallels are the translation of St. Nicaise's head at Reims Cathedral in 1213; see R. Branner, "Historical Aspects of the Reconstruction of Reims Cathedral, 1210–1241," *Speculum* 36 (1961), 23–37; and the translation of St. Quentin in 1228, which probably included a separation of his head; see E. M. Shortell, "Dismembering Saint Quentin: Gothic Architecture and the Display of Relics," *Gesta* 36 (1997), 32–47, esp. 38. For the general background, see J. Braun, *Die Reliquiare des christlichen Kultes und ihre Entwicklung* (Freiburg, 1940), 413–34, figs. 475–508; E. Kovács, *Kopfreliquiare des Mittelalters* (Budapest, 1964); F. Souchal, "Les bustes reliquiares et la sculpture," *Gazette des beaux-arts*, ser. 6, 67 (1966), 205–16; B. D. Boehm, "Medieval Head Reliquaries of the Massif Central" (Ph.D. diss., New York University, 1990); B. Falk, "Bildnissreliquiare im Mittelalter," *Aachener Kunstblätter* 59 (1991–93), 99–238; S. B. Montgomery, "The Use and Perception of Reliquary Busts in the Late Middle Ages" (Ph.D. diss., Rutgers University, 1996); id., "Mittite Capud Meum . . . ad Matrem Meam ut Osculetur Eum: The Form and Meaning of the Reliquary Bust of Saint Just,"

Gesta 36 (1997), 48–64.

[36] For a detailed account of the sources for the translation and circumstances surrounding it, including the surviving translucent enamel fragments, see Brown, "Philippe le Bel" (as in note 34), 175–82.

[37] This subject is particularly prominent in the Yale manuscript; see A. Stones, "The Illustrations of B.N. Fr. 95 and Yale 229: Prolegomena to a Comparative Analysis," in *Word and Image in Arthurian Romance*, ed. K. Busby (New York, 1996), 203–83, at 209–11.

[38] Paris, B.N.F. fr. 1391, f. 174r, and Brussels, B.R., 10212, f. 233r; see Folda, *Saint-Jean d'Acre* (as in note 27), pls. 183 and 100, respectively. While the latter is clearly one of Folda's Hospitaler Group manuscripts, I would date B.N.F. fr. 1391 very much earlier than Folda (93), who puts it in the last quarter of the thirteenth century. I agree that it is north French in origin. Its small historiated initials remind me of those in another classical compendium, Edinburgh, Univ. Lib., Ms. 20, which probably dates in the second quarter of the thirteenth century; see C. R. A. Borland, *A Catalogue of the Western Mediaeval Manuscripts in Edinburgh University Library* (Edinburgh, 1916).

[39] Brussels, B.R., 10168-72, painted in Rome in 1293: Folda, *Saint-Jean d'Acre* (as in note 27), 93, pl. 184.

[40] F. 15v, illustrated with a line drawing in C. Raynaud, *La Violence au moyen âge, IIIe–XVe siècle* (Paris, 1990), 200, fig. 99. I thank Jeremy Jacobs for drawing my attention to this book.

young Henry, son of Henry II, against his father.[41] Hagiography offered much earlier instances of severed heads; that of St. Edmund was one of the best known and was visually narrated across several episodes in the twelfth-century *Vita* from Bury St. Edmunds now in New York, Morgan Lib., Ms. M. 736.[42] Another particularly appealing example is found in Besançon, B.M., Ms. 677, f. 56v.[43]

Not surprisingly, however, it is in the iconography of battle that the severed head is most frequently depicted outside the context of hagiography. The battle scenes in the Old Testament Picture Bible in New York, Morgan Lib., Ms. M. 638,[44] which was probably made a generation or two earlier in the same region as Madame Marie's book, abound in severed heads and limbs on the ground. Executioners raising swords or killing people are to be found on ff. 13v (Jephtha sacrifices his daughter and Abimelech slays his brethren), 14r (Abimelech's head cut off by his armour-bearer so that it should not be said he was killed by a woman, who had mortally crushed him with part of a millstone), 25r (Agag hewn in pieces by Samuel), 28v (David and Goliath), 30r (David and his companions offer Saul the severed heads of 200 Philistines, of whom twelve are shown), 35r (Philistines cut off Saul's crowned head and bear it on a spear), 36r (David orders the slaying of the Amalekite), 38v (Ishbosheth's assassins offer his head to David), and 46v (Sheba executed and his head thrown to Joab).

Contemporary beheadings in the turbulent last years of the thirteenth century might have lent added poignancy to Madame Marie's pictures of severed heads, although hanging, rather than decapitation, would seem to have been the preferred form of capital punishment in France and England. Beheading was relegated to battle scenes or to the realms of literary hyperbole. The Annals of Ghent, for instance, exemplify the brutality of Robert of Artois and the French in Flanders in 1302 by noting that they even decapitated the images of saints in the churches as though they were alive.[45] The chronicler also describes the beheading of Bouchard d'Avesnes, despite his clerical status as archdeacon of Laon, as punishment for having ravished his ward, Margaret of Flanders.[46] According to the chronicler, his head was paraded through all the towns of Flanders and Hainaut, no doubt on a spear, like that of Saul in the Old Testament Picture Bible, although Bouchard seems in fact to have died not by execution, but of illness.[47]

Decapitation was a form of death that was seen to be brutal, ignominious, and effective, yet it could be accomplished and depicted with considerable decorum. All of the victims of decapitation in Madame Marie's book remain fully clothed, with the distasteful element of spewing blood confined to their necks and barely splattering out onto their elegantly modelled garments. But Madame Marie's book also includes several images which focus explicitly on the torments inflicted upon the naked bodies of the saints. They were based to some extent on the Mocking, Scourging,

<hr>

[41] Dante, *Inferno* XXVIII. See P. Brieger, M. Meiss, and C. S. Singleton, *Illuminated Manuscripts of the Divine Comedy*, 2 vols. (Princeton, 1969), pls. 277c, d; 278c, 279a, b, c; 280a, b; 281a, b; 282; 283a, b.

[42] C. M. Kauffmann, *Romanesque Manuscripts, 1066–1190* (A Survey of Manuscripts Illuminated in the British Isles 3) (London, 1975), no. 34. The head episodes are on pp. 26–31 and 191 of the manuscript.

[43] Raynaud, *Violence au moyen âge* (as in note 40), 210, fig. 104.

[44] *Old Testament Miniatures*, ed. S. Cockerell, preface by J. Plummer (New York, n.d. [1969]).

[45] *Annales Gandenses*, ed. H. Johnstone (London, 1951), 28–29.

[46] She gave the county of Hainaut in 1256 to Jean d'Avesnes, son of the elder of her two sons by Bouchard, while the county of Flanders came at her death in 1280 to Guy de Dampierre, her son by her second husband, Guillaume de Dampierre.

[47] Johnstone, *Annales Gandenses* (as in note 45), 81, cites Funck-Brentano's edition on this point.

and Crucifixion of Christ, episodes which in just this period were coming to be the focus of special attention in devotional books made in Flanders and Brabant, accompanied by images of Christ as Man of Sorrows and of the Instruments of the Passion.[48] Madame Marie's images include neither the Man of Sorrows nor the Instruments of the Passion, yet her pictures of flaying, nipple removal, and the disgorging of entrails are particularly innovative and evocative, and, like the severed heads, depart from the Passion of Christ into the realm of spectacular and unusual torture. The revulsion expressed by those who see these images for the first time is often striking.

FLAYING

The flaying of St. Bartholomew (f. 67v, Fig. 4) offers an unusual form of martyrdom, recounted by Isidore (PL 3:1291) and Bede (PL 94:1016),[49] making him a sort of Christian parallel to the Marsyas of classical mythology. Marsyas was flayed by Apollo for having dared to compete with him in a pipe-playing competition,[50] and is usually depicted in Roman sculpture as hanging by his wrists.[51] Bartholomew, according to the *De ortu et obitu patrum* and the *Breviarium apostolorum*, preached in Lycaonia and was martyred in Armenia by flaying.[52] It was in Persia that Herodotus, and, later, Valerius Maximus, state that flaying was the punishment meted out by the Persian ruler Cambyses to the judge Sisamnes for accepting bribes. Sisamnes' skin was stretched out over the chair upon which his son and successor as judge would sit.[53] A rare depiction of these subjects is on the twin panels commissioned by the burghers of Bruges from Gerhard David in 1491 and 1498–99.[54] In the context of the thirteenth and early fourteenth centuries, however, flaying is a topic more actual than one might imagine. Torture in general was at first restricted to slaves and was legally justified in the Roman Empire by the concept of *maiestas*, or crime against the state. Attitudes to torture during the Middle Ages are characterized by a pattern of condemnation by both

---

[48] Such as the Rothschild Canticles (Hamburger, *Rothschild Canticles*, as in note 21), the Hours of Margaret of Beaujeu, and the ivory book at the Victoria and Albert Museum. See R. Berliner, "'Arma Christi,'" *Münchener Jahrbuch für bildende Kunst* 3 (1955), 33–152; R. Suckale, "'Arma Christi': Überlegungen zur Zeichenhaftigkeit mittelalterlicher Andachtsbilder," *Städeljahrbuch* 6 (1977), 177–208; L. F. Sandler, "Jean Pucelle and the Lost Miniatures of the Belleville Breviary," *ArtB* 46 (1984), 74–96; M. A. Stones, in Wace, *"La Vie de sainte Marguerite"* (Tübingen, 1990), 195–96.

[49] *BSS*, cols. 852–77; *LCI*, vol. 5, cols. 320–26 (Bartholomäus)."

[50] Ovid, *Metamorphoses* VI.382–400.

[51] H. A. Weis, *The Hanging Marsyas and Its Copies: Roman Innovations in a Hellenistic Sculptural Tradition* (Rome, 1992).

[52] Both the *Breviarium* (of which the earliest extant copy is eighth century) and Isidore may depend on the earlier of the two recensions of the *De ortu et obitu patrum*, ca. 600, according to which Bartholomew preached in Lycaonia, then in India with St. Matthew, and was martyred by flaying in Armenia. See Baudouin de Gaiffier, "Le *Breviarium Apostolorum* (*BHL* 652): Tradition et oeuvres apparentées," *Analecta Bollandiana* 81 (1963), 89–116, at 106–7.

[53] Herodotus V.21–5; Valerius Maximus VI.3; see also John Hoccleve, *The Regiment of Princes*, ed. F. J. Furnivall (EETS, ES 72) (London, 1897), ll. 2675–88. Another incidence of flaying in the context of Persia is that of Julian the Apostate, who was flayed after death and his skin nailed to the palace door by order of King Shapur, recounted in John Lydgate, *The Fall of Princes*, ed. H. Bergen (EETS, ES 121–24) (London, 1918–19), ll. 1632–38; the Hoccleve and Lydgate references are cited by W. R. Barron, "The Penalties for Treason in Medieval Life and Literature," *Journal of Medieval History* 7 (1981), 187–202, at 194.

[54] Bruges, Stadtmuseum 182, 159. See Eberhard Freiherr von Bodenhausen, *Gerard David und seine Schule* (Munich, 1905), 127–37. The panels have been connected with payments to David of 1491 and 1498–99 for official paintings of unspecified subjects.

church and state, with exceptions made due to particular circumstances. Cases of treason were the most common justification for torture, of which flaying, particularly in France, and drawing and quartering, especially in England, were the most notorious.[55]

"He flayed his Lord to spread his board" says the chronicler of the Annals of Ghent of Guy de Dampierre, count of Flanders 1280–1304,[56] and he uses the skin motif again, with the Flemish burghers fearing for their skins as Jacques and Pierre Flote and their men enter Bruges in 1302.[57] No actual incident of flaying is recorded in the Annals of Ghent, however. As a punishment it was unusual in that period and was a fate reserved only for particularly heinous criminals. An infamous instance of flaying in early fourteenth-century France was that of Philippe and Gaultier d'Aulnay, lovers of the king's daughters-in-law Marguerite de Bourgogne[58] and Blanche de Bourgogne.[59] Arrested by Philippe le Bel (r. 1285–1314) at Pontoise, the two men were flayed alive on 12 April 1314, their heads and genitals were cut off, and their bodies left suspended as carrion for birds and beasts of prey.[60] Marguerite and Blanche were imprisoned at Château-Gaillard; Marguerite died shortly afterward in prison, while Blanche remained a prisoner until she was permitted to retire to Maubuisson in 1325, where she died in 1326.[61] This flaying episode was considered sufficiently striking for it to enter the illustrated tradition of the *Fleurs des chroniques*, notably, again, in the four-

[55] The most useful general survey is E. Peters, *Torture* (Oxford, 1985). See also A. Mellor, *La Torture: Son histoire, son abolition, sa réapparition au XXe siècle* (Paris, 1949). P. Fiorelli, *La tortura giudiziaria nel diritto comune*, 2 vols. (Milan, 1953), was not available to me. On punishments for treason, particularly flaying, see especially Barron, "Penalties for Treason" (as in note 53), 194.

[56] Johnstone, *Annales Gandenses* (as in note 45), pp. 4–5.

[57] "Pelli sue timentes"; ibid., pp. 22–23.

[58] Daughter of Robert II, duc de Bourgogne, married in 1305 to Louis, the future Louis X le Hutin (r. 1314–16) and King of Navarre (1307–16). At her death, Louis married (1315) Clementia of Hungary (d. 1328) who bore him a posthumous son, Jean, on 15 November 1316; Jean died a few days later (19 November). Marguerite and Louis's daughter Jeanne (1312–49) survived both her parents and her half-brother, but whatever rights to the throne she might have enjoyed were usurped by her uncle Philippe V (r. 1316–22). However, she and her husband Philippe, comte d'Evreux, succeeded Charles IV to the kingdom of Navarre at the latter's death in 1328; she ruled alone after her husband's death in 1343 until her own death in 1349. See Anselme de Sainte-Marie (Pierre de Guibours), *Histoire de la maison royale de France et des grands officiers de la couronne*, rev. P. Ange and P. Simplicien (Paris, 1726–33; repr. New York, 1967), vol. 1, 92, 282; and Mas Latrie, *Trésor de chronologie* (as in note 17), col. 1523, noting that in Mas Latrie, col. 1734, she is given as the daughter of Philip V, not of Louis le Hutin. For much useful material, see E. A. R. Brown, "'The Prince is Father of the King': The Character and Childhood of Philip the Fair of France," *Medieval Studies* 49 (1987), 282–334, repr. in ead., *Monarchy of Capetian France* (as in note 34), vol. 2,

290 n. 23. For more on the adultery and its ramifications, see the forthcoming monograph by E. A. R. Brown and her contribution to *Fauvel Studies*, ed. M. Bent and A. Wathey (Oxford, 1998).

[59] Blanche, married in 1308 to Louis's brother, Charles de la Marche (Charles IV le Bel, r. 1322–28), and her sister Jeanne, were the daughters of Mahaut d'Artois and Othon, comte de Bourgogne. Jeanne, married in 1307 to Philippe V le Long (r. 1316–22) was accused of complicity in the affair but was exonerated and released after a brief imprisonment in the castle of Dourdan. Charles divorced Blanche in 1322 on the grounds that her mother, Mahaut d'Artois, was his godmother (adultery not at the time constituting cause), and married Marie de Luxembourg, daughter of Emperor Henry VII (Anselme, *Histoire de la maison royale* [as in note 58], vol. 1, 96–97).

[60] *Chronique latine de Guillaume de Nangis de 1113 à 1300 avec les Continuations de cette chronique de 1300 à 1368*, ed. H. Géraud, 2 vols. (Paris, 1843; repr. New York and London, 1965), vol. 1, 404–6; *Recueil des historiens des Gaules et de la France*, vol. 20, ed. J. Naudet and P. C. F. Daunou (Paris, 1840) 609–10 (see also 691); vol. 21, ed. J. D. Guigniaut and J. N. de Wailly (Paris, 1855), 658; *Ly Myreur des histors: Chronique de Jean des Preis dit d'Outremeuyse*, ed. A. Borgnet and S. Bormans, 7 vols. (Brussels, 1864–87), vol. 6, 197–98; *La Chronique métrique attribué à Geffroy de Paris*, ed. A. Diverrès (Publications de la Faculté des lettres de l'Université de Strasbourg 129) (Paris, 1956), 203.5936–40.

[61] The Continuation of Guillaume de Nangis's *Chronicle* simply says "miserabiliter finirent" (p. 404); according to Anselme, *Histoire de la maison royale* (as in note 58), vol. 1, 92, Marguerite was strangled with a winding-sheet.

teenth-century copy in Besançon, B.M., 677, f. 76r, where both victims are shown roped to oppo-site ends of the same table, one attacked in the belly, the other on the right arm.[62]

Madame Marie's painters were working two decades or more before the episode of 1314 oc-curred and may have seen models of the flaying of St. Bartholomew emanating from elsewhere in the empire. Depictions of his flaying are found by the early twelfth century, in the Stuttgart Pas-sional (Stuttgart, Württembergische Landesbibliothek, Cod. hist. 2° 56, f. 67a),[63] and a century later on the Maurinus shrine in Cologne.[64] More decorous models for the depiction of St. Bartholomew were also available by the early thirteenth century, suggesting that the painters (per-haps guided by Madame Marie's spiritual advisor) had made the deliberate choice to depict the ac-tual activity of flaying. At Chartres, the saint is shown fully clothed and holding his attribute, a knife.[65] It was also the attribute, rather than the activity, that the metalworkers of Hainaut depicted on the copper-gilt panel now in the British Museum.[66] On the Three Kings Shrine in Cologne Cathedral, the fully clothed saint holds his epidermis in his hand,[67] as he does in the Oscott Psalter (London, B.L. Add. 50000, f. 10v), made in England ca. 1275.[68] This type almost anticipates the skin man of Henri de Mondeville's medical treatise, transmitted in the illustrated French transla-tion of 1314, in which a naked flayed man carries his skin on a stick over his shoulder (Fig. 5).[69]

---

[62] Raynaud, *Violence au moyen âge* (as in note 40), 192, fig. 93. Another historical case of flaying is that of Hugues Géraud, bishop of Cahors, flayed and burnt at Avignon in July 1317, for having attempted to poison Pope John XXII. See Barron, "Penalties for Treason" (as in note 53), p. 192, citing *Vitae Paparum Avionensium*, ed. S. Baluze, re-ed. G. Mollat (Paris, 1914), 185. Barron fur-ther cites (193) the examples of Guillaume des Baux, prince of Orange, in 1218; the chamberlain of Robert, count of Rouen, partially flayed in 1360; and Bertrand, comte d'Armagnac, constable of France, in 1418. Liter-ary hyperbole accounts for other references, at variance with fact, surrounding the death of Richard Coeur de Lion; in the moral tale recounted by Geoffroy de la Tour-Landry ca. 1371–72, and in the romances of *Sir Firumbras, The Sowdon of Babylon, The Prose Merlin, Layamon's Brut, King Horn, Guy of Warwick*, Chrétien's *Cligès* and *Lancelot*, the *Roman du comte d'Anjou*, the prose *Lancelot, Havelock the Dane*, the *Book of the Knight of the Tower*, Lydgate's *Pil-grimage of the Life of Man*, and the *Siege of Jerusalem*, cited by Barron (193–95).

[63] A. Boeckler, *Stuttgarter Passionale* (Augsburg, 1923), fig. 78.

[64] *Ornamenta Ecclesiae* (Cologne, 1985), vol. 2, 296–302, no. E.79, dated there ca. 1170. There are also instances in liturgical books of the region, such as the Martyrology of Notre-Dames-des-Prés, Douai, Valenciennes, B.M., 838.

[65] *LCI*, vol. 5, col. 326; not clear in W. Sauerländer, *Die Gotische Skuptur in Frankreich, 1140–1270* (Munich, 1970), pl. 111.

[66] British Museum, inv. 1906.7-17.2: *L'Art et la cour* (Ot-tawa, 1972), no. 43, pl. 61; *Schatz aus den Trümern* (Co-logne, 1996), no. 22.

[67] *Ornamenta Ecclesiae* (as in note 64), vol. 2, 216–24, no. E.18, dated there ca. 1180–ca. 1230.

[68] Reproduced in colour in D. H. Turner, *Early Gothic Illuminated Manuscripts* (London, 1965), pl. IV, dated ca. 1270; N. J. Morgan, *Early Gothic Manuscripts*, pt. 2, *1250–1285* (London, 1988), no. 151.

[69] Court physician to Philippe le Bel (d. 1314) and Louis le Hutin (d. 1316), and responsible for their em-balming, Mondeville lectured at the universities of Mont-pellier and Paris. He was reputedly the first to use large-size illustrations in his lectures, of which the small miniatures in Paris, B.N.F. fr. 2030 are supposedly a reflection. See J. L. Pagel, *Leben, Lehre und Leistungen des Heinrich von Mondeville (Hermondaville): Ein Beitrag zur Geschichte der Anatomie und Chirurgie, Theil I, enthaltend den Text der Chirurgie des H. von Mondeville nach Berliner, Er-furter und Pariser Codices, Vorrede und Einleitung* (Berlin, 1892); *Thiel II, Die Anatomie* (Berlin, 1899); K. Sudhoff, *Ein Beitrag zur Geschichte der Anatomie im Mittelalter* (Leipzig, 1908; repr. Hildesheim, 1964), 82–89, pl. 23:1–13. Sudhoff's reproductions of the drawing in the Berlin and Erfurt manuscripts show that they are treated as diagrams, unlike those in B.N.F. fr. 2030, which are drawings based on entire human figures; F. Weindler, *Geschichte der gynäkologisch-anatomischen Abbildungen* (Dres-den, 1908), figs. 40–51; L. Choulant, *History and Bibliogra-phy of Anatomic Illustration in Its Relation to Anatomic Science and the Graphic Arts*, trans. and ed. M. Frank (Chicago, 1920), figs. on pp. 58–59; P. Huard and M. D. Grmek, *Mille ans de chirurgie en Occident: V^e–XVe s.* (Paris, 1966), figs. 104–9; R. Margotta, *The Story of Medicine*, ed. P. Lewis (New York, 1967), 118; R. Herrlinger, *History of Medical Il-lustration from Antiquity to 1600*, trans. G. Fulton-Smith

This motif survives into the sixteenth century in the statue of Marco d'Agrate in the transept of Milan Cathedral of ca. 1552–56, and in the related anatomical statues in Cracow.[70] What characterizes Madame Marie's version is the L-shaped posture of Bartholomew's naked body lying, unusually, on its front, with the torso raised erect,[71] and the emphasis on the skin peeled off, similar to the version on the Maurinus shrine. This depiction anticipates the still more brutal treatment of flayed skin in the early fourteenth-century Hungarian Legendary.[72]

NIPPLES AND ENTRAILS

If the treatment of the flaying and the severed heads in Madame Marie's book do no more than add dramatic and realistic detail to models that were not particularly unusual, the depictions of Sts. Agatha and Vincent have a different agenda. Both force the viewer to confront directly, but in a transmuted form, the bodily functions of delivery and nurture, and thus are particularly appropriate to the married and maternal state of their patron.[73]

Remarkable attention is paid by the artist of Madame Marie's book to anatomical detail, and it is the nipples, as opposed to the breast as a whole, which are the focus of the torturer's attentions (f. 97v, Fig. 6). Perversely reminiscent of the baby teeth which would have attacked the nipples of the medieval nurse,[74] whether mother or wet nurse,[75] the toothed pliers, further highlighted by the use of gold, wrench the nipples off the breasts, causing blood to flow from the wounds

<hr>

(Nijkerk, 1967), 40–41, figs. 37a, 37b; *La Médecine médiévale à travers les manuscrits de la Bibliothèque nationale*, ed. A. Gourdon and J.-C. Sournia (Paris, 1982), no. 37; M. C. Pouchelle, *Corps et chirurgie à l'apogée du Moyen Age: Savoir et imaginaire du corps chez Henri de Mondeville, chirurgien de Philippe le Bel* (Paris, 1983).

[70] *BSS*, 871. See Z. Ameisenova, *Problem Modeli Anatomicznych "Écorchés" i Trzy Statuetki w Bibliotece Jagiellońskiej* (Wrocław, 1963), fig. 22.

[71] This pose anticipates to some degree Stephan Lochner's treatment of the same subject a century and a half later; see *Stefan Lochner, Meister zu Köln: Herkunft, Werke, Wirkung*, ed. F. G. Zehnder (Cologne, 1993), no. 91, Berlin, Staatliche Museen zu Berlin, Preussischer Kulturbesitz, Kupferstichkabinett, Inv. Nr. KdZ 778 (workshop copy); and no. 117, Apostles Altar, Frankfurt am Main, Städelsches Kunstinstitut, Inv. Nr. 821-832. It is markedly different from the supine pose in which he is usually depicted; see Sotheby's, 2 December 1997, lot 52.

[72] Rome, Bibl. Vat., Ms. Lat. 8541; New York, Morgan Lib., Ms. M. 360; The Hermitage Museum, St. Petersburg (E 16 930-4); and Bancroft Library, University of California at Berkeley (2 Ms. A2 M2 1300: 37). See *Magyar Anjou Legéndarium*, ed. L. Ferenc (Budapest, 1973); *Ungarisches Legendarium, Vat. Lat. 8541*, ed. G. Morello, H. Stamm, and G. Betz (Stuttgart, 1991); *Biblioteca Apostolica Vaticana: Liturgie und Andacht im Mittelalter*, ed. J. M. Plotzek

and U. Surmann (Stuttgart, 1992), no. 48; J. Bader and G. Starr, "A Saint in the Family: A Leaf of the Hungarian Anjou Legendary at Berkeley," *Hungarian Studies* 2 (1986), 1–11. The St. Bartholomew image is in Morgan Lib., Ms. M. 360, f. XXI (Ferenc, pl. XIII). See Stones, *Livre d'images* (as in note 1), fig. 50.

[73] For the ways in which Agatha's martyrdom was exploited in medieval hagiography by a male audience, see M. Easton, "Saint Agatha and the Sanctification of Violence," *Studies in Iconography* 16 (1994), 83–114. The agenda here, I think, is different, aimed at female viwers.

[74] I thank Bernard S. Bachrach for this observation.

[75] The practice of nursing continued well into the childhood of medieval infants, unlike their modern counterparts, although in aristocratic families the nursing was generally not done by the mother. Elizabeth A. R. Brown notes that Philippe le Bel and his brothers were tended both by a nurse (*nutrix*) and a cradle rocker (*cunabularia*) (see "Philip the Fair" [as in note 58], 318). For the belief that the mother's milk was especially suitable for her children, Brown cites Gilles de Rome, *De Regimine Principum Libri III* (Rome, 1482), 2.2:15; and M. M. McLaughlin, "Survivors and Surrogates: Children and Parents from the Ninth to the Thirteenth Centuries," in *The History of Childhood*, ed. L. de Mause (New York, 1974), 115–16.

inflicted.[76] It is likely that the focus on the nipples which is evident in this elegant and realistic depiction was intended to stress the self-referential aspects of Madame Marie's identification with the saint and to call direct attention to the nurturing function of Agatha's attacked breasts as a reversal of the nursing model of motherhood. Other depictions of the tortures of St. Agatha tend to show the removal of the entire breast, as in the Pamplona Bible of the late twelfth century,[77] the Carpentras leaves of the middle of the thirteenth century (Fig. 7),[78] the Antiphonary of the Cistercian abbey of Cambron of the 1270s (Fig. 8),[79] and the Breviary of Philippe le Bel of 1285.[80]

Other female saints, such as Margaret,[81] are also frequently shown in medieval hagiographical illustration as victims of torture aimed at the breasts or the upper torso in general, but it is significant that the image of St. Margaret preserved here (f. 100r) shows the saint emerging fully clothed from the dragon that had swallowed her. This is the incident from her life that made her the patroness of women in childbirth. It is unlikely that the second image of Margaret, now missing, would have shown her being tortured, since the titulus at the beginning of the book mentions that Madame Marie was present in the picture, and there are no images in the book where she looks directly at tortures, either female or male.

The evisceration of St. Vincent (f. 78r, Fig. 9) is perhaps the most unusual miniature in the entire book. The nature of St. Vincent's martyrdom is unknown.[82] He is more usually shown martyred on a gridiron like his fellow Iberian and deacon St. Lawrence, who in this manuscript (f. 77v) is in fact shown being roasted, with particular attention given to details such as pitchfork, bellows, spikes on the grill, and exotic hats worn by the torturers. Lawrence's image remains undamaged, while Vincent's face has been obliterated. This may be another case of pious kissing, of which there

---

[76] I have not found an exact parallel among medieval surgical tools. Those depicted in Latin copies of the *Liber cirurgia* of Albucasis (936–1013) provide the best examples; see, for instance, Paris, B.N.F. lat. 7127, f. 38r (illustrated in Gourdon and Sounia, *Médecine médiévale* [as in note 69], no. 50); Sotheby's, 2 December 1997, lot 98, attributed to Italy, perhaps the Veneto, ca. 1300; and particularly the saw-toothed instruments (with but a single blade) in New Haven, Yale Medical Library, Cod. Paneth 28, p. 576, reproduced in L. McKinney, *Medical Illustrations in Medieval Manuscripts* (London, 1965), no. 60; but none is exactly comparable to this distinctive tool. Judith Golden suggested to me that farm implements, such as those used to remove the testicles of animals, might provide better parallels, but no such examples are included in the famous rent books, the *Rentier d'Audenarde*, Brussels, B.R., 1175 (L. Verriest, *Le Polyptyque illustré dit "Vieil Rentier" de Messire Jehan de Pamele-Audenarde [vers 1275]* [Brussels, 1950]), and the rentier of the bishop of Cambrai, Lille, A.N.D., 3 G 1208 (*La Partie cambrésienne du Polyptyque dit "Terrier de l'Evêque" de Cambrai*, ed. A. Hjorth, 2 vols. [Romanica Gothoburgensia 12 and 16] [Stockholm, 1971, and Kungväl, 1978]).

[77] F. Bucher, *The Pamplona Bibles* (New Haven, 1971), pl. 530.

[78] The martyrdoms of the saints is one of a series of full-page miniatures (presumably cut from a psalter or book of hours) that have been inserted into a fifteenth-century book of hours. Reproductions are at the Institut de Recherche et d'Histoire des Textes, Section iconographique, Orléans, and the Photo Study Collection at the J. Paul Getty Museum, Los Angeles.

[79] A. Stones and J. Steyaert, *Medieval Illumination, Glass, and Sculpture in Minnesota Collections* (Minneapolis, 1978), no. 4; A. von Euw and J. Plotzek, *Die Handschriften der Sammlung Ludwig* (Cologne, 1979), no. VI, 5; Christie's, 9 December 1981, lot 229; E. Teviotdale, "750 Years in the Life of a Pair of Cistercian Antiphonals," *Pastoral Music* 20, no. 2 (December 1995–January 1996), 38–40.

[80] See note 29 above. Another example that shows the torturers attacking the nipples of St. Agatha is the so-called Psalter-Hours of Yolande of Soissons, New York, Morgan Lib., Ms. M. 729, f. 260r, in a historiated initial illustrating the suffrage to St. Agatha.

[81] *Passio Kiliani, Ps. Theotimus, Passio Margaretae, orationes, vollständige Faksimile-Ausgabe im Originalformat des Codex Ms. I 189 aus dem Besitz der Niedersächsischen Landesbibliothek Hannover*, commentary by C. J. Hahn; introduction, transcription, and translation by H. Immel (Graz, 1988); Stones, in *Wace* (as in note 48).

[82] *BSS*, cols. 1149–55; Stones, *Livre d'images* (as in note 1), 82–83.

are many in the book,[83] and may indicate a special veneration on someone's part. Only one other depiction of the evisceration of Vincent is known to this writer. It is in the early fourteenth-century Hungarian Legendary,[84] and is in the context of his roasting, suggesting that the pouring out of the entrails is due not to the intervention of the torturers, who raise stones and a pick to attack the saint, but rather to spontaneous explosion caused by the heat of the fire beneath him. This is a different case than that in Madame Marie's book, where the torturers are directly responsible for the removal of the entrails. It is not out of the question that a lost model linked these two works. Not only is the Bartholomew flaying similar in dramatic effect, but another of Vincent's tortures in the Hungarian Legendary shows sharp points used to make holes all over his body, as happens in Madame Marie's book to Quentin (f. 82v), whereas Quentin's *Passio* relates that sharp points were rammed not all over his naked body, but between his finger and finger nails, and between his shoulder blades.[85]

Evisceration is a torture which is otherwise only occasionally meted out to saints. The tasteful martyrdom of St. Amphibalus, companion of St. Alban, which M. R. James compared to a punishment described in the *Njalssaga*, is worth mentioning here.[86] It anticipates the equally delicate evisceration of St. Erasmus, bishop of Formiae in Campania, which was popular in the fifteenth century and features notably in the Hours of Catherine of Cleves (New York, Morgan Lib., Ms. M. 945, p. 258)[87] and in Dirk Bouts's panel painting of 1458 in St. Peter's, Leuven.[88] Madame Marie's version is less polite and bears witness to a mentality that did not shrink from blood and guts, but rather exploited both.

The late tenth-century Menologion of Basil II (Bibl. Vat. gr. 1613, p. 336) provides a case from the East showing the entrails of St. Basilidis of Greece spewing (to a limited extent) from his body.[89] In the West, the only parallel in hagiography that I know for a comparably revolting spilling out of the entrails (unlike the delicacy reserved for Amphibalus and Erasmus) is that of St. Mamas, patron of the cathedral of Langres since the eighth century. His cult was fuelled by the acquisition of an arm relic from the emperor in 1075,[90] and a statue was commissioned in 1341 by King Philip VI (r. 1328–50) from the Parisian sculptor Evrard d'Orléans for the tympanum of the north portal of the cathedral. Now in the treasury, it shows the headless and fully clothed saint with his entrails spewing forth through his garments (Fig. 10).[91]

The battles of the Old Testament shown in the Old Testament Picture Bible, New York, Morgan Lib., Ms. M. 638, also reflect a similar mentality.[92] The Bible as a whole offers close analogies to Madame Marie's book in its realistic depiction of implements, arms and armour, and objects of

[83] Stones, *Livre d'images* (as in note 1), 107–8.

[84] See note 72 above.

[85] Illustrated in W. Cahn, *Romanesque Manuscripts: The Twelfth Century* (London, 1996), no. 94.

[86] Dublin, Trinity College E.i.40, f. 45r; and London, B.L., Ms. Royal 2.B.VI, f. 10v. See M. R. James, *Illustrations to the Life of St. Alban in Trinity College, Dublin, Ms. E.i.40* (Oxford, 1924), fig. 49; see also N. J. Morgan, *Early Gothic Manuscripts*, pt. 1, *1190–1250* (London, 1982), nos. 85 and 86, ill. 286.

[87] *The Hours of Catherine of Cleves*, introduction and commentaries by J. Plummer (New York, n.d.), 125.

[88] M. Friedländer, *Early Netherlandish Painting*, trans. H. Norden, 14 vols. (Leiden and Brussels, 1967–76), vol. 3 (1968), 20, pls. 14, 15.

[89] *Il Menologio di Basilio II (Cod. Vaticano greco 1613)*, 2 vols. (Turin, 1897), vol. 2, 336.

[90] *BSS*, vol. 8, cols. 592–608; *LCI*, vol. 7, cols. 483–86.

[91] I thank Lois Drewer for this important reference. See F. Baron, "Le Maître-autel de l'abbaye de Maubuisson au XIVᵉ siècle," *Monuments Piot* 57 (1971), 129–51, at 145, 148, fig. 13.

[92] See note 44 above.

everyday life. Entrails disgorged from bodies pierced by swords and lances feature in the capture of Hai (f. 10v), the subduing of the Moabites (f. 12r), Deborah encouraging Barak to attack the army of Jabin (f. 12r), Amasa slain by Joab (f. 46v), and, a particularly interesting example, the Levite hewing the corpse of his dead and violated wife in pieces (f. 16v). This is the only case I know, apart from the medical examples mentioned below, of spewing entrails associated with a woman.

Historical cases of disembowelment happen to men and are usually punishment for treason. The fate of Judas, betrayer of Christ, commonly shown in medieval sculpture and painting as hanging from a tree with his entrails cascading forth, is an obvious parallel. If flaying was the supreme form such punishment took in medieval France, drawing and quartering, which included evisceration, was the English punishment for comparable crimes.[93] Famous victims in the late thirteenth and early fourteenth centuries were Prince Davydd III (d. 1283) and Llywelyn Bren (d. 1317), leaders of Welsh resistance to Edward I and II; William Wallace (d. 1305), leader of the Scots against Edward I; and Andrew Harclay, Earl of Carlisle (d. 1323), who joined Robert the Bruce against Edward II. The sentence against William Wallace includes the notation "for your burning churches and relics your heart, liver, lungs, and entrails from which your wicked thoughts came shall be burned . . . ."[94] None of these incidents seems to have entered the illustrations of the Chronicles, but the illustrated copies of the *Divine Comedy* show Dante in hell, observing the Sowers of Discord, who are continually split apart, with accompanying disgorging of guts. This was a punishment for the instigators of scandal and schism, such as Mahomet, Mosca dei Lamberti, Bertrand de Born (who, already mentioned as holding his severed head, is attended by evil-looking torturers, one of whom hangs out his tongue), and Geri del Bello.[95]

The inclusion of Vincent's evisceration in a book made for a married woman may suggest another dimension of interpretation. One might see this torture inflicted on a man not only as a suffering saint for whom to feel pity and fear, but also as a reversal of the particular fears proper to a woman, and a focus for reifying them. Conception and childbirth held many terrors until the second half of the twentieth century. Nor could female saints embody those fears, only the positive outcome of childbirth, not its pain nor the death that so often resulted. The Virgin Mary, St. Anne, and St. Elizabeth all successfully gave birth, and St. Margaret bursting forth from the dragon also presented, and interceded for, a positive outcome. The opening of the Virgin's womb would reveal the presence of the Godhead either as the embryo of the Christ Child [96] or as the Trinity, as in the opening Virgin and Child statues which were popular as devotional images in Germany in the early fourteenth century.[97] One would certainly not see the Virgin's blood and guts revealed: she could not be literally vested with the fears surrounding childbirth.

However, the ripped-open stomach of Vincent might certainly allude, in reverse, to the fear of a caesarian section, as is shown for the birth of Julius Caesar in the Princeton, University Library,

[93] See Barron, "Penalties for Treason" (as in note 53); and D. M. Walker, *The Oxford Companion to Law* (Oxford, 1980), 377, 1232, articles on drawing and quartering, and treason, to which Janelle Greenberg kindly drew my attention.

[94] The passage is quoted in the entry in *Dictionary of National Biography*, ed. L. Stephen (London, 1885–1901), from *Chronicles of Edward I and Edward II*, Rolls Ser., 137.

[95] *Inferno* XXVIII; see note 38 above.

[96] For instance, in the early fourteenth-century Gradual of Wonnenthal in Karlsruhe, Badische Landesbibliothek U.H.i.

[97] G. Radler, *Die Schreinmadonna "Vierge ouvrante": Von den bernhardinischen Anfängen bis zur Frauenmystik im Deutschordensland, mit beschreibendem Katalog* (Frankfurt am Main, 1990).

Garrett 128, *Histoire ancienne* (Fig. 11).[98] This is one of the first, if not the earliest, illustrated copies (ca. 1300), as is indicated by the presence of marginal notes for the illuminator.[99] Worse still, conception in the late thirteenth century could even result in dissection.[100] Madame Marie's artist may well have known models like the puzzling dissection or autopsy scene in Oxford, Bodl., Ms. Ashmole 399 (Fig. 12),[101] or the anatomical studies which were coming into prominence in medical circles at the end of the thirteenth century in Montpellier and Paris. Alongside the skin man illustration in Henri de Mondeville's *Anatomy* (Paris, B.N.F. fr. 2030), mentioned above, are several other drawings where the human figure, both male and female, is opened up at front or back to show the internal organs or the spinal cord (Fig. 13).[102]

If the Mondeville translation was undoubtedly made in the orbit of the Parisian court, there was also a keen interest in a similar kind of medical diagram centred on the human body, female and male, in the south of France, to which Basel, Univ. Bibl. D.II.11 bears witness. It includes an anatomical treatise in Provençal accompanied by five full-page drawings, one of which shows a woman with uterus revealed, the others, of men, showing the skeleton, veins, male sexual organs, and arteries.[103] The medical school at Salerno is the setting for the central episode in Hartmann von Auwe's *Arme Heinrich,* where the heroine offers her body to be dissected by a surgeon in order to cure Heinrich of leprosy. He hears the surgeon sharpening his knife in a neighbouring room; looking at the scene through the keyhole, he sees the girl's naked beauty, and realizes he cannot allow this sacrifice to occur.[104] The story would seem to lend itself to illustration, yet no illustrated

[98] A. Bennett, J. F. Preston, and W. P. Stoneman, *A Summary Guide to Western Medieval Manuscripts at Princeton University* (Princeton, 1991), 43.

[99] I read the accompanying notes next to the miniature as: "famez a oevre/ventre dune fame/a coutia(us) & e(n)traie(n)t/i effa(n)t qui a gr(an)s/shouens (?)."

[100] The earliest reference to a dissection of a human corpse noted by M. N. Alston, "The Attitude of the Church towards Dissection before 1500," *Bulletin of the Institute of the History of Medicine* 16 (1944), 221–38, at 226, is of 1286, in the chronicle of Salimbene, cited from MGH, *Scriptores* (1905–13), 613.

[101] Discussed in McKinney, *Medical Illustrations* (as in note 76), 100–1, no. 96, citing earlier interpretations; see also Huard and Grmek, *Mille ans de chirurgie* (as in note 69), fig. 128; Margotta, *Story of Medicine* (as in note 69), 132; Morgan, *Early Gothic Manuscripts*, pt. 2 (as in note 68), cat. 117, ills. 99, 100, with full bibliography, to which may be added L. Dixon, *Perilous Chastity: Women and Illness in Pre-Enlightenment Art and Medicine* (Ithaca, 1995), 26–38. The miniatures are an added bifolio without accompanying text, and consequently open to varying interpretations, summarized by McKinney, 100–1. I think the hat worn by the dissectionist is significant: close to a Jewish hat in shape, it may well suggest that a Jewish abortionist or dissectionist is being caught in the act by the woman's physician. An interesting parallel situation involving a Jew is recounted in the mid-thirteenth-century

chronicle of Richer of Senones in relation to a window with the Life of Saint Dié at the Collegiate Church of Saint-Dié (Vosges), which depicts episodes from the story of a Christian girl, hired as a domestic servant by a Jewish necromancer who drugged her and removed her uterus. She survived, Christian matrons determined what had happened, and caused the Jew to be convicted and hanged. See M. P. Lillich, *Rainbow Like an Emerald: Stained Glass in Lorraine in the Thirteenth and Early Fourteenth Centuries* (University Park and London, 1991), 78–81, pl. IV.14. I thank Marcia Kupfer for drawing this example to my attention. There is no formal link with the scene of dissection in Bodl., Ashmole 399, nor, apparently, is the removal of the uterus actually shown in the glass.

[102] Sudhoff, *Geschichte der Anatomie* (as in note 69), pl. 23, nos. 5, 6, 9, 11, 12, 13 and the references cited in note 69 above.

[103] Sudhoff, *Geschichte der Anatomie* (as in note 69), 11–29, pls. 1–5; Herrlinger, *History of Medical Illustration* (as in note 69) pl. 2, fig. 39; Choulant, *Anatomic Illustration* (as in note 69), 50–52, 55–60.

[104] Hartmann von Aue, *Der arme Heinrich*, ed. H. Paul, 15th ed. (Tübingen, 1984), ll. 1049–1284. I thank Deborah Gatewood for this reference. The separation of the heart from the body also found literary expression in stories of married women unknowingly eating the hearts of their lovers, as in the *Lai de l'ignaure* and the *Roman du Châtelain de Coucy,* also unillustrated so far as I know. See

copies have survived. It was another two centuries before pictures showing Nero watching the dissection of the naked body of his mother Agrippina, whom he had had assassinated, entered the illustrative tradition of Laurent de Premierfait's translation of Boccaccio's *Cas des nobles hommes et femmes*.[105]

Madame Marie's book was made just at the time when the kings and queens of France were providing for separate heart, entrails, and body tombs in different churches,[106] despite Pope Boniface VIII's edict against the boiling of the dead body to separate flesh from bones.[107] Philip IV obtained an indult allowing him separate heart and body burials, the former at Poissy and the latter at Saint-Denis,[108] whereas Louis X was buried intact at Saint-Denis. Both bodies were prepared for burial by Henri de Mondeville.[109] The degree to which they were embalmed, if at all, is a question on which the sources are unclear. The process can hardly have been as it is described in the thirteenth-century versions of the story of Troy, whether in the French edition of Benoît de Sainte-Maure[110] or the Latin of Guido delle Colonne.[111] Both featured the embalming of the body of Hector, accomplished by pouring embalming fluid into his body through a hole in the head and distributing it through a series of tubes.[112] An illustrative tradition in Italy shows that this episode had attracted particular attention there in the late thirteenth and early fourteenth centuries.[113]

Le Roman du castelain de Couci et de la dame de Fayel, par Jakemes (Société des anciens texts français), ed. M. Delbouille and J. E. Matzke (Paris, 1936); *Le Roman du Chastelain de Coucy et de la dame de Fayel* (Lille, Bibliothèque municipale, fonds Godefroy 50), ed. A. M. Babbi (Fasano, 1994). These romances are quite different in their macabre and moralizing overtones from the other famous heart romance, René of Anjou's *Le cuer d'amours espris*, of which three illustrated copies survive: see *King René's Book of Love (Le Cueur d'Amours Espris), the National Library, Vienna (Cod. Vind. 2597)*, ed. F. Unterkircher (New York, 1975); see also F. Avril and N. Reynaud, *Les Manuscrits à peintures en France 1440–1520* (Paris, 1993), no. 209.

[105] Such as Paris, Arsenal 5193, f. 290v, reproduced in colour on the cover of paperback edition of Pouchelle, *Corps et chirurgie* (as in note 69). This incident is not in Suetonius.

[106] Alston, "Attitude of the Church" (as in note 100), at 230–38; C. A. Bradford, *Heart Burial* (London, 1933); A. Erlande-Brandenbourg, *Le Roi est mort: Étude sur les funérailles, les sépultures et les tombeaux des rois de France jusqu'à la fin du XIIIᵉ siècle* (Bibliothèque de la Société française d'archéologie 7) (Geneva, 1975); E. A. R. Brown, "Death and the Human Body in the Later Middle Ages: The Legislation of Boniface VIII on the Division of the Corpse," *Viator* 12 (1981), 221–70, repr. in ead., *Monarchy of Capetian France* (as in note 34), no. VI; ead., "The Ceremonial of Royal Succession in Capetian France: The Double Funeral of Louis X," *Traditio* 34 (1978), 227–71, repr. ibid., no. VII; ead., "The Ceremo-

nial of Royal Succession in Capetian France: The Funeral of Philip V," *Speculum* 55 (1980), 266–93, repr. ibid., no. VIII.

[107] 27 September 1299, published in *Les Registres de Boniface VIII*, ed. G. Digard et al. (Bibliothèque des Écoles françaises d'Athènes et de Rome, ser. 2, no. 4) (Paris, 1884–1939), no. 3409; A. Potthast, *Regesta Pontificum Romanorum inde ab Anno post Christum Natum 1198 ad Annum 1304*, 2 vols. (Berlin, 1874–85), no. 24881.

[108] Brown, "Death and the Human Body" (as in note 106), 256, citing C. Baudon de Mony, "La Mort et les funérailles de Philippe le Bel d'après un compte rendu à la court de Majorque," *Bibliothèque de l'École des chartes* 58 (1897), 11–12.

[109] Brown, "Death and the Human Body" (as in note 106), 257, citing Pagel, *Leben, Lehre und Leistungen* (as in note 69), 392. Brown notes that the term used, "preparavimus," need not imply embalming.

[110] *Le Roman de Troie, par Benoît de Sainte-Maure*, ed. L. Constans (Paris, 1904–12).

[111] Guido delle Colonne, *Historia destructionis Troiae*, ed. N. E. Griffin (Cambridge, Mass., 1936); trans. M. E. Meek (Bloomington and London), 1974.

[112] Book XXII; trans. Meek (as in note 111), 170–71.

[113] H. Buchthal, *Historia Troiana: Studies in the History of Mediaeval Secular Illustration* (Studies of the Warburg Institute 32) (London and Leiden, 1971), pl. 44b, Madrid, Biblioteca Nacionale, 17805, f. 97v. See also id., "Hector's Tomb," in *De Artibus Opuscula XL: Essays in Honor of Erwin Panofsky*, ed. M. Meiss (New York, 1961), 29–36.

CONCLUSION

We can only speculate as to whether Madame Marie or her husband, Wautier d'Enghien, actually had a personal physician, and if so what medical pictures he might have owned and used and been able to pass to her illuminators, or whether those illuminators might themselves have produced such pictures for the medical market, and made these striking images for Madame Marie as a partial by-product. Although her library list is not extant, Marie de Rethel is known for commissioning a Book of Monsters and it is likely that her library did contain other literary works, perhaps some of whose texts or pictures mirrored aspects of these devotional images.

The battered state of the book is a clear indication that it was actually used. Its pages, torn and repaired with strips of parchment, are splattered with wax, some faces have been erased through kissing or pious erasure, and Madame Marie herself has been deliberately covered up. Generations of users reacted and responded in various ways to these images. The precise function of the book in Madame Marie's pious exercises cannot be known for certain in the absence of accompanying text and without documentation of the kind that is more readily available in the fifteenth century, for Cecily of York and her daughter and cousin,[114] for example. Their books and devotional practices clearly owed much to monastic models of prayer, homilies, meditation, and reading.

This picture book may originally have been accompanied by a volume of suffrages and prayers, or perhaps Madame Marie knew these by heart or had her Franciscan confessor say them for her. But Madame Marie's pictures do seem to add another dimension to what we know of late thirteenth-century private devotion. They seem to discourage too much mystical meditation, to focus instead on the female patron's own experience, transmuted to that of the saints, and so encourage her to transcend her present state. The book appears to have been a one-off job; its pictures are not like any other pictures. It was a special book for a special person, with its particular circumstances only hinted at, and that through the pictures themselves. The late thirteenth century was a period of experimentation, in which each of the major devotional books stands on its own: the Rothschild Canticles, the Psalter-Hours of Yolande of Soissons, the Nürnberg Hours. Each of these is a special case and none a duplicate of any other. Not until the fifteenth century did standard patterns emerge as foci for private devotion: the panel painting and the book of hours. Madame Marie's book anticipates both.[115]

---

[114] See *Margaret of York, Simon Marmion, and the Visions of Tondal*, ed. T. Kren (Malibu, Ca., 1992), with extensive references.

[115] It is a pleasure to acknowledge the unparalleled resources of the Index of Christian Art and the generous assistance of its staff, especially Adelaide Bennett Hagens and Lois Drewer.

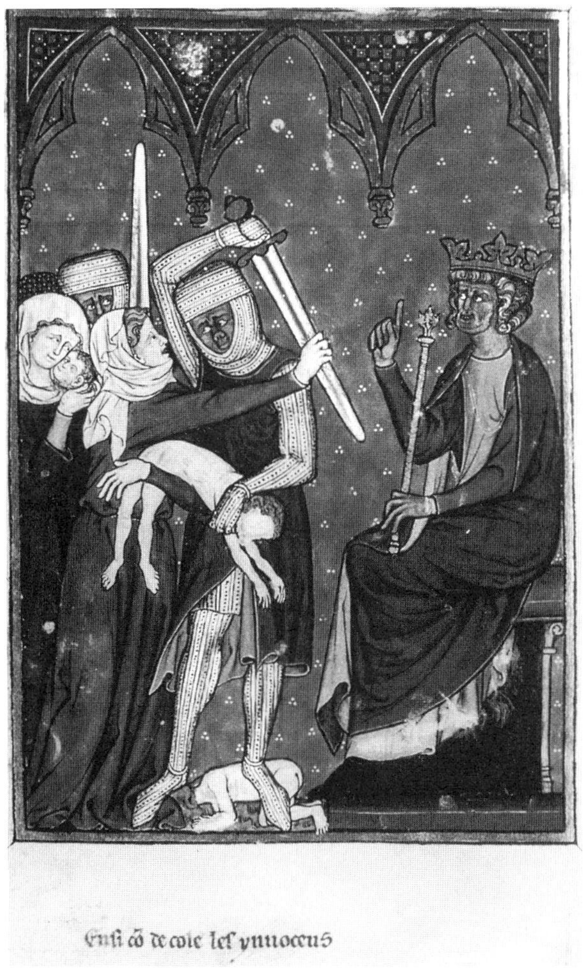

1. Paris, Bibliothèque Nationale de France, Ms. nouv. acq. fr. 16251, f. 24v. Massacre of the Innocents

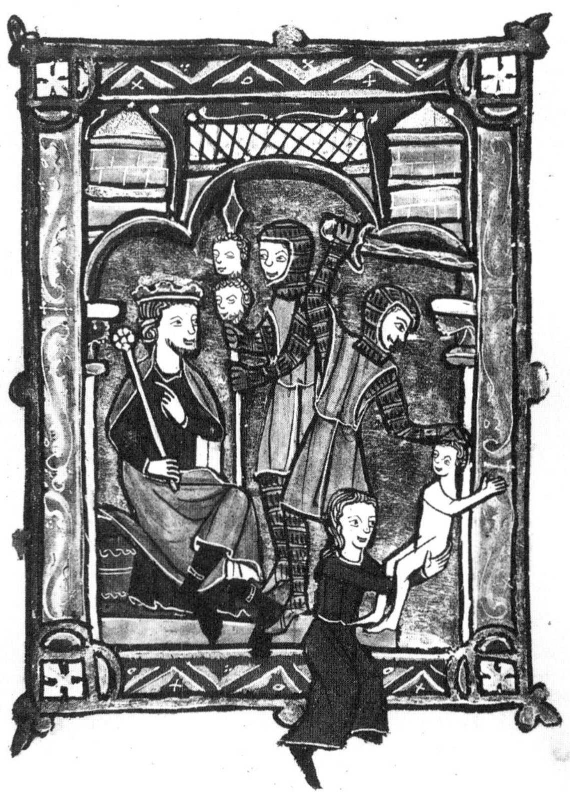

2. Aix-en-Provence, Bibliothèque Méjanes, Ms. 15, f. XI. Massacre of the Innocents

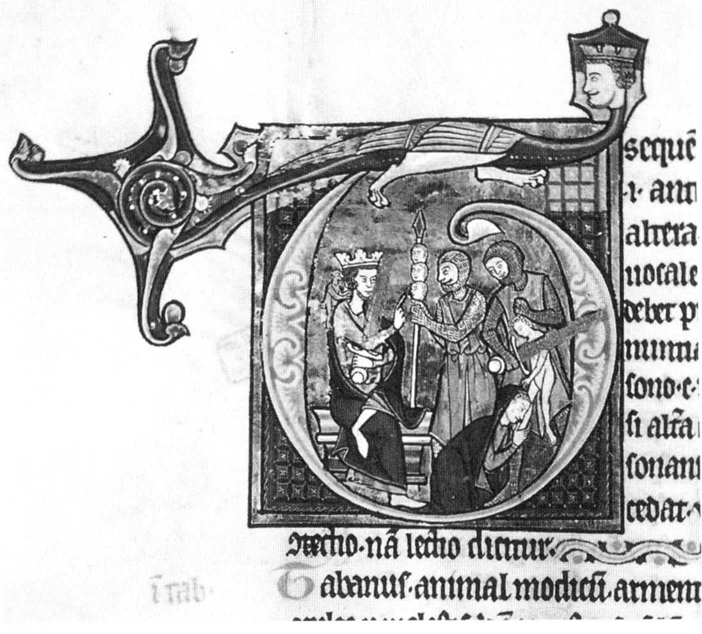

3. Valenciennes, Bibliothèque Municipale, Ms. 397, f. 90v. Epitome of Tyranny

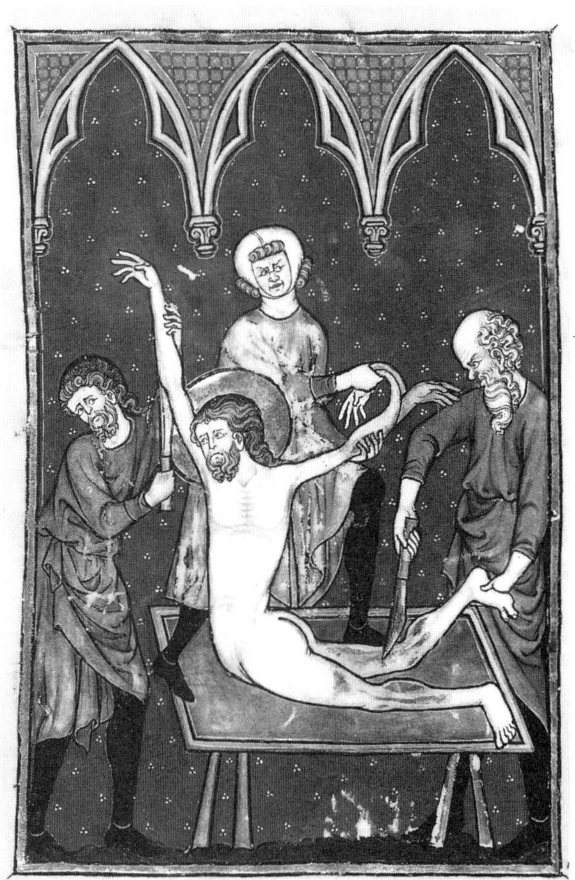

4. Paris, Bibliothèque Nationale de France, Ms. nouv. acq. fr. 16251, f. 67v. Flaying of St. Bartholomew

5. Paris, Bibliothèque Nationale de France, Ms. fr. 2030, f. 10v. Skin man

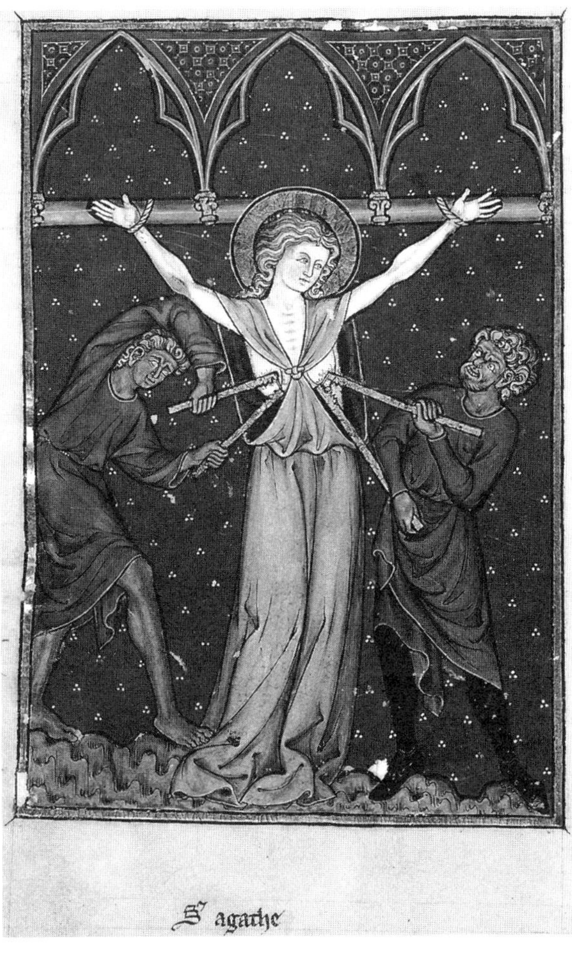

6. Paris, Bibliothèque Nationale de France, Ms. nouv. acq. fr. 16251, f. 97v. Torture of St. Agatha

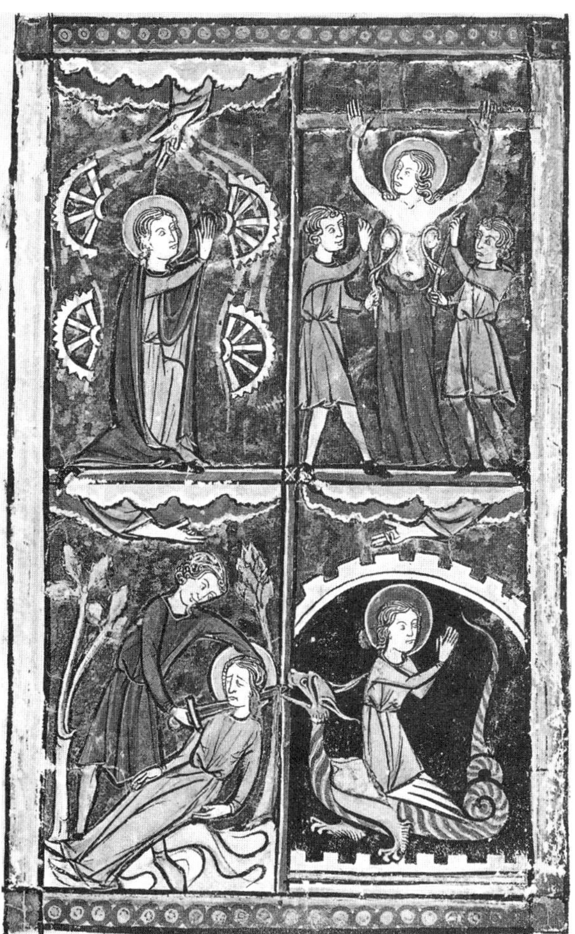

7. Carpentras, Bibliothèque Inguimbertine, Ms. 77, f. 178v. Torture of St. Agatha

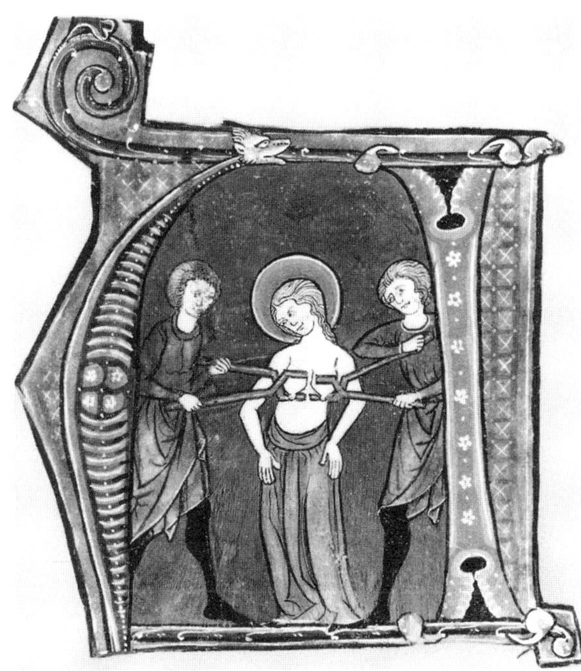

8. Collegeville, Minnesota, St. John's University, Ms. 44 (Bean Ms. 3), f. 24a. Torture of St. Agatha

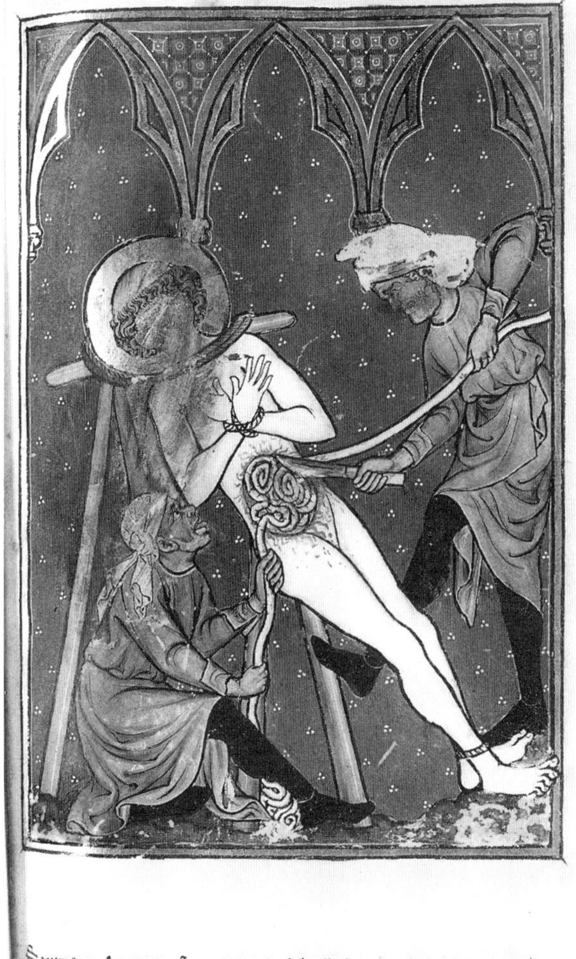

9. Paris, Bibliothèque Nationale de France, Ms. nouv. acq. fr. 16251, f. 78r. Evisceration of St. Vincent

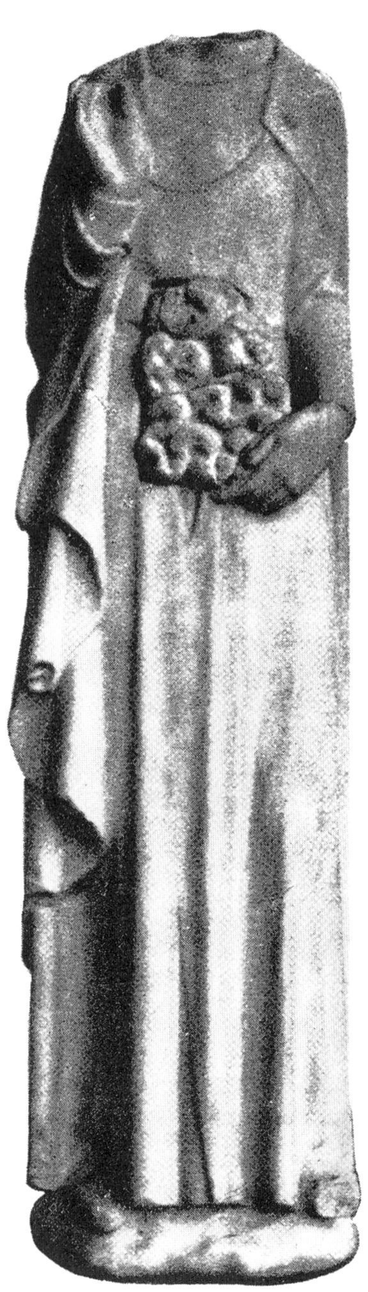

10. Langres, Cathedral Treasury, St. Mamas

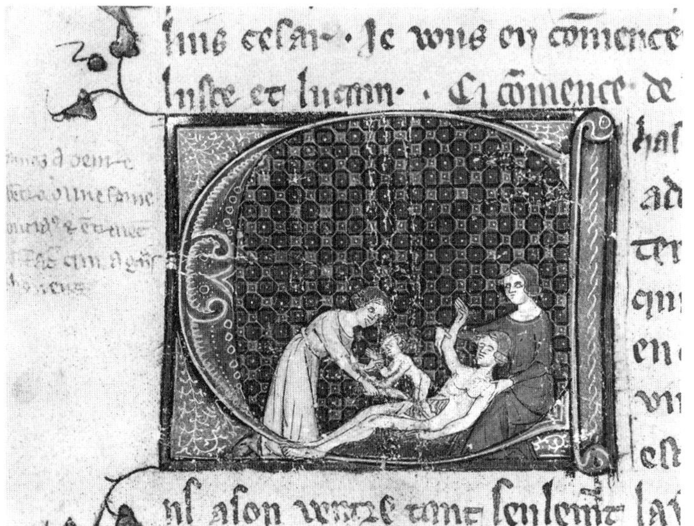

11. Princeton, University Library, Ms. Garrett 128, f. 144r. Birth of Julius Caesar

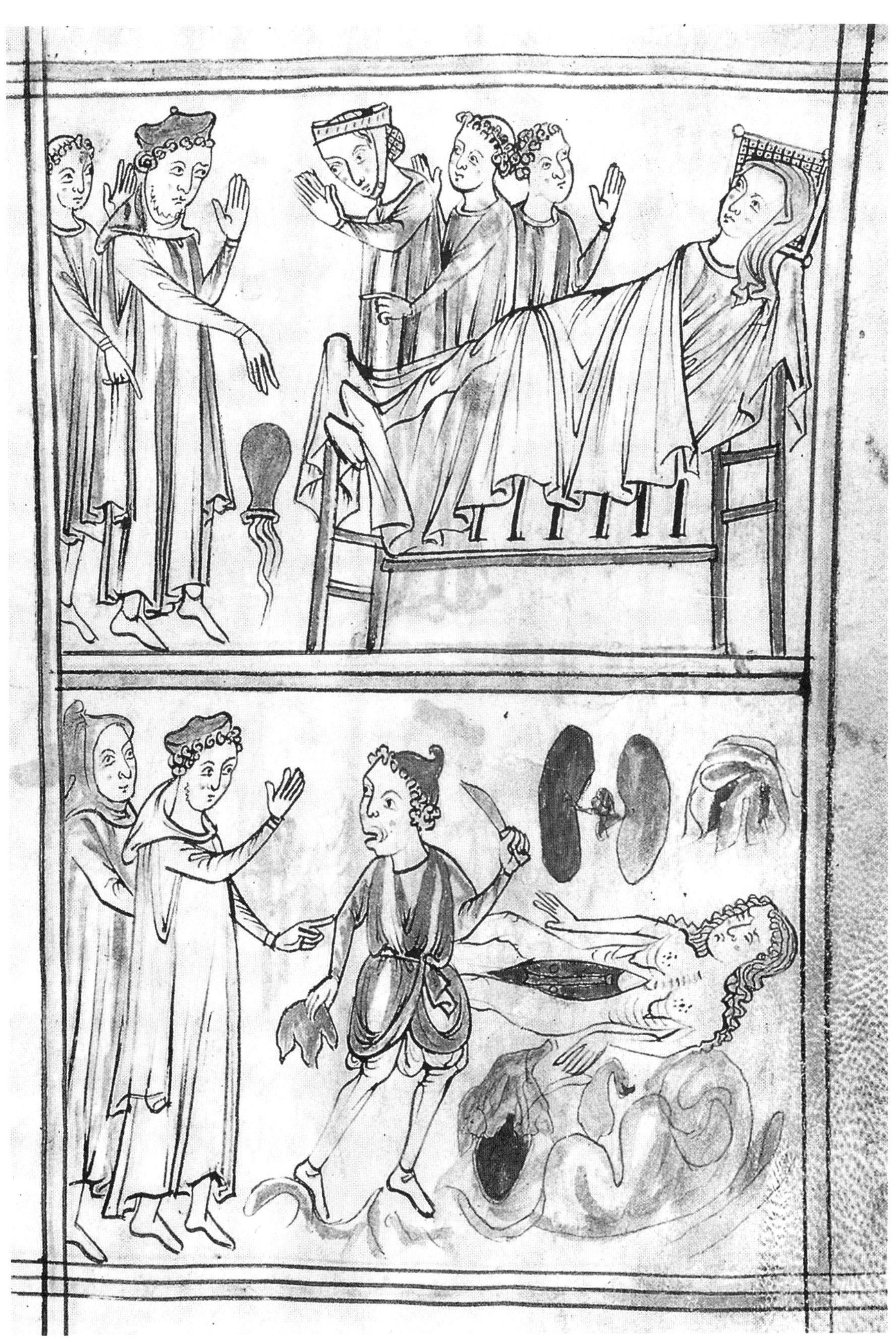

12. Oxford, Bodleian Library, Ms. Ashmole 399, f. 34r. Dissection or autopsy scene

entiers dont lun aparra en lune
partie de lacoille et lautre en lautre

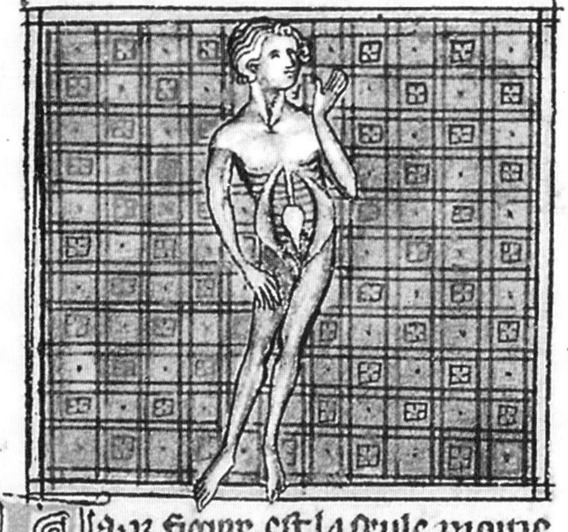

La .13. figure est la seule moitie
dedens de lame des la isintu
re delespine qui est ou milieu des
costes dur aus doit des pies trenche
par lemilieu du ventre de la toute
du stomach due aucul en la quele
apert lammatrique gesant sus
le longation. Et les .2. coillons de
dens lie entre le col delie et la grat
concauite. et apert la vessie estat
sur le col delie dedens entre les gro
silles de la queue et les os des han
ches.

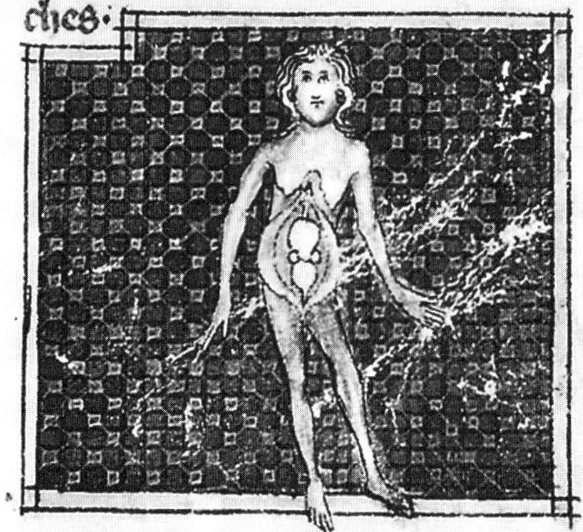

13. Paris, Bibliothèque Nationale de France, Ms. fr. 2030, f. 29r. Anatomical drawing

Moral Structure in
the Ashburnham Pentateuch

.

DOROTHY HOOGLAND VERKERK

THE IDIOSYNCRATIC arrangement of scenes on the folios of the late sixth-century Ashburnham Pentateuch (Paris, B.N.F. nouv. acq. lat. 2334), is the most perplexing of the many questions surrounding the manuscript.[1] Noted for their color and rich details, the illustrations appear on eighteen folios of the manuscript, and none of them follows any consistent pattern of organization. Folio 6r, for example, shows no relation to the narrative sequence related in Genesis 3 and 4, the story of Cain and Abel (Fig. 1). At the left of the top register, Adam and Eve, dressed in their animal skins, stand under a bower. Directly below, in the second register, Eve dandles Cain on her lap while Adam tills the ground. In the top register, Eve nurses her second son, Abel. Abel tends his flocks in the bottom register on the left, and Cain tills the soil in the bottom right register. The two brothers offer their gifts to God in the top right register. In the center, the hand of God rejects Cain's blemished offering and accepts Abel's perfect offering. Cain kills Abel in the bottom center of the folio. The sequence concludes with God questioning Cain in the middle register to the far right. If the scenes are read in correct narrative order, it must be concluded that they are placed in an incoherent manner that jumps erratically around the folio.

To decipher what the reasoning behind the placement and selection of illustrations may have been, it is necessary to abandon many personal assumptions. One must set aside, for the moment, the reconstruction of the prototype and focus instead on the existing illustrations. Secondly, the chronology of the biblical narrative has to be relinquished. The chaos created by the illustrations' sequence is the result of trying to read them according to the biblical narrative; in other words, a textual structure that moves in a strict chronological order, with one scene leading to the next. Pic-

---

[1] O. von Gebhardt, *The Miniatures of the Ashburnham Pentateuch* (London, 1883) publishes black-and-white plates and the inscriptions; R. Sörries, *Christlich-antike Buchmalerei im Überblick* (Wiesbaden, 1993), 26–33, publishes small color plates. An origin in Rome is suggested in D. H. Verkerk, "Roman Bible Illumination 400–700 A.D. and the Ashburnham Pentateuch," in *Imaging the Early Medieval Bible*, ed. J. Williams (University Park, Pa., 1999). Discussions of the origins proposed for the manuscript—northern Africa, Spain, Germany, northern Italy, Dalmatia, Syria—are found in F. Rickert, *Studien zum Ashburnham Pentateuch (Paris, Bibl. Nat. NAL. 2334)* (Ph.D. diss., University of Bonn, 1986); and D. Verkerk, "Liturgy and Narrative in the Ashburnham Pentateuch," (Ph.D. diss., Rutgers, The State University of New Jersey, 1992), 17–36. See also I. R. Gill, "The Orthography of the Ashburnham Pentateuch and Other Latin Manuscripts of the Late Proto-Romance Period—Some Questions of Palaeography and Vulgar Latin Linguistics," *Institute of Classical Studies Bulletin* 23 (1976), 27–44; H. J. van Ginhoven, "Le Miniaturiste du Pentateuque de Tours ou Pentateuque d'Ashburnham et se méthode de travail (Paris, Bibliothèque nationale, Nouv. acq. lat. 2334)," *CahArch* 42 (1994), 65–74.

tures are not limited to this strict chronology and narrative sequence. These illustrations invite a viewing as a visual and oral structure. The illustrations' layout on the folios becomes more comprehensible when seen from the viewpoint of storytelling with a didactic function.

The codex originally had sixty-nine illustrated folios interspersed throughout the text.[2] The eighteen extant illustrations generally begin chronologically in the upper left, and then revert to a compact series of scenes scattered over the folio. Complicating this, the multipartite format is not consistent throughout the manuscript. Scenes such as the Deluge and the Crossing of the Red Sea occupy the entire folio or most of it (Figs. 2, 3). In addition, the combination of text and illustration is found on folios 21r, 30r, and 127v: the meeting of Isaac and Rebecca, Laban searching the tents for his household gods, and Moses conferring his spirit to the seventy elders.[3] The manuscript also contains a full-page decorated frontispiece and six folios of *capitula* lists that resemble canon tables.[4] Although little more than one quarter of the original illustrated folios survives, it is enough to allow some notion of how essential the illustrations were for the manuscript. The richness and variety of the illustrations are unprecedented in surviving early medieval manuscripts.

While the organization of the scenes has been questioned persistently, the attempts to account for it remain problematic. Within the methodological frame of his recension theory, Kurt Weitzmann found the out-of-narrative order puzzling, noting "the . . . scenes which the illustrator distributed over the surface in a purely decorative manner with utter disregard for the correct sequence."[5] According to Weitzmann, the artist, working from a larger pictorial cycle, placed the scenes willy-nilly and used an excessive amount of "filler" such as the wheat in the lower right corner of folio 6r (Fig. 1). When confronted with a lengthy series of pictures from which to select and reorganize, the artist of the Ashburnham Pentateuch resorted to a haphazard jumble.

Joseph Gutmann proposed a Jewish, Syro-Palestinian prototype for the Ashburnham Pentateuch,[6] arguing that a model with either an Aramaic or a Hebraic text, reading from right to left, would explain the narrative movement from right to left in folios 21r, 22v, 25r, and 44r.[7] In the lower right of folio 21r, for example, Rebecca parts from her family, and the action then moves to the left. On folio 22r, Rebecca asks for God's guidance in the upper right and then gives birth to twins in the lower left. Most of the folios, however, do not follow a right-to-left sequence.

Neither Weitzmann nor Gutmann was concerned with the details of each illustrated folio. They placed the Ashburnham Pentateuch's illustrations within the frame of larger overarching

---

[2] B. Narkiss, "Reconstruction of Some of the Original Quires of the Ashburnham Pentateuch," *CahArch* 22 (1972), 19–38; H. Quentin, "La Critique de la vulgate," *Revue bénédictine* 36 (1924), 424–25, calculates sixty-two; D. Wright, review of *Early Medieval Painting from the Fourth to the Eleventh Century*, by A. Grabar and C. Nordenfalk, in *ArtB* 43 (1961), 251, sixty-five.

[3] Sörries, *Buchmalerie* (as in note 1), pls. 6, 8, 12.

[4] J. C. Sloane, "The Torah Shrine in the Ashburnham Pentateuch," *Jewish Quarterly Review* 25 (1934), 1–12; J. Gutmann, "The Jewish Origin of the Ashburnham Pentateuch Miniatures," *Jewish Quarterly Review* 44 (1953–54), 55–72. On the *capitula* lists, see D. Wright, "The Canon Tables of the Codex Beneventanus and Related Documents," *DOP* 33 (1979), 137–55.

[5] K. Weitzmann, *Late Antique and Early Christian Book Illumination* (New York, 1977), 118–25, esp. 118.

[6] Gutmann, "Jewish Origin" (as in note 4), 55–72. Gutmann followed C. R. Morey, "Lecture Notes on Early Latin Manuscripts" (New York University, n.d.), 54, that the disturbed order derives from copying a rotulus or codex. Joseph Gutmann, in response to Rickert, *Studien* (as in note 1) reversed his position, no longer maintaining his hypothesis for the influence of Jewish legends in the Ashburnham Pentateuch; see his "The Dura Europos Synagogue Paintings and Their Influence on Later Christian and Jewish Art," *Artibus et Historiae* 17 (1988), note 9. I am deeply indebted to Joseph Gutmann for sharing his wide-ranging bibliographic knowledge and for his encouragement.

[7] Sörries, *Buchmalerie* (as in note 1), pls. 6, 7, 8, 9.

theses: the evolution of pictorial recensions and the influence of rabbinical traditions on Christian art. There are two fundamental problems with both of these approaches to examining the arrangement of scenes in the book. First, they look to a previous model for answers without considering the contemporaneous issues that may have shaped the codex: the function of the manuscript in large part determines its format. Secondly, both are based in a textual, or written, structure defined by the biblical narratives. They assume that the chronological sequence of narrative determined the order of the scenes, and that illustration was subordinate to the written text.

I find it difficult to accept the underlying assumption that the makers of this manuscript resorted to merely decorative devices or were confined by a model when it came to selecting scenes from a larger cycle and then arranging those scenes on a folio. They could create complex iconographical meanings. The Crossing of the Red Sea, for example, can be understood as a narrative of the Hebrews escaping Pharaoh's wrath by crossing the Red Sea on dry land. The visual cue on folio 68r (Fig. 3), however, shows that the illustration differs from the text and interprets this scene typologically, not historically.[8] The pillar of fire and cloud (*columna nubis*) is depicted as a large candle held by two hands,[9] not as a flaming architectural column or a burning cypress tree, the two standard portrayals of the pillar in medieval art.[10] During the Easter Vigil, the deacon held a candle while the celebrant led the catechumens to the waters of baptism. In the manuscript the hand-held candle is a visual prompt to remember the meaning of the Red Sea crossing for the Christian: it was a foreshadowing of Christian baptism. Through the inclusion of the candle, Jewish history is appropriated and transformed into Christian history in the Ashburnham Pentateuch. The candle is thus a simple insertion that profoundly changes the text's meaning. The illustrations show a complex, imaginative, and rich pictorial iconography that does not hesitate to invent by incorporating contemporary imagery. The sophistication of this iconography argues against a less competent handling of format and argues for a more profound structure.

The detailed and lively paintings also argue for more than a decorative or haphazard approach. Rich domestic details, such as Rebecca making a savory dish, as well as architectural details are among the most appealing aspects of the illustrations (Fig. 4).[11] The makers of manuscripts were not lacking in creativity when asked to arrange scenes on a page. After all, by this time illustrators of manuscripts had been creating varied solutions for at least two hundred years.[12] A grid format that accommodated many scenes was used in the Corpus Christi Gospels (Cambridge, Cor-

[8] This argument is fully developed in D. H. Verkerk, "Exodus and Easter Vigil in the Ashburnham Pentateuch," *ArtB* 77 (1995), 94–105.

[9] Cf. M. Avery, *The Exultet Rolls of South Italy* (Princeton, 1936), pls. XIX, XIII, XIV, L, LVI, LXVI; see also T. F. Kelly, *The Exultet in Southern Italy* (New York and Oxford, 1996).

[10] For the architectural column, see J. Wilpert, *I sarcophagi cristiani antichi* (Rome, 1929 and 1932), vol. 1, pl. LXXXXVII(4); vol. 2, pls. CCIC (3), CCX (1,2), CCXI (1,2), CCXVI (8); G. Jeremias, *Die Holztür der Basilika S. Sabina in Rom* (Tübingen, 1980), pls. 26, 28; S. Dufrenne, *L'Illustration des psautiers grecs du moyen âge* (Paris, 1966), pls. 14, 23, 39, 55; M. Metzger, *La Haggada enluminé* (Lei-

den, 1973), 288–301, pls. 357, 381, 384. For the burning cypress, see J. Lowden, *The Octateuchs: A Study in Byzantine Manuscript Illumination* (University Park, Pa., 1992), 134–37; A. Cutler, *The Aristocratic Psalters in Byzantium* (Paris, 1984), figs. 107, 155, 229, 253, 326, 369; Avery, *Exultet Rolls* (as in note 9), pls. LXXIV, CLIX.

[11] F. Rickert, "Zu den Stadt- und Architekturdarstellungen des Ashburnham Pentateuch (Paris, Bibl. Nat. NAL 2334)," in *Actes du XIe Congrès international d'archéologie chrétienne* (Studi di antichità cristiana, 41) (Rome, 1989), 1341–54.

[12] J. Lowden, "The Beginnings of Biblical Illustration," in *Imaging the Early Medieval Bible*, ed. J. Williams (University Park, Pa., 1999).

pus Christi College, Cod. 286)[13] and the Quedlinburg Itala (Berlin, Staatsbibl., Ms. Theol. Lat., f. 485, and Quedlinburg, Cathedral Treasury).[14] Considering the number of illustrations on the multipartite folios, it is unusual that the illustrator did *not* choose the grid format. It signals that another rationale may be behind the curious configuration. Rather than being decorative or imposed by a textual model, the organization should be viewed as intentional and creative. The number of illustrated folios, the lavish detail, and the iconographical complexity suggest that the illuminations were valuable and carefully considered.

Physical evidence in the Ashburnham Pentateuch supports the idea that the illustrations were the *raison d'être* for the manuscript. For example, a lengthy *titulus* accompanies each scene and figure, ensuring that the illustrations are clearly identified. No matter how familiar the reader may be with the story, the *tituli* provide the correct biblical texts. The scene of the midwives before Pharaoh in the upper right of folio 56r, for example, shows the second interrogation, not the first (Fig. 5).[15] The *titulus* tells the reader that the midwives are protesting that they have done their job, but the Hebrew women continue to bear many children. Because the scenes are not in narrative sequence, the *tituli* provide a check. Furthermore, below the painted *tituli* is another set of ink *tituli*. The ink *tituli* were derived from an Old Latin (*Vetus Latina*), or pre-Vulgate, text and accompanied the pen-and-ink underdrawings. This type is found on folio 56r where water damage has washed away the gouache to reveal the pen and ink.[16] When the thick gouache was applied over the ink drawings and inscriptions, the ink *tituli* were translated and written in goauche, in Vulgate Latin. Obviously, some trouble was taken to change the wording of the *tituli*, but the order of the episodes was kept intact.

In summary, the number of illustrations, the complexity of detail, the sophistication of the iconography, and the clarity provided by the *tituli* argue that the idiosyncrasies of the Pentateuch's illustrations are intentional. Furthermore, simpler solutions to illustrating the Bible were available. The explanation does not lie in the relationship of hypothetical exemplar to surviving manuscript, but in the use of the codex itself. Pope Gregory's now famous dictum that pictures were books for the illiterate exemplifies the Church's understanding of how pictures could bring to mind Bible stories.[17] Pope Gregory was not suggesting that the illiterate learn the Bible stories from pictures, but that the pictures remind them of stories they had already learned. It was a matter of memory and oral repetition.[18]

[13] F. Wormald, *The Miniatures in the Gospels of St. Augustine (Corpus Christi College Ms. 286)* (Cambridge, 1954); E. A. Lowe, *Codices Latini Antiquiores,* vol. 2 (Oxford, 1935), no. 126; P. McGurk, *Latin Gospel Books from A.D. 400 to A.D. 800* (Paris and Brussels, 1961), no. *3; Sörries, *Buchmalerie* (as in note 1), 34–36.

[14] H. Degering and A. Boeckler, *Die Quedlinburger Italafragmente* (Berlin, 1932); Lowe, *Codices Latini* (as in note 13), vol. 8, no. 1069; I. Levin, *The Quedlinburg Itala: The Oldest Illustrated Biblical Manuscript* (Leiden, 1985); Sörries, *Buchmalerie* (as in note 1), 23–25.

[15] Exod. 1:15–16; 1:18–20.

[16] Cf. M. Grant, *Dawn of the Middle Ages* (New York, 1981; reprint, New York, 1986), 13.

[17] In general see: M. Camille, "Seeing and Reading: Some Visual Implications of Medieval Literacy and Illiteracy," *Art History* 8 (1985), 26–49; L. Duggan, "Was Art Really the 'Book of the Illiterate?'" *Word and Image* 5 (1989), 227–51; C. M. Chazelle, "Pictures, Books and the Illiterate: Pope Gregory I's Letters to Serenus of Marseilles," *Word and Image* 6 (1990), 138–53; idem, "Memory, Instruction, Worship: 'Gregory's' Influence on Early Medieval Doctrines of the Artistic Image," in *Gregory the Great: A Symposium* (Notre Dame Studies in Theology 2), ed. J. Cavadini (Notre Dame, Ind. and London, 1995), 181–215.

[18] In general, see M. J. Carruthers, *The Book of Memory: A Study of Memory in Medieval Culture* (Cambridge, 1990).

Art historians traditionally understand Gregory to be referring to church murals, such as those that once adorned Old St. Peter's.[19] Herbert Kessler coined the term "painted primer" to suggest that illuminated books were the inspiration for wall paintings.[20] On the other hand, John Lowden suggests that the appreciation of wall paintings led to the illuminated Bible in the fifth century.[21] Whether book illuminations inspired wall painting, or vice versa, the emphasis in this paper is on the fact that illustrations could inform an audience about the truth of scripture, that the illustrations in the Ashburnham Pentateuch comprise a "painted primer," and that they were aids in teaching church history. More importantly, the stories taught the right order of life. Even more than for recollection, Christians mined the stories for their moral lessons.[22]

Both Augustine and John Chrysostom wrote catechisms or short pamphlets on teaching church history. Augustine's *De catechizandis rudibus* was written about A.D. 400.[23] Augustine, who wrote in response to Deogratias's letter asking for advice on teaching inquirers seeking to enter the catechumenate,[24] gives pedagogical advice and two model catechismal instructions: a longer and a shorter version of church history. Augustine's profound understanding of human psychology is evident throughout the work. No doubt it was his sound pedagogical advice that made his work the fundamental catechism from the fourth to the twentieth century.[25] Almost his contemporary, John Chrysostom wrote *Address on Vainglory and the Right Way for Parents to Bring up Their Children* in the late fourth century.[26] Using specific examples, Chrysostom paraphrases Bible stories and gleans morals from them for young boys. These two texts contain valuable information about how bibli-

[19] S. Waetzoldt, *Die Kopien des 17. Jahrhunderts nach Mosaiken und Wandmalereien in Rom* (Vienna and Munich, 1964), figs. 463–485; W. Tronzo, "The Prestige of Saint Peter's: Observations on the Function of Monumental Narrative Cycles in Italy," in *Pictorial Narrative in Antiquity and the Middles Ages*, ed. H. L. Kessler and M. S. Simpson (National Gallery of Art, Studies in the History of Art 16) (Washington, D.C., 1985), 93–112; H. L. Kessler, "Passover in St. Peter's," *Journal of Jewish Art* 12–13 (1986–87), 169–78.

[20] H. L. Kessler, "Pictorial Narrative and Church Mission in Sixth-Century Gaul," in *Pictorial Narrative* (as in note 19), 75–91; idem, "Pictures As Scripture in Fifth-Century Churches," *Studia Artium Orientalis et Occidentalis* 2 (1985), 17–31; idem, "*Facies Bibliothecae Revelata*: Carolingian Art as Spiritual Seeing," in *Testo e immagine nell'alto medioevo: Settimane di studio del centro italiano di studi sull'alto medioevo*, vol. 41 (Spoleto, 1995), 533–94.

[21] Lowden, "Biblical Illustration" (as in note 12).

[22] Origen, *Hom. Ex.* 2.3: "Think rather that you are being taught through these stories that you may learn the right order of life, moral teachings, the struggles of faith in virtue" (*Homilies on Genesis and Exodus* [Fathers of the Church, vol. 71], trans. R. E. Heine [Washington, D.C., 1982], 245).

[23] *The First Catechetical Instruction [De Catechizandis Rudibus]*, translated and annotated by J. P. Christopher (An-

cient Christian Writers 2) (Westminster, Md., 1946); W. Harmless, *Augustine and the Catechumenate* (Collegeville, Mn., 1995), 107–54, gives the fullest discussion; see also B. Capelle, "Prédication et catéchèse selon saint Augustin," *Questions liturgiques et paroissiales* 33 (1952), 55–64; L. J. Van der Lof, "The Date of the *De Catechizandis Rudibus*," *Vigiliae Christianae* 16 (1962), 198–204; F. van der Meer, *Augustine the Bishop: The Life and Work of a Father of the Church* (London and New York, 1961), 453–67; A. E. Cruz, "El *De Catechizandis Rudibus* y la metodologia de la ebangelización agustiniana," *Augustinus* 15 (1970), 349–68; T. T. Rowe, *Saint Augustine: Pastoral Theologian* (London, 1974), 41–43.

[24] L. D. Folkemer, "The Study of the Catechumenate," in *Conversion, Catechumenate, and Baptism in the Early Church* (Studies in Early Christianity, vol. 11), ed. E. Ferguson, D. M. Scholer, and P. C. Finney (New York and London, 1993), 244–65.

[25] *Catechetical Instruction*, trans. Christopher (as in note 23), 8–10; Harmless, *Augustine* (as in note 23), 108; W. Burghardt, "Catechetics in the Early Church: Program and Psychology," *Living Light* 1 (1964), 100–18.

[26] M. L. W. Laistner, *Christianity and Pagan Culture in the Later Roman Empire Together with an English Translation of John Chrysostom's Address on Vainglory and the Right Way for Parents to Bring up Their Children* (Ithaca, N.Y., 1951).

cal stories were taught to those unschooled in scripture and church history.[27] Augustine and John Chrysostom outline the pedagogy and then apply the theory with concrete scriptural examples. The Ashburnham Pentateuch does not illustrate these literary works, but it does seem to put into practice, by means of the visual arts, the same pedagogical principles. The mode of thinking, or the writing of history, that shaped the catecheses is the same conceptual framework that shaped the illuminations.

Although Augustine is traditionally viewed as ambivalent toward the visual arts, he uses an astounding number of visual metaphors in his catechismal instruction. He employs a popular Ciceronian metaphor that the development of an idea is like the evolving or unrolling of a manuscript.[28] Augustine was also pedagogically and psychologically aware of who the catechumens were likely to be. Students of rhetoric, for example, should learn humility and not scoff at their teacher's mispronunciations; and, while others need further instruction, " . . . it is enough for the more intelligent to be told what [the sacrament] signifies, while with slower minds we should use somewhat more words and illustrations, that they may not consider lightly what they see."[29] Although Augustine may have had in mind verbal illustrations, we know from Gregory's letters that pictures were used to recall the truths found in the biblical stories.[30]

Augustine was acutely aware of the student who cannot tolerate a lengthy verbal discourse. Concerning the dullard, Augustine exhorts his fellow catechists to pray for the slow-witted students rather than give them too much verbal instruction, "rather, say much on his behalf to God, than say much to him about God."[31] Using another visual metaphor, Augustine reminds the weary and bored teacher that a familiar landscape becomes a delight when seen through fresh eyes. For Augustine the words must become an image in the mind because these imprints aid in memory retention. "Anger" is a different word, or sign, in Hebrew, Greek, and Latin, but everyone understands the meaning of an angry face.[32]

In his instructional pamphlet, John Chrysostom, like Augustine, invokes mental images to teach parents how to raise their children. Using a metaphor that compares a child with a city, he warns parents to guard the gate of their sons' eyes. He should not view the theater or bathe with women, but should be shown beautiful things: sky, sun, flowers, meadow, and *fair books*.[33] That John Chrysostom intended "fair books" to signify illustrated books is a likely interpretation and supports the notion of "painted primers." In summary, Augustine understands that images in the mind aid the memory.[34] Chrysostom also refers to visual images, and perhaps even illustrated books, that were suitable for the moral enlightenment of young eyes.

---

[27] B. Stock, *Augustine the Reader: Meditation, Self-Knowledge, and the Ethics of Interpretation* (Cambridge, Mass., 1996), esp. 181–90; W. M Green, "Augustine on the Teaching of History," *University of California Publications in Classical Philology* 12 (1944), 315–32.

[28] *De cat. rud.*, 3.5.

[29] *De cat. rud.*, 9.13.

[30] See also Paulinus of Nola, *The Poems of St. Paulinus of Nola*, trans. P. G. Walsh (Ancient Christian Writers, vol. 40) (New York and Paramus, N.J., 1975), 291–93.

[31] *De cat. rud.*, 13.18.

[32] *De cat. rud.*, 2.3.

[33] *An Address*, 59; Laistner, *Christianity and Pagan Culture* (as in note 26), 138, n. 32 agrees with S. Haidacher, *Des hl. Johannes Chrysostomus Büchlein über Hoffart und Kindererzieheng* (Freiburg im Breisgau, 1907) that fair books may be understood as illuminations in manuscripts.

[34] In general, see Carruthers, *Book of Memory* (as in note 18); W. Kemp, "Visual Narratives, Memory, and the Medieval *Esprit du System*," in *Images of Memory: On Remembering and Representation*, ed. S. Küchler and W. Melion (Washington, D.C., and London, 1991), 87–108; Stock, *Augustine the Reader* (as in note 27).

In both John Chrysostom and Augustine, biblical stories function on two levels. Old Testament stories were not only to be interpreted literally as historical accounts, but also to be taken as prophetic or moral tales.[35] Those unschooled in the meaning of Jewish history for Christians need instruction.[36]

Some illustrations in the Ashburnham Pentateuch do just that: they explain the story's meaning for the Christian. Besides the Crossing of the Red Sea discussed previously, the illustrations on folio 76r show ample typological interpretation (Fig. 6). According to Exodus 24, Moses went up Mount Sinai, then built an altar, offered holocausts (sacrifices that are completely consumed by fire), and read the covenant to the Israelites. The *tituli* make these events clear: *hic moyses edificabit altare ex lapidibus et leget populo librum federis* (here Moses will build an altar out of stone and reads the books of the covenant to the people); *hic ubi offerent olocausta* (here is where they offer holocausts); *hic filii isrl. dicunt ad moysen omnia que precepit dns faciemus* (here the children of Israel say to Moses, "We will do all the things the Lord has instructed"). The words give the proper scriptural scenario; however, the images circumvent the *tituli* and interpret Exodus 24 for Christians.[37] A careful examination shows that the artist is referring to contemporary practice. Gender, for example, divides the Israelites, the veiled women on the left and men on the right, as they would be in a sixth-century church. The holocausts are portrayed as a eucharistic sacrifice of bread and wine, not as animal sacrifices. Moses is depicted as a celebrant of the mass surrounded by seven deacons, or Levites as they were referred to, dressed in white robes. As the Israelites offered holocausts, so early medieval Christians offered their gifts during the mass.[38]

Below the Exodus 24 scene is an enigmatic representation of the Tabernacle. Joshua, Moses, Aaron, Nadab, and Abihu—standing in white pitched tents—pull back the curtains and gesture to the viewer to enter the Tabernacle. This scene cannot be attributed to any particular text. Although others have interpreted the tent in the context of Jewish exegesis,[39] it is also possible to interpret it within the framework of contemporary Christian exegesis: the tent is the Israelite Tabernacle that anticipated the New Testament church—"the tent of the priesthood not made by heavenly hands"—which in turn anticipates the Heavenly Tabernacle, or the Heavenly Jerusalem.[40] The biblical text provides the history. The illustration provides the typological meaning, visually manifested in the eucharistic sacrifice and Tabernacle (Israelite, New Testament, and Heavenly).

[35] Augustine, *De doct. crist.*, 3.20.

[36] R. M. Grant, "Development of the Christian Catechumenate," in *Made, Not Born: New Perspectives on Christian Initiation and the Catechumenate* (Notre Dame, In., 1976), 32–49; M. Dujarier, *A History of the Catechumenate: The First Six Centuries*, trans. E. J. Haasl (New York, 1979); L. Turck, "Aux origines du catéchuménat," and J. Daniélou, "La catéchèse dans la tradition patristique," in *Conversion, Catechumenate, and Baptism* (as in note 24), 266–77 and 279–92.

[37] For a complete discussion, see Verkerk, "Exodus and Easter Vigil" (as in note 8), 99–105.

[38] K. Stevenson, *Eucharist and Offering* (New York, 1986), 74–98.

[39] K. Schubert (with an introduction by D. Flusser), "Jewish Pictorial Traditions in Early Christian Art," in *Jew-* *ish Historiography and Iconography in Early and Medieval Christianity* (Compendia Rerum Iudaicarum ad Novem Testamentum, vol. 2), ed. P. J. Tomson and P. A. Cathey (Assen/Maastricht and Minneapolis, Minn., 1992), 247–49; K. Schubert and U. Schubert, "Marginalien zur 'Sinai-Szene' in der Katacombe der Via Latina in Rom," *Kairos* 17 (1975), 300–2.

[40] Ps. 51:9; Isa. 1:8; Acts 7:44–50; Heb. 9:1–12; Rev. 15:5–6; Ambrose, *De myst.*, 7.34, 36; see also B. Kühnel, "Jewish Symbolism of the Temple and the Tabernacle and Christian Symbolism of the Holy Sepulchre and the Heavenly Tabernacle," *Journal of Jewish Art* 12–13 (1986–87), 147–68; eadem, *From the Earthly to the Heavenly Jerusalem: Representations of the Holy City in Christian Art of the First Millennium* (Freiburg im Breisgau, 1987).

The illustrator has given visual expression to the pedagogy outlined by Augustine's catechetical instruction. The images interpreted the text for contemporary Christians.

The distribution of the illustrations within the manuscript also needs to be addressed, particularly the emphasis on certain narratives and not on others. Why does the Deluge, for example, occupy a full page, while other folios have more than one illustration squeezed onto them? The biblical episode of Moses before the burning bush was given prominent and repeated artistic representation in Early Christian art,[41] but Moses and the bush are shunted to the far right in the Ashburnham Pentateuch (Fig. 5). Moses and the burning bush is an outstanding theophany, a special moment where the deity is made visually manifest. As a moment in *history*, however, it is less important. The answer to the question of emphasis provides the framework to understand why the placement is chaotic.

Augustine, employing the rhetorical technique of *narratio*, instructs the catechist to make selections from history: emphasize the highlights and move rapidly through the lesser stories.[42] Augustine underscores this advice repeatedly: "these [cardinal points in history] we ought not to present as a parchment rolled up and at once snatch them out of sight, but we ought by dwelling somewhat upon them to untie, so to speak, *and spread them out to view, and offer them to the minds of our hearer to examine and adore*" (emphasis mine).[43] The remaining details should be woven into the catechetical narrative in a rapid survey. In this way the catechumen is not exhausted and the memory is not confused. The Ashburnham Pentateuch spreads out the pictures of those cardinal points in history, allowing the viewer to examine them for their prophetic meaning.

Which key moments in history should one emphasize when teaching the catechism? The Deluge, Abraham's Sacrifice, the Crossing of the Red Sea, and the Heavenly Jerusalem are key moments in Augustine's model catechetical instruction. With the exception of Abraham's Sacrifice, which did not survive, these stories are also given the greatest emphasis in the Ashburnham Pentateuch. The manuscript's illustrations thus provide a visual parallel to the pedagogy outlined by Augustine. The cardinal moments are emphasized by receiving most of the compositional space, the lesser narratives are woven into a rapid survey of scenes.

This seems quite straightforward, but the question of the chaotic placement remains. John Chrysostom's instruction may be viewed as an interpretive tool for the lesser scenes. For Chrysostom, Bible stories teach moral lessons. Although he is thinking of children, his ultimate goal and his pedagogy are remarkably similar to Augustine's: tell the Bible stories in simple terms, paraphrasing certain parts, and always emphasize the moral lessons. The child should memorize the story, so that when he hears it in church he will be delighted because he can recall the words.[44] In retelling the story for moralizing purposes, John Chrysostom, like the illustrator of the Ashburnham Pentateuch, does not follow the chronology of the Genesis text. Chrysostom gives two stories about two brothers as examples: the story of Cain and Abel and the story of Jacob and Esau. Rather than beginning with the birth of the brothers, he begins: "Once upon a time, there were two sons of one father, even two brothers . . . one was a shepherd and one was a farmer."[45] John Chrysostom

---

[41] Cf. synagogue, Dura Europos (K. Weitzmann and H. L. Kessler, *The Frescoes of the Dura Synagogue and Christian Art* [Dumbarton Oaks Studies 28] [Washington, D.C., 1990], fig. 74); now-lost fresco, San Paolo f.l.m., Rome (Waetzoldt, *Kopien* [as in note 19], fig. 355); wooden door, Sta. Sabina, Rome (G. Jeremias, *Die Holztür der Basilika S. Sabina in Rom* [Tübingen, 1980], pl. 20).

[42] Harmless, *Augustine* (as in note 23), 126–33.

[43] *De cat. rud.*, 3.5 (*Catechetical Instruction*, trans. Christopher [as in note 23], 18).

[44] John Chrysostom speaks only of a male child.

[45] *An Address*, 39.

even provides instructions on when to pause for emphasis. During the paraphrasing of the stories about two brothers, he is quick to point out the morals and the useful lessons. The murder of Abel, for example, tells us that the Christian dead are taken to heaven. Although the Ashburnham Pentateuch does not illustrate John Chrysostom's instructional pamphlet, it is clear that he provides a parallel textual model for the way in which the folios were meant to be viewed: not as strict chronological illustrations of Jewish scriptures, but reworked as moral lessons for contemporary Christians. The folios are arranged with an eye to moral, didactic lessons.

The visual cues are interesting. Firstly, the broad swaths of color organize and group the scenes. Secondly, the rich domestic and vegetal details often provide interesting commentary on the tableaus. Reading meaning into them is fully in keeping with contemporary exegetical practice. For Augustine, knowledge of Palestine's plants and animals was essential in grasping the meaning of scripture.[46] Just as there were onomastic treatises on biblical names,[47] Augustine wanted an onomasticon for all the stones, trees, herbs, animals, and metals mentioned in the Bible. Through such humble herbs as hyssop, for example, the student of scripture could learn about the love of Christ and the purging of pride (Ex. 12:22; Ps. 51).

To demonstrate how this may have worked, we may follow John Chrysostom's lead and chose two folios depicting the story of two sets of brothers: Cain and Abel, Jacob and Esau (Figs. 1, 4). Kurt Weitzmann noted that these scenes were arranged according to areas of color.[48] The color swaths may, in fact, have been more than formal devices. They direct the viewer to group persons and actions together, since, as discussed above, the standard format of left to right and top to bottom lacks cohesion. The dominant purple area on folio 6 sets the stage for the pictorial representation of two opposing brothers, one a farmer and one a shepherd. Kurt Schubert observed that the two confronting rams at the top of the purple swath and in the center of the folio underscore the conflict between the two brothers, which resulted in the shedding of Abel's innocent blood.[49] Although Schubert interpreted the white and brown rams as ultimately reliant on a Jewish Midrash, the concept of the two rams as clues to understanding the story's conflict and the color areas as organizing aids is worthy of further study.

The purple color swath dominates almost half the folio, yet contains only the two brothers at their work and the murder. The emphasis in the illustration is not on history, but on the conflict between two brothers. Secondly, there is the theme of "reaping what you sow." In addition to Adam and Cain tilling while Eve and Abel tend children or sheep, wheat is ripening and a palm tree bears large fruits. The palm and the wheat call attention to themselves, since the artist normally depicts vegetation in the stylized manner customary in sixth-century art.[50]

Palms as indicators of Paradise had enjoyed a long artistic tradition in a variety of media.[51] They were used in scripture to illustrate a moral. Psalm 91(92) contrasts the evil-doers who will be

---

[46] *De doct. christ.*, 2.39,59.

[47] Cf. D. E. Groh, "The 'Onomasticon' of Eusebius and the Rise of Christian Palestine," *Studia Patristica* 18, pt. 1 (1986), 23–31; T. D. Barnes, "The Composition of Eusebius' *Onomasticon*," *Journal of Theological Studies* 26 (1975), 412–15; ha-Onomastikon: The Onomastikon of Eusebius, trans. E. Z. Melamed (Jerusalem, 1966); *Eusebius, Das Onomastikon der biblischen Ortsnamen*, ed. E. Klostermann (Hildesheim, 1966).

[48] Weitzmann, *Late Antique* (as in note 5), 118.

[49] Schubert,"Jewish Pictorial Traditions" (as in note 39), 249–53.

[50] Cf. the apse mosaic of S. Apollinare in Classe and the creation of plants in the Cotton Genesis (*Age of Spirituality: Late Antique and Early Christian Art, Third to Seventh Century*, ed. K. Weitzmann [New York, 1977], nos. 409, 505).

[51] Cf. mosaic floor, synagogue of Hamman-Lif, Tunisia; *Traditio legis* apse mosaic, Sta. Constanza, Rome; gold glass bowl, Toledo Museum of Art, Toledo, Ohio; silver

scattered and "the righteous [who] flourish like a palm tree."[52] This psalm is referred to in Matthew 12, where Jesus refers to good trees and bad trees as a metaphor for good and evil men.[53] The contrast between the straight palm tree and the figure of Cain echoes the psalm and the parable. Abel was taken to Paradise, while Cain was cursed and forced to wander in the wilderness. Augustine in his catechetical instructions repeatedly refers to wheat and chaff as the signs of the believer and unbeliever.[54] In the Ashburnham Pentateuch, the seemingly inconsequential details such as candles, wheat, and palms are often visual clues on how to interpret the story.

In the illustrations of Jacob and Esau on folio 25, the grouping of scenes by background color is particularly evident, since the color areas are not horizontal, suggesting registers, but are irregular in formation, suggesting intention. Framed by white architecture, the brown backdrop contains four episodes, which move from right to left. On the far left, Rebecca eavesdrops on Isaac instructing Esau, who wears a brown tunic, to hunt venison. Rebecca then hastily bids Jacob, who wears a white tunic, to obtain the blessing instead of his elder brother Esau. Moving to the right, Jacob serves Isaac the savory dish and then receives the blessing from Isaac.

The second group of scenes also takes place within a white architectural frame, but with a salmon-colored background. Jacob, clad in his white tunic, carries two black kids for the pot Rebecca stirs. Below is a brick-walled pen containing sheep and goats. To the right, Isaac gestures to Esau, who brings in his dish, which will be rejected. Below, Rebecca and Isaac send Jacob away, fearing Esau's wrath and urging Jacob to find a proper wife among his father's people.

The final group is placed against a green backdrop with minimal reference to architecture. Walking in from the right margin, Esau carries a slain deer on his shoulder. He then cooks the venison for his father, Isaac. Below, Jacob dreams. The angel ascends and descends, while the head of God is contained within a blue swath of color at the top of the ladder. Finally, Jacob, turning back while pointing ahead, walks out of the red frame and into the wilderness of the margin.

The illustration directs our viewing by color groupings and by providing commentary by means of embellishments. Within the salmon-colored group, the brick pen occupies fully one quarter of the compositional field. Curiously, the pen contains two black goats, two brown sheep, and four white sheep. The juxtaposition of sheep and goats, especially black goats, suggests the parable of the blessed and the damned (Matt. 25:32–33). The parable is given its fullest expression in a sarcophagus lid from Rome (Fig. 7). Christ, flanked by processions of goats and sheep, raises his left hand to reject the goats and lowers his right hand to bless the sheep.[55] Similar gestures are seen in the salmon-colored grouping in the Ashburnham Pentateuch: Isaac raises his hand to reject Esau's dish, while below he sends Jacob away with his blessing. Paired together, one above the

---

reliquary, now in the Louvre, Paris (*Age of Spirituality* [as in note 50], no. 344[a], fig. 74, nos. 503, 571).

[52] "I listen for the downfall of my cruel foes. The righteous flourish like a palm-tree, they grow tall as a cedar on Lebanon; planted as they are in the house of the Lord" (NEB, Ps. 92:11–13).

[53] "Either make the tree good and its fruit good, or make the tree bad and its fruit bad; you can tell a tree by its fruit . . . . A good man produces good from the store of good within himself; and an evil man from evil within

produces evil." See also Matt. 3:10; 7:15–20; Luke 3:9; 6:43–45; Jude 12.

[54] *De cat. rud.*, 7.11, 17.26, 19.31, 27.54. Chaff is blown in the wind: Job 13:25; 21:18; Pss. 1:4; 35:5; 83:13; Isa. 13:17; 29:5; 33:11; 41:15; Jer. 13:24; Dan. 2:35; Hos. 13:3; Zeph. 2:2. In the New Testament chaff symbolizes those who are burned as worthless after the righteous (wheat) are gathered into the granary: Matt. 3:12; Luke 3:17.

[55] *Age of Spirituality* (as in note 50), 558, no. 501.

other, the posture and dress of Isaac are identical in both episodes; only the gesture varies, which is a telling detail. As in the sarcophagus, where Christ's gestures are pivotal, Isaac's gestures tell the story in the manuscript. By circumventing the chronological sequence of the scenes, the illustrator is able to create a meaningful juxtaposition between the two brothers.

Expounding on this story of two brothers, John Chrysostom finds that the moral lessons are plentiful. He contrasts, with great relish, the behavior of the two brothers: from Jacob the child learns to strive for his father's blessing, to despise the belly, and to obey his parents by making a proper marriage. From Esau, on the other hand, a child learns the foolishness of greed, the wickedness of hatred, and the folly of marrying against a parent's wishes.[56] John Chrysostom's point is not to impart the story, but to convey an adapted version filled with clues and hints at useful lessons. Using the language of color and association, the Ashburnham Pentateuch illustrator also constructs visual comparisons and provides visual clues in order to bring out the morals embedded in the biblical story.

In conclusion, I believe that the creators of this manuscript were remarkably adept in directing the viewer to the deeper meanings and morals to be found in the illustrations. In doing so, the illustrations function independently from the text. They tell different stories and are organized on different principles not bound by textual chronology. The Ashburnham Pentateuch challenges us to set aside preconceived notions of narrative structure and the relationship of image to text. The illuminations, by being bound within sacred scripture, occupy a privileged position from which they can appropriate the text, comment upon it, and, ultimately, reveal the truth within the text.

[56] *An Address*, 44–51.

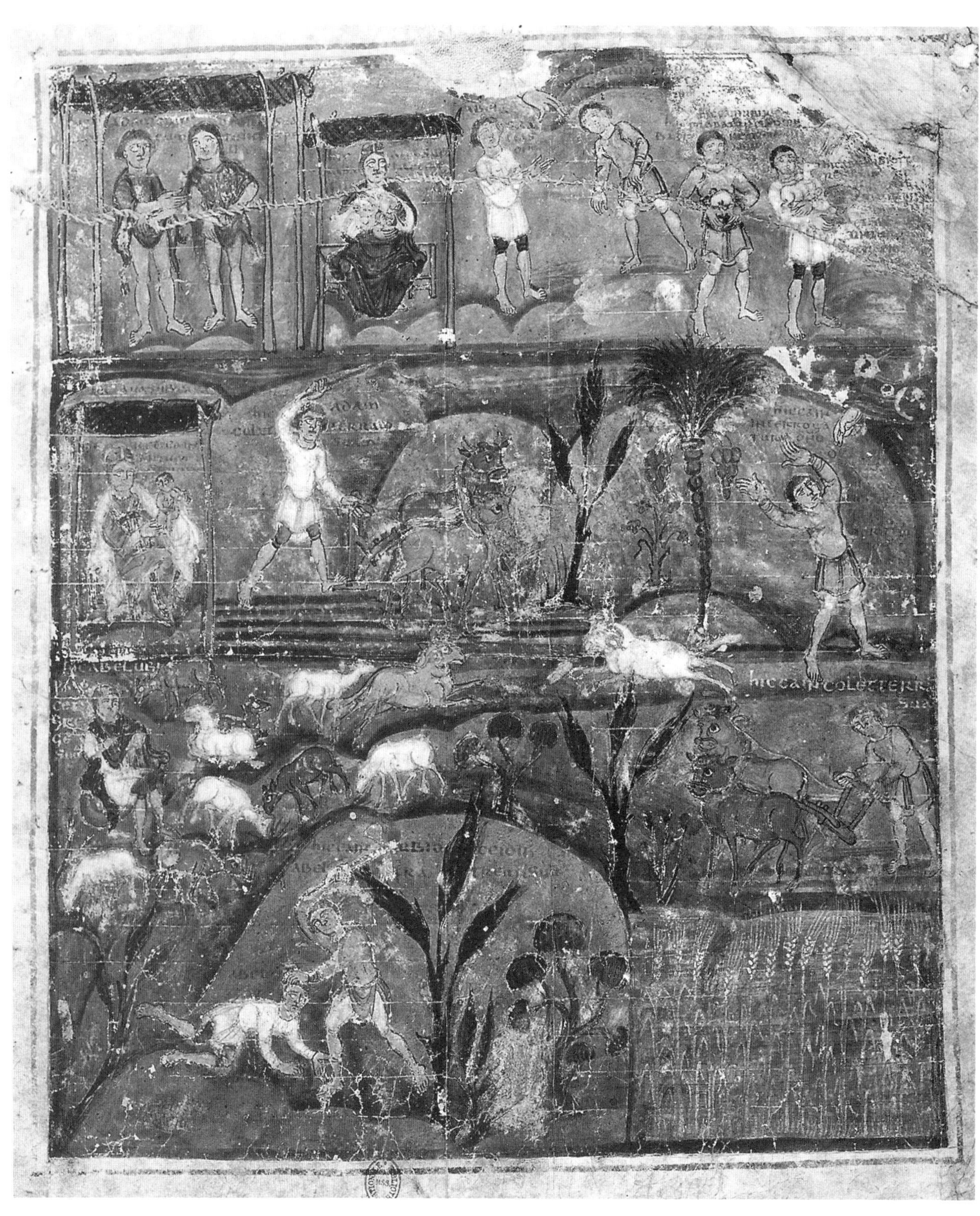

1. Paris, Bibliothèque Nationale de France, nouv. acq. lat. 2334, Ashburnham Pentateuch, f. 6r. Cain and Abel

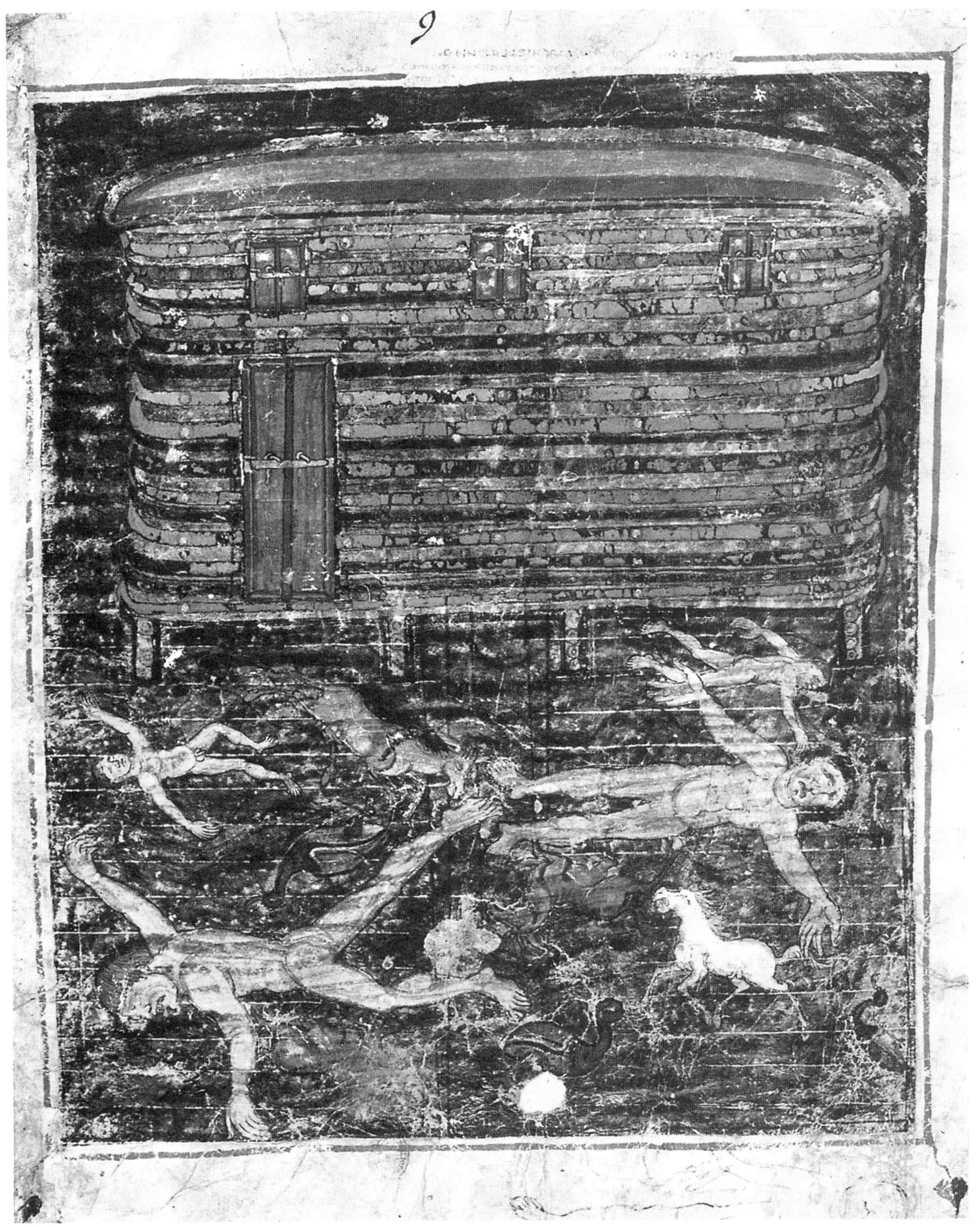

2. Paris, Bibliothèque Nationale de France, nouv. acq. lat. 2334, Ashburnham Pentateuch, f. 9r. Deluge

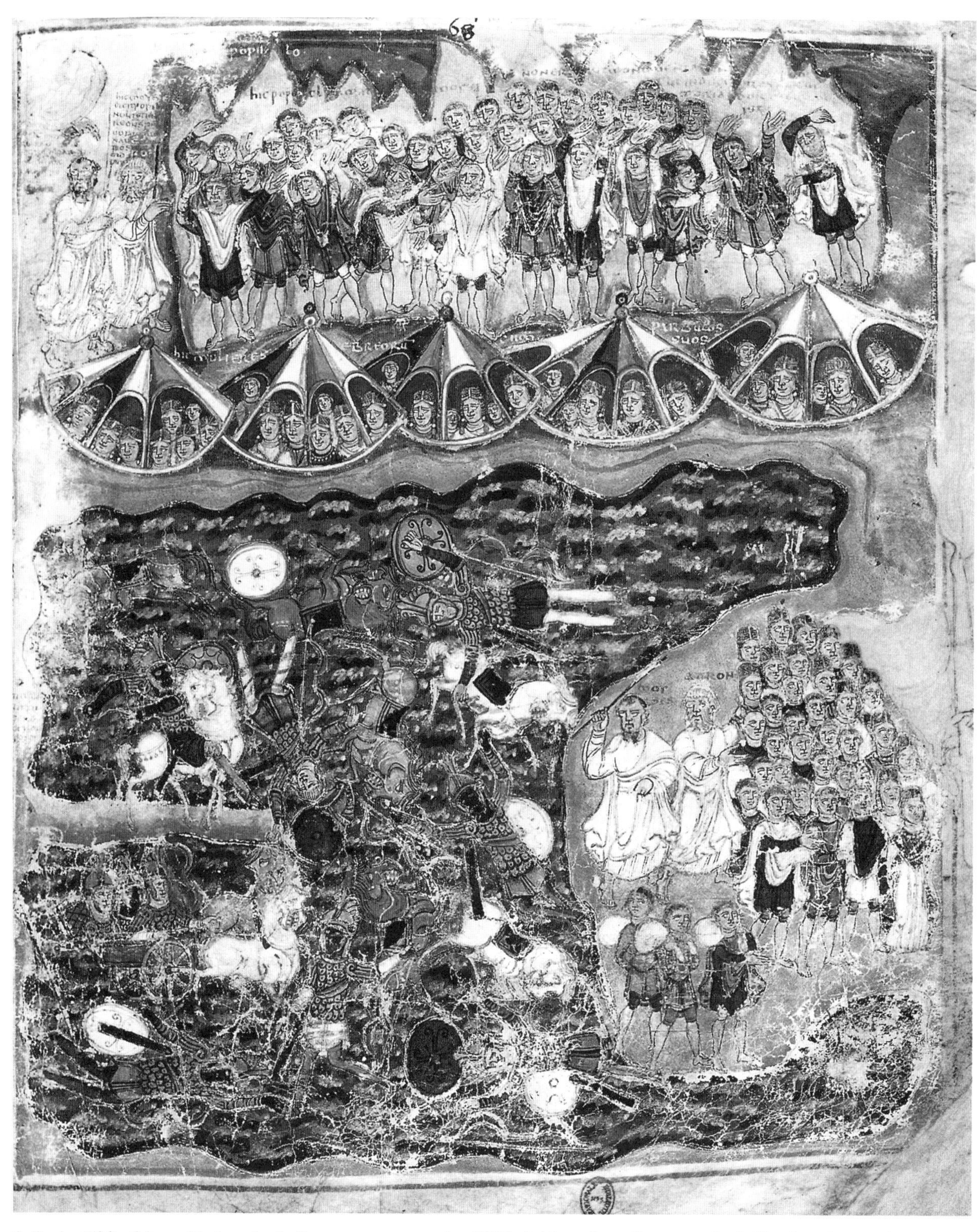

3. Paris, Bibliothèque Nationale de France, nouv. acq. lat. 2334, Ashburnham Pentateuch, f. 68r. Crossing of the Red
Sea

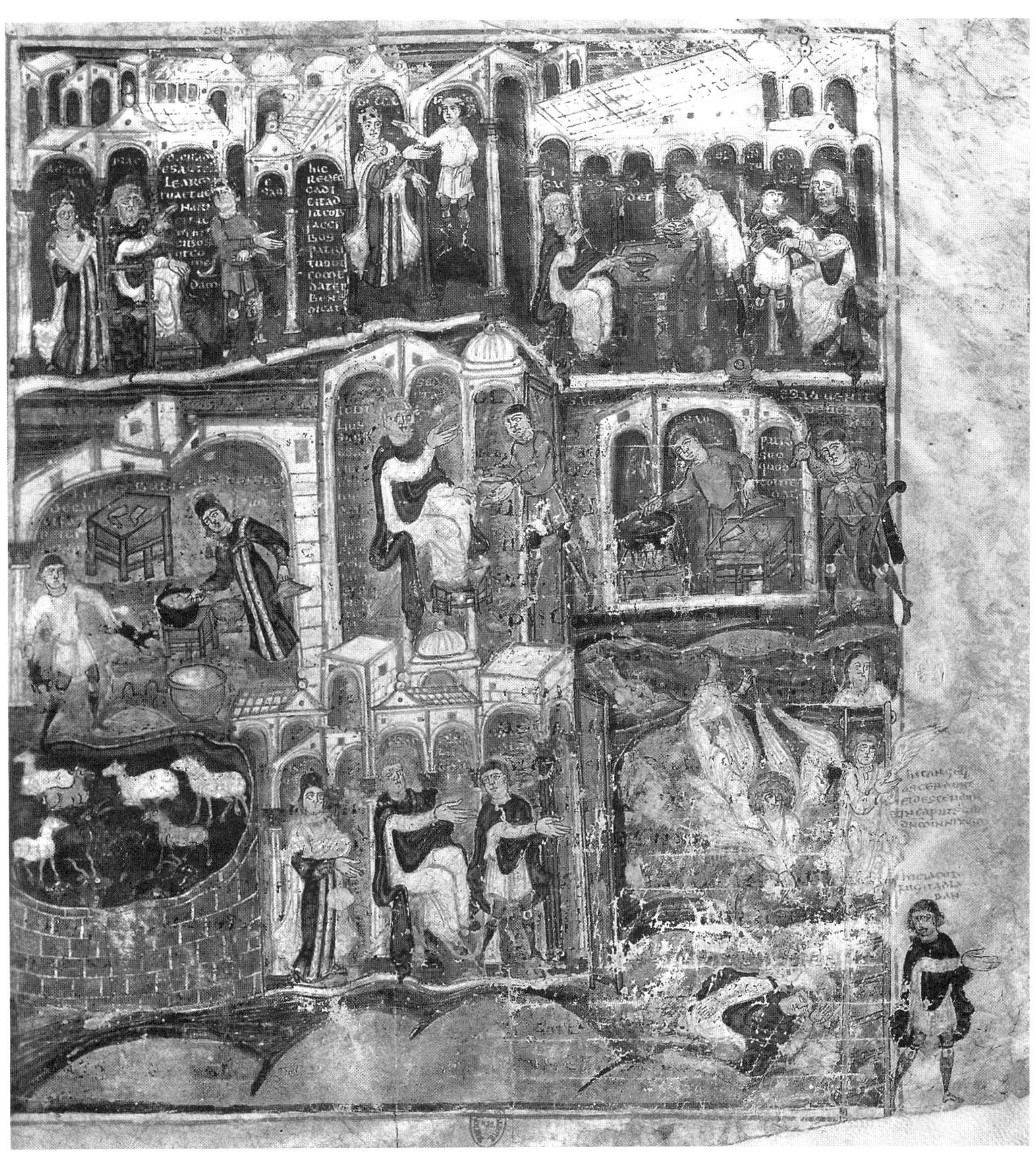

4. Paris, Bibliothèque Nationale de France, nouv. acq. lat. 2334, Ashburnham Pentateuch, f. 25r. Jacob and Esau

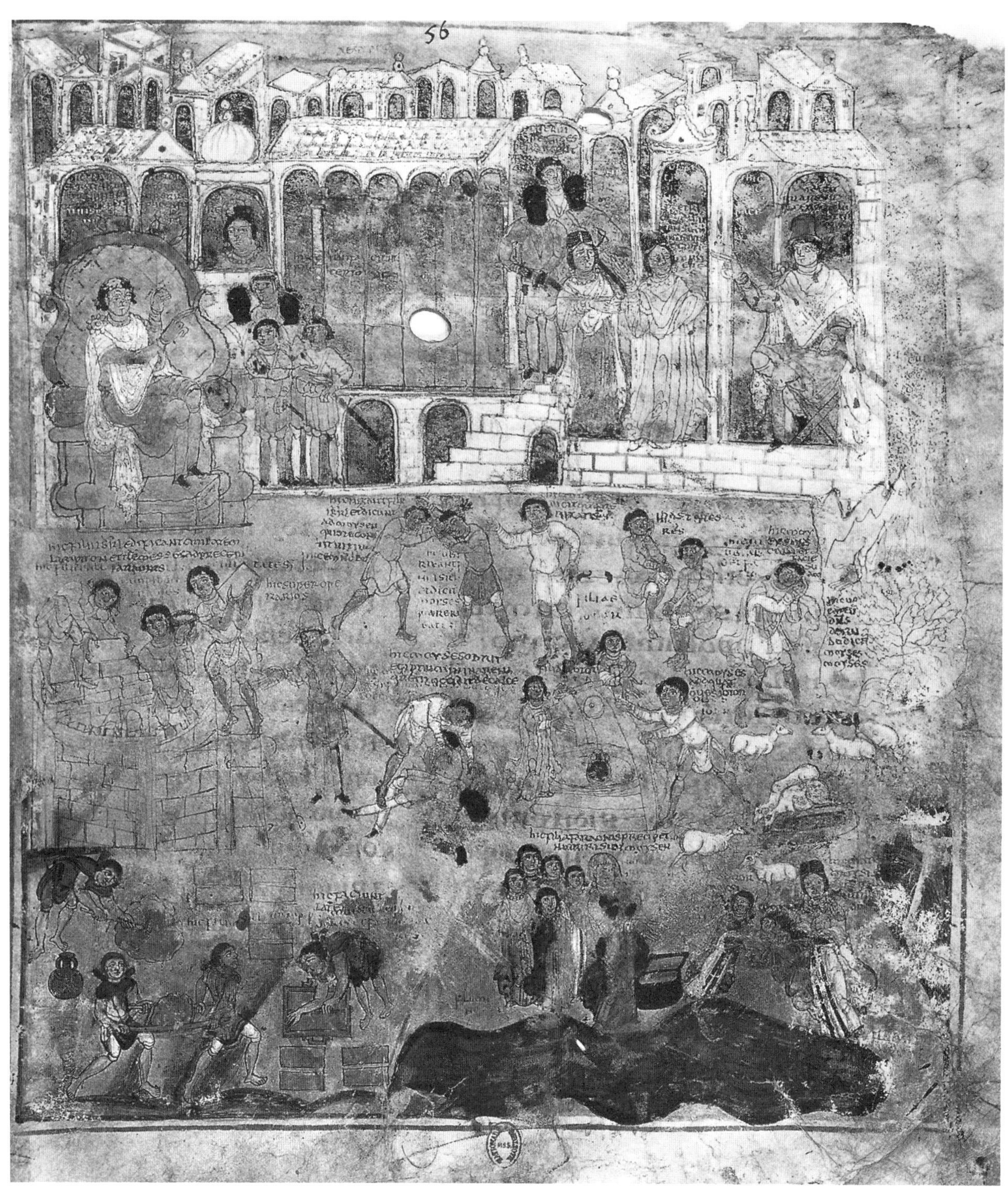

5. Paris, Bibliothèque Nationale de France, nouv. acq. lat. 2334, Ashburnham Pentateuch, f. 56r. Egyptian captivity

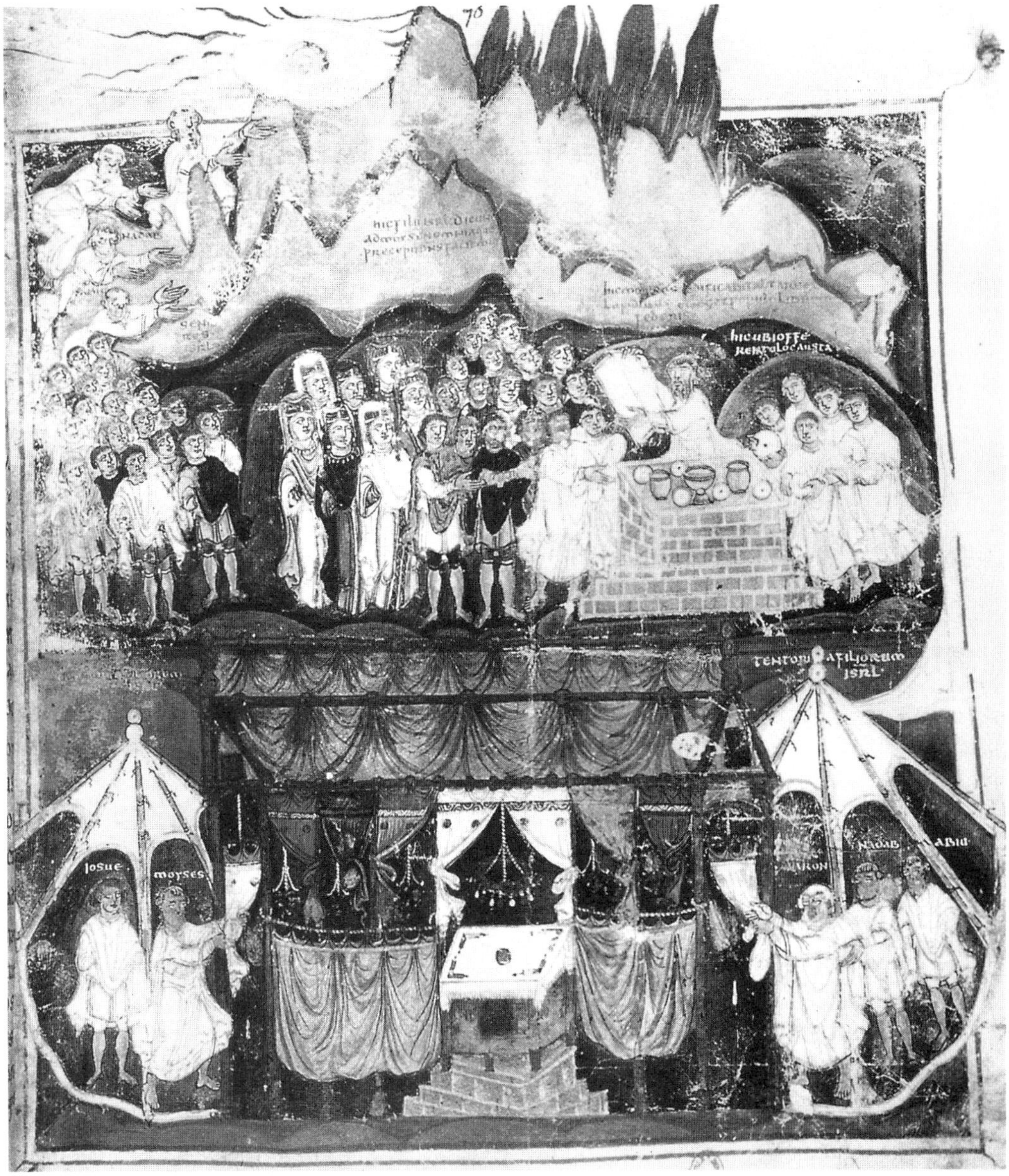

6. Paris, Bibliothèque Nationale de France, nouv. acq. lat. 2334, Ashburnham Pentateuch, f. 76r. Mount Sinai

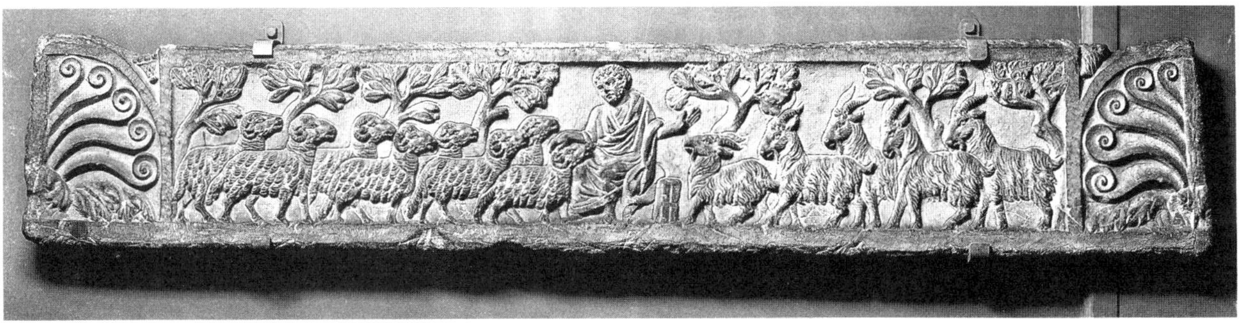

7. New York, The Metropolitan Museum of Art. Sarcophagus lid with Last Judgment

A Woman's Power of Prayer versus the Devil in a Book of Hours of ca. 1300

·

ADELAIDE BENNETT*

IN NORTHERN France and the Francophone regions of Flanders and Hainaut, the book of hours was the prevalent book of prayers for the laity from the mid-thirteenth century on. It was used as a manual to practice daily devotions, but also to guide the conscience along the path of righteousness. One notable example which functioned as a penitential handbook is a northeastern French manuscript of ca. 1300 or the early fourteenth century in Cambrai (Bibliothèque Municipale, Ms. 87).[1] It is well known for its full-page All Saints miniature between the calendar and

* I thank Ms. Bénédicte Terouanne, the conservateur of the Bibliothèque Municipale, Cambrai, for her courteous permission to examine Ms. 87.

[1] A. Durieux, *Les Miniatures des manuscrits de la Bibliothèque de Cambrai* (Cambrai, 1861), text, pp. 83–84; plates, pl. 8; A. E. L. M. Molinier, *Catalogue général des bibliothèques publiques de France, Départements XVII, Cambrai* (Paris, 1891), 21–22; G. von Vitzthum, *Die Pariser Miniaturmalerei von der Zeit des hl. Ludwig bis zu Philipp von Valois und ihr Verhältnis zur Malerei in Nordwesteuropa* (Leipzig, 1907), 146; London, New Palaeographical Society, *Facsimiles of Ancient Manuscripts*, ed. E. Maunde Thompson et al., ser. 2 (London, 1913–30), text; pls. 42a (f. 17v), 42b (f. 217r); E. G. Millar, *The Library of A. Chester Beatty: A Descriptive Catalogue of the Western Manuscripts*, 2 vols. (Oxford, 1930), vol. 2, 105–6; P. Neveux and E. Dacier, *Les Richesses des bibliothèques provinciales de France* (Paris, 1932), vol. 1, 94, color pl. XXVII (f. 17v); J. Billioud, "Très anciennes Heures de Thérouanne à la bibliothèque de Marseille," *Trésors des bibliothèques de France* 5 (1935), 178 n. 2, 179 n. 3, 184; Arras, Musée d'Arras, *L'Art du moyen âge en Artois* (Arras, 1951), no. 68, pl. XX (f. 60r, not f. 65r); Paris, Bibliothèque Nationale, *Manuscrits à peintures du XIIIe au XVIe siècle* (Paris, 1955), no. 69; B. Gagnebin, "Le Livre d'heures d'Agnès de Savoie, comtesse de Genève," *Genava*, n.s., 11 (1963), 328–29, fig. 3 (f. 16v); B. Blumenkranz, "Représentations de Synagoga en France," in *Mélanges offerts à René Crozet*, ed. P. Gallais and Y.-J. Rious, 2 vols. (Poitiers, 1966), vol. 2, 1149, 1155; B. Blumenthal and D. Bozo, "Synagoga méconnue–Synagoga inconnue," *Revue des études juives* 125 (1966), 38, pl. 2 (f. 17v); L. M. C. Randall, *Images in the Margins of Gothic Manuscripts* (Berkeley and Los Angeles, 1966), 30, fig. 141 (f. 30r); *The Celebrated Library of the Late Major J. R. Abbey*, London, Sotheby's, 1 December 1970, lot 2868; M. A. Stones, "The Illustrated French Prose Lancelot in Belgium, Flandres and Paris" (Ph.D. diss., University of London, 1970), 24, n. 28, 111, 212, 268; Ottawa, National Gallery of Canada, *Art and the Courts* (Ottawa, 1972), no. 18, pl. 26 (f. 17v); F. O. Büttner, "'Ad Te, Domine, Levavi Animam Meam': Bildnisse in der Wortillustration zu Psalm 24:1," in *Miscellanea Codicologica F. Masai Dicata MCMLXXIX*, ed. P. Cockshaw, M.-C. Garand, and P. Jodogne, 2 vols. (Ghent, 1979), vol. 2, 335; P. de Winter, "Une Réalisation exceptionelle d'enlumineurs français et anglais vers 1300: Le Bréviaire de Renaud de Bar, évêque de Metz," in *Actes du 103e Congrès national des Sociétés savantes, 1978* (Paris, 1980), 38–39, 41, fig. 7 (f. 29r); P. Verdier, *Le Couronnement de la Vierge: Les Origines et les premiers développement d'un thème iconographique* (Montreal, 1981), 10, 147, fig. 72 (f. 17v); A. von Euw and J. Plotzek, *Die Handschriften der Sammlung Ludwig*, 4 vols. (Cologne, 1979–84), vol. 2, 80; A. Stones, "Notes on Three Illuminated Alexander Manuscripts," in *The Medieval Alexander*

the hours of the Virgin.[2] Less familiar are the remarkable and extensive pictorial programs for the various texts that constitute this book of hours.

The manuscript contains both Latin and French texts, with rubrics.[3] It begins with the calendar, followed by the hours of the Virgin, the hours of the Cross, devotional prayers including the Five Joys of the Virgin, the Seven Penitential Psalms with the litany, suffrages, more prayers, the office of the dead, and thirty-four Ave prayers to Christ. The texts are in Latin except those of the calendar and the hours of the Cross, which are in French. The last third of the book consists mainly of vernacular devotional material, such as the prayer to the Guardian Angel, the Seven Requests to the Lord, the Nine Joys of the Virgin, and the Sorrows of the Virgin on the Passion.

Evidence for liturgical use of the Cambrai manuscript is composite. The calendar includes predominantly Parisian saints and a few from northeast France. Only two mendicants, Peter Martyr and Francis of Assisi, are included. Saint Louis of France, who was canonized in 1297, is added for August 25th. The hours of the Virgin and the office of the dead follow the use of Reims. The litany is not distinctive, but it enlists a few Parisian saints, such as Denis, Germaine, and Geneviève, as well as one Franciscan, Elizabeth of Hungary. Two Dominicans, Peter the Martyr and Dominic of Bologna, appear in suffrages or prayers to saints, which number twenty-six. Two female penitents, Mary Magdalen and Mary of Egypt, head the list of fourteen virgins in the litany. Both are included in suffrages addressed to six virgins, as well as in the calendar.

Cambrai Ms. 87 measures 250 × 180 (165 × 113) mm, which is large for a book of hours. It is written in black formal script of textura semiquadrata in a single column of fifteen lines. The decoration in 239 folios encompasses twelve calendar pictures, two full-page miniatures on separate leaves, and 234 historiated initials. Cambrai Ms. 87 is one of the few early books of hours with an elaborate program in which historiated initials introduce nearly all of the psalms, hymns, lessons,

---

Legend and Romance Epic: Essays in Honor of David J. A. Ross, ed. P. Noble, L. Polak, and C. Isoz (Millwood, N.Y., 1982), 204 n. 20; J. H. Oliver, *Gothic Manuscript Illumination in the Diocese of Liège (c. 1250–c. 1330),* 2 vols. (Leuven, 1988), vol. 1, 150 n. 1; A. Stones, "Commentaire des enluminures du Ms. Troyes 1905," in *La Vie de sainte Marguerite* (Tübingen, 1990), 188 n. 8, 195 n. 32; P. Hoegger, "The Fourteenth-Century Gradual of Wettingen," in *1000 Years of Swiss Art,* ed. H. Horat (New York, 1992), 37, fig. 41 (f. 113r); A. Bräm, "Buchmalerei des 13. und 14. Jahrhunderts in Frankreich, Flandern, Hennegau, Maasland und Lothringen: Literaturbericht 1970–1992," *Kunstchronik* 47 (1994), 81–82; A. Stones, "Madame Marie's Picture-Book: A Precursor of Flemish Painting around 1400," in *Flanders in a European Perspective: Manuscript Illumination around 1400 in Flanders and Abroad* (Proceedings of the International Colloquium, Leuven, 7–10 September 1993), ed. M. Smeyers and B. Cardon (Leuven, 1995), 431 n. 10; Cologne, Schnütgen-Museum, and Paris, Musée National du Moyen âge–Thermes de Cluny, *Schatz aus den Trümmern: Der Silberschrein von Nivelles und die europäische Hochgotik/Un Trésor gothique: La Châsse de Nivelles* (Cologne and Paris, 1996), no. 51, pp. 265, 267, 378, color fig. 64 (f.

17v); A. Stones, *Le Livre d'images de Madame Marie* (Paris, 1997), 17 and nn. 2, 3; A. Bräm, *Das Andachtsbuch der Marie de Gavre, Paris, Bibliothèque Nationale, Ms. nouv. acq. fr. 16251: Buchmalerei in der Diözese Cambrai im letzten Viertel des 13. Jahrhunderts* (Wiesbaden, 1997), 31, 70, 75, 177–79, 222, figs. 59 (f. 17v), 60 (f. 65v, Flagellation, erroneously included instead of f. 64v), 61 (f. 217r, not f. 217v); Paris, Galeries nationales du Grand Palais, *L'Art au temps des rois maudits Philippe le Bel et ses fils: 1285–1328* (Paris, 1998), no. 210, color fig. p. 311 (f. 17v).

The only known provenance of this book of hours since the sixteenth century is the Benedictine Abbey of Saint Sépulchre, Cambrai.

[2] The All Saints miniature (f. 17v) has been reproduced at least eight times in publications; illustrations of a few other folios (ff. 16v, 29r, 30r, 60r, 65v, 113r, 217r) have been published once, to my knowledge; see the bibliography in note 1.

[3] A full codicological description with the list of texts and subjects will be given in the forthcoming study on Cambrai Ms. 87 by Adelaide Bennett and Alison Stones.

chapters, and collects that form essential components of the eight canonical hours of the Virgin, as well as of the office of the dead.

The identity of the user or owner of this richly illuminated *Horae* is problematic, but its textual and visual evidence provides some answers. A number of prayers, such as the *O intemerata*, are in the feminine gender.[4] There are also 108 representations of a laywoman throughout. In contrast, a male devotee appears a mere seven times, and then only toward the end. It is in the last third, the French section, of Cambrai Ms. 87 that both the woman and the man dress in heraldic garments, but their identities cannot be established with certainty.[5] Clearly the couple was privileged and wealthy. The textual and pictorial contents of the Cambrai book are geared to probing this noblewoman's conscience, and to promoting her appropriate conduct as a pious Christian. One obvious example of this intent is the repetitive portrayal of her within initials and in margins as a devotee, often kneeling and with her joined hands raised. In the vernacular portion of Cambrai Ms. 87, the Nine Joys of the Virgin underscore her prominence in relation to the Virgin. The prologue to the Joys (f. 200v, Fig. 1) shows the lady outside the initial T, enclosing the Annunciate Virgin, who epit-

[4] (1) "Deus qui uoluisti pro nostra redemptione . . . *me miseram peccatricem*," ff. 70v–71r; (2) "Deprecor te domina sancta maria mater dei pietate plenissima summi regis filia . . . *pro me peccatrice famula tua . . . michi peccatrici*," ff. 106r–107r; (3) "Sancta maria mater domini nostri ihesu xpi in manus tuas et in manus filii tui commendo hodie . . . *famulam tuam indignam et miseram*," ff. 107r–108r; (4) "O intemerata et in eternum benedicta singularis . . . *michi peccatrici . . . peccatrix*," ff. 108r–110v; (5) "Misericordiam tuam quesumus domine interueniente beato cendonio confessore tuo nobis placatus impende et *michi peccatrici*," f. 112v.

[5] (1) On f. 200v (Fig. 1), a female devotee's blue mantle shows in the lower part three small shields (gules missing because it was rubbed off or never applied), *3 pales vair, on a chief or a lion issuant sable*, and in the upper part two small shields, *or a lion rampant sable*, and her robe displays small shields, *sable a lion rampant argent, crowned or*.

(2) On f. 203r (Fig. 3), a kneeling knight in surcoat and ailettes of *gules 3 pales vair, on a chief or a lion issuant sable*.

(3) On f. 217r, a couple in heraldic garments: a kneeling man's mantle and ailettes with the charge of *gules 3 pales vair, on a chief or a lion issuant sable*, and a kneeling woman's mantle with the same charge, except that *lion in chief* is not visible.

(4) On ff. 207v, 208r, 209r, 211r, 212v, 215r, and 229v, in initials for vernacular prayers to the Virgin, coats of arms bear the same charges, *quarterly, 1 and 4, gules 3 pales vair, on a chief or a lion rampant sable, 2 and 3, sable a lion rampant argent, crowned or*. Molinier, *Catalogue* (as in note 1), 22, wrongly gives *gules* for *sable* in the second and third quarters and omits the *crowned or*.

Prominently displayed is the distinctive Châtillon charge of *gules 3 pales vair on a chief or a lion rampant sable* of Flanders, Hainaut, and Avesnes. On the basis of this heraldry, scholars and cataloguers have sought to identify

the couple. (1) Mahaut of Brabant (d. 1288), wife of Guy of Châtillon, Count of S. Pol, was mentioned first by Molinier, *Catalogue*, 22, and accepted most recently by Bräm, *Das Andachtsbuch der Marie de Gavre* (as in note 1), 222. But her date of death is too early for the general style of Cambrai Ms. 87, and the arms of Brabant, *sable a lion or*, are not in the manuscript. (2) Isabel of Rumigny was proposed by S. C. Cockerell in 1909 when he examined Cambrai Ms. 87; he later gave his notes to Millar (*Library of A. Chester Beatty* [as in note 1], vol. 2, 105); this identity has been accepted in most subsequent publications. Her spouse was thought to be Gauthier d'Austresche, but in fact she was the third wife of Gauthier of Châtillon (1250–1329), Count of Porcien, constable of France, whom she married in 1312. The Rumigny charge of *gules a lion rampant argent*, however, does not appear in Cambrai Ms. 87. (3) Beatrice of Flanders (d. 1303), wife of Hugh of Châtillon, Count of Blois, was first suggested by George Warner in *Facsimiles of Ancient Manuscripts* (as in note 1), text for pl. 42. The counts of Blois bore the arms of *gules 3 pales vair, on a chief or a lion rampant sable*, but this manuscript shows a variant charge in ff. 200v, 203r, 217r: *gules 3 pales vair, on a chief or a lion issuant sable*, pointing to the cadet family of Châtillon, Gauthier d'Austresche (fl. 1302), châtelain of Bar and solicitor of Vic-sur-Aisne, whose wife remains unidentified (Porcher in his 1955 catalogue, *Manuscrits à peintures* [as in note 1], no. 69). In view of these particular heraldric bearings, not previously described in the literature, Gauthier d'Austresche seems to be the most promising candidate, a proposal that would accord well with the stylistic appearance of the Cambrai book of hours as well as related manuscripts dating around 1300. For the particulars on heraldry, I am most grateful to Alison Stones and Pierre Bony. Details of these heraldic matters will be discussed by Stones in the forthcoming study of the Cambrai *Horae*.

omizes humility. The Joys illustrate Marian episodes, such as the Visitation for the second Joy, the Nativity for the third Joy, the Adoration of the Magi for the fourth, and so on. But the picture for the first Joy (f. 201r, Fig. 2) is quite personalized: the female devotee prays to the standing Virgin for her intercession. In fact, the postscript to the Joys in red rubrics (f. 203r, Fig. 3) tells the user to repeat the Ave Maria nine times in honor and remembrance of the Virgin, who will aid, advise, and ward off temptations of the enemy. The lady seeks the Virgin's protection from her enemy.

To identify the enemy and her temptations it is necessary to turn to the beginning of the woman's book, the hours of the Virgin. This is the most essential text in any book of hours, and was to be recited, read, or meditated upon eight times a day, from Matins to Compline. By the early fourteenth century pictures for the canonical hours of the Virgin were often the chief events from the childhood of Christ. A pertinent example is the Ruskins Book of Hours (Los Angeles, The J. Paul Getty Museum, Ms. Ludwig IX.3), contemporary with and stylistically related to Cambrai Ms. 87, in which the Annunciation is the introduction for Matins, the Visitation for Lauds, the Nativity for Prime, and so forth.[6] The Cambrai illustrations instead focus on the noblewoman's use of the hours as an aid to examining her conscience. Matins is the only hour which depicts the Marian episode of the Annunciation (f. 19r, Fig. 4). From Lauds to Compline, the five-line historiated initials form an unusual moralizing cycle concerning the devil and a woman, who is most likely the owner of the book.

At Lauds (f. 29r, Fig. 5), the devil in the guise of a two-faced man in a red tunic plays the role of a tempter, with his right hand raised toward the well-dressed woman and his left hand pointing to an empty bed. His left countenance is black-skinned and not visible to the woman, and his right is white and glances at her. The standing lady avoids him and the bed by turning and looking toward the clouds at the right; with her joined hands raised high, she implores the heavens. The luxuriously vair-lined bed must symbolize the desires of the flesh. It could be a pictogram for one of manifold sins, such as adultery, often illustrated by a couple embracing in bed.[7] In one medallion of the mid-thirteenth-century Moralized Bible in Oxford (Bodl. Lib., Ms. Bodley 270b, f. 36r), a devil at the right entices a couple to sinful activities in bed, picturing the typological commentary on the vice of *luxuria*, in addition to those of avarice and cupidity.[8] In the Cambrai initial, the bed may serve to warn the noblewoman of the need to be chaste and not commit illicit love.[9] In the right margin, a youth plays a gittern and dances a step, with his right leg crossed over his standing left, stressing the pleasantries of daily life. He also may represent allurement to erotic adventures

[6] Euw and Plotzek, *Sammlung Ludwig* (as in note 1), vol. 2, 74–83: f. 37v, Matins, Annunciation (color pl. p. 81); f. 63v, Lauds, Visitation (fig. 28); f. 76r, Prime, Nativity (fig. 31); f. 81v, Terce, Annunciation to the Shepherds (fig. 33); f. 85v, Sext, Massacre of the Innocents (fig. 32); f. 89r, None, Adoration of the Magi (fig. 34); Vespers (missing); and f. 98v, Compline, Flight into Egypt (fig. 36).

[7] For the iconography of the bed in the Middle Ages, see K. Lerchner, *'Lectulus Floridus': Zur Bedeutung des Bettes in Literatur und Handschriftenillustration des Mittelaltars* (Cologne, Weimar, and Vienna, 1993). Of particular interest to this paper is her analysis of Psalms 4:5, 6:7, and 35:5, which view the bed as emblem of sins or as prick of

conscience: ibid., 81–99. Biblical references are from the Latin Vulgate and, if quoted in English, from the Douai version.

[8] A. de Laborde, *La Bible moralisée*, 5 vols. (Paris, 1911–27), vol. 1, pl. 36. The adjoining exegesis reads: "Hoc significat quod diabolus per tria genera peccatorum populum dei destruit per luxuriam per superbiam per cupiditatem."

[9] In literature, the Picardian text *Songe du Castel*, written in the second half of the thirteenth century, describes one of the vices, Lechery, assailing the castle only by night (suggesting that illicit nocturnal activities are committed on beds); see M. W. Bloomfield, *The Seven Deadly Sins* (East Lansing, Mich., 1952), 135 and n. 101.

through sound and sight. The vice of *luxuria* is linked with music and dancing, considered to be the twin evils of excess which corrupt one's soul.[10]

Though the initial to Prime is gone, it is probable that its illustration formed part of the didactic program.

For Terce (f. 43v, Fig. 6), the bicephalic figure reappears. In this depiction the left, black face looks demonic, with a protruding horn, and the right, white face wears bangs and a cap. The figure sways slightly to the left, raises a container of objects resembling coins in his left hand, and holds what is probably a money bag in his right. These attributes typify the vice of avarice, as do the chest and money bags, for example, in an early thirteenth-century Parisian psalter in Albenga (Biblioteca Capitolare, Ms. s.n., f. 72r).[11] The devil tempts the lady with material goods; she resists greed by turning her back on him and kneeling in prayer toward the heavens. In the lower border, a mounted trumpeter on a red lion seemingly sounds a warning to the woman.[12]

In Sext (f. 47r, Fig. 7), the fifth canonical hour, which usually coincides with noontime, the double-faced man dresses more grandly in gray and orange-red with vair-lined creases, a bicolored garment that complements his two-sided appearance and accentuates his deceitful character.[13] Holding a bowl of food and a jug, he represents gluttony. In the late thirteenth-century *Verger de Solas* from Arras (Paris, B.N.F., Ms. fr. 9220, f. 6r), the top left roundel drooping from the Tree of

[10] This association is traditional, as evidenced in a late tenth-century copy of Prudentius's *Psychomachia*, Paris, B.N.F., Ms. lat. 8318, f. 52v; see R. Stettiner, *Die illustrierten Prudentiushandschriften*, 2 vols. (Berlin, 1895–1905), vol. 1, 309 [verse 340]; vol. 2, pl. 413. Two other examples of the *Psychomachia* show Luxuria reclining on a couch behind a banquet table, beside a group of men, including one blowing a horn: ninth-century copy, Leiden, Bibliotheek der Universiteit, Ms. Burm. Q. 3, f. 132r (ibid., vol. 1, 300–2 [verse 310]; vol. 2, pl. 95[1]; and tenth-century copy, Brussels, B.R., Ms. 9987-91, f. 109r (ibid., vol. 1, 300–2 [verse 310]; vol. 2, pl. 95[5]).

For the role of the devil in musical and dancing activities, such as those performed by Luxuria and Salome, see R. Hammerstein, *Diabolus in Musica: Studien zur Ikonographie der Musik im Mittelalter* (Berne and Munich, 1974), 50–58, figs. 34–62 (including the Paris Prudentius Ms. mentioned above, fig. 43); B. Fassbender, *Gotische Tanzdarstellungen* (Frankfurt am Main, 1994); H. Steger, "Der unheilige Tanz der Salome: Eine bildsemiotische Studie zum mehrfachen Schriftsinn im Hochmittelalter," in *Mein ganzer Körper ist Gesicht: Groteske Darstellungen in der europäischen Kunst und Literatur des Mittelalters* (Freiburg im Breisgau, 1994), 131–69; and J. J. G. Alexander, "Dancing in the Streets," *JWalt* 54 (1996), 151, 155, figs. 5, 6; however, Alexander discusses the more positive and social aspects of dancing as his main theme; see the full bibliography in his notes 29–33.

For views of the medieval secular musician, see also W. Salmen, *Der Spielmann im Mittelalter* (Innsbruck, 1983); and G. Foster, "The Iconology of Musical Instruments

and Musical Performance in Thirteenth-Century French Manuscript Illuminations" (Ph.D. diss., City University of New York, 1977), 65–76.

[11] A. De Floriani, *Miniature parigine del Duecento: Il salterio di Albenga e altri manoscritti* (Genoa, 1990), color pl. X, p. 37. This iconography is not unique to Psalm 51. A miser depositing a sack into a chest appears in another French psalter, use of St. Omer now in Baltimore (Walters Art Gallery, Ms. W. 112, f. 82r), illustrated in L. M. C. Randall et al., *Medieval and Renaissance Manuscripts in the Walters Art Gallery*, vol. 1, *France, 875–1420* (Baltimore and London, 1989), 89, no. 38, fig. 77; it is stylistically related to the Cambrai group of the Bute Psalter (Los Angeles, The J. Paul Getty Museum, Ms. 46). The long-haired Avarice of the Albenga Psalter recurs with similar attributes, pose, gesture, and appearance in the stained-glass west rose window of Notre-Dame, Paris, ca. 1220, reproduced in M. Aubert, L. Grodecki, et al., *Les Vitraux de Notre Dame et de la Sainte Chapelle de Paris* (Corpus Vitrearum Medii Aevi, France) (Paris, 1959), pl. 4 (L5), and in M. Friedman, "Sünde, Sünder und die Darstellungen der Laster in den Bildern zur 'Bible moralisée,'" *Wiener Jahrbuch für Kunstgeschichte* 37 (1984), 166, fig. 26. Cf. J. J. G. Alexander, "Iconography and Ideology: Uncovering Social Meaning in Western Medieval Christian Art," *Studies in Iconography* 15 (1993), 26, 28, fig. 18.

[12] See note 15 below.

[13] For negative connotations of particolored or bicolored garments, see R. Mellinkoff, *Outcasts: Signs of Otherness in Northern European Art of the Late Middle Ages*, 2 vols. (Berkeley and Los Angeles, 1993), vol. 1, 7–31.

Vices shows a two-faced personification of gluttony who drinks and eats at the same time.[14] The lady in the Cambrai initial also dresses more elaborately, with a broad headdress and a vair-lined mantle. In rejecting the man's encouragement, she pleads to the heavens above. Her prayer for help is echoed above by the words of the collect of the previous hour at Terce, "Protege domine famulos tuos," which shows the Virgin with her mantle protecting two men from others who are armed. A kneeling man looking toward the heavens is shown below the two-line initial for the hymn *Veni creator*. The menace of evil and violence lurks in the lower periphery, where a red lion attacks a white horse, whose rider tries to ward it off with his sword.[15]

At None (f. 50v, Fig. 8), the tempter reveals his true appearance, which is a full-fledged dark devil with claws and with red horns sprouting from his head, body, and legs. This diabolical archer aims his deadly arrow at the lady's back.[16] This activity is reminiscent of the image in the Lambeth Palace Apocalypse of ca. 1264–67 (London, Lambeth Palace, Ms. 209, f. 53r),[17] which shows a hairy demon bending his bow and shooting an arrow of temptation at a seated personification of penitence, depicted as a noble lady armed with the shield of faith. Wearing a wimpled veil, she may well be the book owner Eleanor de Quincy, a widow who is portrayed wearing the heraldic mantle (Ferrers and de Quincy) of her husband Roger, second Earl of Winchester (d. 1264) on folio 48r. In Lambeth Ms. 209, the spiritual warfare between the two protagonists elaborates upon Ephesians 6:11 ("Put you on the armour of God, that you may be able to stand against the deceits of the devil") and 16 ("taking the shield of faith where with you may be able to extinguish all the fiery darts of the most wicked one"). In Cambrai Ms. 87, however, the standing lady is defenseless; she directs her appeal to heaven for deliverance from this treacherous creature. The devil assaulting her with an arrow may denote several meanings, ranging from the general to the specific. Psalms evoke vivid imagery of demon-archers shooting at people who fell to temptation, especially in the illustrated Utrecht Psalter of the ninth century and its later English copies.[18] One eleventh-century

---

[14] M. Evans, "Laster," *LCI*, vol. 4, fig. col. 25.

[15] In the Bible, 1 Peter 5:8 compares the lion to the devil. Cf. Psalm 7:3: "Lest at any time he seize upon my soul like a lion."

[16] For the lowly and often despised status of the archer in medieval society, see J. Bradbury, *The Medieval Archer* (Woodbridge, Suffolk, and Rochester, N.Y., 1985), 1–3, 159–60, 169–70; and M. Camille, *Image on the Edge: The Margins of Medieval Art* (Cambridge, Mass., 1992), 106–8.

[17] S. Lewis, *Reading Images: Narrative Discourse and Reception in the Thirteenth-Century Illuminated Apocalypse* (Cambridge, 1995), 292–93, fig. 228; N. Morgan, *The Lambeth Apocalypse: Manuscript 209 in Lambeth Palace Library*, with a contribution by Michelle Brown, 2 vols. (London, 1990), vol. 1, 61–65; vol. 2, pl. f. 53r. Morgan mentions also Psalm 90:5–6, especially on the arrow of the devil, as influential for the iconography of the Lambeth picture. Aiding the woman are her two guardian angels, whose presence clearly relates to verses 10–11 of the same psalm (ibid., 62).

[18] E.g., illustrations of Psalm 10:3 ("the wicked have bent their bow") showing two archers drawing their bows in the mid-ninth-century Utrecht Psalter, Bibliotheek der Universiteit Utrecht, Ms. 484/32, f. 6r (E. DeWald, *The Il-*

lustrations of the Utrecht Psalter [Princeton, 1932], pl. IX; and *Vollständige Faksimile-Ausgabe im Original Format der Handschrift 32, Utrecht-Psalter, aus dem Besitz der Bibliotheek der Rijksuniversiteit te Utrecht* [Graz, 1982], vol. 1, f. 6r); the Harley Psalter of ca. 1000, London, B.L., Ms. Harley 603, f. 6r (T. H. Ohlgren, *Anglo-Saxon Textual Illustration: Photographs of Sixteen Manuscripts with Descriptions and Illustration* [Kalamazoo, Mich., 1992], pl. p. 156 [2.10]); the Canterbury psalter of the mid-twelfth century, Cambridge, Trinity College Library, Ms. R.17.1, f. 19r (M. R. James, *The Canterbury Psalter* [London, 1935], pl. f. 19r); and three archers in the later Canterbury psalter of 1180–90, Paris, B.N.F., Ms. lat. 8846, f. 19r (H. Omont, *Psautier illustré [XIIIᵉ siècle]: Reproduction des 107 miniatures du manuscrit latin 8846 de la Bibliothèque Nationale* [Paris, 1906], pl. 19). In the Bury St. Edmunds Psalter of the second quarter of the eleventh century, also from Canterbury, Christ Church (Rome, Bibl. Vat., Ms. Reg. lat. 12, f. 27v), the archer becomes a hairy demon, drawing arrows from a quiver (Ohlgren, *Anglo-Saxon Textual Illustration*, pl. p. 254 [3.6]). For the background of the fiendish archer in biblical imagery (e.g., Psalms 7, 10, 36, 59, 63, and 90, and Ephesians 6:11 and 16), see F. Reitinger, *Schüsse, die Ihn nicht erreichten: Eine Motifgeschichte des*

bilingual psalter, in Latin and Anglo-Saxon, now in Paris (B.N.F., Ms. lat. 8824, f. 6r), pictures a wild-haired demon targeting his arrows at an embracing couple seated inside an edifice within the column after the Latin text of Psalm 7:14, *sagittas suas argentibus effecit,* "he hath made ready his arrows for them that burn." In the adjoining column, the Anglo-Saxon prose describes the devil firing his arrows at the couple who burn with lust and other vices.[19] A late tenth-century copy of Prudentius's *Psychomachia* probably from Tours (Paris, B.N.F., Ms. lat. 8318, f. 53v) labels the archer as Fornication shooting at Chastity.[20] In the Cambrai manuscript, the arrow may signify lust striking at the lady who averts her glance from the devil. The bottom margin illustrates a horseman armed with a sword galloping away from a snail, which often represents cowardice.[21] To counteract this negative message, the lady must exert her courage to resist the devil through prayer.

The Vespers initial (f. 53v, Fig. 9) expands the drama to include two well-attired temptresses flanking the petitioner in the center. On the left, the hairy devil jabs the supplicant's back with a black hook and stands by a woman so close as to suggest a two-sided tempter, like the Prince of this World, as in Strasbourg Cathedral, or the Woman of this World, as in Worms Cathedral, both of whose backs are studded with serpents and toads.[22] In the initial on the right, a female gittern player represents frivolous revelry pursued by women.[23] In contrast, in the two-line initial B of the None collect on the same page, clerics performing sacred chants to the Lord or the Virgin are deemed praiseworthy. In the bottom margin, the image of two horsemen running lances at each other would add jousting to the list of pleasures frowned upon by the Church.[24]

Gottesattentats (Paderborn, Munich, Vienna, and Zurich, 1997), 12–18.

[19] B. Colgrave, *The Paris Psalter: Ms. Bibliothèque Nationale Fonds Latin 8824* (Early English Manuscripts in Facsimile 8) (Copenhagen, 1958), pl. f. 6r; Ohlgren, *Anglo-Saxon Textual Illustration* [as in note 18], pl. p. 302 [4.11]. For specific discussion of this pictorial rendering of the Latin (Roman) version of Psalm 7:12–14 and its Anglo-Saxon text, see R. Harris, "An Illustration in an Anglo-Saxon Psalter," *JWarb* 26 (1963), 255–57, pl. 31(b). Related to Ms. lat. 8824, but less relevant for my argument, is the Bury St. Edmunds Psalter, ff. 24–25 (Harris, 257; Ohlgren, *Anglo-Saxon Textual Illustration,* pls. pp. 252–53 [3.4–3.5]).

[20] Stettiner, *Prudentiushandschriften* (as in note 10), vol. 1, 7–8; vol. 2, pl. 8.

[21] L. M. C. Randall, "The Snail in Gothic Marginal Warfare," *Speculum* 37 (1962), 358–67.

[22] W. Stammler, *Frau Welt: Eine mittelalterliche Allegorie* (Freiburg, 1959), 24–25, figs. 1, 2 (Strasbourg, Cathedral, west facade, on the left embrasure of the right portal [Last Judgment], in the company of the Foolish Virgins, 1280–85), and 53, fig. 10 (Worms, Cathedral, south exterior, wall of the Annakapelle, early fourteenth century). For Strasbourg, see also O. Schmitt, *Gotische Skulpturen des Strassburger Münsters,* 2 vols. (Frankfurt am Main, 1924), vol. 2, pl. 131; and H. Reinhardt, *La Cathédrale de Strasbourg* (Paris, 1972), 127, fig. 111; for Worms, see R. Kautzsch, *Der Dom zu Worms* (Berlin, 1938), pl. 106c. For general discussion of other examples in Basel, Nurem-

berg, Regensburg, and Bamberg, see Stammler, *Frau Welt,* 24–27, figs. 3–8. For an overview, see G. Gsodam, "Welt, Fürst Welt, Frau Welt," *LCI,* vol. 4, 496–98. Biblical citations for the Prince of this World are John 12:31, 14:30, and 16:11.

[23] For the long-standing negative views expressed by Christian writers of the patristic age and more recently, see, in addition to the references cited for the medieval musician in note 10 above, J. McKinnon, "The Meaning of the Patristic Polemics against Musical Instruments," *Current Musicology* 1 (1965), 69–83; idem, "Musical Instruments in Medieval Psalm Commentaries and Psalters," *Journal of the American Musicological Society* 21 (1968), 3–20; and G. Henderson, "The Musician in the Stocks at Higham Ferrers, Northamptonshire," in *England in the Thirteenth Century: Proceedings of the 1989 Harlaxton Symposium,* ed. W. M. Ormrod (Stamford, 1991), 135–47.

[24] S. Painter, *French Chivalry: Chivalric Ideas and Practices in Mediaeval France* (Baltimore, 1940), 153–65; R. Barber and J. Barker, *Tournaments: Jousts, Chivalry and Pageants in the Middle Ages* (Woodbridge, Suffolk, 1989), 138–49; for general background, see J. R. V. Barker, *The Tournament in England 1100–1400* (Woodbridge, Suffolk, 1986), 70–83; see also the list of manuscripts under "Knights tilting" in Randall, *Images* (as in note 1), 140. For specific examples of illustrated manuscripts with moral connotations, see A. Bennett, "A Thirteenth-Century French Book of Hours for Marie," *JWalt* 54 (1996), 25–27.

At the last canonical hour of Compline (f. 60r, Fig. 10), the two-faced devil resumes his disguise, in this instance as a falconer. With a lure in his right hand, a purse at his waist, and a falcon or hawk on his gloved left hand, he embodies the courtly pleasures of falconry, enjoyed by both men and women. The standing lady invokes help from heaven. The bottom margin adds a pictorial gloss on a sport of two gladiators, a practice which was also condemned by ecclesiastical authorities.[25]

Falconry was long regarded as a royal or noble sport, a view that can be traced in early medieval imagery of kingship, and symbolized the pleasures of the hunt, as commonly depicted in calendar illustrations for May.[26] In representations of the Three Living and Three Dead, for example, in the Robert De Lisle Psalter (London, B.L., Ms. Arundel 83 II, f. 127r), one of the three kings sports a falcon in pursuing his transitory pastime.[27] Falconry is also associated with sins, as pictured earlier in the twelfth-century Saint Albans Psalter (Hildesheim, Sankt Godehard, p. 315) for Psalm 118:37: "Turn away my eyes that may not behold vanity."[28] The psalmist points below to sins and vanities of the world: the left group of a hawker and a woman holding a flower, signifying the delights of the world, and an apple, reminding us of Eve's fall to sin; and the right group of a man proffering a coin and drawing a woman to him, denoting avarice or cupidity and lust. Moralized Bibles of the thirteenth century frequently link falconers with the sins of lust and greed.[29]

For the hours of the Virgin, the major historiated initials are extraordinary in detail and in program. First among these is the portrayal of the devil with two masks, one of which is half-human and the other half-diabolical.[30] Normally the creature appears bestial and naked, as illustrated in the None and Vespers initials above (Figs. 8, 9). But four other initials show the two-faced devil in different human disguises and in full attire (Figs. 5–7, 10), so appropriate to his cunning nature. Pertinent comparisons with this two-faced representation are few. There is, of course, the tradition of the pagan god Janus, whose two faces gazed in opposite directions, east and west, toward the

[25] See note 24.

[26] For example, The Hague, K.B., Ms. 76 F 13, f. 5v, illustrated in *Schatten van de Koninklijke Bibliotheek: Acht eeuwen verluchte handschriften, Tentoonstelling in het Rijksmuseum Meermanno-Westreenianum/Museum van het Boek 17, december 1980–15 maart 1981* (The Hague, 1980), no. 18, color pl. II, fig. p. 46.

[27] L. F. Sandler, *The Psalter of Robert De Lisle in the British Library* (New York, 1983), 42, color pl. 5. For other examples of a falconer as one of the Three Living, see W. Rotzler, *Die Begegnung der drei Lebenden und der drei Toten: Ein Beitrag zur Forschung über die mittelalterlichen Vergänglichkeitsdarstellungen* (Winterthur, 1961), with earlier bibliography.

[28] O. Pächt, C. R. Dodwell, and F. Wormald, *The St. Albans Psalter (Albani Psalter)* (London, 1960), 250–51, pl. 77 (p. 315/f. 158r); *Der Schatz von St. Godehard*, ed. M. Brandt (Hildesheim, 1988), 160, color fig. 161.

[29] E.g., London, B.L., Ms. Harley 1526-1527, II, f. 29r, illustrated in Laborde, *Bible moralisée* (as in note 8), vol. 3, pl. 500, picturing three couples, the first embracing, the second giving a goblet to falconer, and the third making

music, all seated behind a banquet table, beside the typological commentary "Dies festus iste in quo saltatrix placuit prosperitatem mundi significat que spiritum carni subicit." For other examples of falconry associated with sins, especially in Moralized Bibles, see Friedman, "Sünde, Sünder und die Darstellungen der Laster" (as in note 11), 157–71; and H.-W. Stork, *Die Wiener französische Bible moralisée Codex 2554 der Österreichischen Nationalbibliothek* (St. Ingbert, 1992), 303–9.

[30] The literature on the devil is extensive. For a recent major discussion, see P. Dinzelbacher, *Angst im Mittelalter. Teufels-, Todes- und Gotteserfahrung: Mentalitätsgeschichte und Ikonographie* (Paderborn, 1996). R. Mellinkoff, *The Devil at Isenheim: Reflections of Popular Belief in Grunewald's Altarpiece* (Berkeley, Los Angeles, and London, 1988), 28, discusses Pope Gregory the Great's popularization of Satan's deception (also elaborated in D. I. Wee, "The Temptation of Christ and the Motif of Divine Duplicity in the Corpus Christi Cycle Drama," *Modern Philology* 72 [1974], 7: "the medieval world conceived of the devil as a cunning, petty, mischievous, trick-playing imposter").

doors of his temple.[31] Originally a Roman deity, he metamorphosed into a christianized figure in the Labors of the Months cycle for January, which is called after him.[32] Manuscript calendars, for instance, show him facing two doors, one closed and the other open, signaling the end of the old year and the beginning of the new.[33] Age sometimes differentiates the two faces or heads, one elderly and one youthful, as in the January calendar of the Ingeborg Psalter, of around 1200 (Chantilly, Musée Condé, Ms. 9/1695, f. 3v).[34] More frequently, though, Janus eats and drinks simultaneously at a banquet table.[35] Sometimes this double-faced image is employed for the personification of gluttony and is shown feasting, as in the aforementioned *Verger de Solas* from Arras.[36] Aside from Cambrai Ms. 87, a hairy, horned, two-faced devil of the Janus type rarely appears. Of the vast numbers of devil depictions in the thirteenth-century Moralized Bibles, one demon with twin countenances and protruding tongues appears in the typological scene for Moses, Plague of Boils (Ex. 9:9–10), in the Vienna Moralized Bible of the 1220s (Vienna, Ö.N.B., Ms. 1179, f. 27r). At the center, he glances left at a man seated with his legs crossed and caressing the chin of a youth, and right at a hooded horseman trampling a fallen man.[37]

A second uncommon feature is the color distinction for the two faces of the devil which stress his deception. His white human face looks innocent, but his black diabolical face, which is averted,

[31] See H. Buchthal, *Miniature Painting in the Latin Kingdom of Jerusalem* (Oxford, 1957), 77, pls. 128a–c (two-headed), 153b, 153c (two-faced), for manuscript illustrations of the *Histoire universelle*. Based largely on Isidore of Seville's *Etymologiae*, the 1023 copy of Hrabanus Maurus, *De universo*, at Montecassino (Biblioteca del Monumento nazionale di Montecassino, Ms. Cod. Casin. 132, p. 386, lib. 15:6, "De diis gentium") shows Janus as a two-faced pagan god with Saturn, Jupiter, and Neptune (A. Amelli, *Miniature sacre e profane dell'anno 1023 illustranti l'enciclopedia medioevale di Rabano Mauro* [Montecassino, 1896], pl. CVIII; M. Reuter, *Text und Bild im Codex 132 der Bibliothek von Montecassino, "Liber Rabani de Originibus Rerum": Untersuchungen zur mittelalterlichen Illustrationspraxis* [Munich, 1984], 178, fig. 114).

[32] J. C. Webster, *The Labors of the Months in Antique and Medieval Art to the End of the Twelfth Century* (Princeton, 1938), 62–63, 132–33, 136, 141–42, 144, 146, 156, 165, 171. Isidore of Seville describes the two-faced appearance of Janus in his verse for January, in *Etymologiae* 5:33 (PL 82:219): "Unde et bifrons idem Janus pingitur ut introitus anni et exitus demonstretur." Apparently one of the earliest calendar examples of a two-headed Janus is in a late tenth-century Ottonian Sacramentary from Fulda: Berlin, Staatsbibl., Ms. Theol. lat. f. 192, cover (Webster, *Labors*, pl. XIV; *Zimelien: Abendländische Handschriften des Mittelalters aus den Sammlungen der Stiftung Preussischer Kulturbesitz Berlin* [Wiesbaden, 1975], no. 34, color pl. p. 57).

[33] Examples appear in both English and French calendar manuscripts from the twelfth and thirteenth centuries; the bicephalic Janus between two doors is especially popular in early thirteenth-century Parisian and northeast French psalter calendars. For other media, see, for instance, the mosaic floor of the early twelfth century in the Cathedral of Aosta (Webster, *Labors* [as in note 32], 136, no. 35, pl. XXI), and the medallions painted on the arch in Panteon de los Reyes, San Isidore, León (ibid., 165).

[34] F. Deuchler, *Der Ingeborgpsalter* (Berlin, 1967), pl. 1; idem, *Der Ingeborg Psalter* (Graz, 1985), pl. f. 3v.

[35] E.g., Missal of Saint-Nicaise, Reims (1285–97), St. Petersburg, Public Library, Ms. lat. Q.v.I.78, f. 4r (I. Mokretsova and V. Romanova, *Les Manuscrits enluminés français du XIIIe siècle dans les collections soviétiques, 1270–1300* (Moscow, 1984), color fig. p. 200. See also Webster, *Labors* (as in note 32), 170–72, nos. 90, 92, 93, 95, 96, pls. 56, 58, 59, 61, 62.

[36] See note 14 above. Other two-faced or two-headed examples are, for instance, the Creator of the World, sometimes in the presence of the dove of Holy Spirit (forming the Trinity), notably in Italian Trecento art, especially in Neapolitan manuscripts (J. Zahlten, *Creatio Mundi: Darstellungen der sechs Schöpfungstage und naturwissenschaftliches Weltbild im Mittelalter* [Stuttgart, 1979], figs. 103, 135, 136, 189, 190, 209, 262, 316, 365, 366, 378, 400); or the two-faced personification Prudence in Italian art, e.g., Giotto's fresco, Padua, Scrovegni Chapel (C. Semenzato, *Giotto: La capella degli Scrovegni* [Milan, 1983], pl. 58); and Florence, Or San Michele, Tabernacle of the Virgin, north socle (1359) (*Orsanmichele a Firenze/Orsanmichele Florence*, ed. D. Finiello Zervas, 2 vols. (Modena, 1996), vol. 2, fig. 639. In both instances, age differentiates the two countenances.

[37] The typological commentary reads as follows: "Hoc significat prauos homines qui uulnerantur in puluere peccatorum et post mortem ueniunt ad infernum." A reproduction of f. 27r is in the photograph collection at the Department of Art and Archaeology, Columbia University, an important research center for French Gothic manuscripts.

appears sinister. White, of course, stands for purity, and black symbolizes evil.[38] The Latin Father Ambrose comments on the devil turning from white to red to black, the last denoting sin. Connected with this notion, the triune devil (Satan or Lucifer) exists in Italian representations of hell, and even appears tricolored in white, red, and black.[39] Portrayals of a two-faced personification of fortune appear commonly enough, mainly in fifteenth-century French Boethius manuscripts.[40] The light and dark countenances reflect her dual but capricious nature, determining fortune and misfortune. Manuscripts of Christine de Pisan's *La Mutacion de Fortune* around 1403–4, for example, in Chantilly (Musée Condé, Ms. 494, f. 16r) illustrate a bicolored, two-faced crowned Fortune standing on the wheel of fate on the ground.[41] Her composite appearance apparently goes back to descriptions of Boethius.[42] It is not until the twelfth century that a double-headed Fortuna appears, for example, in the Virtues and Vices cycle of a Regensburg manuscript of 1165 (Munich, Bayer. Staatsbibl., Ms. Clm. 13002, f. 3v).[43]

The Cambrai moralistic cycle follows no standardized categories or schematic programs of Virtues and Vices, such as Prudentius's *Psychomachia* with Vices battling Virtues, or Virtues trampling Vices.[44] It also differs from the didactic treatise *La Somme le Roi* composed in 1279 for the

[38] For the devil as black, see L. Link, *The Devil: The Archfiend in Art from the Sixth to the Sixteenth Century* (New York, 1995), 52–53. For a survey of black figures as diabolical, see J. Devisse, *L'Image du noir dans l'art occidental*, 2 vols. (Paris, 1978–79), vol. 2, pt. 1, 62–69; Mellinkoff, *Outcasts* (as in note 13), see index under "Blacks," vol. 1, 343, and under "Skin colors, dark," vol. 1, 358. For the role of blacks as persecutors of Christ and executioners of saints, see K. Gould, "Jean Pucelle and Northern Gothic Art: New Evidence from Strasbourg Cathedral," *ArtB* 74 (1992), 53–55, with full bibliography on p. 53, n. 12.

[39] Devisse, *Image du noir* (as in note 38), vol. 2, pt. 2, 76 and n. 54 (with earlier bibliography), fig. 83 (Dante's *Inferno*, Rome, Bibl. Vat., Ms. Urb. lat. 365, f. 934, by Guglielmo Giraldi, after 1474); P. Brieger, M. Meiss, and C. S. Singleton, *Illuminated Manuscripts of the Divine Comedy*, 2 vols. (Princeton, 1969), vol. 1, 155–57; vol. 2, pls. 317–26 (Inferno XXXIV). J. B. Russell, *Lucifer: The Devil in the Middle Ages* (Ithaca, N.Y., 1984), 232, refers to J. Freccero, "The Sign of Satan," *Modern Language Notes* 80 (1965), 11–26, esp. 15–16, in connection with Ambrose of Milan on the tricolors of the devil in his commentary on Luke 17:6 (*Expositionis in Lucam Liber VIII* [PL 15:1864, no. 29]).

[40] P. Courcelle, *La Consolation de philosophie dans la tradition littéraire: Antécédents et postérité de Boèce* (Paris, 1967), 149, pl. 78 (Paris, B.N.F., Ms. fr. 809, f. 40r, light and dark faces); 151, pls. 82.2 (Paris, B.N.F., Ms. fr. 24307, f. 35v, light and dark faces), 83 (Paris, B.N.F., Ms. fr. Réserve 488, f. XXXIXv, large and small faces), and 85 (Paris, B.N.F., Ms. néerl. 1, f. 58v, two heads); 152–54, pls. 87, 91 (London, B.L., Ms. Harley 4336, f. 1v, and Ms. Harley 4438, f. 1v, light and dark skin), and pls. 88, 92 (Paris, B.N.F., Ms. lat. 6643, ff. 76r, 227r, light and dark skin).

[41] M. Meiss, *French Painting in the Time of Jean de Berry: The Limbourgs and Their Contemporaries*, 2 vols. (New York,

1974), vol. 1, 9, 11; vol. 2, figs. 19–22 (The Hague, K.B., Ms. 78 D 2, f. 16v; Chantilly, Musée Condé, Ms. 494, f. 16r; Brussels, B.R., Ms. 9508, f. 17v; and formerly Paris, Collection of Pierre Berès, f. 16); Devisse, *Image du noir* (as in note 38) vol. 2, pt. 2, 76, fig. 82 (Chantilly Ms.).

[42] Boethius, *The Consolation of Philosophy*, translated, with introduction and notes by R. Green (Indianapolis and New York, 1962), 22 (Book II, prose 1: "You have merely discovered the two-faced nature of this blind goddess"); compare, however, with the Latin, "Deprehendisti caeci numinis ambiguous uultus," in two editions: Anicius Manlius Severinus Boethius, *Philosophiae consolatio*, (Corpus Christianorum Series Latina 94), ed. L. Bieler (Turnholt, 1957), 18, no. 11; and Boethius, *The Consolation of Philosophy*, with the English translation of "I. T." (1609), rev. H. F. Stewart, Loeb Classical Library (London, 1968), p. 174 (translated as: "Thou hast discovered the doubtful looks of this blind goddess," p. 175).

[43] Courcelle, *Consolation* (as in note 40), 144, pl. 66; E. Klemm, *Die romanischen Handschriften der Bayerischen Staatsbibliothek*, pt. 1, *Die Bistümer Regensburg, Passau und Salzburg*, 2 vols. (Wiesbaden, 1980), vol. 1, 60–64 (no. 87), vol. 2, fig. 158; *Regensburger Buchmalerei von frühkarolingischer Zeit bis zum Ausgang des Mittelalters, Ausstellung der Bayerischen Staatsbibliothek München und der Museen der Stadt Regensburg* (Munich, 1987), no. 34, color pl. 25. This cycle was copied in the 1241 Scheyern codex, Munich, Bayer. Staatsbibl., Ms. Clm. 17403, f. 6r (R. Kroos, "Die Bildhandschriften des Klosters Scheyern aus dem 13. Jahrhundert," in *Wittelsbach und Bayern I: Die Zeit der frühen Herzöge, von Otto I. zu Ludwig dem Bayern: Beiträge zur bayerischen Geschichte und Kunst 1180–1350*, ed. H. Glaser [Munich, 1980], 490–91, fig. 174).

[44] Stettiner, *Prudentiushandschiften* (as in note 10); H. Woodruff, "The Illustrated Manuscripts of Prudentius,"

French king, Philip III, and used by the laity.[45] This has quadripartite miniatures with attributes and labels identifying personifications of virtues and vices, and their biblical exempla appearing below, as in the late thirteenth-century British Library copy attributed to Honoré.[46] Not all the vices in Cambrai Ms. 87 are associated with the seven deadly sins as they are in one psalter-hours of ca. 1280 from Liège, now in New York (Morgan Lib., Ms. M. 183, f. 9v). The top left medallion of the mariological miniature shows a haloed female displaying above a male supplicant the seven roundels of the initials for the acrostic SALIGIA: *superbia, avaricia, luxuria, ira, gula, invidia,* and *accidia.*[47] The saint, wearing a berbette, is probably Mary Magdalen, whose seven devils, i.e., sins, were cast out, as mentioned in the Gospels of Mark and Luke.[48] The Cambrai illustrations are not vignettes of vices, such as Gluttony vomiting or Sloth asleep, for instance, which are portrayed in the circular diagram of the five septenaries in a Peter of Poitiers roll in Oxford (Bodl. Lib., Ms. lat.th.c.2, f. 16r).[49] These deeds of sin at the rim of the wheel are to be corrected by thoughts of prayers, in four series of seven, inscribed in the inner circles: Petitions of the Pater Noster, Gifts of the Holy Spirit, the Virtues, and the Beatitudes. Significantly, this notion of sins remedied by prayers is not unlike that of the Cambrai manuscript. But the Cambrai initials depict the personal encounters of a specific woman, who is probably the book owner, with her tempter, much like the biblical story of Christ with Satan,[50] and they mainly concern carnal sins that typically tempted women. The devil indicates or bears attributes that advocate sins of the flesh, such as adultery for

---

Art Studies 7 (1929), 33–79; A. Katzenellenbogen, *Allegories of the Virtues and Vices in Medieval Art from Early Christian Times to the Thirteenth Century* (London, 1939; reprint, New York, 1964); R. B. Green, "Virtues and Vices in the Chapter House Vestibule in Salisbury," *JWarb* 31 (1968), 148–58; J. O'Reilly, *Studies in the Iconography of the Virtues and Vices in the Middle Ages* (New York and London, 1988), 1–82.

[45] E. Kosmer, "A Study of the Style and Iconography of a Thirteenth-Century Somme le Roi (British Museum Ms. Add. 54180) with a Consideration of Other Illustrated Somme Manuscripts of the Thirteenth, Fourteenth and Fifteenth Centuries," (Ph.D. diss., Yale University, 1973); O'Reilly, *Virtues and Vices* (as in note 44), 163–211.

[46] For reproductions of this manuscript in London, B.L., Ms. Add. 54810, see E. G. Millar, *An Illuminated Manuscript of La Somme le Roy Attributed to the Parisian Miniaturist Honoré* (Oxford, 1953); idem, *The Parisian Miniaturist, Honoré* (London, 1959).

[47] A. Watson, "Saligia," *JWarb* 10 (1947), 148–50, fig. p. 149 (reproduction of only the medallion, showing the female and the seven disks of capital sins); Bloomfield, *Seven Deadly Sins* (as in note 9), 86; Oliver, *Gothic Manuscript Illumination* (as in note 1), vol. 1, 106.

[48] Both Watson, "Saligia" (as in note 47) and Oliver, *Gothic Manuscript Illumination* (as in note 1) identify the haloed figure as Virgin Mary. Nevertheless, the Virgin does not wear a berbette. For discussion of Mary Magdalen, see p. 101 below.

[49] The wheel diagram is based on Hugh of Saint-

Victor's *De quinque septenis,* illustrated in full page in P. Sicard, *Diagrammes médiévaux et exégèse visuelle: Le 'Libellus de Formatione Arche' de Hugues de Saint-Victor* (Paris and Turnhout, 1993), 145, pl. 2 (Grover Zinn kindly gave me this reference), and partially reproduced in O. Pächt and J. Alexander, *Illuminated Manuscripts in the Bodleian Library Oxford,* 3 vols. (Oxford, 1966–73), vol. 3, no. 430, pl. XXXVII (430). For a detailed description of a similar wheel of the vices in a contemporary rotulus (London, B.L., Ms. Royal 14. B. IX), see N. Morgan, *Early Gothic Manuscripts,* vol. 2, *1250–1285* (London, 1988), 108. For more examples of the Victorine wheel of the vices, see Katzenellenbogen, *Allegories* (as in note 44), 63–64 n. 2; and A. De la Mare, *Catalogue of the Collection of Medieval Manuscripts Bequeathed to the Bodleian Library, Oxford, by James P. R. Lyell* (Oxford, 1971), 254–56 (Lyell Ms. 84, *Septenarium Pictum*).

[50] Unlike the Cambrai woman and her tempter, Christ confronts and engages in dialogues with Satan. Sometimes Satan appears as a fully-dressed human being, as in a Carolingian ivory bookcover of 830–50 on Ms. Barth. 180, Ausst. 68, Frankfurt a.M., Stadts- und Universitätsbibliothek (Link, *Devil* [as in note 38], 77–79, fig. 27). Cf. Eleanor de Quincy and the Devil in the Lambeth Apocalypse, discussed above and in note 17. Illustrations of the penitential Legend of Theophilus's involvement with the devil and his compact are popular in devotional books of the thirteenth century. His triumph over the devil was achieved, however, through the Virgin's intercession. In the Cambrai tempter cycle, the Virgin is absent.

Lauds and lust for None (Figs. 5, 8), and sins of the world, such as greed in the Terce initial (Fig. 6), gluttony for Sext (Fig. 7), music-playing for Vespers (Fig. 9), and sporting games in Compline (Fig. 10). Instead of being merely traditional, these sins are personalized for the female owner who sought to vanquish the devil's temptations. She turns away from the devil in prayer and averts her eyes from beholding material wants or carnal pleasures.

Reciting and contemplating the key devotional text for daily penance, the Seven Penitential Psalms, would also help the noblewoman in her quest for redemption. Only the first psalm of the penitential series is normally illustrated in books of hours, and this illustration often depicts David's repentance, the owner in prayer, or Christ the Judge.[51] In Cambrai Ms. 87, all the initials of the seven psalms are historiated, and their images are personalized. They concentrate on the woman's resolve to do penance and to attain salvation for her soul. For Psalm 6 (f. 73r, Fig. 11), the female owner kneels outside the initial D. She confronts what will be her destiny if she fails to repent. With her lowered right hand she points to the fiery pains of hell, which are presided over by two devils who would imprison her forever. With her other hand she points above to her future salvation as promised by the figure of Christ the redeemer of the world, with a globe in his left hand. This will all happen only if she performs her daily penance with diligence, sincerity, and contriteness. The subsequent penitential psalms mainly repeat pictures of her alone begging for mercy (Psalm 31, f. 74r; Psalm 37, f. 75v; Psalm 101, f. 79v; Psalm 129, f. 82v), or sometimes petitioning the crucified Christ (Psalm 50, f. 77v). The last psalm (142, f. 83r) pits the lady once more against the devil with his grapnel of torture, if she fails to do penance. Her constant recitations of the seven psalms and the sights of herself envisioning dangers and doing penance are remedial performances of contrition to lessen her guilt.

The selection of the tempter's cycle for the hours of the Virgin, and not for the Seven Penitential Psalms, is interesting. The focus on sin is of course appropriate to these psalms, for example, as is found in the images of the seven deadly sins paired with virtues in the border medallions of the frontispiece to Psalm 6 in the Bedford Hours, of the 1420s (London, B.L., Ms. Add. 18550, f. 96r).[52] In the Cambrai book the penitential cycle forms a natural sequel to the devil's allurements in the hours of the Virgin. This is also true of the penitential psalms, in which the number seven in the hours of the Virgin appears significant. The large initials from Lauds to Compline begin with the same incipits from Psalm 69: *Deus in adiutorium meum intende. Domine ad adiuuandum me festina*, "O God, come to my assistance; O Lord, make haste to help me." The Cambrai illustrations of these verses reflect this concern with prayer in time of temptation and persecution. They focus on the female petitioner whose remedial power thwarts the devil's temptation. The prayers

<hr>

[51] For David's repentance, see, e.g., the late thirteenth-century Psalter-Hours of Yolande de Soissons, New York, Morgan Lib., Ms. M. 729, f. 346r (photograph, Index of Christian Art); for an owner (female) in prayer, e.g., the late thirteenth-century Thérouanne Book of Hours, Marseilles, B.M., Ms. 111, f. 40r (Billioud, "Très Anciennes Heures de Thérouanne" (as in note 1), pl. LXII [5]); for Christ the Judge, e.g., the Hours of Marie of the early 1270s, New York, Metropolitan Museum of Art, The Cloisters, Ms. L.1990.38, f. 66v (Bennett, "Thirteenth-Century French Book of Hours" [as in note 24], fig. 18).

[52] J. Backhouse, *The Bedford Hours* (London, 1990), color fig. 22. Another good example is a French book of hours of ca. 1475, attributed to Robinet Testard, Poitiers (New York, Morgan Lib., Ms. M. 1001), in which each penitential psalm is illustrated with a male personification of a deadly sin, mounted on an animal (W. Voelkle, "Morgan Manuscript M. 1001: The Seven Deadly Sins and the Seven Evil Ones," in *Monsters and Demons in the Ancient and Medieval Worlds: Papers Presented in Honor of Edith Porada*, ed. A. E. Farkas et al. [Mainz, 1987], 101–14, pls. XXXVII–XL [1–7]).

she might have said would surely have included the seven paternosters, and she would have recited the crucial words "Lead us not into temptation." Cues for paternosters abound in the text of the canonical hours of the Virgin. The Cambrai program goes beyond that of earlier thirteenth-century books of hours in emphasizing figures in prayer. These are mainly women, as they are, for instance, from Lauds to Vespers of the hours of the Virgin in a Parisian book of hours of the 1260s in Baltimore (Walters Art Gallery, Ms. W. 40).[53] The Cambrai pictures instead dwell on the hope and power of prayer as crucial instruments against the devil's temptations of the soul, and the vices and sins of the world, in the life of this lady.

There are biblical precedents for the septenary concept of sinning and praying.[54] Peter Damian in the eleventh century correlated the seven sins with the seven canonical hours by citing Proverbs 26:16, "For a just man shall fall seven times and shall rise again but the wicked shall fall into evil."[55] In the New Testament, Luke 17:4 correlates sinning with seven times of the day, and adds that if one repents seven times daily, he is forgiven. This heptad surely provides the ideological basis for the Cambrai program in that the devil tempts the woman to sin but her repentance frustrates him. Mark 16:9 and Luke 8:2 mention the healing of Mary Magdalen, whose seven spirits in the form of devils were cast out, as illustrated in the mid-thirteenth-century Moralized Bible in Paris (B.N.F., Ms. lat. 11560, f. 37v).[56] Though regarded as the first witness to Christ's resurrection, Mary Magdalen later was transformed to a penitent whore. In his homily on Luke 7:36–50, which recounts the anointing of Christ's feet by a woman in the house of Simon the Pharisee, Gregory the Great identified the woman as Mary Magdalen whose seven sins were exorcised. Thus the pope associated her with the sinner whose act of anointing the feet of Christ absolved her and transformed her role to the model of one performing penance.[57] So, like Mary Magdalen in the Liège psalter-hours and the Paris Moralized Bible, the lady in the Cambrai hours could have been perceived as a paragon of repentance; she sought forgiveness for her sins. As mentioned earlier, the two penitents, Mary Magdalen and Mary of Egypt, are prominent in the calendar, litany, and suffrages of the Cambrai book.[58]

Penance was one of the seven sacraments and clearly the most important for the laity. It was one's duty to confess to a priest at least annually, as was dictated by the Fourth Lateran Council of

[53] Randall et al., *Medieval and Renaissance Manuscripts* (as in note 11), no. 29 (ff. 57v, 69v, 75r, 78v, 82r, 85v), fig. 60 (f. 75r); for other French books of hours, see Bennett, "Thirteenth-Century French Book of Hours" (as in note 24), 24–30.

[54] For the background of the seven-part symbolism of sins in the Bible, I owe much to Bloomfield, *Seven Deadly Sins* (as in note 9), 34.

[55] *De horis canonicis* I (PL 145:221–32, esp. 223).

[56] Laborde, *Bible moralisée* (as in note 8), vol. 2, pl. 261. The medallion picture of Christ casting out the seven devils, representing the seven "deadly" sins, from Mary Magdalen, is correlated with the typological commentary on Psalm 142 (the last of the Seven Penitential Psalms): "Hic psalmus septimus est de psalmis penitentialibus qui sunt vii quia peccata nostra delentur septenari numero et isti psalmi sunt contra vii mortalia peccata." No pictorial examples of Christ expelling the seven devils from Mary

Magdalen were cited in the major study by S. Haskins, *Mary Magdalen: Myth and Metaphor* (New York, San Diego, and London, 1993).

[57] Bloomfield, *Seven Deadly Sins* (as in note 9), 73; and V. Saxer, *Le Culte de Marie Madeleine en Occident des origines à la fin du moyen âge*, 2 vols. (Auxerre and Paris, 1959), vol. 1, 2–3 and n. 12 (list of authors in agreement with Gregory the Great). Gregory the Great, *XL Homiliarum in Evangelia*, lib. II, hom. 33 (PL 76:1238–46, esp. 1239: "Septem ergo daemonia Maria habuit, quae uniuersis uitiis plena fuit"). Mary Magdalen is also considered the first apostle and a preacher. On this connection with penance, see K. L. Jansen, "Mary Magdalen and the Mendicants: The Preaching of Penance in the Late Middle Ages," *Journal of Medieval History* 21 (1995), 1–25.

[58] Of all the illustrated suffrages to the named saints, only the initials to Dominic of Bologna (f. 97v) and Mary Magdalen (f. 99v) enclose the female devotee with the

1215.[59] In the Cambrai book of hours, the lady was persistently reminded of the need to examine oneself and to confess sins committed. The initials in the hours of the Virgin are, however, not illustrations of the sacrament of penance, which would have involved the presence of a confessor seated before a kneeling penitent.[60] Rather, they were like a mirror held up to the beholder, who would have recognized her flaws. She was to avoid worldly pleasures which would keep her away from service to God, or at least modify her taste for such things: musical entertainment (Fig. 9), coveting of material goods (Fig. 6), excess food and drink (Fig. 7), sporting events of jousting or gladiators (Figs. 9, 10), and falconry (Fig. 10). And she was to avoid seduction, adultery, and lustful desires (Figs. 5, 8). The book owner sought help through obedience, chastity, penitence, and humility.

The Annunciation (Fig. 4), which was retained for the Matins initial of the hours of the Virgin, was considered the archetype of the Virgin's humility and her most important virtue. Below the Matins invitatory is the Ave Maria, addressed by Gabriel to the Virgin, whose ardent wish was to be the humble servant of God. In accordance with the incipit for the first hour of the day, *Domine labia mea aperies*, the lady would have opened her lips to the Lord and to the Virgin. Her enactment of prayer would help her to overcome pride, that is, falling into temptation, which was equated with rebelliousness against God and was thus regarded as the foremost sin. The ensuing major initials of the hours of the Virgin would serve as mnemonic guide to her endeavors to prevail over demonic influences.

Numerous images of the female devotee throughout and references to her as the *peccatrix* in prayers remind her of the need to pray for release from her sins. The program which is so insistent on maintaining morals may not have been done at her request. Perhaps it was her husband who commissioned the book to be used not only as a personal manual of devotions but also as a means of promoting and ensuring his spouse's virtuous behavior and proper conduct.[61]

The Cambrai program for the hours of the Virgin appears to be specifically tailored as a penitential guide for an individual laywoman. Though apparently exceptional for books of hours, the portrayals of her personal encounters with the devil highlight her daily struggles to lead an upright Christian life.

---

saint. The suffrage initial to Mary of Egypt (f. 101r) illustrates the woman owner only.

[59] Canon 21: "Omnis utrius sexus fidelis, postquam ad annos discretionis pervenerit, omnia sua solus peccat aconfiteatur fideliter, saltem semel in anno proprio sacerdoti, et iniunctam sibi poenitentiam studeat pro viribus adimplere . . . "; printed in *Conciliorum Oecumenicorum Decreta*, ed. J. Alberigo et al., 3d ed. (Bologna, 1973), 245.

[60] For iconography proper to the sacrament of penance, see A. E. Nichols, *Seeable Signs: The Iconography of the Seven Sacraments 1350–1544* (Woodbridge, Suffolk, and Rochester, N.Y., 1994), 222–41.

[61] Some books of hours may have been intended as wedding gifts, as proposed by S. Bell, "Medieval Women Book Owners: Arbiters of Lay Piety and Ambassadors of Culture," *Signs: Journal of Women in Culture and Society* 7 (1982), 742–67, esp. 757 and 763–64 (reprinted in *Women and Power in the Middle Ages*, ed. M. Erler and M. Kowaleski [Athens, Ga., and London, 1988], 149–87, and in *Sisters and Workers in the Middle Ages*, ed. J. Bennett et al. [Chicago and London, 1989], 135–61). For some French examples of thirteenth- and early fourteenth-century books of hours, see Bennett, "Thirteenth-Century French Book of Hours" (as in note 24), 29 (a mother's gift to her daughter in the 1270s, New York, Metropolitan Museum of Art, The Cloisters, Ms. L.1990.38); M. H. Caviness, "Patron or Matron?: A Capetian Bride and a Vade Mecum for Her Marriage Bed," *Speculum* 68 (1993), 333–62; and J. Holladay, "The Education of Jeanne d'Evreux: Personal Piety and Dynastic Salvation in Her Book of Hours at the Cloisters," *Art History* 17 (1994), 585–611 (gift of Charles IV of France to his spouse between 1324 and 1328, New York, Metropolitan Museum of Art, The Cloisters, Ms. 54.1.2). As for the more convincing identification of the Cambrai couple, the forthcoming study (see note 3) will establish more detailed circumstances surrounding the production of Cambrai Ms. 87.

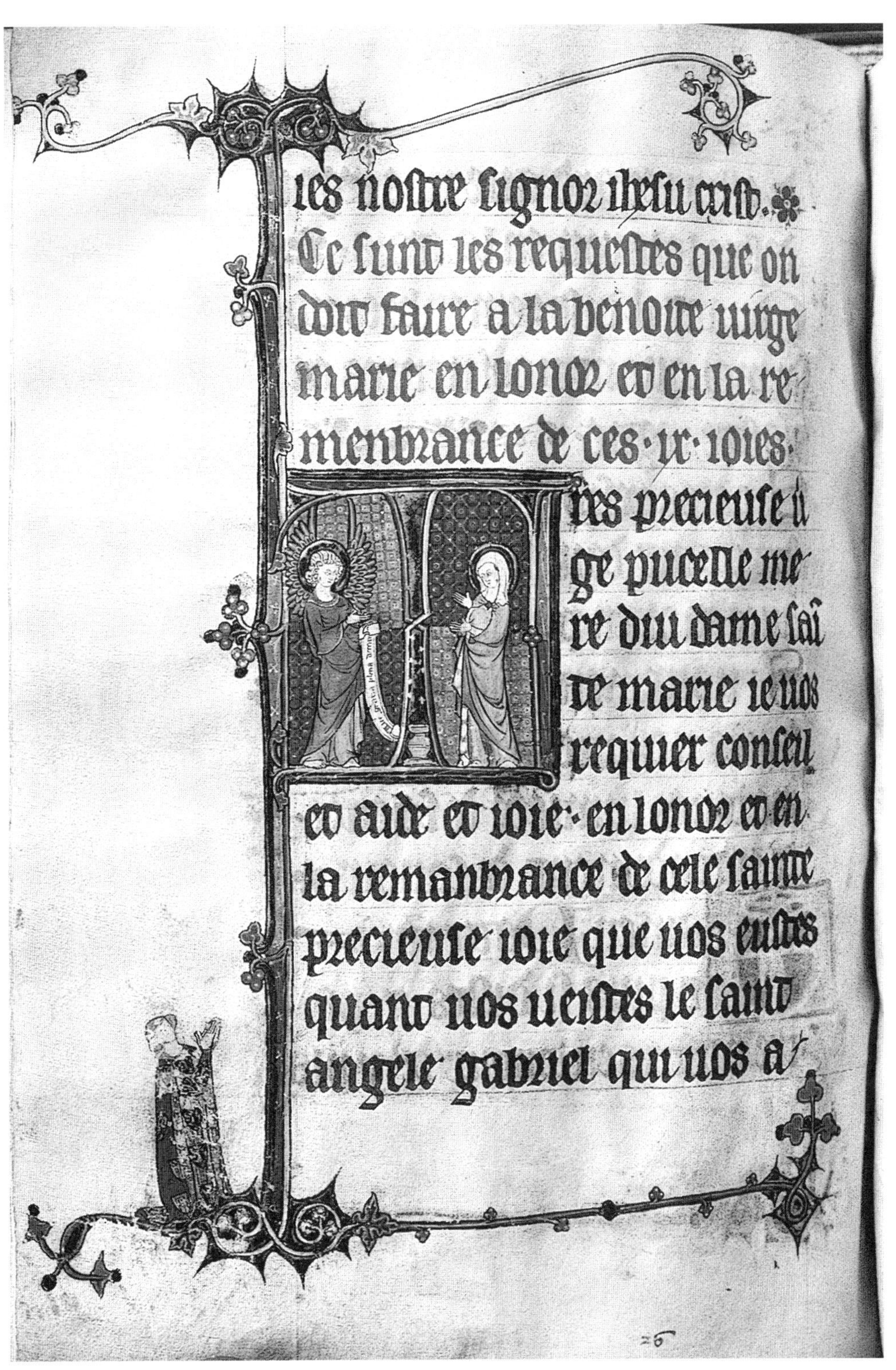

1. Cambrai, Bibliothèque Municipale, Ms. 87, f. 200v. Prologue to the Nine Joys of the Virgin

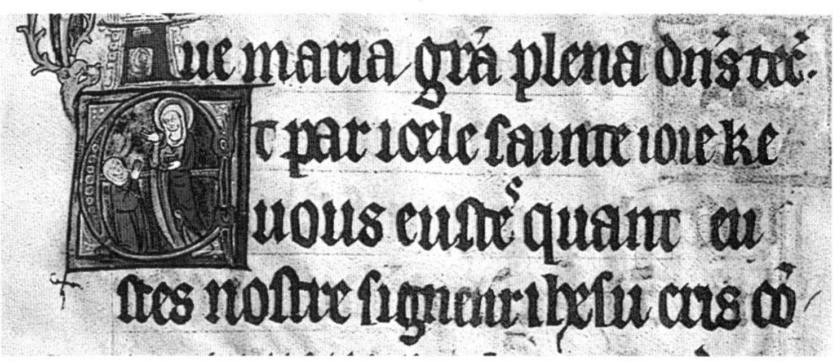

2. Cambrai, Bibliothèque Municipale, Ms. 87, f. 201r. First Joy of the Virgin

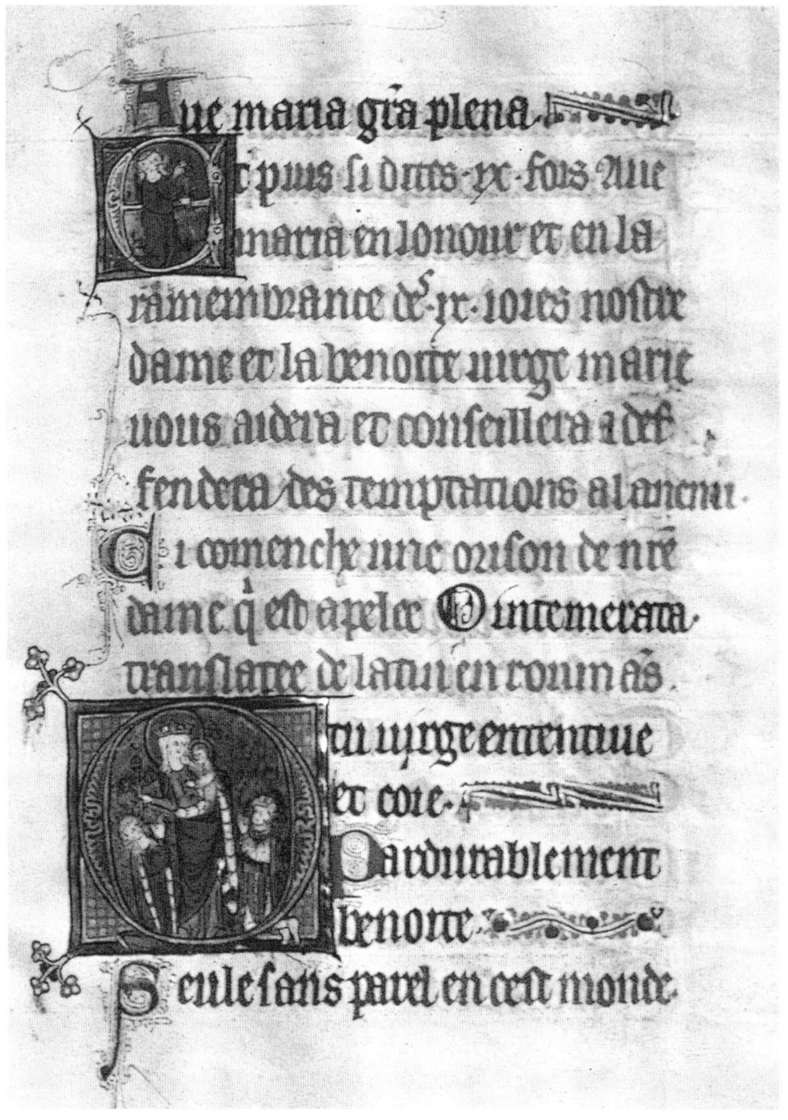

3. Cambrai, Bibliothèque Municipale, Ms. 87, f. 203r. Postscript to the Nine Joys, and Prayer of *O intemerata* in French

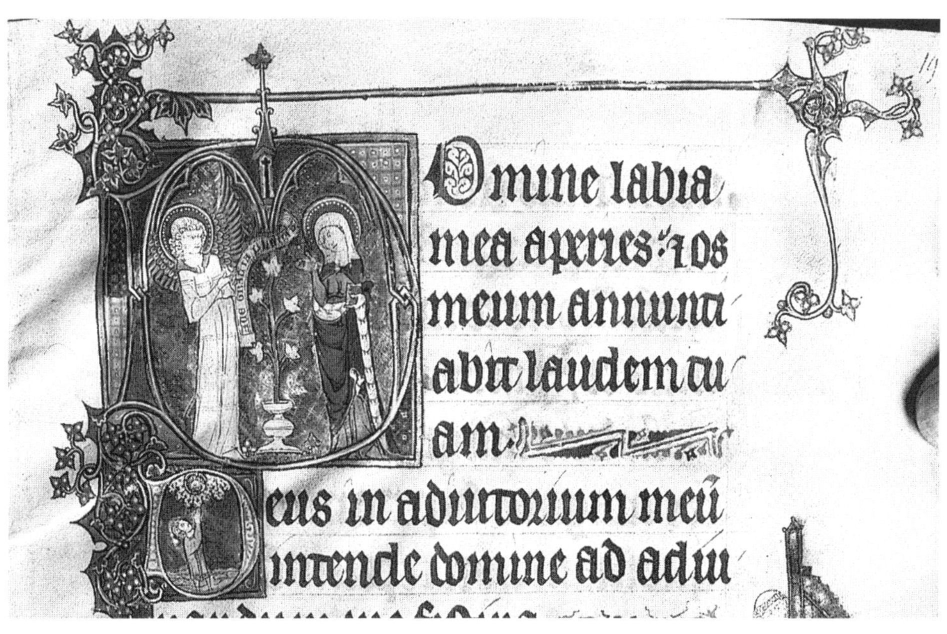

4. Cambrai, Bibliothèque Municipale, Ms. 87, f. 19r. Hours of the Virgin, Matins

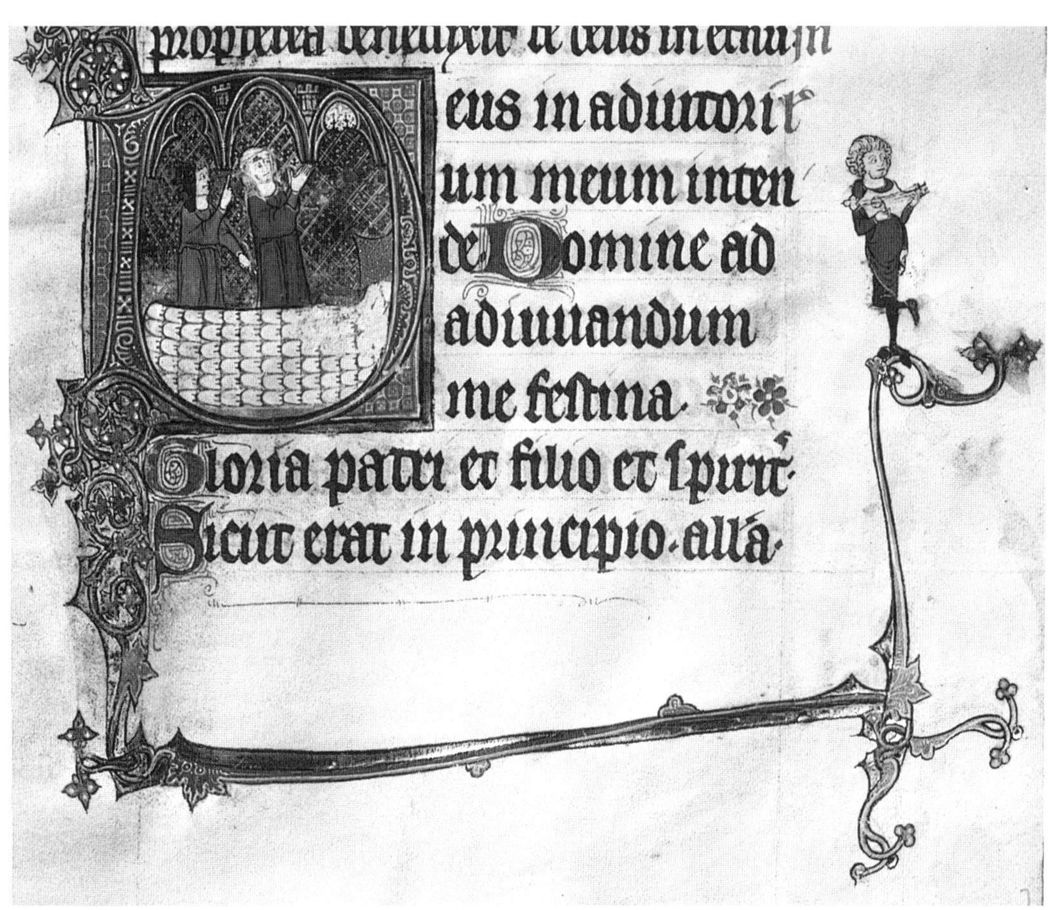

5. Cambrai, Bibliothèque Municipale, Ms. 87, f. 29r. Hours of the Virgin, Lauds

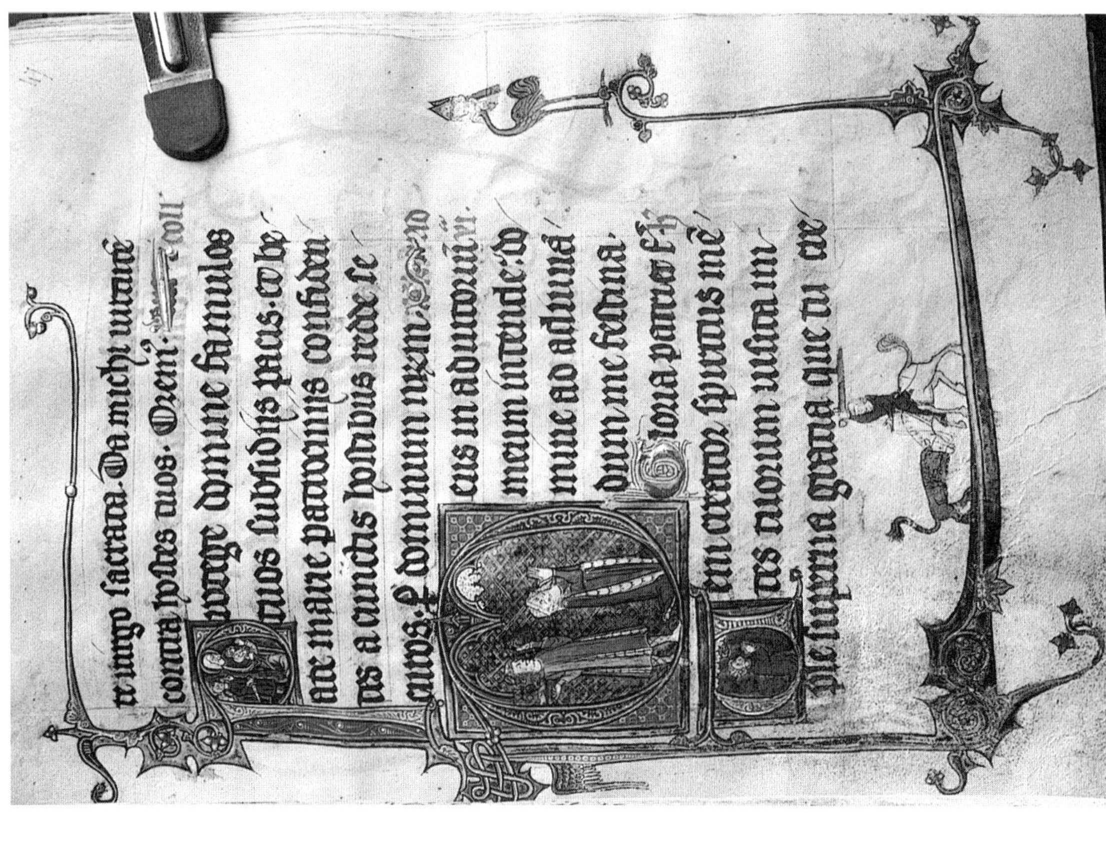

7. Cambrai, Bibliothèque Municipale, Ms. 87, f. 47r. Hours of the Virgin, Sext

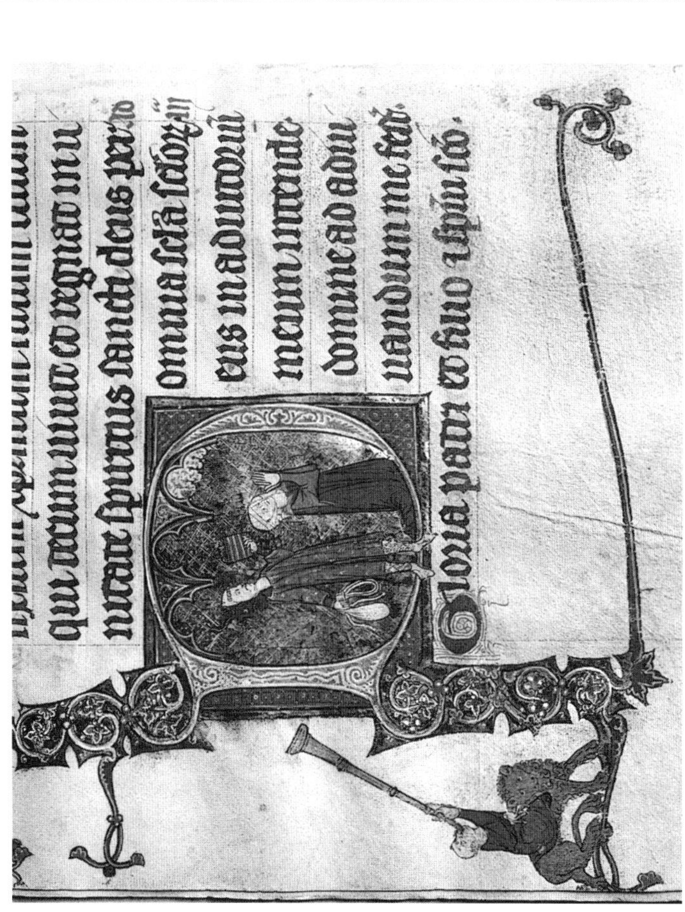

6. Cambrai, Bibliothèque Municipale, Ms. 87, f. 43v. Hours of the Virgin, Terce

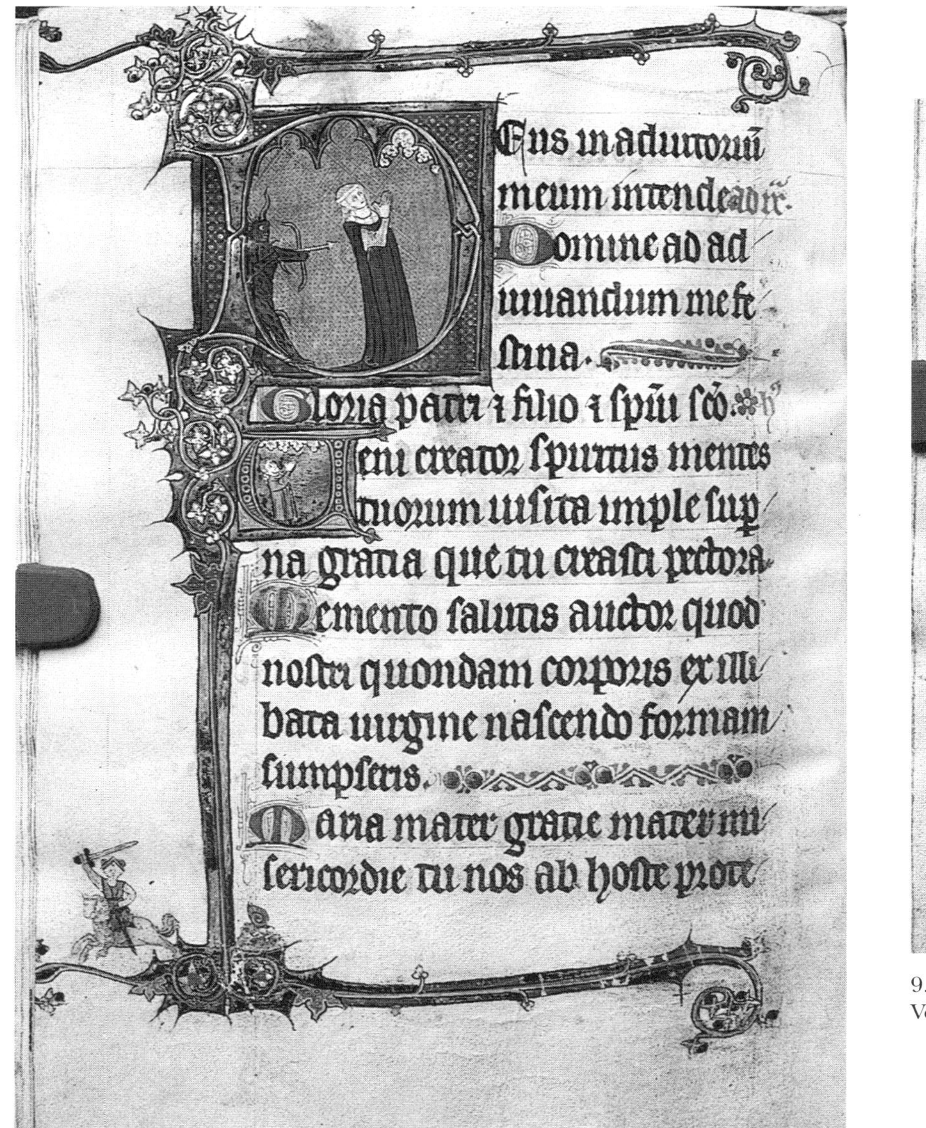

8. Cambrai, Bibliothèque Municipale, Ms. 87, f. 50v. Hours of the Virgin, None

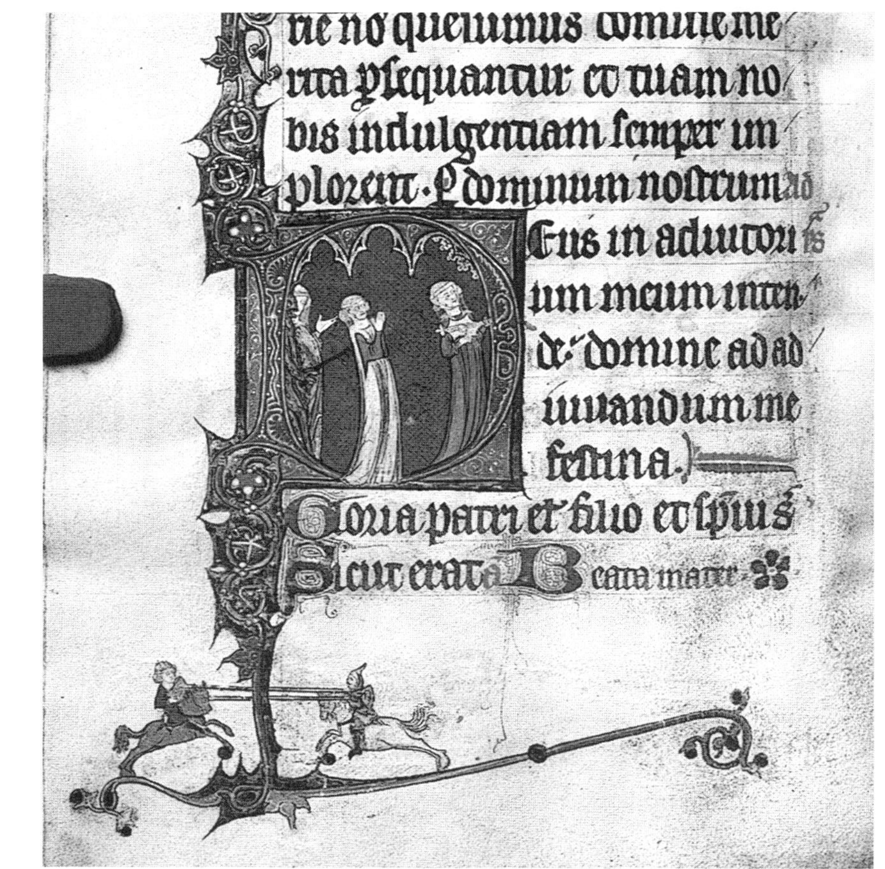

9. Cambrai, Bibliothèque Municipale, Ms. 87, f. 53v. Hours of the Virgin, Vespers

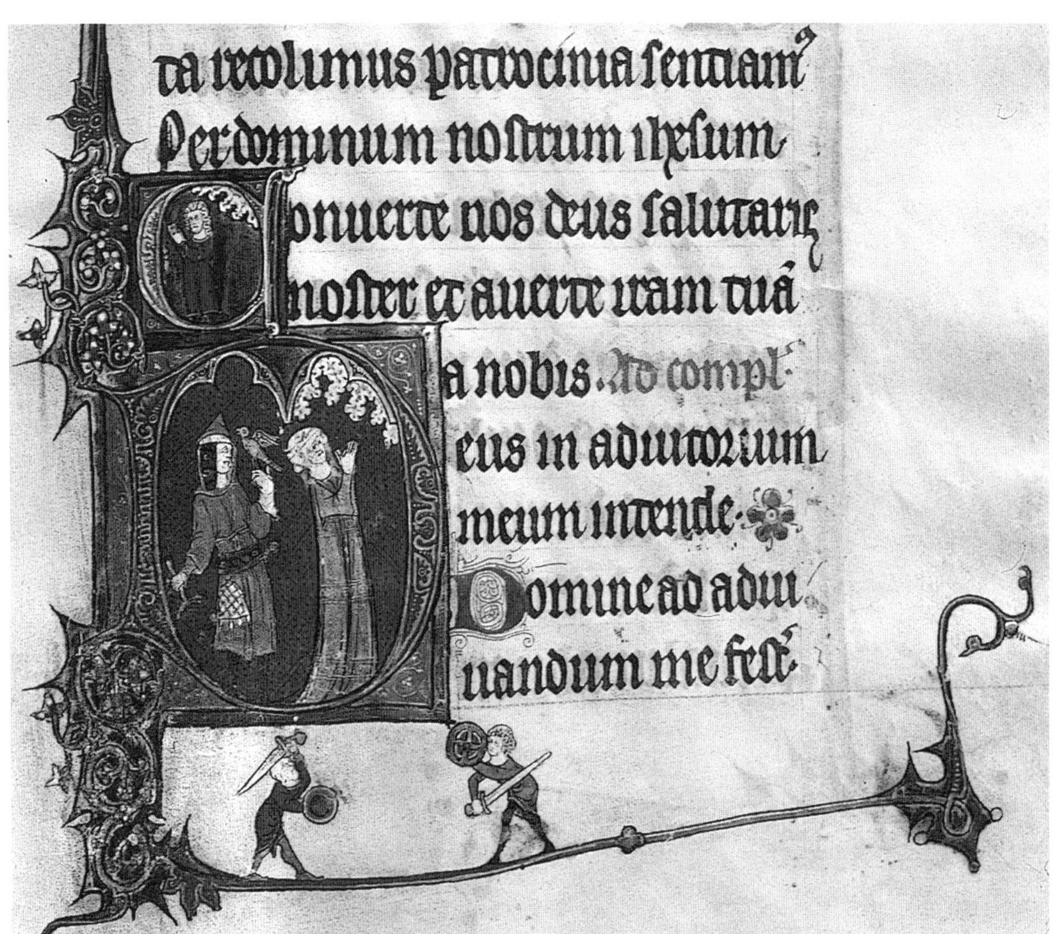

10. Cambrai, Bibliothèque Municipale, Ms. 87, f. 60r. Hours of the Virgin, Compline

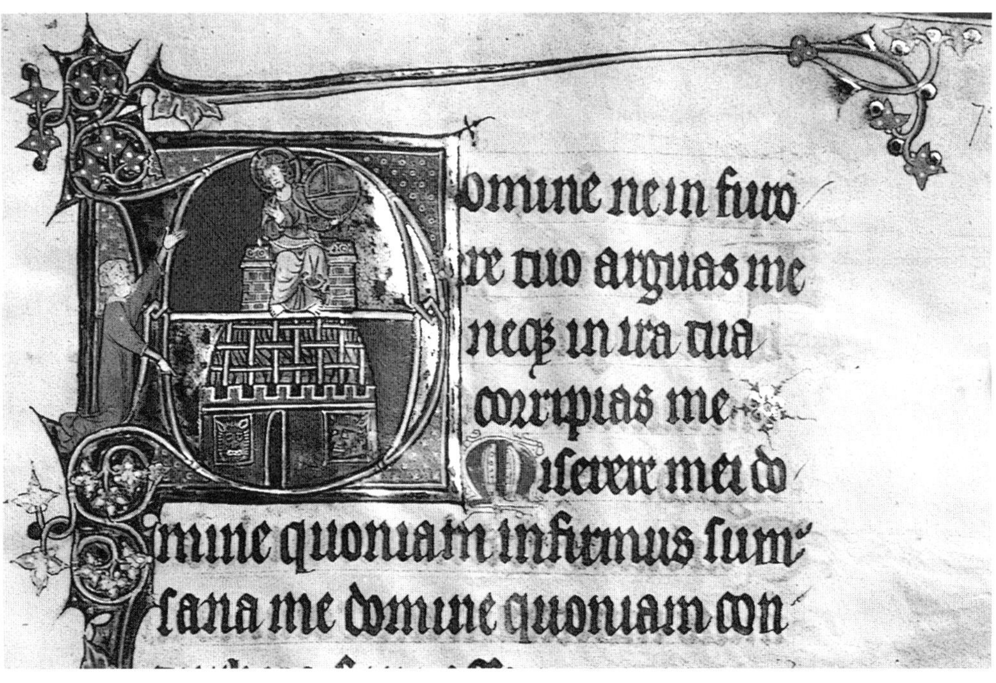

11. Cambrai, Bibliothèque Municipale, Ms. 87, f. 73r. Psalm 6 of the Seven Penitential Psalms

Interpictoriality in the Limoges Chasses
of Stephen, Martial, and Valerie

·

CYNTHIA HAHN

RECENT EXHIBITIONS at the Louvre and the Metropolitan Museum of Art highlighted the unusual and happy coincidence of the survival of three reliquaries representing the three principal saints of the city of Limoges: Stephen, Martial, and Valerie (Figs. 1–4). All three are early, of exceptional quality, and have the relatively unusual form of chasses with narrative scenes as ornament.[1] Unfortunately, not one of these three reliquaries remains in Limoges—they are now in Gimel, the Louvre, and St. Petersburg—and thus we can only surmise about their specific provenances and possible use in the city itself. Nevertheless, a wealth of historical and liturgical evidence from Limoges can be provocatively juxtaposed with a reading of these three objects. A unique opportunity is thus afforded to consider the visual dynamics and viewer reception of the imagery of reliquaries.

The three narratives on the chasses have little specific imagery in common, and the conventional iconographic genealogies of the individual saints do not offer much insight. Nevertheless, each chasse makes use of narrative strategies and significant detail to emphasize differences and similarities among the three saints. The primary operation of viewing, rather than being concerned with locating fixed meaning, takes on the quality of an interpretive act. By means of an "interpictoriality" each chasse focuses on the importance of its hagiographic cult through a sort of visual dialogue.

The term "interpictoriality" is offered here to refer to these visual dynamics by analogy to a literary phenomenon that has particular relevance to this discussion.[2] The notion of intertextuality asserts that readers respond to textual references and cues by bringing previously read texts to bear on current acts of reading. This activity may implicate connotations, innuendoes, even arguments. I will argue that in order to generate meaning, each of these three chasses similarly depends upon viewers' recollections of and responses to imagery and stories during the act of viewing.[3]

Admittedly, there is no hope of recovering the full range of visual reference that may have come into play in the act of medieval "viewing," since too much has been lost of that visual world

---

[1] *Enamels of Limoges: 1100–1350*, exh. cat., Metropolitan Museum of Art, New York, 5 March–16 June 1996 (New York, 1996), nos. 16, 17, and 20. First published as *L'Oeuvre de Limoges: Émaux limousins du Moyen Age*, ed. E. Taburet-Delahaye and B. Drake Boehm (Paris, 1995).

[2] For example, see the discussions in J. Culler, *The Pursuit of Signs: Semiotics, Literature, Deconstruction* (Ithaca, 1981), esp. part 2.

[3] For further exploration of recollection in the case of the Valerie chasse, see C. Hahn, "Valerie's Gift: A Narrative Enamel Chasse from Limoges" in *Reading Medieval Images*, ed. E. Sears and T. Thomas (Ann Arbor, in press).

and too little is known about such viewing. In this brief treatment it would not be feasible to recover all the meaningful, banal, or obscure pictorial references to New Testament imagery, to gestural significance, or to other saints that the chasses might make. Instead, the focus is restricted to the interaction among the three Limoges chasses, which are treated as a case study of the sort of relationships that interpictorial consideration can bring to the fore.

Even if the iconography of St. Stephen's Life is familiar through its many representations, which would have established the narrative on his chasse as conventional (perhaps a copy in one or more sense, Fig. 1), there is still more to be learned by juxtaposing it with the two other chasses from Limoges.[4] In contrast, the reliquaries in the Louvre and St. Petersburg may have no precedents as visual narratives of the lives of Martial and Valerie. Nevertheless, they do make direct reference to earlier material. There is evidence that they refer both to one another and to narratives and ornament on other reliquaries of various saints.

To recapture some of these interactions, it is necessary to readjust our viewpoint to mimic the more engaged perspective of medieval viewers. Rather than viewing the chasses as static art objects, twelfth- and thirteenth-century spectators would have had a chance to compare reliquaries in action during the processions and relic meetings for which Limoges is famous.[5] In that context, the interaction of the imagery and status of the reliquaries would have been highlighted. Moreover, because each of these three particular saints was a powerful local patron, his or her cult and story would have been well known to any Limousin viewer. Instead of a simple group of singular objects, the three reliquaries assume charged positions in relation to one another. Furthermore, attention to what might be called the conversation among the images recovers evidence that is not fully apparent in the surviving historical or literary record.

The "charges" of the pictorial narratives may be summarized as follows: the Stephen reliquary presents, in the relatively new and sumptuous technique of enamel, a magnificent hagiographic argument for the prestige of the Cathedral of Limoges through its possession of the relics of a universal martyr, indeed, the protomartyr of all Christendom. In response, the Martial reliquary focuses not on the universal but on the local significance of the Life of a confessor and the specific prestige of the apostolic saint Martial. In its turn, the Valerie chasse attempts to have the last word on things Limousin and holy, offering a conciliatory gesture that was intended to make a special peace between the two great male powers of Limoges.[6]

Before we can recover the particularities of these interpictorial dynamics, we must understand the discourse in which the arguments are expressed. This consists primarily of a shared approach to structure and narrative disposition. It also includes the common use of dynamic figures animated by exaggerated gestures to create easily-read dramatic characterizations. Each reliquary begins its narrative on the body of the chasse, completes it on the roof, and takes each surface as a

---

[4] M.-M. Gauthier, *Émaux limousins champlevés des XIIᵉ, XIIIᵉ et XIVᵉ siècles* (Paris, 1950), 30–152, compares the stoning of Stephen to the image on f. 20 of Paris, B.N.F. Ms. lat. 9438, a Sacramentary from Saint-Étienne.

[5] A. Perrier, "Ostensions," *Société archéologique et historique du Limousin* 100 (1974), 119–56; and R. Landes, *Relics, Apocalypse and the Deceits of History: Ademar of Chabannes (989–1034)* (Cambridge, Mass., 1995).

[6] My argument here will follow the sequence of the traditional dating of these three objects, but it would not be severely disturbed by a bit of shuffling. I am only concerned that the Valerie reliquary is the last of the series, and there is every reason to think that it is. Furthermore, even though we cannot be sure that these reliquaries were visible in Limoges, it is relatively certain that their iconography was known to Limoges audiences in some fashion.

succinct narrative field.[7] The narratives generally read from left to right, and divergences from this pattern are meaningful. The Stephen and Valerie reliquaries display even more precise similarities: both show the saint's ultimate sacrifice on the right portion of the front of the roof. Other similarities are obvious, but the differences, as we will see, are more subtle. A more detailed reading of the narrative on the three chasses will suggest many resonances among narratives, characters, and images.

For the purposes of this argument, I will assume that the Stephen chasse (Fig. 1), which before the seventeenth century belonged to the church of Saint-Étienne de Braguse (Corrèze), represents iconography known in Limoges. Perhaps this or another image like it was used at Saint-Étienne of Limoges.[8] (As we will see, it was not unknown for reliquaries to be copied virtually without change.[9]) The reliquary, which is now in Gimel, is the largest and earliest of the three discussed here. It is 25.4 cm high and has been dated to ca. 1160–70. Its narrative relies on the text of Acts.

On the body of the chasse at the left, Stephen preaches, but his audience "cried out with a loud voice and stopped their ears" (Acts 7:57), as one figure does. Only one listener, at the far right of the scene, points to the vision of God that Stephen witnesses: "Full of the Holy Spirit, [he] gazed into heaven and saw the glory of God . . . and . . . said, 'Behold, I see the heavens opened, and the Son of man standing at the right hand of God'" (Acts 7:55–56). A scroll held by Stephen contains a few letters that seem to read "Vox Ihesus," that is, the voice of Jesus. At the right, the saint is led out of the gates of Jerusalem. Above, in a scene that spreads across the roof of the chasse, he kneels and is stoned by a group of seven enraged persecutors. At the left, Saul on a thonelike seat witnesses the stoning and makes a blessing gesture. Above, the divine hand, marked with a cruciform halo, accepts the saint's sacrifice. The iconography is comparable to earlier imagery of Stephen, for example, that in the Carolingian frescoes at Saint-Germain in Auxerre. We should recall that Stephen's cult was widespread after the recovery of his relics in 415, and that St. Augustine himself served as his hagiographer, recording his miracles.[10]

The chasse of St. Martial, now in the Louvre, is dated ca. 1165–75 (Figs. 2 and 3).[11] It is the smallest of the three chasses, only 12.5 cm high. The iconography is original and does not clearly follow a single text, although most elements are close to the *Vita prolixior*, a text that was probably written in the eleventh century by Ademar of Chabannes, a monk with close ties to Saint-Martial. The cycle seems to begin with an exorcism in which the principal figure's arms are bound (Fig. 2). In the *Vita prolixior*, only once is a single demoniac so bound. He belongs to the household of

---

[7] This is similar to the direction of the narrative on the Ambrose altar, a precedent for the use of hagiographic narrative on a reliquary. See C. Hahn, "Narrative on the Golden Altar of Sant'Ambrogio in Milan: Presentation and Reception," *DOP*, in press.

[8] *Enamels of Limoges* (as in note 1), 106–8. If this reliquary really was made for Braguse, I would suppose that it might be a copy of an original made for Limoges. Like the misleading specificity of body-part reliquaries (see C. Hahn, "The Voices of the Saints: Speaking Reliquaries," *Gesta* 36 [1997], 20–31), this chasse might seem, given its imagery, to contain a major Stephen relic. In fact, it contains a vial of his blood and the relics of a number of other saints, Peter, Paul, and Andrew among them. This cluster of apostles may, however, explain the figures of the apostles on the back of the reliquary.

[9] See the discussion of the British Museum's copy of the Valerie reliquary in St. Petersburg below.

[10] D. H. Farmer, *The Oxford Dictionary of Saints*, 2d ed. (Oxford, 1987), 391–2; for Auxerre, see C. Hahn, "Seeing and Believing: The Construction of Sanctity in Early-Medieval Saints' Shrines," *Speculum* 72 (1997), 1101–4; see also Augustine, *City of God*, xxii, ch. 8.

[11] *Enamels of Limoges* (as in note 1), 109–11.

Suzanne, where Martial was received upon entering the city of Limoges.[12] On the chasse, Martial cures the violently insane man with the sign of the cross, as he does in the text. The saint holds a long staff and the scene is witnessed by a togate, nimbed figure who stands behind him. Martial also wears a toga and nimbus. These attributes identify Martial and his companion as missionary apostles, indicating that the second figure is Austriclinian.

The second scene on the register shows Martial arrested and beaten by the pagan priests at Limoges, an event that occurred immediately after the exorcism and Suzanne's conversion. In an earlier beating, the *Vita prolixior* specifies that Martial followed his teacher Peter's advice: "If some-one hits you on the right cheek, offer him the other."[13] The artist has made Martial twist about dur-ing his beating, and thus this figure neatly echoes and reverses the image of the saint at the oppo-site end of the register.

The next scene, on the lid on the opposite side of the reliquary (Fig. 3), does not come from the *Vita prolixior*. It represents events subsequent to the fall of the idols in the earthquake at the pagan temple of Limoges, in which two hiding men were killed by lightning. These two men were converted upon their resurrection by the saint. In the image, Martial uses a staff to raise two figures wearing episcopal miters. The anachronistic miters are proleptic in more than one sense. One of these men, Aurelian, succeeded Martial as bishop of Limoges. The other, Andrew, became the first "abbot" of Saint-Martial.[14]

The narrative continues with Martial's fulfillment of his role as missionary with his conversion of the virgin Valerie. Once again Austriclinian witnesses, although his presence is not specified in the texts at this time. The somewhat ambiguous scene may represent the moment of conversion, may metaphorically represent baptism as the saint blesses Valerie, or may represent his acceptance of her vow of virginity. The *Vita prolixior* emphasizes Valerie's vow and specifies that she made it be-fore the death of her mother.[15] Therefore, the veiled woman presenting Valerie to Martial must be Suzanne, Valerie's mother. The man behind her must be Leocadius, Valerie's father. He is not mentioned in the *Vita prolixior*, but his presence here balances the scene, making Valerie the cen-tral figure. This arrangement is reminiscent of the carefully balanced depictions of marriage vows. It seems likely that Valerie is depicted here as a bride of Christ, given into marriage by her parents. However, when her fiancé Stephen hears that she has "married a different spouse,"[16] he orders her

---

[12] *Naissance d'apôtre: La Vie de saint Martial de Limoges*, ed. R. Landes and C. Paupert (Turnhout, n.d.), i.e., *Vita prolixior*, 58. The *Vita prolixior* is literally filled with demo-niacs and demons, but most are not bound. In one case, nine are presented bound to the saint: *Vita prolixior*, 82.

[13] *Vita prolixior*, 56.

[14] Of course, Saint-Martial was not yet an abbey at this time, but the *Vita prolixior* (ch. XIV) notes that he be-came the head of the church in which Martial was buried, which to a twelfth-century reader meant Saint-Martial. See the argument by Taburet-Delahaye, *Enamels of Limo-ges* (as in note 1), 109, 111, n. 4. Gauthier has asserted that the figures are Austriclinian and Alpinian, Martial's companions (in M.-M. Gauthier and G. François, *Émaux méridionaux: Catalogue international de l'oeuvre de Limoges*, vol. 1, *Époque romane* [Paris, 1987], 100–2, no. 94), but this

is less likely for a few reasons. First, only Austriclinian was resurrected. Second, that would make this the first scene of Martial's Life, and the second would then be on the re-verse of the shrine on the lower part. Finally, Austriclin-ian is characterized as an apostle in toga without miter.

[15] *Vita prolixior*, 61–62.

[16] The preserved *vitae* are printed in the volumes of *Cat-alogus Codicum Hagiographicorum Latinorum Antiquiorum Saeculo XVI Qui Asservantur in Bibliotheca Nationali Pari-siensi*, edited by the Bollandists (Brussels, 1889), vol. 1, 41–44, 196–98; vol. 2, 2–5, 401–3. They vary in terms of the amount of detail that is given. That in volume 1, 41–44, is relatively full; that in volume 2, 2–5, is a frame added to the first and seems to be written to praise Martial rather than Valerie. A sermon on the occasion of her translation is de-scribed and her miracles printed in "Miracula Sanctae Va-

execution. The chasse shows this scene on the right. The register closes, however, with the executioner's sword ominously held upright: the martyrdom itself is not depicted.

Finally, the roof of the chasse depicts the culmination of the narrative in Martial's own death. He is wrapped in a shroud and placed in a tomb by two men. A mitered bishop blesses the body while pronouncing the burial office, reading from a book held out to him by a third man. A fourth man holds a long-handled cross. As none of the four men is characterized as a cleric or monk, they must represent the mourning laity. However, because the bishop must be Aurelian, his appearance here serves to represent the continuity of the episcopal office in Limoges. The two censing angels on the ends of the shrine turn toward this side of the chasse and may be meant to accompany this scene and represent Martial's welcome into heaven.

It is worth underlining the ways in which the narrative on the chasse of St. Martial is unusual. First, it jumps about the chasse from one side to the other. In addition, the chasse is almost unique among Limoges reliquaries in having two sides that seem equally important. Out of the aptly named *Vita prolixior*, the artist has chosen only a few scenes, largely from the midportion of the Life. These scenes are neither the most significant hagiographically nor the most exciting in terms of story, but they did take place in Limoges. Finally, the artist almost never represented what might seem to be the critical moments of his chosen episodes but dwells on the early parts of stories. The exorcism of the possessed man is shown, but not the conversion of Suzanne and her household. We see Martial's beating, but not his imprisonment and the subsequent miracles: divine light, breaking of chains, earthquake, and the death of his persecutors. Valerie's blessing is depicted, but not her works of charity, and the order for her execution but not the martyrdom itself. In perhaps the most significant scene on the reliquary, Martial is shown resurrecting the dead, but the eyes of the corpses are still closed. Finally, Martial is buried and his shroud is given a bright white color that gleams on the surface of the shrine, but the miracles that the shroud accomplished are not depicted.

These peculiarities, so different from the Stephen chasse with its hieratic quality and its representation of Stephen's vision and death, result in the Martial reliquary seeming much more engrossed in the process of story-telling. It has, in a sense, shifted narrative modes. One can well imagine that it is suitable for viewing from all sides during a procession or exhibition, rather than only as a static object on an altar. It was also suitable for explication to viewers. Each of the stories could be completed by the monk who displayed the object.

The chasse of St. Valerie, the third in the series (dated ca. 1175–85), is again large and elaborate like the Stephen chasse, measuring 23.2 cm in height (Fig. 4).[17] On this reliquary, the virgin Valerie's Life is treated in detail, taking up where the Martial Life left off. A number of very short *vitae* of Valerie survive. Details of the pictorial narrative come from these and the *Vita prolixior*.[18] The narrative on the main face begins on the lower left. Duke Stephen has condemned Valerie to death and she is eagerly leading the executioner away. In the second scene, the executioner cuts off the Virgin's head while citizens, converted by her martyrdom, watch from one of the portals of the city. Valerie catches her severed head in her covered hands, and the hand of God blesses the event. The narrative resumes in the center of the roof of the shrine with a scene in which Valerie,

---

leriae," *Analecta Bollandiana* 8 (1889), 279–84. The reference to the spouse is given in *Catalogus*, vol. 1, 41.

[17] *Enamels of Limoges* (as in note 1), 116–18.

[18] See note 16 above.

in the most astounding event of her passion, carries her own head after her death. Thus, as a cephalophore guided by an angel, Valerie presents her head to Martial, who is fully vested rather than togate and serves the mass in front of portals representing the church of Saint-Étienne. The last scene chronologically, on the upper left, represents Valerie's executioner struck down before Duke Stephen by a bolt of heavenly fire, rather than by the avenging angel mentioned in the text.[19]

A number of questions arise about this narrative. Why is the narrative's chronology distorted? Why are there changes in details, especially in costume, from the bottom to the roof? And, finally, why are these scenes chosen to the exclusion of others that seem just as significant: where is Valerie's conversion and blessing (represented on the Martial chasse), and where is the apotheosis of her soul? Where is the avenging angel of the executioner's death and the miracle of his resurrection? Where are Valerie's footprints, the lasting relic-testimony to her headless walk? Is this a purposefully incomplete narrative, as on Martial's chasse? Instead of appealing to authority and convention, or to issues of local significance, we will have to answer these questions primarily in terms of interpictoriality.

The first and most obvious manipulation of the standard narrative order is the chiastic reorganization of the pictorial representation. This is both a more organized diversion from chronological order than is the achronological structure on the Martial chasse, and is a purposeful contrast to the usual arrangement of most chasses, which generally read from left to right within registers. As such, it is charged with meaning. Valerie's movement in the first scene, at the bottom left, is picked up and continued in her progress toward the altar, at the top right. Likewise, the decapitation in the lower right is punished in the death of the executioner in the upper left. As has been argued elsewhere, this organization reflects the hagiographic structure of reversal and may match liturgical response patterns.[20] However, it also creates a focus on the center—Valerie's position in the narrative—and aligns certain significant events.

A related manipulation lies in changes in the costume of the figure of the executioner. The soldier wears the same exotic clothing in both lower scenes: a leather cuirass with *pteryges* complemented by a ribbon tied high on his chest. One of these unexpected classical elements, the chest-level ribbon, is paralleled in depictions in slightly earlier Byzantine art, such as the executioners in the Menologion of Basil II.[21] His headdress is somewhat more unusual and may, in its exoticism, refer to new enemies of Christendom, the Saracens. Oddly, the executioner seems to exchange gestures with God, looking up and perhaps admitting the inevitability of his sin.

The peculiar ribbons on the pagan executioner's headdress, although a small detail, provide an insight. They are reminiscent of such ribbons that are rightfully attached to the bishop's miter (as on Martial's directly above). Such ribbons are called *infulae* and are symbolic of ancient rituals of sacrifice. Thus, the decapitation is cast as a pagan sacrifice, and only at the last moment does the executioner, Hotarius (the name is derived from *hostia*, "sacrifice"), realize that the sacrifice is made to God—that peculiar exchange of gestures noted above.[22] Valerie's sacrifice is properly re-

---

[19] *Catalogus* (as in note 16), vol. 1, 43. The soldier's name is given as Hotarius (vol. 1, 42).

[20] Hahn, "Valerie's Gift" (as in note 3).

[21] C. Stornajolo, *Il Menologio de Basilio II* (Codices e Vaticanis Selecti 8) (Turin, 1907), passim.

[22] Furthermore, the soldier who executed Valerie re-

turns to Duke Stephen and reports the miracles that he has seen. At that moment he is struck dead as Valerie had prophesied, but not by the angel of the text. Rather, the chasse shows a tongue of flame descending from the sky to strike down the soldier. This is yet another reference to sacrifice, one that comes in contrast to voluntary godly

located directly above in the upper register, and given its full significance because it is reiterated on an altar by a servant of God, the bishop Martial.

In the upper left scene, the executioner is punished and realigned with the secular power of the duke. In addition to other changes in his costume, he no longer wears the *infulae*. The "sign" that he was properly engaged in sacrifice is now removed, and his role in the story has changed. Now, as he is miraculously punished by death, his narrative function has shifted and he has become the impetus for the conversion of the duke.

These alignments at the left and the right ultimately serve to call attention once again to Valerie's position in the center and to her action of carrying her head. As the so-called protomartyr of the Limousin, Valerie was said to have sanctified the land with her blood. According to her legend, she was buried in the tomb intended for Martial himself, a situation that recalls Ambrose of Milan's strategy of sanctifying his episcopacy through the burial of the relics of Gervaise and Protaise in his tomb in Milan.[23] However, in order to strengthen Valerie's cult as worthy and separate from Martial's, her body was subsequently moved to Chambon and her cult was celebrated independently from that of Martial.[24] On the reliquary, Valerie's cephalophory has a narrative function, but because by the twelfth century she was no longer buried in Limoges, it cannot serve as confirmation of the location of her burial. Nor does it represent divine speech delivered miraculously through a talking head, another function that this miracle has served in the lives of head-carrying saints.[25] Rather, Valerie's cephalophory represents a different and equally significant gesture: the virgin's voluntary sacrifice of her body.[26] The gesture is purposefully placed as a sacrifice in a mediating position between the two great powers of her time, royalty and church. Valerie takes the center, Stephen the left, and Martial the right.

In other words, Valerie's body may be crucial in establishing the authority of Christianity through her blood, but her sacrifice and the attendant miracles were also instrumental in converting the duke Stephen to Christianity and led to his subsequent founding of a Christian state. The gift of the princess's head is a sort of conciliatory offering cementing the relationship between church and state. Hereafter, according to the *Vita prolixior*, Stephen supported the church with his money and his power.

Unlike on the Martial chasse, the aspects of the narrative that have gone unrepresented on the Valerie chasse are finally unimportant to the reading of the imagery. Hers seems to be a narrative that closes in on its center, complete and resolved. Its narrative and pictorial core is found in Valerie, who, rather than take action herself, submits to her own sacrifice and thereby galvanizes miracle and the resolution of strife. The narrative mode might be characterized as one emphasizing balance and conciliation.

Despite their seeming similarity, the three narratives read very differently. As noted at the outset, the Stephen chasse represents a universal saint and his martyrdom in a faraway place. His story follows the Acts text closely and is formal and hieratic, with few elements of narrative anecdote. It

<hr>

sacrifice. In I Kings 18–38, Elijah prophesied that fire from heaven would immolate the bullocks that the pagan priests had failed to sacrifice. For further discussion, see Hahn, "Valerie's Gift" (as in note 3).

[23] Hahn, "Narrative on the Golden Altar" (as in note 7).

[24] Landes, *Relics* (as in note 5), 51.

[25] M. Coens, "Nouvelles recherches sur un thème hagiographique: La Céphalophore," in *Recueil d'Études Bollandiennes* (Subsidia Hagiographica 37) (Brussels, 1963), 9–31.

[26] C. Hahn, *Engraved on the Heart: Narrative Effect and Pictorial Hagiography of the Central Middle Ages* (in press).

is dominated by paired visions before and at Stephen's death. It speaks to Stephen's eternal and universal importance and his status as spokesman and witness for the church as a well-established narrative of antique authority. In striking contrast, Martial is portrayed in a much less formal or dogmatic fashion, and his narrative is full of anecdotal detail and local references. Martial is represented as the quintessential local patron, engaged in ongoing work for his community. The episodes of his narrative are incomplete, implying continuation. Valerie, in contrast, is neither authoritative nor active. She is the still and balanced center of action—local, yet as powerful as any martyr in her sacrifice which leads to resolution. Only by looking at the stories together do these narrative qualities and modes emerge in contrast to one another.

This visual reading thus has produced stories that seem neatly enclosed, almost isolated from one another in different narrative modes. However, these chasses were never viewed within the hermetically sealed hagiographic reality that has been discussed here. Even if hagiographers attempt to control and construct reception, stories are not cut off from more general processes of storytelling. In the case of the three Limoges chasses, impinging upon the finite stories of the pictures and the *vitae* were the infinite stories known to the viewer concerning each saint's historical, political, and even liturgical position in the city. A consideration of this material creates somewhat different readings of the reliquary narratives. In particular, developments in Martial's cult are shown in details of his story on his chasse.

Martial's depiction as an apostle on the Louvre reliquary emphatically suggests that he should not be mistaken for a humble and local confessor. Martial was promoted to apostolic status in the eleventh century through the controversial efforts of Ademar of Chabannes, a status that was only officially sanctioned by papal decree in the twelfth century.[27] On the chasse, the apostolic rank is reenforced by the toga and elaborate halo that Martial wears in preference to a miter.[28] Even more emphatically, his status as an apostle is represented by the staff which the saint carries and with which he effects the resurrection of the two dead men. That long thin staff topped by a small sphere must be the staff purportedly given to Martial by St. Peter himself.

According to the *Vita prolixior*, Peter gave his staff to Martial so that the missionary could resurrect Austriclinian. Martial carried it thereafter and used it for other miracles including, as this artist has surmised, for his other resurrections. It was also used to accomplish a miracle at Bordeaux and was preserved there as a relic into the seventeenth century.[29] The staff was described in treasury inventories as a long rod, and it seems likely that the twelfth-century artist is recalling just this object in the long rod with a cross represented in the burial scene.

More important than its preservation as an authentic relic is the significance of this object for the issue of Martial's role as apostle (and therefore Limoges's primacy).[30] As Tom Head has demonstrated, the staff of Peter held by Egbert in Trier was an important enough demonstration of the primacy of Trier's bishopric to merit encapsulation in a sumptuous reliquary and prompt

---

[27] Landes, *Relics* (as in note 5), 329.

[28] As does Austriclinian, his companion, whose cult is represented almost equally in the crypt at Saint-Martial. His reliquary was also often paraded along with that of Martial's, but we do not know what it looked like. J.-M. Desbordes and J. Perrier, *Limoges: Crypte Saint-Martial* (Limoges, 1990), fig. on p. 56.

[29] *Vita prolixior*, ch. XX, 85. The Bordeaux relic had a

"main de justice" at the top: see C. Jouhanneaud, "La Crosse de Saint Martial," *Bulletin de la Société archéologique et historique du Limousin* 60 (1910), 367–70. For Bordeaux's political position in the eleventh century as a ducally controlled archbishopric, see Landes, *Relics* (as in note 5), 119.

[30] Landes, *Relics* (as in note 5), 209.

the composition of a group of spurious supporting documents. The significance of the Trier staff was disputed by Cologne, a city that also claimed both the possession of Peter's staff and the primacy.[31] Clearly any staff of Peter was a potent relic. In the case of Martial, the staff itself may have been held by Bordeaux, but the monastery of Saint-Martial held the shroud and the body of the bishop, the man who had wielded the staff as a missionary apostle. Its representation on the chasse makes a subtle but powerful claim for Martial's authority and his local and even regional prestige.

However, in Limoges itself the historical record reveals that the cathedral canons of Saint-Étienne were ambivalent about the power devolving to the monastery in accord with its possession of the body of Martial. Such records suggest that we should read the relationship between the chasses as not only "charged" but competitive. For example, processions by the canons to Saint-Martial on the feast day were a public symbol of ecclesiastical accord, but at least once a whispering member of the bishop's entourage corrected the improper celebration of the liturgy during one of these exercises, presumably to the embarrassment of the monks.[32] Although the bishops of Limoges were for the most part evenhanded in their treatment of the canons and the monks, beginning in the eleventh century the bishops were no longer buried in Saint-Martial, and they at times tried to use the power of Martial's apostolic rank for themselves without the support of the monks.[33] The monks jealously defended their prerogatives, winning the right to help elect bishops after Ademar led a violent demonstration against one election for which he was pointedly not consulted.[34]

Nevertheless, despite such attempts at posturing and positioning, the balance of power between canons and monks remained remarkably even. The canons and bishop claimed rights through the episcopal office and the prestige of their universal patron, the protomartyr Stephen, a saint who has been demonstrated to be a particular patron of bishops and canons throughout western Europe.[35] The monks in their turn were host to the powerful relic body of Martial and a thriving pilgrimage. Furthermore, as lay power grew it was generally invested on the side of the monks. Not only did the lay nobility make many donations in favor of the monastery in order to be included in their prayers (as did, in fact, the bishops themselves),[36] but the count's castle was also situated next to the monastery, and the two were eventually surrounded by a common defensive wall, as was the original *Cité* of Limoges. That is, Limoges in the twelfth century consisted of two walled enclosures, one dominated by the palace of the episcopal lord and including the Cathedral of Saint-Étienne, and the other dominated by the count's palace and including the monastery church of Saint-Martial.[37]

Sharon Farmer has carefully articulated the political developments and machinations of proponents of two similar "cities" in Tours, and surely the story of saintly patronage is equally complex

[31] T. Head, "Art and Artifice in Ottonian Trier," *Gesta* 36 (1997), 72.

[32] J. Becquet, "Les Évêques de Limoges aux Xᵉ, XIᵉ et XIIᵉ siècles," *Bulletin de la Société archéologique et historique du Limousin*, 105 (1978), 63–90; 106 (1979), 79–104, 85–114; 107 (1980), 109–26; 108 (1981), 98–116. The incident occurred under Bishop Itier: 105 (1978), 87.

[33] Becquet, "Les Évêques" (as in note 32), 105 (1978), 92 (again under Itier in 1068–69).

[34] Becquet, "Les Évêques" (as in note 32), 105 (1978), 103. The contested bishop was Humbaud; the revolt was

led by Ademar.

[35] R. Bauerreiss, *Stefanskult und frühe Bischofsstadt* (Munich, 1963).

[36] Becquet, "Les Évêques" (as in note 32), 107 (1980), 134 (Gerard II, 1139–77, was inscribed in the monks' prayers in 1150); B. Barrière, "Une agglomération double (XIᵉ–XIIᵉ siècles)," in *Histoire de Limoges*, ed. L. Perouas (Toulouse, 1989), 67ff.

[37] Barrière "Agglomération double" (as in note 36), 61–82.

in Limoges.[38] But in twelfth-century Limoges, despite or perhaps because of outbreaks of violence, the clergy did finally make attempts to resolve their differences and find a common goal. That goal is perhaps best seen as an offshoot of the idealistic project of the so-called Peace of the Church originating before the millennium. In that utopian venture, clergy joined together to attempt to channel the power and stop the violence of unpredictable lay lords. They used relics and relic displays to rally popular and noble support for their efforts. The movement had a remarkable (even if short-term) effectiveness.[39]

Narratives of historical "context" thus seem to encourage the viewing of the reliquaries of Stephen and Martial as actively contending for status and power in Limoges. If so, it may even be possible to read a pictorial counterclaim on the Stephen chasse concerning the exclusivity of Martial's apostolic prestige. On the chasse, Stephen's vision of and speech with Christ are emphasized (*Vox Ihesus*). In another case of saintly contention, a similar bodily vision and dialogue was claimed to be equivalent to the "apostolic" experience of Christ in the flesh.[40] These narrative details may thus actively counter notions of Martial's apostolicity with pointed reference to Stephen's special prestige. Nevertheless, it cannot be said that either chasse wins the debate. Neither narrative mode, hieratic or process-oriented, is clearly dominant. Furthermore, as we have seen, Valerie's story seems to argue actively for resolution, which is a narrative mode and strategy that seem to continue to support the "Peace" and, in fact, as we will see, is strengthened by the stories that survive concerning the development of her cult.

In Limoges, Valerie was perhaps most vigorously promoted by Ademar and the monks of Saint-Martial. In Ademar's *Vita prolixior*, Valerie neatly supports Martial's importance, as she does on his chasse. In the period with which we are concerned, the monastery of Saint-Martial at Chambon controlled Valerie's *corpus*, but the memory of her burial in Saint-Martial survived. In the crypt of Saint-Martial she occupies a loculus opposite the paired tombs of Martial and Austriclinian and near that of Duke Stephen.[41]

Nevertheless, despite her prominence at Saint-Martial, Valerie also found her place in the *Cité*. Her "marriage ring," a remarkable object first heard of in the twelfth century and now lost, was used in the ceremony of investiture of the Duke of Aquitaine in the cathedral.[42] Finally, in a third locale, the bishop in 1165 consecrated a miracle-producing chapel that had been spontaneously constructed between and slightly north of the two "cities" at the site of the saint's martyrdom. This chapel represents not only a new geographic location but also a new group of devotees. It was reputedly built by a group of jongleurs and street urchins![43]

The St. Petersburg chasse may show Valerie's gift of her head accepted and controlled by Martial. Nevertheless, on that chasse he is depicted as the mitered bishop presiding at Saint-Étienne, a bishop who, according to the Christian legend of the area, had a remarkably productive and peace-

---

[38] S. Farmer, *Communities of St. Martin: Legend and Ritual in Medieval Tours* (Ithaca, 1991).

[39] See the essays in *The Peace of God: Social Violence and Religious Response in France around the Year 1000*, ed. T. Head and R. Landes (Ithaca, 1992); see also Landes, *Relics* (as in note 5), 27–37.

[40] T. A. Dale, "Inventing a Sacred Past: Pictorial Narratives of St. Mark the Evangelist in Aquileia and Venice ca. 1000–1300," *DOP* 48 (1994), 65–66.

[41] Desbordes and Perrier, *Crypte Saint-Martial* (as in note 28), fig. on p. 56.

[42] M.-M. Gauthier, "La Légende de sainte Valérie et les émaux champlevés de Limoges," *Bulletin de la Société archéologique et historique du Limousin* 86 (1955), 76.

[43] Becquet, "Les Évêques" (as in note 32), 107 (1980), 128. The beginnings of construction occurred in 1161. This may also represent a different social class, other than clerics or the nobility, that turned to Valerie for assistance.

ful accord with the duke. Furthermore, both duke and bishop preside in front of important gates and impressively constructed walls which are surely the two cities of Limoges. In addition to the truce narrated in Valerie's *vita*, that between Martial and Duke Stephen, the chasse, when read against history, seems to argue for a new and parallel truce, now between the two cities of the twelfth century, between the monastery and the cathedral. Valerie's sacrifice of her head thus serves in yet another story as a symbol of peace. Indeed, in at least one instance, in 1183, the bishop and abbot were said to have made just such a "peace."[44]

It should come as no surprise that this powerful vision of saintly peace-making is not a unique statement. The St. Petersburg chasse is not the sole surviving pictorial "telling" of Valerie's story. A second reliquary, in the British Museum, of virtually equal workmanship and size, replicates the iconography almost exactly.[45] Furthermore, some twenty other medieval enamel chasses depicting more or less abbreviated versions of the Valerie narrative are now scattered throughout France. One even turns up as far away as Lincoln. This mass-production of chasses recalls a similar situation in the case of Thomas à Becket, where fifty-two chasses of Limoges manufacture helped to spread the relics and cult of the saint throughout Christendom.[46] Valerie's cult was more localized than that of Thomas, surviving primarily in the Limousin. Nevertheless, this duplication and multiplication suggests that the cult of this legendary and yet little-known virgin must also have been promoted for political reasons, just as was that of Thomas. In the *Vita prolixior* Martial was said to have brought peace to the Limousin; it seems that Valerie in her virginal humility was pleased to carry its message with her martyr's body and its relics.

In sum, the three chasses interact in complex ways: they share narrative structure and some minor elements of iconography, but display purposeful reordering and varying narrative modes, thus establishing what can be termed an effective and specific interpictoriality. Furthermore, as medieval Limousin viewers considered the stories depicted on the chasses with full knowledge of the status and historical position of each of these local saints, other narratives began to intersect with the visual ones. In the interpretive process that followed, it is as if the chasses present the vying narratives of a sort of saintly competition. A claim is made, countered, and a possible resolution is offered. The power of dogma of a universal martyr is specifically challenged by the ongoing story of a local and apostolic confessor. The challenge remains but is defused by a model of narrative resolution: the definitive rejoinder of the sacrifice of a local martyr's life. Peace is proposed.

In concluding, it should be noted that the Valerie reliquary presents two particularly interesting and interrelated effects of interpictorial narrative. First, although the chasse represents a narrative that is founded on the same discourse of miracle, martyrdom, and divine approval as those of Stephen and Martial, it reconfigures the direction and drive of those narratives. Instead of the charisma of personality or the effects of decisive action, Valerie's story relies upon her power as the still center of miracle. Through her passive yet efficacious sacrifice she purportedly reconfigures the structure of power and proposes resolution as a narrative strategy. She and her cult may have had little actual power, but she is portrayed as being at the very center of power and may therefore have served as a particularly powerful symbol because of this visual formulation.

---

[44] Becquet, "Les Évêques" (as in note 32), 108 (1981), 98.

[45] Gauthier and François, *Émaux méridionaux* (as in note 14), no. 91.

[46] *Enamels of Limoges* (as in note 1), 162.

As a second aspect of interest, it is important to note that the visual record represented by the Valerie chasse and its versions is far more informative than is the historical record. Given the medieval success of her cult, primarily attested in the production of narrative reliquaries, Valerie's story must have had some success. Nevertheless, and surprisingly, that success is not well recorded in the verbal documents of Limousin history nor in accounts by modern historians. Richard Landes even went so far as to suggest that Valerie's cult was moved to Chambon in the tenth century to reduce saintly competition with Martial.[47] In his important book on the apostolic promotion of Martial, he virtually ignores Valerie's later history and cult at Saint-Martial despite clear evidence that even in her bodily absence, she was an important part of Martial's cult as celebrated by the monks. Visiting canons from Lincoln demanded a bit of the powerful body along with relics of Martial,[48] and, in addition to holding and distributing bits of her relics, the monks also elaborated her office and her *vitae*.[49] Even more than the sparse but suggestive historical documents, the St. Petersburg reliquary, when read in conjunction with the Martial, Stephen, and other Valerie chasses, informs us of Valerie's power. In the end it is interpictoriality that gives some indication as to why Valerie was important, why bishops, monks, canons, dukes, and even street urchins may have cared about her cult and told and read her story, along with the stories of other saints in Limoges.

[47] Landes, *Relics* (as in note 5), 51.

[48] Unfortunately for our purposes, they received the relics in an ivory reliquary: J. Levet, *Histoire de Limoges* (Limoges, 1974), 114.

[49] J. Emerson, "Two Newly Identified Offices for Saints Valeria and Austriclinianus by Ademar de Chabannes (Ms. Paris, B.N. lat. 909, fols. 79–85v)," *Speculum* 40 (1965), 31–46.

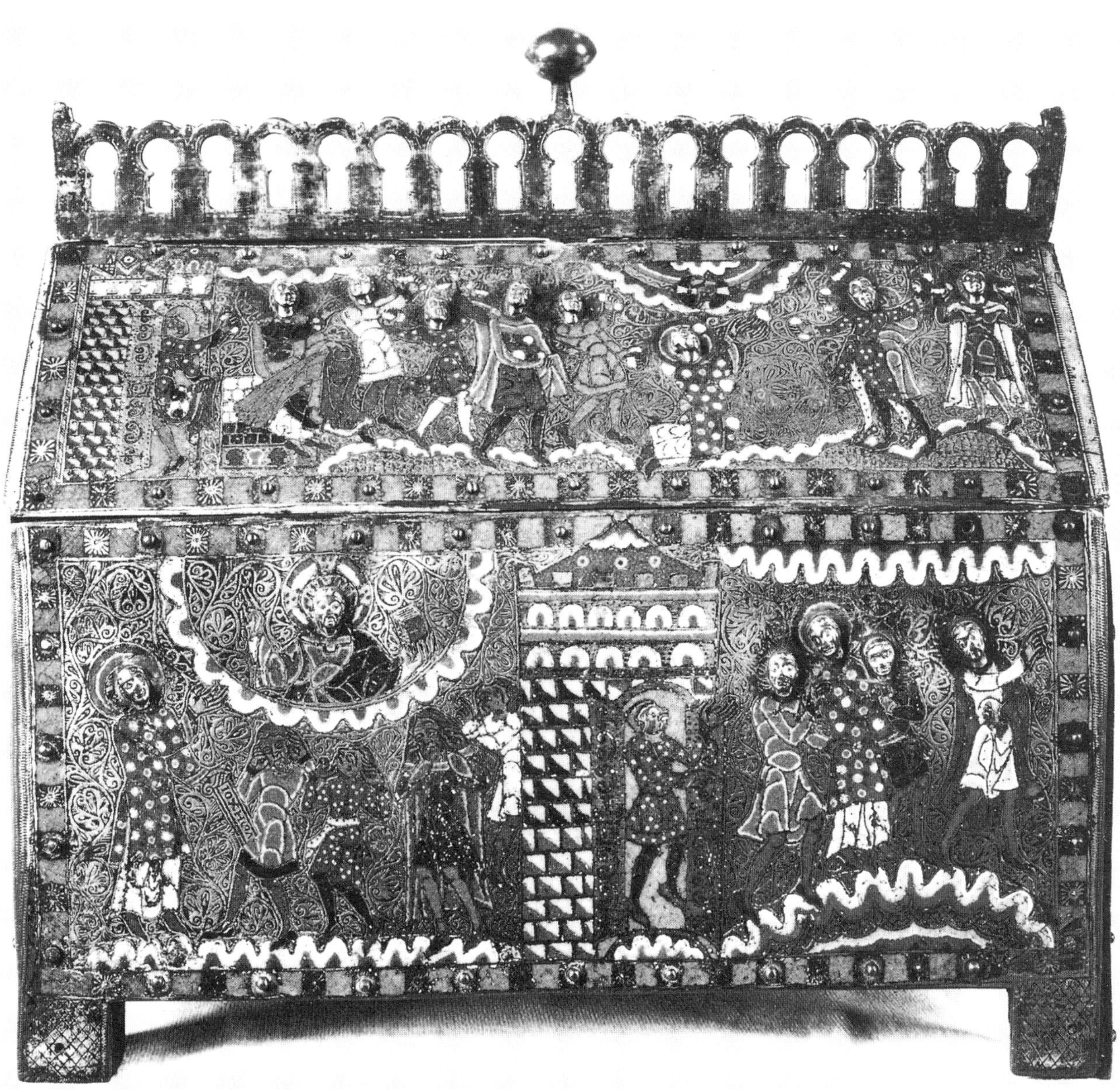

1. Church of Saint-Pardoux, Gimel (Corrèze). Reliquary of St. Stephen

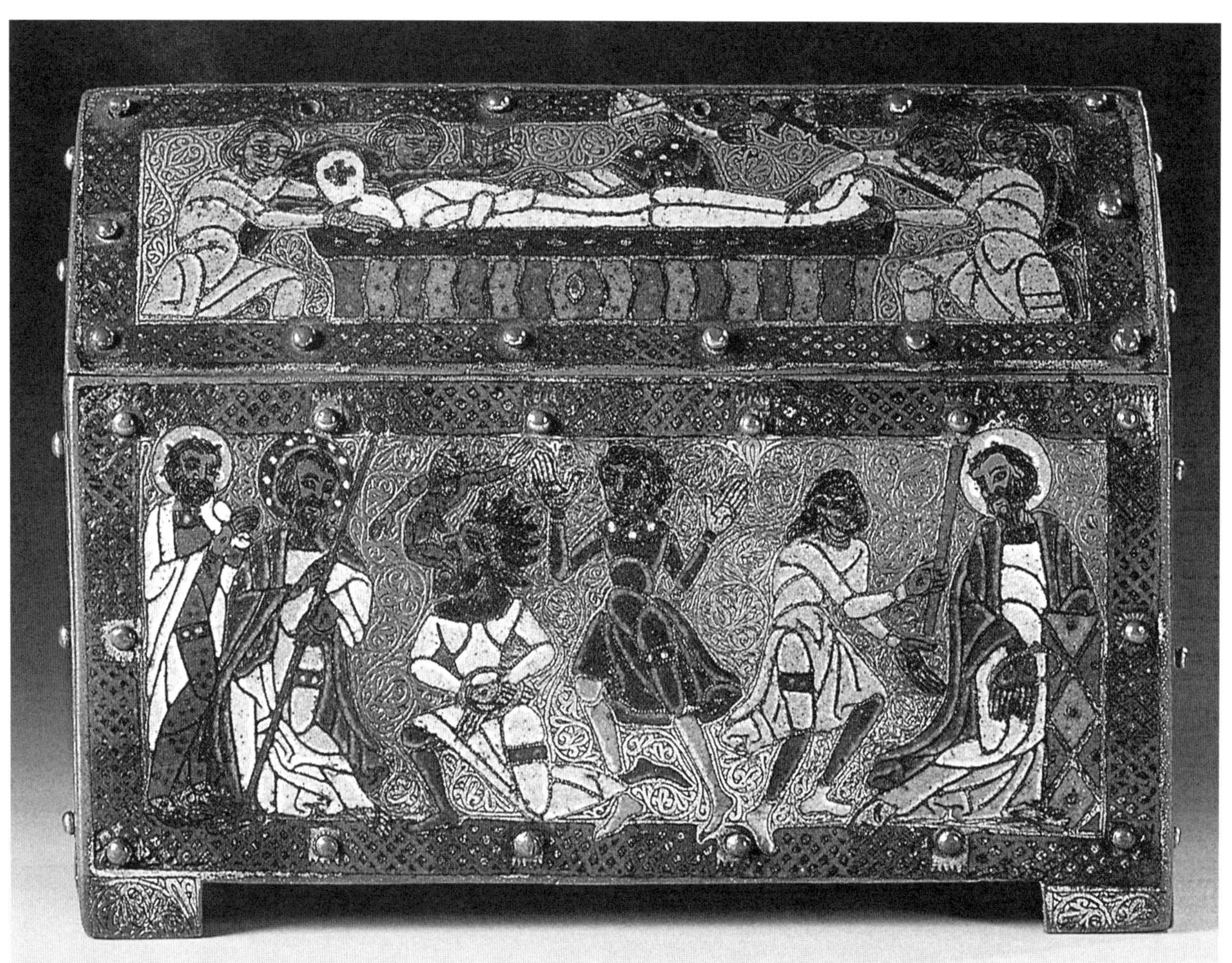

2. Paris, Musée du Louvre, OA 8101. Reliquary of St. Martial, front

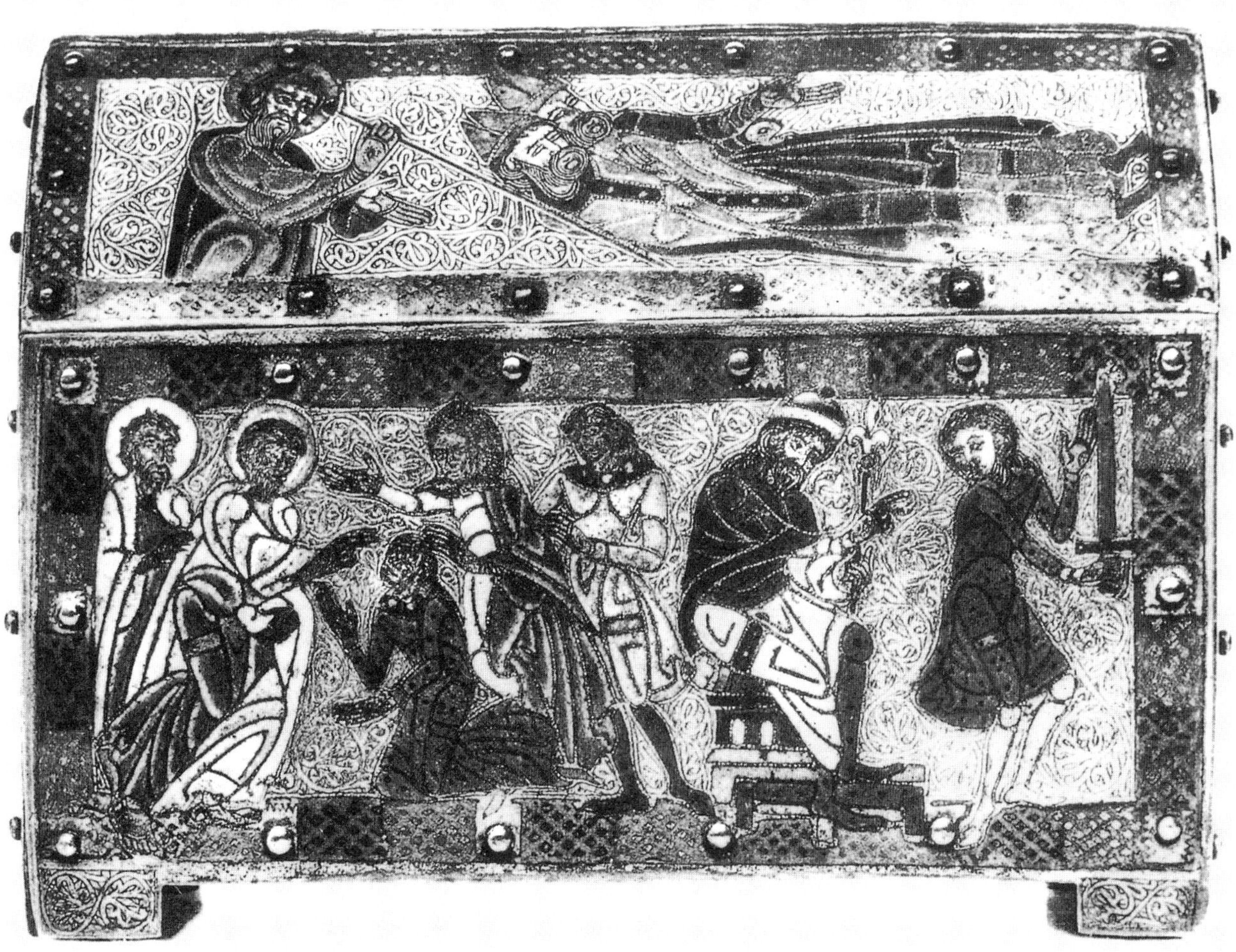

3. Reliquary of St. Martial, back

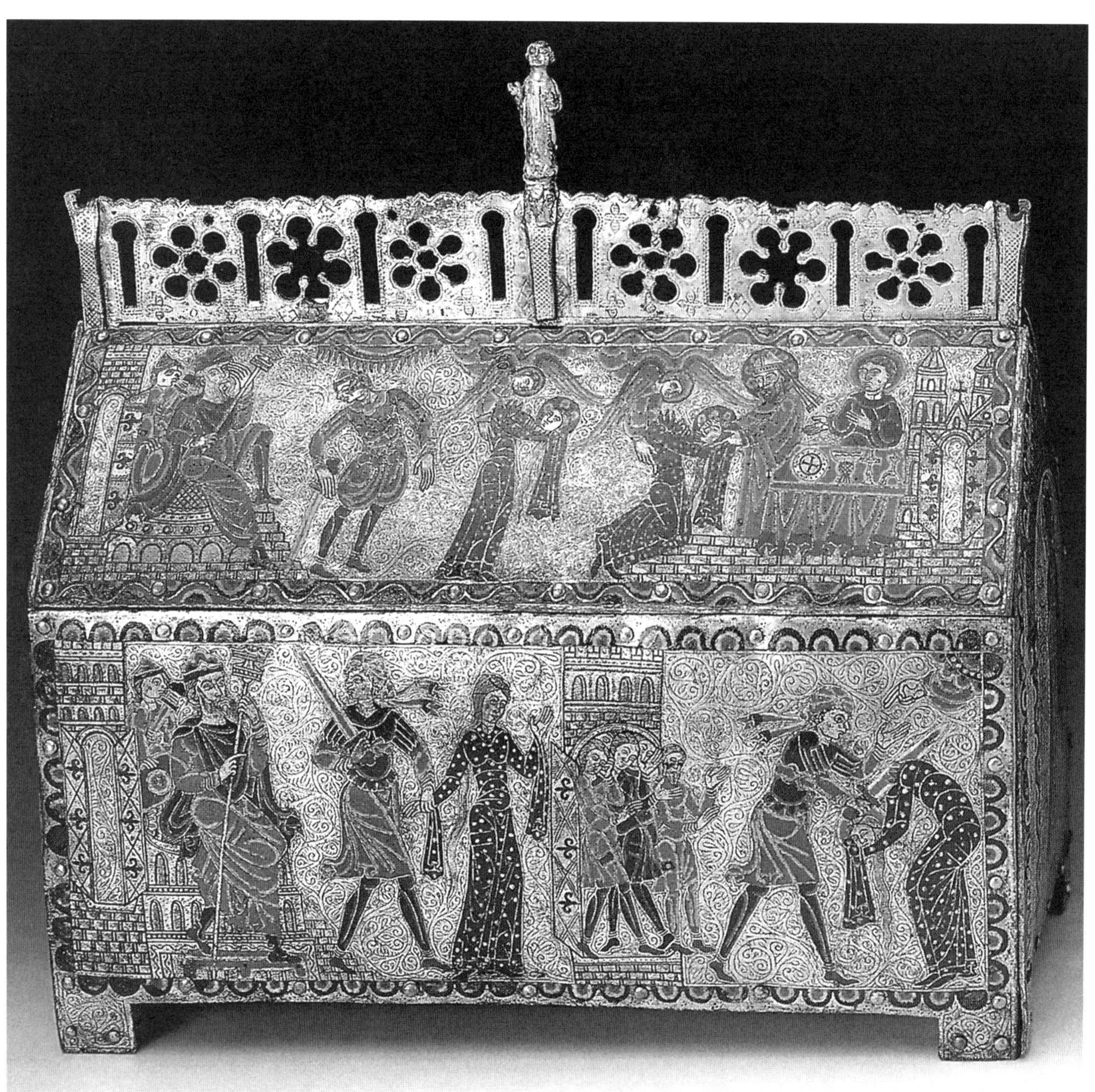

4. St. Petersburg, State Hermitage Museum, Φ 175. Reliquary of St. Valerie

"Of the Significance of Colours":
The Iconography of Colour in Romanesque
and Early Gothic Book Illumination*

·

ANDREAS PETZOLD

ANNA JAMESON'S seminal and influential study on Christian iconography, *Sacred and Leg-endary Art*,[1] first published in 1848, contains a section entitled "Of the Significance of Colours." In this she provides the reader with a list of colours which, in her opinion, were regarded as "appropriate to certain subjects and personages" in Christian art of the Middle Ages. Her observations are principally concerned with garment colours; she notes, for example, with characteristic perspicacity, that Judas is generally represented dressed in "dirty yellow."[2] Implicit in her account is the assumption that artists in their use of colour followed precedent and adhered to convention; this is, of course, to ignore obvious constraints on the artist which may include such factors as the availability and cost of pigments, the specifications of the patron, aesthetic considerations, the syntax of colour relationships, and the degree to which colours within the arena of the pictorial image imitate external appearances and have their basis in social practice. She also assumes that the colours used by the artist had a symbolic or interpretative significance which would have been understood by contemporary spectators.

Later historians of art have tended, in general, not to engage themselves in questions to do with the use of colour in medieval pictorial art, least of all its meaning. One reason for this may lie in the predominance until comparatively recently of the black-and-white photograph as a vehicle for the recording and analysis of artistic images. But with the greater availability of high-quality coloured images in books, facsimiles, and, more recently, via computer applications such as CD-ROMs and the Internet, it is inevitable that questions concerning the use of colour will come more to the foreground.

Nor has the notion of a fixed canon of colour iconography[3] operating in the high Middle Ages, as suggested by Jameson, been widely accepted within art-historical discourse. In the Ro-

---

* This article is a revised version of the final chapter of my Ph.D. thesis: A. Petzold, "The Use of Colour in English Romanesque Manuscript Illumination" (University of London, 1987). A version of the article was given as a paper at the Association of Art Historians Annual Conference in London in April 1997 and again in May of 1997 at the Index of Christian Art as one of a series of lectures on medieval studies. The final version has benefited from comments made by Michael Kauffmann, Sandy Hes-lop, and Barbara Deimling.

[1] A. Jameson, *Sacred and Legendary Art* (London, 1857), vol. 1, 35.

[2] Ibid., 36.

[3] On the iconography of colour in general, see J. Gage, "Colour in History: Relative and Absolute," *Art History* 1 (1978), 104–9; see also the pioneering studies of M. Pastoureau, who emphasises an interdisciplinary approach: most importantly, *Couleurs, images, symboles* (Paris, 1989).

manesque and early Gothic periods it cannot be substantiated by observation; colours for the most part appear to be used in an arbitrary manner, with the principal dramatis personae of Christian art represented in garments of varying colours, though regional factors appear to play a role, with certain schools of illumination, such as the so-called Liuthar school,[4] having distinctive colour schemes. But there are cases of specific characters who are so frequently represented in garments of the same colour that these can be termed colour conventions. One such convention is that of representing Christ in a purple-red mantle, which is generally found in German and Flemish eleventh-century illumination, and is taken up in England in the 1120s in the St. Albans Psalter.[5] There are also certain colour conventions which can be traced back to the Romanesque period and remain tenaciously in use well into the late Middle Ages. One such example is the convention of representing St. John the Evangelist in either a red garment or a combination of red mantle and green undergarment (Fig. 1).[6]

In its ubiquitousness this convention assumes the function of an attribute which assists in identifying the apostle. Colour conventions tend, in general, to be used to a greater extent and in a more systematic way in the late Middle Ages, particularly in northern European art, as can be seen by perusing the illustrations to Ruth Mellinkoff's recent book, *Outcasts*.[7] In the earlier period they can assist in looking at questions of artistic transmission.

Colour conventions such as these have not aroused much comment. They function as a code facilitating the identification and recognition of a character, particularly in a sequence of images. They may have an interpretative function, as suggested by Jameson, or, alternatively, their basis may perhaps lie in social practice.

Colour is an all-pervasive but at the same time elusive aspect of an artistic image which is frequently difficult to describe. It consequently falls outside the scope of traditional iconographic analysis which aims to identify, describe, and collect examples of specific visual imagery, trace their traditions, and then elucidate them by means of contemporary textual sources. In looking at the question of colour iconography, a broader and more relativistic approach needs to be adopted which treats colour as a culturally encoded phenomenon.

In the first part of this article certain methodological guidelines for looking at this question are provided, focusing in turn on both image and text, and in the second a specific case study is examined. The focus here is on garment colours; the question of what colours are used in representations of symbolically significant objects such as crucifixes is not explored, nor is that of skin and hair colour. The representation of these "natural" colours can be as conventionalised and as sus-

---

[4] On this school, see C. R. Dodwell, *The Pictorial Arts of the West, 800–1200* (London, 1993), 142ff.

[5] E.g., Munich, Bayer. Staatsbibl., Ms. Clm. 4453 (*Das Evangeliar Ottos III*, ed. F. Dressler and F. Mütherich [Frankfurt, 1973]): out of the thirty-five scenes in which Christ is present in this manuscript, he wears a purple mantle in twenty-nine; Nuremberg, Germanisches Nationalmuseum, Ms. 156142, Codex Aureus (*Das goldene Evangelienbuch von Echternach: Eine Prunkhandschrift des 11. Jahrhunderts*, ed. R. Kahsnitz [Frankfurt, 1982]): in most cases in this manuscript Christ wears a purple mantle. For colour illustration of a relevant miniature from the St. Albans

Psalter, see Dodwell, *Pictorial Arts* (as in note 4), fig. 336.

[6] Stuttgart, Württembergische Landesbibliothek, Ms. HB. II 24, f. 73v. On this, see the recent facsimile and accompanying commentary (*Der Landgrafenpsalter* [Graz, 1992]). An early example of this convention can be seen in the memorable Crucifixion miniature in Ms. M. 709 (f. 1v) in the Pierpont Morgan Library, New York; for colour illustration, see E. Temple, *Anglo-Saxon Manuscripts, 900–1066* (London, 1976), pl. 289.

[7] R. Mellinkoff, *Outcasts: Signs of Otherness in Northern European Art of the Late Middle Ages* (Berkeley, 1993).

ceptible to ideological construction as that of the colour of fabricated objects, as Mellinkoff has demonstrated in the case of Judas's red hair.[8]

One factor which needs to be taken into account when interpreting colour is its cultural context. Conventions and developments in the use of colour in art can only be understood within the broader social, economic, and intellectual context of the period. Developments in trade, fashion, technology, and language may be particularly significant in this regard.

The valorisation of the colour blue during the Romanesque period can be cited as an illustration of the importance of cultural context. By the end of the twelfth century, saturated blue had superseded purple as the favoured prestige colour in art. By this date it had become the primary colour in which to represent Christ, and later in the thirteenth century it was of course to become the prerogative of the Virgin Mary. This shift from purple to saturated blue as the favoured prestige colour can be seen clearly by comparing the image of Christ in Majesty in the late eleventh-century Stavelot Bible,[9] where Christ wears a purple mantle, with that in an early thirteenth-century English psalter (Fig. 2), where he is represented in a saturated blue mantle combined with a pale, matt red undergarment.[10]

This valorisation of the colour blue may in part be explained by an artistic factor: the conscious emulation of Middle Byzantine models, where it is normally thought appropriate to represent Christ in saturated blue.[11] But it may also be related to broader cultural trends. One factor is the opening up of trade routes, which resulted in the greater availability in northern Europe of high-quality ultramarine, the precious pigment necessary for obtaining this saturated blue, and of which the only mine was in Badakshan, in present-day Afghanistan.

Another factor is a change in fashion: from the second half of the twelfth century saturated blue came increasingly to be used for fashionable and ceremonial dress. This can be seen, for example, in a number of the illustrations in the late twelfth-century Fécamp Psalter,[12] where the youthful, aristocratic falconer in the illustration to the month of May and the aristocratic lady in the striking donor portrait are both dressed in a distinctive saturated blue garment.

The ability to manufacture high-quality, saturated blue cloth may be linked to technological developments in the dyeing industry which took place during this period.[13] By the thirteenth century, the kings of France came to choose saturated blue, in preference to the earlier crimson, as

---

[8] Ibid., vol. 1, 150ff. It would be interesting to look at the question of skin colour in connection with some of the christological illustrations in a group of early and mid-thirteenth-century English manuscripts where certain of the miscreants are singled out by having blackened faces, e.g., Cambridge, St. John's College, Ms. 262; Venice, Biblioteca Marciana, Ms. lat. I.77; Manchester, John Rylands Library, Ms. lat. 24 (for colour illustrations, see Mellinkoff, *Outcasts* [as in note 7], vol. 2, pls. VII.34 and 35); London, B.L., Ms. Royal 1 D.X; London, B.L., Ms. Add. 48985 (for colour illustration, see Mellinkoff, vol. 2, pl. VI.26). In general on this subject, see *The Image of the Black in Western Art*, ed. L. Bugner (New York, 1976), vol. 2.

[9] London, B.L., Ms. Add. 28107, f. 136r. For colour illustration, see W. Cahn, *Romanesque Bible Illumination* (New York, 1982), 129.

[10] London, B.L., Ms. Royal I.D.X, f. 8v (N. Morgan, *Early Gothic Manuscripts*, pt. 1, *1190–1250* [London, 1982], 75).

[11] An example is the striking portrait of Christ in an eleventh-century Gospel Book at the monastery of St. Catherine at Mount Sinai (cod. 204, p. 1). For a colour illustration, see K. Weitzmann and G. Galavaris, *The Monastery of St. Catherine at Mount Sinai: The Illuminated Greek Manuscripts*, vol. 1, *From the Ninth to the Twelfth Century* (Princeton, 1991), colourplate 3.

[12] The Hague, K.B., Ms. 76 F 13, f. 5v (the cloak appears to be lined in squirrel fur, called vair) and f. 28v (*Schatten van de Koninklijke Bibliotheek* [The Hague, 1980], pl. 2).

[13] Pastoureau, *Couleurs, images, symboles* (as in note 3), 24ff.

the colour for their coronation mantles,[14] and their heraldic arms came to consist of golden fleur de lyes superimposed on a deep blue background. The predominant choice of saturated blue for Christ's garment in the numerous illustrations to the luxurious Ingeborg Psalter[15] may in this connection have had overt ideological overtones, reinforcing the association of celestial with temporal kingship, as the psalter was commissioned for Princess Ingeborg, wife of the French king Philip Augustus. Linguistic developments also appear to have played a role. The colour term "azur," which enabled this saturated blue to be named, only emerged in the vernacular at the end of the eleventh century. The first written reference to it is found in the earliest extant French epic, *The Song of Roland*[16] which was written down in the late eleventh century.

An additional aspect which is essential to take into account in interpreting colour conventions is their physical context. The importance of this factor in interpreting sign systems has been emphasised by the French semiotician Émile Benveniste, who noted that "the value of a sign is defined only in the system which incorporates it."[17] By "physical context" is understood not only the object or figure to which the colour is attached, but also the iconographic image in which this is incorporated, and, if there are a series of images, its placement within this sequence. Within a series of images colour may play a narratological function serving to isolate, distinguish, and characterise the principal actants and to draw linkages between different scenes. This can be seen very clearly in christological cycles in twelfth- and thirteenth-century luxury psalters, where the variation in the colour of Christ's garments (particularly his outer garment) from one image to another can be significant and may reflect liturgical, theological, or ideological considerations. There is frequently, for example, a variation in the colour of Christ's garments in scenes to do with the Resurrection. In these, Christ is often represented in either green, which had obvious associations with rebirth, or bright red, or occasionally both these colours.[18]

In this context in the twelfth century, bright red would have had strong connotations of kingship. It was customary for coronation mantles at this date to be an intense, bright red, usually man-

[14] P. E. Schramm, *Der König von Frankreich*, vol. 1 (Darmstadt, 1960), 160.

[15] Chantilly, Musée Condé, Ms. 9 (olim 1695); see the commentary by F. Deuchler, *Der Ingeborgpsalter* (Berlin, 1967), 113 n. 126, and the colour illustrations in the accompanying facsimile.

[16] *Le Chanson de Roland*, ed. F. Whitehead (Oxford, 1970), l. 1557.

[17] See É. Benveniste, "The Semiology of Language," *Semiotica* (special supplement) (1981), 5–23. This article was reprinted in *Semiotics: An Introductory Reader*, ed. R. E. Innes (London, 1986), 228–46. Beneviste (p. 234) comments on four characteristics of secondary signifying systems of relevance to colour symbolism: (1) mode of expression; (2) domain of validity: (3) nature and number of signs; (4) type of operation. He cites as an example the system of traffic lights: its domain of validity is vehicular traffic; its signs are constituted by the chromatic opposition red/green; its type of operation is a relationship of alternation signifying stop/go. He further notes (p. 235)

that two signifying systems may use the same sign without this having the same signification. He again cites the example of traffic lights, where red has nothing in common in terms of signification with the red found, for example, in the French tricolour flag.

[18] Green: in all the scenes in the Codex Egberti, for example, to do with the Resurrection, Christ wears a greyish green mantle, in contrast to the purple worn in earlier scenes (*Codex Egberti: Das Perikopenbuch des Erzbischofs Egbert von Trier*, ed. F. Ronig [Trier, 1977]). Red: in the Harrowing of Hell (f. 91v) and the Ascension (f. 109v), for example, in the Landgrafen Psalter (Stuttgart, Württembergische Landesbibliothek, Ms. HB. II 24), Christ wears a bright red mantle which contrasts with the saturated blue worn by him in the Crucifixion and Trinity scenes. For an example of red combined with green, see Wolfenbüttel, Herzog August Bibliothek, cod. Guelf. 65 Helmst (for colour illustration, see *Heinrich der Löwe und seine Zeit*, ed. J. Lackhardt and F. Niehoff [Braunschweig, 1995], vol. 1, 581).

ufactured from the dye kermes or a similar substance, as can be seen in the surviving coronation mantle of Roger II, dated 1133–34, or that of Otto IV, dated to the end of the twelfth century.[19]

These colour conventions may possibly be interpreted further by recourse to contemporary textual sources, where colours are frequently invested with a symbolic significance. These sources include patristic and exegetical texts, lapidary verses, treatises on heraldry and liturgy, and vernacular literature such as thirteenth- and fourteenth-century German lyric poetry, in which reference is made to the so-called *Minnegewandfarben*, as well as the writings of religious mystics such as Hildegard of Bingen and Elizabeth of Schoenau. In certain cases the choice of colour is specified in the textual source which the artist is illustrating: an example of this is the color specified in the New Testament for the robe of Christ in the mock, regal Crowning of Thorns. In this case, however, the colour differs in the two gospel accounts describing this event: St. Matthew (27:28) specifies scarlet and St. Mark (15:17) purple. Christel Meier and Rudolph Suntrup are in the process of compiling a comprehensive dictionary of medieval colour symbolism; as a preview to this they have published a survey of references to the colour red found in patristic and exegetical texts, which isolates and enumerates the principal associations attached to this colour.[20] Colours are also frequently invested with symbolic significance in popular culture, and this may have provided another source for artists.[21]

However, there is no textual source in the Middle Ages which functions as an iconographic guide comparable to Anna Jameson's account, listing the colours appropriate to certain characters and elucidating their significance. The only medieval technical treatise to contain references to iconographic colour conventions, albeit following biblical accounts, is the Byzantine Mount Athos Handbook,[22] which has come down to us only in a seventeenth-century transcription.

This significance can, therefore, only be surmised at indirectly by drawing inferences from references which interpret colour in related textual sources. One potential source for establishing what colours are appropriate to specific dramatis personae is provided by stage directions to liturgical plays when they specify in what colours characters should be dressed. In certain cases the

[19] For colour illustration of the mantle of Roger II, see A. Petzold, *Romanesque Art* (London, 1995), 154; and for that of Otto IV, see *Heinrich der Löwe* (as in note 18), vol. 1, E9 and 341. Barbara Deimling ("Medieval Church Portals and Their Importance in the History of Law," in *Romanesque*, ed. R. Toman [Cologne, 1997], 324–27) discusses the association of the color red at this period with the judiciary and judgment. She comments on the practice of painting church doors in northern Europe, particularly Germany, in red and notes that Theophilus, in *De diversis artibus* (I.20) devotes an entire chapter to describing how to do this. She further notes that it was customary for the Holy Roman Emperor to mark the enfeoffment of his jurisdiction by the handing over of a red banner; one example of this custom, which she cites, recorded in 1195, took place when Henry IV enfeoffed the town of Cremona with his regalia.

[20] C. Meier and R. Suntrup, "Zum Lexikon der Farbenbedeutungen im Mittelalter," *Frühmittelalterliche Stu-*

dien 21 (1987), 390–478; Meier has also produced a separate study on the subject of gemstones (*Gemma spiritalis: Methode und Gebrauch der Edelsteinallegorese vom frühen Christentum bis ins 18. Jahrhundert* [Munich, 1977]) in which she discusses the symbolism of their colour. On colour and liturgy, see R. Kroos and F. Kobler, "Farbe (liturgisch)," *Reallexikon zur deutschen Kunstgeschichte*, vol. 7 (1981), cols. 54–139. On Hildegard of Bingen's rich colour imagery, see C. Meier, "Die Bedeutung der Farben im Werk Hildegards von Bingen," *Frühmittelalterliche Studien* 6 (1972), 245–355. On colour imagery in literary sources in general, see the important article by P. Dronke, "Tradition and Innovation in Medieval Western Colour-Imagery," *Eranos Yearbook* 41 (1972), 51–107.

[21] See O. Lauffer, *Farbensymbolik im deutschen Volksbrauch* (Hamburg, 1948).

[22] See P. Hetherington, *The "Painter's Manual" of Dionysius of Fourna* (London, 1974).

significance of colour conventions may also be inferred from textual sources. In the case of St. John the Evangelist it is, for example, entirely consistent with his characterisation in medieval exegesis, as exemplified by Hugh of St. Victor's description of him as the fire of love,[23] to represent him in red, as Christian love (*caritas*) is one of the main associations attached to this colour in the literary sources;[24] accordingly, it was normally thought appropriate to represent the personification of the cardinal virtue Caritas in red.[25] Similarly, the green garment, which St. John also frequently wears, may allude to his faith, as this was one of the main associations to be attached to this colour. Both these associations are made explicit in a letter written by Innocent III in 1198 to Richard II, accompanying the gift of four gemstones, where he relates the redness of the garnet stone to love and the greenness of the emerald to faith.[26]

However, interpreting the colour terms referred to in medieval textual sources in modern English frequently poses problems. Caution needs to be taken in blandly equating medieval colour terms with modern English ones, since the classification and linguistic codification of colours are relative to different cultures and different periods. John Gage[27] has emphasised that in modern colour terminology priority is given to hue, but that earlier systems of colour terminology place greater emphasis on other attributes of colour, particularly its light-dark axis, or may refer to the material which embodies the hue. A study of colour terms in classical Latin[28] would appear to substantiate this view, though the way in which these terms developed in medieval Latin has not been fully investigated. In the eleventh and twelfth centuries colour terms, such as "azur" mentioned earlier, also emerge in the vernacular. In the course of the later Middle Ages a more abstract colour terminology appears to have emerged. One would expect, conversely, that the mental picture which a person had of a specific colour term would coincide with the meaning which that term had at that time and not to the modern colour term which it approximates. This has implications when interpreting medieval visual colour conventions, which may have been named by terms that do not have a precise equivalent in modern, hue-based colour terminology. It would be interesting, for example, to know what colour term was used to describe the pale matt red used for the Virgin's mantle in the Crucifixion in the Landgrafen Psalter (Fig. 1) and Christ's undergarment in the English psalter discussed above (Fig. 2).

Another problem encountered when interpreting medieval colour symbolism is its multivalent nature, with a broad range of interpretations, both positive and negative, being attached to specific colours. Nor are these interpretations constant; they may change during the course of time. The choice of a colour by an artist in a specific artistic context might have been informed by one of the relevant interpretations attached to that colour, and this in turn might have been comprehensible to an informed spectator.

The same multivalency in colour symbolism which is evident in textual sources can be seen equally in visual ones. It has been noted, for example, that Judas is frequently represented in yellow, but this colour is also seen as appropriate for the mantle of St. Peter, where it has no negative

<hr>

[23] PL 176:1112. Latin: "Joannes ignem amoris."

[24] Meier and Suntrup, "Lexikon der Farbenbedeutungen" (as in note 20), 446ff.

[25] See, for example, Ambrogio Lorenzetti's *Maestà* at Massa Marittima (for colour illustration, see J. Gage, *Colour and Culture* [London, 1993], pl. 56).

[26] PL 214:180. Latin: "Porro smaragdi viriditas fidem . . . granati rubicunditas charitatem . . . significat."

[27] See J. Gage, "Colour in Western Art: An Issue?" *ArtB* 72 (1990), 518–41.

[28] J. André, *Étude sur les termes de couleur dans la langue latin* (Paris, 1949).

associations. In the Pericopes Book of Henry II,[29] for example, St. Peter in the majority of cases wears a pale, but full yellow mantle. Another example is the colour green. On the one hand, it was one of the most praised colours in the twelfth century. Hugh of St. Victor went so far as to describe it as "beautiful beyond all colours."[30] It was seen as a symbol of faith, immortality, and eternity, and used in artistic contexts, as has been noted, as a symbol of resurrection and eternity. It was frequently associated with Christ, and, according to one popular legend, the eyes of Christ were green.[31] On the other hand, green was associated in folklore with the demonic;[32] it may be this association that underlies its use for the faces of Christ's tormenters in the scene of the Mocking of Christ (Fig. 3) in one of the prefatory leaves to the mid-twelfth-century Eadwine Psalter.[33]

There were also in the Middle Ages specialised, recondite codes of colour symbolism with their own specific domain of validity. Of these the most elaborate to be devised was that of heraldry.[34] In the period covered by this survey the language of heraldry was not fully developed and had not been properly codified,[35] though there are by the mid-twelfth century elaborate examples of shields emblazoned with heraldic devices in manuscript illumination.[36] It was not until the early fifteenth century that Sicily Herald[37] compiled an extensive treatise in which he set out the symbolic significance of colours used in heraldry.

JUDAS AND SYNAGOGUE IN YELLOW

This part of the paper looks at a specific colour iconographic convention which can be traced back to the Romanesque period. This is the practice, noted by Jameson, of representing Judas,[38] and also Synagogue, the female personification of the Jewish religion, in yellow. The yellow is often distinguished from that assigned to St. Peter by having an "off" or dark appearance.

The convention of representing Judas in at least one distinctive yellow garment can first be seen in northern European book illumination of the late twelfth and early thirteenth centuries; an

[29] Munich, Bayer. Staatsbibl., Ms. Clm. 4452, ff. 77v, 78r, 105r, 136r, 152v, 162r (for colour illustrations, see *Zierde für ewige Zeit: Das Perikopenbuch Heinrichs II*, ed. H. Fillitz [Frankfurt, 1994]).

[30] PL 176:820D–821B. Latin: "Postremo super omne pulchrum viride."

[31] See Dronke, "Tradition and Innovation" (as in note 20); and J. Puertolas, "Legendas cristianas primitivas en las obras," *Hispanic Review* 38 (1970), 376.

[32] See D. W. Robertson, "Why the Devil Wears Green," *Modern English Notes* 69 (1954), 470–72; and H. Bächtold-Stäubli, *Handwörterbuch des deutschen Aberglaubens* (Berlin, 1930), vol. 3, 1182.

[33] London, Victoria and Albert Museum, Ms. 661, recto. Other examples of the same date are: (a) the demons and damned in the scene of hell's mouth in the Winchester Psalter (London, B.L., Cotton Ms. Nero C.IV, f. 39r) and (b) the figure of Satan in a stained glass panel from Tours in the Victoria and Albert Museum (C. 107:1909).

[34] On colour in heraldry in general, see M. Pastoureau, *Traité d'héraldique* (Paris, 1993), 101ff.

[35] On this see A. Ailes, "Heraldry in Twelfth-Century England: The Evidence," in *England in the Twelfth Century (Proceedings of the 1988 Harlaxton Symposium)*, ed. D. Williams (Woodbridge, 1990), 10ff.

[36] They can be seen, for example, in the first volume of the mid-twelfth-century Dover Bible (Cambridge, Corpus Christi College, Ms. 3). In the initial on f. 102v, for example, Joshua and Caleb hold emblazoned shields. Their striped and chequered designs are probably based on actual textiles used to cover shields, and they likely adhere to heraldic conventions.

[37] Sicily Herald, *Le Blason des couleurs en armes, livres et devises*, ed. H. Cocheris (Paris, 1860).

[38] On this convention, see Mellinkoff, *Outcasts* (as in note 7), vol. 1, 51ff.; and Pastoureau, *Couleurs, images, symboles* (as in note 3), 50 and 76. For a summary of colours used in representations of Judas, see P. Dinzelbacher, *Judastraditionen* (Vienna, 1977), 23–26.

early example is in the Betrayal scene in the Copenhagen Psalter,[39] dated ca. 1170, where Judas's main garment is a pale, dehydrated yellow (Fig. 4). At this period yellow is only one of the main colours to be assigned to Judas, with bright red and gaudy green being equally popular. The most memorable example in the history of art of Judas represented in yellow is in the Arena Chapel, where in the central image of the Betrayal Judas is dressed entirely in an all-encompassing yellow cloak with which he envelops Christ.[40] By the late Middle Ages in northern European art, yellow had become by far the most common, but not the only colour, bright red being another favourite, with which to designate the disgraced apostle.[41] Justas Jonas (1493–1555), a contemporary of Luther, referred to this convention when he described how painters characteristically depicted Judas with a red beard and yellow garment.[42] The convention remained in use well into the seventeenth century, as can be seen in Philippe de Champaigne's memorable image of the Last Supper in the Louvre.

The convention of representing Synagogue in yellow again dates back to the late twelfth century. One of the earliest examples can be seen in the Crucifixion miniature to a sumptuous Gospel Book[43] made in the last decade of the twelfth century probably at Braunschweig. In this, Synagogue, who stands to the left of Christ, wears a dark yellow mantle and a blue veil;[44] she contrasts with the female personification of the Church, Ecclesia, who stands to Christ's right and wears a red mantle. Another early example of the convention can be seen in the Crucifixion miniature in the early thirteenth-century Landgrafen Psalter (Fig. 1). At the base of this miniature, beneath the crucifix and enclosed within a roundel, is the diminutive and emblematic figure of Synagogue who holds a goat's head and is dressed entirely in pale yellow. In contrast, the triumphant and crowned figure of Ecclesia stands at its apex. She holds in one hand the resurrection banner and in the other a chalice, and is dressed in deep red, which may in this context both have a eucharistic significance and refer to the cardinal virtue Caritas. The chromatic, binary opposition is one that continues to be used as late as the fifteenth century, as can be seen in the famous pendant images by Conrad Witz of Synagogue and Ecclesia,[45] who are rendered respectively in gaudy yellow and blood red.

---

[39] Copenhagen, Royal Library, Ms. Thott 143 2º, f. 14r. Other early examples are: London, B.L., Ms. Add. 17738, f. 4r; Gnesen Gospel Book, Gnesen, Cathedral Library, Ms. 2, f. 138v; Karlsruhe, Badische Landesbibliothek, Ms. Cod. Bruchsal 1, f. 28r; Paris, B.N.F., Ms. Lat. 17961, f. 113v (see Mellinkoff, *Outcasts* [as in note 7], vol. 2, pl. VII.3: Judas is dressed in this entirely in yellow).

[40] For illustrations, see Mellinkoff, *Outcasts* (as in note 7), vol. 2, pl. II.38; and M. Lisner, "Die Gewandfarben der Apostel in Giotto's Arenafresken: Farbgebung und Farbikonographie," *Zeitschrift für Kunstgeschichte* 7 (1990), 334 and 343, who notes that the convention of dressing Judas in yellow occurs earlier in Florentine art and cites as an example the betrayal scene in a painted cross in Pistoia Cathedral dated ca. 1274. This is unlikely to have furnished Giotto's source. As the convention was rarely used in earlier Italian art, it is conceivable that Giotto derived it from northern art.

[41] See Mellinkoff, *Outcasts* (as in note 7), vol. 2, pls.

I.30, 45; II.40, 41, 42; III.52; VI.52, 53, 55; VII.7, 11, 13, 14, 15, 16, 17, 19, 20, 21; VIII.17, 18; IX.4, 33.

[42] Dinzelbacher, *Judastraditionen* (as in note 38), 24: "ein solch rotbärtig . . . in einem gelben Rock."

[43] Trier, Domschatz, cod. 142, f. 90v (for colour illustration, see *Heinrich der Löwe* [as in note 18], vol. 2, 448). Other early examples occur in: (a) the Picture Bible of Petris de Funes, dated 1197 (Amiens, B.M., Ms. 108, f. 193r); (b) a mid-thirteenth-century German paste-down inserted into a missal (Wolfenbüttel, Herzog August Bibliothek, Ms. cod. Guelph 522 Helmst); and (c) one of the stained glass windows in the Elizabethkirche at Marburg, dated to the second quarter of the thirteenth century.

[44] According to papal legislation instituted in the thirteenth century, Jewish women had to wear a long veil with two blue stripes on it (see A. Rubens, *Jewish Costume* [London, 1973], vol. 1, 91).

[45] Mellinkoff, *Outcasts* (as in note 7), vol. 2, pls. II.33 and 34.

These pictorial conventions are occasionally referred to in the stage directions to liturgical plays, though the references tend to be late. Both the fifteenth-century *Dresden JohannesSpiel* and the *Lucerne Play* of 1588 specify that Judas should be dressed in yellow.[46] The late fifteenth-century *Donauschingen Passionplay* specifies that Synagogue should be dressed in the Jewish manner and hold a yellow banner with a black idol on it.[47] The thirteenth-century French poem *Desputoison de la Sina-gogue et de Sainte Eglise* specifies that Ecclesia should be dressed in bright red (*vermeille*) and Synagogue in "brune,"[48] though whether this term includes shades of dark brown is difficult to establish.

The practice of representing Judas and Synagogue in yellow has a social basis, as Jews were frequently compelled to wear one distinct item of clothing which was yellow in colour. This practice of differentiating Jews by their dress is one that goes back as far as the eighth century in regions under Islamic rule; it normally took the form of a distinctive item of clothing, usually the head-dress, which had to be yellow. In the West, from as early as the eleventh century, Jews normally wore of their own accord a distinctive type of pointed hat which was also usually yellow in colour. At the Fourth Lateran Council in 1215 it was stipulated that Jews had to further distinguish themselves by means of their dress. The nature of this distinction was not specified, but at an early date it came increasingly to take the form of a badge, most commonly, though not exclusively, yellow in colour.[49] This practice continued in use in certain areas of Europe into the eighteenth century, and was revived by the Nazis in the twentieth. Yellow had various additional nefarious associations attached to it; it was used as a mark to distinguish other marginalised groups such as prostitutes,[50] heretics,[51] and felons. In certain regions of France and Italy it was customary to daub the doors of the homes of felons in yellow.[52]

Though it was customary for Jews to be dressed in one distinctive item of yellow clothing, they do not appear to have worn actual yellow robes comparable to those of Judas and Synagogue described above. Artists must, therefore, have exercised a degree of artistic licence in representing Judas and Synagogue in this way. In the case of Synagogue, the yellow robe serves to further identify her with the Jews, and, in the case of Judas, it serves a dual function, both reinforcing his identification with the Jews (with whom his very name was etymologically linked) and as a felon. Colour thus plays a crucial role in the construction of identity.

Conclusion

The question of colour in art and its meaning is more complex than Anna Jameson's perceptive formulations would suggest. The verbal culture of the High Middle Ages is saturated with colour

---

[46] See, respectively, O. Richter, "Das JohannesSpiel zu Dresden," *Neues Archiv für sächsische Geschichte und Alter-tumskunde* 4 (1883), 111; and M. Blakemore Evans, *The Passion Play of Lucerne: An Historical and Critical Introduc-tion* (New York, 1943), 182: "ein gelen rock."

[47] See P. Webber, *Geistliches Schauspiel und kirchliche Kunst* (Stuttgart, 1894), 87.

[48] Ibid., 86ff.

[49] For a summary of colours used, see Mellinkoff, *Out-casts* (as in note 7), vol. 1, 46; and Rubens, *Jewish Costume* (as in note 44), vol. 1, 81ff. On legislation relating to the Jewish badge, see S. Grayzel, *The Church and the Jews in the Thirteenth Century* (New York, 1961), 61.

[50] See J. Bumke, *Courtly Culture, Literature, and Society in the High Middle Ages* (Berkeley, 1991), 154; and Bächtold-Stäubli, *Handwörterbuch* (as in note 32), vol. 3, 581ff.: "Gelb ist unter den Farben wohl die auffallendste."

[51] Mellinkoff, *Outcasts* (as in note 7), vol. 1, 42, 242 n. 39.

[52] M. Bulard, *Le Scorpion, symbole du peuple juif* (Paris, 1935), 32.

imagery, and one would expect this to be pressed into service by artists and be mirrored in the visual art of the period. But the traditional approach to iconography is one that does not do justice to colour. The notion of a fixed canon of colour iconography with precise correspondences between colours and concepts mirrored in visual art is one that is predicated on a monolithic conception of medieval learning and does not adequately take into account the dynamics of cultural interchange. Nor does it adequately take into account the specific artistic contexts in which colours are used. Furthermore, it ignores the issue of colour terminology, as the terms used to describe colours which had symbolic associations do not necessarily have their precise correspondence in modern, hue-based colour terminology. But it does seem that in specific artistic contexts artists represented figures in colours which had associations attached to them consistent with the characterisation which it was wished to promote of that figure.

The question of colour and its meaning is not one for which it is easy to provide neat answers. However, to ignore colour in the analysis of medieval pictorial art is to deny a dimension of the image which was valued at the time, and to allow a tool of art history, namely the black-and-white photograph, to determine the results of art-historical enquiry.

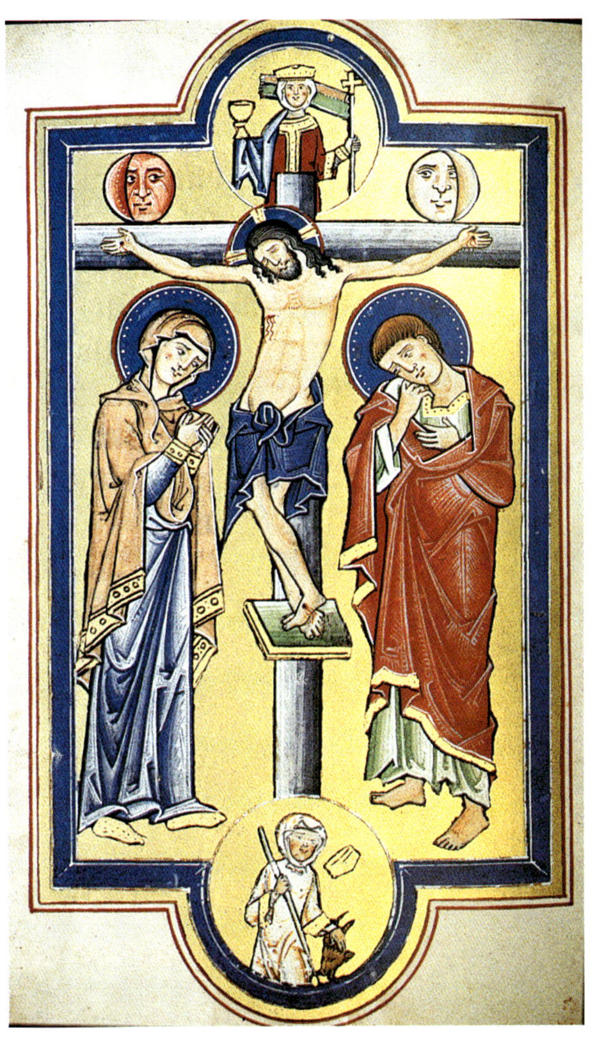

1. Stuttgart, Württembergische Landesbibliothek, Ms. HB. II 24, f. 73v. Crucifixion

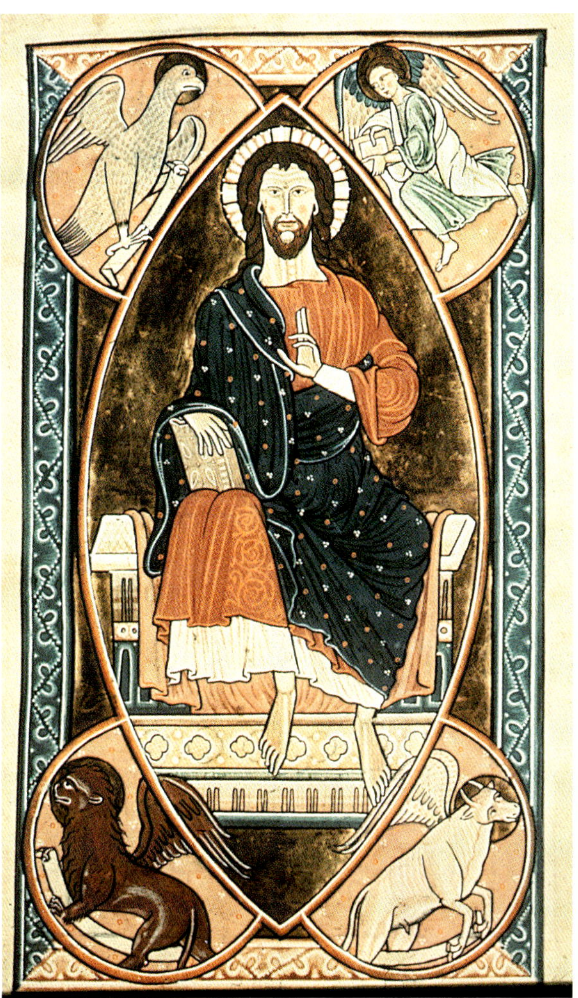

2. London, British Library, Ms. Royal 1.D.X, f. 8v. Christ in Majesty

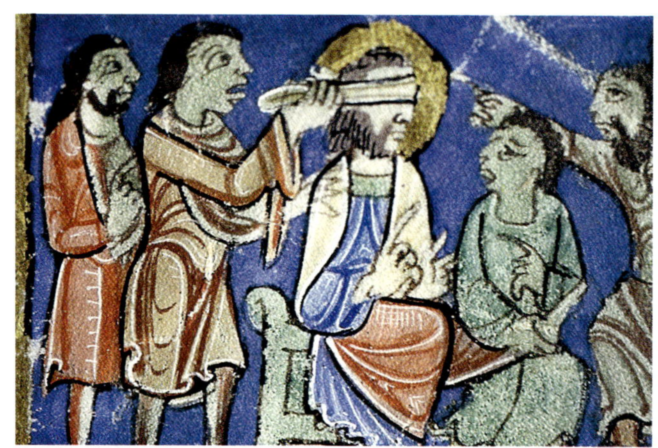

3. London, Victoria and Albert Museum, Ms. 661, recto.
Mocking of Christ

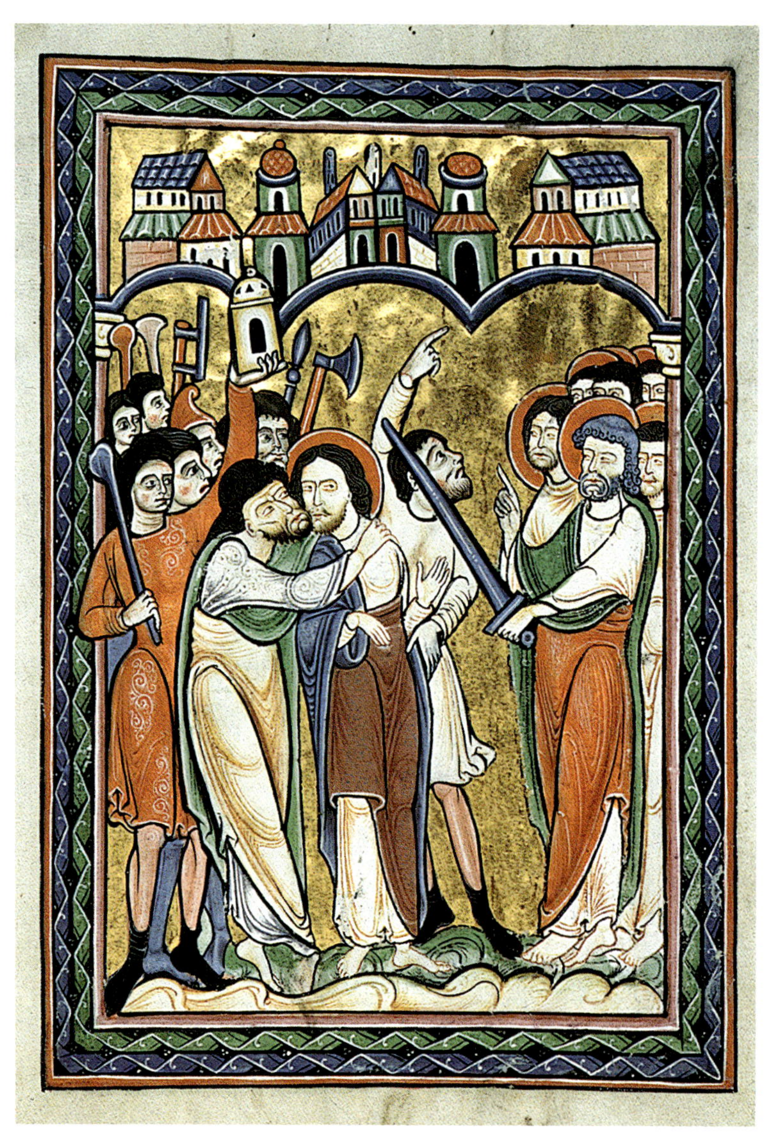

4. Copenhagen, Royal Library, Ms. Thott 13 2°, f. 14. Betrayal

Looking Eastward: The Story of
Noe at Monreale Cathedral

·

J A M E S   D ' E M I L I O

FROM the late eleventh through the thirteenth century, Old Testament narrative cycles formed an important part of church decoration in central and southern Italy as well as in Sicily. These cycles have been linked to the fifth-century paintings in the naves of St. Peter's and St. Paul's in Rome, and their popularity explained by the artistic influence of Rome and Montecassino, and the authority and prestige of the early Roman churches in the age of the reform papacy.[1] Studies of their iconography have explored their relationship to the early Roman cycles and used them to complete our knowledge of those lost works.[2]

That these cycles preserve iconographic features of the fifth-century decoration of the Roman churches has drawn them into the broader discussion of Old Testament illustration and the supposed sources for monumental works in early manuscript illumination. Of course, at the head of this recension of scholarly studies lay Tikkanen's discovery of the relationship between the Cotton Genesis and the mosaics of the narthex of San Marco in Venice.[3] Time was to prove that an exceptional case in monumental art, but the study of Old Testament illustration has been driven by efforts to reconstruct such extensively illustrated early manuscripts and trace their recensions

[1] Discussions of these cycles and their context include: J. Garber, *Wirkungen der frühchristlichen Gemäldezyklen der alten Peters- und Pauls-Basiliken in Rom* (Berlin, 1918), 28–54; O. Demus, *The Mosaics of Norman Sicily* (London, 1949), 205–9, 250–57; R. Bergman, *The Salerno Ivories: Ars Sacra from Medieval Amalfi* (Cambridge, Mass., 1980), 4–14; E. Kitzinger, "The Arts as Aspects of a Renaissance: Rome and Italy," in *Renaissance and Renewal in the Twelfth Century*, ed. R. L. Benson and G. Constable (Cambridge, Mass., 1982), 637–70; W. Tronzo, "The Prestige of St. Peter's: Observations on the Function of Monumental Narrative Cycles in Italy," in *Pictorial Narrative in Antiquity and the Middle Ages* (Studies in the History of Art 16), ed. H. L. Kessler and M. S. Simpson, (Washington, D.C., 1985), 93–112; H. Kessler, "'Caput et Speculum Omnium Ecclesiarum': Old St. Peter's and Church Decoration in Medieval Latium," in *Italian Church Decoration of the Middle Ages and Early Renaissance* (Villa Spelman Colloquia 1), ed. W. Tronzo (Bologna, 1989), 119–46; H. Toubert, *Un art dirigé, réforme grégorienne et iconographie* (Paris, 1990),

93–362; W. Tronzo, "I grandi cicli pittorici romani e la loro influenza," in *La pittura in Italia: L'altomedioevo*, ed. C. Bertelli (Milan, 1994), 355–68.

[2] For the cycles of St. Peter's and St. Paul's and the seventeenth-century drawings and watercolors which partially recorded them: Garber, *Frühchristlichen Gemäldezyklen* (as in note 1), 3–28; J. White, "Cavallini and the Lost Frescoes of S. Paolo," *JWarb* 19 (1956), 84–95; S. Waetzoldt, *Die Kopien des 17. Jahrhunderts nach Mosaiken und Wandmalereien in Rom* (Vienna, 1964), 55–72, pls. 328–408, 484–85; H. Kessler, "Pictures as Scripture in Fifth-Century Churches," *Studia Artium Orientalis et Occidentalis* 2 (1985), 17–31.

[3] J. J. Tikkanen, *Die Genesismosaiken von S. Marco in Venedig und ihr Verhältnis zu den Miniaturen der Cottonbibel* (Helsinki, 1889). Cf. the discussions in E. Kitzinger, "The Role of Miniature Painting in Mural Decoration," in *The Place of Book Illumination in Byzantine Art* (Princeton, 1975), 99–109, 120–21; O. Demus, *The Mosaic Decoration of San Marco, Venice*, ed. H. Kessler (Chicago, 1988), 127–78.

through later works thought to be dependent upon them.[4] For a generation, Kurt Weitzmann set the scholarly agenda in this area, as he developed a method based upon text criticism for studying illuminations, establishing family relationships among them, and reconstructing the extensively illustrated archetypes that he imagined at the head of the recensions.[5]

Such efforts emphasized the development of the iconography of individual scenes over time and gave less attention to the principles behind their selection and arrangement within single cycles. Admittedly, the study of whole fresco cycles is often frustrated by their fragmentary state and the difficulty of appreciating their overall layout from photographs.[6] By contrast, photographic archives like the Index of Christian Art encourage the analysis of individual scenes and create a context for them that their makers could never have imagined.[7] As scholars sought to fit these Old Testament cycles into large families of related illustrations, they highlighted their similarities, explaining differences in terms of mechanical processes, like contamination or conflation, within an essentially conservative tradition of copying. The novice who stumbles across lists of allegedly related cycles in scholarly footnotes on this or that iconographic peculiarity might be quite surprised to see how different many of these cycles appear; in fact, someone not already seduced by the power of their lost models might hardly recognize their similarities at all.[8]

After all, these frescoes and mosaics decorate churches ranging in scale and importance from the abbey of Montecassino and the royal foundations of Norman Sicily to modest chapels and convents hidden in the hills of Latium and the Abruzzo. The placement and arrangement of the Old Testament cycle, its physical and thematic relationship to New Testament cycles, the selection of scenes and the density of the narrative all vary considerably from site to site, even while the iconography of particular scenes may retain remarkable similarities. Consider, for a moment, the placement of some cycles commonly considered together: Old Testament scenes once decorated the atrium at Montecassino; on the aisle walls at Sant'Angelo in Formis, they envelop the christologi-

---

[4] On San Marco: O. Demus, "A Renascence of Early Christian Art in Thirteenth Century Venice," in *Late Classical and Mediaeval Studies in Honor of Albert Mathias Friend, Jr.* (Princeton, 1955), 348–61; J. Lowden, *The Octateuchs: A Study in Byzantine Manuscript Illustration* (University Park, Pa., 1992), 99–100. One comparable case is provided by André Grabar's discovery of links between the Ashburnham Pentateuch and eleventh-century frescoes at Tours: "Fresques romanes copiées sur les miniatures du Pentateuque du Tours," *CahArch* 9 (1957), 329–41.

[5] K. Weitzmann, *Illustrations in Roll and Codex: A Study of the Origin and Method of Text Illustration* (Studies in Manuscript Illumination 2) (Princeton, 1970); idem, *Studies in Classical and Byzantine Manuscript Illumination* (Chicago, 1971); idem, "The Study of Byzantine Book Illumination: Past, Present, and Future," in *The Place of Book Illumination* (as in note 3), 1–60; K. Weitzmann and H. L. Kessler, *The Cotton Genesis, British Library Codex Cotton Otho B.VI* (The Illustrations in the Manuscripts of the Septuagint 1: Genesis) (Princeton, 1986). Other studies illustrating the application of his method include: L. Kötzsche-Breitenbruch, *Die neue Katakombe an der Via*

Latina in Rom: Untersuchungen zur Ikonographie der alttestamentlichen Wandmalereien (*Jahrbuch für Antike und Christentum*, Ergänzungsband 4) (Münster, 1976); Bergman, *Salerno Ivories* (as in note 1); H. Kessler, *The Illustrated Bibles from Tours* (Studies in Manuscript Illumination 7) (Princeton, 1977).

[6] Cf. the comments of Marilyn Lavin, *The Place of Narrative: Mural Decoration in Italian Churches, 431–1600* (Chicago, 1990), 3–4.

[7] John Lowden draws attention to how the working methods of modern scholars shape views of manuscript illuminators' uses of sources: *Octateuchs* (as in note 4), 91. Cf. Willibald Sauerlander's observations on how Porter's photography of Romanesque monuments, aided by the automobile, created a "motorized representation of Romanesque monumental art": "La cultura figurativa emiliana in età romanica," in *Nicholaus e l'arte del suo tempo*, ed. A. M. Romanini, vol. 1 (Ferrara, 1985), 53–55.

[8] Cf. the lists in Demus, *Mosaics of Norman Sicily* (as in note 1), 205–6, 250–51; Bergman, *Salerno Ivories* (as in note 1), 7–8; or Kessler, "Old St. Peter's" (as in note 1), 126–27.

cal cycle of the nave; they appear on the north wall and—as a prelude to a christological cycle— on the upper register of the south wall at San Pietro in Valle, in the upper register of a three-tiered arrangement on both walls of the nave at San Giovanni a Porta Latina in Rome, and in two registers in the naves of the Palatine Chapel in Palermo and Monreale Cathedral.

Without denying the remarkable persistence of iconographic features of individual scenes, the quotation of prominent elements of prestigious models, or the family relationships among these Old Testament cycles, we might give more attention to how artists responded creatively— and critically—to their models as they adapted them to architectural contexts, integrated them into overall schemes of decoration, and enriched them with new meanings.[9] Recent studies illustrate the possibilities of such an approach. For the late twelfth-century frescoes in the Becket Chapel at Anagni, Herbert Kessler described "the manipulation of . . . the narratives to focus on the altar" and analyzed how the borrowed imagery served as a "means for integrating a new saint into the established church hierarchy."[10] In the mid-thirteenth-century decoration at the Basilian monastery of Grottaferrata, he showed how the Old Testament narratives were integrated into an overall program shaped by the writings of Basil the Great and thirteenth-century debates over the Trinity.[11]

Potentially more far-reaching are the remarks of William Tronzo in his study of one of the distinguishing features of the New Testament cycles linked with St. Peter's: the monumental crucifixion whose size and format disrupt the regular arrangement of tiered scenes.[12] In recovering the original liturgical setting for this image, Tronzo distanced it from its copies and recognized the originality of the later artists' efforts "to create an artistically and conceptually unified whole out of what was a pastiche: the two chronologically disparate and unrelated decorations in the nave of Saint Peter's."[13]

The work of Marilyn Lavin and others affords new insights into the overall disposition of cycles of frescoes and the strategies that artists and viewers relied upon to make them communicate their meaning.[14] In fact, studies of visual narratives in diverse media and settings—stained glass windows, bronze doors, cloister capitals, carved portals and painted altarpieces—encourage investigation of the narrative strategies and disposition of fresco cycles that have too long been viewed in the shadow of their more prestigious models or mined for their contribution to the understanding of the iconography of individual scenes.[15]

Comparison of the Old Testament cycles in the naves of the Palatine Chapel at Palermo and of Monreale Cathedral offers an opportunity to watch artists responding critically and creatively to

---

[9] For the study of Old Testament illustration in manuscripts, one can cite the exemplary work of John Lowden, *Octateuchs* (as in note 4), in shifting our attention from the reconstruction of recensions and imagined archetypes to an intimate look at the working practices and choices of scribes and illuminators.

[10] Kessler, "Old St. Peter's" (as in note 1), 132–34.

[11] Ibid., 135–44.

[12] Tronzo, "Prestige of St. Peter's" (as in note 1).

[13] Ibid., 108–9.

[14] Lavin, *Place of Narrative* (as in note 6); M. Kupfer, *Romanesque Wall Painting in Central France* (New Haven, 1993), 59–147.

[15] Such studies include: F. Deuchler, "Le Sens de la lecture: A propos du boustrophédon," in *Études d'art médiéval offertes à Louis Grodecki* (Paris, 1981), 251–58; K. Horste, "The Passion Series from La Daurade and Problems of Narrative Composition in the Cloister Capital," *Gesta* 21 (1982), 31–62; L. Seidel, "Installation as Inspiration: The Passion Cycle from La Daurade," *Gesta* 25 (1986), 83–92; J. White, "The Bronze Doors of Bonanus and the Development of Dramatic Narrative," *Art History* 11 (1988), 158–94; K. Nolan, "Narrative in the Capital Frieze of Notre-Dame at Etampes," *ArtB* 71 (1989), 166–84; W. Kemp, *The Narratives of Gothic Stained Glass* (Cambridge, 1997).

a nearly contemporary work as they sought to reproduce it in a new setting.[16] The artists at Monreale adapted the cycle to the huge scale of the cathedral, altered the relationship of the scenes to the nave arcade, and, most interesting of all, adjusted it to prevent the westward movement of the narrative on the south wall from competing with the progression toward the apse, the focal point of the cathedral's decoration. Viewing these scenes in their architectural setting—and not under their subject headings—suggests new explanations for the choice, arrangement, and composition of individual scenes.

The mosaic decoration of the Palatine Chapel of Roger II was underway by 1143—the date that appears in the mosaic inscription around the base of the crossing dome, but was only completed under his son and successor, William I (1154–66).[17] The building is an architectural hybrid, combining a Western basilica with the characteristic forms of the centrally planned Middle Byzantine church.[18] To the west, a nave of five bays is flanked by aisles and, to the east, the domed choir and lateral bays of the raised sanctuary each terminate in an eastern apse. The royal functions of the two-storied chapel complicated its design and shaped the layout of its lavish decoration.[19] A raised throne platform against the west wall of the nave and a hypothetical royal balcony in the north bay of the crossing created focal points and privileged viewpoints of the decoration of the chapel.[20]

The mosaic decoration falls into two groups which match the architectural divisions of the building. The eastern choir offers a variant of the Middle Byzantine system centered on the dome, where the bust of the Pantocrator is ringed by angels, prophets, and evangelists in a hierarchy of descending orders, and completed by a christological feast cycle in the lateral bays.[21] As Kitzinger demonstrated long ago, that feast cycle has been arranged in deference to the view from a royal balcony, once set in the north wall of the crossing.[22] To the west, narratives of Genesis from the

---

[16] Cf. the remarks of Ernst Kitzinger on the unusual degree of correspondences between the two monumental cycles: *The Mosaics of Monreale* (Palermo, 1960), 33–43, 50–63.

[17] For a recent summary of sources for the building history with additional bibliography: W. Tronzo, *The Cultures of His Kingdom: Roger II and the Cappella Palatina in Palermo* (Princeton, 1997), 15–16. Other recent studies of the building and its decoration include: E. Borsook, *Messages in Mosaic: The Royal Programmes of Norman Sicily (1130–1187)* (Oxford, 1990), 16–50; N. N. Nersessian, "The Cappella Palatina of Roger II: The Relationship of Its Imagery to Its Political Function" (Ph.D. diss., University of California at Los Angeles, 1981).

[18] This commonplace view of the design has recently been modified by Tronzo, *Cultures of His Kingdom* (as in note 17), 19, 104. Precedents for the design have also been cited in the plans of Basilian monastic churches in eastern Sicily: B. Brenk, "Il concetto progettuale degli edifici reali in epoca normanna in Sicilia," *Quaderni dell'Accademia delle arti del disegno* 2 (1990), 8.

[19] S. Ćurčić underscored the importance of the two-storied arrangement within a Byzantine palatine tradition: "Some Palatine Aspects of the Cappella Palatina in Palermo," *DOP* 41 (1987), 126–27.

[20] William Tronzo has recently argued for the existence of a balcony at the east end of the north wall of the nave for viewing the king and hearing the liturgy: *Cultures of His Kingdom* (as in note 17), 49–54, 98–99, 122–23. For the western throne platform, the uses of the nave as a royal ceremonial hall, and the decoration of the west wall: Ćurčić, "Some Palatine Aspects" (as in note 19), 140–43; Borsook, *Messages in Mosaic* (as in note 17), 20–22; B. Brenk, "Zur Bedeutung des Mosaiks an der Westwand der Cappella Palatina in Palermo," in *Studien zur byzantinischen Kunstgeschichte: Festschrift für Horst Hallensleben zum 65. Geburtstag* (Amsterdam, 1995), 185–94; Tronzo, *Cultures of His Kingdom* (as in note 17), 68–78, 95, 99–104, 122–24, 130–33.

[21] Demus, *Mosaics of Norman Sicily* (as in note 1), 210–12, 218–19; E. Kitzinger, "The Mosaics of the Cappella Palatina in Palermo: An Essay on the Choice and Arrangement of Subjects," *ArtB* 31 (1949), 271–76; idem, "Mosaic Decoration in Sicily under Roger II and the Classical Byzantine System of Church Decoration," in *Italian Church Decoration* (as in note 1), 147–58.

[22] Kitzinger, "Mosaics of the Cappella Palatina" (as in note 21), 279–88.

Creation to the story of Jacob wrap around the nave in two tiers (Figs. 1–5), while stories of Sts. Peter and Paul decorate the aisle walls.

The relationship of the nave mosaics to the overall program of the Palatine Chapel remains a matter of debate. There is widespread agreement that they represent the last phases of the decorative program, and their execution has commonly been attributed to local craftsmen.[23] Whether they were planned from the start is another matter.[24] Whatever its place in the initial program, the use of an Old Testament cycle has been explained by reference to Italian traditions, based upon the cycles at Rome and Montecassino.[25]

Although Demus acknowledged that the choice of an Old Testament cycle reflected Italian practices, he attributed the iconographic links among these cycles to common models in the Greek tradition of Old Testament illustration.[26] He so stressed the importance of these models that he flatly rejected the idea of any programmatic intent in the Sicilian cycles. "The illustrative cycle," he wrote, "has no deeper meaning: both the choice and the manner in which the narrative was treated were conditioned only by influences from outside . . . ."[27] Recent scholarship has been less friendly to such passive notions of artistic influence, and scholars have looked for meaning in distinctive features of the Genesis cycle at Palermo: the representation of the seven days of Creation, the prominence of the stories of Noe and Jacob, and the closing of the narrative with Jacob's wrestling with the angel.[28]

These features were retained at Monreale Cathedral, where the Genesis cycle follows the same path around the nave, begins and ends with the same episodes, and repeats nearly all the scenes from Palermo, often with similar iconography and tituli. In fact, the close relationship between these two cycles represents but one of the links between the Palatine Chapel and William II's foundation at Monreale, where many features of the decoration and architecture of the small chapel were reproduced and brought into harmony on an immensely larger scale.[29]

The relationship between the two Genesis cycles often extends to minor details of the iconography and composition of individual scenes. Consider, for example, the two versions of the Judgment of Adam and Eve (Figs. 4, 10). Beyond their overall similarities, they share minor details: Eve's X-shaped hair net; her right hand pointing at the serpent; Adam's right hand placed over his breast; the pattern of trilobate leaves, fruit, and branches in the round crown of the tree; the form of the bushes; and the separation of the two types of foliage by the serpent.

---

[23] Demus, *Mosaics of Norman Sicily* (as in note 1), 55–57; Kitzinger, "Mosaic Decoration in Sicily" (as in note 21), 153–54; Borsook, *Messages in Mosaic* (as in note 17), 39–40.

[24] Demus, *Mosaics of Norman Sicily* (as in note 1), 46–58; Kitzinger, "Mosaic Decoration in Sicily" (as in note 21), 153–54. For two recent, contrasting views with ample references to older literature: Borsook, *Messages in Mosaic* (as in note 17), 17–50; Tronzo, *Cultures of His Kingdom* (as in note 17), 62–68, 94–96.

[25] Demus, *Mosaics of Norman Sicily* (as in note 1), 205–9, 223–25; Tronzo, *Cultures of His Kingdom* (as in note 17), 63.

[26] Demus, *Mosaics of Norman Sicily* (as in note 1), 250–57.

[27] Ibid., 245.

[28] Nersessian, "The Cappella Palatina of Roger II" (as in note 17), 48–93; Borsook, *Messages in Mosaic* (as in note 17), 31–33.

[29] For the history of the foundation and the chronology of Monreale Cathedral and its decoration: Kitzinger, *Mosaics of Monreale* (as in note 16), 17–19; Borsook, *Messages in Mosaic* (as in note 17), 51–53. For the close relationship between the two buildings and their decoration: Demus, *Mosaics of Norman Sicily* (as in note 1), 227–28; Kitzinger, *Mosaics of Monreale*, 25–26; W. Krönig, *The Cathedral of Monreale and Norman Architecture in Sicily* (Palermo, 1965), 172–75; Tronzo, "Grandi cicli pittorici" (as in note 1), 363–65; V. Pace, "La pittura medievale in Sicilia," in *La pittura in Italia: L'altomedioevo* (as in note 1), 314.

Style and scale account for the most obvious differences. At Monreale, for example, God strides swiftly forward; his robe is broken into stylized forms by swirling lines, and the fluttering folds of the hem are repeated three times, all accenting his motion. This stock figure of the new dynamic style reappears in whole or in part throughout the church. In the Old Testament cycle, the new workshop at Monreale energized the scenes at Palermo with the nervous idiom of late twelfth-century Byzantine painting.[30]

Other changes respond to the greater scale of the decoration at Monreale. In the Judgment of Adam and Eve, the artist added a second tree and widened the scene. Now, God's hand is completely to the left of the tree, and the figures of Adam and Eve no longer overlap. Similar changes appear throughout the cycle as the artists exploited the vast expanse of wall space: individual scenes spread over a larger area; secondary figures and props multiply; episodes combined at Palermo earn separate panels at Monreale; new scenes complete the cycle.

Besides the changes attributable to style and scale, Demus noted several new features of significance at Monreale: the Creator seated on a globe, the voice of Abel's blood, and Noe pressing grapes in the vineyard.[31] He argued that the artists in the two churches relied on different model books for monumental decoration composed at Constantinople.[32] For Kitzinger, the artists at Monreale responded flexibly to the cycle in the Palatine Chapel, using it as a compositional skeleton which they enlarged by drawing freely upon other sources.[33] In effect, Demus reduced the iconographic changes at Monreale to the mechanical reproduction of new models and removed the problem of interpreting them to Constantinople. Kitzinger's approach focuses on the two surviving monuments, and, by inviting us to turn from sources to choices, he offers a starting point for an inquiry into the concerns which guided the responses of the artists at Monreale to the cycle at Palermo.

In the Palatine Chapel, the tall stilted arches of the nave left small, awkwardly shaped spaces for the lower scenes.[34] The artists treated these like rectangular panels cut by the arcade. As a result, figures are partly cut off and the odd effect of the cropped scenes is heightened by the thinness of the border lining the arcade. As the artists crowded figures into the cramped scenes, those in successive episodes overlapped, while their orientation and the direction of their movement changed from one scene to another (Figs. 3, 5).[35] In addition, the narrative was interrupted by the medallions crowning each arch and the prominent void of the arcades, which threatened to swallow up the moving figures.

This arrangement seems unsatisfactory when compared with the registers of panels laid out on the ample walls of other Italian basilicas, but the lack of a clear orientation in the narrative might have been less jarring in the Palatine Chapel. After all, the west-east axis was but one—and not the most important—of those along which the mosaicists organized their decoration. The dome of the crossing, the royal view from the north balcony toward the south wall of the crossing,

---

[30] Kitzinger, *Mosaics of Monreale* (as in note 16), 69–84.

[31] Though cited by Demus as a difference between the two cycles, the absence of the figure of Abel's blood at Palermo could be a result of the almost complete restoration of that section of the cycle.

[32] Demus, *Mosaics of Norman Sicily* (as in note 1), 246–61, 331–34.

[33] Kitzinger, *Mosaics of Monreale* (as in note 16), 54–63.

[34] Various authors have commented on the awkward fit of the scenes in the lower register at Palermo: Demus, *Mosaics of Norman Sicily* (as in note 1), 204–5, 261–62; Tronzo, *Cultures of His Kingdom* (as in note 17), 65–67.

[35] On the combining of scenes in single panels at Palermo: Demus, *Mosaics of Norman Sicily* (as in note 1), 247–48.

the mosaic above the throne platform of the west wall, and the mosaic of the Nativity at the east end of the south aisle—visible to those entering from the principal doorway in the south aisle—offered competing focal points which diminished the importance of the modest apse of the chapel.[36] The western throne platform and the marked divisions between the nave and choir made it appropriate for the mosaics of the small five-bay nave to turn inward without asserting a strong longitudinal thrust.[37]

At Monreale, the artists fit the rectangular scenes comfortably above the nave arcade.[38] Demus, characteristically, suggested that the change might have been "brought about by the influence of South Italian prototypes."[39] It is better understood as part of the careful rethinking of the relationship between the architecture and mosaics at Monreale, as these were planned and carried out together in one swift campaign.[40] Not only did this unity of design set Monreale apart from the Palatine Chapel, but the architecture and decoration at Monreale were powerfully focused on one point: the Pantocrator of the eastern apse.[41]

On the north wall of the nave, the artists exploited the rhythms of the arcade, as the rolling landscapes and moving figures accelerate the rightward progress of the narrative toward the sanctuary (Figs. 10, 11).[42] There is little respite from this motion. The two panels with Rebecca and the servant draw us rapidly forward, and the contrast with the Palatine Chapel could not be greater. There, the camels face in different directions, and Rebecca and the servant ride off into the void (Fig. 5). In the story of Isaac, Jacob, and Esau, the artists added new scenes and placed two in each panel to quicken the pace (Fig. 11).[43] No leftward movement is allowed: as Isaac speaks to him, Esau faces the viewer as a bridge to the next figure of him striding up the curve of the arch (Fig. 11).

The artists' success at speeding the narrative on the north wall of the nave has been noted by Kitzinger and others, but it has overshadowed the clever handling of the opposite problem on the south wall: how to arrest the rightward movement of the narrative away from the sanctuary (Figs. 6–8).[44] In three of the seven full panels, the ark provides a central focus, while in two others the

---

[36] Cf. notes 20–22. The redundant image of the Pantocrator in the central apse has been widely regarded as evidence of a change of plan in which it may have replaced an earlier image of the Virgin: Demus, *Mosaics of Norman Sicily* (as in note 1), 53–55; Kitzinger, "Mosaics of the Cappella Palatina" (as in note 21), 272–73, 288; Tronzo, *Cultures of His Kingdom* (as in note 17), 92–94. Borsook, however, views it in relationship to the mosaics of the west wall: *Messages in Mosaic* (as in note 17), 20–22. Tronzo discusses the importance of the view of the mosaic of the Nativity from the entrance in the south aisle: *Cultures of His Kingdom*, 56, 112–19.

[37] Tronzo describes the decoration of the nave as turned in upon itself: *Cultures of His Kingdom* (as in note 17), 67.

[38] Kitzinger, *Mosaics of Monreale* (as in note 16), 92; Tronzo, *Cultures of His Kingdom* (as in note 17), 66–67.

[39] Demus, *Mosaics of Norman Sicily* (as in note 1), 204–5, 237.

[40] The unity of the architecture and decoration at

Monreale and the effort there to bring into harmony diverse elements of the Palatine Chapel have been stressed by several authors, e.g., Kitzinger, *Mosaics of Monreale* (as in note 16), 19, 67–68, 95–103; Tronzo, *Cultures of His Kingdom* (as in note 17), 66–67.

[41] Demus, *Mosaics of Norman Sicily* (as in note 1), 103–4, 227; Kitzinger, *Mosaics of Monreale* (as in note 16), 26, 105–10; Krönig, *Cathedral of Monreale* (as in note 29), 44–45.

[42] O. Demus, *Byzantine Mosaic Decoration: Aspects of Monumental Art in Byzantium* (London, 1948), 63; Kitzinger, *Mosaics of Monreale* (as in note 16), 92.

[43] Demus explains the expanded cycle at Monreale as a more faithful rendering of a model that was awkwardly compressed at Palermo, rather than conceding the possibility of an ad hoc expansion of the cycle at Monreale: *Mosaics of Norman Sicily* (as in note 1), 248.

[44] This posed less of a problem in the upper register where the windows broke the flow of the narrative and the Creation cycle may have been conceived of as, appro-

Tower of Babel or Noe's family weight the center of the composition. In the scene of the animals entering the ark, four poles even anchor the ark to the nave arcades (Fig. 6). This scene, like that of Isaac and Esau on the north wall, represented an addition to the Palatine cycle. On the south wall, however, such additions increased the number of centralized compositions.

The designers of the scenes on the south wall were not content to slow the narrative with static compositions. They altered the rightward movement that marked some of these scenes at Palermo and weighted the left side of several compositions.[45] In the new scene of the animals entering the ark, the two principal figures of Noe and one of his sons face left, forcing Noe to pull the animals awkwardly into the left side of the ark. In fact, Noe faces left from the left side of the ark in three successive scenes (Fig. 6). By contrast, in both corresponding scenes at Palermo, Noe peers from the right door of the ark, and, behind him, nearly all of the figures look to the right through the windows in the ark (Fig. 1). Even the placement of the inscriptions orients the narrative to the left at Monreale. In the three easternmost scenes of the Noe story, the inscriptions occupy two or three lines at the left, an arrangement that is unparalleled on the north wall (Fig. 6).

More important iconographic changes take place in the scenes of Noe's offering, his drunkenness, and the building of the Tower of Babel; these, too, represent efforts to slow the rightward movement of the narrative. In the new scene of Noe's offering—not shown at Palermo—the artists centered the composition on the compact group of Noe and his family (Fig. 7). The inscription fills five lines at the left, while, to the right, the figure of God is reduced to a bust, in contrast to the standing figure beneath the rainbow in the conflated scene of Noe leaving the ark at Palermo (Fig. 1). In the larger setting at Monreale, the smaller figure of God is exceptional, but its use is consistent with other efforts to draw attention away from the right side of the panels.

In the scene of Noe's drunkenness, two crucial changes occur at Monreale (Fig. 7). First, a seated figure of Noe pressing grapes replaces the two youths gathering grapes, lending more importance to the left side (Fig. 2). Secondly, Ham now stands over Noe, pointing down at him, instead of standing at the left and looking rightward at his father and brothers. In his new position, Ham looks leftward and solidly frames the right side of the scene. More interestingly, Shem and Japheth look toward their father pressing grapes. In this clever composition, their backward gaze—no longer interrupted by Ham—seems to create a scene oriented from right to left, though two separate episodes are represented.

In the scene of the Tower of Babel, the artists removed the episode of the confusion of tongues, although it is still mentioned in the inscription (Figs. 8, 2). A stonecutter bending toward the left has replaced the group of men on the right in Palermo. Formally, his placement recalls that of Noe's son in the entry of the animals into the ark (Fig. 6). It is the only episode that is richer in detail in the Palatine Chapel, and the only omission at Monreale of an episode from the Palatine Genesis cycle.[46] While the artist doubled episodes in single panels on the north wall to accel-

<hr>

priately, emanating from the sanctuary. Demus recognized the potential conflict between "the intended progression from west to east" and "the opposite decoration of the narrative" for the decorators of basilicas, but he did not observe its handling at Monreale: *Mosaics of Norman Sicily* (as in note 1), 201.

[45] Marilyn Lavin provides examples of the use of com-

positions oriented from right to left as "braking mechanisms" to bring the rightward flow of a narrative to a halt at the end of registers in the Florentine Baptistery and the Scrovegni Chapel: *Place of Narrative* (as in note 6), 41, 45.

[46] Demus attributes the differences to the use of different models, *Mosaics of Norman Sicily* (as in note 1), 250; Kitzinger, *Mosaics of Monreale* (as in note 16), 62, 86–87.

erate the narrative, he sacrificed this episode to create a centralized composition with key figures facing the left.

The tiny figure of God sending the rainbow to Noe, the addition of Noe in the vineyard, and the elimination of the confusion of tongues represent substantive iconographic changes motivated by the same effort to arrest the westward progress of the narrative that shaped lesser details of compositions all along the south arcade. This effort to slow the movement and create static compositions is all the more remarkable and, evidently, purposeful, as it runs counter to these artists' stylistic tendency to infuse their scenes with agitated movement. Nor is it likely to be explained by Italian traditions of nave decoration. After all, several early churches presented parallel streams of scenes moving toward the entrance along both walls.[47] In such cases, the leftward progress of the narrative on the north wall may have prompted the leftward orientation of individual scenes to support the flow of the narrative.[48] By the twelfth century, the "wrap-around" arrangement of the cycle at Monreale had become a common form of nave decoration, and its popularity might well be due, in part, to the easy harmony between the left-to-right progress of the narrative on each wall and a left-to-right reading of the individual scenes.[49]

The formal adjustments at Monreale suggest the concerns of Byzantine artists, accustomed to a hierarchy of images rather than to long, continuous narratives. Through these changes, they expressed their critique of the multiple viewpoints and diffused focus of the Palatine Chapel. Instead, at Monreale the figures were used to direct the spectator's attention toward the dominating image of the Pantocrator in the eastern apse. Indeed, the Old Testament figures themselves seem oriented toward the Pantocrator, as if to emphasize their typological role as prefigurations of the New Testament.[50] That the artists were concerned not just with the viewer, but with presenting the figures themselves as populating an illusionistic space oriented toward the sanctuary, is underscored by the extraordinary skill they displayed throughout the church in relating figures across space around corners and curving surfaces.[51]

This discussion of the Genesis cycles at Palermo and Monreale began with Demus's remark on their total dependency upon their models and the lack of meaning in the choice of scenes or handling of individual episodes. At Monreale, at least, the thoughtful adaptation of the cycle in different ways to the north and south arcades belies that view of passive reception. In fact, the handling of the cycle not only reveals formal concerns with the layout of the narrative, but, as one last example suggests, it combines a sensitivity to that architectural setting with an effort to draw new meaning from the model in the Palatine Chapel.

The west wall at Monreale includes four scenes of the Genesis cycle in two superposed registers flanking the large window (Fig. 9). The upper register presents the Creation of Eve and the Introduction of Eve to Adam. The latter is one of three scenes in this section of the cycle that the artist has added to those at Palermo. The addition of Adam in Paradise at the end of the south wall

---

[47] Lavin, *Place of Narrative* (as in note 6), 15–27.

[48] Cf. Herbert Kessler's comments on the reversal of the composition of the Crossing of the Red Sea at Grottaferrata, "Old St. Peter's" (as in note 1), 136. Marilyn Lavin offers examples of sixteenth-century cycles in which the leftward orientation of individual scenes supports leftward or counterclockwise movement of the narrative: *Place of Narrative* (as in note 6), 241.

[49] Lavin, *Place of Narrative* (as in note 6), 27–28; Demus, *Mosaics of Norman Sicily* (as in note 1), 201.

[50] The relationship between the two testaments was also stressed by the placement of the scenes of the Presentation in the Temple and Christ among the Doctors above the western arch of the crossing: Kitzinger, *Mosaics of Monreale* (as in note 16), 31.

[51] Borsook, *Messages in Mosaic* (as in note 17), pls. 113–15.

advanced the Creation of Eve to the west wall. At the west end of the north wall, the artist further expanded Eve's role with the scene of Eve and the serpent. Her prominence suggests the traditional typological contrast with Mary, titular of the church and subject of the mosaic cycle once represented on the exterior face of the west wall and the side walls of the western porch.[52]

The second register of the west wall displays the Visit of the Angels to Lot and the Destruction of Sodom. The latter scene initiated the series above the north arcade at the west end of the nave at Palermo (Fig. 4). At Monreale, it is dominated by the figure of Lot's wife turned into a pillar of salt, and its displacement to the west wall, a traditional site for the Last Judgment, alludes to typological interpretations of the destruction of Sodom and Gomorrah as the Last Judgment, developed from Luke's Gospel (Lk. 17:28–32). Together, Eve, the destruction of Sodom, and Lot's wife create a constellation of images on the interior of the west wall that represent the antithesis of the progress from the Old Testament toward the New that is expressed by the sequence of cycles culminating in the sanctuary. Like Jesus' admonitions in the Gospel of Luke (Lk. 9:62, 17:32), they provide, as it were, a warning for those who would, like Lot's wife, look backward.

[52] Borsook, *Messages in Mosaic* (as in note 17), 62; for the destroyed mosaics of the porch, Demus, *Mosaics of Norman Sicily* (as in note 1), 122–23; Krönig, *Cathedral of Monreale* (as in note 29), 35.

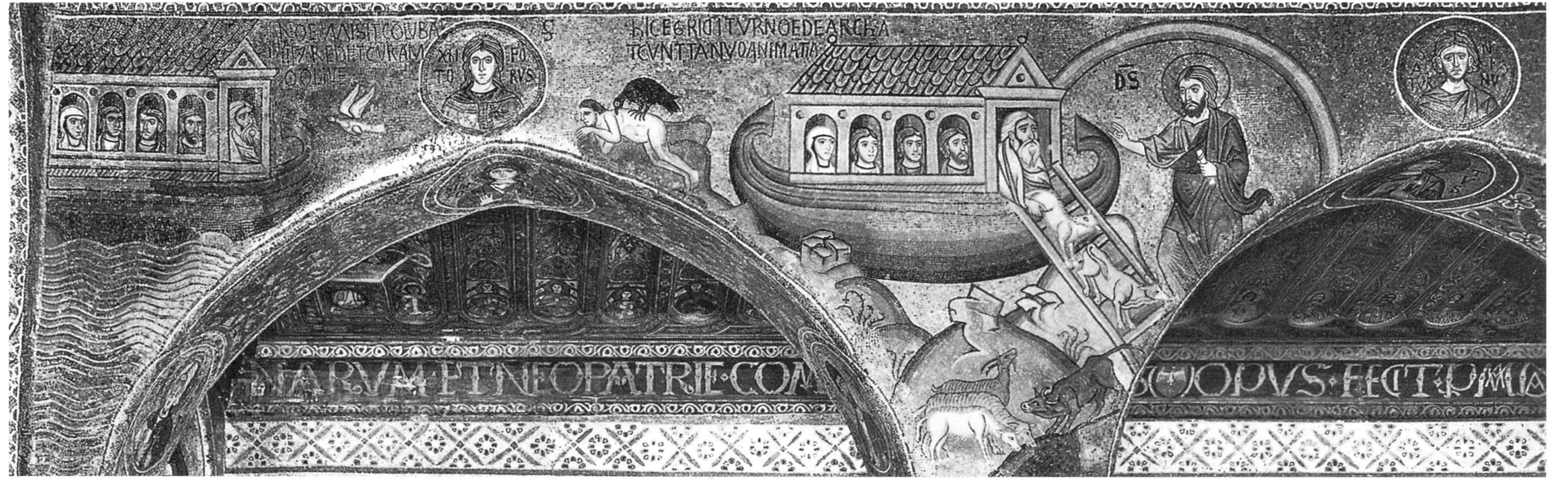

1. Palermo, Palatine Chapel, south wall of nave, east end

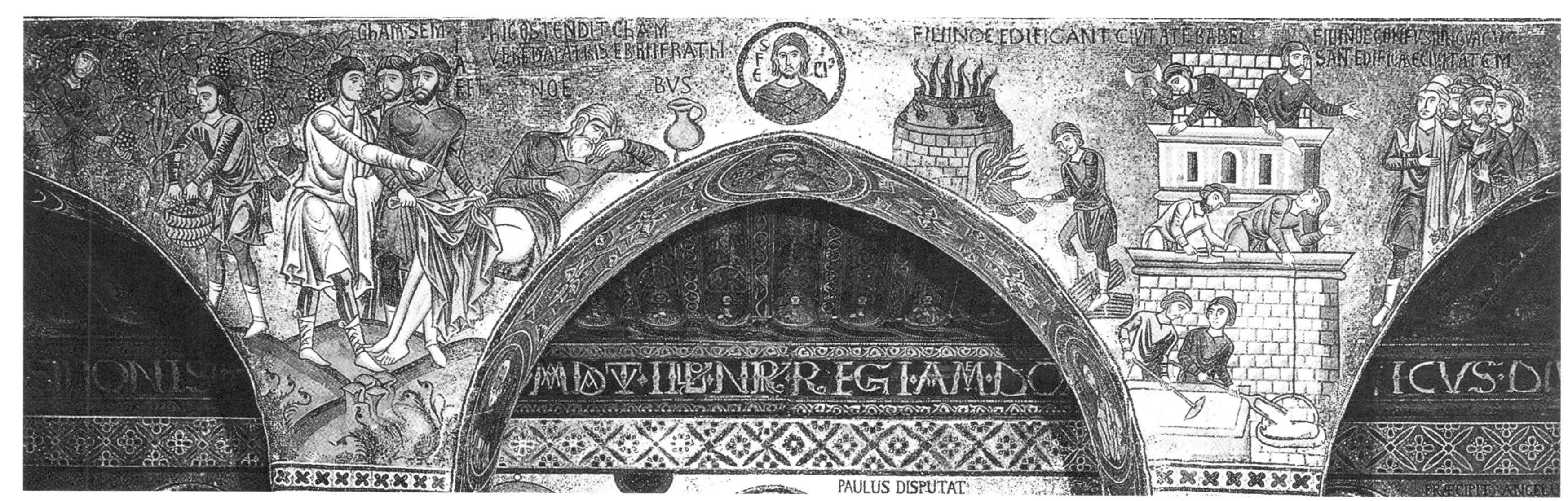

2. Palermo, Palatine Chapel, south wall of nave, central section

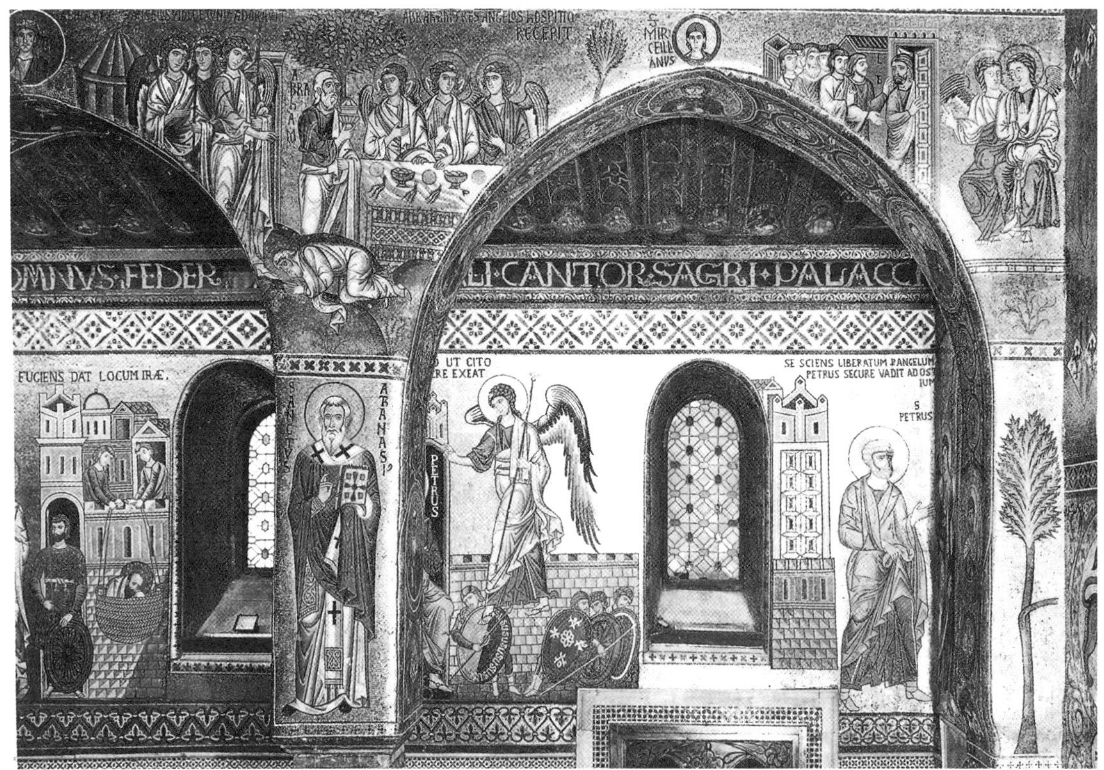

3. Palermo, Palatine Chapel, south wall of nave, west end

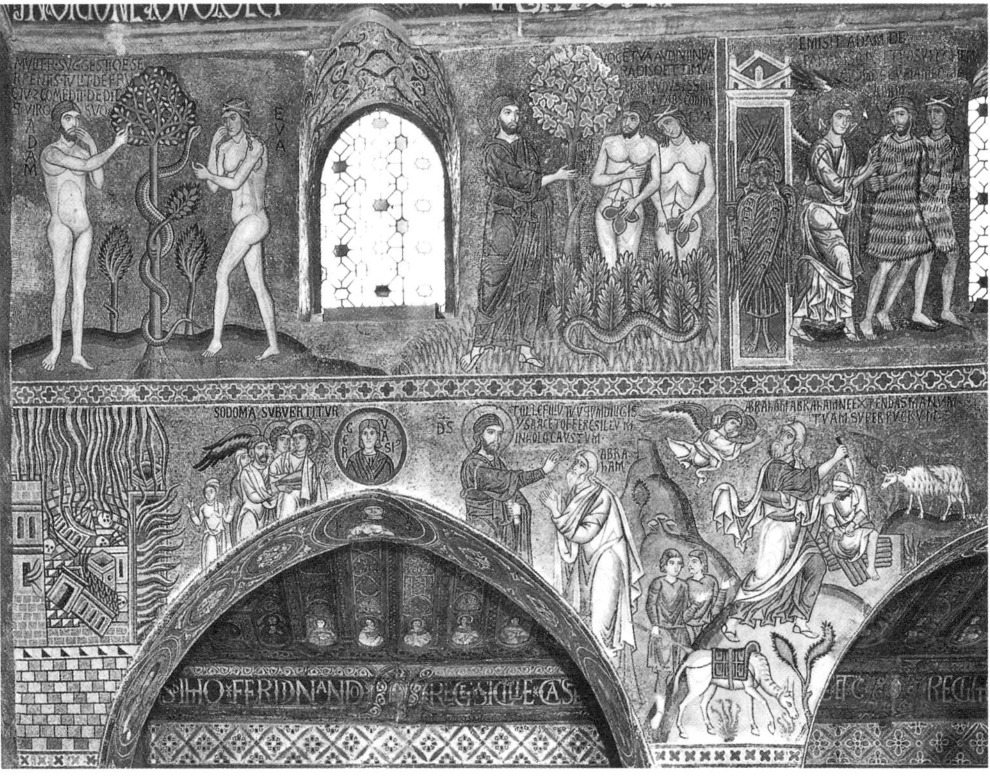

4. Palermo, Palatine Chapel, north wall of nave, west end

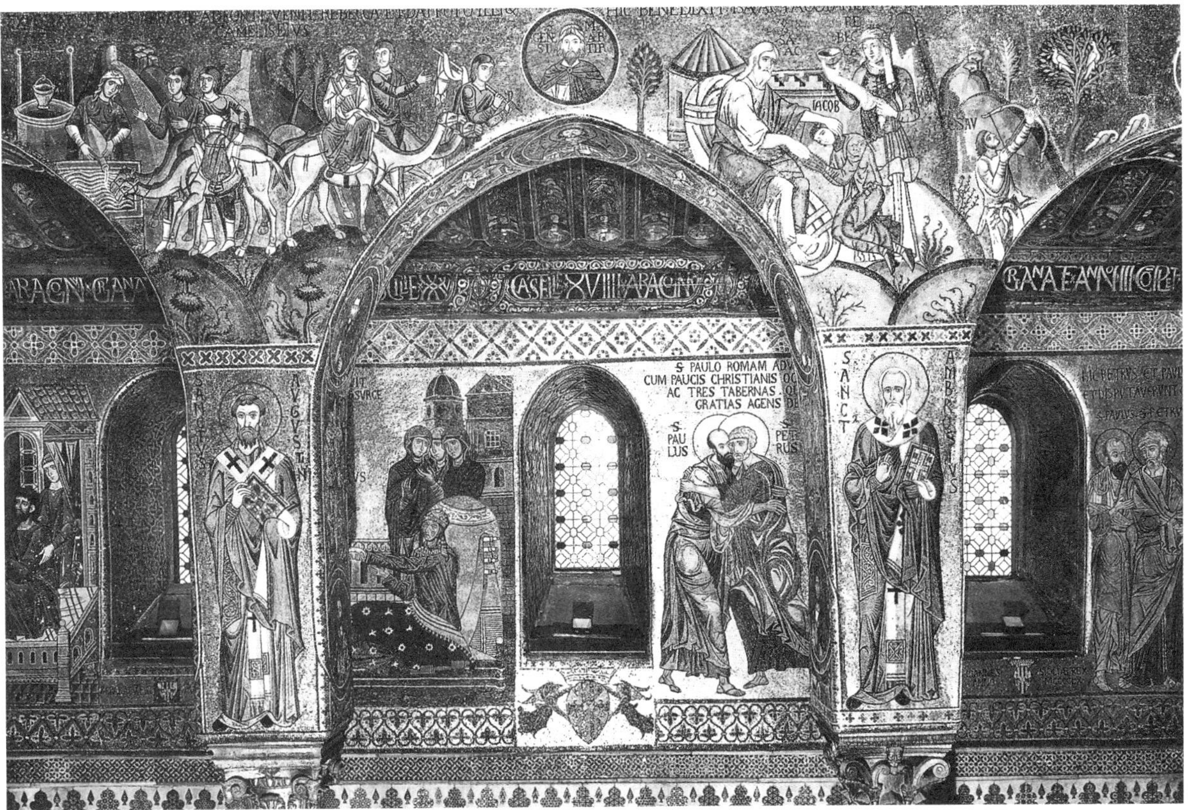

5. Palermo, Palatine Chapel, north wall of nave, central section

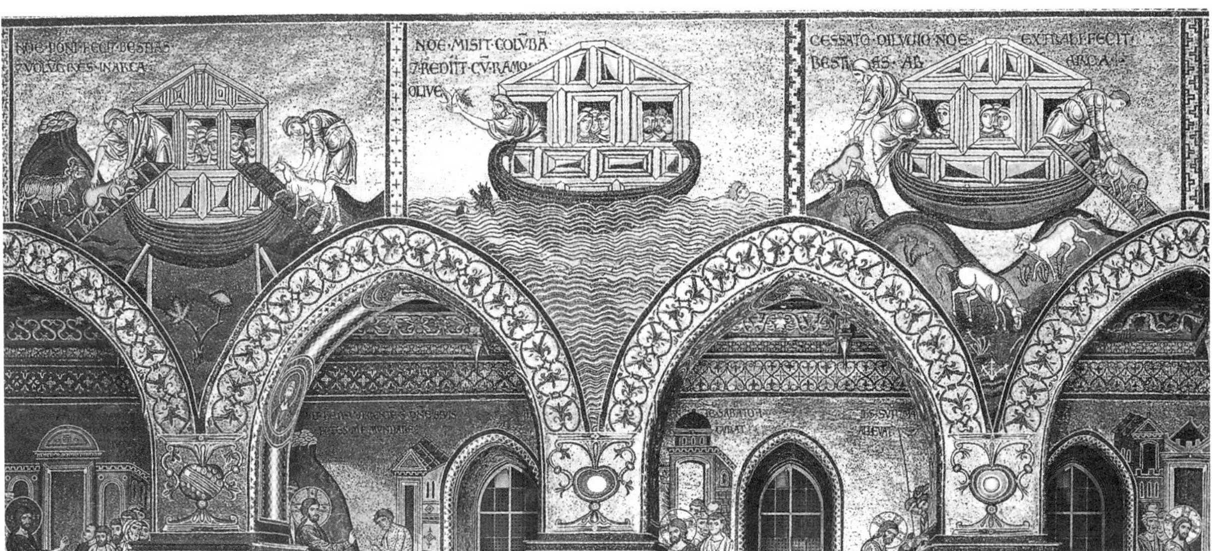

6. Monreale, Cathedral, south wall of nave, eastern section

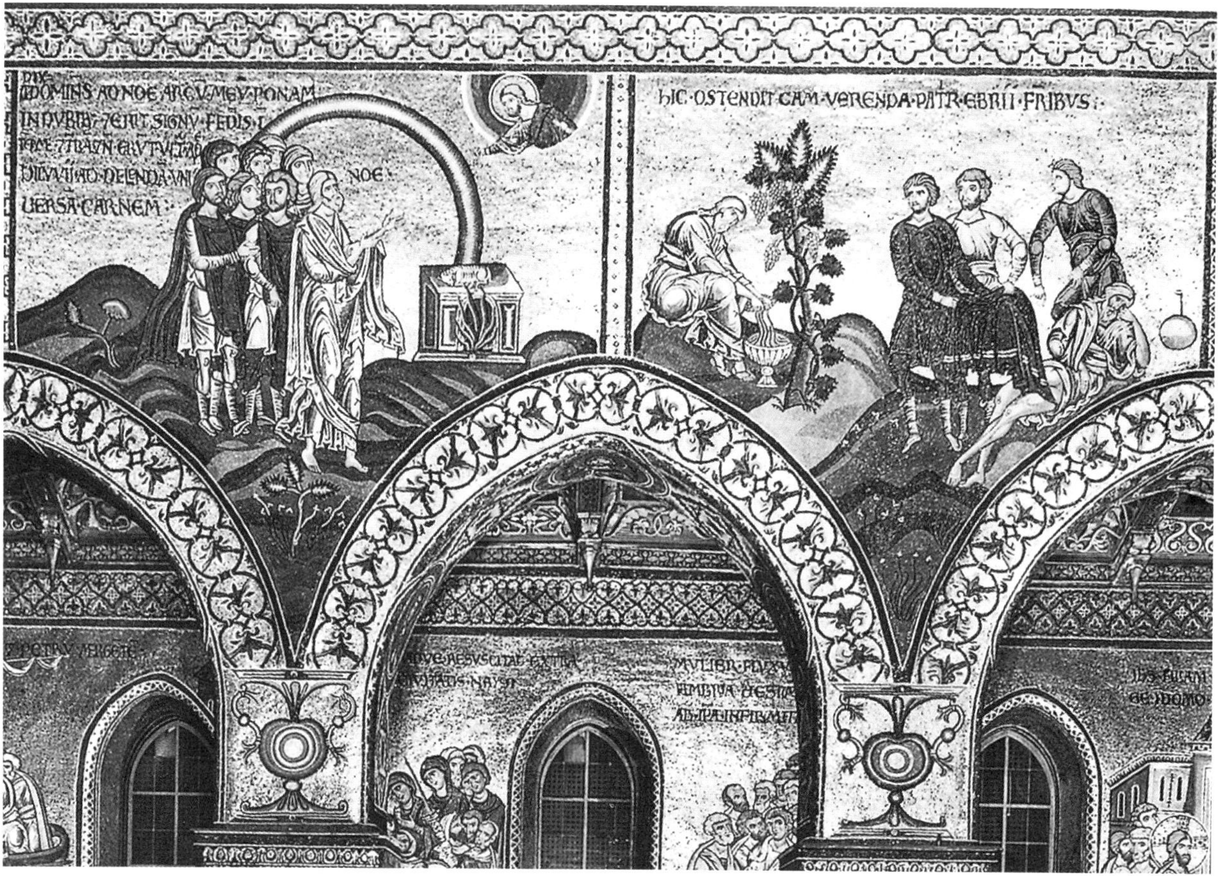

7. Monreale, Cathedral, south wall of nave, central section

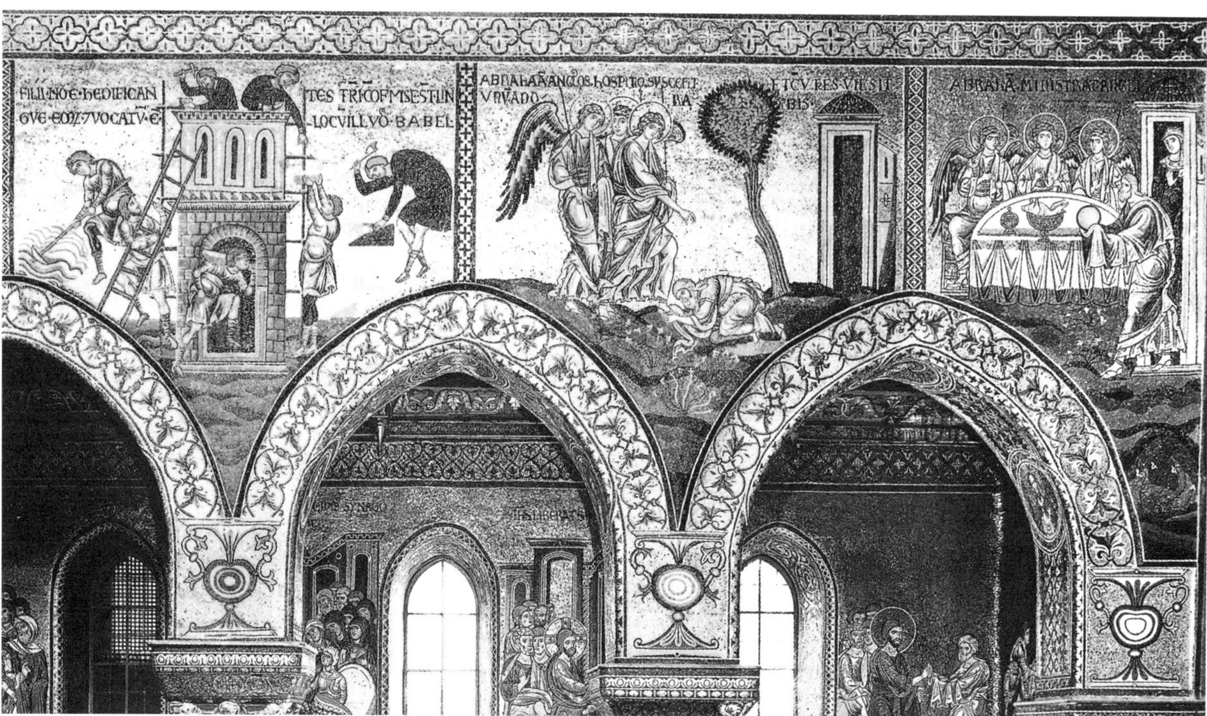

8. Monreale, Cathedral, south wall of nave, west end

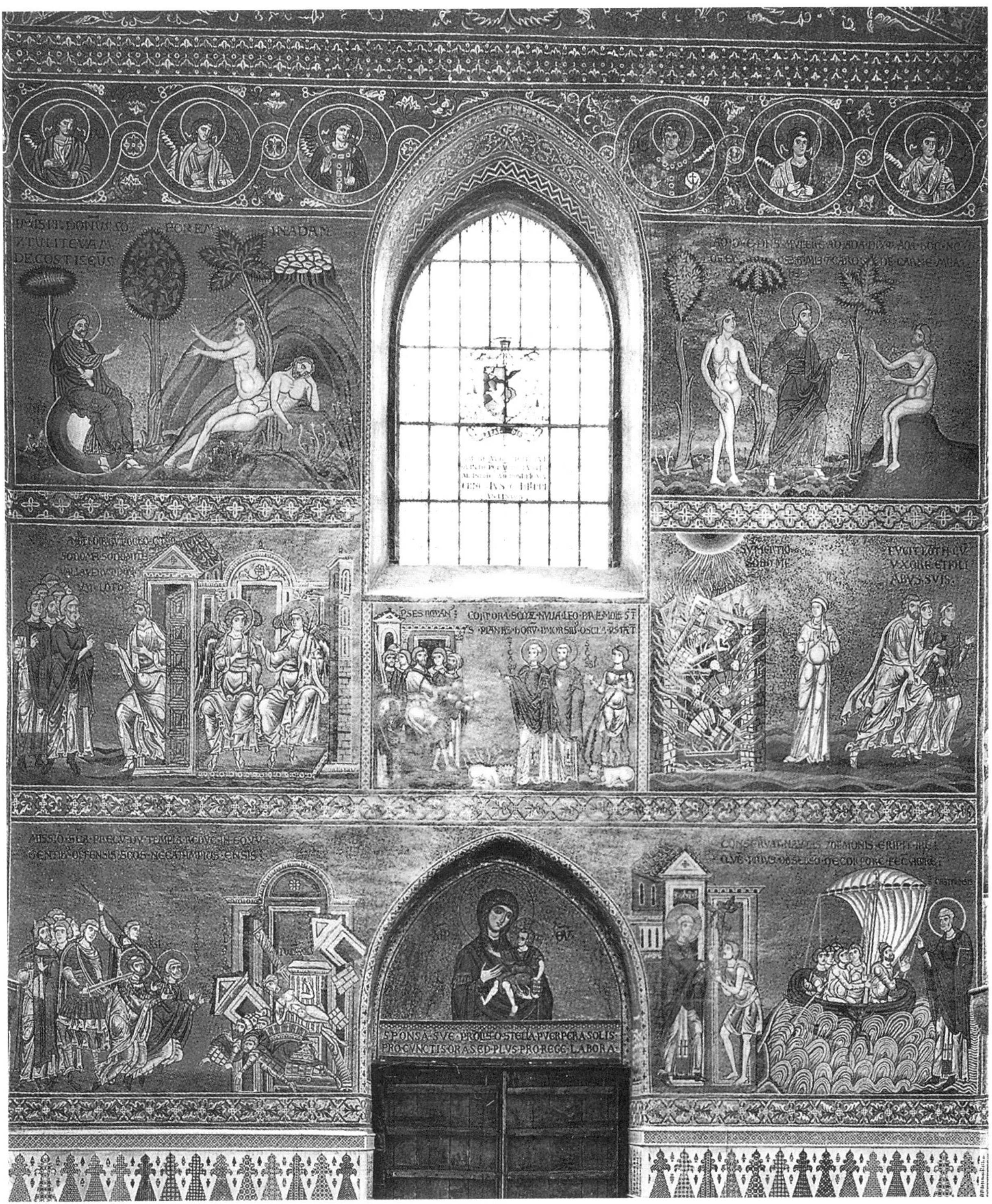

9. Monreale, Cathedral, west wall of nave

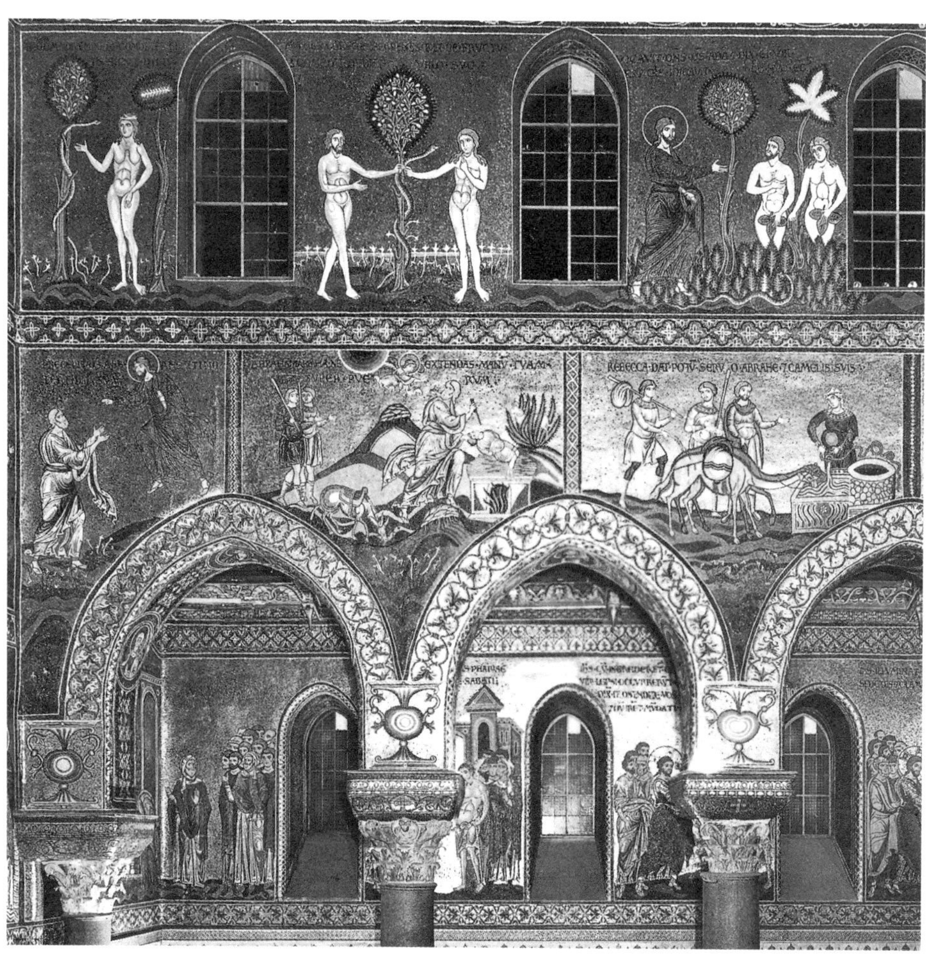

10. Monreale, Cathedral, north wall of nave, west end

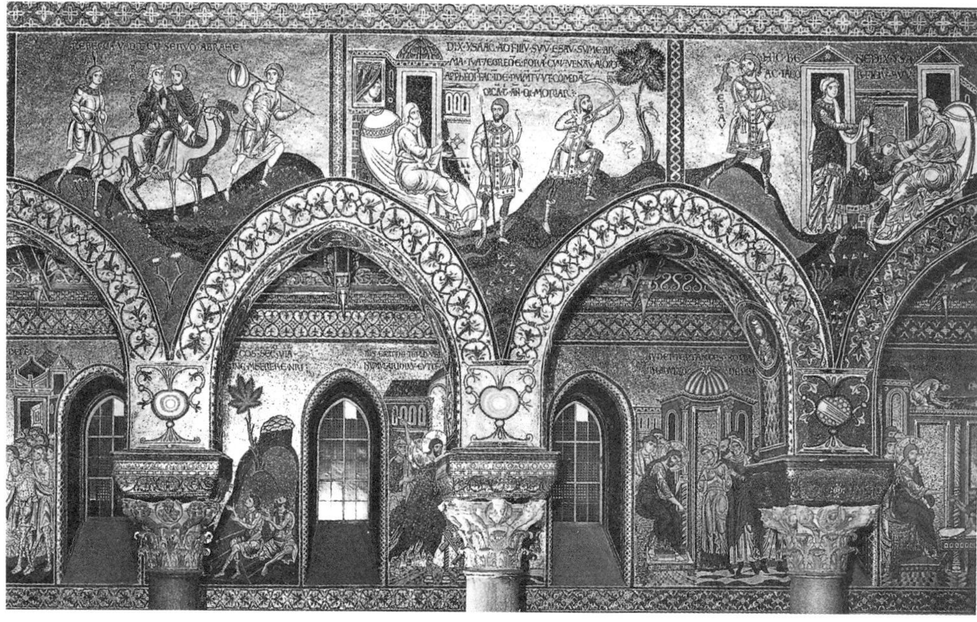

11. Monreale, Cathedral, north wall of nave, central section

The Architecture and Sculpture of the Portal
of the South Side of Arezzo Cathedral

·

GIOVANNI FRENI

THE PORTAL on the south side of the Cathedral of Arezzo is the only surviving fourteenth-century portal of the building still in situ. The portals on the facade together with the facade itself, started circa 1327, were never finished; the remains were demolished at the beginning of this century, when a new, neo-Gothic facade, designed by Dante Viviani, was built (1910–14). Only a few pieces of sculpture survive from the original Gothic facade and they are now on display in the Museo d'Arte Medievale e Moderna of Arezzo. Another portal, on the north side of the cathedral, was demolished when the chapel of the "Madonna del Conforto" was built at the end of the eighteenth century. This portal is documented in the 1760 plan of the cathedral, but no trace of it has survived.[1] There are no records of its structure or design, nor do we know whether it was built at the same time as the one on the south side.

Despite the fact that the south portal is central to understanding the building history of the duomo, few scholars have studied its architecture and sculpture. The portal on the south side is unusual in having architectural and sculptural decoration on both the exterior and the interior of the cathedral, which appears to be a rarity in Italy. Their architectural and decorative layouts differ considerably from each other. The external portal (Fig. 1) is placed on a high socle and is framed by two plain pilasters arranged in two sections. The first of these frames the portal, while the second flanks the tympanum. A second inner pair of pilasters, also arranged in two sections, juts out from the first one. The upper section of the inner pilasters protrudes more than the lower one, and is supported by a pair of corbels placed on top of the cornice which forms the base of the tympanum in the centre. The entire front surface of the inner pilasters is decorated with a series of reliefs (Figs. 2, 3) representing the Virtues and Vices, along with other allegorical figures and scenes which are not always identifiable due to weathering.[2] In the embrasures beside the portal, a double curved moulding, which follows a concave and then a convex pattern (*gola*), is decorated with large acanthus leaves arranged with their main veins set diagonally.

---

[1] This plan is preserved in the Sala Capitolare of the duomo. It was published in M. Armandi, "Vescovi e committenza, il caso della cattedrale aretina," in *La battaglia di Campaldino, Atti del convegno* (Arezzo, 1989), 234–57, esp. 242; and S. Casciu, "Pianta della cattedrale," in *Mater Christi: Altissime testimonianze del culto della Vergine nel territorio aretino*, ed. A. M. Maetzke (Arezzo, 1996), 104.

[2] The reliefs are arranged on both the upper order and the lower sections of the pilasters. Each section of the pilaster is decorated with four large panels depicting an allegory. A smaller rectangular panel with a scene or a symbolic animal is placed below each allegorical figure. Since the reliefs are considerably damaged, it is possible to recognize only a small number of the allegorical figures and scenes of the cycle.

This moulding is followed by a series of undecorated pilasters and colonnettes which enclose a large diagonal pilaster with classicizing rinceaux scrolls. The pilasters and the order of the embrasures are surmounted by large-leafed capitals. A cornice runs above the capitals, dividing the lower from the upper part of the portal. The archivolts, framed by a spiral moulding, continue the order of the embrasures. The cornice of the gable is supported by a series of leafed corbels which form trifoliate arcades. Two badly damaged statues (two angels or an anomalous Annunciation, with the Virgin on the left side) are placed outside the archivolts and beside the upper order of pilasters. A group of sculptures in "cocciopesto,"[3] with a Madonna *lactans* (Fig. 4) before a pair of angels bearing curtains, and flanked by two bishop saints (possibly St. Donatus and St. Satyrus), stands on the projecting cornice, partly within the tympanum and partly outside it.

The roof which covers the portal is not original. It is likely that two stump structures on top of the second section of the decorated pilasters, visible in an old photograph of the portal, were what remained of the original pinnacles or of the bases of two statues (Fig. 5).[4] The lintel of the door is supported by two corbels with large acanthus leaves placed on top of the plain jambs. The lintel is composed of a series of trapezoidal elements wedged into each other, constituting a self-supporting structure. This same type of lintel was also used in the original portals of the facade of the cathedral.[5]

The pilasters have been damaged by weathering, and several figures and scenes of the allegorical cycle have completely disappeared or are hardly recognisable. Some original parts of the portal, which in photographs of the 1960s appear severely eroded, have been reconstructed. These include the frame of the gable and some frames of the reliefs with allegorical figures in the upper section of the decorated pilasters.[6]

The structure of the "internal portal" consists of a simple frame (Fig. 6). This is made up of two thin semi-octagonal pilasters, each of which terminates in a capital which supports an impost joined to the frame continuing in the lintel. Above the imposts and behind each of the statues of the Annunciation are short, thin, semi-octagonal pilasters ending in a pair of capitals joined to the triangular gable. In the space between the lintel and the gable a lowered arch is framed by a thin

[3] Kreytenberg, reporting an oral communication from A. M. Maetzke, affirms that the group of the Madonna *lactans* with the two angels and the two bishop saints is in "cocciopesto," a special technique which employs a mass of smashed bricks with a binding medium. According to Maetzke's information, the whole group is a single piece worked in situ (G. Kreytenberg, "L'Annunciazione sopra la Porta del Campanile nel Duomo di Firenze," *Prospettiva* 27 [1981], 52–62, esp. 58).

[4] That the roof is not an original part of the portal is confirmed by the condition of the original decorative mouldings of the tympanum, and of the reliefs of the upper order of the sculpted pilasters, which were recently restored and partly reconstructed. In fact, some 1960s pre-restoration photographs in the Conway Library, Courtauld Institute of Art, London, show that the original carvings had been severely damaged by the weather. This would not have happened if the portal had been protected by such a roof. I do not know of any other four-

teenth-century portal in a Tuscan church that was provided with such a roof covering its gable.

[5] One of the original doorways of the facade, with such a lintel, was saved from the demolition of the Gothic facade at the beginning of this century and is now kept in one of the sculpture rooms of the Museo d'Arte Medievale e Moderna of Arezzo. On the architraves of the doorways of the Cathedral of Arezzo, see G. Martelli, "Gli architravi delle antiche porte della cattedrale di Arezzo," *Bollettino del Centro studi di storia dell'architettura* 9 (1955), 33–36.

[6] Comparison of recent photographs and the 1960s pre-restoration photographs in the Conway Library, Courtauld Institute of Art, London, testifies to the rapid deterioration of the sandstone sculptures of the portal of the Cathedral of Arezzo over the course of the last decades. Some earlier photographs, published by Kreytenberg ("Annunciazione" [as in note 3], figs. 16, 18, 19), show the reliefs in even better condition.

moulding. Another round moulding, which constitutes the internal border of a stone arch touching the side pilasters and the gable frame, encloses a space which contained a painted decoration, now entirely faded.

The capitals are the only decorated architectural pieces of the whole inner portal. They are covered with elongated, pointed water-leaves. This type of design is found on some of the capitals in the north aisle of the cathedral, but the style and the execution of those on the portal are very different. Here the leaves are gathered in tighter groups, and the design appears more simplified. An Annunciation (Figs. 7, 8), whose figures of the angel and the Virgin are placed on top of imposts above the water-leaf capitals, completes the decoration of the inner portal. Both of these statues, together with the capitals which support them, have been damaged by weathering. This happened because the inner portal and its sculptures remained exposed for a long time. The section of the south wall corresponding to the fourth bay of the church, where the portal is located, was built up to the top of the portal by 1337. But the inner portal and the Annunciation group lacked any protection because this part of the duomo was not vaulted and roofed until the completion of the building during the last campaign of work between 1471 and 1511.[7]

The first study which dealt with the south portal of the duomo was that by the Pasqui brothers, authors of the first monograph on the Aretine cathedral. They attributed the making of the external portal to the sculptors who, in the second half of the fourteenth century, were active in the yard of the palace of the Fraternità dei Laici of Arezzo.[8]

Salmi, in his first study on the cathedral in 1915, dated the portal ca. 1380 on the basis of the similarity between the design of the Aretine portal and the so-called Porta dei Canonici of the Florentine duomo, which was also finished at that time.[9] To re-enforce his thesis, Salmi confirmed Venturi's attribution of the allegorical cycle of the pilasters to the Florentine Betto di Francesco and the Aretine Giovanni di Francesco, the masters who carved the Arca di San Donato between the late 1360s and the early 1370s.[10] In a later study, Salmi reaffirmed this dating and the attribu-

---

[7] This is confirmed by the homogeneity of the masonry and by two funerary inscriptions dated 1337 and 1339 on the stone of the wall. The documents, which testify to the resumption of work on the cathedral between 1471 and 1511, confirm that this section of the wall was completed during the fourteenth century; see M. Salmi, "La cattedrale d'Arezzo," *L'Arte* 18 (1915), 373–91, esp. 380ff.; and my forthcoming study on the public patronage and the building phases of the cathedral, based on unpublished documentation, which is part of my Ph.D. thesis on art and patronage in fourteenth-century Arezzo.

[8] A. Pasqui and U. Pasqui, *Il duomo di Arezzo* (Arezzo, 1880), 25.

[9] Salmi, "Cattedrale" (as in note 7), 381; see also id., "L'Architettura nell'aretino: Il periodo gotico," in *Atti del XII Congresso di storia dell'architettura: L'Architettura nell'aretino, Arezzo 10–15 Settembre 1961* (Rome, 1969), 70–103, esp. 86. Salmi, in these studies and in his subsequent essays on the cathedral, did not take into account the complex history of the "Porta dei Canonici," which was completed in two different phases. In fact, the Florentine door was originally conceived as a portal without

a gable, and was completed by 1378. Subsequently, the gable with its sculpted decoration was added to the door. The added gable was probably designed by Giovanni Fetti, chief master of the Opera del Duomo between 1378 and 1382. The gable and its sculpted decoration is convincingly attributed to him by Kreytenberg; see G. Brunetti, "Osservazioni sulla Porta dei Canonici," *Mitteilungen des kunsthistorischen Instituts in Florenz* 8, nos. 1–4 (Oct. 1957–May 1959), 1–12; G. Kreytenberg, "Giovanni Fetti und die Porta dei Canonici des Florentiner Doms," *Mitteilungen des kunsthistorischen Institutes in Florenz* 20 (1976), 127–58.

[10] A. Venturi, *Storia dell'arte italiana*, vol. 4, *La scultura del Trecento e le sue origini* (Turin, 1906), 388. On the controversial matter of the identity of the sculptors of the Arca di San Donato, see M. Salmi, "Berichte über die Sitzungen des Instituts, 26. Sitzung, 23 Mai 1930," *Mitteilungen des kunsthistorisches Institutes in Florenz* 3 (1930), 359–60; Kreytenberg, "Giovanni Fetti" (as in note 9), 151, n. 33; E. Agnolucci, "L'Arca-Altare di San Donato nella cultura artistica del Trecento aretino," *Antichità viva* 27 (1988), 32–38.

tion of the external part of the portal, and dated its internal part to the 1330s. He assigned it to a Sienese master due to the use of the thin polygonal pilasters and the style of the Annunciation group, which he judged to be close to the sculpture of Giovanni d'Agostino.[11]

Salmi's attribution of the external portal to the masters of the Arca di San Donato is not convincing, especially if the proportions, the drapery, and the character of the personifications are compared with the reliefs of the Arca. Moreover, the dating of the portal to ca. 1380 is questionable. At that time Arezzo was passing through the most tragic period of its history. Between the late 1370s and the early 1380s the city was divided by internal factional struggles. It was sacked twice and occupied by the troops of Enguerrand de Coucy, who in 1384 sold the city to the Florentines. The Aretines eventually accepted Florentine domination as the only way to gain peace and stability, and they never subsequently regained their autonomy. It is extremely unlikely that the sculptors' yard of the cathedral was kept open during such a traumatic period.[12] Salmi's attribution of the internal portal to a Sienese master who was a follower of Giovanni d'Agostino is thus uncertain, but his study of the features of the internal portal is convincing.

The most recent study on the Aretine portal is by Kreytenberg, who attempted to reconstruct the work of an assistant and follower of Giovanni di Balduccio active in the Baroncelli chapel in Santa Croce in Florence.[13] The German scholar, studying the "Porta del Campanile" of the Cathedral of Santa Maria del Fiore and the Annunciation in that portal, confirmed a thesis originally proposed by Schmarsow in 1887,[14] which attributed the angel and the Virgin to two different masters. Kreytenberg attributed the angel to Iacopo di Piero Guidi, documented in Florence between 1379 and 1385, and the Virgin to an earlier sculptor, an assistant of Giovanni di Balduccio, who collaborated with the master in the making of the sculpture of the Baroncelli chapel in Santa Croce.

Kreytenberg dated the Virgin ca. 1330, and to support his argument he accepted a suggestion made by Schmarsow, who attributed the group in "cocciopesto" in the tympanum of the portal of Arezzo to the master of the Virgin Annunciate in Florence. On the basis of two inscriptions on the external wall of the Arezzo Cathedral, and of a presumed coat of arms of the Tarlati on the base of the sculptural group of the tympanum or in the tympanum itself, Kreytenberg dated the Aretine portal to the period between 1330 and 1340. He also attributed to this master the reliefs with the allegorical personifications on the pilasters. Kreytenberg therefore gathered together a consistent

[11] M. Salmi, "Il duomo di Arezzo," *Fede ed arte*, 1962, 134–47; republished in *Atti e Memorie dell'Accademia Petrarca* 48 (1986), 247–74, esp. 257.

[12] On the historical situation in Arezzo in the second half of the fourteenth century, see M. Falciai, *Storia d'Arezzo dalle origini alla fine del granducato lorenese* (Arezzo, 1928), 177–83; U. Pasqui, *Documenti per la storia della città di Arezzo nel medio Evo*, vol. 3 (Florence, 1937), xi–xv; D. Bini, "Il conflitto secolare tra i comuni di Arezzo e di Firenze fino all'assoggettamento del primo al secondo," *Atti e Memorie dell'Accademia Petrarca* 30–31 (1941), 55–73, esp. 67–71; M. Luzzati, "Firenze e l'area toscana," in *Storia d'Italia*, ed. G. Galasso, vol. 3, pt. 1 (Turin, 1987), with bibliography on medieval Arezzo, 687–88; R. Black, *Benedetto Accolti and the Florentine Renaissance* (Cambridge, 1985), esp. 1–3, and p. 1 n. 1 for further bibliography; A. Antoniella, "Affermazione e forme istituzionali della do-

minazione fiorentina sul territorio di Arezzo (secc. XIV–XVI)," *Annali aretini* 1 (1993), 173–203, passim, but esp. 173–92.

[13] Kreytenberg, "Annunciazione" (as in note 3). On the sculpture in the Baroncelli chapel, see Venturi, *Storia* (as in note 10), vol. 4, 544; W. F. Volbach, in G. Vitzthum von Eckstädt and W. F. Volbach, *Die Malerei und Plastik des Mittelalters in Italien* (Handbuch der Kunstwissenschaft) (Wildpark-Potsdam, 1924), 150 (quoted by Valentiner, below); R. W. Valentiner, "Una statua ignota di Tino di Camaino in Santa Croce in Firenze," *L'Arte*, 1933, 83–107, esp. 89–93; id., "Giovanni Balducci a Firenze e una scultura di Maso," *L'Arte*, 1935, 3–29, esp. 14–15; P. Toesca, *Il Trecento* (Turin, 1951), 268–69.

[14] A. Schmarsow, "Vier Statuetten in der Domopera zu Florenz," *Jahrbuch der Königlich Preussischen Kunstsammlungen* 7 (1887), 145ff.

catalogue of sculptures which he considered to be by this unnamed assistant of Giovanni di Balduccio, which includes the Virgin Annunciate of the "Porta del Campanile" in Florence, a relief of the Redeemer and another with the symbol of the evangelist John in the Cappella Baroncelli in Santa Croce in Florence, the "cocciopesto" group in the tympanum of the south portal of the Cathedral of Arezzo (Fig. 4), the reliefs of the allegorical cycle of the same portal, and the statue of St. Luke with his symbol in a niche originally in the facade of the duomo of Arezzo (Fig. 11).

Kreytenberg's dating of the portal appears to be correct, but his attribution poses difficulties. He did not take into account the presence of the internal portal, and some of the assumptions and facts he used to date the Aretine door and the Madonna *lactans* group are questionable. Before discussing the attribution, it is necessary to examine the arguments used by Kreytenberg to date the portal. Kreytenberg's dating of the Madonna *lactans* group (Fig. 4) is based on the assumption that the sculptures in the tympanum were made specially for the south side portal. Thus, he concluded that the presence of the coat of arms of the Tarlati, who ruled Arezzo up to 1337, in the tympanum or the Madonna group could be used to confirm a date in the 1330s for both the portal and the sculpted group. The presence of such a coat of arms is uncertain,[15] and it is doubtful that the Madonna *lactans* group was made specifically for this portal. This is reinforced when the dimensions of the sculptures and those of the tympanum are compared: the Madonna with the two angels hardly fits the tympanum, the two bishop saints stand in front of it below the archivolts, and the base of the sculpted group protrudes from the lower cornice. It is necessary, therefore, to consider the portal and the sculpture independently.

Kreytenberg also considered two inscriptions, one, dated 1337, to the left of the portal and the other, dated 1338, to its right. He argued that both of them were evidence for the dating of the portal. Vertical junctures in the masonry of the south wall make it possible to identify the sections which belong to a specific building phase. The inscription dated 1337 is the only one which belongs to the same section of wall as the portal. This may be considered as a terminus ante quem for the building and the decoration of the portal.

The sculptural and architectural styles conform to such a date. The external portal was built in a single building phase by a workshop very keen on a fourteenth-century classicizing style. The acanthus leaves on the concave-convex moulding immediately inside the figurative pilasters, the large-leafed capitals, and the scroll decoration of the diagonal pilasters were certainly carved by a single workshop. The pilasters with the allegorical cycle can also be ascribed to the same workshop. They are an integral part of the portal as a whole, both in structure and style. This is demonstrated

---

[15] The first mention of the coat of arms is in Pasqui and Viviani's guide to Arezzo (U. Pasqui and U. Viviani, *Guida illustrata storica, artistica e commerciale di Arezzo e dintorni* [Arezzo, 1925], 79, 80–81). The authors refer to it twice. The first time the coat of arms is considered to be part of the portal, the second time as placed on the base of the Madonna group. It is not recorded in the Pasquis's earlier monograph on the duomo (Pasqui and Pasqui, *Il duomo* [as in note 8]). The second and last reference to the Tarlati arms is by Tafi, who considers it to be an immediately detectable part of the portal, without specifying its position (A. Tafi, *Arezzo: Guida storico-artistica* [Arezzo, 1978], 227, quoted by Kreytenberg, "Annunciazione" [as in note 3], 62 n. 39). None of the other authors who have written studies on the duomo, such as Salmi and Armandi, mentioned this coat of arms. Examining the portal directly, I could not see it at all. The Tarlati arms are not visible on the front of the base of the sculpted group of the Madonna in the tympanum, the most likely setting for such a family shield, nor on its right side. On the left side of the base there is something barely visible which may be a shield, but the observer, even using binoculars or a telephoto lens, cannot determine that it is a coat of arms, and even less whether it is the Tarlati's.

by the joining of the capitals and by the coherent classicizing conception of the figures of the allegorical cycle. The frame of the gable, recently restored with newly carved pieces, together with the design of the cornice base of the tympanum were conceived in conjunction with the earlier decoration of the south wall of the cathedral.

The original design of the Arezzo portal, without the later addition of the roof and with its original top pinnacles, is similar to certain examples of Sienese miniature architecture, such as the tabernacle of the church of Sant'Eugenia a Monastero (Siena), or the tabernacle of the church of Sant'Alessandro in Castel Nuovo Berardenga, which Garzelli dated to 1340.[16] The composition of the tabernacles and the Aretine portal share several features despite a difference in the proportions of the gable and the use of pointed-arch tympana in the tabernacles and a round-arch tympanum in the portal. Parallels include the setting of the outer pilasters and embrasures on a high socle, the presence over the capitals of the cornice which forms the base of the tympanum, the articulation of the outer pilasters in two sections (the first framing the door and the second the tympanum and the archivolts), the direct joining of the side pilasters and the upper frame of the gable, and the arrangement of the jambs and lintel of the door. Many of these characteristics are also found elsewhere, such as in the "Petroni monument" in the convent of San Francesco in Siena, dated 1336 by an inscription, and attributed to Agostino di Giovanni assisted by his son Domenico or Agnolo di Ventura.[17]

Other features of the Aretine portal are comparable to the Baroncelli monument in Santa Croce (Fig. 9), which is dated 1327 and attributed to Giovanni di Balduccio. The use of protruding corbels to support the pilasters beside the arch in the Florentine monument is very similar to that in the Arezzo portal. The arrangement of the pilaster decoration with rectangular panels carved with reliefs representing seated prophets is also similar to the Aretine examples.[18] The concave-convex moulding with the large diagonal acanthus leaves of the Arezzo portal (Fig. 10) is common to the portals of the Cathedral of Orvieto[19] and that of the Palazzo dei Priori of Perugia (dated between 1333 and ca. 1353).[20] Although these decorated mouldings cannot be attributed

[16] A. R. Garzelli, *Sculture toscane nel Dugento e nel Trecento* (Florence, 1969), 160–61, nos. 20, 21, figs. 142, 143.

[17] R. W. Valentiner, "Studies in Italian Gothic Plastic Art," *Art in America* 13, no. 1 (1924), 3–18, esp. 17–18; W. Cohn Goerke, "Scultori senesi del Trecento," *Rivista d'arte*, 1938, 242–89, esp. 281–82, and 1939, 1–22; Toesca, *Trecento* (as in note 13), 296–97; A. R. Garzelli, "Problemi di scultura gotica senese, 3," *Critica d'arte* 14, no. 88 (1967), 36–50, esp. 42–47; Garzelli, *Sculture toscane* (as in note 16), 99, 156–57; E. Carli, *L'Arte nella Basilica di San Francesco a Siena* (Siena, 1971), 15–16; id., *Gli scultori senesi* (Milan, 1980), 20, 22, 110–11; R. Bartalini, "Agostino di Giovanni e Compagni, I: Una traccia per Agnolo di Ventura," *Prospettiva* 61 (1991), 21–28.

[18] Kreytenberg, "Annunciazione" (as in note 3). See also note 13 above.

[19] According to the documents, the colonnettes and the mouldings which decorate the splay of the portals were carved beginning in 1321, and further works are recorded between 1337 and 1339; see L. Fumi, *Il duomo*

d'Orvieto e i suoi restauri (Rome, 1891), 41 (XII), 43 (XXIX), 53–59 (XCI, CI, CXIV, CXL, CXLIII). For a comparison of the sculpted decoration of the facade of the Cathedral of Orvieto and the portal of the Palazzo dei Priori of Perugia, see Garzelli, *Sculture toscane* (as in note 16), 207–11. On the portals of the Cathedral of Orvieto, see J. White, "The Reliefs on the Facade of the Duomo at Orvieto," *JWarb* 22 (1959), 254–302 (with a thorough discussion of the previous bibliography), esp. 265–69; E. L. Schlee, "Problemi cronologici della facciata del Duomo di Orvieto," in *Il Duomo di Orvieto e le grandi cattedrali del Duecento*, ed. G. Barlozzetti (Turin, 1995), 99–167, esp. 116–18 (a study which puts forward a very idiosyncratic hypothesis on the facade of the Orvieto duomo).

[20] Toesca, *Trecento* (as in note 13), 370 (dating it to the mid-fourteenth century); A. R. Garzelli, "Scultura del Trecento a Siena e fuori Siena," *Critica d'arte* 15, no. 94 (1968), 55–65, esp. 64–65; id., *Sculture toscane* (as in note 16), 207–11 (the author supposes that the portal was executed over a very long period, possibly between 1319 and

to the same hand, the vigorous and naturalistic treatment of the foliage is noteworthy in all of them.

The allegorical figures in the pilasters are badly eroded. All the seated personifications of virtues, allegorical figures, and bishops are of classical proportions. There is no hint of "gothicization," either in the dimensions of the figures or in their poses, which have an air of solemn stillness. Even the movement of the standing figure on the lower section of the left pilaster, identified as Inconstancy (Fig. 2), is overwhelmed by the balanced position of its arms suspended on the strong fulcrum of its body. All of these Aretine allegories are classic and Giottesque in character, and are similar to the considerably earlier Virtues and Vices of the Cappella degli Scrovegni in Padua. Other characteristics that typify these Aretine reliefs are the heavy drapery falling vertically in deep, wide, articulated folds, together with the rather short necks. Some of the figures, such as Meekness on the lower section of the right pilaster (Fig. 3) or Despair on the upper section of the left one, have rounded faces. In other cases, such as that of the bishop saint seated on a dragon, possibly St. Donatus, the face has slightly more elongated proportions. The strong facial features with deeply hollowed cavities for the oval protruding eyes, the fleshy eyelids and lips, and the strong, short noses indicate the work of a single hand.

The heavy drapery folds falling vertically are reminiscent of the "Florentine style" of Tino di Camaino, as it appears in pieces of sculpture such as the statue of Bishop Antonio degli Orsi, or in the lower part of the drapery of the *Madonna Sedes Sapientiae*, both from the sepulchral monument of the Florentine prelate (ca. 1321). Parallels can also be seen in the drapery of the Virtues in the bronze portal of Andrea Pisano. The drapery of the Aretine Justice, for example, shows the same pattern as the folds of its homologue Virtue in the Florentine series.

The layout of the Aretine reliefs (Figs. 2, 3) and the carved panels of the Baroncelli monument in Santa Croce in Florence (Fig. 9) are also similar. However, the style of the Florentine prophet reliefs differs considerably from the Aretine allegories in their dynamic postures and the treatment of the drapery. Only a vague similarity can be found between the facial features of the Redeemer in the Baroncelli chapel and the features on some of the allegorical personifications in Arezzo. This, however, is not sufficient to attribute the Aretine sculptures to the master of the Florentine reliefs.

The similarities between the reliefs of the Aretine portal and the group in "cocciopesto" in the tympanum of the same portal proposed by Kreytenberg must be rejected. The proportions of the "cocciopesto" Madonna *lactans* group (Fig. 4) are characterised by a Gothic elongation. The Virgin and her court of angels and saints have thin, oval faces and they are all wrapped in excessively folded drapery. The figures in "cocciopesto" and those in the relief panels of the pilasters are not by the same hand. The slim, thin trunk of the Virgin, for example, is not comparable to that of any of the seated allegorical figures. The sculptor of the tympanum group therefore cannot be identified as the master of the pilasters. However, as discussed above, the architectonic structure of the portal and its sculpted decoration confirm a dating in the 1330s.

Salmi considered the internal portal briefly in a 1962 paper on the cathedral,[21] affirming that it should be attributed to a Sienese follower of Giovanni d'Agostino, who also sculpted the group

---

1353, and that its sculpture was influenced by the reliefs of the facade of the Cathedral of Orvieto); G. Previtali, "Sviluppi Perugini: Per il Maestro della Madonna di Sant'Agostino," *Prospettiva* 32 (1983), 12–20, repr. in id., *Studi sulla scultura gotica in Italia* (Turin, 1991), 57–69.

[21] Salmi, "Duomo" (as in note 11), 257 (1986 reprint).

of the Annunciation. He pointed out the thin, elongated polygonal pilasters or shafts of the portal, which are similar to the shafts used in the Tarlati cenotaph and in the chapel of Ciuccio Tarlati, both in the duomo of Arezzo.[22] This, however, may not be sufficient to advance an attribution to a Sienese master. It is true that between the 1320s and the 1330s the use of such thin polygonal pilasters recurs mostly in the work of Sienese sculptors, such as Agostino di Giovanni and his son Giovanni, or Tino di Camaino, as in the Angevin tombs in Naples. Moreover, the use of polygonal shafts is also found in Sienese drawings, such as that by the architect-sculptor who designed the front of the Baroncelli chapel in the *tramezzo* of Santa Croce, or another preserved in three parchment fragments in the Archive of the Opera del Duomo of Orvieto, the British Library (1899-6-17-2), and the Staatliche Museum in Berlin (Kupferstichkabinet, Kdz. 3392), possibly representing a pulpit by an anonymous Sienese master.[23] Polygonal shafts became widely used in central Italian Gothic architecture at a later date, and this feature was also popular in Arezzo. This is confirmed by the instruction Bertoldino di Baldovino gave to a Florentine Master, Francesco Talenti, in the contract for the building of his chapel in the duomo of Arezzo, expressly requesting him to follow the design of the shafts made by Giovanni d'Agostino and his father Agostino in the Tarlati chapel in the duomo and in the chapel of the sons of Ghino di Puccio Grassi in the Pieve di Santa Maria.[24] In contrast to the pilasters in the Aretine portal, the shafts which are used in Sienese architecture are usually arranged in two or more sections and are joined together by a protruding shaft-ring. Plain octagonal piers had been used earlier in Santa Croce, and semi-octagonal pilasters already formed the structure of the piers of the Cathedral of Arezzo.

The Sienese origin of the master responsible for the internal portal cannot be confirmed with certainty, but it is clear at the very least that he was working from a Sienese model. The general design of the frame of the portal, with a gable enclosing a round arch and supported by a pair of polygonal pilasters, is similar to that of the Tarlati cenotaph (1328–30), and to that of the chapel of Ciuccio Tarlati, all of them originally in the south aisle.[25] Moreover, the structure, including the

[22] On the Tarlati cenotaph and for further bibliography, see Cohn Goerke, "Scultori senesi" (as in note 17), 1 (1938), esp. 260–78; A. R. Garzelli, "Problemi di scultura gotica senese, 2," *Critica d'arte* 13, no. 79 (1966), 17–28; id., *Sculture toscane* (as in note 16), 77ff. (on the piers, see esp. 81–82); Carli, *Scultori senesi* (as in note 17), 19, 100–4 (with extensive bibliography). Two recent studies of the iconography of the tomb are E. W. Harrison, "A Study of Political Iconography on Six Italian Tombs of the Fourteenth Century" (diss., Northwestern University, 1987); and G. A. S. Pelham, "The Political and Philosophical Programme of the Tomb of Guido Tarlati" (M.A. diss., Courtauld Institute of Art, London, 1995).

[23] On the Sienese drawings mentioned here, see B. Degenhart and A. Schmitt, *Corpus der italienischen Zeichnungen, 1300–1450* (Berlin, 1968), vol. 1, 88–89, 99–102, and vol. 3, pls. 65, 71–75; M. Hall, "The *Tramezzo* in Santa Croce, Florence, Reconstructed," *ArtB* 56 (1974), 325–41 (differing from Degenhart's opinion, the author thinks that the drawing for the chapel in Santa Croce is not necessarily Sienese: see esp. 334–36); A. R. Garzelli, *Il Museo dell'Opera del Duomo di Orvieto* (Bologna, 1972), 39–41; A. R. Calderoni Masetti, "Sui disegni figurati trecenteschi

del Museo dell'Opera del Duomo di Orvieto," in *Ori e Tesori d'Europa, Atti del convegno di studio, Castello di Udine, 3–5 Dicembre 1991*, ed. G. Bergamini and P. Goi (Udine, 1992), 245–54 (the author, attributing the drawings to Ugolino di Vieri, proposes an interesting new hypothesis about the object represented, which could be a piece of goldsmithery rather than architecture).

[24] The document was originally transcribed and published by Pasqui (U. Pasqui, "La cappella Bertoldini nel Duomo di Arezzo," *Numero unico di arte e storia aretina* [Arezzo, 1914], v–vi) but with some mistakes and a few omissions. I have edited a new transcription from the original which will be included in my forthcoming Ph.D. thesis. The contract for the chapel of Ciuccio Tarlati in the duomo has been published in S. Borghesi and L. Banchi, *Nuovi documenti per la storia dell'arte senese* (Siena, 1898), 21. The contract for the Ghini chapel in the Pieve has been published in G. Milanesi, *Documenti per l'arte senese* (Siena, 1854), 200–3.

[25] The chapel of Ciuccio Tarlati is still standing in its original position in the south aisle as the portal; the Tarlati cenotaph was moved to the north aisle in 1783.

flat tympanum and the gable of the portal of the duomo, is similar to the door carved in the panel "Fatto Vescovo" on Guido Tarlati's tomb.

The design of the internal portal of the duomo is similar to that of the Gothic portal of Santa Maria Maggiore in Florence. Although the Florentine portal is more elongated, the use of pointed arches in the tympanum and in the archivolts, together with a deep embrasure and the general design of its frame, is similar to that of the Arezzo portal. The use of polygonal pilasters, the simple design of the frame of the gable, and the capitals decorated with water-leaves are features common to both portals. Unfortunately, the date of the Florentine portal is uncertain. Paatz hypothesised that the Florentine portal was built during the fourteenth-century renovation of the church, which was carried out in the course of the second third of the century.[26] More recently, Kreytenberg attributed the Madonna and Child originally in the tympanum of the portal of Santa Maria Maggiore to Zanobi di Bartolo, documented in Florence between 1366 and 1376, and dated the portal to ca. 1380 on the basis of its similarity with that of San Carlo.[27]

More solid dating evidence for the internal portal comes from the Annunciation group (Figs. 7, 8). It is likely that the statues were originally conceived for the portal because of its imposts, which were designed to support such carvings, and its similarities with the chapel of Ciuccio Tarlati (Fig. 12), which shows a similar Annunciation. Both figures of the Annunciation are by the same master, who does not appear to have been a follower of Giovanni d'Agostino. The Annunciation in the Tarlati chapel shows both the Virgin and the angel as emotional and communicative. The figures are characterised by a slim and elongated elegance, their movement is solved in a slight "hanchement," and the construction of their bodies and of the folds of their garments is conceived in the synthetic style of Giovanni, which makes his Annunciation completely different from that of the Aretine portal.

A work which is similar to the style of the angel of the Annunciation on the south portal is St. Luke with his symbol (Fig. 11), now in the Museo d'Arte Medievale e Moderna of Arezzo, which was originally placed in the lower niche of the south buttress of the facade of the duomo. St. Luke has been severely eroded, but the proportions of the figure, the shape of his face, and the pattern of his drapery are still recognisable, and all of them suggest that the work was executed by the same classicizing sculptor who carved the angel of the Annunciation of the south portal.

Vasari attributed St. Luke and the group of the Madonna *lactans* in the tympanum of the south side portal to Niccolò d'Arezzo. He also incorrectly gathered under the name of Niccolò d'Arezzo the work of another artist, the younger Niccolò di Pietro Lamberti, called Il Pela, from Florence, and recorded that this artist took part in the competition for the second door of the Florentine baptistery.[28] Adolfo Venturi did not believe that the Madonna *lactans* group was the work of Niccolò di Pietro Lamberti.[29] Procacci, after a careful reading of Ghiberti's *Commentari* and with the

[26] W. Paatz, *Die Kirchen von Florenz*, vol. 3 (Frankfurt a.M., 1952), 615–55, esp. 615, 617–19, 621, 625, 635, 636 n. 6. Paatz argued that an earlier model for the portal of Santa Maria Maggiore was the portal of the right nave of Santa Maria Novella, opened in the Chiostro dei Morti (ibid., 621). It shows, indeed, the use of a pair of plain, thin polygonal pilasters framing the doorway, which supports a heavy gable (see also A. Busignani and R. Bencini, *Le chiese di Firenze: Il quartiere di Santa Maria Novella* [Florence, 1979], 64).

[27] G. Kreytenberg, "La Madonna di Santa Maria Maggiore a Firenze," *Antichità viva* 20, no. 2 (1981), 16–20.

[28] G. Vasari, *Le vite*, ed. G. Milanesi, vol. 2 (Florence, 1878), 135–42.

[29] Venturi (*Storia* [as in note 10], vol. 4, 388) attributed the group in the tympanum to Agostino di Giovanni and his workshop. Subsequently, he considered the matter again and confirmed that two masters named Niccolò were active in Florence at the beginning of the fifteenth century. Both of them were mentioned in Ghiberti's *Com-*

help of newly-discovered archival records, managed to separate the Florentine Niccolò di Pietro Lamberti from the Aretine Niccolò di Luca Spinelli.[30] According to the archival records, the latter was the brother of Spinello Aretino and lived between 1350–52 and 1420–27. Procacci therefore confirmed Vasari's attribution of St. Luke and the Madonna *lactans* group to Niccolò di Luca Spinelli d'Arezzo on the basis of the Gothic features, which could fit the personality of an artist active in the second half of the fourteenth century. No certain work by Niccolò Spinelli is known, and the attribution of the Madonna *lactans* group and the St. Luke to the same artist becomes even less tenable once the association is made between the evangelist statue and the Annunciation on the portal.

The Aretine statutes of 1327 testify that the building of the facade was imminent or had already started at that time.[31] The niche for St. Luke was placed in the south side buttress of the facade, which, being an important supporting structure, must have been one of the first parts of the front to be built. The design of the niche for St. Luke, as reconstructed from the fragments in the Museo d'Arte Medievale e Moderno and old pre-demolition photographs, shows features similar to the internal frame of the south side portal. The use of round arches in a network of thin elongated shafts and frames suggests that the design was similar to the frame of the south portal. Old photographs show a second niche on top of St. Luke's. Its design, characterised by a thin gable frame supported by thin pilasters ending in a pair of pinnacles and enclosing a round arch, is directly related to that of the internal frame of the south portal.[32] All of these elements suggest a date for the internal frame of the south portal between 1327 and 1337, the period when the south pilaster of the facade with its niches was presumably built.

The structure of the internal portal and the style of the Annunciation suggest that they were executed in the same period as the external part of the portal. It is, however, difficult to establish whether the master or the workshop responsible for the Virtues and Vices and the decoration of the embrasures and the archivolts is the same hand responsible for the Annunciation group.[33] A comparison of the Annunciation and the reliefs of the allegorical cycle is problematic because of the differences in format and the bad condition of the sculptures in the external part of the portal. The sober decoration of the internal portal does not show any direct stylistic relationship with the external portal.

---

mentari and in a document of 1404 concerning the *fabbrica* of Santa Reparata as "Nicholaus de Aretio Aurifex" and "Nicholaus Pieri Lamberti" (A. Venturi, *Storia dell'arte italiana*, vol. 6, *La scultura del Quattrocento* [Turin, 1907], 2 n. 1). See also the Milanesi commentary on G. Vasari, *Le vite* (Florence, 1878), vol. 2, 139 nn. 2 and 3.

[30] U. Procacci, "Niccolò di Pietro Lamberti, detto Il Pela di Firenze e Niccolò di Luca Spinelli d'Arezzo," *Il Vasari* 4 (1928), fasc. 4, 300–16.

[31] "... ut dicta ecclesia clarius elucescat et prospectum habeat clariorem et citius compleatur ...," *Statuto di Arezzo, 1327*, ed. G. Marri Camerani (Florence, 1946), lib. II, ch. XLVIIII, p. 107. While this article was in press I found a new document which suggests that the lower part of the facade with the portals was at least partly built by 1336.

[32] See Salmi, "Cattedrale" (as in note 7), 383; id., "Duomo" (as in note 11), 260; id., "Architettura" (as in note 9), 90; Alinari no. 9382.

[33] An additional sculpture can be attributed to the master of the Annunciation. It is a statue of the enthroned Madonna with Child in the Museo Diocesiano of Cortona, from the church of Santa Margherita, Cortona. Kosegarten has correctly pointed to the Virgin with Child in the Museo dell'Opera del Duomo of Siena, originally in the frame of the rose window of the facade of the duomo, as the model for the Cortona Madonna (A. Kosegarten, "Einige sienesische Darstellungen der Muttergottes aus dem frühen Trecento," *Jahrbuch der Berliner Museen* 8 [1966], 96–118, esp. 98, 114). She dated the Madonna in the Museo Diocesiano not later than 1320, but a slightly later date within the 1320s would be acceptable.

The sculpture of the Aretine portal is evidence of the activity of a group of artists whose distinctive figurative culture is different from that of the Sienese masters who worked in Arezzo during the same period: Agnolo di Ventura, Agostino di Giovanni, and his son Giovanni. The quality of their work is considerably more refined than that of the rough followers of Giovanni Pisano who executed the series of Madonna statues originally placed on the city gates.[34] This gives a new perspective to the study of sculpture in fourteenth-century Arezzo. The archival records testify to an intense period of artistic activity in the city, linked to the building of family chapels in the cathedral, the Pieve, the churches of the mendicant orders, and certain hospitals. Several documents expressly mention the sculptural decoration of the family chapels. In other cases, the presence of rich furnishing is confirmed by the amount of the dowry of the pious foundations.[35] Unfortunately, almost all of these foundations were lost in the sixteenth- and seventeenth-century renovation of the religious buildings. The surviving architecture and sculpture of the south portal is, therefore, significant and important evidence for the intense artistic activity in fourteenth-century Arezzo.

[34] Agnolucci, "Arca-Altare" (as in note 10), 32–33; M. Armandi, "Le Madonne delle porte urbiche aretine," in *Mater Christi* (as in note 1), 17–21.

[35] S. K. Cohn, *The Cult of Remembrance and the Black Death: Six Renaissance Cities in Central Italy* (Baltimore, 1992), passim. I have undertaken extensive research, still in progress, in the Arezzo archives and in the Archivio di Stato di Firenze, in the course of which I have collected a large amount of documentation concerning patronage in Arezzo and the foundation of family chapels.

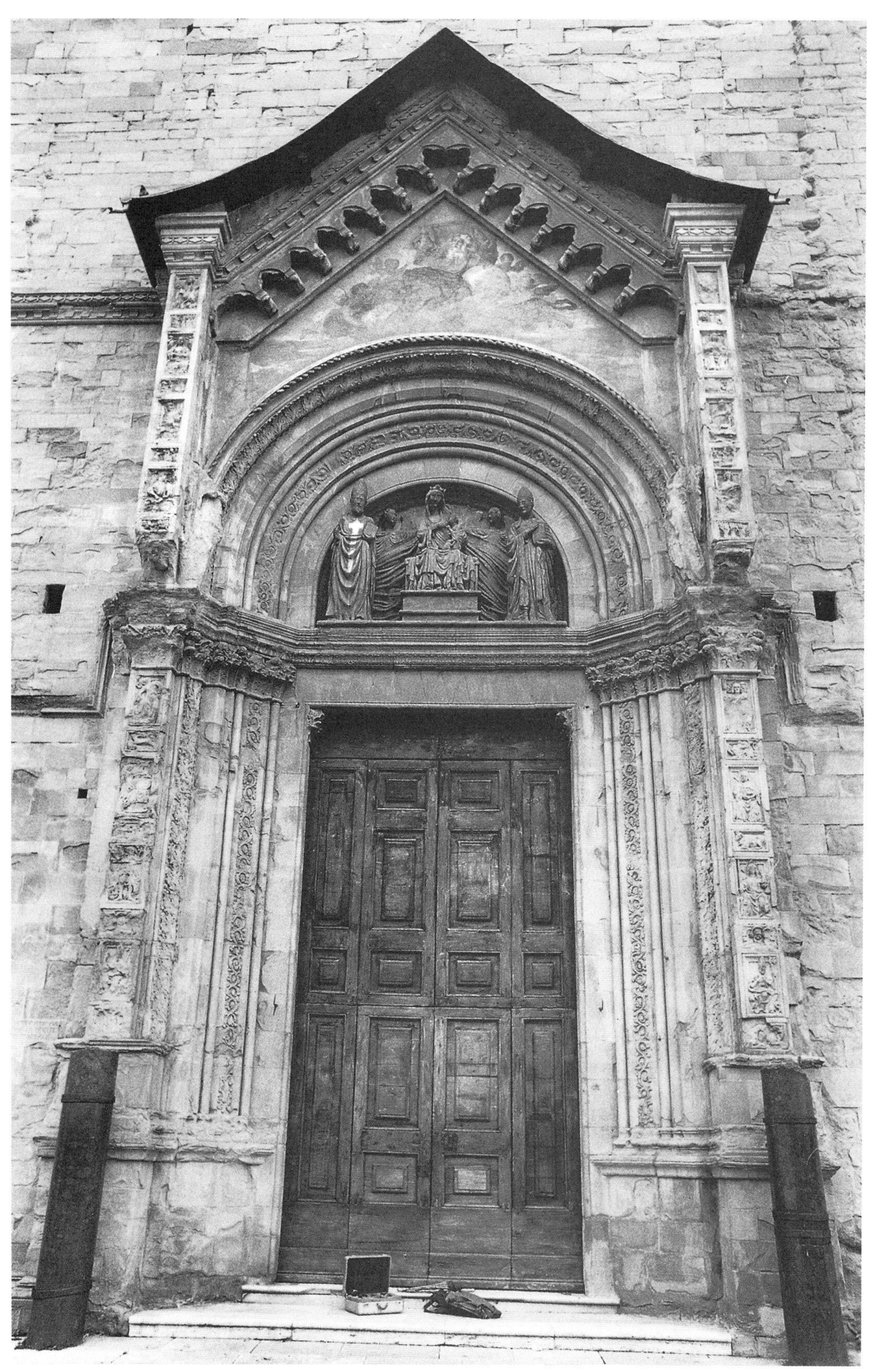

1. Arezzo, Cathedral, south side, portal

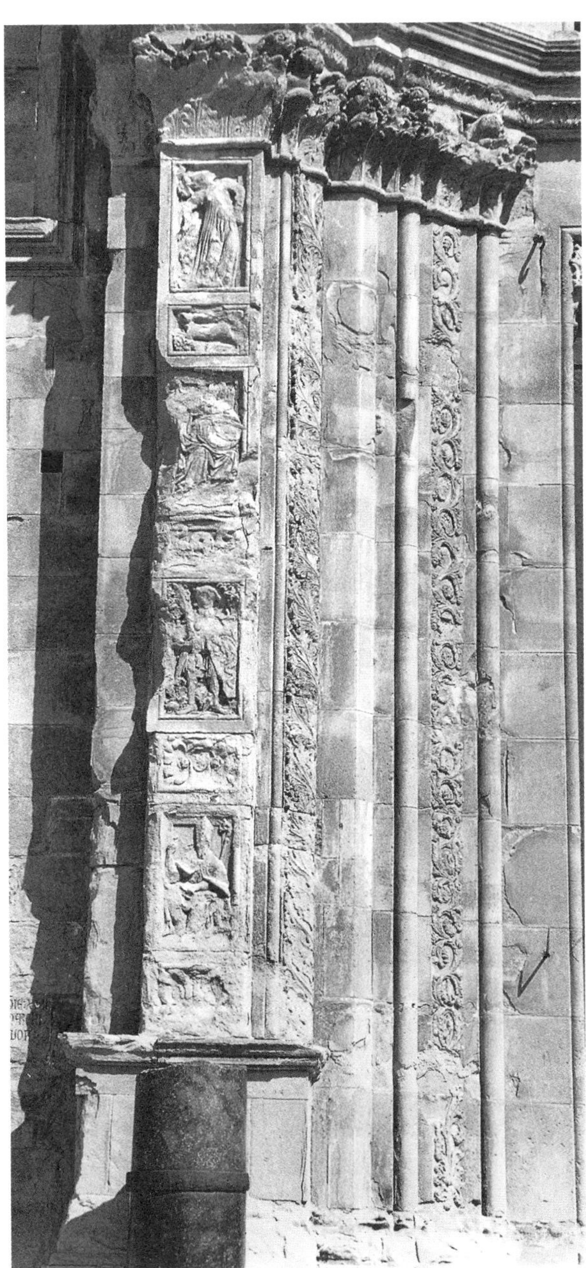

2. Arezzo, Cathedral, south side, portal, detail of the lower section of the left pilaster

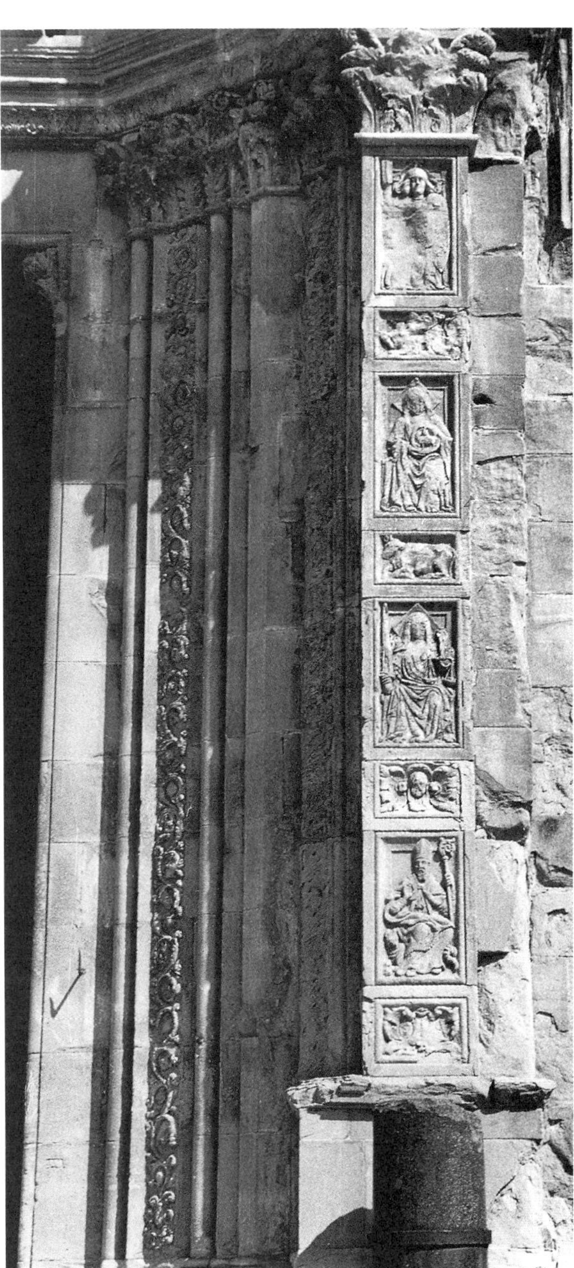

3. Arezzo, Cathedral, south side, portal, detail of the lower section of the right pilaster

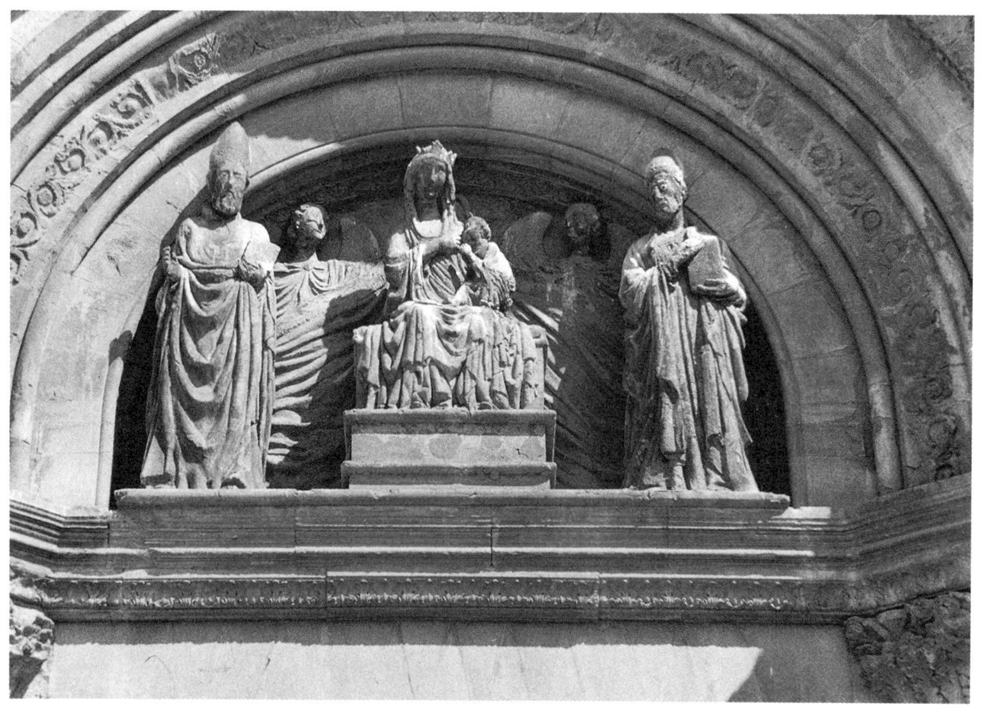

4. Arezzo, Cathedral, south side, portal, detail of the Madonna *lactans* group

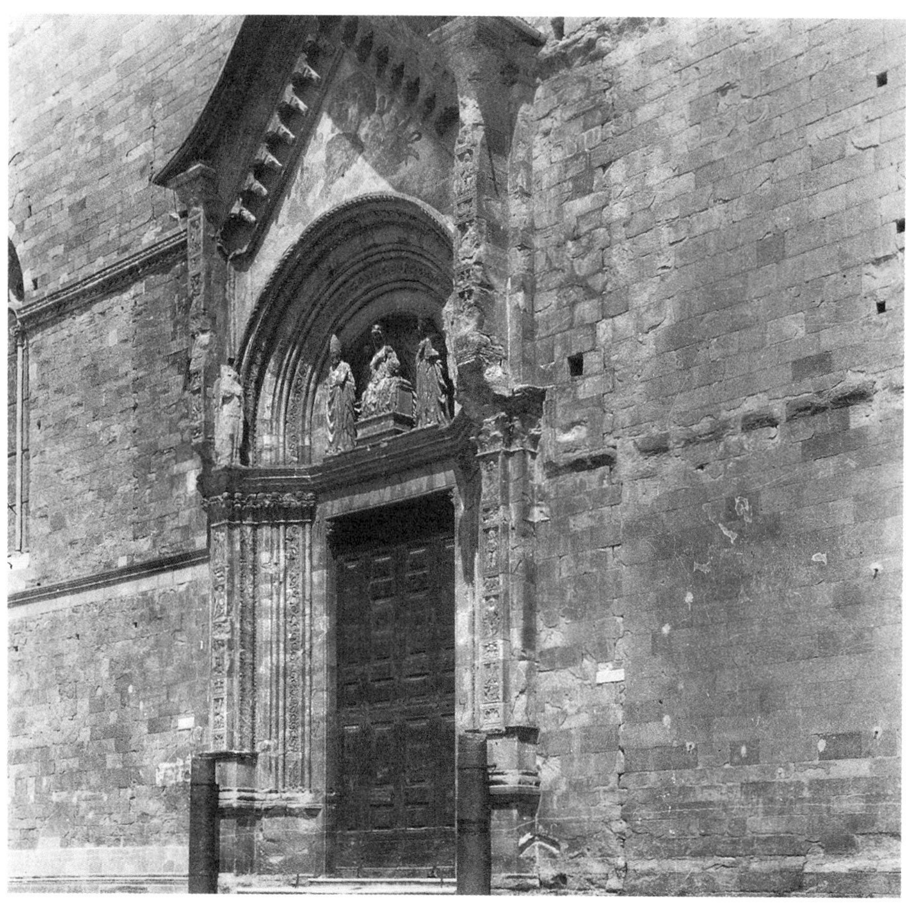

5. Arezzo, Cathedral, south side, portal, before restoration

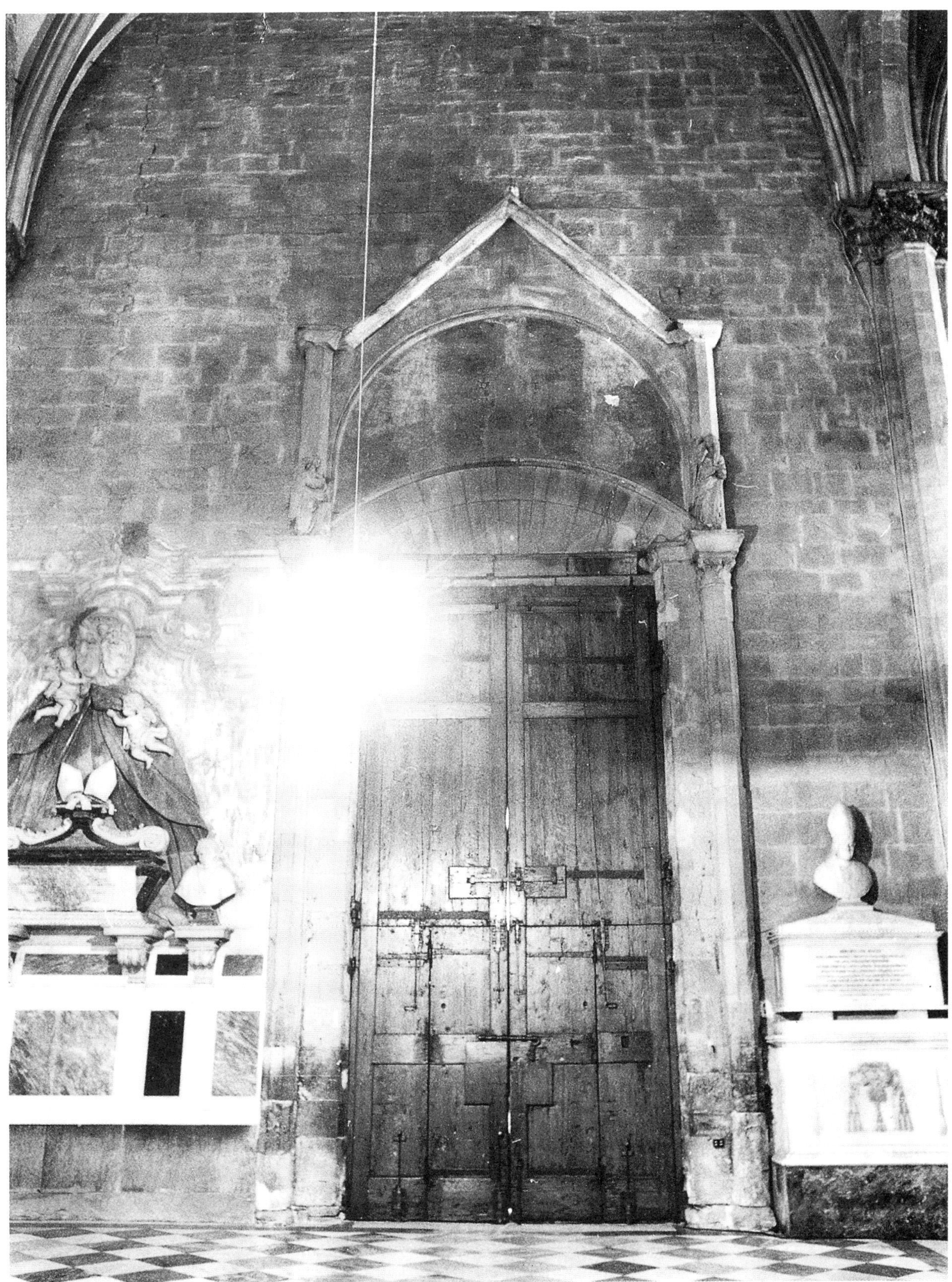

6. Arezzo, Cathedral, south side, portal, interior decoration

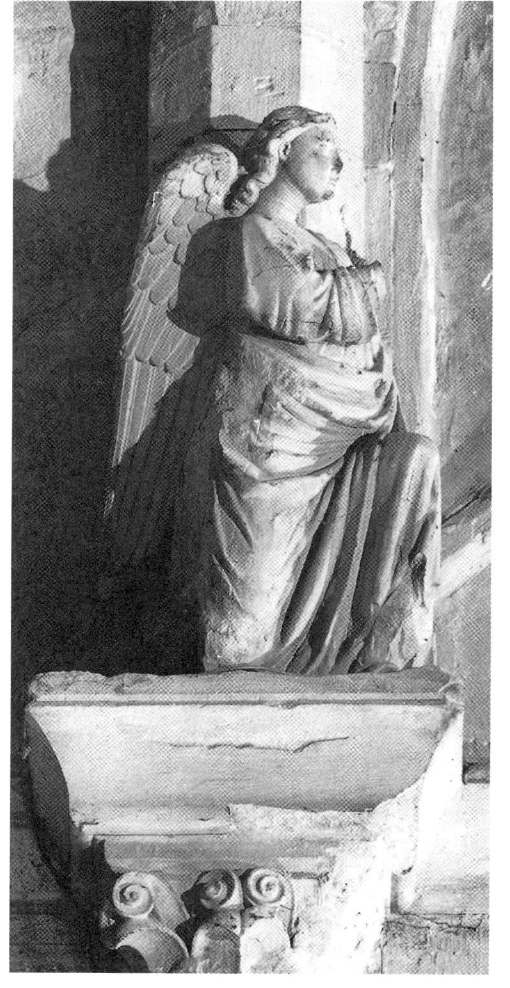

7. Arezzo, Cathedral, south side, portal, interior, angel of the Annunciation

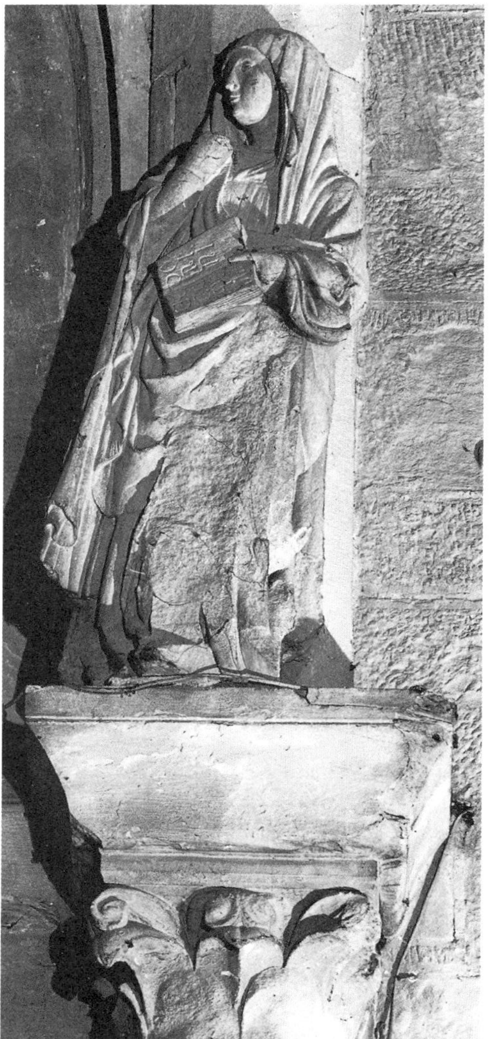

8. Arezzo, Cathedral, south side, portal, interior, Virgin of the Annunciation

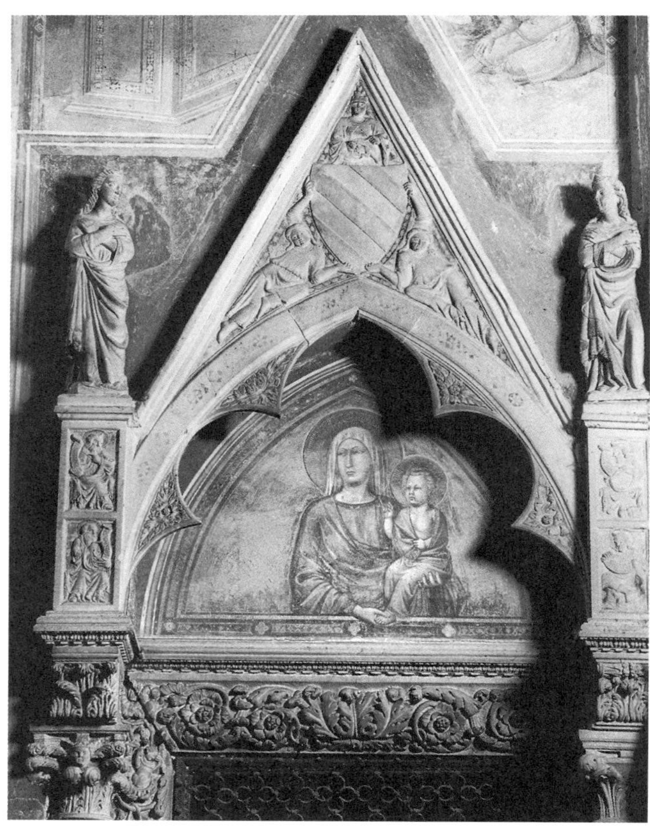

9. Florence, Santa Croce, Baroncelli monument, detail

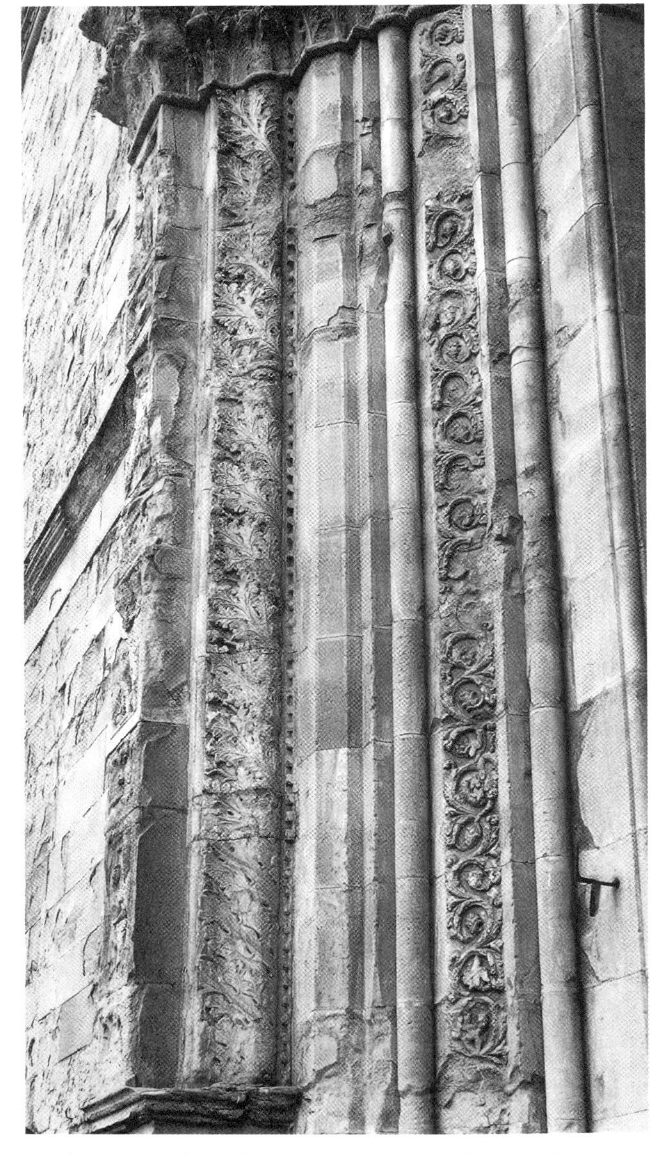

10. *Arezzo, Cathedral, south side, portal, detail of the decoration of the embrasure*

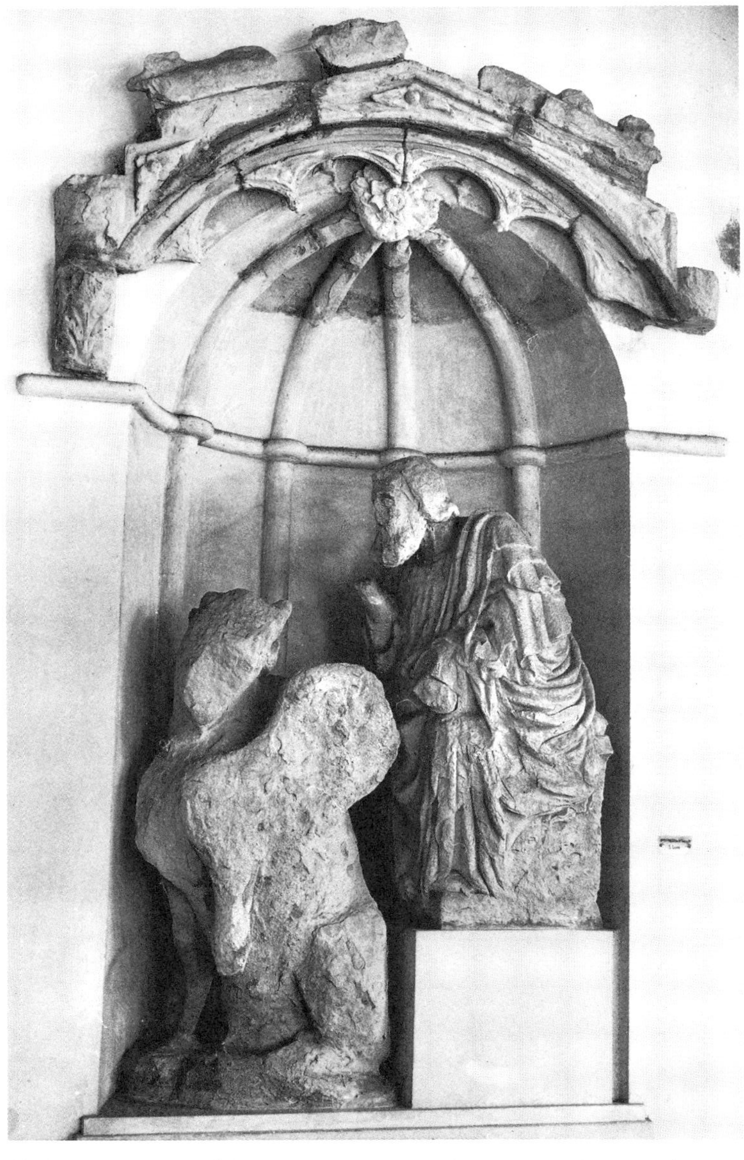

11. *Arezzo, Museo d'Arte Medievale e Moderna, St. Luke from the Gothic facade of the cathedral*

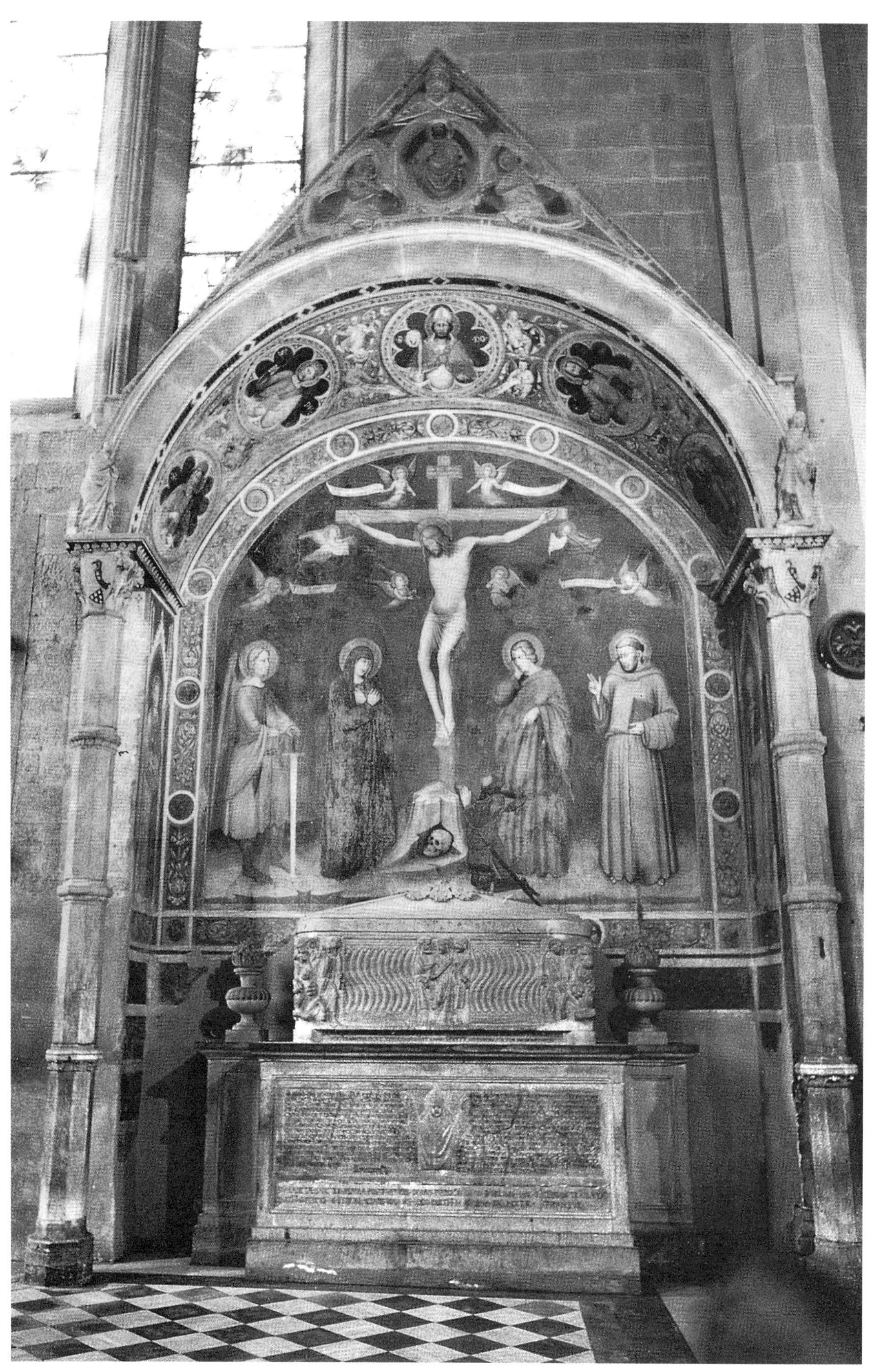

12. Arezzo, Cathedral, chapel of Ciuccio Tarlati

Daring Conflation? A Difficult Image in the Genesis Sequence of the Eton Roundels (Eton College, Ms. 177, f. 2r)*

·

AVRIL HENRY

THE SCENE in the central roundel of Windsor, Eton College, Ms. 177, f. 2r, has been tentatively identified as God with Cain (Fig. 1).[1] It is impossible to identify with certainty.[2] This paper suggests that ambiguity is the whole point of the image, and that it consciously conflates several scenes which might be expected in the position which the roundel holds in a sequence. If true, this would imply a remarkable level of visual literacy in certain thirteenth-century readers, and a use of conflation (a common enough phenomenon in itself) which is unusually complex and daring. On the other hand, it may also suggest that such a level of conflation is commoner than we think, particularly among images hitherto regarded as "unidentified."

The problematic roundel cannot depict anything very unusual; indeed, it should show something deeply familiar to its medieval readers, for it is part of a totally text-free opening. The first double-spread (Figs. 2a, 2b) presents the basic Genesis story which requires the Redemption outlined in the typological section that forms the rest of Eton Roundels and ends with the Coronation of the Bride/Virgin/Church/Soul (Fig. 3). Indeed, the manuscript as a whole is essentially a religious *picture* book: the roundels are followed by the work which occupies most of the book, an illustrated Apocalypse with brief Anglo-Norman text under each large illumination (Fig. 4). The manuscript as a whole thus begins with the material world's creation, and ends with its apocalyptic destruction followed by the vision of the New Jerusalem. Throughout Eton Ms. 177, the parts of which were apparently bound together from the outset, text is subordinate to image.

Yet the subject of the problem roundel resists identification. Its design is devoid of any distinctive attribute which would limit it to one scene. It is distinguished by the very absence of such

* This article is based on work carried out at the Index of Christian Art at the University of Utrecht with the unstinting assistance of its Curator, Drs. Dirk Jacob Jansen. I also thank the Director of the Princeton Index, Dr. Colum Hourihane, whose personal kindness and support, as well as his highly successful organisation of the conference "Iconography at the Index: Celebrating Eighty Years of the Index of Christian Art," it is my pleasure to acknowledge. Permission for re-publication of images from *The Eton Roundels* has been graciously granted by the Provost and Fellows of Eton College.

[1] *The Eton Roundels: Eton College Ms. 177: "Figurae Bibliorum,"* ed. A. Henry (Aldershot and Brookfield, Vermont, 1990), 107 (full-colour facsimile of the first work in Eton Ms. 177, with an introduction, transcription of the Latin, translation, commentary, notes, and bibliography).

[2] C. Chavannes-Mazel, *Quaerendo* 23.2 (1993), 120, an otherwise positive reviewer, objected, not without good reason, to the proposed identification, but confessed to being unable to suggest a plausible alternative. Dr. Chavannes-Mazel told me that she has a research student at work on the image: I await the outcome with interest.

attributes. If this is a deliberate refusal to accept the limitations of one scene, the roundel's ambiguous multiplicity may have been intended to promote prayerful contemplation.

The alternative to multiple conflation is that the roundel is the product of incompetence or artistic decline. It has been rightly observed that there was "development of iconographic types in the late twelfth and thirteenth centuries which are not highly individualized, and are so reduced that any can with little change stand for a wide variety of scenes; there is corresponding diminution of the meanings and hence of the importance of the individual scene."[3] I believe that in its context, the problematic Eton roundel shows precisely creative use of this reduced individualisation of scenes, and so paradoxically multiplies meanings.

To understand the possible scenes represented in the roundel, we need to consider various evidence: the patterns of narrative sequence on the first opening; possible links between the Genesis "narrative" and the typological sequence following it; the condensation of both the Genesis and the typological sequences; conflated imagery elsewhere in the roundels; the meaning of depicted gestures; and, lastly, external precedents for suggested readings. The evidence of the narrative on the Genesis opening will be treated first, by itself. The other evidence will be considered under each possible identification.

READING THE GENESIS OPENING

To identify the image, one needs to know whether the problematic roundel begins or ends the page. However, there may be more than one reading order,[4] for the reading order on the double-spread as a whole is not simple. Leaving the problematic roundel aside for the moment, the opening presents the familiar, essential Genesis story in logical form. The verso (Fig. 2a) holds the Creation. Similar sequences are commonplace, for example, in Lambeth Palace Library, Ms. 3, f. 6v: the initial I of *In principio* at the start of the Book of Genesis is composed of eight roundels, six for the days of Creation, and roundels at the top and bottom showing the Creator, his hands in the latter at rest on the edge of the roundel. The recto of the Eton Genesis opening (Fig. 2b) shows the Fall and its consequences.

The first page begins in the centre, with the creation of the world, but normal reading order of this page does *not* give us Genesis 1:1–2:25's:

> Day 1. Creation of heaven and earth, light
> Day 2. Separation of heaven and earth
> Day 3. Separation of land and water, creation of plants
> Day 4. Creation of stars, sun, and moon
> Day 5. Creation of animals (of air, water)
> Day 6. Creation of animals (of land) and man/woman
> Day 7. God's rest

---

[3] J. H. Plummer, "The Lothian Morgan Bible: A Study in English Illumination of the Early Thirteenth Century" (Diss., Columbia University, 1953; University Microfilms, Ann Arbor, Publication 6685), 81.

[4] Such multiple reading is common, for example, in

the contemporary works examined by Wolfgang Kemp, *The Narratives of Gothic Stained Glass*, trans. C. D. Saltzwedel (Cambridge Studies in New Art History and Criticism) (Cambridge, 1997).

The layout is not narrative but thematic: Adam and Eve are on God's dexter side, the animals on his less important side. The designer may similarly play with readers' expectations in the disputed image.

We cannot, without some explanation, read events on the recto in biblical order either. The biblical order is:

    a. The Fall (Gen. 3:6)
    b. Adam and Eve (clothed) labour (Gen. 3:17–21)
    c. The Expulsion (Gen. 3:24)
    d. Cain kills Abel (Gen. 4:8)

Leaving aside the controversial centre roundel for a moment, the verso, reading left to right, presents:

    a. The Fall
    b. The Expulsion
    c. Adam and Eve labour
    d. Cain kills Abel

Adam and Eve are naked in the Expulsion, although in the Bible they are clothed before they leave Paradise, but this particular disturbance of sequence is not unusual: the Expulsion often shows Adam and Eve shielding their nakedness with leaves.[5] The right-hand page offers us neither the biblical order nor events in the same order as those on the opposite page, which would end the right-hand page with Adam and Eve Labour, instead of Cain Kills Abel. The designer expects the reader to think, not merely to follow simple reading habits.[6] Conceivably, comparable demands are made on the interpreter of the roundel. For some possible identifications we need to read our roundel first on its page, and for others, last, so that it closes the Genesis sequence.

The disputed scene must by definition show something which an educated medieval reader would expect in a Genesis series, but the fact that such series vary widely both in their selection of scenes and in their degree of iconographic complexity is central to the argument, for it is that tradition which makes the adumbrated conflation possible.

Genesis with New Testament

The problematic roundel relates not only to Genesis but also to what follows in the manuscript: a highly condensed typological sequence beginning with the Nativity. A leap from Genesis to New

---

[5] This tradition may derive from the fact that it is not unreasonable to associate Eve's spinning, in Adam and Eve Labour, with the provision of clothes. L. Réau, *Iconographie de l'art chrétien*, vol. 2, pt. 1 (Paris, 1955), 90, lists examples of the Expulsion in which Adam and Eve are both clothed or naked, but the latter is the ubiquitous norm: examples include a capital at Clermont Ferrand and a relief in the outer porch of the north porch at Chartres Cathedral (A. Gardner, *Medieval Sculpture in France* [Cambridge, 1931], figs. 135, 252); see also Mu-

nich, Bayer. Staatsbibl., Clm. 835, f. 8v, illustrated in N. Morgan, *Early Gothic Manuscripts*, vol. 1, *1199–1250* (A Survey of Manuscripts Illuminated in the British Isles 4) (London and Oxford, 1982), fig. 76.

[6] This playing with expected reading sequence is not unusual. An interesting example is the Carew-Poyntz Book of Hours (Cambridge, Fitzwilliam Museum, Ms. 48) of about a hundred years later, in which the reading order of the elements forming upper and *bas-de-page* images is very varied.

Testament is common because, as Augustine says, "the whole narrative of Genesis, in the most minute details, is a prophecy of Christ and of the Church."[7] Both literal and typological functions are relevant here.

As shown in the edition, the Genesis opening and the typological openings together form seven thematically unified double-spreads:

VERSO	RECTO	THEME
1. Creation	Fall	Genesis
2. [blank]	Nativity	Jesus' childhood
3. Presentation	Baptism	Jesus and the Law
4. Carrying of the Cross	Crucifixion	The Cross
5. Resurrection	Harrowing of Hell	Conquest of death/hell
6. Ascension	Synagogue Unveiled	Holy Spirit
7. The Coronation of the Bride	[blank]	Vision of God

Like the other double-spreads, the first, containing the Genesis sequence, is a unit.[8] Its lack of caption is in contrast to the ten illuminated typological pages which follow it, where captioned roundels present selected events from, and prophecies of, the life of Christ and the Church. The Genesis opening, the typological sequence, and the illustrated Apocalypse all treat the battle with evil, and the founding of new eras. (The apocalyptic vision of the celestial city of the New Jerusalem may be peculiarly relevant to our reading of the problematic roundel.)

The roundels as a whole are highly condensed. Conflation is a means of condensation.[9] It is worth digressing to consider the supporting evidence for conflation in our problematic scene. The following examples are explained in detail in the edition, so a brief outline will suffice here. The multiple conflations in the Coronation of the Bride at the end of the Eton Roundels will be discussed below (p. 178). On the same folio, Abraham Tithes to Melchizedek includes the commoner Melchizedek Offers Bread and Wine. The caption of the Circumcision and its marginal reference to Exodus 4[:23–26] indicate the Circumcision of Moses, or, if the marginal reference was an error for Exodus 12:44–49, the Law of Circumcision. The roundel, however, shows a conventional Circumcision of Christ, mother and son nimbed, Mary distracting her son with her breast—an action attributed to the Virgin.[10] The caption thus recalls not only that the Old Law's rite of purification,

---

[7] *Contra Faustum* (CSEL 25, sect. 6, pt. 1) (Prague, 1891), 337–44; translated in "Reply to Faustus the Manichæan," *Writings in Connection with the Manichæan Heresy,* Book 12, trans. R. Stothert, vol. 5 of *The Works of Aurelius Augustine, Bishop of Hippo: A New Translation,* ed. M. Dods (Edinburgh, 1872), 209. Ruth Mellinkoff's work on this text ("Cain and the Jews," *Journal of Jewish Art* 6 [1979], 16–38) will be much cited below.

[8] The unity in double-spreads is particularly important in typological works designed for meditation: the manuscripts and printed versions of *Biblia Pauperum,* for example, are so designed (see *Biblia Pauperum: A Facsimile Edition [of the Forty-Page Blockbook],* ed. A. Henry [Aldershot and Ithaca, 1987], 4–8), and so are those in most versions of *Speculum Humanae Salvationis.*

[9] Well-known examples of visual conflation include the central scene on f. 3v, an entirely normal fusion the Presentation (of Jesus by Joseph), Simeon's Recognition of Christ, and the Purification of Mary (D. Shorr, "The Iconographic Development of the Presentation in the Temple," *ArtB* 28 [1946], 23–32). Ideas associated with victory, debt, repayment, sacrifice, purification, and recognition thus flow together in this traditional conflation (*Eton Roundels* [as in note 1], 112–13). Conflation of the complexity suggested in our problematic roundel is an extension of this tradition.

[10] See Nicholas Love, *The Mirrour of the Blessed Lyf of Jesu Christ: A Translation of the Latin Work Entitled "Meditationes Vitae Christi" Attributed to Cardinal Bonaventura, Made before the Year 1410 by Nicholas Love,* ed. L. F. Powell (Oxford, 1908), 53.

circumcision, is replaced by baptism,[11] but also that Christ's circumcision foreshadowed his own baptism, through the link provided by martyrdom conceived as a "baptism of blood." If this curious melding of Old and New Testament elements is not due to incompetence, it may be an adventurous conflation. The practice of using a New Testament scene as a "type" is not without parallel even in this manuscript: on f. 7r John the Baptist is a New Testament prophet, even if he is also the last prophet of the Old. These details are more likely to indicate sophistication than solipsism.

To return to the leap from Genesis to New Testament: a typical example is Paris, B.N.F. Lat. 15472, f. 8r, where the initial I to the Book of Genesis is comprised of seven small niches holding the days of Creation; the lowest shows the creation of Eve, while in a larger, bipartite unit below that, God is seated at rest on the left, with the Crucifixion on the right. (In context, the great butterfly or moth hovering nearby may suggest resurrection). Similarly, the initial letter of the Book of Genesis on London, B.L., Ms. Royal 1.D.1, f. 5r contains, reading from the top, four rectangular sections covering the days of Creation; under that three sections deal with the Fall and its consequences; at the bottom, one shows the Crucifixion (Fig. 5). The Genesis sequence in the initial letter of the Book of Genesis in the thirteenth-century Arras, Bibliothèque de la Ville, Ms. 561, f. 4v, is a wonderful example of the productive juxtaposition of Old and New Testament events. The capital contains eight roundels, each of five mini-roundels arranged as a quatrefoil with one in the centre, rather like the roundels on an Eton page. God is in the centre of all the roundels but the last: thirty-two Old Testament scenes are thus shown, reading from 9 o'clock clockwise, unless the central roundel is described first. The first four roundels include:

1. The Prohibition; the Fall; the Nakedness of Adam and Eve; the Expulsion
2. Adam and Eve Labour; an Angel Addresses Adam; Eve and Cain; Cain's Sacrifice
3. Cain Kills Abel; the Condemnation of Cain; unidentified (a bearded standing man raises his right hand towards a standing youth on his sinister side: ? Lamech); Noah Receives God's Instructions from an Angel.
4. Noah's Nakedness; Noah Builds the Ark; the Ark; Noah Digs Vines

(The last four roundels contain parts of the stories of Abraham, Jacob, and Joseph.) There are also historiated semicircles in the spandrels between roundels, containing not demi-figures as in Eton Ms. 177, but full figures holding empty scrolls. In addition, twenty-four further roundels showing New Testament scenes fill the spaces between the two columns on the page.[12]

Possible Identifications

Such is the tradition of linking a Genesis sequence to the New Testament, the variety of Genesis sequences, and the fluidity of medieval ways of reading a page, that nine subjects might be shown in our roundel:

[11] *Eton Roundels* (as in note 1), 59–62 and 19, n. 30.

[12] The image deserves an illustration, but unfortunately it has proved impossible to obtain a photograph of publishable quality, as the manuscript is on extended tour in France.

1. God Addressing Adam: the Prohibition
2. God Addressing Adam as Man on the Seventh Day
3. God Rests on the Seventh Day
4. Father and Son Discuss the Incarnation
5. Trinity and the Right Hand of the Father (Ps. 109)
6. The King Triumphs over His Enemies (Ps. 109)
7. The Condemnation of Cain
8. God Instructs Noah (Gen. 6)
9. God's Covenant with Noah (Gen. 8:21–11:17)

Each is partly suggested and partly contradicted by the roundel, in its resistance to single identification. For this very reason, art offers no exact analogue, but a plethora of near-analogues, each relevant at that point in the work as a whole.

If the roundel *starts* the page and the Fall story, there are only three scenes which it can hold: the Prohibition, God Addressing Adam as Man on the Seventh Day, God Rests on the Seventh Day.

1. The Prohibition

One's natural inclination is to read the central roundel first, and so to expect the Prohibition—God forbidding any tampering with the apple tree seen at the top left—as M. R. James did.[13] But the roundel cannot simply hold the Prohibition. First, the figure in the central roundel (hereafter referred to as X) is unlikely to be Adam under edict, for three reasons. X is bearded, whereas Adam is beardless elsewhere on the opening (but consistency in such details is not always to be found in narrative illumination). Second, Adam in the Prohibition normally stands (see the Bible of Robert de Bello [Fig. 11], the first half of the first roundel in the horizontal member). More importantly, Adam was, of course, naked before the Fall, and X is clothed. This is highly unlikely to be the result of designer error on a page where the clothing of Adam and Eve clearly bears moral significance. Nevertheless, the natural inclination to read the central roundel first, as on the opposite page, does momentarily bring the Prohibition to mind. That is very different from *identifying* the scene as the Prohibition.

2. God Addressing Adam as Man

One would expect X's clothed state to rule out the scene's being God and Adam. In fact, there is some rare precedent for Adam being shown clothed, *as he represents Man,* on the Seventh Day. The frontispiece of the early twelfth-century Verdun, B.M., Ms. 1, f. Jr, is a Creation. Its central wheel shape is divided into parts representing six days, the sixth being at the top, where Adam is a naked demi-figure. The centre is reserved for the seventh day, where God sits on his throne, while to the right, on the step, kneels Adam as Man, clothed and stretching up his hands in prayer. Adam is unusually small compared with God, who puts his left arm round Adam's shoulder and blesses him with his right hand.[14]

---

[13] M. R. James, *A Descriptive Catalogue of the Manuscripts in the Library of Eton College* (Cambridge, 1895), 95.

[14] A. Heiman, "The Six Days of Creation in a Twelfth-Century Manuscript," *JWarb* 1 (1937), 270.

The body language and gestures in the problematic Eton roundel are, however, very different. With his dexter hand the Father makes "le geste de l'enseignement et de l'ordre."[15] A gesture of command towards Adam as Man is not the same as a gesture of protection, but might be appropriate.

There are four objections to identifying the scene as God Addressing Adam as Man. First, the scene is rare; it would not be an *expected* part of a Genesis sequence. Second, indicators vital to recognition of the subject, such as Adam's small size and God's protective gesture to him, are absent. Third, the harmony between creator and creature implicit in God Addressing Adam as Man is barely appropriate on a page devoted to unpleasant consequences of the Fall. Fourth, the gesture of the Father's sinister hand is inappropriate. It makes a forceful and unusual gesture—the open hand lifted, *thumb outward*, to shoulder level: a gesture not found elsewhere in this manuscript, and rare anywhere. Garnier illustrates it by only one illumination, where it signifies "opposition, négation, refus, abandon."[16]

3. God Rests on the Seventh Day

The design of our roundel is in some ways close to that of a Trinity often associated with pictorial Genesis cycles in contemporary English and French Bibles. One particularly relevant example is in the contemporary English Bible of Robert de Bello, London, B.L., Ms. Burney 3 (Fig. 11), where the initial L of *Liber* at the start of the Book of Genesis takes us down through seven large, overlapping roundels containing the six days of Creation (the first including the Fall of the Angels). This time, God's rest on the seventh day is represented by a Trinity, Father and Son seated side-by-side with the dove between them. The horizontal member of the L is then filled by six roundels showing the Prohibition, the Fall, God Rebukes Adam, the Expulsion, Adam and Eve Labour, Noah's Ark, the Tower of Babel, the Journey of Abraham and Isaac, and the Sacrifice of Isaac. The junction of the Creation story and that of the Fall and its consequences is thus marked by the Trinity, and so it might be in Ms. 177, our problematic roundel briefly recalling God resting on the seventh day.

But there is no dove in our roundel. There might be two explanations for this. First, dove notwithstanding, de Bello's Bible represents the plural (not necessarily triple) deity of Genesis 1:2: "Faciamus hominem ad imaginem et similitudinem nostram," Genesis 3:22: "Ecce Adam quasi unus ex nobis," and John 1:1: "In principio erat Verbum, et verbum erat apud Deum . . . ."[17] Second, the dove might be "taken as read." That possibility will be discussed under the next heading.

REMAINING INTERPRETATIONS

Just as we cannot use the left-hand page's sequence of minor roundels as a guide to reading those on the right-hand page, neither can we use the priority of the left-hand central roundel on its page

---

[15] F. Garnier, *Le Langage de l'image au moyen âge: Signification et symbolique*, 2 vols. (Paris, 1982), vol. 1, 165: "Dieu, le pape, l'évêque ou le maître font souvent le geste de l'enseignement et de l'ordre avec deux doigts au lieu d'un."

[16] Garnier, *Langage de l'image* (as in note 15), vol. 1, 173. In view of the suggestion below that our roundel might show the Condemnation of Cain, it is a curious coincidence that Garnier's sole example of this gesture shows Cain, both his hands making this gesture as he rejects God's accusation: "par cette position, peu naturelle, il manifeste qu'il ne veu pas reconnaître sa culpabilité et rejette l'accusation divine. Présenter le dos de la main, c'est refuser, repousser" (Garnier, vol. 1, 179–80, fig. G [144]).

[17] J. Zahlten, *Creatio Mundi: Darstellungen der Sechs Schöpfungstage und naturwissenschaftliches Weltbild im Mittelalter* (Stuttgarter Beiträge zur Geschichte und Politik 13) (Stuttgart, 1969), 6.

as an argument for the priority of the right-hand central roundel on its page. If, instead of beginning the Genesis sequence, our roundel ends it, the scene in question might be any of the following: Father and Son Discuss the Incarnation, the Right Hand of the Father, the King Triumphs over His Enemies, the Condemnation of Cain, God Instructs Noah, or God's Covenant with Noah. Each makes considerable sense in the sequence as a whole, and can be partly defended in terms of the roundel's design. All would normally contain identifying elements which are in fact absent. These six remaining possible subjects will be considered in turn.

4. Father and Son Discuss the Incarnation

A scene showing the persons of the Trinity discussing the imminent Incarnation would be highly appropriate, for the Nativity is overleaf. One recalls the way in which, in "The Parliament of Heaven" play, discussion between all three divine persons (and their personified attributes, the Four Daughters of God) is immediately followed by the Annunciation.[18] Similar, too, is the wonderful moment in *Piers Plowman* where Piers, at that stage embodying mankind's recognition of human need of Christ, attacks the devil (who is stealing the tree's soul-fruit) by hurling the Second Person, one of the Trinity of three props supporting the Tree of Charity—and at once Christ is conceived:

> And Piers, for pure tene, that a pil he laughte,
> And hitte after hym, happe how it myghte,
> *Filius* by the Faderes wille and frenesse of *Spiritus Sancti*,
> To go robbe that rageman and reve the fruyt fro hym.
> And thanne spak *Spiritus Sanctus* in Gabrielis mouthe
> To a maide that highte Marie . . . .[19]

Unfortunately, I have found no direct pictorial, as opposed to dramatic and literary precedent for the Father and Son Discuss the Incarnation. Visual recognition of it could hardly have been relied upon in the medieval reader. In addition, the Holy Spirit is by definition part of such divine discussion, he being, to put it mildly, essential to the Incarnation.

However, we might be meant to "read in" the dove. There are precedents for the dove being absent from our problematic roundel because it had, as it were, left to implement the Incarnation implied in the Nativity overleaf. In Psalm 109 in Oxford, Magdalen College Library, Ms. 100, f. 134r, the dove is on its way from Father and Son, not to the Incarnation but to Pentecost. The dove occupies a wavy area indicating the heavens, and is relevant to both scenes, the Trinity in the upper section and the Pentecost below. It hovers between the two worlds, and two conventions. This leaves the two seated male figures of the Trinity readable as the Right Hand of the Father.

---

[18] The scene, with all three persons present as one would expect, is familiar in late medieval English drama (*The N-Town Play: Cotton Ms. Vespasian D. 8*, ed. S. Spector, vol. 1 [EETS, SS 11] [Oxford, 1991], 111–18). See also *The Mary Play from the N. Town Manuscript*, ed. P. Meredith (London, 1987), 72–73.

[19] William Langland, *The Vision of Piers Plowman: A Critical Edition of the B-Text Based on Trinity College Cambridge Ms. B.15.17*, ed. A. V. C. Schmidt (London, 1995), XVI.86–91.

5. *Trinity, the Right Hand of the Father, and the Worcester Connection*

The Right Hand of the Father is the only one of the nine possible subjects that normally contains two male figures seated side by side. The scene is extremely common by the thirteenth century, though versions of it occur as early as the ninth. It is usually associated with Psalm 109:1: "The Lord said to my Lord: Sit thou at my right hand until I make thy enemies thy footstool."[20] The image known as the Right Hand of the Father is technically different from that of the Trinity, in which the dove of the Spirit is suspended between Father and Son; but because of the possibility that we are to "read in" a dove, we need to recall the standard Trinity, which is the commonest image in thirteenth-century historiated initials of Psalm 109.

TRINITY: The norm shows Father and Son seated, both bearded (as the Father and X are in our roundel), the dove descending, all three persons, or at least Father and Son, commonly cross-nimbed (Figs. 6–8).[21] Sometimes the Son is still standing, accepting the Father's invitation to be seated at his right hand (Fig. 19).[22]

The dove is sometimes such a small part of the design that it is easy to miss, as in London, B.L., Ms. Harley 2839-40, f. 310v (Fig. 9). Sometimes the dove "separated out" in a different way, being contained by an element which visually separates it from Father and Son—paradoxically, this is often a device intended to represent the unity of the Trinity, the dual procession of the Spirit from Father and Son. For example, the initial D to Psalm 109 in the late twelfth-century B.L., Ms. Royal 2.A.XXII, f. 132r (Fig. 10) shows the dove in a kind of mandorla formed by two overlapping circles round Father and Son. In the thirteenth-century Brussels, B.R., Ms. 9961-2, f. 74r, the dove is in the spandrel between the two figures. These forms make it easier to regard the dove as a separable element.

THE RIGHT HAND OF THE FATHER: Indeed, the absence of a dove from what is otherwise a Trinity identifies the scene formally known as the Right Hand of the Father, the closest visual analogue to the design in the problematic roundel (Figs. 13–17).[23] This identification of the subject is attractive in the context of the page. In some examples of the Trinity, both figures hold books (Fig. 9), and sometimes the Son's book is inscribed "Ego sum bonus pastor novus" (I am the new Good Shepherd), so that he is presented as an Abel figure.[24] There is no book in our roundel, but this connotation of the scene would be appropriate after the death of the father in Cain Kills Abel in the bottom right-hand roundel (Fig. 2b).

<hr>

[20] "Dixit Dominus Domino meo: Sede a dextris meis, donec ponam inimicos tuos scabellum pedum tuorum." The popularity of the quotation is partly due to its being quoted in Mt. 12:44, Luke 20:43, Acts 2:35, and Heb. 1:13.

[21] Further such examples of the Right Hand of the Father associated with Psalm 109 are in the following thirteenth-century manuscripts: New York, Morgan Lib., Ms. M. 283, f. 126r; Ms. M. 440, f. 106r; Ms. G. 42, f. 176r; Oxford, Bodl., Ms. Laud. Lat. 114, f. 148r; and Baltimore, Walters Art Gallery, Ms. W.115, Psalterium Plenum, French, ca. 1318, f. 153r. Sometimes Father and Son are both unbearded, as in the thirteenth-century Arles Psalter, Bordeaux, B.M., Ms. 7, f. 183r.

[22] This posture also occurs in the Right Hand of the Father associated with Psalm 109 in an English Psalter and Sarum Hours, ca. 1300, f. 101r (once Christie's, 23–24 October 1974, Lot 1477; this is now in a private collection in London).

[23] Further examples of this form of the Right Hand of the Father associated with Psalm 109 are in London, B.L., Ms. Lansdown 383, early twelfth century, f. 108r; Oxford, Bodl., Ms. Douce 293, f. 100v; and Oxford, Ms. Auct. D. 2. 8, f. 241r.

[24] R. Calkins, *Illuminated Books of the Middle Ages* (London, 1983), 220 and pl. 123.

Appropriate also is the notion of reclamation inherent in this event; in the initial D of Psalm 109 in the Amesbury Psalter (Oxford, All Souls', Ms. 6, f. 126r) this is made explicit: the Father's seizing of the Son's wrist indicates the latter's being brought back to his rightful place (Christ is often depicted using the same gesture in pulling Adam out of hellmouth).[25]

Interpretation of the Father and Son as the Right Hand of the Father is also attractive in terms of the parallel this would create between this roundel, at the end of the Old Testament sequence, and the central roundel of the last page of the New Testament typological sequence, the Coronation of the Bride (Fig. 3). In both, the person honoured is seated at God's right hand. This is why both the Right Hand of the Father and the Coronation of Ecclesia (subsumed in the Coronation of the Bride) are so often found in the historiated first initials of Psalm 109 (Figs. 19, 20, 21).[26]

THE WORCESTER CONNECTION: It is just possible that the scenes in these two roundels—one ending the Genesis and one the typological sequence—might once have been physically juxtaposed. If there is a link from our roundel to the Coronation of the Bride, the link may reflect Ms. 177's lost source—or analogue, since no direct link can be proved, and it is likely that a pattern-book was involved. M. R. James found thirteenth-century captions scribbled on the flyleaf of a twelfth-century Worcester Cathedral manuscript.[27] The captions, closely echoed by those in the roundels' ten typological pages, are thought to be those of images once running round the decagonal Norman chapter house of Worcester Cathedral, remodelled in the thirteenth century. Of course, if a Genesis sequence in that chapter house had, like that in our book, been without captions, the manuscript record found by James would bear no trace of it. However, if the Genesis sequence was at Worcester, its ten roundels might have been distributed round the ten bays, one over or under each of the ten typological "pages." Interesting juxtapositions would result. The order of the Creation sequence is debatable, but what matters here is the tenth juxtaposition that would result: the problematic roundel and the Coronation of the Bride/Virgin/Church/Soul would have been together:[28]

1. Creation: world	Nativity (a re-creation)
2. Creation: birds (seeking heaven)	Presentation (to God)
3. Creation: land animals	Baptism
4. Creation: Adam	Carrying of the Cross
5. Creation: Eve from Adam's side	Crucifixion (blood from side)
6. The Fall (death let loose)	Resurrection (death conquered)
7. The Expulsion (banishment)	Harrowing of Hell (release)
8. Adam and Eve Labour (on earth)	Ascension (to heaven)
9. Cain Kills Abel (Jews kill Christ)	Synagogue Unveiled (Jews enlightened)
10. X Seated by God the Father	Coronation of the Bride (enthronements)

[25] Garnier, *Langage de l'image* (as in note 15), vol. 1, 199, 201: the appropriate meaning here is "protection."

[26] Calkins, *Illuminated Books* (as in note 24), 220, who also mentions the Last Judgment, with the Blessed on God's right, as a subject found in these initials.

[27] M. R. James, "On Two Series of Paintings Formerly at Worcester Priory, I," *Proceedings of the Cambridge Anti-*

quarian Society 10, n.s. 4 (1898–1904), 99–110.

[28] *Eton Roundels* (as in note 1), 31–51 for details. The edition points out that one aspect of the manuscript suggests that the Genesis sequence may have been an early afterthought by the roundels' designer or patron: the first bifolium is separate from the following six-leaf quire. This afterthought is not, of course, incompatible with the

The Trinity and the Coronation of the Bride are in fact juxtaposed in the historiated capital to Psalm 109 in London, B.L., Ms. Add. 54179, f. 110r (Fig. 19). More commonly, the Coronation of the Bride alone is found (Fig. 20);[29] sometimes the bride is unambiguously Ecclesia, identified by being dressed exactly like Christ to signify their mystical marriage, or by a gloss, or by her carrying a model church.[30]

On Eton Roundels f. 7v (Fig. 3), the three Old Testament types of the Coronation of the Bride show that the Coronation is conventionally conflated with the Assumption, the Church as Bride of Christ, the Coronation of the Soul, and, more adventurously, with the Chariot of Aminadab (the bride as Synagogue, with connotations which will be relevant in the section below devoted to the Condemnation of Cain). The triumphant or reconciled bride is thus Virgin, Church, Soul, and Synagogue: a fitting parallel to the Son's enthronement in the Right Hand of the Father.

There are other precedents, too, for witty echoes of the Right Hand of the Father composition. In the fourteenth-century Breviary of Charles V (Paris, B.N.F., Ms. Lat. 1052, f. 261r), the initial of Psalm 109 contains King Charles V Acknowledged by the Father (Fig. 18): the kneeling king on the Father's right indicates the king's view of the importance of his position.[31]

There are, however, serious objections to interpreting the roundel as the Right Hand of the Father. (They apply also to the Father and Son Discuss the Incarnation, if that is not already discounted for being without exact precedent in art.) First, X is unnimbed, while the Father has a crossed nimbus.[32] There are precedents for both Father and Son having plain nimbuses (Figs. 14, 16); for both being nimbed, only the Son having a crossed nimbus;[33] and for both having crossed nimbuses, which is the norm, but it is almost inconceivable that the Father should be shown nimbed while the Son is not.

Second, typical thirteenth-century representations of the Persons of the Trinity manifest the persons' equality (which is why Father and Son are so often almost identical),[34] yet in our roundel various postural devices suggest subordination of X to the Father. Some Trinities, such as that in the Lothian Morgan Bible, follow a different theology and do show a subordinate Son, but no humiliation is implied: the Father has precedence as *tota substantia* while the Son is subordinated as *derivatio*, and even in the Lothian Morgan image, Father and Son are both cross-nimbed.[35] How-

---

Genesis sequence's pre-existence at Worcester and in a pattern-book which was the common source of Worcester and Eton 177. However, if the Genesis sequence is a contemporary afterthought, it is hard to reconcile the consciousness of content which that implies with careless production of the roundel.

[29] For further examples of the Coronation of the Bride associated with Psalm 109, see Archief Grootseminarie Brugge, Ms. 55/171, second half of thirteenth century, f. 110v; Dublin, Chester Beatty Library, Ms. 61, late thirteenth century, f. 156v; London, B.L., Ms. Lansdown 431, f. 85r.

[30] She is dressed like Christ in the Coronation of the Bride associated with Psalm 109 in Cambridge, St. John's College, Ms. D. 6, Hours-Psalter, thirteenth century, f. 132r, and she holds a model church in Imola, Biblioteca Comunale di Imola, Ms. 100, thirteenth century, f. 132v.

[31] Calkins, *Illuminated Books* (as in note 24), 230, 234.

[32] The Father often has a crossed nimbus even when he appears alone: "Gottvater mit Kreuznimbus," J. Schmidt, *Religion und Kunst II: Der Kreuznimbus im Christusbild. Eine kunstgeschichtliche Betrachtung trinitarische Theologie um Gottesbild und Herrschaftsglaube* (Denken und Handeln 10) (Bochum, 1989), figs. 10, 12, 13, 23, 27, 28.

[33] Psalm 109: Cambridge, Trinity College, Ms. R. 17.1, f. 199v, thirteenth century.

[34] "Les personnes de la Trinité, le roi appelé à siéger à la droite de Dieu, le pape et l'empereur, sont assis sur un même trône ou banc pour marquer des égalités et des rapprochements de nature ou de dignité" (Garnier, *Langage de l'image* [as in note 15], vol. 1, 87).

[35] New York, Morgan Lib., Ms. M. 791, Lothian Morgan Bible, ca. 1215–20, f. 4v, Trinity and Creation. J. H. Plummer, "The Lothian Morgan Bible: A Study in English Illumination of the Early Thirteenth Century" (Ph.D. Diss.,

ever, X is lower than the Father; X is in three-quarter view, while the Father is drawn parallel with the picture plane, so taking precedence;[36] X is partly out of frame; and X's foot seems to be trodden on by the Father, a gesture which "traduit une domination complète, la victoire sur un ennemi, l'écrasement du mal"—a meaning based on Psalm 109:1, so that we seem to have Christ made a footstool instead of his enemies.[37] X and the Father are separated by a stylised tree, which, since space is at a premium, is certainly not a space-filler, but represents a deliberate separation of figures by a vertical object to signal their difference;[38] indeed, the Father is *framed* between trees which create, as it were, an exclusion zone. (The convention is perhaps most familiar in Annunciation compositions, where Gabriel and the Virgin are separated by a lily, a column, a corridor, or other architectural feature, the separating feature often being significantly breached by the scroll bearing the angel's greeting.)

Third, the event depicted in the Right Hand of the Father is not in the Book of Genesis, and although the similar Trinity is found at the end of Genesis sequences, as we have seen, I have not found a Right Hand of the Father in that position. Finally, the Father's gestures are not easy to reconcile with the Right Hand of the Father. The Father's sinister hand's gesture of *refus* might, perhaps, refer to the Old Law, about to be replaced by the New, but his dexter hand's gesture of command is inappropriate to agreement that the Son be incarnate, or to enthronement of the Son as an equal.

6. The King Triumphs over His Enemies (Psalm 109)

This is relevant because X's foot seems to be trodden on by the Father, recalling Psalm 109's enemies made a footstool (see note 20), and because other aspects of the design suggest X's subjection. Indeed the Right Hand of the Father is often associated with the King Triumphs over His Enemies. Sometimes the "enemies" are underfoot, as in Oxford, Bodl., Laud. Lat. 114, f. 148r, or Oxford, Bodl., Douce 293, f. 100v. The enemy may also be in a separate scene: in the Winchester Bible, variants of the same composition illustrate parallel versions of Psalm 109 (Fig. 12). The roundel on the left illustrates "sede a dextris meis" by a conventional Trinity. The roundel on the right illustrates the next clause, "ponam inimicos tuos scabellum pedum tuorum": the bearded king on the right grasps the wrist of the unbearded king on the left, the gesture here indicating capture or constraint.[39] The late twelfth- or early thirteenth-century London, B.L., Ms. Harley 5102, f. 104r, illustrates both scenes, too: the dove is in a roundel held by Father and Son half way between themselves and the King Triumphs over His Enemies below. Perhaps both subjects are also echoed in our roundel. They would lead well from Fall to Incarnation.

The main difficulty is that Eton 177 is not Psalm 109: the reader has to recognise first the Right Hand of the Father and then its corollary, the King Triumphs over His Enemies.

Columbia University, 1953; University Microfilms, Ann Arbor, Publication 6685), 55. Plummer describes the Trinity on the Bible's famous frontispiece as showing this subordination in direct contrast to much of twelfth-century speculation on the Son as *aequalitas*.

[36] Garnier, *Langage de l'image* (as in note 15), vol. 1, 124, n. 1.

[37] Ibid., vol. 1, 232–33.

[38] Ibid., vol. 1, 102–3.

[39] Ibid., vol. 1, 199, 203.

7. The Condemnation of Cain

If, on the other hand, the scene is the Condemnation of Cain, all the signs of X's subjugation to the Father make sense, the absence of the dove is explained, and *le refus* clearly refers to God's rejection of Cain. X's dexter hand makes the "open hand turned towards outside, arm bent" gesture which according to Garnier indicates acceptance, agreement, or attention.[40] X's sinister hand is closed on his lap, and it is so drawn that his arms appear crossed, both positions which may, but need not, indicate duplicity.[41]

The Genesis sequence would then present the punishment of the sins both of our first parents and of the first murderer, whose condemnation immediately follows his sin, and rounds off the Genesis page. The recto would then consist of images of separation and disharmony, indicating the need for mankind's salvation, initiated overleaf in the typological sequence.

The scene's suggesting the Condemnation of Cain would also, paradoxically, relate well to the Eton Roundels' strong emphasis on the conversion of the Jews. (It is important to recall that this theme is an echo of the roundels' analogue or source, indicated by the captions discovered by M. R. James;[42] before it was represented in the second half of the thirteenth century in our manuscript, the theme may have been peculiarly relevant in twelfth-century Worcester, a major centre of Jewry.) The "unflattering and odious" equation of the evil Cain with the Jews is traceable to a highly relevant passage by St. Ambrose.[43]

These two brothers, Cain and Abel, have furnished us with the prototype of the Synagogue and the Church. In Cain we perceive the parricidal people of the Jews, who were stained with the blood of their Lord, their Creator, and as a result of the child-bearing of the Virgin Mary, their Brother, also.[44] Ruth Mellinkoff traces the idea through Jerome to its amplification in Augustine,[45] who observes "only when a Jew comes over to Christ, he is no longer Cain"; she then traces it through subsequent exegesis until it was popularised in the twelfth century by Peter de Riga's *Aurora*,[46] which states that, like Cain, the Jew is marked, but by circumcision.[47]

The twelfth century saw not only the *Aurora* but also the terrible anti-Semitic recommendations of Peter the Venerable and Innocent III, culminating in Canon 68 of the Fourth Lateran Council of 1215, requiring Jews to wear a distinguishing mark.[48] Cain's equation with the Jews appears in art in the twelfth century, and by the mid-thirteenth century had become the official attitude to the first murderer. The manuscript was made roughly thirty years before the expulsion of

---

[40] Ibid., vol. 1, 174.

[41] Ibid., vol. 1, 216–21.

[42] See *Eton Roundels* (as in note 1), 42–43, for an account of this emphasis.

[43] Mellinkoff, "Cain and the Jews" (as in note 7), 16–38; see also her *The Mark of Cain* (Berkeley, 1981).

[44] Ambrose, *Hexameron, Paradise, and Cain and Abel*, trans. J. Savage (Fathers of the Church 42) (New York, 1961), 399–409, cited in Mellinkoff, "Cain and the Jews" (as in note 7), n. 3.

[45] Jerome, Letter no. 36, "Ad Damasum," *Lettres*, 8 vols., ed. and trans. J. Labourt (Collection des universités de France) (Paris, 1951), 342; in the Dods translation (see note 4 above), p. 213: cited in Mellinkoff, "Cain and

the Jews" (as in note 7), 17 and nn. 4, 7. Augustine, *Contra Faustum* (as in note 7), 337–44; trans. Stothert (as in note 7), 209–14; both cited by Mellinkoff, n. 5.

[46] *Aurora Petri Rigae Biblia Versificata: A Verse Commentary on the Bible*, pt. 1, ed. P. E. Beichner (Notre Dame, Ind., 1965).

[47] *Aurora* 44, cited by Mellinkoff, "Cain and the Jews" (as in note 7), 18. This saying of Peter de Riga's might give added point to the ambiguity of the Circumcision (f. 4r) discussed below, which may be simultaneously that of Moses and of Christ.

[48] S. Grayzel, *The Church and the Jews in the Thirteenth Century* (New York, 1933; rev. ed. 1966), 308–9, cited in Mellinkoff, "Cain and the Jews" (as in note 7), n. 17.

the Jews from England in 1290. It is surely inconceivable, therefore, that Cain's story could be included in the Eton Genesis sequence (ca. 1260) without Cain's equation with Jewry being implied.
If the central roundel were the Condemnation of Cain, punishment of the first murder would
form a neat contrast with the redemption of mankind obtained by the death, not of Abel, but of
his antitype, Christ.

If the central roundel were the Condemnation of Cain, the last Genesis page would also form
the perfect contrast to the last two pages of the New Testament sequence, on which images of spiritual harmony predominate. The traditional condemnation of Jews as symbolised by Cain would be
offset, in the new order, by Synagogue Unveiled and by the Coronation of the Bride (Fig. 3). In the
text quoted above, Augustine also says of the Jews: "While they will not turn to God, the veil which
is on their minds in reading the Old Testament is not taken away. This veil is taken away only by
Christ, who does not do away with the reading of the Old Testament, but with the covering which
hides its virtue."

The Eton Roundels and its traditional typological patterns may be an agent in this very process: inclusion of Synagogue Unveiled in such a brief and highly selective sequence makes particular sense in a work positing redemption of the Jews. In addition, in the Coronation of the Bride
(Fig. 3), the presence of the chariot in what is otherwise a combined Assumption/Coronation is,
when read with its surrounding types, a clear indication that the woman in the chariot is, among
other things, the Sulamitess addressed by Solomon in the prophecy in the bottom left-hand
roundel of this final page: " . . . my soul troubled me for the chariots of Aminadab. Return, return,
O Sulamitess: return, return, that we may behold thee."[49] She is interpreted in Christian exegesis
as Synagogue addressing Christ (of whom Solomon is a type) when she replies: "I did not know
that you were God . . . . I did not know that you were the Saviour but it was you who blinded me."[50]
On this same page, harmony is shown in the reconciled Four Daughters of God, in the top two
roundels, and in the union of Judah and Edom (Jews and gentiles) in Christ, in the bottom right-
hand roundel.[51] The presence of the Condemnation of Cain at the end of the Genesis sequence
would thus relate to the emphasis on Jewish/Christian reconciliation found in the typological section of the manuscript.

The main objection to the Condemnation of Cain hypothesis is that X is shown *seated* and in
the place of privilege at God's right hand.[52] X's being on God's right-hand side is not, in itself, incompatible with identification of X as Cain. Cain stands on God's dexter side, for example, in a
twelfth-century capital at Chalon-sur-Saône,[53] in an early thirteenth-century Bohemian manuscript,[54] and in a late twelfth- or early thirteenth-century psalter related to the Ingeborg Psalter,

<hr>

[49] Cant. 6:11–12.

[50] The so-called Honorius of Autun (PL 172:454),
cited by P. Verdier, *Le Couronnement de la Vierge: Les origines
et les premiers développements d'un thème iconographique*
(Montreal, 1980), 36–37; see also *Eton Roundels* (as in
note 1), 136–39. The exegesis of the chariot of Aminadab
by Pastor Eerner (ca. 1160/70), and the image's use in
another context, are described in Kemp, *Narratives* (as in
note 4), 48: Aminadab = Christ; his chariot = four
Gospels; horses = Four Evangelists; wheels = four decisive stations of Christ's life: Nativity, Crucifixion, Resurrection, Ascension.

[51] *Eton Roundels* (as in note 1), f. 7v and 136–39.

[52] "Aux XIe, XIIe et XIIIe siècles, la position assise
est réservée à Dieu et aux personnages, réels ou allégoriques, qui jouissent d'une supériorité hiérarchique et
d'un pouvoir: le roi, le pape, l'évêque, le juge exercent
leurs fonctions assis" (Garnier, *Langage de l'image* [as in
note 15], vol. 1, 113).

[53] Mellinkoff, "Cain and the Jews" (as in note 7), fig.
13.

[54] Ibid., fig. 14.

where in two linked historiated initials in Psalm 23, Cain, on the dexter side, holds a scroll inscribed with Genesis 4:9, while opposite Christ-Logos holds a scroll inscribed with another part of
Genesis 4:9.[55] (In this psalter's sequence of historiated initials, this image is preceded by Cain Kills
Abel heading Psalm 23, f. 91v, while initials to Psalms 26–29, 31, 33, and 35 give the Noah story.)[56]
X's being on God's right hand both here and in the problematic roundel might, at one level, be
an example of what Garnier calls the "narrative reason" for placing someone on the sinister side—
to indicate sequence rather than status.[57] We might be looking at the very moment when Cain is
banished from God's presence: he is still (just) seeing God.[58]

The problem of X's being *seated* on God's right is more intractable. Cain in a position suggesting his enthronement is unlikely, and it is not surprising that there is, as far as I can discover,
no iconographic precedent for a Condemnation of Cain so composed. God and Cain usually
stand. The normal composition is found, for example, in Fitzwilliam Museum, Ms. 330.2, a page
from a William de Brailes psalter (Fig. 22)—also English, and at ca. 1240 only a little earlier than
Eton Ms. 177. The page presents eight comparable scenes from Genesis, which, from left to right,
are: the Creation of Adam, God Rebukes Adam and the Serpent (these first two images in small
roundels above the six main scenes), Adam and Eve Clothed by God,[59] Adam and Eve Labour, the
Sacrifices of Cain and Abel, the Murder of Abel, the Condemnation of Cain, and the Death of
Cain. In the De Brailes Condemnation of Cain (bottom left in Fig. 22) God's scroll reads "V*BI
E*ST FR*ATER* TV*VS*: VAG*US* ET P*ROFVG*VS" (Where is thy brother? A fugitive and a
vagabond [shalt thou be upon the earth] [Gen. 4:9,13]). This basic design as it appears in the De
Brailes page is common, expressing the official attitude to the wretched Cain: for example, it appears in the thirteenth-century Salisbury Cathedral chapter house reliefs (Fig. 23). This scene, and
the same as found in a thirteenth-century *Bible moralisée*, are reproduced by Mellinkoff with her
translation of the associated text: "God who cursed Cain signifies Jesus Christ who cursed the Jews,
and all infidels, who like the Jews, are hurrying to eternal damnation."[60]

X's being seated is also a problem because the resulting composition so strongly suggests the
Son enthroned at the Father's right hand. Yet it is hard to ignore the Father's emphatic gesture of
rejection, which, though appropriate to Cain (or to the Noah story discussed below), is less obviously appropriate to Father and Son. There is a conflict between the implications of the figures
being seated or enthroned, and the details which suggest subjugation of X. The result is equation,

---

[55] New York, Morgan Lib., Ms. M. 338, closely related to the Ingeborg Psalter, f. 94r, the Condemnation of Cain, associated with Psalm 23. F. Deuchler, *Der Ingeborgpsalter* (Berlin, 1967), 117, 173.

[56] Ibid., figs. 125–34.

[57] Garnier, *Langage de l'image* (as in note 15), vol. 1, 40, 88–91.

[58] Compare the beautiful stone reliefs in the spandrels of the pulpitum arches of Modena Cathedral, where Judas—still haloed, but with the offered pieces of silver in his outstretched hand—is shown poised at the moment of his full transition to guilt. The series of reliefs is just visible in A. C. Quintavalle, *Il Duomo di Modena* (Forma e colore: I grandi cicli dell'arte 1) (Florence, 1965), pls. 23, 24.

[59] Morgan, *Early Gothic Manuscripts* (as in note 5), 118,

observes that this is very rare, though occurring, in addition, on one of the separate leaves (ca. 1230–40 and also made in Oxford) held in Paris, Collection Wildenstein, Musée Marmottan.

[60] "Deus qui maledixit caym significat ihesum christum qui maledixit iudeos & omnes infideles qui sicut ipsi festinant ad eternam dampnationem": Mellinkoff, "Cain and the Jews" (as in note 7), fig. 15, p. 23 and fig. 2. The *Bible moralisée* cited is Oxford, Bodl., Ms. Bodley 270b, f. 8: see A. de Laborde, *La Bible moralisée illustrée*, 5 vols. (Paris, 1911–27), vol. 1. A similar scene occurs also in another thirteenth-century *Bible moralisée*, Vienna, Ö.N.B., Ms. Vindobonensis 2554, f. 2v: see A. Ulrich, *Kain und Abel in der Kunst: Untersuchungen zur Ikonographie und Auslegungsgeschichte* (Bamberg, 1981), fig. 292.

in the mind, of Cain and Christ. Is this so unthinkable? The familiar typology of Moses Lifting up
the Serpent equates the crucified Christ with a sculpted snake representing those which had been
killing the Israelites: Christ is for a moment sin embodied, so that sin may die.[61] The punishment
of sin in Cain is also overlaid by the sacrifice of Christ.

Is it possible that in the contemporary anti-Jewish climate in Britain the disputed image in the
Genesis sequence designedly presented a fusion of the Condemnation of Cain and the Son Seated
at the Right Hand of the Father, the Jews' "shame" being by implication simultaneously recorded
and redeemed? The two apparently antithetical events would almost present the condemnation of
Cain as the cause of God's plan for the Incarnation—so that we see Cain at the moment of his condemnation, yet seated by God in a design recalling the honouring of the Son "at God's right hand."
To be sure, this gives us a Condemnation of Cain without precedent in its composition, but that is
inevitable in such a fusion. The designer could not combine the traditional iconography of Cain's
condemnation with the imagery of Christ's enthronement, so had to suggest the Cain-identity of
X by other means, including the narrative sequence of the page, the thematic linking of the ends
of the Genesis and typological sequences, and the small pictorial details described above.

This is the point at which to note the half-roundels on this page, which are occupied by angels
who lift joined hands before their faces. All the other half-roundels are occupied by unidentifiable
human beings. Perhaps both angels and human beings merely represent an on-page audience. It
has been objected that the central scene cannot be the Condemnation of Cain since "angels would
never pay homage to such a pair."[62] However, a formal gesture of homage is made with joined
hands held low, so that the receiver of homage may hold them between his own.[63] The high gesture of prayer or adoration made by these angels might mean a number of things if the image is a
multiple conflation. If a fusion of Cain/Christ imagery is intended in the roundel, homage to the
subtlety of the divine plan would be appropriate. The angels might be emphasising the vision of
God which Cain lost, or praying for mankind's redemption, or approving God's action. The latter
would be highly relevant to the next subject possibly present in the roundel.

8. God Instructs Noah

Interpretation of the roundel as God Instructs Noah is attractive for a number of reasons. In Genesis cycles, if Cain Kills Abel (depicted in the bottom right-hand corner of the page) is not followed
by more of the story of Cain, it is frequently followed by God Instructs Noah:[64] "He said to Noe:
The end of all flesh is come before me; the earth is filled with iniquity through them; and I will destroy them with the earth. / Make thee an ark . . . ." (Gen. 6:13–14). A typical example is found in
an English Bible from the first half of the thirteenth century, Oxford, Bodl., Ms. Auct. D.3.4, f. 3v,
in the initial I to the Book of Genesis (Fig. 24); under a mandorla containing the dove of the Spirit,

[61] See *Eton Roundels* (as in note 1), f. 5r, and explanations on 122–24.

[62] See note 2 above.

[63] Garnier, *Langage de l'image* (as in note 15), vol. 1,
206–7.

[64] For example, Noah's Ark performs a similar bridg-
ing function between Old and New Testament sequences
at the end of the first two openings of Paris, B.N.F., Ms.

Lat. 9584 (*Speculum Humanae Salvationis: Being a Reproduction of an Italian Manuscript of the Fourteenth Century*,
ed. M. R. James [Oxford, 1926]): the first two openings
contain the Fall of the Angels, Creation of Eve, Marriage
of Adam and Eve, Eve and the Serpent, then the Fall, the
Expulsion, Adam and Eve Labour, and Noah's Ark, before the third opening begins the New Testament sequence.

five roundels show the Creator and days of Creation up to the creation of Eve, and five more represent the Fall, the Expulsion, Adam and Eve at Labour, the Sacrifices of Cain and Abel, Cain Kills Abel, and at the bottom, Noah's Ark. With the exception of the last, the parallel with the Eton Genesis sequence is close, and it becomes closer when one looks at the scenes in the spandrels. These are sometimes typologically related, at one remove, to scenes in nearby roundels; for example, the spandrels on either side of the Sacrifices of Cain and Abel and Cain Kills Abel, show Eliseus with the Woman of Sarepta, her two crossed sticks representing the Cross, to which both the sacrifice of Abel and his death relate. Sometimes, however, the spandrels bear direct narrative relationship to the roundels, as in the case of the roundel of most interest to us, the lowest one, Noah's Ark, whose four associated spandrels show God Instructs Noah and Builders of the Ark. This is one of many examples of Cain Kills Abel being followed by God Instructs Noah, strong evidence that the latter would be called to mind by our problematic roundel coming after the death of Abel.

The Noah group no doubt symbolises the founding of the Church. Interpretation of the problematic Eton roundel in terms of God Instructs Noah is also attractive because of the ancient equation of Noah with Christ.[65] By the end of the fourth century the flood had an established place in Christian teaching. It was a sign of deliverance, followed by a new Creation, a new start for all people. Noah, like Christ, was the first of a new generation.[66] Exegetical interpretations of Noah as a type of Christ in terms of three concepts—his ending one race and beginning another, his righteousness, and his name's meaning "rest"—have been assembled by Lewis and by Unger.[67] In a metaphor which may be significant later in the argument, Origen actually spoke of Christ as Noah: "our Noah who is alone truly just and perfect, our Lord Jesus Christ."[68]

The ark, of course, anciently signifies the Church.[69] The ark's imminent construction would thus be relevant both to the coming Incarnation and to the culmination of the following typological sequence in a page centred on the much-conflated image of the Church/Virgin/Soul Triumphant (f. 7v).[70] The gesture of *refus* in this case would indicate God's rejection of the sinful world about to be flooded: "he repented him that he had made man on the earth. And being

[65] The parallel with Christ is also repeated by Hugh St. Victor: "Restat nunc ut videamus, quae sit arca Ecclesiae, vel ut expressius loquor, ipsa Ecclesia arca est, quam summus Noe, id est Dominus noster Jesus Christus, gubernator, et portus inter procellas hujus vitae regens per se ducit ad se" (PL 176:629); and: "Tunc namquam fabricata est arca, quando de latere Christi in cruce pendentis in sanguine et aqua profluxerunt Ecclesiae sacramenta. Quando Agnus immolatus est, tunc est sponsa Agni nata" (PL 176:630).

[66] R. W. Unger, "Noah in Early Christian Thought and Art," chap. 3 of *The Art of Medieval Technology: Images of Noah the Shipbuilder* (New Brunswick, N.J., 1991), 35.

[67] J. P. Lewis, *A Study of the Interpretation of Noah and the Flood in Jewish and Christian Literature* (Leiden, 1968). For example, Tertullian noted "a first beginning with Adam, a second with Noah, a third with Christ" (Unger, "Noah in Early Christian Thought" [as in note 66], 31–33, citing *De Monogamia* 5.5; CSEL 76:52). The idea is partly based on interpretation of Genesis 5:28–29: "And Lamech lived a hundred and eighty-two years, and begot a son. / And

he called his name Noe, saying: This same shall comfort us from the works and labours of our hands on the earth, which the Lord hath cursed."

[68] *Hom. in Gen.* ii.3 (GCS 29.30), cited in J. Daniélou, "Déluge, baptême, jugement," *Dieu vivant* (1947), 102–3.

[69] Lewis, *Noah and the Flood* (as in note 67), 162–67, assembles the evidence from Tertullian, Cyprian, Cyril of Jerusalem, Hilary, and Jerome ("this is the ark of Noah, and he who is not in it shall perish when the flood prevails" [*Eph.* 123.11; CSEL 54:63–64).

[70] The ancient equation of ark and Church is well expressed by Hugh St. Victor (PL 176:626): "Ipse est, qui in mari viam ponit, quia corpus suum, id est Ecclesiam suam, quasi arcam in diluvio, sic inter hujus vitae procellas regens usque ad portum quietis aeternae perducit. Si ergo salvari cupimus, oportet nos intrare hanc arcam." A little later, with great relevance to the last image in the Eton Roundels, he says: "Primam vocemus arcam Noe, secundam arcam Ecclesia, tertiam arcam sapientiae, quartam arcam matris gratiae."

touched inwardly with sorrow of heart, / He said: I will destroy man, whom I have created, from the face of the earth, from man even to beasts, from the creeping thing even to the fowls of the air; for it repenteth me that I have made them. / But Noe found grace before the Lord" (Gen. 6:6–8).

The symbolic ark could of course have been unambiguously indicated by the commoner image of the ark under construction, but in that image the parallel between ark and Church would dominate, rather than the parallel between Noah and Christ as founders of new ages and examples of righteousness. The earthly Jerusalem would see the founding of the Church militant (on earth), the celestial city of the New Jerusalem, celebrated in the Apocalypse, would represent the Church triumphant (in heaven).

The main objection to identifying the scene as God Instructs Noah is that in this subject, as in the Condemnation of Cain, both figures usually stand,[71] or Noah stands while God leans from heaven (Fig. 26),[72] or, less commonly, Noah kneels (Fig. 25).[73] Noah is rarely shown seated, but when he is, it is as overseer of workmen building the ark[74] or when he is part of a genealogy of Christ. Curiously, one great English twelfth-century stained-glass figure of him at Canterbury Cathedral, once part of such a genealogy, shows him seated, without attribute or narrative sequence, but identified by name, and making gestures not unlike those of X in reverse, the dexter hand holding a fold of his garment, the sinister hand lifted, thumb upwards. Caviness, presumably interpreting his gesture, says he "speaks with God."[75] God Instructs Noah is usually identified either by unambiguous position within a Noah cycle, or by Noah's carrying a relevant attribute, such as a T-axe, adze, hammer, or pitch-brush.

SIMILARITY OF NOAH AND CAIN IMAGES: It is entirely relevant to the interpretation of our roundel that the Condemnation of Cain and God Instructs Noah (with Noah standing) are often remarkably similar, as well as following each other in the pictorial narrative (though separated by fifty-seven Bible verses). Similarity in the figures' posture occurs often enough to suggest that a process of echo and contrast is intended, marking the transition from a sinful world to one about to be cleansed, and leading us to ponder the very different causes of God's communication with both men. Such similarity might partly explain the easy conflation of these two subjects in the mind.

An early example of such similarity occurs at the end of a sequence Cain Kills Abel, the Condemnation of Cain, God Instructs Noah, in an eleventh-century fresco at Sant'Angelo in Formis

[71] See, for example, God Instructs Noah in Chartres Cathedral, Noah Window, no. 12, ca. 1210 (restored), north side of nave; London, B.L., Ms. Cotton Nero C. IV, Psalter of St. Swithin's Priory, twelfth century, f. 3r; Munich, Bayer. Staatsbibl., lat. 835, f. 10r.

[72] See also Leiden, Rijksuniversiteit, Ms. B.P.L. 76 A, St. Louis Psalter, start of thirteenth century, f. 10v, which shows Cain and Abel Offer Sacrifice, Cain Kills Abel, God Instructs Noah, Noah Builds the Ark, God Instructs Noah; and New York, Morgan Lib., Ms. M. 638, ca. 1250, f. 2v.

[73] Noah half-kneels also in God Instructs Noah, Cambridge, St. John's College, Ms. K. 26, Psalter, thirteenth century, f. 7r.

[74] Unger, "Noah in Early Christian Thought" (as in note 66), 71, observes: "having Noah seated is extremely rare in any illustration." An unusual example of Noah seated while receiving instructions is in the thirteenth-century Flemish Oxford, Bodl., Ms. Canon. Liturg. 393, f. 238v: Noah (with a nimbus) is seated on the left, at work, his left hand raised and an axe in his right; he looks towards God's hand extending from heaven (Unger, fig. 20). Noah enthroned as he directs his labourers belongs to the southern European tradition (Unger, 48).

[75] M. H. Caviness, *The Early Stained Glass of Canterbury Cathedral circa 1175–1220* (Princeton, 1977), 112; see also 51–52 and fig. 66. The window, formerly N:XX in the clerestory, is now in the south window of the southwest transept.

(Fig. 26). Cain condemned stands, not looking up at God, but with his left hand open-fingered on his breast; a bearded Noah also stands, looking up and lifting both his hands to God (represented a second time). The separation of each scene from the next by a tree invites comparison of the similar stances of Cain and Noah.

A third example is found in the late twelfth- or early thirteenth-century Miniature Masson 13 (Fig. 27). The page is read from the bottom, where the serpent-coiled Tree of the Knowledge of Good and Evil is flanked by Adam and Eve, and constrained, perhaps symbolically, by the words of God. This Fall is represented in a quatrefoil which literally as well as metaphorically is the basis of the rest of the image. The central area above is occupied in the lower half by the angel of the Expulsion controlling the closed gates of Paradise. Above him, over the four rivers of Paradise, burgeons the fruiting Tree of Life, its crop (in both senses) Christ. On either side of this central shaft, at the bottom, three pairs of roundels show Adam and Eve labouring; the pair above that shows the sacrifice of Cain and Abel and the death of Abel; the pair above that shows the Condemnation of Cain and God Instructs Noah; two pairs at the top show the story of Noah's ark. The lower part of the whole design is thus devoted to mankind's control of his material environment, while the upper part is devoted to construction of the ark, the symbol of the Church, our spiritual environment. The pair of roundels showing the Condemnation of Cain and God Instructs Noah acts as a visual transition between the two areas and concepts. In both, Christ-Logos is cross-nimbed and holds a scroll, which in the Noah scene is inscribed with Genesis 6:14. Apart from the scroll, only Cain's absence of responsive gesture, and Noah's beard, distinguish the two. The cursing of evil (Cain) and the building of the Church as a bulwark against it fuse in the eye and mind. This page and this process lend weight to the suggestion that a similar fusion is present in the Eton roundel.

9. God's Covenant with Noah

God's Covenant with Noah is the final possible identification:

> Behold, I will establish my covenant with you, and with your seed after you. / And with every living soul that is with you, as well in all birds as in cattle and beasts of the earth, that are come forth out of the ark; and in all the beasts of the earth./ I will establish my covenant with you; and all flesh shall be no more destroyed with the waters of a flood, neither shall there be from henceforth a flood to waste the earth./ And God said: This is the sign of the covenant which I give between me and you . . . / I will set my bow in the clouds, and it shall be the sign of a covenant between me, and between the earth (Gen. 9:9–13).

This interpretation is attractive for a number of reasons. First, it looks backward, representing a kind of second Creation, completing the Genesis opening with a pleasing symmetry. Second, it looks forward, prefiguring the covenant fulfilled in the Incarnation represented overleaf in the manuscript: the Old Testament foreshadows the New. Third, the gesture of *refus* would refer, in this case, either to the destroyed sinful world, or to the flood itself, both rejected now by God. Fourth, parallels between Noah and Christ, and the ark and Church, would be again be implicit.

Unfortunately, the identifying element of this scene—the rainbow—is missing,[76] as is a scroll

---

[76] *LCI*, vol. 4, 618, entry 8, "Bund Gottes m. N[oe]."

suggesting the covenant, or anything apart from context to identify Noah—for though one might expect God Instructs Noah after Cain Kills Abel, it is rather a long leap to God's Covenant with Noah. In this subject, too, God and Noah are usually standing,[77] but at least their being seated while an agreement is made would be more normal than their being seated for God Instructs Noah, a scene presenting Noah's obedience and suggesting imminent activity. Noah is in fact shown seated, though alone, in a picture Bible, Augsburg, Universitätsbibliothek Augsburg, Cod. 1.2.4.15 (formerly Maihingen, Wallerstein Library, Ms. I.2.qu.15), a picture Bible and Vitae Sanctorum, f. 10r, where he gesticulates upwards to the rainbow which identifies the scene.

CONFLATION

Perhaps our roundel is ambiguous so that it functions as a meditational device. X cannot be clothed if he is Adam at the Prohibition; he cannot be unnimbed if he is Christ, or seated if he is Cain, Noah under instruction, or Noah at the Covenant; yet context implies all of them and X must be at least one. It would have been easy to include an identifying nimbus, mark, or tool. The extreme condensation of both the Genesis and the New Testament sections of the book make this compression even more likely: we have eight or nine events for the price of one. Perhaps X was intended to act simultaneously as Adam, as Son, as Cain, and as Noah, in an overlaying of functions no less surprising, perhaps, than the protean shifts of identification embodied in the figure of Piers Plowman, or the multiple layers of interpretation applied to the Bible, or the clear examples of traditional and less traditional conflation elsewhere in Eton Ms. 177.

Perhaps the density and complexity of this English book reflect its audience. The readership of it is not known, but the fact that the manuscript is unique, without the long documented history, wide distribution, or printed forms of *Biblia Pauperum* or *Speculum Humanae Salvationis*, implies a religious audience. The book's being in Latin, and the absence of medieval scribbles, doodles, pen-trials, and personal signatures (the few owners' and readers' contributions are all postmedieval) similarly suggest that it was for a religious house. Its iconographic connections with Worcester Cathedral (described above) may imply a Benedictine origin. The image's complexity, if that is what it has, may also indicate a learned audience.

Conflation in our roundel, if it exists, is innovative, suggesting productive contrasts as well as confirming parallels. If this is so, it suggests a level of intended ambiguity and complexity unusual in medieval English iconography, and a level of theological daring which to our over-fastidious taste is hard to swallow. Perhaps new examples remain to be found of the conflation not only of complementary or related subjects but also of apparently antithetical ones (such as Cain and Christ) fused in the mind's eye and—in the medieval sense of memory and image recall—the imagination.

---

[77] London, B.L., Ms. Cotton Claudius B.IV, f. 16v is unusual in that it shows Noah, his family behind him, *kneeling* before God, a great rainbow over them all (*The Old* *English Illustrated Hexateuch: British Museum Cotton Claudius B IV*, ed. C. R. Dodwell and P. Clemoes (Early English Manuscripts in Facsimile 18) (Copenhagen, 1974).

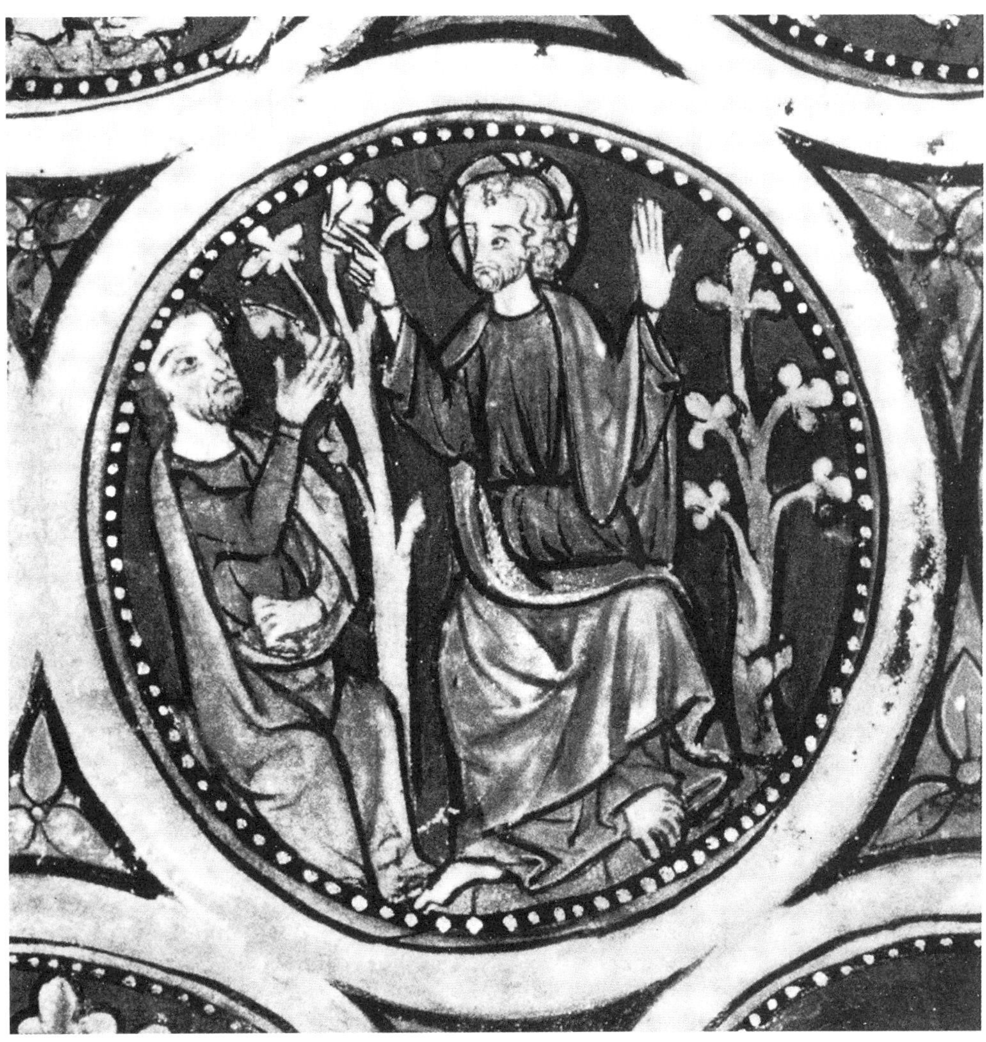

1. Windsor, Eton College, Ms. 177, Eton Roundels, f. 2r. The problematic roundel, detail of Fig. 2b

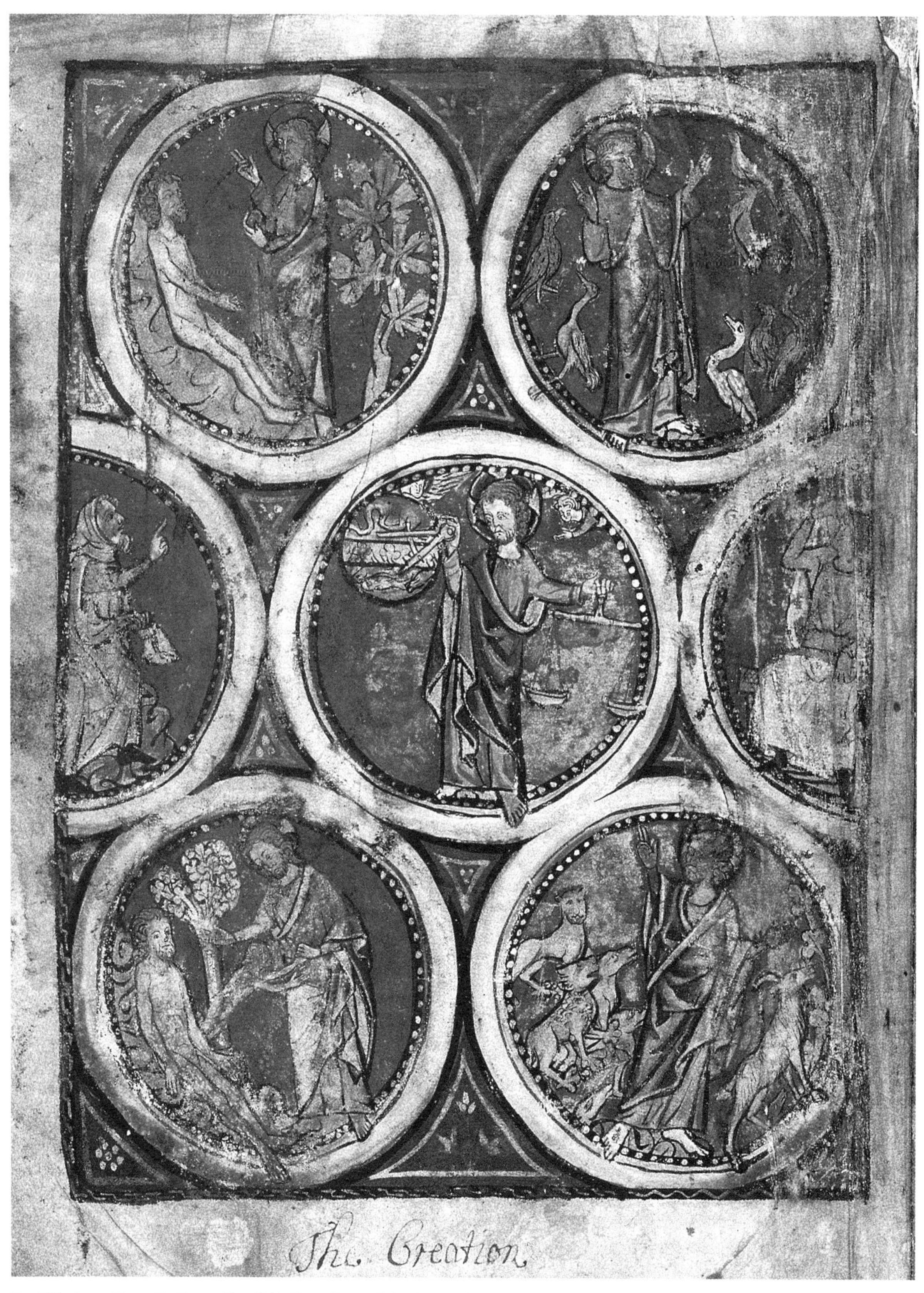

2a. Windsor, Eton College, Ms. 177, Eton Roundels, f. 1v. The Genesis opening: Creation

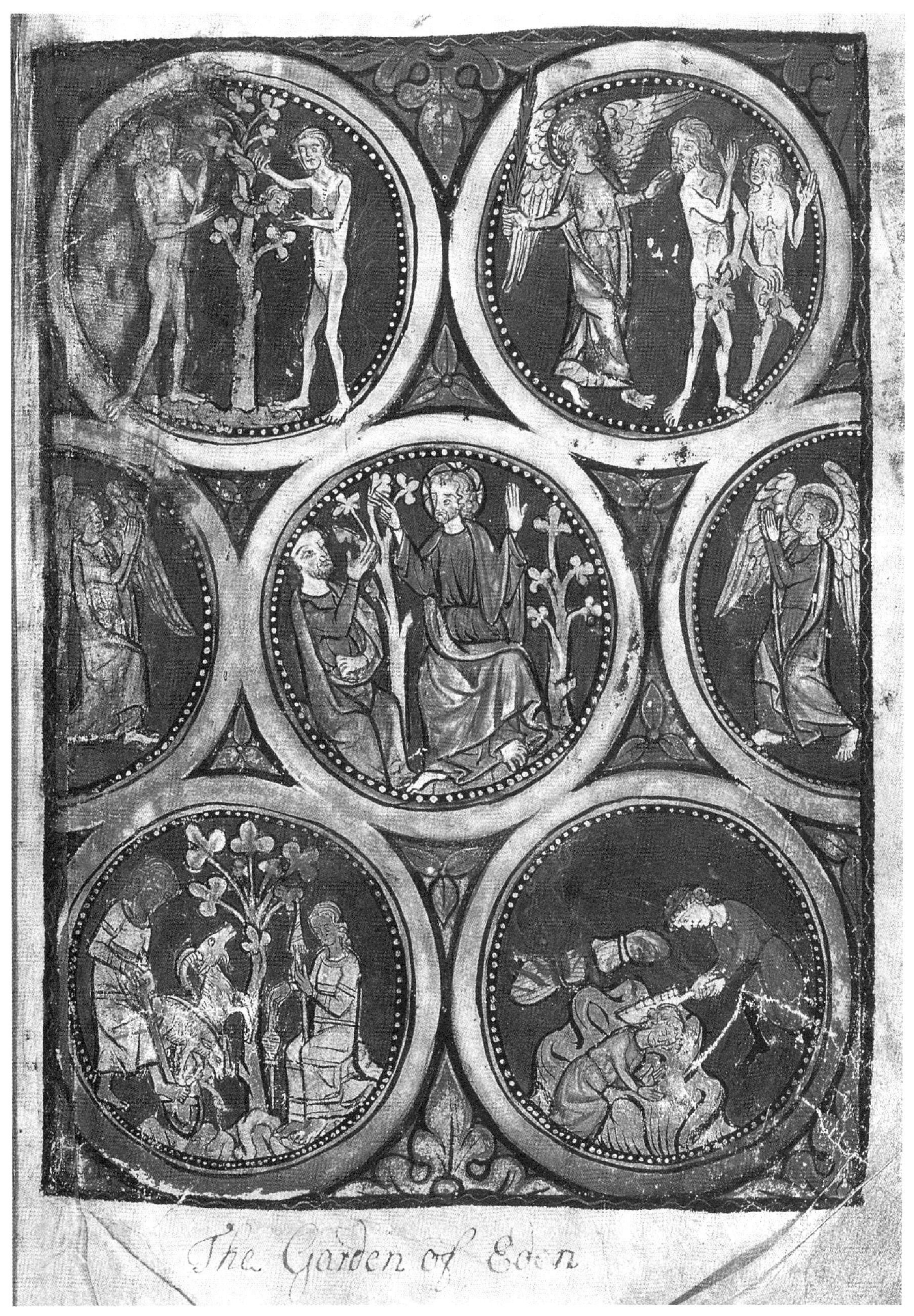

2b. Windsor, Eton College, Ms. 177, Eton Roundels, f. 2r. The Genesis opening: the Fall and its immediate consequences

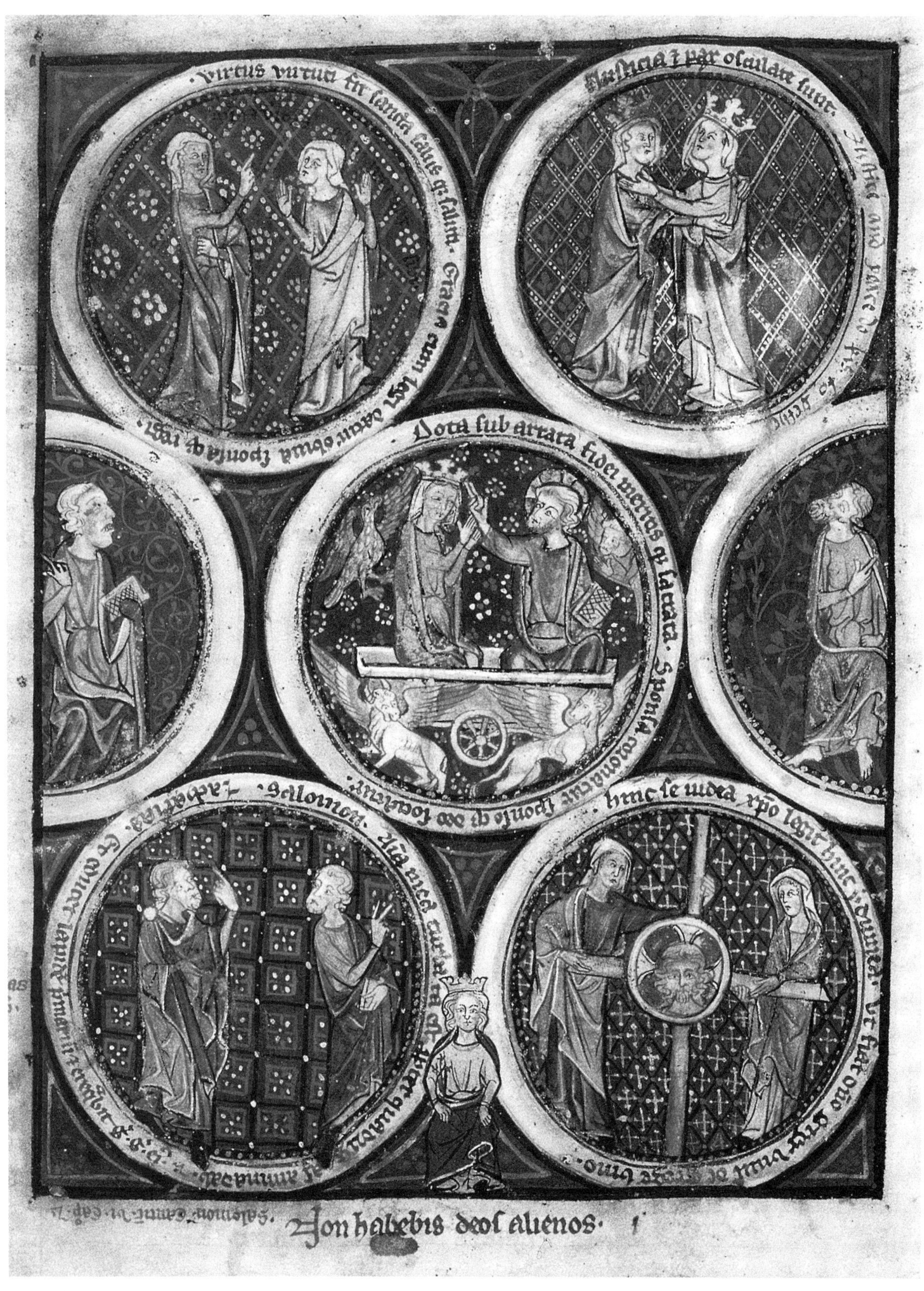

3. Windsor, Eton College, Ms. 177, Eton Roundels, f. 7v. Coronation of the Bride/Virgin/Church/Soul (centre), with Mercy and Truth, Justice and Peace, Sacharias and Solomon, Judah and Edom

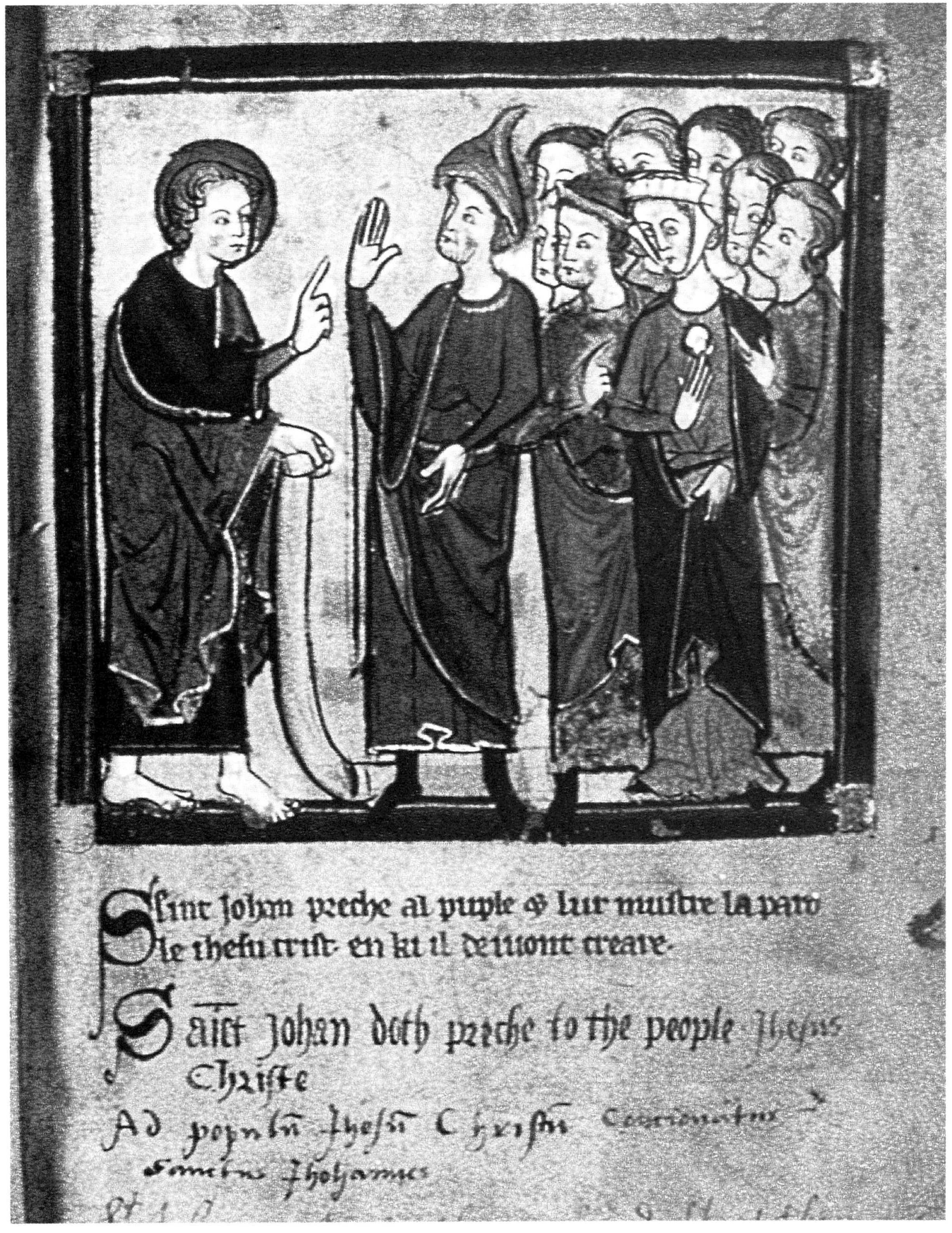

4. Windsor, Eton College, Ms. 177, f. 9r. The beginning of the Life of St. John preceding the illustrated Apocalypse

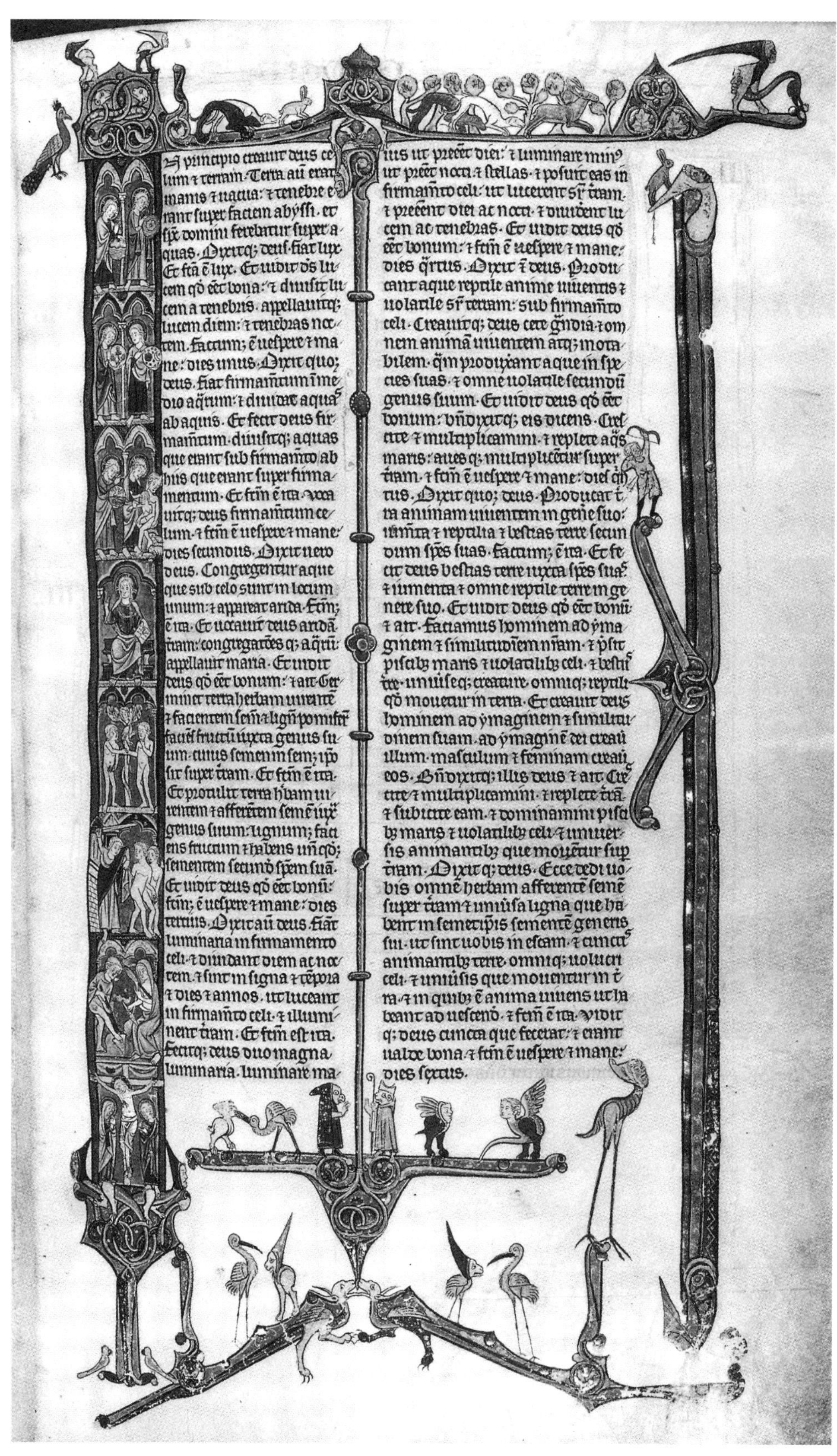

5. London, British Library, Ms. Royal 1.D.1, mid-thirteenth century, f. 5r. Initial I, Book of Genesis

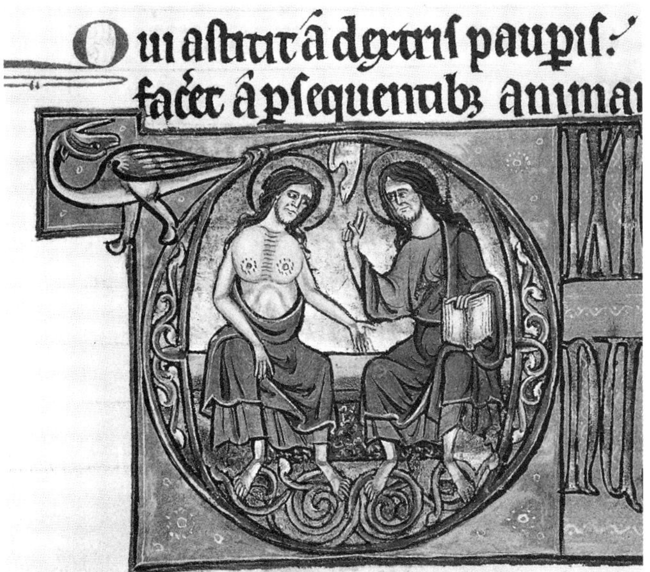

6. New York, Pierpont Morgan Library, Ms. G.25, thirteenth century, f. 121v, Psalm 109. The Right Hand of the Father

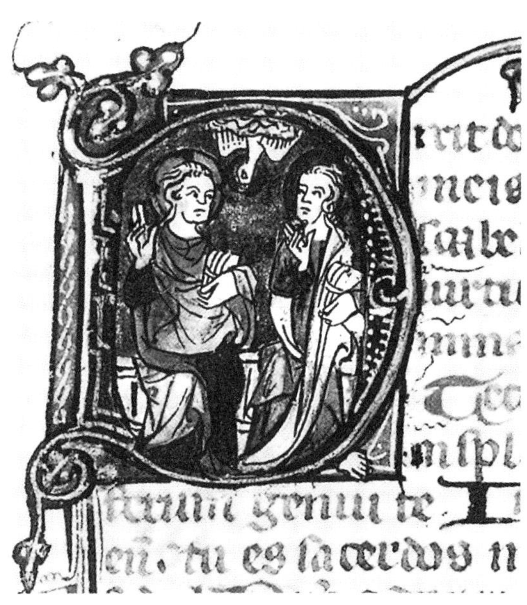

7. Brussels, Bibliothèque Royale, Ms. 8544, Breviary, f. 53r, Psalm 109. The Right Hand of the Father

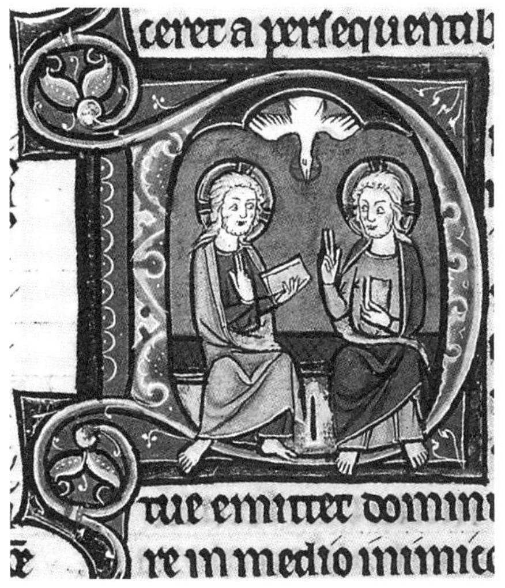

8. London, British Library, Ms. Royal 1.D.I, mid-thirteenth century, f. 252r, Psalm 109. The Right Hand of the Father

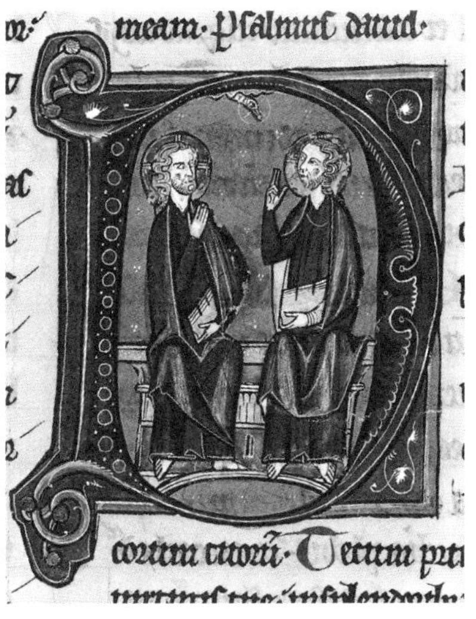

9. London, British Library, Ms. Harley 2839–40, f. 310v, Psalm 109. Trinity

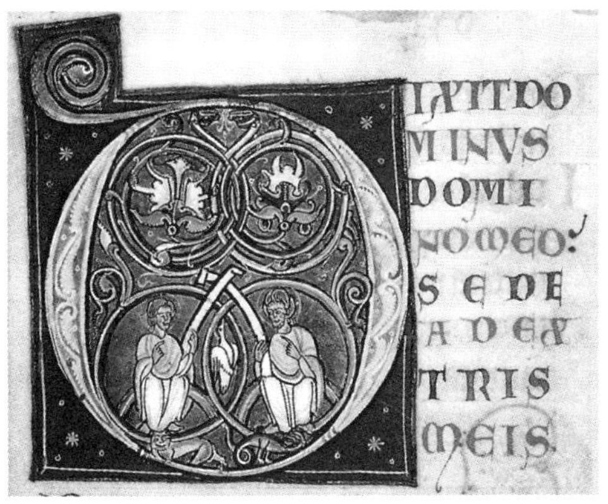

10. London, British Library, Ms. Royal 2.A.XXII, late twelfth century, f. 132r, Psalm 109. Trinity

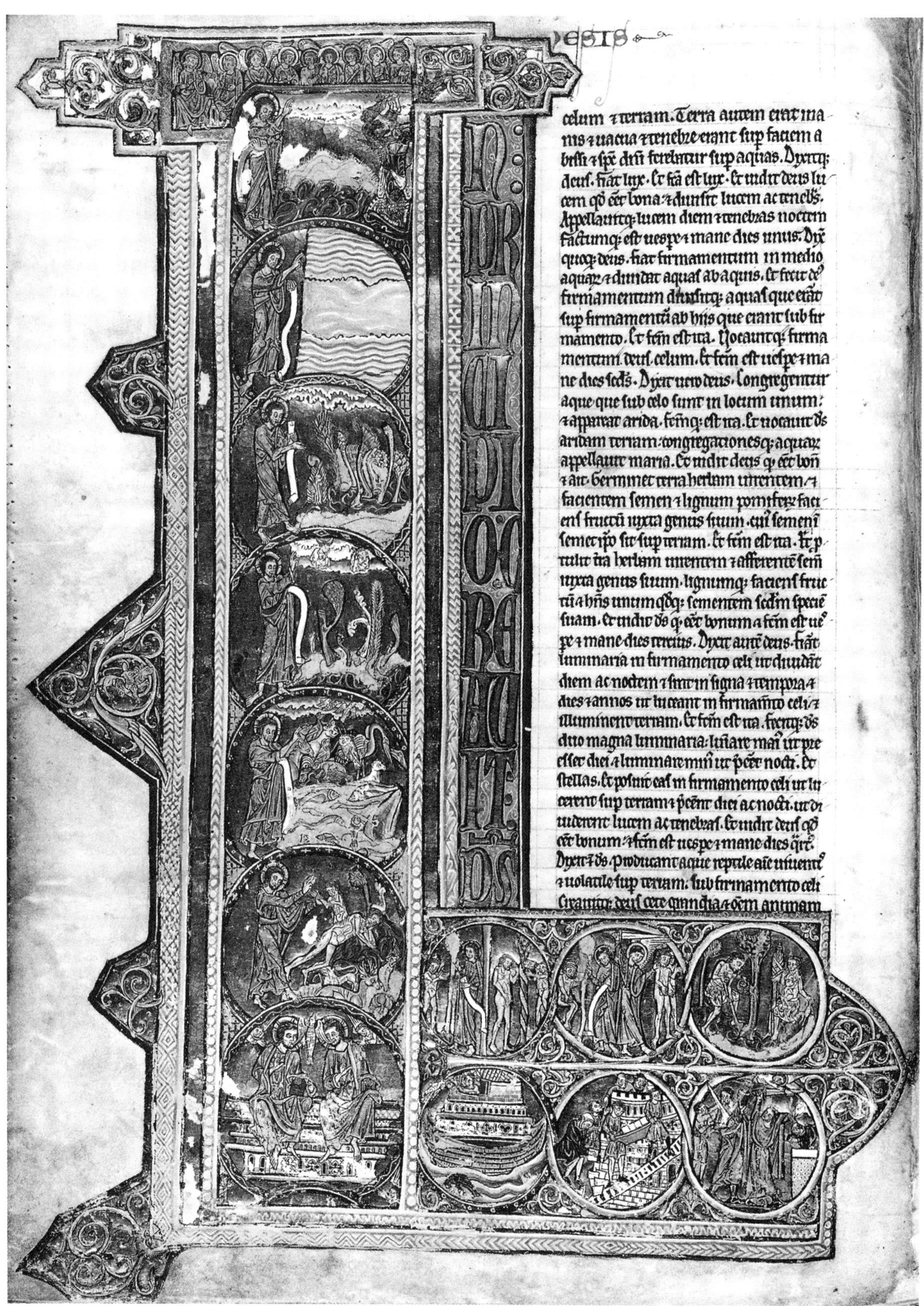

11. London: British Library, Ms. Burney 3, Bible of Robert de Bello, English, f. 5v. Initial L, Book of Genesis

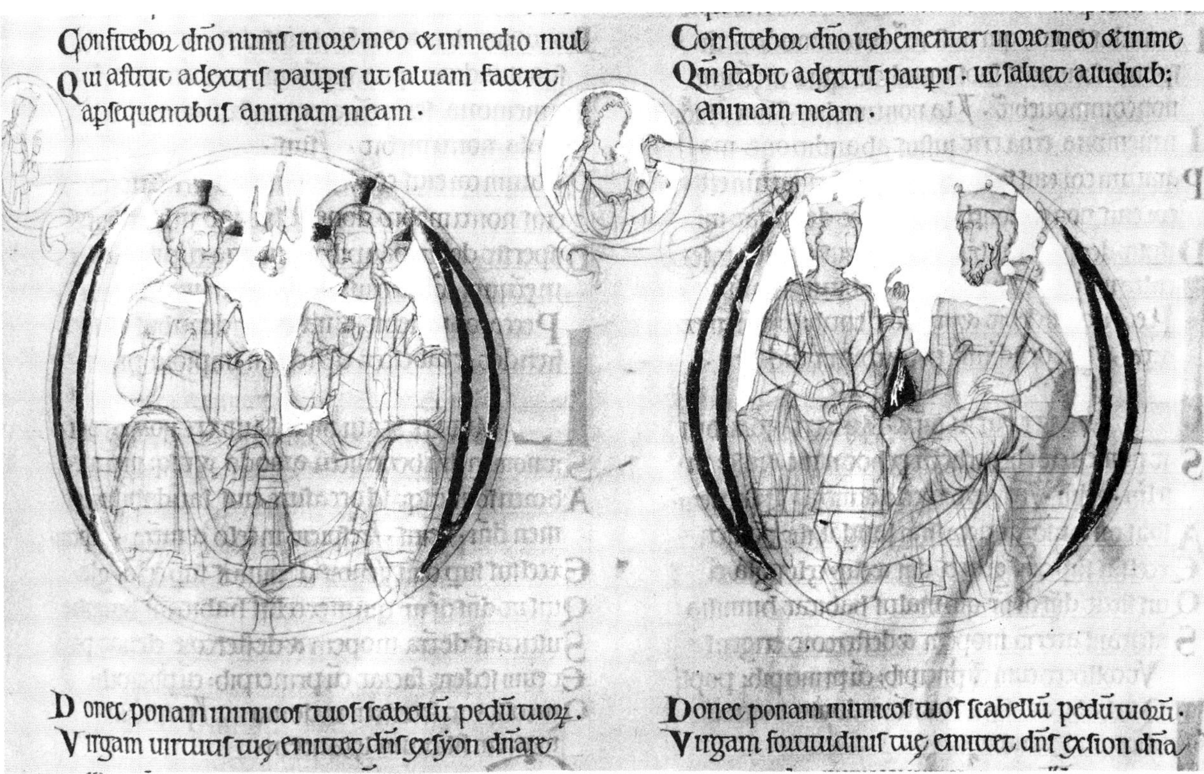

12. Winchester Cathedral, Ms. 17, Winchester Bible, English, twelfth century, the Gothic Majesty Master, f. 250r, Psalm 109, parallel versions. Trinity and the King's Enemy Made His Footstool

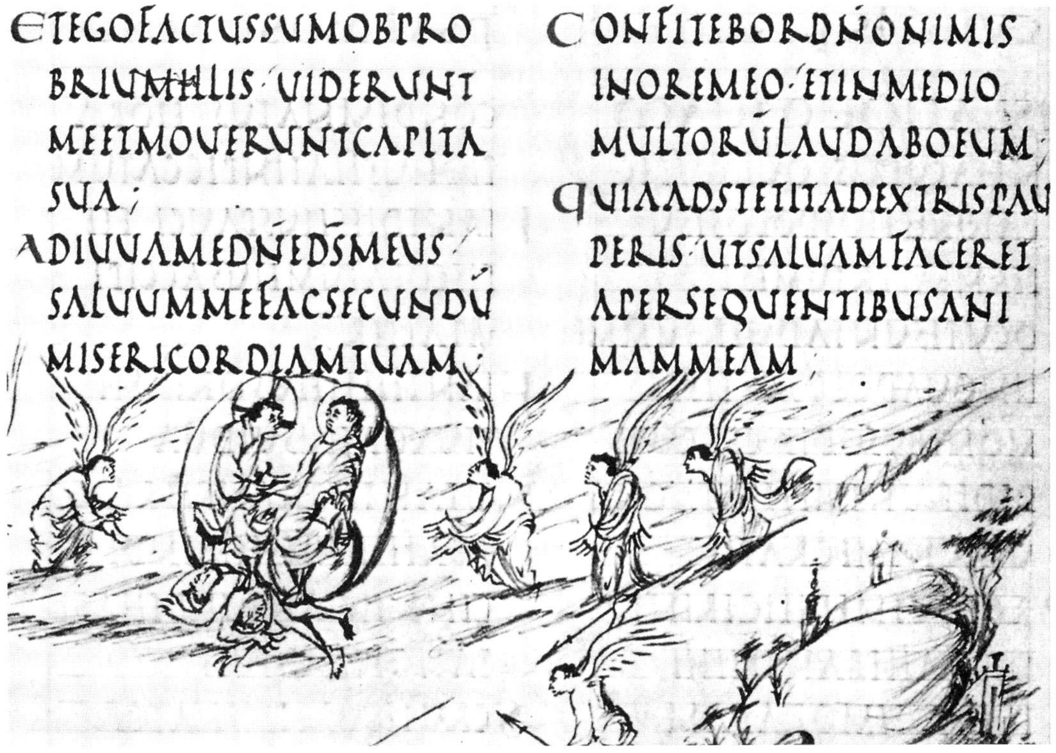

13. Utrecht, Universiteitsbibliotheek, Ms. 32 (was 484), Utrecht Psalter, ninth century, f. 64v, Psalm 109. The Right Hand of the Father

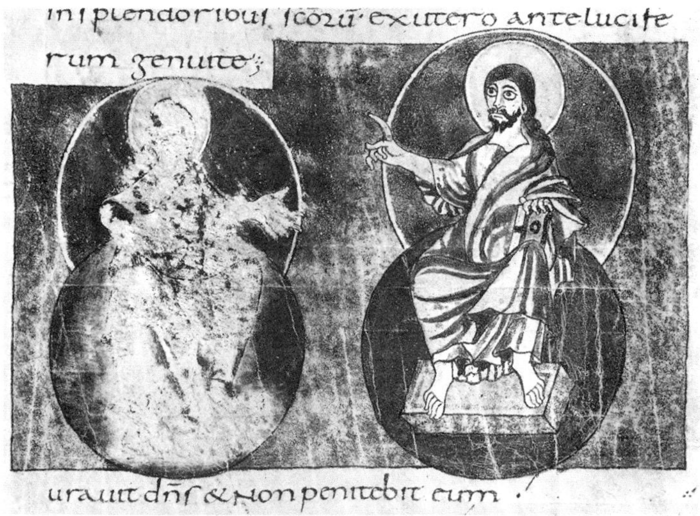

14. Stuttgart, Württembergische Landesbibliothek, Ms. bibl. 2° 23, psalter, twelfth
century, f. 127v, Psalm 109. The Right Hand of
the Father

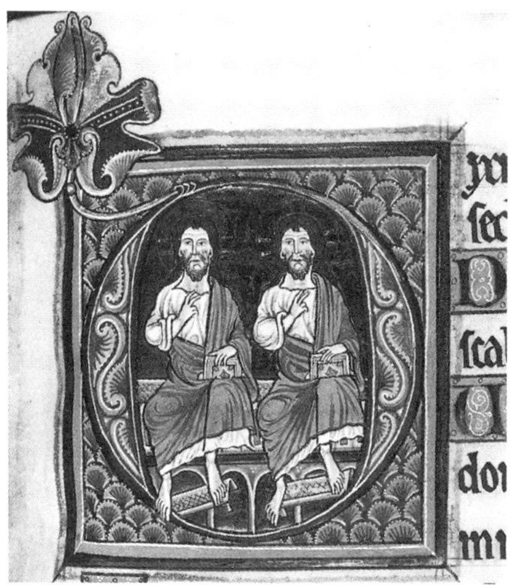

15. London, British Library, Ms. Royal
1.D.X, early thirteenth century, f. 98r,
Psalm 109. The Right Hand of the Father

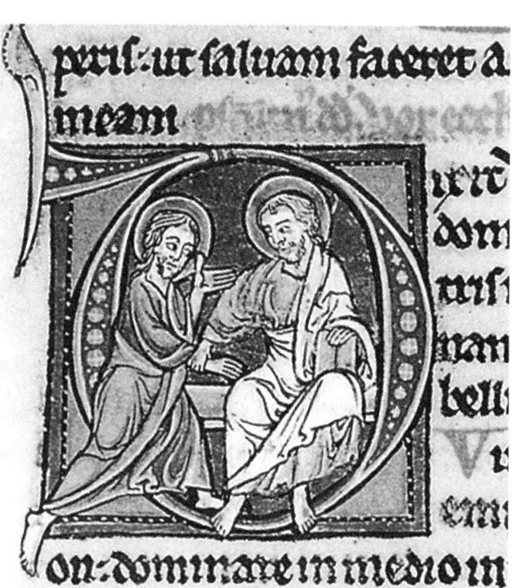

16. Oxford, Bodleian Library, Ms. Kenni-
cott 15, early thirteenth century, p. 397,
Psalm 109. The Right Hand of the Father

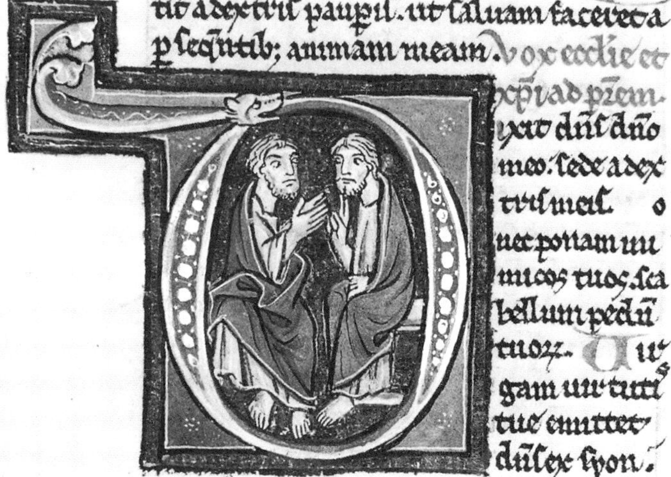

17. Cambridge, Emmanuel College Library,
Ms. 67 (was I.3.15), f. 235v, Psalm 109. The
Right Hand of the Father

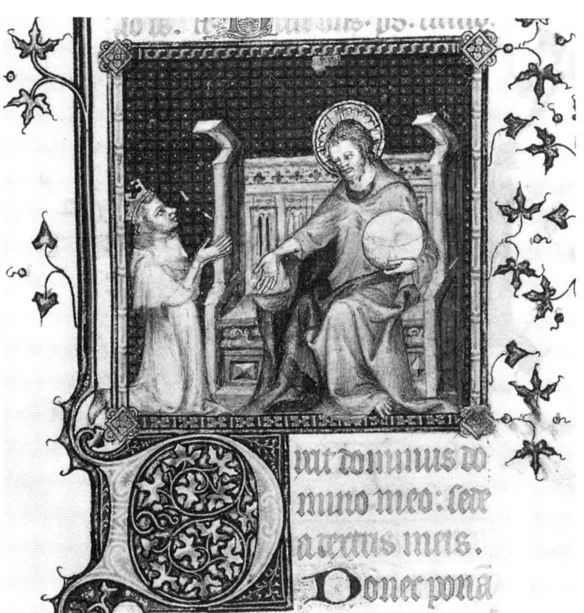

18. Paris, Bibliothèque Nationale de France, Ms. Lat. 1052, Breviary of Charles V, f. 261r, Psalm 109. King Charles V Acknowledged by the Father

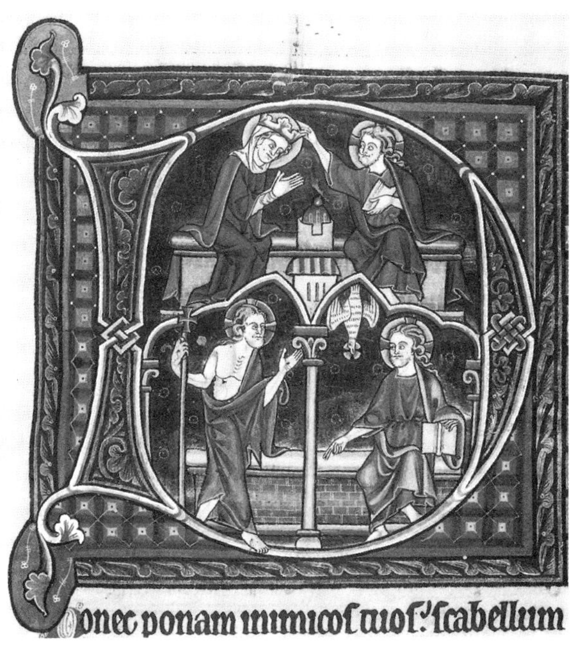

19. London, British Library, Ms. Add. 54179, twelfth century, f. 110r, Psalm 109:1. Coronation of the Bride and Right Hand of the Father

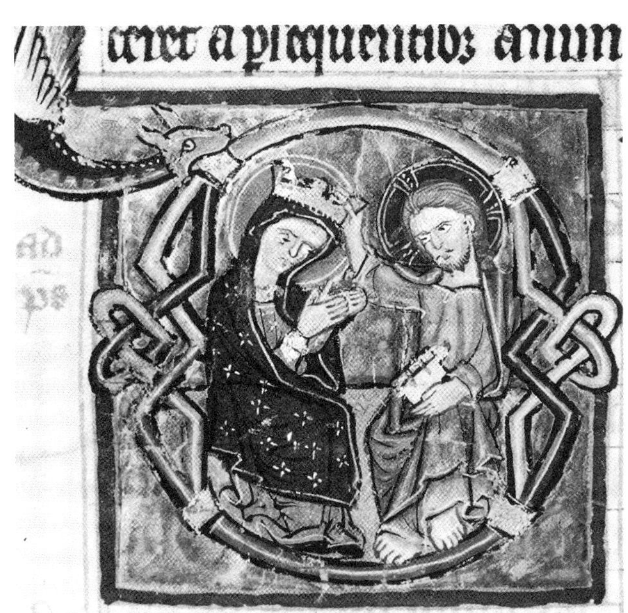

20. Esztergom, Erseki Könyvtár (Bishop's Palace), Ms. II.5, f. 95v. Coronation of the Bride

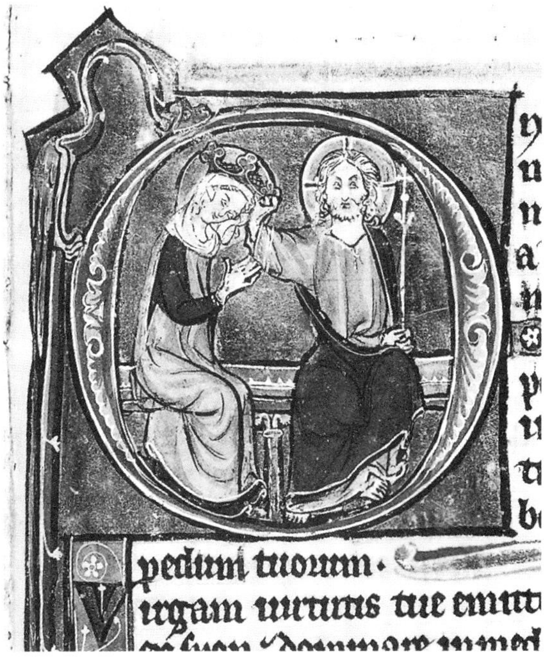

21. New York, Pierpont Morgan Library, Ms. 72, thirteenth century, f. 158r. Coronation of the Bride

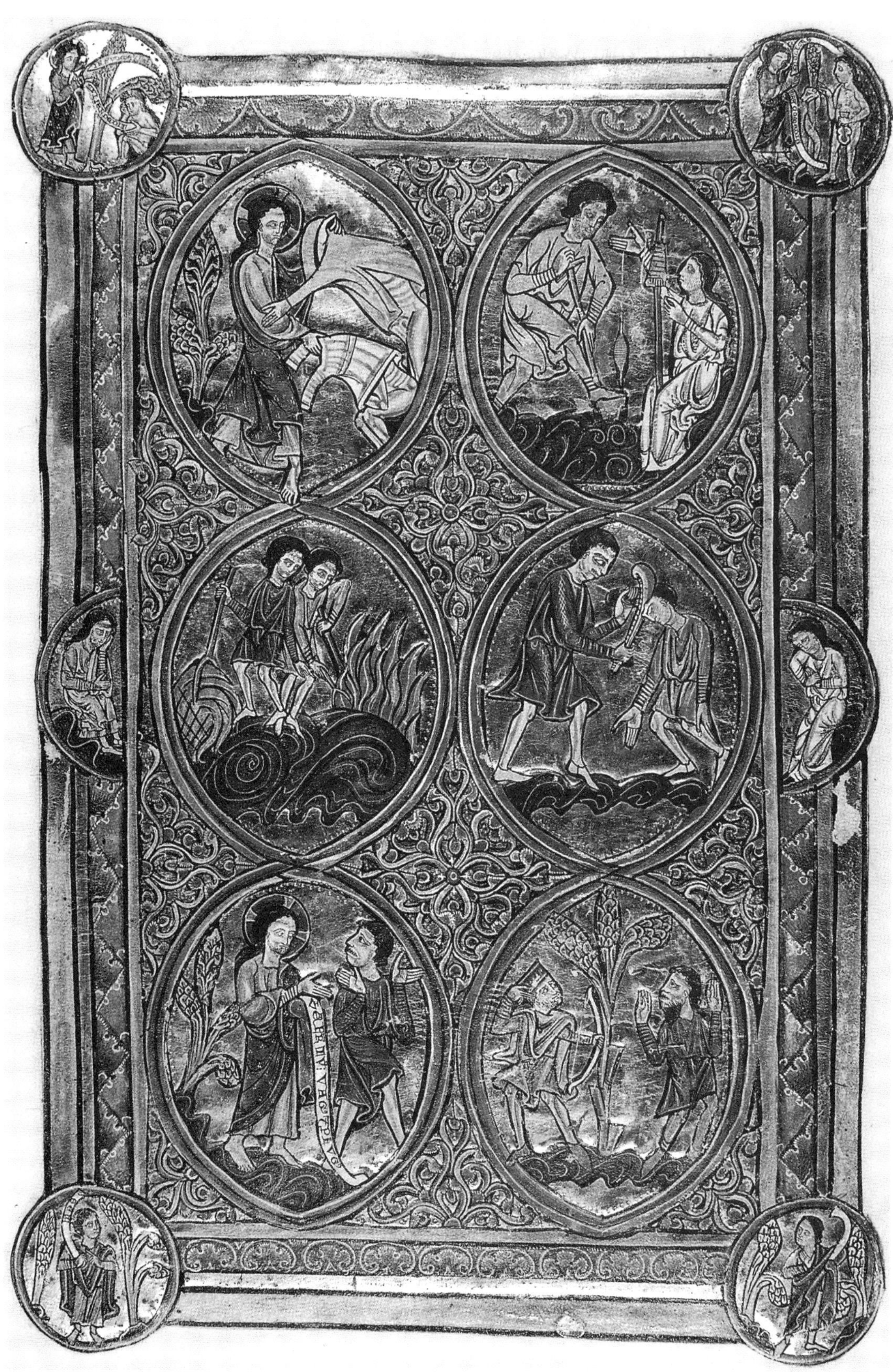

22. Cambridge, Fitzwilliam Museum, Ms. 330.2, leaf from a William de Brailes psalter. Scenes from Genesis

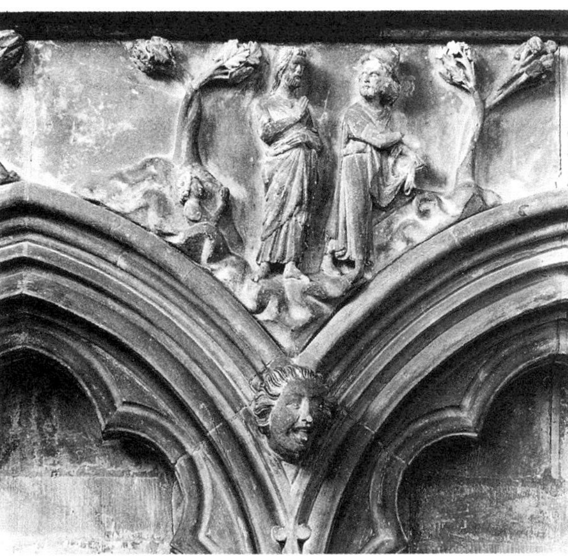

23. Salisbury Cathedral, chapter house, relief. The Condemnation of Cain

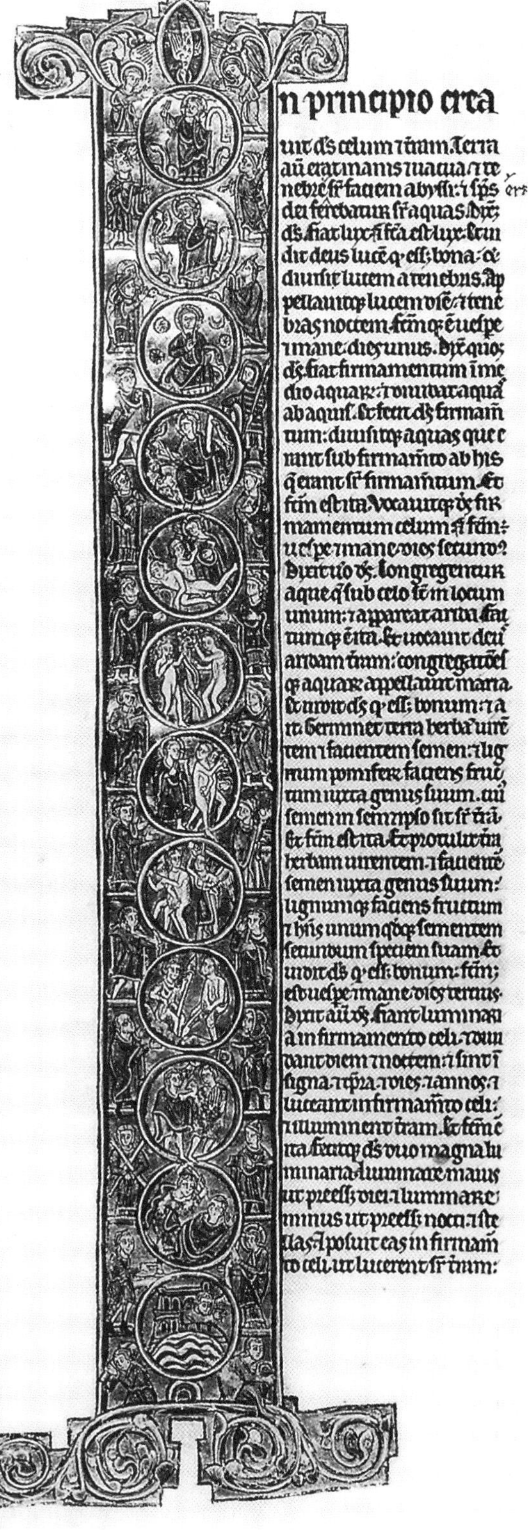

24. Oxford, Bodleian Library, Ms. Auct. D.3.4, Bible, English, thirteenth century, f. 3v. Initial I, Book of Genesis

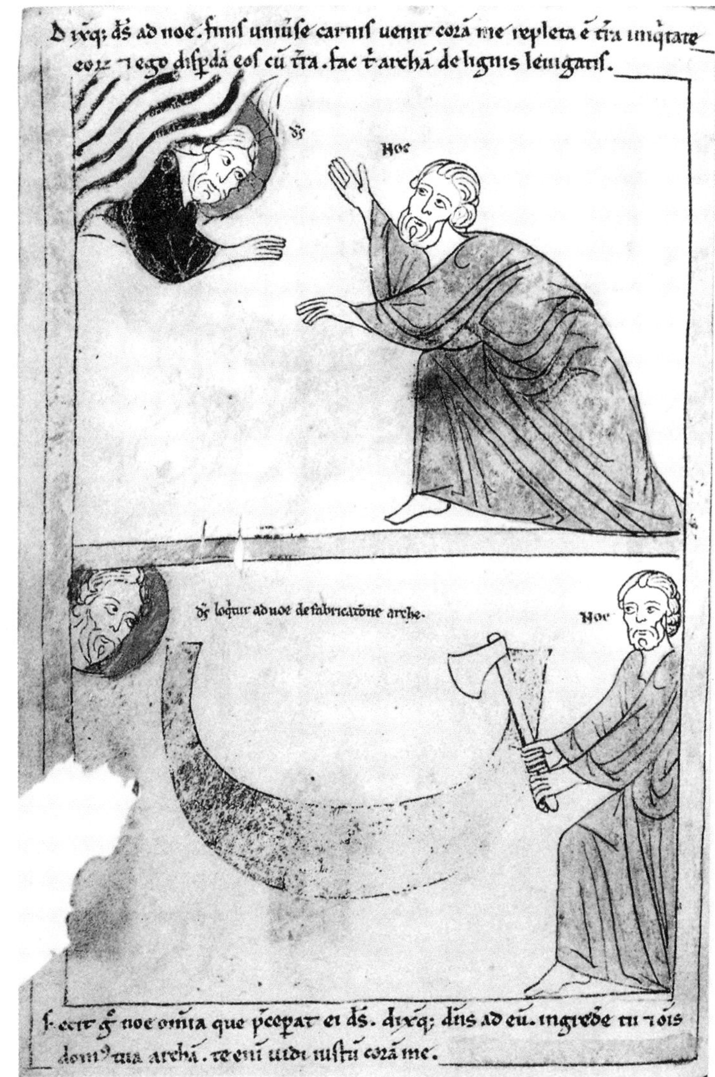

25. Augsburg, Universitätsbibliothek Augsburg, Ms. I.2.4.14 (formerly Maihingen, Wallerstein Library, Ms. I.2.qu.15), picture Bible and Vitae Sanctorum, ca. 1200, f. 8v. God Instructs Noah

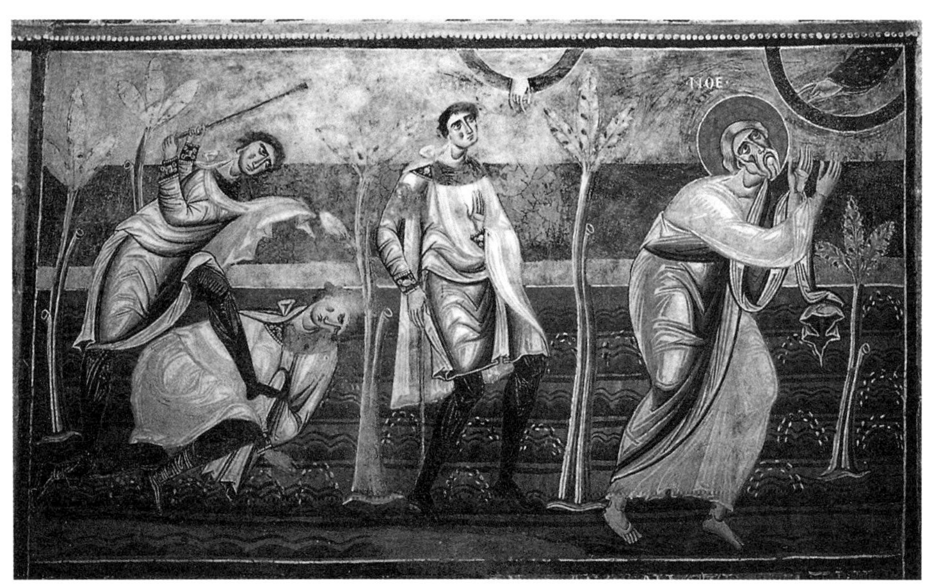

26. Capua, Basilica Benedettina di Sant'Angelo in Formis, left aisle, west wall. Cain Kills Abel, the Condemnation of Cain, and God Instructs Noah, eleventh century

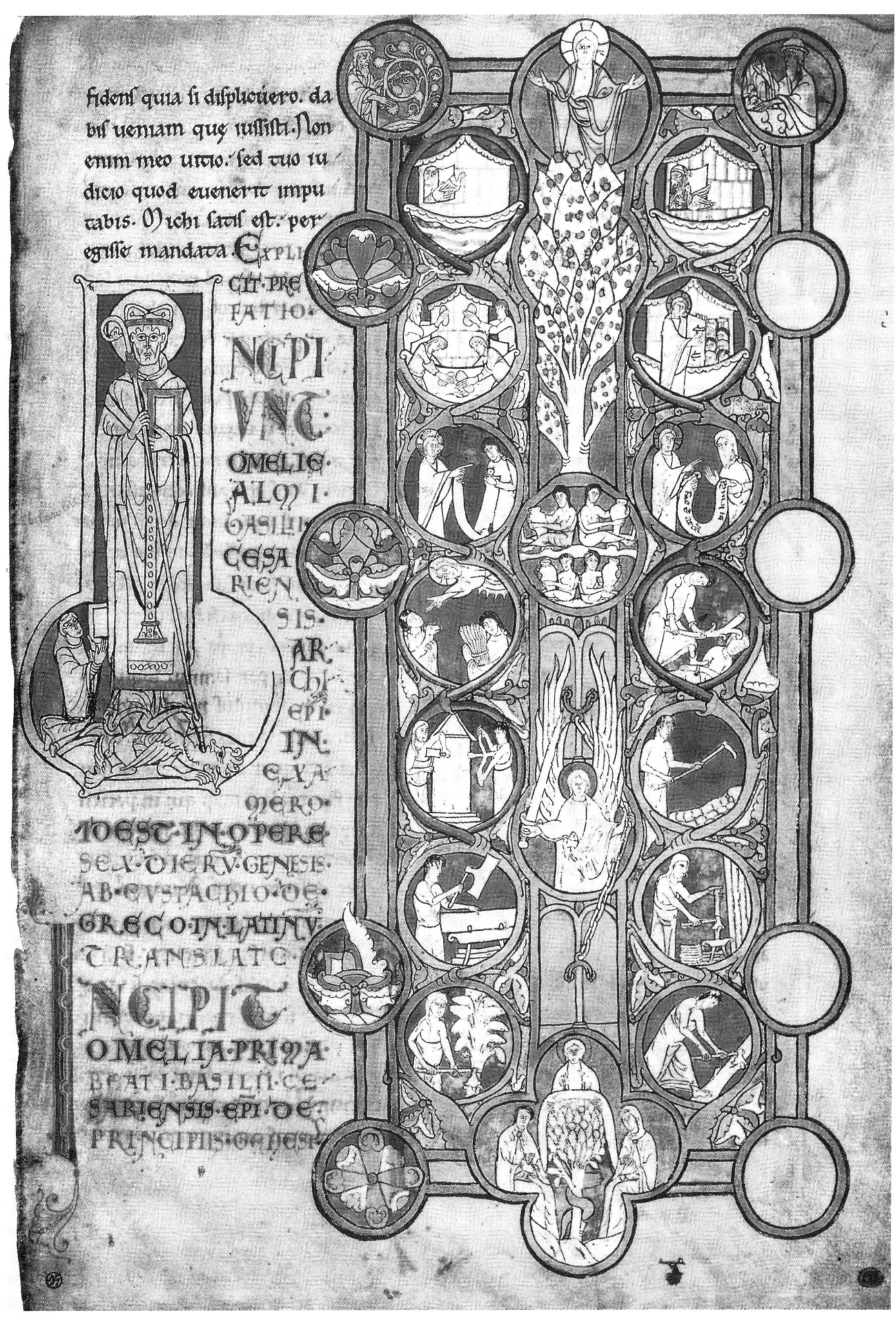

27. Paris, École des Beaux Arts, Miniature Masson 13, French, Abbey of Saint-Lambert de Liesseis (Cambrai), twelfth to thirteenth century. A page from Basil the Great, *Homilies*

The Personal Appropriation of
Iconographic Forms:
Two Franciscan Signatures

·

J O H N   V.   F L E M I N G

THE FIGURAL language of Christian images of the Middle Ages constitutes a sign system necessarily linked with the verbal sign systems of Early Christian literature, and especially that of the Bible. The currently fashionable disparagement of "Panofskian" iconographic study, and the repetitious assurances of certain influential medievalists that their projects are very different from that conducted by Emile Mâle, may usefully remind us that there is, always was, and always will be more to images than simply words translated into paint; but we ignore the textual basis of the Christian iconographic system as a whole only at a very dear cost.

In general, as D. W. Robertson long ago and definitively argued, Christian pictorial iconography constitutes, in Augustinian terms, a system of "conventional signs"; and its analysis usefully follows the pattern outlined by Augustine in *De doctrina christiana*. It may be observed that there is, in Augustinian linguistic analysis, an implicit universality, and this despite the fact that Augustine was a close observer of linguistic particularity and locality. The tropes of the Bible, though plural, polymorphous, and polysemous, yield to the inspired exegete meanings that are definite, definitive, and, perhaps above all, universal. So also is it with pictorial images deriving from those tropes. The familiar emblem of Petrine iconography, Peter's keys, can be taken as an example. They derive from a definite scriptural passage (Mt. 16:19) in which Jesus says to Peter "I give you the keys to the Kingdom of Heaven." But they do not long remain a limited, personal Petrine attribute; in practically all Catholic images that have come down to us, they implicitly bring with them an exegetically based political theory. The crossed keys of Peter, that is, whatever their stylistic expression, utter a universal claim of ecclesial or papal authority. Yet as can be seen in the armorial bearings of various Renaissance popes, there may be an impulse to personalize and individualize the power of the keys. It is also possible, in altered intellectual circumstances, to maintain the outward form of an icon while ignoring or even repudiating its conventional inner meaning. The gospel text says nothing of the number, color, or material composition of Peter's keys. It is possibly implicit that there are two, one to lock and the other to unlock, but the convention of two keys, crossed, the one of gold, the other of iron, became very common in the Middle Ages. Yet when Milton in *Lycidas* introduces Peter—

> Last came, and last did go,
> The Pilot of the Galilean Lake;

> Two massy keys he bore of metals twain
> (The golden opes, the iron shuts amain).

—the last thing he has in mind is a statement of papal authority.

This study seeks to explore two confrontations of the universal and the particular or the personal, from an iconographic point of view. There are few things more "personal" than a man's signature. It is a distinctive sign that denominates the person of the writer. When the word "signature" is used in a metaphorical way, as for instance in the phrase "signature tune," a pointer is made to a unique particularity that distinguishes the individual from the universal. The search for the origins of psychological subjectivity among Europeans, possibly as indeterminate as it is popular, marches ever regressively forward from Rousseau and Jacques Casanova in the eighteenth century to Petrarch in the fourteenth, Abelard and Heloise in the twelfth, and so on. A number of essays seriously claim the discovery of "subjectivity" in the Latin ascetic texts of Late Antiquity.

There has emerged something of a consensus among invigilators of early subjectivity that the evangelical revival of the thirteenth century, and in particular those mendicant movements which were its most articulate institutional expressions, provide a promising field for investigation. Mendicant piety has often been found to be novel in its affective and histrionic qualities, and in its vernacular biblicism, and its augmented appreciation of the world of nature, among other things.

It might be possible, in this context, to examine the fact, remarked upon twice by his biographer, Thomas of Celano, a man who knew him personally, that Francis of Assisi appropriated as his personal signature the sign tau. "The sign Tau was his favorite above all other signs," writes Thomas in one place." It was the only signature that he used at the end of his letters, and he painted the image of all the cells he inhabited."[1] Again Thomas says: "He used the sign tau to sign his letters every time he sent a letter either out of need or out of charity."[2] There is archeological and textual evidence to support this claim. Students of the Franciscan cult are familiar with some of the numerous mural taus claimed to be from Francis's hand. If one is to judge from the inscriptional evidence, Francis appears to have moved restlessly and constantly about Umbria.

There can be no doubt whatsoever about the authenticity of another alleged holograph tau. Perhaps the most famous of Franciscan relics, unchallenged in its authenticity, is the autograph of the blessing which Francis of Assisi wrote out for his friend Friar Leo during their retreat at Alvernia in 1224.[3] It is a *chartula*, a small sheet of vellum which is written in Latin in Francis's hand on both sides. One side contains a quasi-biblical hymn of praise of the kind known in Italian as *lauda*. The other side contains a blessing copied out by Francis following the text of Numbers 6:24–26: "Benedicat tibi Dominus et custodiat te; ostendat faciem suam tibi et misereatur tui. Convertat vultum suum ad te et det tibi pacem." This is nearly a verbatim citation, the difference being that the scriptural verses repeat the subject "Dominus" in the second and third clauses.

Some years ago I published an essay in *Franziskanische Studien* claiming to find in the signature a spiritual cryptogram.[4] Although at the time I feared that the suggestion would command all the authority of the latest revision of the Baconian cipher, it has been widely accepted among Francis-

---

[1] Thomas of Celano, *Tractatus de miraculis*, 3.

[2] Celano, *Tractatus de miraculis*, 159.

[3] English text in *Saint Francis of Assisi: Writings and Early Biographies. English Omnibus for the Sources of the Life of*

Saint Francis, ed. M. G. Habig (Chicago, 1973), 123–26.

[4] J. V. Fleming, "The Iconographic Unity of the Blessing for Brother Leo," *Franziskanische Studien* 63 (1981), 203–20.

can scholars, and I continue to be confident of its correctness. The cryptogram depends upon an authorial and self-conscious juggling of the valences of the "pictorial" and the "graphic" possibilities of the *signum* tau.

In the reading that has traditionally been given to the construct, the tau is an extra-verbal sign of therapeutic protection or a prompt for the manual gesture of benediction with the sign of the cross. The "edition" that Esser gave to it in his definitive publication of Francis's *opuscula* was "Dominus benedicat, frater Leo, te."[5] My study did remark upon the considerable difficulty involved in coming up with that reading, which does violence both to elementary syntactical laws and to widely shared Western conventions of reading. It seems obvious, both on account of the context of the scriptural text invoked and that of the consolatory genre of the *chartula* as a whole, that Francis does indeed mean something very like the sentence "Dominus benedicat, frater Leo, te." Awkward syntax need not negate authenticity of emotion.

But the tau is both a pictorial and a graphic element. It participates, that is, in at least two discrete systems of conventional signs. As a graphic element, the tau is identical to the majuscule Latin "T." This capital "T" is significantly different from most of the minuscule "*t*s," of which there are many in the text of the blessing; however, it is precisely echoed in the "T" which is the second letter in the second line to the right of the large tau. When its graphic nature is realized, an invitation is extended to a second reading of the concluding element of the blessing. It is "Dominus bene fletote dicat"—the meaning of which is "Well may the Lord say, 'You shall weep!'" or "Let the Lord say, 'Well shall you weep!'"

The message of the final line of the Franciscan blessing may, therefore, be said to exemplify precisely the plurality or polysemousness that is the subject of this paper; for it combines the universal with the personal and the particular. The personal and the particular apply to Brother Leo in the circumstances in which he found himself during his retreat at La Verna. Those circumstances, though not definitively particularized, are clear enough in their outline. He was suffering from what he recognized as a spiritual temptation, and he required the spiritual therapies of admonition, comfort, and reassurance to combat it. Francis therefore invoked the Aaronic blessing upon Leo with an articulate particularity: "May the Lord bless *you*, Brother Leo." Implied in the literary form is the intimate relationship between the two friends and brothers that we know did in fact exist. But there was also in Francis's thought an apprehension of the universal function of the Franciscan order. That universal function, which is spelled out in early Franciscan documents many hundreds of times, was to call all men to *penance*.

There are numerous learned studies of the image of the tau. The origins of the therapeutic and prophylactic associations of the *signum* tau have been studied by several scholars and may now be regarded as definitely established. In particular, Damien Vorreux has devoted a brief monograph to its particular Franciscan usages.[6] The image was of mixed parentage, and like many other items in the repertory of Early Christian iconography in that it was derived from a union of pre-Christian associations and patristic exegesis. One biblical interpretation of the word "tau" was simply "sign" or "mark" with the incidental root meaning of the word "signature." The particular mark with which it became associated was the bloody mark daubed on the houses of the Hebrews as a

---

[5] See K. Esser, *Die Opuscula des hl. Franziskus von Assisi* (Grottaferrata, 1976), 134–46.

[6] D. Vorreux, *Un symbole franciscain: Le Tau* (Paris, 1977).

sign to the destroying angel that he should exempt them from the general slaughter of the Passover. Because of its connection with the narrative of the Passover, it took on associations with the mysteries of the Eucharist, of which the Passover feast was taken to be the type. It was also associated with the standard used by Aaron and Moses to hold up the brazen serpent in the desert, and hence because of Jesus' own application of this event to his own "lifting up" it was also applied to the Crucifixion of Christ. However learned its exegetical origins may have been, its principal associations had clearly filtered down into popular culture early in the medieval period. There is a well-known passage in the *Historia Francorum* of Gregory of Tours, in reference to the plague of the year 546, which testifies to the popular belief in the therapeutic power of the *signum* tau, which was marked on the facades of churches and domestic buildings alike. According to Gregory, it was the peasants (*rustici*) who called the sign the "tau."[7]

There is accordingly a wide spectrum of possible "sources" of Francis's experience of the tau, which range from what may be called "high theological art" such as is found in a family of well-known Mosan plaques to popular culture. This paper suggests that the Franciscan use of the tau was implied in various aspects of his spiritual self-identification. The modern study of medieval biblical typology once suffered from the defective supposition that the entire system was artificial, extrinsic, and imposed *a posteriori*. Thus it is a commonplace of medieval exegesis to compare Jesus' delivery of a "new" law from a mountain with Moses' reception of the Law on a mountain. Only comparatively recently has it been generally recognized by scholars of the New Testament that the evangelical presentation of the so-called Sermon on the Mount certainly is invoking that very typological idea even in the moment of literary presentation. Patristic exegetes discovered and perhaps ingeniously elaborated, but they did not invent, the concordances. An analogous suggestion concerning Franciscan apocalypticism could be suggested. It is the consensus of church historians that certain thirteenth-century Franciscans, for example, Brother Gerardo of San Donnino, author of the infamous *Introductorius* to the oeuvre of Joachim of Fiore, madly superimposed an imaginary biography of Francis of Assisi upon the template of the Revelation of Saint John.

He may well have done so. It may well be, however, that the madness was not in the apocalypticism itself, but in the excess. St. Bonaventure, among the most level-headed and politic church leaders of his day, and an unwavering papalist, certainly believed that Francis was the apocalyptic "angel of the sixth seal." The early Franciscans believed in the apocalyptic mission of their order for many reasons; but one of them, clearly, was that Francis himself had believed in it. Apocalyptic expectation is everywhere in the cultural experience of the Golden Age of primitive Franciscanism, as recorded in its literary monuments. This may be concluded as being a genuine and empirical intuition of Francis's own life. Francis probably adopted the sign of the tau as his signature because he had come to believe that he was an "angel"—remembering what for him that word would still mean, namely, a "messenger," or "a man like Aaron."

The ninth chapter of the prophecy of Ezekiel contains a striking apocalyptic image of God's judgment on sinful Jerusalem. Six executioners, each with sword in hand, appear on the road to the upper or northern gate of the city. One of them is a scribe with an inkhorn at his belt—*vestitus lineis et atramentarium scriptoris ad renes*. It is this scribe's office to mark with the sign *Thau* the foreheads of those few who are to be saved from the imminent general slaughter of the unjust. In

---

[7] PL 71:272.

an earlier study by this writer on the *San Francesco nel deserto* of Giovanni Bellini, a chapter was devoted to the learned literary sources that probably directly or indirectly controlled Bellini's iconographic program.[8] The connections among Aaron, the angel of the Passover, and the scribe dressed in linen are widely disseminated in Romanesque exegesis and monumental art. After a comprehensive review of the primitive Franciscan texts, this paper proposes that, although the identification of the "man like Aaron" with Francis was given a learned rationale by Bonaventure and other Franciscan apologists, it had first been intuited in an experiential way by Francis himself. It is impossible to gauge the degree of self-consciousness that this identification would have involved; but it does seem sufficiently clear that, just as he modeled his life after so many other pictorial ideas in the Scriptures, he adopted the signature tau after the tau-writer of the ninth chapter of Ezekiel.

Francis called himself an *idiota*. The usual meaning of this word, ill served by its modern English derivative, is a common, uneducated man. It also may denote an illiterate, that is, one unable to read or write Latin. Francis was not in fact illiterate. He read, wrote, and spoke biblical and cloister Latin competently; and the man who could construct or at least appreciate an amphibology based in the rare verbal form *fletote* might even be said to have a certain amount of Latin learning. But his fundamental and unwavering self-identification, around which also he structured his order, was with *minoritas*—that "lesserness" or radical humility that directed his every conscious gesture. He was being true to an inner humility in his adoption of the "mark" of an illiterate as his signature, as the cross has been legally accepted down to this very day.

From the iconographic point of view, however, the situation is problematical. The famous remark of Gregory the Great that the images in churches were the "biblia pauperum" is often repeated as though it made sense without further explanation. The implication is that pictures, unlike words, are "natural" signs. A survey of that idea as it has appeared and reappeared in Christian thought would make an interesting study. But if pictorial iconography is a system of conventional signs, there is a requirement for "picturacy" in the intellectual apprehension of images no less than for literacy in the intellectual apprehension of words. One way of describing the phenomenon of Francis's tau-signature would be to say that it uses a heavily freighted conventional sign *as though it were* a natural sign.

A cognate problem appears with regard to a second famous Franciscan signature, that of Christopher Columbus."Famous" is perhaps not the *mot juste:* perhaps "notorious" will serve. Only the supposed Baconian cipher in the works of Shakespeare has proved a more powerful magnet for ingenious error. In Umberto Eco's recent novel *Foucault's Pendulum*, two of the characters discuss a manuscript submitted for publication at their publishing house. It is a study of the Columbus signature, and "it analyzes his signature and finds in it a reference to the pyramids. Columbus's real aim was to reconstruct the Temple of Jerusalem, since he was grand master of the Templars-in-exile. Being a Portuguese Jew and therefore an expert cabalist, he used talismanic spells to calm storms and overcome scurvy."[9] This may have been intended as exuberant satire; but it is in fact accurate in two of its claims, and fails only by its timidity to suggest the weirdness of Columbus's mind.

---

[8] J. V. Fleming, *From Bonaventure to Bellini: An Essay in Franciscan Exegesis* (Princeton, 1982), 99–128.

[9] U. Eco, *Foucault's Pendulum* (New York, 1989), 273.

It is a technical liberty to call Columbus a Franciscan, since no specific document, such as a letter of confraternity, exists that would put the question beyond dispute. It would be a distraction in this paper to discuss the fairly extensive evidence that points to a likelihood so great as to fall just short of certainty. At the very least, Columbus's signature shares the spirit of Francis's and is, indeed, probably influenced by it. And though no auto-interpretation of either signature exists, Columbus's detailed and revealing description of *his* does survive. This is in the document of *mayorazgo*, or stipulated primogeniture, in which, under the date of 22 February 1498, he wills his signature to his son Don Diego Colón. He stipulates that his successive heirs, of which Don Diego is the most immediate, shall, when they come into their inheritance, henceforth sign all documents "with the signature that I am accustomed to use now," thus detailed:

> que es una .X. con una .S. encima y una .M. con una .A. romana
>
> encima, y encima d'ella una .S. y despues una .Y. greca con una
>
> .S. encima con sus rayas y bírgulas como agora hago . . .[10]

The literal elements of the signature contain the most matter. This paper is limited to examining the aspect indicated by the terminal prepositional phrase "con sus rayas y bírgulas . . . ." The word "rayas" is problematical. It has been taken to mean "straight lines." This is correct only if the concept of "straight lines" is understood as the geometrical disposition of the "mystical" letters. To grasp the cruciform pictogram outlined or "graphed" by the mysterious letters requires an appreciation for the rectilinearity of the construct. But the word *bírgulas* is less problematical: it means the points of punctuation.

This signature is more modern than Francis's in that it does actually include its author's name, though only in an oblique way. "Columbus" is of course a Latinized version of the admiral's Italian family name: Colombo. The more obvious way for an Iberian to transliterate this Italian name would be Colombo. But the Spanish form of the admiral's name, certainly chosen by himself, is not Colombo but Colón.

There were in classical Latin two different words for dove: *columba* (*columbus* in its masculine form) and *palumbes* (masculine or feminine). The first corresponded to the Greek *peristera*, the latter to the Greek *phatta*. The former often denoted the domestic pigeon, the latter the wood pigeon or ring-dove; but from the ornithological point of view it is usually not possible to distinguish between them in surviving texts. Their etymological history in the modern Romance languages is interesting. Only in the *langue d'Oc* do derivatives from both words survive; all the rest had, by the early modern period, made an unlegislated choice between the *c*-form and the *p*-form, distinguishing between the domestic and wild birds by the help of an ancillary adjective. Thus the modern Italian word is *colomba*; the modern Portuguese word *pombo*. Castillian Spanish, from the very earliest vernacular texts we have, had opted for the *p*-form with *paloma*.

Hence, had the Genovese Cristoforo Colombo wished to have preserved merely his phonology in Castillian Spanish, he could have done so easily enough by leaving his name unchanged. But if he wanted to preserve his onomastic *meaning*, he would have had to change his name to Palumbo. There was another way open to him, however, that allowed him to combine phonology with signification. Columbus spent crucial years in Catalonia. The word for dove in Catalan, which

---

10 "Institución de Mayorazgo," in Cristóbal Colón, *Textos y documentos completos*, ed. C. Varela (Madrid, 1984), 193.

was in the fifteenth century a more important language of the Mediterranean world than was Castillian, was *colon* or *colom.*

This paper is not the first to divagate on the admiral's name. The first was probably by Columbus himself, but the first of textual record is that of his son Fernando, author of his earliest biography. The original of Fernando's book, which must have been in Spanish, has never been found. The first edition is an Italian translation (Venice, 1571). In an early passage in which he sought to correct insults or slights offered to his father by Gonzalo Fernadez de Oviedo in his celebrated *Historia general y natural de las Indías,* Fernando gives a lengthy disquisition on the "mystery" of his father's name. In summary, he says that[11] the admiral bore the name of Colombo because he bore the grace of the Holy Spirit, which in the baptism of John descended upon Jesus in the form of a dove, to faraway nations who knew not God. As for the Colón, "it came to him to adopt the cognomen Colón because in Greek it means 'member.'" The given name "Christopher" is more easily disposed of. Like the legendary Christopher who carried the infant Christ across the water, Christopher Colonus likewise carried the Christ across the Atlantic Ocean.

This is wholly consistent with various documents in which Columbus exposed what might be called his personal, self-reflexive apocalypticism, and especially with the famous letter written to the Reyes in 1501, in which he talks at length about biblical prophecy.[12] Like Francis, Columbus came to see for himself a very special and personal role in the history of salvation. What could be seen as an intellectual gesture of arrogance or audacious impertinence, he would have viewed as a grace of humility. In the letter mentioned above, he wrote thus of those who derided him and his visionary project:

> . . . they laughed at me for not being a learned man, for having the culture of a sailor, for being a layman, and so on. I answer that which Saint Matthew said: "O Lord, who desirest to keep so many things secret from learned men, but reveal them to the innocents." And the same Saint Matthew: "As Our Lord was going to Jerusalem, the children sang out 'Hossanah to the Son of David!' And the scribes to test Him asked him if He heard what they said, and He answered them, Yes, saying 'Do you not know that from the mouths of babes and innocents the truth is spoken?'"[13]

Here is the perfect self-infantilizing gesture of the Franciscan *idiota.*

It is interesting to see how Columbus may have "pictured" these ideas when he constructed his signature. Fernando was entirely correct in saying that in Greek *kolon* means member. Its typical context in Greek, and its only context commonly noted in Latin texts of Columbus's time, is grammatical or rhetorical. The *kolon* is a member or part of a written or spoken statement. The Latin word for the complete expression of more than one thought is a sentence was *periodus.* The smaller unit of the *periodus,* roughly equivalent to the phrase, was the *comma.* Its larger unit, the independent clause, was the *colon.* It will be obvious that these three syntactical units have given their names to three common punctuation marks: the comma (,), the colon (:), and the period (.). The key "mysteries" that Columbus sought to convey in the final line of his signature were two: that he was another Christopher, or Christ-bearer, and that he enjoyed (or groaned beneath) the special

---

[11] Facsimile edition, introduced by G. Bellini (Rome, 1992), 2v–3r.

[12] Ed. in Varela, *Textos y documentos* (as in note 9), 277–81.

[13] Ibid., 278–79.

commission of the Holy Ghost. Had he been a genuine instead of a spiritual *idiota* he might have used an *image* of a Christopher or of a dove. Evidence exists as to how simple sailors signed documents in Columbus's day. But in fact he was a man of "gran ingenio, é gentil Latino," as Oviedo said of him.[14] He knew that there were words, and that there were things, and that sometimes words *were* things. The ambiguous terrain where words, things, and images come together has been provisionally mapped by Jean Céard and Jean-Claude Margolin in their *Rébus de la Renaissance;* but more intensive study, particularly in terms of its relationship to *personal* expression, is needed.[15] Like Francis, whose sacramental and perhaps quasi-mystical view of the world of things he shared, Columbus chose as his thing a scribal emblem as his own personalized emblem of inscription.

There is another witty feature that may have engaged Columbus's imagination. The degree to which Columbus was in any serious way a believer in the prophecies of Joachim of Fiore is a subject of considerable dispute; but there is no doubt that he regarded his personal and divinely inspired discovery one of the defining and unchangeable moments in human history. The heart of the "new law" of Christianity is contained in the fifth chapter of the Gospel of Matthew, in the so-called Sermon on the Mount. The sermon begins with two passages of decisive importance to Francis's own religious imagination and hence to the regular legislation of his "new" order—the Beatitudes and the reinterpretation of the Mosaic Law. Francis found an especial application in the final beatitude, "how blest you are when you suffer insults and persecution and every kind of calumny for my sake." His metaphorical image of *minoritas* is clearly related to two of Jesus's cognate images, which are those of the "salt of the earth" and the city on the hill that cannot be hidden. The link between the Beatitudes and the statement of the new law is this: "Do not suppose that I have come to abolish the Law and the prophets; I did not come to abolish, but to complete. I tell you this: so long as heaven and earth endure, not a letter, not a stroke, will disappear from the Law until all that must happen has happened [Mt. 5:17–18]." The terms "letter" and "stroke," the famous "jot and tittle" of the King James Version, appear in the Vulgate as *iota* and *apex.* Their precise meaning varies in medieval commentaries, but a consensus seems to suggest "dot and stroke." It will be noticed that the colon mark (/.) is in fact composed of an iota and an apex.

[14] G. Fernández de Oviedo y Valdés, *Historia general y natural de las Indías,* ed. J. Amador de los Ríos (Asunción de Paraguay, n.d.), vol. 1, 43.

[15] J. Céard and J.-C. Margolin, *Rébus de la Renaissance: Des images qui parlent,* 2 vols. (Paris, 1986).

2

METHODOLOGY

·

How to Improve Art-Historical Services

·

LUTZ HEUSINGER

IN 1942, a book entitled *The Index of Christian Art at Princeton University* was published at Princeton. This handbook, written by Helen Woodruff, with a foreword by Charles Rufus Morey, records that:

> The Subject File of the Index, the Key to the Titles, and a Key to the Bibliography have been photographed on microfilm and two copies struck off from the negative. One copy has been placed in the Dumbarton Oaks Research Library of Harvard University, located in Washington, D.C., the other in the Library of the Metropolitan Museum in New York City. Once a year all new entries and all corrected or altered ones are filmed, and the prints added to the copies. By a similar process a copy of the photographs has been made, but this is installed at Dumbarton Oaks only. It is hoped that in the near future other copies can be placed in libraries and museums of this country and of Europe, making the Index accessible to a larger number of the students whose investigations have led them into the fields of early Christian and medieval history.[1]

A footnote states: "A charge for this service is made at the rate of $1.00 per hour for the time involved in looking up and recording data. Duplicate photographs can be purchased for 15 cents each for less than five or 10 cents each in larger quantities. Prices are subject to change without notice." The idea, as congenial as it is noble, of making an unpublished research instrument like the Index of Christian Art available in other places as well at minimal cost, could obviously not be pursued during the Second World War. It was not until 1961 that a copy of the Index was installed in the Vatican, and 1962 that the copy in Utrecht was established.

Twelve years later, in 1974, the Witt Library, with the help of the J. Paul Getty Museum, copied its indispensable collection of reproductions onto microfiche and, perhaps inspired by the model of the Index of Christian Art, made five copies available in North America, Australia, and on the European continent in a program of mutual endowments. Another twenty years later, the Courtauld Institute was able to overcome copyright restrictions and produce additional copies of the Witt Library to be sold as a publication. In 1977, the Bildarchiv Foto Marburg began incorporating photographs of art in Germany into a unified form and offering it on microfiche under the title "Marburger Index." Today, this collection, which has now grown to 1.3 million photographs, can be consulted in 120 locations around the world. There followed comparable publications such as those of the Alinari archive, the photographic archive of the Deutsches Archäologisches Institut

---

[1] H. Woodruff, *The Index of Christian Art at Princeton University* (Princeton, 1942), 10.

in Rome, and the Conway Library. Since then, other large libraries with important art-historical material such as the Bibliotheca Palatina and the Cicognara library have been made available on microfiche in many places. Thus the process of not only preserving large collections of important research material in their original locations, but also offering them to potentially interested users elsewhere, has come a long way since its beginnings in the 1930s.

The question now, however, concerns the future. At the present, virtually every museum, library, archive, university, and research institute is working on establishing a presence on the Internet, accessible to all, whether at home or at work. In most cases, however, this has nothing to do with making research materials available. It generally consists only of a kind of trivial advertising for institutions and persons that is neither relevant nor interesting. Nonetheless, we can still learn from positive exceptions like the National Gallery in Washington or the Index of Christian Art. Such examples show that it is now possible to transport important materials and information directly to the researcher, making them more effective than ever before. Four suggestions are proposed in this paper as to how this opportunity should be used and improved.

1. REDUCING THE COST OF RESEARCH MATERIALS

In the thirteenth century, the production of a single manuscript was expensive and time-consuming. As is well known, the production of a printed book was much less costly. The development of digital media has once again reduced the cost of reproducing information by many orders of magnitude. Prevailing circumstances indicate that in the future every small museum and college, despite its modest budget, will finally gain access to the materials needed for genuine research. It is also probable that in all countries development will continue to be concentrated in a few institutions that can afford to take full advantage of the new offerings. At present, there are two main ways in which large collections of material are made available for research. The first of these concerns large publishing houses such as Chadwyck-Healey, which offers monumental collections of information such as The English Poetry Full-Text Database, The American Poetry Full-Text Database, Goethes Werke (Weimarer Ausgabe), the Patrologia Latina, or Art Theorists of the Italian Renaissance, available to anyone who can pay the subscription fee.

Secondly, a group of institutions such as the French national museums, the Library of Congress, the National Gallery in Washington, the Deutsches Historisches Museum, and others, which are public institutions and feel a sense of responsibility for public education, offer their materials at no cost.

As a rule, the literature that Chadwyck-Healey digitizes and sells to libraries in digital form is obtained at no cost from those very libraries; this procedure is legitimate, as libraries should be free-of-charge to users. But this poses the problem as to why the libraries themselves could not digitize their own collections through the division and sharing of labor in order to reduce the cost. The digitization of the materials that form the basis of our social memory and public responsibility par excellence should not be left to the contingencies of the market and commercial constellations. The development of the World Wide Web has made it necessary to reconsider one of the defining standards of art history. Up to now, collections of information have been sold for a price as the products of publishing houses; today this is no longer the only option, and in fact this development is only beginning. More materials will be digitized in the future. New research will probably be digitally published from the start. The deciding question is whether this is something that is desirable or whether it is unimportant.

The Deutsche Forschungsgemeinschaft (German Research Association), in many respects the equivalent of the National Endowment for the Humanities, intends to grant $1.3 million to the Bildarchiv Foto Marburg in order to digitize and prepare the 1.3 million photographs of the Marburger Index to be made available at no cost on the World Wide Web in the best possible quality. The continuing expansion of the Marburger Index by about 60,000 photographs a year has long been financed not least of all by the $60,000 in royalties that we receive annually for the Index from its publishing house. In the coming years, therefore, it will not be possible for the Index to offer additional photographs free-of-charge on the Internet. Nevertheless, the aim is to make the entire body of 1.3 million cost-free photographs, along with the extensions to the database, so attractive that it can be financed entirely from endowments as a kind of national photo archive of art and architecture in Germany. In this way it can be offered free-of-charge to users. If other institutions around the world with large collections of material could make an effort to find similar solutions, it would be easier to find the grants for building up an international and truly great photo archive for Western art.

2. Comprehensively Enriched Offerings of Research Material

There are essentially two obstacles to the effective large-scale dissemination of art-historical information. The primary difficulties are social, and have to do with property rights; technological concerns are secondary. As long as scholarly recognition hangs on the principle of "publish or perish" in printed form, the opportunities for a faster, more comprehensive, and cheaper exchange of information remain drastically limited. Thus it is all the more significant that the technical deficits that have up to now prevented the exchange of large bodies of information are growing smaller on a daily basis.

What began in the 1970s as a small database on a large computer can now be illustrated and offered on the Internet with increasing comprehensiveness, density, and quality. The difficulties that still exist are being overcome with a little imagination. For example, the National Gallery in Washington, D.C. does not simply offer large image files for its paintings, which at present would take too long to download, but rather a larger number of intelligently dimensioned, detailed records. A project which the Bildarchiv Foto Marburg is currently working on for the Deutsche Forschungsgemeinschaft, together with the Staatsbibliothek in Berlin and the Bayerische Staatsbibliothek in Munich, aims to develop this idea even further. The project involves the creation of a complete database of medieval manuscripts in German libraries. This databank is intended to provide a computer-supported instrument for the scholarly study of manuscripts. It will also be made available on the World Wide Web to anyone interested. To expedite the completion of this project, two existing resources will be used.

The first task involves the digitization of a complete set of some 15,000 manuscript catalogues, which has been put together over the last twenty years with the support of the Deutsche Forschungsgemeinschaft. The second source is the digitization of existing photographic reproductions of these manuscripts.

A preliminary method of accessing the material is achieved by incorporating the index entries from the catalogues, in addition to the catalogue texts and the reproductions. The example of the twelfth-century Kollektar Aa35 in Fulda shows that the intent is not simply to provide detailed, structured cataloguing of all the relevant data on the manuscript. A complete, high-quality photographic reproduction will also constitute an important part of the database. The researcher should be able to view the images as precisely as possible and see what has already been written about them in order to form a better judgment. The structured information is merely the finding aid it always was.

Nowadays it is possible to offer large bodies of electronic material, including many high-resolution images and extensive texts, an opportunity of which we should take advantage.

3. Integrated Availability of Research Materials

The advantages of being able to study the holdings of a museum on the World Wide Web are obvious. In the majority of cases, however, researchers investigate not only objects in a single museum, but ones that are widely distributed in different locations, collections, and buildings. It is not enough for every museum, archive, and institution to simply improve accessibility to its own individual collection of material in the future. Interconnection between collections is also necessary, with the goal of enabling researchers to answer overarching questions. This has presented no difficulties for the French national museums. They have catalogued their collections in a unified manner and can now offer them collectively on the World Wide Web.

Computers and computer programs are constantly becoming both more powerful and easier to use. Even when they are made by different companies, they are now working better together. For this reason it is becoming easier to find institutions with compatible computer systems, whose employees possess compatible background knowledge. At the same time, art-historical research tools have been improved. Within days, even a novice can effectively use and even enjoy the new ICONCLASS Browser. Similarly, tools like the Art and Architecture Thesaurus or the Thesaurus of Artists' Names produced in Leipzig are constantly being improved. In recent years many have learned how to transform and modify data collections with little effort and modest resources.

Any institution can acquire an easy-to-use database program, collections of iconographic and artists' biographical information based on international standards, relevant parts of thesauri, and a wealth of further data at almost no cost, and still enjoy considerable individual freedom without endangering the compatibility of the databases. A convergence, whose speed will largely depend on the quality and quantity of the products that will be provided, can be expected in the coming years. Many individual achievements and projects will continue to pave the way for the effective, integrated availability of information.

4. More Detailed Iconographical Access to Research Materials

Anyone who has consulted a large collection of art-historical material like the Index of Christian Art knows the problem of trying to approach iconographic differentiation as the collection grows. In this respect ICONCLASS offers an outstanding vocabulary. But there is still the question as to how this vocabulary can be most effectively used to describe and access works of art in a way that is as deep, multi-faceted, and appropriate as possible. The fourth and final suggestion in this paper has to do with this issue. If ICONCLASS is used to organize a collection of reproductions according to iconography, it is sufficient to supply each reproduction with a single notation. The postcard-sized reproductions of the Decimal Index of the Art of the Low Countries (DIAL) used a number of notations in order to catalogue more thoroughly the representational content of the individual paintings. To do this the syntax that is published in the General Introduction to ICONCLASS in volume 2 (1974) was used. This allows notations to be combined in two ways: on the one hand as an additive sequence of notations with no relational signs between them (the standard case), and secondly where they are connected by a colon to indicate a special relation, the so-called "combined notation."

If the aim was to catalogue representational content in an even more differentiated way, it would be logical to elaborate on this comparatively simple syntax and define more than just two kinds of relationships between iconographical objects. The introduction of a definite and differentiated syntax, as in the *Thesaurus iconographique* of François Garnier,[2] could give rise to compatibility problems. An effort should be made to find a way to indicate whether Joseph or Mary is playing with the Child, whether the man is cutting the woman's hair or the other way around, whether the king has the crown on his head or in his hand, whether the child is sitting on the ground or on a cabinet, etc.

Other possible improvements in the recording of iconographical subjects may be explained using a simple example. In 1520, the humanist Georg Spalatin, privy secretary of Frederick the Wise, elector of Saxony, commissioned Lucas Cranach the Elder to print a portrait of Luther for dissemination. Three trial proofs have been preserved. Two prints are known of the first state. One of these is in Vienna (Fig. 1) and the other in Washington, D.C. Only a single print of the second state is preserved, in the Schlossmuseum in Weimar (Fig. 2). Thirty prints exist of the third and last state (Fig. 3), but as Koepplin demonstrated in his 1974 publication[3] the watermarks indicate that only a few of them date before the years 1570–90. It is revealing that this famous, indeed classic portrait of Luther, which has had a determinative influence on the German image of the Reformer, was originally not meant to be disseminated at all, but instead appears to have been suppressed.

Cranach developed another portrait from his first picture of Luther, which in the same year, 1520, was successfully disseminated from the Saxon court (Fig. 4). When the two pictures are compared it becomes clear, as Warnke[4] suggested in the title of his book on "Cranach's Luther," that we are dealing here with the creation of a political image unsurpassed by any of the present day. The simple bust of a serene, unapproachable reformer has become the half-figure portrait of a pious, inspired, committed monk. How can this event be described with the help of ICONCLASS?

This is possible firstly by using a certain range of information fields, such as:

- primary iconography
- secondary iconography
- local relation

---

[2] F. Garnier, *Thesaurus iconographique: Système descriptif des représentations* (Paris, 1984).

[3] D. Koepplin and T. Falk, *Lucas Cranach, Catalogue*, 2d ed. (Basel, 1974), vol. 1, 92, no. 35.

[4] M. Warnke, *Cranachs Luther: Entwürfe für ein Image* (Frankfurt am Main, 1984).

· iconographical addition
· iconographical subtraction
· associative iconography
· alternate interpretation

Secondly, the notations in every field can be ranked according to the pictorial significance of the characteristics they designate. A picture whose iconography is to be described using the ICON-CLASS vocabulary, therefore, should first be analyzed and understood according to art and art-historical principles before its content can be classified in an appropriate way. Current practice gives reason enough to emphasize this point. When the notations on an image are recorded in a factually justifiable sequence, they can be mechanically numbered within the database and thus retrieved in relation to their importance in the picture. This feature is indispensable for large databases. Results from a search which calls up some 20,000 images without distinguishing the degree of significance are of limited use.

It is possible to go beyond this simple and effective way of differentiating iconographic importance and divide the hierarchically ordered notations into two groups: a first group for iconographic facts of primary significance in the image, and a second one for those of secondary importance, for example, when they appear in the background, are small, or are clearly incidental. The cataloguing of around 130,000 works of art in German museums has proven that this kind of unified and consistent distinction between primary and secondary iconography is possible and is welcomed by database users. A field designated "local relation" could serve for the names of geographic entities which are not represented, but which relate historically to the subject. For the present image, Wittenberg would fall into this category.

Unfortunately, it would be impossible to make the differences between the first and the second Cranach portrait of Luther retrievable in structured cataloguing. The decisive formal alterations in detail (shading, lighting, folds, etc.) cannot be retrievably indicated. It is possible, however, to provide an information field for "iconographical additions" and use it to specify what was added in the later print: the gesture of "hand on heart," the book, and the niche. In this way it may be possible to search for images which, in comparison with their model, have been enriched with the gesture, a book, and a niche. At a later date Cranach's pious portrait of Luther induced Hans Baldung Grien to go a step further. He copied the model in reverse and supplemented it with the dove of the Holy Ghost as well as a kind of halo. In this way, Luther becomes a sacred figure. The resulting image may not actually show a saint, but most definitely evokes the association. In cases like these, in which one is also reminded of Jan Białostocki's iconographic "Rahmenformen," one could, and indeed should provide a field for "iconographical association." This would enable us to search for images which, though they do not actually show a given subject, nevertheless evoke its association. If the researcher came to the conclusion that Baldung wanted to portray Luther not like a saint, but instead and contrary to Luther's own intention, as a saint, one could indicate the notation "Martin Luther as a saint shown with the Holy Ghost" as the primary object of representation.

Conceivably, however, there might be some doubt as to this interpretation. In that case, one could have recourse to a field for notations giving an alternate interpretation. "Martin Luther as a saint shown with the Holy Ghost" would thus be entered, but not preferred.

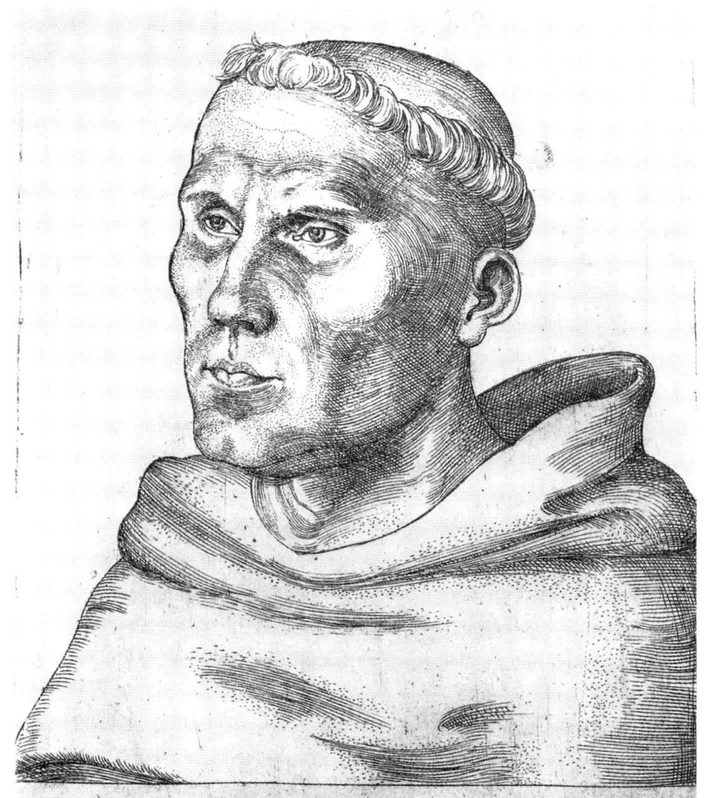

1. Lucas Cranach the Elder, *Martin Luther*, first engraving, first state, 1520, 13.8 × 9.5 cm, Vienna, Graphische Sammlung Albertina, inv. 1929/78

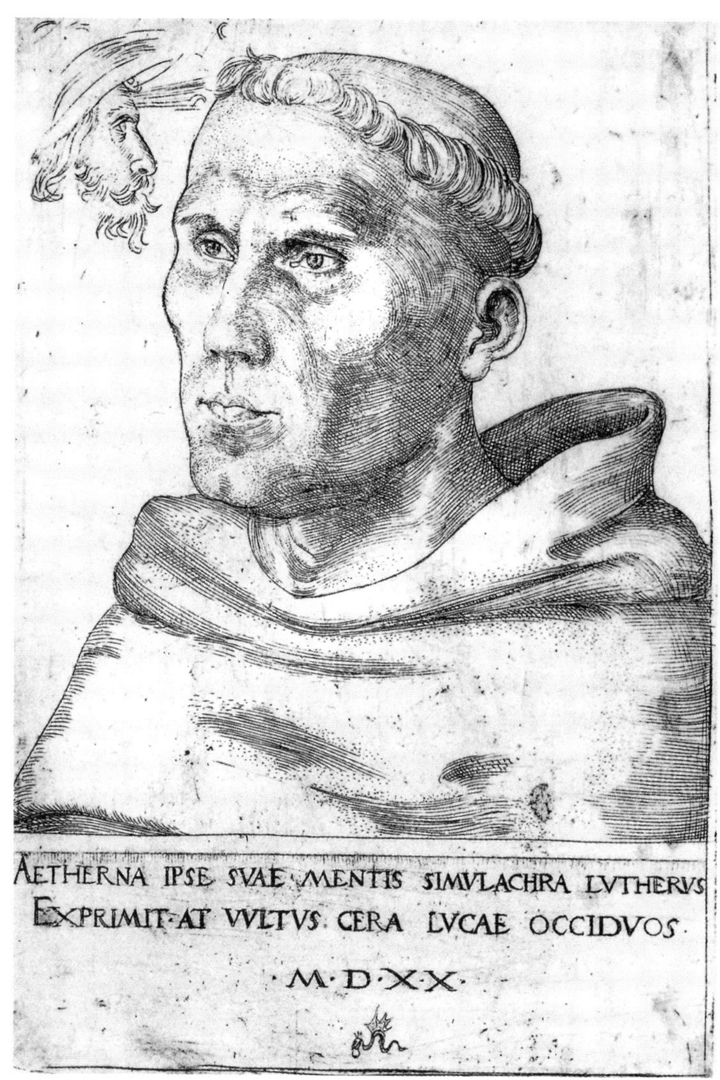

2. Lucas Cranach the Elder, *Martin Luther*, first engraving, second state, 1520, 13.8 × 9.5 cm, Weimar, Schlossmuseum, inv. DK 36/79

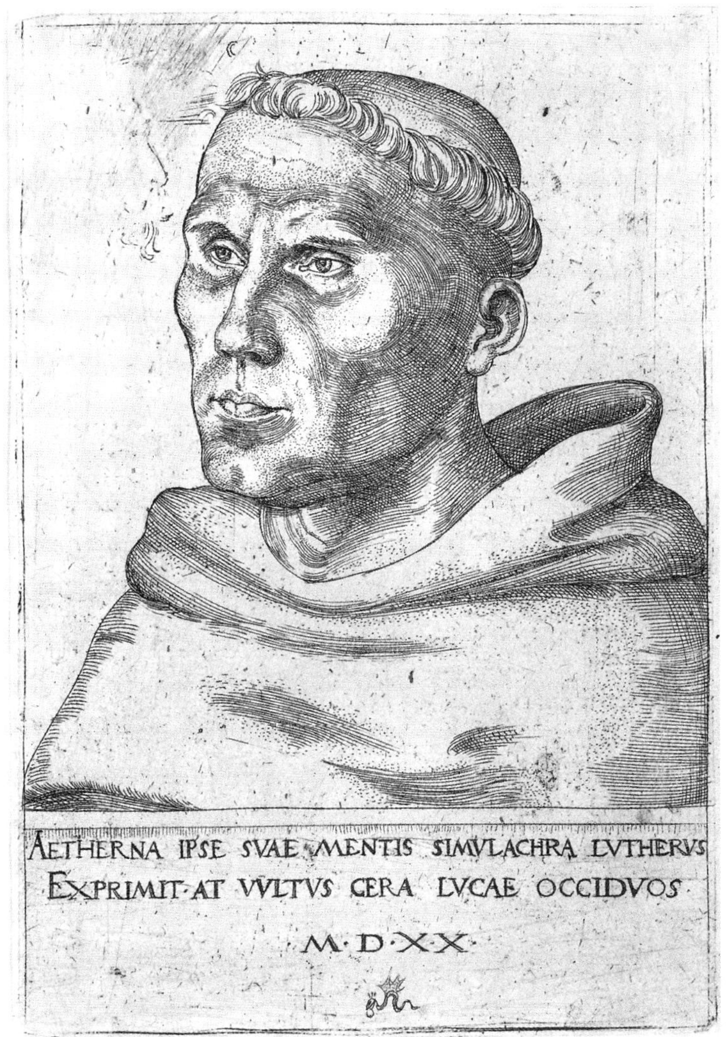

3. Lucas Cranach the Elder, *Martin Luther*, first engraving, third state,
1520, 13.8 × 11.5 cm, Hamburg, Kunsthalle, Kupferstichkabinett (B.5)

PRIMARY ICONOGRAPHY: (1) 11 P 16 41 :
                        (2) 61 B 2 (LUTHER, Martin) 11 (+52 2) :
                        (3) 11 P 31 52 1 (AUGUSTINIANS)

LOCAL RELATIONSHIP: (1) 61 E (WITTENBERG)

This means: (1) the Reformation represented by (2) Martin Luther (bust,
three-quarter view) as (3) an Augustinian monk; the representation is relevant
to the history of Wittenberg.

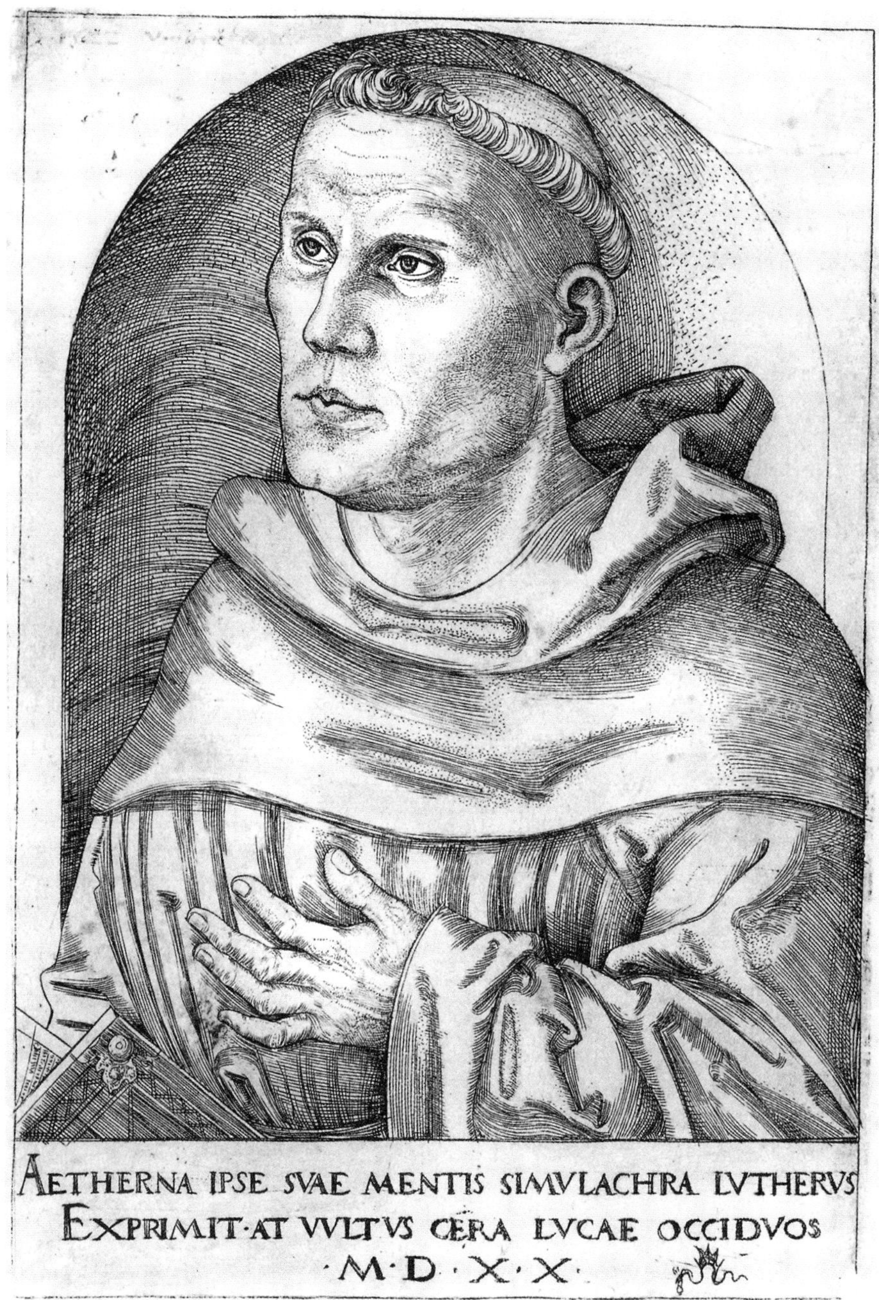

4. Lucas Cranach the Elder, *Martin Luther*, second engraving, 1520, 17.9 × 12.5 cm, Munich, Staatliche Graphische Sammlung, inv. 14448

PRIMARY ICONOGRAPHY: (1) 11 P 31 52 1 (AUGUSTINIANS) :
                                      (2) 61 B 2 (LUTHER, Martin) 11 (+52 2) &
                                      (3) 31 A 25 16 2 &
                                      (4) 49 M 32 &
                                      (5) 48 C 16 22 (NICHE)
LOCAL RELATIONSHIP: (1) 61 E (WITTENBERG)
ICONOGRAPHICAL ADDITION: (1) 31 A 25 16 2 &
                                      (2) 49 M 32 &
                                      (3) 48 C 16 22 (NICHE)

This means: (1) the Augustinian monk (2) Martin Luther (bust, three-quarter view) with (3) his hand on his heart and (4) a book, shown in (5) a niche; the representation is relevant to the history of Wittenberg; to the first engraving have been added (1) the gesture of the hand on the heart, (2) the book, and (3) the niche.

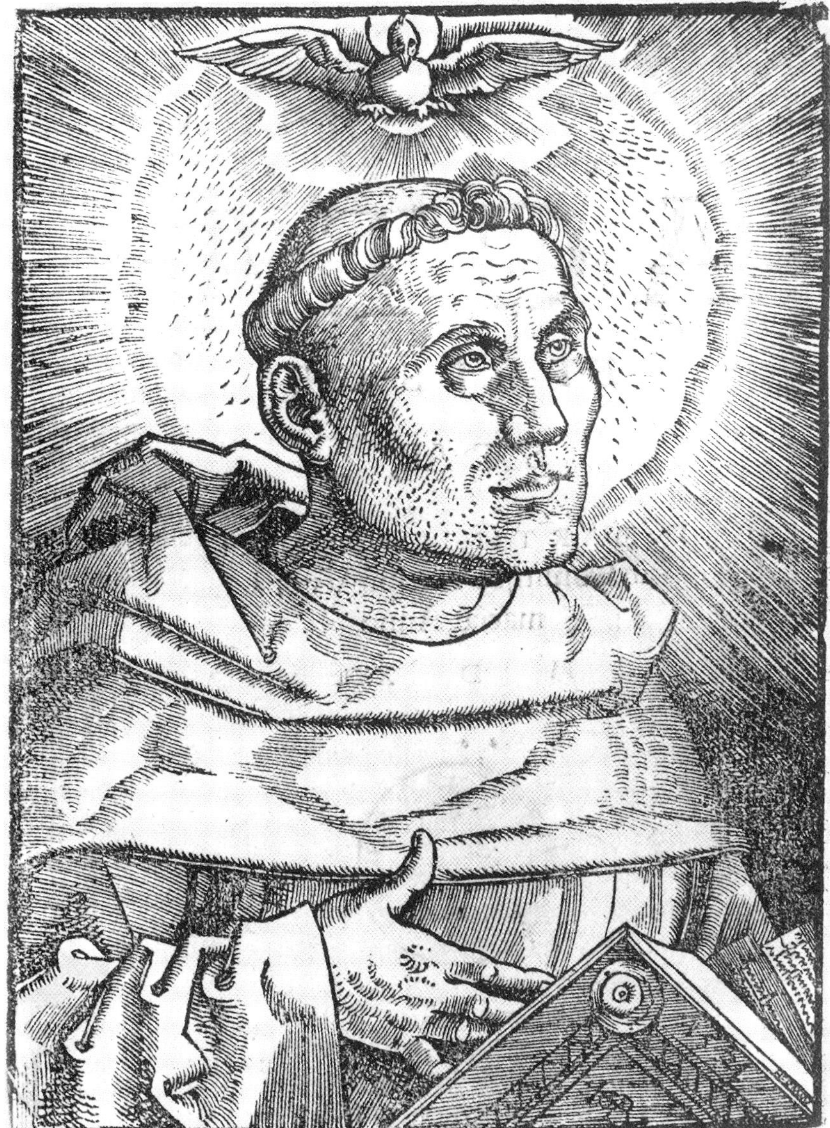

5. Hans Baldung gen. Grien, *Martin Luther*, woodcut, 1521, 15.4 × 11.5 cm,
Württembergische Landesbibliothek

PRIMARY ICONOGRAPHY: (1) 61 B 2 (LUTHER, Martin) 11 (+52 2) :
 (2) 11 P 31 52 1 (AUGUSTINIANS) &
 (3) 11 E 1 &
 (4) 22 C 31

SECONDARY ICONOGRAPHY: (1) 31 A 25 16 2 &
 (2) 49 M 32 &

ICONOGRAPHICAL SUBTRACTION: (1) 48 C 16 22 (NICHE)

ICONOGRAPHICAL ADDITION: (1) 11 E 1 &
 (2) 22 C 31

ICONOGRAPHICAL ASSOCIATION: (1) 11 H (LUTHER, Martin) 9 (+13)

ALTERNATE INTERPRETATION: (1) 11 H (LUTHER, Martin) 9 (+13)

This means: (1) Martin Luther (bust, three-quarter view) as (2) an Augustinian monk with
(3) the Holy Ghost (as a dove) and (4) a radiance; also shown with (1) the gesture of the
hand on the heart and (2) a book; the niche in Cranach's engraving has been replaced by
(1) the Holy Ghost and (2) the radiance. The image evokes the iconographical association
of (1) a portrait of a saint (Martin Luther) shown with the Holy Ghost (as a dove). In
addition, an alternative interpretation could call the image (1) a portrait of a saint (Martin
Luther) shown with the Holy Ghost (as a dove).

The Persistence of Mythological, Religious, and Literary Narratives as Subjects of Works of Art*

.

HELENE E. ROBERTS

"The precedent behind every action, its invisible, ever-present lining"

ROBERTO CALASSO refers to the "precedent behind every action" that forms the "invisible, ever-present lining" near the end of his *Marriage of Cadmus and Harmony*.[1] Harmony voices the thought when she realizes that her future has already been decided, and that she has been living her life as foretold in a myth. These same words could equally apply to the many instances when mythological, religious, and literary narratives provide the common coin of cultural discourse: the "invisible, ever-present lining" of the way we describe and explain our actions and circumstances.

People define themselves through the configurations of the narratives they tell. The "precedent" of a mythic action may be used, or subtly altered, in order to explain actions in a later time and place. When a new story of a great love is told, for example, allusions are often made to the older narratives—Orpheus and Eurydice, Dido and Aeneas, Hero and Leander, Tristan and Isolde, Romeo and Juliet. When a society begins to see itself in a different light, this change is often announced by the recasting of familiar stories.

Classical mythology, religious texts, and literary works provide such a complex texture of relationships, situations, and associations that they have been appropriated for a variety of uses. The narratives describe rape, ruination, empowerment, victimization, and inexplicable changes of fortune, not to mention inescapable guilt, ambition, arrogance, greed, pride, passion, sexual and gender ambiguities, courage, cowardice, love, death, and a host of other universal human predicaments.

With such a rich menu of precedents embedded in our cultural memory, it is not difficult to see why these "ever-present" narratives keep recurring. Take, for example, the story of Orpheus. Several years ago in Boston, in the span of one weekend, there were performances of two operas based on this story: Claudio Monteverdi's *Orfeo*, from the seventeenth century, and Philip Glass's *Orphée*, a twentieth-century work. During the same weekend Jean Cocteau's film *Orphée*, on which the Glass opera was based, could be seen in Boston, as could *Black Orpheus*, the film set in modern Brazil and loosely based on the Orpheus legend. One could also have seen paintings depicting the

---

* Portions of this article appeared in the introduction and the essay "Abandonment" in the *Encyclopedia of Comparative Mythology*, and are reprinted here with the permission of Fitzroy Dearborn Publishers.

[1] R. Calasso, *The Marriage of Cadmus and Harmony*, trans. T. Parks (London, 1994), 383.

story of Orpheus by Giovanni da San Giovanni, Odilon Redon, and George Frederic Watts at the Fogg Art Museum, Harvard University,[2] and, at the Boston Museum of Fine Arts, paintings of Orpheus by Eugène Delacroix and Jan Cox.[3] Twentieth-century artists such as Raoul Dufy, Paul Klee, André Breton, André Masson, Max Beckmann, Oskar Kokoschka, and Pablo Picasso, who depicted the Orpheus myth, are also represented in Boston collections. These examples do not include sculptors, nor the artists whose names are less known, nor the many poems, novels, dramas, and dances based on the theme of Orpheus.[4]

A Greek myth that was the subject of poems in the seventh century before Christ was, twenty-seven centuries later, still intriguing audiences and inspiring artists, novelists, poets, and composers. The Orpheus myth is impressive not only in its ability to endure over this span of time, but also in its ability to sustain metamorphoses into a variety of forms, genres, and interpretations. Although the core of the original story remained recognizable, the presentations, and the meanings to be garnered from them, amounted to transformations.

When early Christians, eager to give their religion a historical background, and wanting to appease their pagan neighbors, looked for an iconography with which to depict their Christ, they chose to pattern their depictions on Orpheus, who had similar attributes—a peaceful nature, spiritual power, reputed monotheism, and a gruesome death. In the catacombs Christ was thus depicted as the Good Shepherd surrounded by animals, as Orpheus had been in Roman mosaics.[5]

In the era of courtly love, Orpheus became a troubadour serenading his lady Eurydice, as in a fifteenth-century manuscript illumination from John Lydgate's *Fall of Princes* in the British Library, London.[6] During and after the Renaissance Orpheus was seen as an embodiment of Neoplatonic love and an emblem of order in the universe, charming the wild animals into peace and harmony, as he does in a seventeenth-century painting by Roelant Savery in the National Gallery, London.[7] In the nineteenth century Orpheus became a symbol of thwarted love and loss, as in Ary Scheffer's depiction of Eurydice's death, painted in 1814, now in the Chateau of Blois.[8] Her second death on the threshold of the return from Hades realized the threatening power of the gaze, as in George Frederic Watts's painting in the Watts Gallery, Compton.[9]

[2] E. P. Bowron, *European Paintings before 1900 in the Fogg Art Museum* (Cambridge, Mass., 1990), pls. 83 (Watts), 406 (Redon), 725 (Giovanni da San Giovanni).

[3] A. R. Murphy, *European Paintings in the Museum of Fine Arts, Boston: An Illustrated Summary Catalogue* (Boston, 1985), 67 (Cox), 79 (Delacroix).

[4] Claudio Monteverdi, *Orfeo* (1607); Philip Glass, *Orphée* (1993); Jean Cocteau, *Orphée* (1950); *Black Orpheus*, directed by Marcel Camus (1959). More works of art inspired by the Orpheus myth are discussed and reproduced in J. E. Bernstock, *Under the Spell of Orpheus: The Persistence of a Myth in Twentieth-Century Art* (Carbondale, Ill., 1991); J. B. Friedman, *Orpheus in the Middle Ages* (Cambridge, Mass., 1972); D. M. Kosinski, *Orpheus in Nineteenth-Century Symbolism* (Ann Arbor, 1989); and *Les Metamorphoses de Orphée*, exhib. cat., Tourcoing (France), Musée des Beaux-Arts (Brussels, 1995).

[5] Examples include Orpheus as musician, Roman mosaic, Antakya, Archaeological Museum: *LIMC*, vol. 7, 91, no. 103; and Christ as Good Shepherd, wall painting, third century, Rome, Catacomb of Domitilla: A. Grabar, *Early Christian Art* (New York, 1968), fig. 84.

[6] Orpheus and Eurydice Courting, in John Lydgate, *Fall of Princes*, manuscript, ca. 1450, London, B.L., Ms. Harley 1766, f. 76r; Friedman, *Orpheus in the Middle Ages* (as in note 4), 170, pl. 24.

[7] Roelant Savery, *Orpheus Charming the Animals*, seventeenth century, London, National Gallery: *The National Gallery Complete Illustrated Catalogue* (London, 1995), 618.

[8] Ary Scheffer, *Death of Eurydice*, 1814, Blois, Chateau: L. Ewals, *Ary Scheffer, 1795–1858: Gevierd romanticus* (Dordrecht, 1995), 78.

[9] George Frederic Watts, *Orpheus and Eurydice*, 1860, Compton, Watts Gallery: G. Reynolds, *Victorian Painting* (New York, 1966), 135.

In the modern era Orpheus became the symbol of the anguish and despair of the artist, a prisoner of his gift and of his love. In Ossip Zadkine's sculpture of 1914, the lyre is not held by Orpheus, but is a part of him; in fact, it is literally tearing him apart.[10] Orpheus also became the victim of the possessive love of a Eurydice, with narrowed eyes and grasping hands, in Pierre and Gilles's painted photograph of 1990.[11] Paintings of Orpheus's journey to the underworld contain fewer variations over the span of time and are perhaps based more on artistic and theatrical conventions of the portrayal of Hades than on the perceived character of Orpheus. Typically he is shown playing a lyre or other instrument to charm Persephone and Pluto and gain the release of Eurydice. There are many examples of the scene, ranging from Apulian kraters to twentieth-century paintings.[12]

The incident that intrigued every age was that of Orpheus's death at the hands of the maddened Maenads. Variations occur, but the intense fury of the Maenads bent on their gruesome task and the helplessness of Orpheus seem to be shared by all. They perhaps reveal more about each age's weapons for killing and its attitude toward the depiction of violence, than about its attitude toward Orpheus. Only in a twentieth-century example by Felix Vallotton do the Maenads actually tear Orpheus's body with their hands, as described in the Greek texts. In Gustave Moreau's *The Young Thracian,* and in other examples, Orpheus's severed head continued to sing and prophesy after his death. Like his severed head and his enshrined lyre, his story continues to speak to the contemporary world.[13]

One way to show both the pervasiveness and the changing nuances of familiar narratives is to trace their recurrences and transformations, as has just been done here ever so briefly and simplistically with the story of Orpheus. Several books and exhibitions have traced the frequent reappearances of the Orpheus myth with much greater detail and sophistication.[14]

One might also take an action or circumstance and trace how it has been depicted in terms of these well-known narratives, or show how the narratives have been used to define a particular set of actions and situations. The *Encyclopedia of Comparative Iconography,* a recently published reference work using this method, seeks to show both the consistency and the variety of the use of these narratives and other themes in the history of art.[15] The essays compare similar actions and circumstances described in mythological, religious, and literary narrative scenes. Under the letter

[10] Ossip Zadkine, *Orpheus,* bronze, 1948, Antwerp, Open Air Museum: S. Lecombre, *Ossip Zadkine: L'Oeuvre Sculpté* (Paris, 1994), 477.

[11] Pierre and Gilles, *Orpheus,* painted photograph, 1990, Vienna, private collection; *Metamorphoses de Orphée* (as in note 4), 207, no. 163.

[12] Orpheus in the underworld, Apulian volute-krater, Karlsruhe, Badische Landesmuseum B 4: A. D. Trendall, *Red Figure Vases of South Italy and Sicily* (London and New York, 1989), fig. 151. In many later works of art Orpheus is playing a viol, as in François Perrier (Bourguignon), *Orpheus before Pluto and Persephone,* seventeenth century, Paris, Louvre: *Metamorphoses de Orphée* (as in note 4), 128, no. 25.

[13] Examples include Orpheus killed by the Thracian women, Attic stamnos, Basel, Antikenmuseum BS 1411: *LIMC,* vol. 7, 86, no. 35; Death of Orpheus, from John Lydgate, *Fall of Princes,* manuscript, ca. 1450, London, B.L.,

Ms. Harley 1766, f. 76v: Friedman, *Orpheus in the Middle Ages* (as in note 4), 171, pl. 25; Albrecht Dürer, *The Death of Orpheus,* pen drawing, ca. 1494, Hamburg, Kunsthalle: *Metamorphoses de Orphée* (as in note 4), 65; Emile Lévy, *Death of Orpheus,* 1866, Paris, Musée d'Orsay: R. Rosenblum, *Paintings in the Musée D'Orsay* (New York, 1989), 53; Felix Vallotton, *Orpheus Dismembered by the Maenads,* 1914, Paris, private collection: *Metamorphoses de Orphée,* 193, no. 133; Gustave Moreau, *The Young Thracian,* 1865, Paris, Musée d'Orsay: Rosenblum, *Musée D'Orsay,* 79. More works of art on the theme of Orpheus are listed in J. Davidson Reid, *The Oxford Guide to Classical Mythology in the Arts, 1300–1990s* (New York and Oxford, 1993), vol. 2, 773–801.

[14] See note 2.

[15] *Encyclopedia of Comparative Iconography,* ed. H. E. Roberts (Chicago and London, 1998), 2 vols., 1200 pp.

"A," for example, the *Encyclopedia of Comparative Iconography* includes entries on the themes of abandonment, abduction, abundance, and adultery; and the entries continue through to zodiac, discussing the narratives and iconographic attributes relevant to each theme and the treatment of the theme in different ages, cultures, and media. The relation of the narratives to real historical situations is also investigated.

The action of abandonment, for example, usually concerned with the weak and dependent, especially women and children, deserted by the strong and ruthless or the irresponsible and improvident, is often demonstrated by the reiteration of familiar narratives. Children like Oedipus, whose ruthless father ordered him to be left to die on a mountain top, or women like Ariadne, abandoned on an island by her ambitious lover Theseus, are well-known examples of abandonment from classical mythology. Moses, left afloat in a basket in the bulrushes, or Hagar and Ishmael, thrust out by Abraham to wander in the wilderness, are examples from the Bible.

The historian John Boswell, in his book *The Kindness of Strangers*, describes how the circumstances of abandonment in myth and art reflected the realities of existence throughout most of human history.[16] Until the nineteenth century children were regularly abandoned as a method of family limitation. In some ages as many as a third of the children born were exposed, sometimes to die, but often with the not unrealistic hope that they would be taken in, perhaps adopted, by other families. Before the medieval period children were also regularly sold into slavery or prostitution, and later into the not always much improved condition of servitude.

To establish an iconography of abandoned children, one turns to Moses and Oedipus who were the abandoned figures most often depicted in works of art. In an unusual classical red-figured vase painting in Paris, the small Oedipus clings to a shepherd, although it is unclear whether it is the shepherd who was sent to expose him or the one who rescued him.[17] On the lid of an Adonis sarcophagus of the third century A.D. in the Vatican, the exposed child Oedipus, curled up under a tree, is found by the Corinthian shepherd and his goat.[18] Two medieval manuscript illuminations of the subject, one from a thirteenth-century manuscript in Pommersfelden, the other a fourteenth-century example in Munich, depict the abandoned child as naked and hung upside down by his feet, an expedient which, while looking extremely painful, apparently was actually used in an attempt to protect abandoned children from animals (Fig. 1).[19] These scenes, repellent to modern eyes, were only the understood references indicating the common practice of abandonment. This uncomfortable position became an attribute of the iconography of the abandoned Oedipus. Even though the best-known Greek text of the Oedipus story, Sophocles' drama *Oedipus the King*, has King Laius's herdsman disobeying his orders and giving the child to a Corinthian shepherd rather than actually exposing him, the iconographic attribute of the abandoned child in a tree continued to be used in later centuries. A print of 1663 by Salvator Rosa entitled *The Rescue of the Infant Oedipus*, for example, shows the abandoned child bound by his feet in a tree (Fig. 2).[20]

---

[16] J. Boswell, *The Kindness of Strangers* (New York, 1988).

[17] Euphorbus with the child Oedipus, red-figured vase painting, Paris, Cabinet des Médailles 372: *LIMC*, vol. 7, 3, no. 3.

[18] Oedipus discovered by the shepherd from Corinth, sarcophagus lid, third century A.D., Rome, Vatican: G. Koch and H. Sichtermann, *Römische Sarkophage* (Munich, 1982), 170, fig. 142.

[19] Pommersfelden, Schlossbibliothek, Cod. 295, thirteenth century, f. 52v, the Story of Oedipus; Munich, Staatsbibliothek, Ms. gall. 6, fourteenth century, f. 21, Oedipus.

[20] Salvator Rosa, *The Rescue of the Infant Oedipus*, etching and drypoint, 1663, second state, Boston, Museum of Fine Arts. With thanks to Norman Doenges for translating the Latin inscription.

Here, as the inscription states, Oedipus's feet, pointing to the celestial signs in the sky, reveal his destiny. The scene was repeated in the 1847 painting of the theme by Jean-François Millet, *Oedipus Untied from the Tree* (Fig. 3), in which two peasants have just found the abandoned child and are releasing him.[21] Honoré Daumier also painted this scene, following the same basic iconography.[22]

The Old Testament, in Exodus 2:3–10, tells the story of how Moses was set adrift by his family on an ark of bulrushes. A thirteenth-century illumination from the Oxford *Bible moralisée* represents the baby Moses swaddled and set adrift in a boatlike basket by his grieving family.[23] In this manuscript Moses is associated with a prefiguration of the Nativity of Christ, who is shown similarly bound in swaddling clothes. In the nineteenth century Gustave Moreau pictured the infant no longer swaddled but prematurely displaying his shining horns and floating blissfully on the basket of woven reeds.[24] Although the paintings showing Moses being set adrift in the bulrushes can be found in all periods, their number is far outweighed by the more popular scene of Moses being rescued by the Pharaoh's daughter.

These paintings of a mythic and a biblical hero reflect the haphazard circumstances awaiting the abandoned child. Little is known about the early institutional efforts to preserve these children. Sometime in the medieval period the Church began to establish foundling homes. A manuscript exists depicting the circumstances leading to the founding of an early hospice, the Hospital of the Holy Spirit in Rome, in the twelfth century. One miniature shows mothers dropping their children into the Tiber: one swaddled, but with a weight attached to it, another naked. Another mother, furtively glancing around, seems about to join the two mothers at the bridge. Another miniature from the same manuscript shows fishermen on the Tiber finding more babies than fish in their nets.[25] They took these babies to the Pope, who, under God's direction, founded the Hospital of the Holy Spirit as a foundling home.

In the Renaissance, secular and civic organizations began to care for abandoned children. One of the most enduring was the Hospital of the Innocents founded in Florence in 1419. Designed by Filippo Brunelleschi, the building is still regarded as a model of functional and aesthetic design. Its care for the deserted children was charmingly expressed in a series of roundels by Andrea della Robbia on the facade. Installed in 1487, they show the infant foundlings emerging from their swaddling clothes into the new life offered by the hospital.[26] Swaddling, though not unique to them, became a common attribute of abandoned children.

Another foundling hospital, this one established in London in 1739, also united artistic expression with the care of abandoned children, and illustrates a conscious use of iconographic precedents. Thomas Coram, a successful sea captain, was moved by the number of abandoned children left to die in the streets, roads, and dung heaps of England, and by the high death rate of chil-

[21] Jean-François Millet, *Oedipus Untied from the Tree*, 1847, Ottawa, National Gallery of Canada.

[22] Honoré Daumier, *Oedipus and the Shepherd*, 1847, New York, Thanhauser Collection: K. E. Maison, *Honoré Daumier: Catalogue Raisonné of the Paintings, Watercolors, and Drawings*, vol. 1, *The Paintings* (Greenwich, Conn., 1967), pl. 1.

[23] Abandonment of Moses, illumination from the *Bible moralisée*, Oxford, Bodl., Ms. Bodl. 270b, f. 176: Boswell, *Kindness of Strangers* (as in note 16), pl. 5.

[24] Gustave Moreau, *The Infant Moses*, 1878, Cambridge, Mass., Harvard University, Fogg Art Museum: P.-L. Mathieu, *Gustave Moreau* (Paris, 1994), 136.

[25] *Manuscript dur la fondation*, twelfth century, Rome, Hospital of the Holy Spirit, miniatures 3, 6: Boswell, *Kindness of Strangers* (as in note 16), pls. 15, 16.

[26] Filippo Brunelleschi, architect, Ospedale degli Innocenti, Florence, 1419; Andrea della Robbia, Infants Freed from Their Swaddling Clothes, terracotta roundels, ca. 1419, Florence, Ospedale degli Innocenti.

dren in poorhouses. He enlisted the help of the artist William Hogarth and others in founding a home for these children. Hogarth played a number of roles in the new institution, but the one that is now remembered most often is the portrait he painted of the founder.[27] In the Baroque tradition, Captain Coram is depicted seated by a large pillar, the sea beyond showing ships in full sail. At his feet a globe and a book, perhaps his logbook, further refer to his seafaring background. He has now cast these aside to concentrate on the project of the Foundling Hospital. On a table by his right hand lie rolls of paper, one inscribed "The Royal Charter" of the founding of the hospital, the others probably the plans for it. In his hand he holds the seal of his new institution, with the scene of the Pharaoh's daughter finding Moses visible on its surface. Another painting of Thomas Coram, this one by Balthazar Nebot, is not as artistically adroit as Hogarth's but has an awkward charm nevertheless, and also harks back to the story of Moses. It shows the compassionate founder standing over the familiar sight of a reed basket at the side of the road, in which a foundling child raises its little arms imploringly (Fig. 4).[28]

Hogarth interested other artists in contributing paintings to the new institution, many of them portraits of supporters of the hospital, others on themes related iconographically to the abandonment and rescue of children. The sumptuous Court Room (Fig. 5), for example, where the governors and guardians held their deliberations, contained James Wills's *Little Children Brought to Christ* to the right of the mantlepiece. Joseph Highmore's painting of the outcast *Hagar and Ishmael* was on the right of the door, and John Michael Rysbrack's relief *Charity* was located over the mantlepiece. Decorative roundels contained paintings of other charitable institutions including Chelsea Hospital, the Charterhouse, and Bethlehem Hospital, better known as Bedlam. On the other side of the room were Francis Hayman's *The Finding of the Infant Moses in the Bulrushes* and Hogarth's *Moses Brought before Pharaoh's Daughter*.[29] The hospital soon owned one of the few art collections open to the public, a circumstance that led to its becoming a fashionable meeting place, attracting a generous endowment of funds for its charitable work. Artists held exhibitions in the hospital, and Handel conducted one of the early performances of the *Messiah* there, as well as other concerts. Other artists who continued to support the hospital included Benjamin West, whose *Christ Presenting a Little Child* was placed in the chapel in 1801.[30]

In the mid-nineteenth century, Emma Brownlow King, whose own father had been a foundling at the hospital and rose to become one of its officials, painted an interesting series of

[27] William Hogarth, *Thomas Coram*, 1740, London, Thomas Coram Foundation: B. Nicolson, *The Treasures of the Foundling Hospital* (Oxford, 1972), frontispiece and pl. 45 (detail: the royal charter).

[28] Balthazar Nebot, *Thomas Coram*, ca. 1741, London, Thomas Coram Foundation: Nicolson, *Treasures* (as in note 27), pl. 46.

[29] James Wills, *Little Children Brought to Christ*, oil on canvas, 1746, London, Thomas Coram Foundation for Children: *Catalogue of Paintings in British Collections* (London, 1993), 551, no. 1756; Joseph Highmore, *Hagar and Ishmael*, oil on canvas, 1746, London, Thomas Coram Foundation for Children: ibid., 535, no. 1704; John Michael Rysbrack, *Charity*, white marble relief, 1746, London, Thomas Coram Foundation for Children; Richard

Wilson, *London: Foundling Hospital*, 1746, London, Thomas Coram Foundation for Children: D. H. Solkin, *Painting for Money: The Visual Arts and the Public Sphere in Eighteenth-Century England* (New Haven and London, 1992), 168, pl. 64; Francis Hayman, *The Finding of the Infant Moses in the Bulrushes*, oil on canvas, 1746, London, Thomas Coram Foundation for Children: *Catalogue of Paintings*, 534, no. 1700; William Hogarth, *Moses Brought before Pharaoh's Daughter*, oil on canvas, 1746, London, Thomas Coram Foundation for Children: ibid., 537, no. 1707.

[30] Benjamin West, *Christ Presenting a Little Child*, oil on canvas, before 1801, London, Thomas Coram Foundation for Children: *Catalogue of Paintings* (as in note 29), 551, no. 1755.

paintings of activities at the Foundling Hospital during the 1850s and '60s, including *The Christening*, *The Sick Room*, *Taking Leave*, and *The Foundling Restored to Its Mother*.[31] Some of the institution's collection of paintings can be seen in the backgrounds of these works. The hospital's distinctive way of dressing the children became a marker used by painters to indicate foundling status, as in Emma Brownlow King's *The Foundling Girl at Christmas Dinner*, Harold Copping's *Foundling Girl* and *Foundling Boy*, and Sophie Anderson's *Foundling Girls in the Chapel*.[32] Although most of the buildings of the Foundling Hospital were destroyed in the 1920s, the Court Room was dismantled and erected again in Brunswick Square, where it and the art collection, still largely intact, can be seen by arrangement. The present activities of the Thomas Coram Foundation, although changed since its inception, continue to focus on child care and education. Throughout its history the Foundling Hospital not only used the traditional iconography of abandonment, as in its seal, to help define its purpose, but through its art collection also employed that same iconography to establish an ambience that promoted its social and fund-raising activities. Especially in the theme of the finding of Moses, the iconographic "precedent" was used as a "lining" or reference point for its charitable deeds.[33]

David Alfaro Siqueiros painted a twentieth-century child victim of abandonment in 1937 in his *Echo of a Scream* (Fig. 6). A screaming child, his anguished cry echoed in a second larger head, sits in the midst of a debris-strewn, war-ravished landscape. He is not the passive victim, like Oedipus or Moses, who were perhaps quieted by a sense of their forthcoming rescue foretold in myth and sacred text, but is screaming his protest at a violent and uncaring modern world which does not ensure his rescue.[34]

The adult victim of abandonment most frequently depicted in art is Ariadne, abandoned on the island of Naxos by her lover Theseus, whom she had helped to defeat the Minotaur and escape from the Labyrinth on Crete. Artists have depicted scenes of Ariadne's abandonment in various ways, reflecting the concerns of society at differing times and places. The Greek vase paintings devoted to the scene concentrated on exonerating Theseus from blame for deserting the woman who saved his life. The Athenians, who had adopted Theseus as their national hero, seemed eager to explain this potential moral failing as caused by the intervention of the gods. Athena is the culprit on a stamnos in Boston, driving the alarmed Theseus to his ship while Hypnos, the small winged figure on the right, drops a sleeping potion on the recumbent Ariadne (Fig. 7).[35] The in-

---

[31] Emma Brownlow King, *The Christening*, 1863: Nicolson, *Treasures* (as in note 27), pl. 95; *The Sick Room*, 1864: R. H. Nichols and F. A. Wray, *The History of the Foundling Hospital* (London, 1935), fig. facing p. 127; *Taking Leave*, 1858–64; *The Foundling Restored to Its Mother*, 1858: Nicolson, *Treasures*, pl. 94.

[32] Emma Brownlow King, *A Foundling Girl at Christmas Dinner*, 1868: Nicolson, *Treasures* (as in note 27), pl. 97; Harold Copping, *Foundling Girl* and *Foundling Boy;* Sophie Anderson, *Foundling Girls in the Chapel*, oil on canvas, ca. 1855–71: Nicolson, *Treasures*, pl. 96. All are in the Thomas Coram Foundation for Children, London.

[33] For more information about the Foundling Hospital, see R. K. McClure, *Coram's Children: The London Foundling Hospital in the Eighteenth Century* (New Haven,

1981); Nicolson, *Treasures* (as in note 27); J. Orr and W. Barnes, *The Story of the Thomas Coram Foundation for Children and Its Art Collection* (London, 1997); Solkin, *Painting for Money* (as in note 29), chap. 5, "Exhibitions of Sympathy," 157–74. The paintings mentioned are reproduced in these books. A catalogue of the art collection is included in Nicolson.

[34] David Alfaro Siqueiros, *Echo of a Scream*, 1937, enamel on wood, 121.9 × 91.4 cm, New York, The Museum of Modern Art.

[35] The following Greek vase paintings also show Theseus being directed to leave, or led away from, the abandoned Ariadne: lekythos, Taranto, *ARV*[2] 560, no. 5: *LIMC*, vol. 3, 1057, no. 52; cup, manner of the Foundry Painter, 500–475 B.C., Tarquinia, Museo Nazionale, RC

tervention of the gods in promoting the destiny of heroes at the expense of women is a theme repeated in the desertion of Dido by Aeneas in Virgil's *Aeneid.* "The epic hero," the literary historian Lawrence Lipking reminds us, "tends to define himself by leaving a woman behind," one he may or may not return to, and usually abandons without dire consequences to himself.[36] It is often the abandoned woman, her anger and pain, which interest the poet and the painter.

Medieval, Renaissance, Baroque, and nineteenth-century artists frequently painted the abandoned Ariadne and her suffering as she realizes that her lover has deserted her. In a medieval illumination from an Ovid manuscript (*Heroides,* Oxford, Ms. Balliol 383), a startled Ariadne watches her lover's ship sail away.[37] In Carlo Saraceni's painting, several centuries later, a nearly naked Ariadne on the far left throws out her arms in distress as she sees Theseus's ship sailing off into the distance. The rocky landscape looms over her despairing figure.[38] In the late eighteenth century, Angelica Kauffmann painted more compact versions of this scene. In the Dresden version, Ariadne, in dishabille and partially silhouetted against a stormy sky, gestures with raised arms toward the departing ship; a putto hides his tearful face (Fig. 8).[39] Patrons from the Renaissance to the modern period, and especially in the eighteenth century, demanded paintings that were beautiful and free of all that was ugly and distasteful. This made it difficult to create heroines in the act of expressing any emotions that would disfigure the beauty of their faces. Angelica Kauffmann solved this dilemma by displacing the expression of emotion onto the putto. Furthermore, his face, contorted with crying, is largely hidden by his bowed head, his curly locks, and his pudgy little hands.

The theme of the abandoned Ariadne was extremely popular in the nineteenth century. In most of the depictions the distressed Ariadne appears as a recumbent nude, dazed and exhausted by her emotions. John Vanderlyn's *Ariadne* remains the premier example of a painting of the nude in nineteenth-century America (Fig. 9).[40] In England paintings of Ariadne shared academic exhibition walls with a number of other abandoned women, including Psyche, Clytie, and Calypso. It seemed a theme of particular import for this period, and one related to many genre paintings showing the rescue of women in distress.

Another sense of the word "abandonment" occurs in the abandonment of restraints as one gives oneself up to intense emotion, such as grief, or religious ecstasy. Among the many examples are scenes, both ancient and modern, of bacchanalia. Maenads (Bacchants), female followers of the cult of Dionysus (Bacchus), were given to abandoned frenzy characterized by the drinking of wine, wild dancing, and the rending and killing of animals. Euripides, in his play the *Bacchae,* describes the nightmarish and grotesque abandonment of normal restraint when events provide an

---

5291, *ARV*[2], 405, no. 1: *LIMC,* vol. 3, 1057, no. 53; skyphos by the Lewis Painter, 475–450 B.C., Vienna 1773, *ARV*[2], 972, no. 2: *LIMC,* vol. 7, 948, no. 312; hydria by the Syleus Painter, 500–475 B.C., Berlin 2179, *ARV*[2], 252, no. 52: *LIMC,* vol. 2, 1000, no. 489.

[36] L. Lipking, *Abandoned Women and Poetic Tradition* (Chicago and London, 1988), xvi.

[37] Ariadne Watching Theseus's Ship Sailing Away, illumination in Ovid, *Heroides,* Oxford, Bodl., Ms. Balliol 383, f. 72r: T. H. Ohlgren, *Illuminated Manuscripts: An Index to Selected Bodleian Library Color Reproductions* (New York and London, 1977), 113 (no illustration).

[38] Carlo Saraceni, *The Abandoned Ariadne,* ca. 1680, Naples, Gallerie di Capodimonte: *Museo e Gallerie Nazionali di Capodimonte, La Collezione Farnese* (Naples, 1995), vol. 2, 44.

[39] Angelica Kauffmann, *Ariadne,* 1782, Dresden, Gemäldegalerie: O. Sandner, *Hommage au Angelika Kauffmann* (Milan, 1992), pl. 27.

[40] John Vanderlyn, *Ariadne,* 1874, Philadelphia, Pennsylvania Academy of the Fine Arts: K. C. Lindsey, *The Works of John Vanderlyn* (Binghamton, N.Y., 1970), 82–83, fig. 57.

outlet for women's hostility and an escape from their frustrated lives. By preying on Pentheus's curiosity and perhaps on his unrecognized voyeuristic or transvestite longings, Dionysus lures him to dress in women's clothing in order to spy on the women's secret rites. It is a trap, and when Dionysus reveals the spy to the Maenads, including Pentheus's own mother, they don't recognize him, and tear him limb from limb.

A fresco in the House of the Vettii at Pompeii depicts the death of Pentheus, but it hardly does justice to the grotesque frenzy of Euripides' play.[41] The faces of the Maenads are intense, though calm, but nevertheless the swirling rhythms and the concentration with which they begin their ghastly dismemberment capture some of the diabolic fury of their act. In the nineteenth century, the Swiss painter Charles Gleyre took up the same theme at an earlier point of the narrative in his *Pentheus Pursued by the Maenads*.[42] In the foreground the fleeing Pentheus (a classical nude with a cape) makes an agonized gesture of despair as he desperately looks for a place to hide in the rocky landscape. The possessed Maenads, silhouetted against the sky, abandoned to unreasoning fury, have spotted their prey. Thracian Maenads roaming in the mountains also killed Orpheus in a similar frenzy.

Dorothea Tanning, a twentieth-century painter associated with the surrealists, also evoked the abandonment of the bacchanalia, creating drawings of Maenads, including *Maenad II* in 1986.[43] A similar manic energy and ecstatic abandon suggestive of sexual encounters and rapturous couplings inform many of Tanning's paintings. In his review of her exhibition, Donald Kuspit aptly called her a "Maenad."[44] *Reality*, painted between 1973 and 1983, mirrors the surrender to grief Tanning experienced during her husband Max Ernst's illness and after his death in 1976, but also the despair of being abandoned by her dying husband (Fig. 10).[45] The configurations of ecstatic abandon of the Maenad have collapsed into exhaustion and desolation. The woman's own leaden dejection is mirrored in the dead, stonelike gaze of the dog, who, like Angelica Kauffmann's putto, expresses the emotional state of the forsaken woman. Tanning often used this dog, Kachina, to symbolize herself.

The theme of abandonment, in its different meanings, continues to be expressed using references to the familiar age-old stories and their earlier depictions. These narratives have, indeed, become the "precedent behind every action, its invisible, ever-present lining," permeating the way we think about and describe ourselves. In applying the use of the comparative method, the *Encyclopedia of Comparative Iconography* analyzes the way narratives relate to specific actions and how actions are communicated through text and image. Essays describe how the narratives and their depictions change over time, and in different styles and circumstances. In addition, the contributors investigate how the narratives correspond to historical reality and how they translate into different media. Since there was no reference source that grouped narratives according to the actions and

<hr>

[41] *Death of Pentheus*, Roman fresco, Pompeii, House of the Vettii: G. Cerulli Irelli et al., *Pompejanische Wandmalerei* (Stuttgart, 1990), pl. 57.

[42] Charles Gleyre, *Pentheus Pursued by the Maenads*, 1865, Basel, Kunstmuseum: W. Hauptmann, *Charles Gleyre, 1806–1874*, vol. 2, *Catalogue Raisonné* (Zurich and Princeton, 1996), no. 850.

[43] Dorothea Tanning, *Maenad II*, crayon on paper, 1986, collection of the artist: J. C. Bailey, *Dorothea Tanning*

(New York, 1995), 253, pl. 257.

[44] *Dorothea Tanning; Hail Delirium: A Catalogue Raisonné of the Artist's Illustrated Books and Prints, 1942–1991*, ed. R. Waddell and L. W. Ruby, with an essay by Donald Kuspit (New York, 1992), n.p.

[45] Dorothea Tanning, *Reality*, oil on canvas, 1973–83, private collection: Bailey, *Dorothea Tanning* (as in note 43), 139, pl. 112.

circumstances contained in them, the identification of the narratives with the actions and circumstances forming the themes of the essays had to come from the backgrounds, expertise, and knowledge of the contributors.

Works such as the *LIMC* (*Lexicon Iconographicum Mythologiae Classicae*),[46] which includes comprehensive articles on a group of narratives, as well as reproductions of many of the works of art listed, are the most useful of all reference works, but unfortunately are rather rare, and given the state of publishing today and the increasing costs of permissions for reproductions, it is unlikely that such massive undertakings will be financed with any great frequency in the future. Moreover, with a much larger number of images and texts to deal with, can later periods ever be treated as comprehensively? The collections of photographic images of works of art indexed iconographically, such as the Princeton Index of Christian Art, the Marburger Index, the Index Iconologicus, and the Witt Library, can be of immense help, but few contributors had the time or finances to visit them.

In undertaking a project such as the *Encyclopedia of Comparative Iconography* one needs extensive sources of texts and illustrations. One telling of a narrative, or one depiction of a theme, is like taking a snapshot in time. The collection of such snapshots from different ages, genres, and cultures forms a body of material that is rather like an album of photographs. From such an album one can compare, analyze, contrast, discover patterns, and make generalizations about how different artists and societies have appropriated narratives and concepts. Only through the comparison and analysis of many individual instances can patterns be isolated. That is why it is so crucial to be able to view a comprehensive number of depictions, along with relevant information about them.

As we can now hope to supplement textual sources with electronic ones, the situation for comparative research in iconography looks hopeful. Projects which index extensive collections of visual materials iconographically and disseminate them electronically will change the course of iconographic research, making it not only more thorough, but also much more efficient. Without the prohibitive expenses of travel, researchers can finally have access to the world's cultural inheritance. Such undertakings will allow the identification of the shape, condition, and meaning of that "invisible lining" which underlies and helps define our culture.

---

[46] *Lexicon Iconographicum Mythologiae Classicae* (Zurich, 1981–), 8 vols.

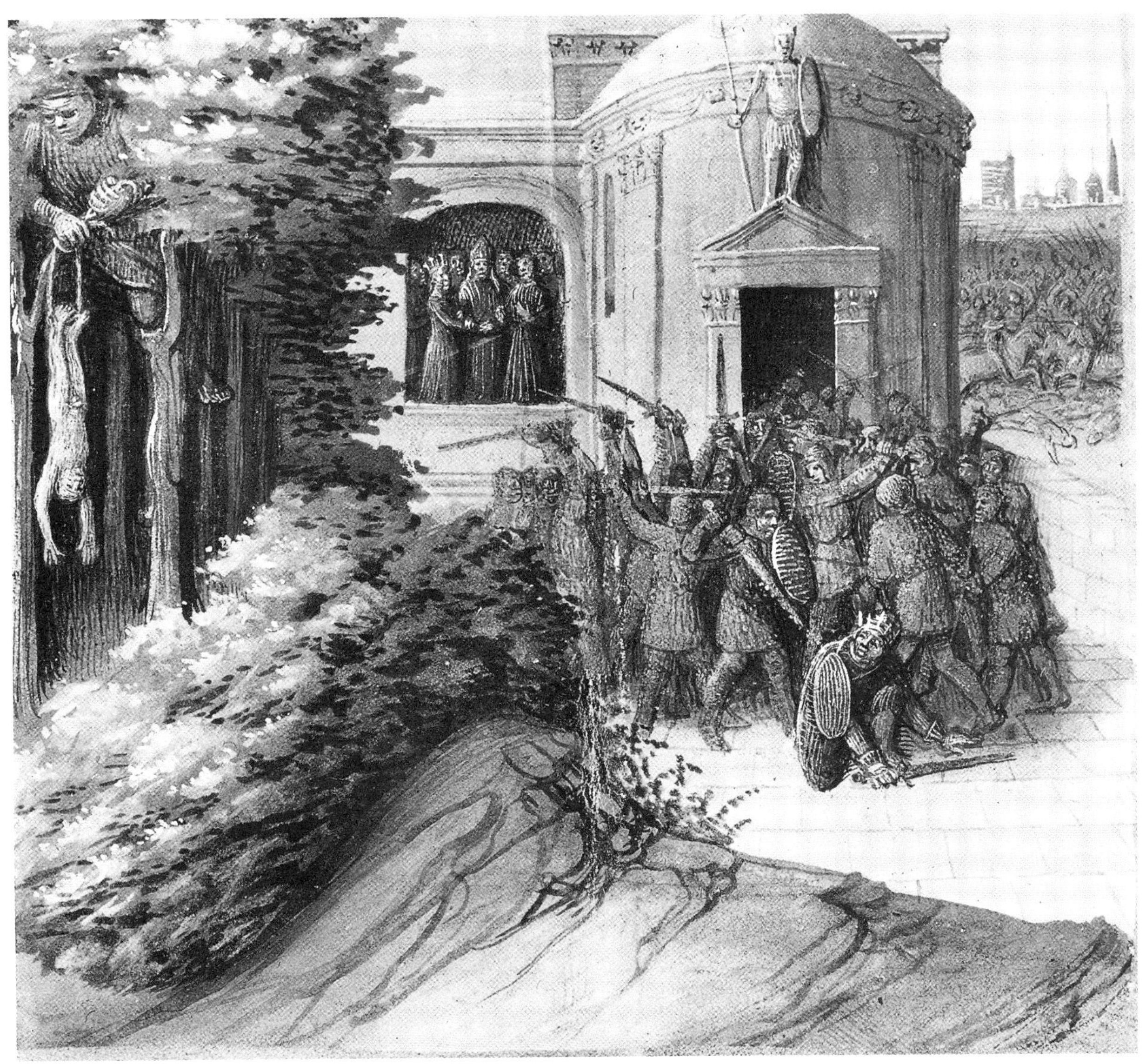

1. Oedipus, manuscript, fourteenth century, Munich, Staatsbibliothek, Ms. gall. 6, f. 21

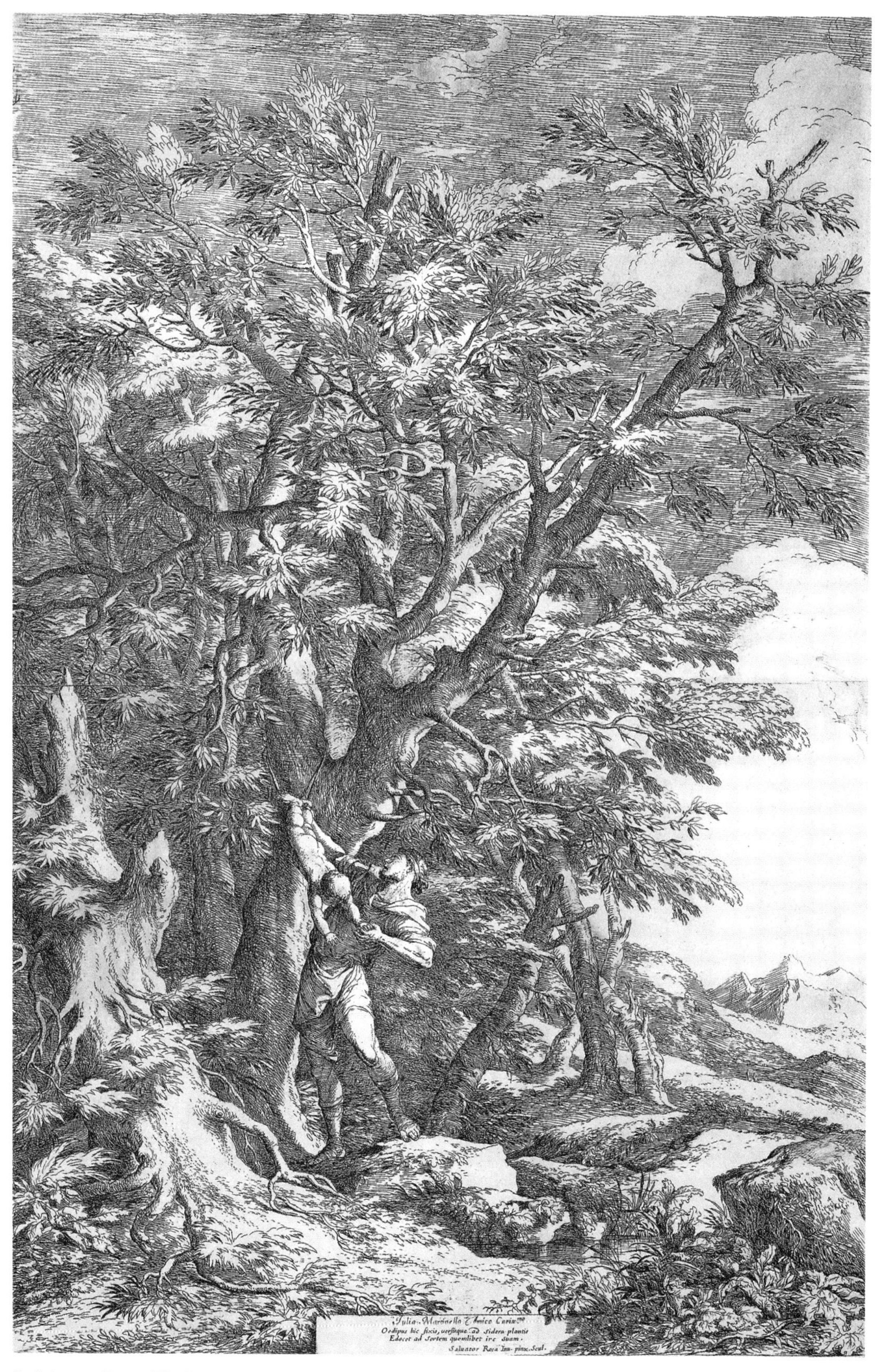

2. Salvator Rosa, *The Rescue of the Infant Oedipus*, etching and drypoint, 1663, second state, Boston, Museum of Fine Arts

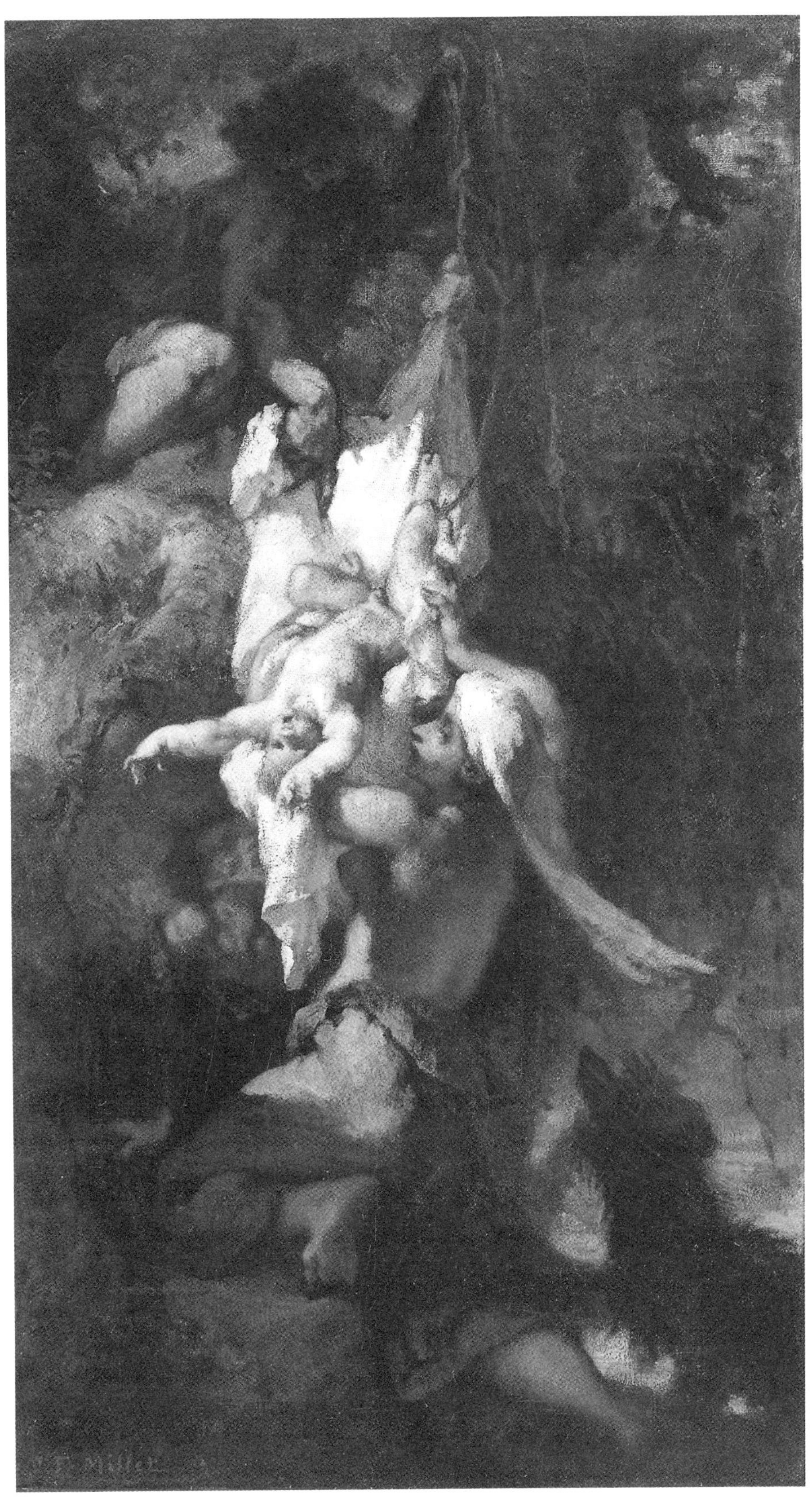

3. Jean-François Millet, *Oedipus Untied from the Tree*, 1847, Ottawa, National Gallery of Canada

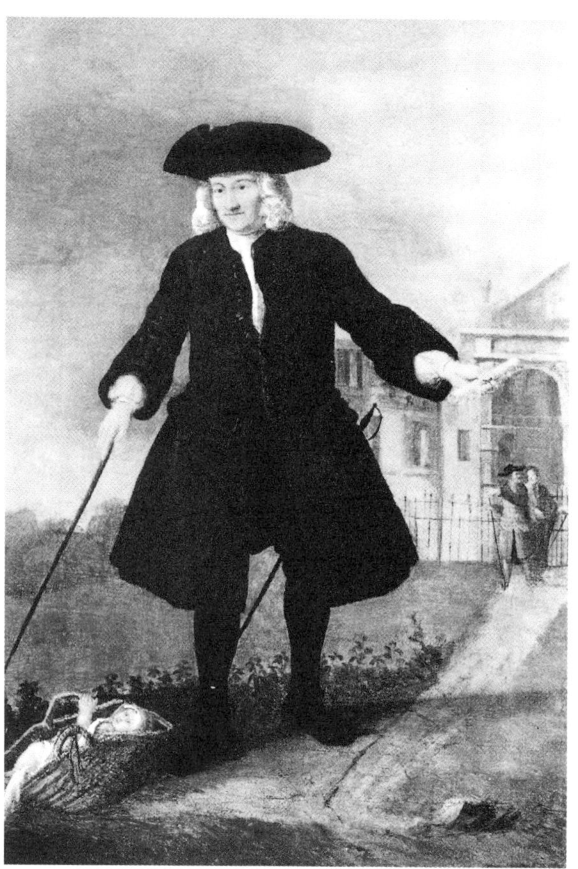

4. Balthazar Nebot, *Thomas Coram*, ca. 1741, London, Thomas Coram Foundation

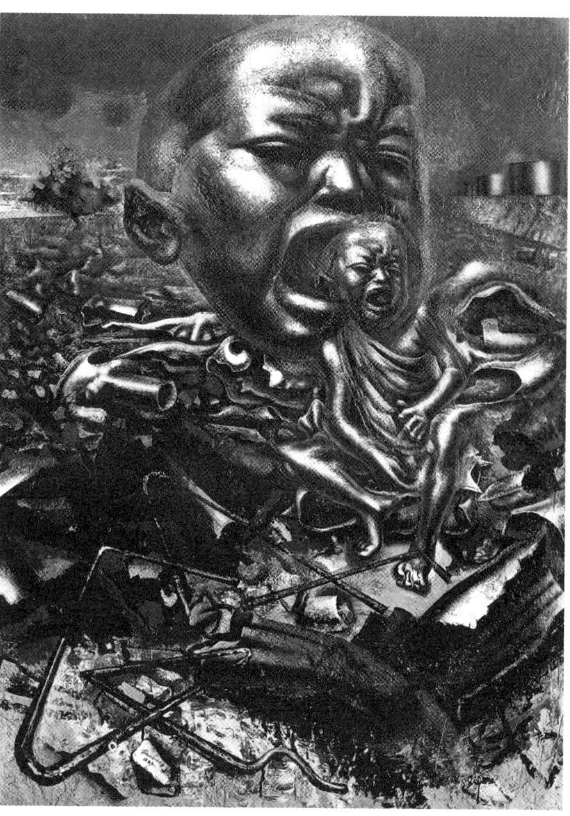

6. David Alfaro Siqueiros, *Echo of a Scream*, 1937, enamel on wood, New York, The Museum of Modern Art

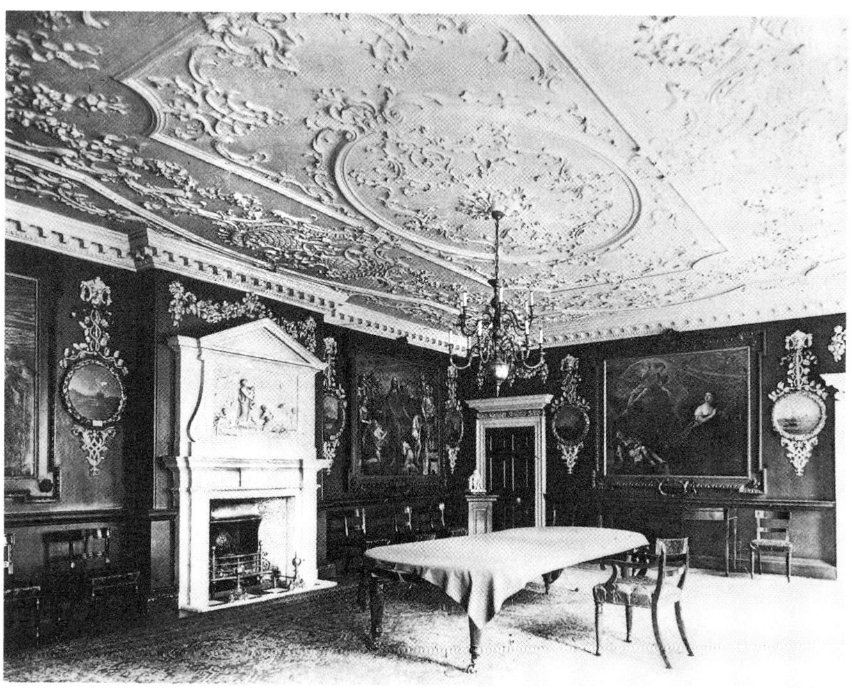

5. The Court Room of the Foundling Hospital, London

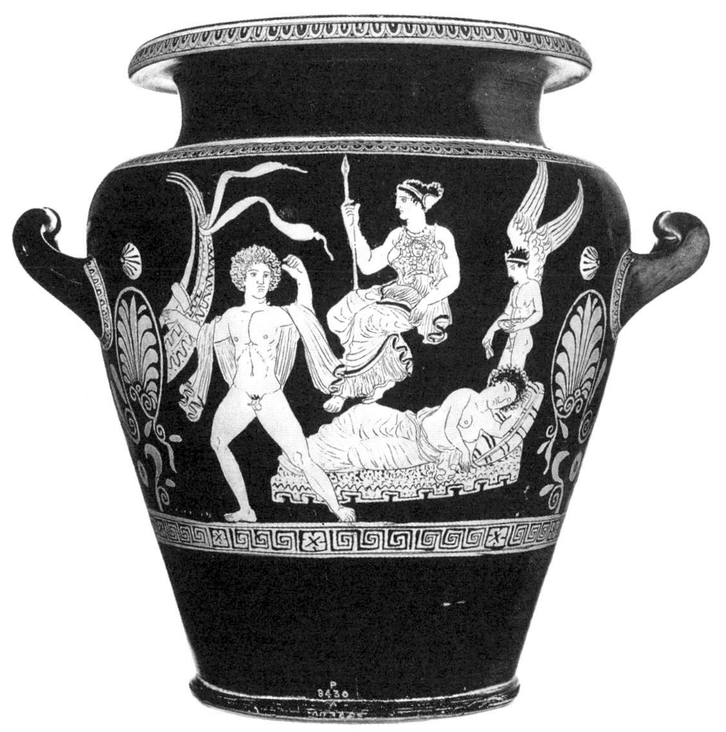

7. Stamnos, Boston, Museum of Fine Arts 00.349, H. L. Pierce Fund

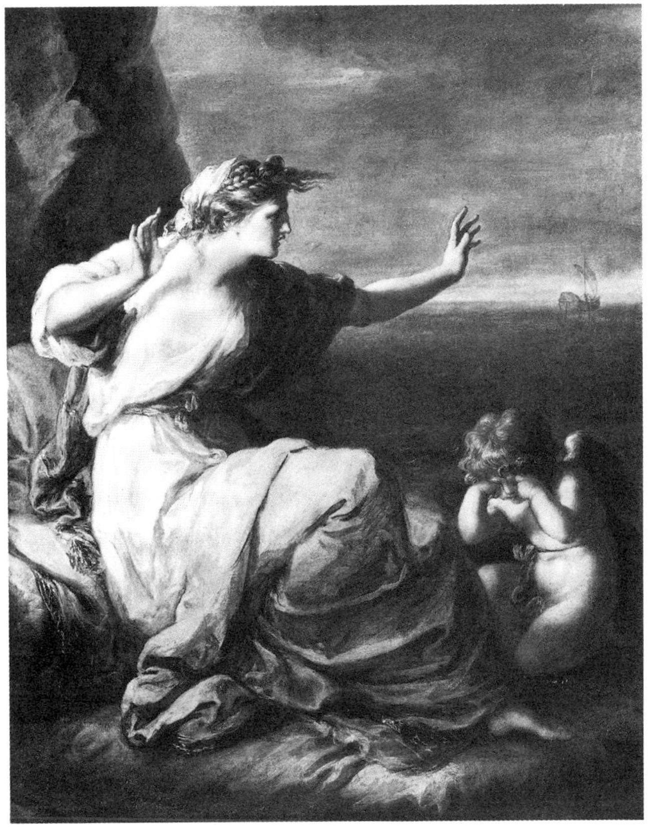

8. Angelica Kauffmann, *Ariadne*, 1782, Dresden, Gemäldegalerie

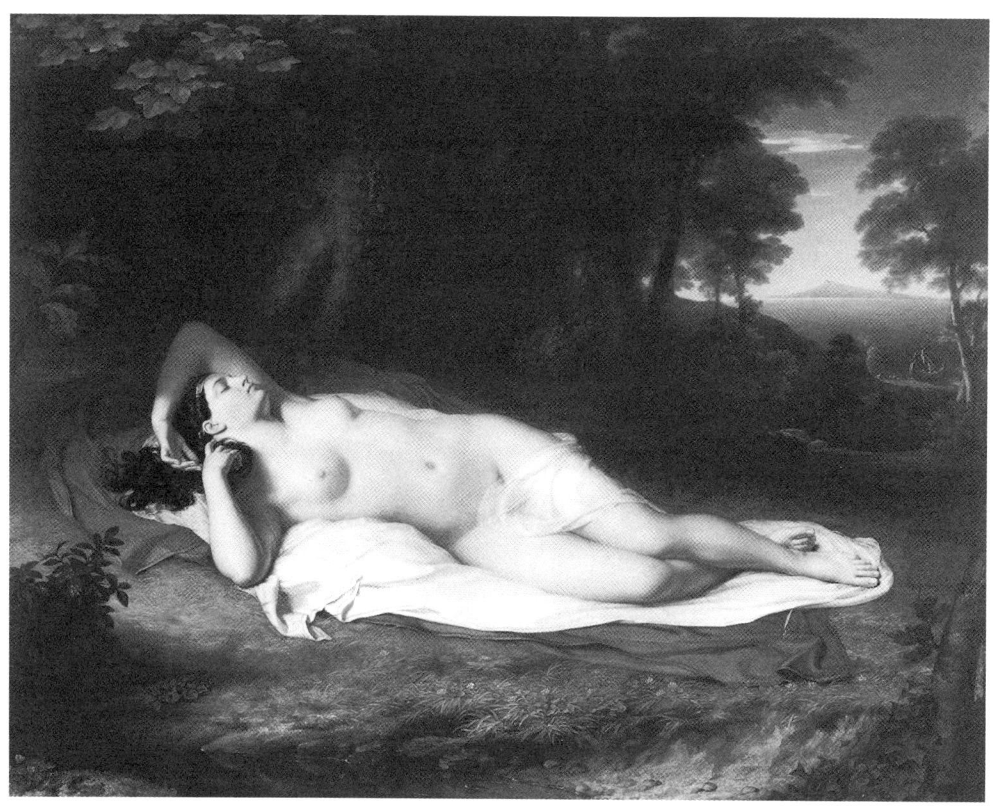

9. John Vanderlyn, *Ariadne*, 1874, Philadelphia, Pennsylvania Academy of the Fine Arts, gift of
Mrs. Sarah Harrison

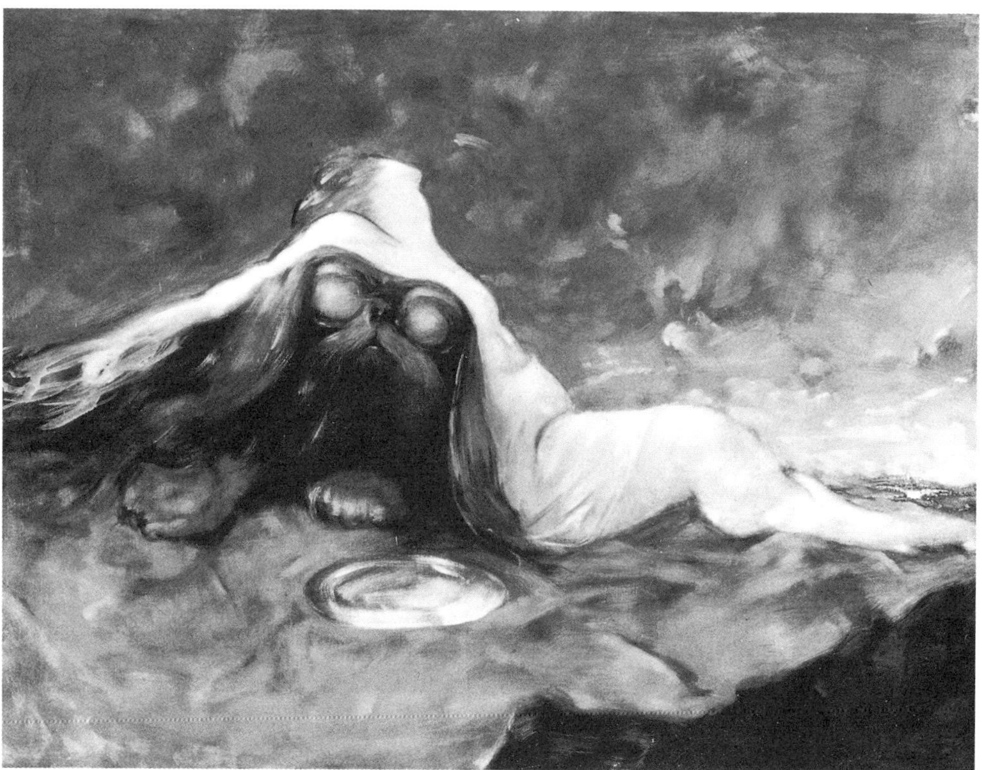

10. Dorothea Tanning, *Reality*, oil on canvas, 1973–83, collection of the artist

The Iconography of *The Ship of State*
by Peter Paul Rubens: A Variant on
the Theme "Hercules am Scheidewege"

·

PETER VAN HUISSTEDE

IN THIS ARTICLE a new interpretation is proposed for the iconography of a painting by Rubens often referred to as *The Ship of State* or *The Coming of Age of Louis XIII* (Fig. 1). The work is part of a series consisting of twenty-four paintings commissioned in 1622 by Maria de' Medici for the Luxembourg Palace. The paintings are presently in the Musée du Louvre, Paris.

This new interpretation is based on research undertaken using the electronic databases of the Corpus of Dutch Fifteenth-, Sixteenth-, and Seventeenth-Century Printers' Devices and the collection of sixteenth-century emblem books in the holdings of the Royal Library in The Hague. Printers' devices, which are small marks used by printers and booksellers to identify their work, often consist of an image and a motto. The images contained in these two sources have been described in a detailed manner using the ICONCLASS system.

ELECTRONIC RESOURCES AND RESEARCH

Research on this computerized project has concentrated on the study of Dutch printers' devices against the background of what has been called the "emblematic game." This is described in more detail at a later point in this article.

The database includes nearly 15,000 printers' devices, and these have been electronically catalogued in considerable detail. The organization of the data is simple and affords the user multiple ways of handling searches. For example, it is possible to list all printers' devices that depict a lion with a column or to list all devices that were used in Rotterdam during the second half of the seventeenth century, or to list all devices used by members of the Waesberge family. It is also possible to use the applied ICONCLASS notations to group material according to the visual content of the printers' devices.

In the 1930s a Belgian researcher, Maurice Sabbe, made a typology of fifteenth- and sixteenth-century printers' devices from the southern Netherlands. This typology clearly showed that during the sixteenth century printers' devices developed from rather simple commercial ownership marks not unlike those used by other craftsmen into devices that were clearly influenced by emblems. The development of printers' devices into small emblems during the sixteenth century is not surprising.

The first emblem books were printed and published at that time by the same people, printers, and booksellers who used printers' devices. Sabbe's typology is, albeit with minor changes, also valid for printers' devices from the northern Netherlands up to the seventeenth century. This can be easily shown by ordering the records in a chronological sequence, and then dividing them into groups according to elements of their visual content with the help of ICONCLASS notations.

Printers' devices are best studied against the background of the "emblematic game." The emblematic game can be defined as being about *copia*, that is, abundance, riches, or wealth. Miedema[1] was the first to assert that at the heart of the emblematic genre lies embellishment, a concept encompassing activities like searching, explaining, changing, enriching, adapting, and paraphrasing. The purpose in practicing *copia* was to produce *cornucopia:* something that is rich and full, but also adequate and of suitable form and content in a given context.

The emblematic game has a context of change, adaption, visual synonyms, mirroring, etc. Printers' devices are an example of applied emblematics. As such, they allow us to study the "emblematic game" in a well-defined context: that of the printing and selling of books. In this context, details such as words or parts of images are very important. Things that are the same are not so much of interest, as is often the case in iconographic research, but rather similar objects, whereby different images are related to one idea or to similar images that denote different ideas, are of particular interest. To fully understand the nature of this material and to enable research to be undertaken it is necessary to have access to large numbers of emblems, words and images from the same cultural context which has been consistently catalogued in a detailed manner. The computer, SGML, and ICONCLASS have proved to be invaluable instruments in this kind of study.

THE SHIP OF STATE BY PETER PAUL RUBENS

It is against such a background and with such a wealth of catalogued material that this paper proposes a new interpretation of the painting known as *The Ship of State* or *The Coming of Age of Louis XIII*, as it is sometimes referred to. It is necessary to examine this work in iconographic and textual detail. *The Ship of State* is particularly interesting to any researcher who may be interested in printers' devices, because one of the shields at the side of the boat depicts a lion holding a column. This was a well-known printers' device in the northern Netherlands during the first half of the seventeenth century.

In the summer of 1968, Professor Van de Waal, the *auctor intellectualis* of the ICONCLASS system, wrote that when applying ICONCLASS it was necessary to "use combined notations (signatures as he then called them)[2] for something depicting the Church symbolized by a sailing vessel,

---

[1] H. Miedema, "The Term 'Emblema' in Alciati," *JWarb* 31 (1968), 234–50.

[2] H. van de Waal, *Decimal Index of the Art of the Low Countries (DIAL): Abridged Edition of the ICONCLASS System*, 2d rev. ed. (The Hague, [1968]), 11: "Combined signatures. As a means of further classification when subjects are more specific or more complex, the separate indications of different aspects of these subjects can be written down together as combined signatures. The two (or more) parts of these combined signatures are divided by a colon, which means in general 'in relation to', and more specifically may mean 'as a symbol of'. An example: 11L:46C24 [. . .]. This method makes it also possible to enter the material from more than one side. The combination 11L:46C24 may be important not only for Christian iconography but also from a documentary point of view (in a series of 'pictures of sailing vessels')."

like (using the notations then in use): 11L:46C24." This, he goes on to say, has the great advantage of allowing the material to be approached from more than one angle. The importance of this concept in opening up visual material in a more detailed way, will, I hope, be shown in the following sections.

Previous Interpretation of This Work

Susan Saward provides the following description of the painting:

> The *gubernaculum navis* travels through turbulent waves from out of the storm-tossed clouds blown by a wind god, towards more serene waters. France stands vigilantly at the mast with the *orbis mundi* and the flaming sword of divine Justice; Maria de' Medici at the helm offers her son the tiller; the ship is rowed by four vigourous female figures, who can be identified by the *imprese* on the shields on the side of the bark. They are the virtues and blessings of the king, with which the ship is guided safely through the troubled waters of government: the first is a personification of the *Fortitudo* and *Magnaminitas* of the king upholding the *securitas* of the state; the second is watchful *Providentia* guarding the *salus*; third is *Aequitas*, assuring the people of a just and fair administration; and lastly, a personification of the symbol of *Pax*, the blessing inherent in the administration as a whole. The two other female figures, who have no distinguishing attributes, trim the sails; they also must refer to the felicitous administration of Louis XIII and are there to keep the vessel running smoothly. Perhaps they represent *Patientia*, the hard-working endurance of the emperor under the burden of government, and the related *Constantia*, the imperial virtue of perseverance, of "sticking to a position or a course" despite obstacles. The twin stars Castor and Pollux, Saint Elmo's fire, appear above the ship to ensure its safe voyage. Below in the rough seas, the dolphin guides the craft through the dark nights.[3]

Millen and Wolf[4] published a study which is interesting for several reasons. They are critical of Saward's analysis; they present a methodological point of view; and, rather curiously in the light of the two previous points, they fail to present a new interpretation of this particular painting. They object to the overall interpretation of the cycle by Saward, but they particularly criticize her use of classical textual and visual material to study the paintings, without making it plausible that these two strains indeed made up the appropriate context in which to study the paintings.

When Millen and Wolf sketch the context of their research, they stress the particular historical and personal circumstances that are important for their interpretation of the cycle. These include the idea that the paintings were commissioned by Maria de' Medici, daughter of Johanna of Austria and Grand Duke Francesco de' Medici, in difficult personal and political circumstances in France; they list the contemporary sources that Rubens was aware of; and they acknowledge that "Rubens' Medici cycle is too vast and multiform in its sources and allusions, too humanly biographical, too fully bound up with what the Queen herself wished to convey, too wily, and, in short, too *witty* to be straitjacketed into a painter's exegesis on Classical literary and archaeological materials."[5]

[3] S. Saward, *The Golden Age of Maria de' Medici* (Ann Arbor, 1982), 159–60.

[4] R. F. Millen and R. E. Wolf, *Heroic Deeds and Mystic Figures: A New Reading of Rubens' Life of Maria de' Medici* (Princeton, 1989).

[5] Ibid., 7.

It is interesting to note that Millen and Wolf's views paraphrase this writer's description of what in this paper is called the "emblematic game." They discuss a collection of manuscripts in a Florentine archive entitled "Impresas, Emblems, Crests, Reverses of Medals, and Other Symbols Used on Various Occasions by Personages of the Most Serene House of the Medici in Tuscany."[6] In these lists, which are without illustrations or commentary, they found the device of Maria de' Medici, which was a caduceus with the motto *Pax optima rerum*, "Peace is the highest good." The authors acknowledge the importance of the so-called emblem literature in order to interpret the Luxembourg cycle, and they take a liberal stance toward what emblem literature is, stating that "for convenience throughout the book 'emblem' is used generically for the entire category which includes also impresas, devices, ciphers, hieroglyphs, and any other aphoristic or metaphorical signs, whether referring to persons, places, events, or ideas."[7] It is possible to include in this list a category of what could be called "applied emblematics" such as printers' devices, and literary sources like Erasmus's *Adagia*, *Parabolae*, and *Apothegmata*, that often seem to have furnished the raw material for aphoristic and metaphorical signs.

It is interesting to see what Millen and Wolf were able to discover about the iconography of *The Ship of State*. Their main argument is that the scene does not depict the historical, ceremonial event that took place on 27 September 1614 (an event that would place Louis XIII in the spotlight), but is an emblematical reduction of the event for which Rubens mainly used, according to the authors, medals, coins, and other devices.[8] They state that for the basic idea,

> he [Rubens] went back to Horace's ship of state and produced another of his unseaworthy boats likely to be swamped between the left and the right banks of the Seine at its narrowest. This gilded parade float is dragon-powered and adorned on its stern with dolphins and the inevitable swag of fruit. It is propelled by eight decidedly buxom and muscular blowzy viragos [we see only four] who look for all the world as if in a rowboat alongside, with no room for their legs. Two other members of the all-female crew tend to the sails. Overtopping all is the familiar personification of France with flame-shaped sword (like a Malay kriss) in one hand and the orb of government in the other. At the tiller is young Louis in full regal panoply including the Order of the Holy Spirit. A lamb-like early adolescent, he dutifully looks to his mother for instruction on steering the ship of state. She is the very image of modesty, humility even: an iron will in net fichu and satin gown. In the stormy sky are two Fames, one with a coiled Roman buccina, the other (difficult to make out) with a straight trumpet. Above the cross arm of the mast, twin stars: Castor and Pollux. In the sea, Louis's titular dolphin and an occasional coy fish.[9]

The prosaic description of the painting quoted above is followed by a more urbane description of the main persons visible in the painting. Millen and Wolf believe that, according to the Baluze manuscript, a kind of working outline drawn up for Rubens, the vessel is propelled by Force (*Fortitudo*), Prudence (*Prudentia*), and Justice (*Justitia*), with Temperance (*Temperantia*) lowering the sails as the boat enters port. There is also a pen-drawing by Rubens which is a study for this painting, and in it the figures are identified in writing as: Prudenza (*Prudentia*), Constanza (*Con-*

---

[6] Ibid., 7.

[7] Ibid., 7.

[8] Ibid., 169–70.

[9] Ibid., 170.

stantia), Forza (*Fortitudo*), and, in the air, Fama (*Fama*). This pen sketch and the oil sketch show shields at the side of the boat, but only the finished painting has shields with a visible content (Fig. 2). Millen and Wolf state that these shields have been variously interpreted and offer, with some reservations, their suggestions.[10]

The different readings of the four shields are as follows:

1. This emblem has been read as "a lion overthrowing a column,"[11] "a lion with column,"[12] "a lion biting into a column,"[13] and "the lion is exerting its full strength to hold up the column and set it upright, making the subject Fortitude . . . ."[14] All authors agree that the shield signifies Force (*Fortitudo*); only Saward's interpretation, which is based on classical sources, differs; she interprets the shield as *Fortitudo* and *Magnaminitas* of the king upholding the *securitas* of the state.[15] Millen and Wolf quote Ripa's entry for *Fortezza:* "Armed woman . . . leans on a column, because of the parts of an edifice this is the strongest which supports the others; at her feet a lion will lie."

2. On the second shield a flaming altar is shown with four sphinxes on its base and a serpent coiling around the shaft; above the altar is an open eye. The scene is interpreted as Piety by Held[16] and Grossmann,[17] and as Religion by Von Simson.[18] Millen and Wolf go somewhat further, stating that: "On many Roman coins a snake coiled around an altar has the significance of Salus Augusti, the health of the emperor, and this is certainly something Maria might wish for her sickly son who few thought would live to complete his reign and many (probably Maria herself) hoped would be superseded or succeeded by his thriving younger brother Gaston."[19] They also show that they have reservations when they state that "we have seen that the serpent has manifold meanings, and perhaps this emblem is yet to be deciphered." Strangely enough, the authors do not mention the interpretation of this shield by Saward. She identifies the woman with the shield as watchful *Providentia* guarding the *salus.*[20]

3. All authors agree that the third shield shows a pair of scales held by a hand emerging from the clouds, and that this signifies Justice or Equity.

4. The last shield shows crossed cornucopias held by clasped hands and flanked by a caduceus. Held interprets the scene as signifying Concord (*Concordia*);[21] Grossmann believes that it signifies *Fides*;[22] Von Simson argues for Good Faith;[23] and Mautour thinks of Felicity or Concord.[24] Millen and Wolf[25] once again omit Saward's[26] interpretation (*Pax*), but they do provide us with some additional material that makes them follow the interpretation of Mautour.

---

[10] Ibid., 170.

[11] K. Grossmann, *Die Gemäldezyklus der Galerie der Maria von Medici von Peter Paul Rubens* (Strassburg, 1906), 77.

[12] O. G. von Simson, *Zur Genealogie der weltlichen Apotheose im Barock, besonders der Medicigalerie des P. P. Rubens* (Strassburg, 1936), 367.

[13] J. S. Held, *The Oil Sketches of Peter Paul Rubens: A Critical Catalogue*, 2 vols. (Princeton, 1980), vol. 1, 118.

[14] Millen and Wolf, *Heroic Deeds* (as in note 4), 170.

[15] Saward, *Golden Age* (as in note 3), 159–60.

[16] Held, *Oil Sketches* (as in note 13), vol. 1, 118.

[17] Grossmann, *Gemäldezyklus* (as in note 11), 77.

[18] Von Simson, *Genealogie* (as in note 12), 367.

[19] Millen and Wolf, *Heroic Deeds* (as in note 4), 170–71.

[20] Saward, *Golden Age* (as in note 3), 160.

[21] Held, *Oil Sketches* (as in note 13), vol. 1, 118.

[22] Grossmann, *Gemäldezyklus* (as in note 11), 78.

[23] Von Simson, *Genealogie* (as in note 12), 367.

[24] Ph. B. Moreau de Mautour, *Description de la galerie du Palais de Luxembourg* (Paris, 1704), cited by Millen and Wolf, *Heroic Deeds* (as in note 4), 171.

[25] Millen and Wolf, *Heroic Deeds* (as in note 4), 171.

[26] Saward, *Golden Age* (as in note 3), 160.

Millen and Wolf argue that emblematic sources, besides inspiring details of Rubens's painting, also played a major role in the composition as a whole. They present two emblems of Maria de' Medici which are both based on coins and show Maria de' Medici in a boat.[27] One depicts Maria as Cybele calming the waves, with the motto *Servando dea facta deos*. This is translated by Millen and Wolf as "Serving the gods, she herself become goddess." The other shows Maria steering the ship of state, with Louis XIII at the bow; the motto reads: *Tanti dux femina facti*, "A woman has directed this important action."

Castor and Pollux are interpreted as denoting the two brothers Louis and Gaston d'Orleans, the latter being the favorite of Maria for the kingship.[28] They interpret the figure of Maria de' Medici, who seems to invite the young king to take over the steering of the ship of state, as "a deliberate and perhaps not entirely well-meant bit of special pleading."[29]

It is intriguing that in Millen and Wolf's whole interpretation they do not seem to have acquired enough access to those emblematic sources they themselves claim to be necessary to unravel the iconographic details of the painting. They state that "the hunt was on. It called for running three trails. One led through the thickets and sometimes mazes of emblematics and thus into the related fields of antique and modern numismatics, goldsmiths' designs, book illustrations, prints, popular imagery."[30] They don't succeed in bringing into play enough textual and visual evidence from the cultural context known to Rubens and to those who commissioned him; this would have enabled them to track down the different meanings that viewers sharing this cultural context could attach to the painting.

A New Interpretation

The interpretation of the painting in this paper was sparked by the shield depicting the lion holding a column. That image was found in the database as a printers' device, especially in connection with members of the Waesberge family, where it was accompanied by the motto *Ingenio superatur* (Fig. 3). It was clear that Rubens scholars were unaware of this interpretation and association. All of the above scholars, except Saward, had interpreted the first shield as denoting "Force," an interpretation that led some authors to interpret the other shields as depicting related virtues: *Prudentia, Justitia*, and *Temperantia*. A study of the three other shields led to an examination of the unusual overall composition of the painting. The final area of research, and one which is still on-going, was an attempt to discover if there were any clues in *picturae* of the emblems of Alciati for this particular composition.

The first shield depicts a motif that was used in the southern and the northern Netherlands as a printers' device. The printers' device depicting a lion holding a column also has a motto: *Ingenio superatur*, "He (or she) is overcome by ingenuity" (Fig. 3). It is the motto which leads to the meaning of the device. The column stands for "Force," but the lion plays the role of "ingenio" lifting the column, thus representing the idea that "ingenio" overpowers sheer force.

The second shield on the side of the ship of state is an emblem taken directly from Andrea Alciati's *Emblemata*. It is number 150 (using the number of the Tozzi edition, Padua, 1621), with the

---

²⁷ Millen and Wolf, *Heroic Deeds* (as in note 4), figs. 39, 40.
²⁸ Ibid., 172–73.
²⁹ Ibid., 173.
³⁰ Ibid., 8.

motto *Salus publica* (Fig. 4). The *pictura* shows a snake on an altar; in front of it are people kneeling, or possibly praying, with a landscape and city in the background. The explanation is: "Phoebigena erectis Epidaurius insidet aris, Mitis, & immani conditur angue Deus. Accurunt agri, veniatque salutifer orant. Annuit, atque ratas efficit ille preces." Daly translates this epigram as: "The Epidaurian son of Apollo, Aesculapius, sits on an elevated altar, and the gentle god is disguised in the form of a huge snake. The sick flock to him and pray that he come as a healer. He nods his assent, and fulfills their prayers."[31]

The theme *Salus publica* is important, but so also are the other elements in this explanation. Aesculapius heals the sick that come to him. Here the eye in the sky seems to place the scene in a Christian context. This change of context is easily believed by looking at an emblem from Claude Paradin's *Devises heroïques*.[32] The third emblem or device in Paradin's volume, with the motto *Secum feret omnia mortis*, depicts a cross with a snake coiled around it, and draws a parallel between Moses who erected the brazen serpent to heal the adder-bitten Jews, and the cross referring to Christ who with his death saved us from eternal death. The two-layered typology touching on the Old Testament (Moses and the snake) and the New Testament (Christ and the cross) is augmented with a third layer from classical antiquity (Aesculapius as a snake). Public welfare, and, attached to that, the role of the king in acquiring it, appears to be the theme of the second shield.

The third shield, depicting a hand from the clouds holding a pair of scales, is a familiar motif referring to such concepts as Justice, *Aequabiliter* (the equality of justice). Henkel and Schöne give two examples of this emblem.[33]

The fourth shield depicts a caduceus with two hands and two cornucopiae. Apart from the two hands, the elements of this image are also a familiar emblem from Alciati. It is emblem 119 (in the 1621 Padua edition) with the motto *Virtuti fortuna comes*, "Fortune the comrade of excellence" (Fig. 5). The explanation is as follows: "Angvibvs implicitis, geminis caduceus alis inter Amalthea cornua rectus adest. Pollentes sic mente viros, fandique peritos indicat, ut rerum copia multa beat." In Daly's translation: "A caduceus with two snakes entwined about it and two wings stands upright between the horns of Amalthea. Thus it suggests that a rich abundance of things blesses men powerful in mind and skilled in speaking." The two hands usually refer to such concepts as *Amicitia* and *Concordia*. It would appear, then, that the shield can be interpreted, at least with the emblem of Alciati in mind, as men who are powerful in mind, skilled in speaking, directed toward whatever is the message of the two hands (*Amicitia, Concordia*, etc.), and who generate rich abundance. It is interesting to note that Alciati's emblem was used as printers' device in the northern Netherlands by Jan I van Turnhout ('s-Hertogenbosch, 1527–69).[34] In the southern Netherlands the *pictura* of Alciati's emblem was used by Petrus Bellerus (Antwerp, 1575–1600) and his widow and heirs, with a different motto: *Concordia fructus*. The shield painted by Rubens seems to incorporate the meaning of the device (*Concordia* pays off), referred to by the motto of Bellerus, by way of the two hands.

[31] P. M. Daly and S. Cuttler, *Andreas Alciatus*, vol. 2, *Emblems in Translation* (Toronto, Buffalo, and London, 1985), emblem 150.

[32] C. Paradin and G. Siméon, *Princeliicke Deviisen . . . Wt franschen in onse tael verduytscht* (Leiden, 1615); this edition also includes a Dutch translation of the work of Gabriello Simeoni.

[33] A. Henkel and A. Schöne, *Emblemata: Handbuch zur Sinnbildkunst des XVI. und XVII. Jahrhunderts* (Stuttgart, 1976), 1434–36.

[34] In Georgius Macropedius, *Epistolica . . . Quae . . . Quicquid ad Prima Rhetorices Elementa Attinet* (Sylvaeducis, 1556).

The second and fourth shields depict emblems taken from Alciati's *Emblemata.* The first of these depicts a motif that is known as a Dutch printers' device (the motif of the fourth shield was also used as a printers' device). The first and fourth shield carry a certain didactic undertone. The third shield is related to another painting in the series: *The Felicity of the Government of Maria de' Medici.*

It is clear that the "emblematic game" is being played. This perception is reinforced if the composition of the painting is examined. A large and plump dragon-headed boat which is small in relation to the figures aboard has the first oarswoman doing something which is not clear (pushing off?). Millen and Wolf,[35] as well as Warnke[36] and Saward,[37] make extensive use of (antique) medals related to the theme of the ship of state. All of them see the rather peculiar composition of the painting by Rubens as a result of the influence of these medals. However, since this new interpretation shows that two of the shields on the side of the boat are emblems taken from Alciati, it would be worthwhile to have a closer look at *picturae* of emblems from Alciati that depict ships. Two particularly interesting emblems are to be found by querying the electronic Padua edition of Alciati, published in 1621, using the ICONCLASS notation for ship: 46C21.

Emblem 43 in the 1621 Padua edition bears the motto *Spes proxima* (Fig. 6). The *pictura* shows a ship in a rough sea, blown by the wind with the twin stars of the Dioscuri in the sky. The explanation is as follows: "In nvmeris agitur Respublica nostra procellis, et spes venturae sola salutis adest: Non secus ac navis medio circum aequore, venti quam rapiunt, salsis iamque fatiscit aquis. Quod si Helena adueniant, lucentia sidera, fratres, Amissos animos spes bona restituit." Daly translates this as: "Our state is buffeted by countless storms, and there is only one hope for its future safety; and not unlike a ship in the midst of the sea which the winds snatch, it is already breaking up in the salt water. But if the shining stars, the brothers of Helen—Castor and Pollux—should appear, good hope restores the sinking spirits."[38] Although the ship at sea in high winds, which is a significant part of the emblem, is missing, it is important to note the visual reference to the emblem *Spes proxima* by way of the ship (of state) and the twin stars.

Emblem 83 in the 1621 Padua edition of Alciati (Fig. 7) is even more important in looking at the composition and iconographic content. The motto is *In facile à virtute desciscentes,* which has been translated by Daly as "On those who easily fall from virtue." The *pictura* closely resembles the composition of the painting by Rubens. In fact, the resemblance is so striking that it is possible to speculate whether Rubens echoes the *pictura* of Alciati's emblem to develop the association between his painting and Alciati's emblem. This idea does not appear to be too farfetched when it is possible to see that even the *remora* depicted in the *pictura* of Alciati's emblem is visible in the painting of Rubens, albeit replaced by a dolphin.[39] This is a play of words on "dauphin," crown prince and dolphin.

[35] Millen and Wolf, *Heroic Deeds* (as in note 4), 171.

[36] M. Warnke, *Laudando Praecipere: Der Medicizyklus des Peter Paul Rubens* (Groningen, 1993), 23.

[37] Saward, *Golden Age* (as in note 3), pls. 89 and 92.

[38] Daly and Cuttler, *Andreas Alciatus* (as in note 31), emblem 43.

[39] Pliny in his *Historia naturalis* mentions the legendary *remora* as *echeneis remora* or *odinolytes* (*Natural History, with an English Translation in Ten Volumes* [Loeb ed.], ed. W. H. S. Jones, vol. 8, *Books XXVIII–XXXII* [London and Cambridge, Mass., 1963], 464ff.). Roemer Vischer, a Dutch emblem writer, remarks dryly that the slowness of a ship is not caused by the "remoras" attached to its sides, but rather by the drinking habits of its crew (R. Vischer, *Sinnepoppen,* pt. 1 [Amsterdam, 1614], emblem 48).

The explanation of the emblem is as follows: "Parva velut limax spreto Remora impete venti, Remorumque, ratem sistere sola potest: Sic quosdam ingenio & virtute ad sidera vectos Detinet in medio tramite caussa levis. Anxia lis veluti est, vel qui meretricius ardor Egregiis iuuenes seuocat à studiis." This has been translated by Daly as: "The remora, tiny as a snail, can by itself cause a ship to stop, disdaining the force of the wind and oars. So does a petty cause hold back in mid-course those drawn to the stars by their talent and virtue. It is like a worrisome lawsuit or passion for a harlot, which draws youths from outstanding studies." The *remora* and its substitution, the dolphin, draw us into the domain of the well-known adage *Festina lente*. In the Dutch translation of the devices of Gabriello Simeoni it is possible to read:

> Vespasianvs, die in't rijck, en oock in deuchden Augustum volgde nae, hem altijt meer verheuchden In sijn voorsichticheyt, dan in sijn groote macht, En achte dat verstant was boven wapens cracht. De haesticheyt, dat is, het Dolfins snellick swemmen, Ginck hij met traecheyt, als met eenen Ancker, temmen. Een Prins die dees gewoonte in alles onderhouwt, Doet niet veel dat misluct, veel min dat hem berouwt.[40]

In translation, this reads as "Vespasian followed Augustus's prudence rather than his power; he valued intellect more than force. Rashness (like the swimming dolphin) he coupled with slowness (the anchor). A prince who acts accordingly does not make many mistakes, and has to regret things even less."

If the interpretation is based on the sources presented above, it is possible to arrive at a conclusion which is close to that of Millen and Wolf, of the work as a "spectacular riposte, no less political than personal."

The overall composition of the painting led to the two emblems of Alciati, *Spes proxima* (emblem 48) and *In facile à virtute desciscentes* (emblem 83), which seem to constitute the main theme of the painting. This is the theme of *Hercules am Scheidewege:* with Louis XIII at the helm, the ship of state could go either in the wrong direction (led by someone who easily falls from virtue) or in the right direction (*Spes proxima*). Iconographers have debated whether Rubens's boat is leaving harbor or about to enter it.[41] Of course, the answer is neither. This boat is going nowhere, because the composition visually expresses the central theme of the painting, that it can go either way. The joke of replacing the *remora* with a dolphin ("dauphin"), that is, a force opposite from that of *Festina lente,* adds another layer to the painting. This refers to the rashness of Louis XIII, the dauphin, who might lead the ship of state into dangerous waters. The shields on the side of the boat seem to present the views of Maria on how to steer the ship of state into safe waters. They range from clear and bitter warnings to suggestions for a political course. The first shield, when interpreted as *Ingenio superatur,* expands on the first overall theme, that is, the ability of man's ingenuity to overcome sheer force. It presents an ironic lesson for the young king. The second shield, *Salus publica,* illustrates the power of the king to bring about safety for the state. The third shield, related to the theme of justice, refers to Maria de' Medici. By way of the motif of the scales, the shield refers to another painting in the cycle, *The Felicity of the Government of Maria de' Medici.* The fourth shield is also an emblem taken from Alciati. The shield can be interpreted, with the emblem

---

[40] Paradin and Siméon, *Princeliicke Deviisen* (as in note 32), emblem 184.

[41] Millen and Wolf, *Heroic Deeds* (as in note 4), 170.

of Alciati in mind, as referring to men who are powerful in mind, skilled in speaking, directed toward whatever is the message of the two hands (*Amicitia, Concordia*, etc.), and generating rich abundance. But the shield also contains, by way of the caduceus depicted, a reference to the personal device of Maria de' Medici: *Pax optima rerum*, "Peace is the highest good."

The second and third shields seem to refer to the more general concepts and lessons. The second shield depicts *Salus publica*, a common objective for any ruler. In the case of the French king Louis XIII, there are two remarks to be made. Firstly, like his father, Henry IV, Louis XIII possessed healing powers. As Marc Bloch explained in his book, *Les Rois thaumaturges*, "Dans la monarchie française du XVIIe siècle, le toucher des écrouelles a définitivement pris rang parmi les pompes solennelles dont s'entoure la splendeur du souverain. Louis XIII et Louis XIV y procèdent régulièrement aux grandes fêtes, Pâques, Pentecôte, Noël ou le Jour de l'An, parfois la Chandeleur, la Trinité, l'Assomption, la Touissaint."[42] Secondly, Louis XIII himself suffered from poor health. In the words of Madeleine Foisil, "A plusieurs reprises, il a été malade sans que l'on puisse dire s'il s'agit d'épreuves passagères ou des allertes annonciatrices d'un état incurable qui fera de Louis XIII le roi malade."[43] It is not clear if this shield is intended to carry an ironic meaning, as suggested by Millen and Wolf.[44]

The third shield refers to *Justitia*. But the motif of the scales is predominant in another painting from the cycle, *The Felicity of the Government of Maria de' Medici*. This puts forward the idea that by honoring justice the young king would follow in the footsteps of his mother. It is also possible that this shield could be interpreted as an ironic message. In the course of the troubles in 1614, Louis XIII became referred to as Louis the Just. Moote notes that "In the midst of the troubles of 1614, and frustrated with his wayward tongue, Louis noted this sobriquet, commenting wryly that he wanted people to call him Louis the Just and not Louis the Stammerer."[45] If the proposed interpretation is accepted, and especially the visual reference from this shield to the painting *The Felicity of the Government of Maria de' Medici*, then the advice to honor the course of his mother toward justice, can be seen as a clever turnaround of the images and messages displayed at the glorious entry of Louis and Maria into Paris from Nantes. Moote records that "As thousands of happy subjects cheered, Louis passed through arches of triumph that bore references to all the royal virtues. But the most striking message was emblazoned on an immense tableau depicting Louis in full regalia at the bow of the ship of state and Marie at its helm as it triumphed over the storms of political turmoil. For those who might miss the message, the accompanying mottoes proclaimed Louis XIII a 'peaceful' and 'most just' king, and the queen regent as 'moderate in peace and war.'"[46]

But the first and the fourth shields put forward the strongest lessons for the young king. The fourth shield depicts, as has been shown earlier, an emblem taken directly from Alciati, (emblem 119): *Virtuti fortuna comes*, "Fortune the comrade of excellence." This emblem, about a rich abundance of things that blesses men who are powerful in mind and skilled in speaking, clearly holds an ironic, if not bitter, message. Even though Louis XIII appears to have had the ability, he was not very powerful either mentally or intellectually and was more drawn toward practical, mechanical

---

[42] M. Bloch, *Les Rois thaumaturges: Étude sur le caractère surnaturel attribué à la puissance royale particulièrement en France et en Angleterre* (Paris, 1983), 360–61.

[43] M. Foisil, *L'Enfant Louis XIII: L'Éducation d'un roi (1601–1617)* (s.l., 1996), 201.

[44] Millen and Wolf, *Heroic Deeds* (as in note 4), 171.

[45] A. Lloyd Moote, *Louis XIII, the Just* (Berkeley and Los Angeles, 1989), 56.

[46] Ibid., 57.

subjects. Particularly appropriate to this point is the fact that he had a tremendous stutter. Moote records that even though he "was not born with the legendary teeth that his father, Henry IV, and his son Louis XIV reputedly inflicted on their nurses, the dauphin had an appetite greater than his ability to feed. An attending surgeon tried to help by cutting the membrane under his tongue when he was two days old. That physical handicap contributed to a dangling royal tongue and, through emotional tensions, to a frustrating lifelong stammer that appeared by his third year."[47]

The first shield is often interpreted as simply denoting *Fortitudo,* but it could actually denote the victory of "ingenio" over sheer force. This is, once again, a clear "riposte" from the mother to her son, who was a rash ruler relying on force and who, in a short period of time, upturned much of the carefully plotted politics of his mother.

This new interpretation of the painting by Rubens must be seen in the light of that troublesome period, 1615–24, when, according to Moote, "Louis searched for a mode of governing as he overthrew his mother and began his personal rule."[48] This period saw an end to the so-called *Pax hispanica* enjoyed by Maria de' Medici. Louis XIII was declared of age in an official ceremony on the 2 October 1614. Maria de Medici commissioned the paintings from Rubens in 1622. The years between 1614 and 1622 brought civil war, tensions between mother and son, and short reconciliations. At the end of this period Louis was estranged, if not at outright war, with his mother, his brother, and his wife. The concepts of *Amicitia* and *Concordia* clearly did not enter into personal relations. Millen and Wolf describe this relationship with the following:

> We began with the idea that the paintings were commissioned for her private residence not by the Dowager Queen of France, acting in the name and for the purposes of the country she could now only counsel and never again rule, but by Maria de' Medici, daughter of Johanna of Austria (a Habsburg queen by birth) and Grand Duke Francesco de' Medici, ruler over Tuscany; that Maria de' Medici had been humiliated by the royal husband she loved but had then, slowly and by force of circumstances and no small diplomatic skill, won his respect for her capabilities; that after a regency it took the coolest of heads to steer through, she was repaid with ingratitude and even exiled by the royal son she could scarcely love but forced herself to tolerate . . . .[49]

As with any iconographic interpretation, it is necessary for the iconographer to ask if too much is being read into the work. The answer is not simple in this case, as in so many other examples, but circumstantial evidence does exist that reinforces the above suggestions.

Knowledge of the emblems has certainly added to this new interpretation. There is no objection whatsoever to the more traditional reading of the painting by Rubens as a ship of state, with the shields denoting the traditional virtues *Fortitudo, Prudentia, Justitia,* and *Temperantia.* The interpretation by Saward is more problematic. She fails to make it plausible that the classical sources she unearthed with such care constituted a common pool from which Maria de' Medici, Rubens, as well as others, could draw. This new interpretation depends solely on knowledge of the emblems by Alciati, and the existence of what we have called the "emblematic game." The combination of the two emblems from Alciati, *Spes proxima* and *In facile à virtute desciscentes,* together with the replacement of

[47] Ibid., 21.   [49] Millen and Wolf, *Heroic Deeds* (as in note 4), 5.

[48] Ibid., 3.

the *remora* with a dolphin, constitutes the central theme of the painting. This is a variant of the *Hercules am Scheidewege* theme, whereby Maria de' Medici offers the helm of the ship of state to her son, but not without some ironic, venomous lessons, which are concealed in the depictions on the shields. This ship is capable of going either way, as is France. This could be a bumpy ride on rough seas due to rash, all-powerful politics by a king not powerful in mind or speech, or "hope might be near at hand" (*Spes proxima*), if he would adopt the politics his mother practiced during the years of her regency. Rubens even came up with a very clever composition that transcends historical boundaries. In trying to interpret the direction of the boat, whether it was leaving or arriving at port, iconographers were, without actually realizing it, visualizing the main theme of the work. This was centered on the doubts of Maria de' Medici as to where her son might lead France.

Knowledge of the emblems of Alciati proved necessary in arriving at this new interpretation. The extent to which such emblems were understood by people in the first part of the seventeenth century is not known. Rubens probably did understand them, since he undertook some work for Christoffel Plantin, the famous Antwerp printer and publisher, who published several emblem books, like the *Omnia Emblemata* by Alciati, with a commentary by Claude Mignault, in 1577 and 1581. But even Louis XIII could perhaps have grasped the disguised meaning of the painting. Foisil records that:

> Il [that is, Héroard] a dans sa bibliothèque de beaux grands livres devenus rares et qui font maintenant la fierté des collections publiques et privées de notre temps et que l'on ne mettrait, certes pas, entre les mains d'un petit garçon de trois ans. Il a les ouvrages d'histoire naturelle de Conrad Gessner, *La Cosmographie* de Merula, *Le Livre des bâtiments* de Vitruve, *Les Emblèmes* d'Alciat, etc. Ouvrages austères pour ceux qui ne sont point des humanistes, des lecteurs entraînés. Mais ils sont illustrés de belles gravures dont on peut admirer la beauté, la verité. Alors, grâce à l'art et à l'invention d'Héroard pour les montrer, les livres savants deviennent, par la magie d'un instant, des livres d'enfant.[50]

This new interpretation of *The Ship of State* as a painting that contains several layers of meaning is an example of how knowledge of emblems as well as so-called applied emblems, like printers' devices, together with the idea of the existence of something like an "emblematic game," can provide insights into the historical meaning of a painting. It cannot be proven that the substitution of a dolphin for a *remora* would have been noted by someone of the early seventeenth century as a playful way to change the meaning of the emblem used. Even the existence of the "emblematic game" which is suggested as an underlying context for this research cannot be proven. However, additional research outside of this particular painting, which cannot be dealt with in the context of this paper, does reinforce the existence of this "emblematic game."

The images contained in the emblem books which are at present incorporated in the electronic corpus are all described in detail with the help of the ICONCLASS system. The value of Van der Waal's practical advice, mentioned at the beginning of this article, can be inferred from the results obtained in this paper. A simple query with the ICONCLASS notation for ship (46C21) in the database first directed attention to the two emblems from Alciati that are crucial in understanding the contents and composition of Rubens's painting.

---

[50] Foisil, *L'Enfant Louis XIII* (as in note 43), 95.

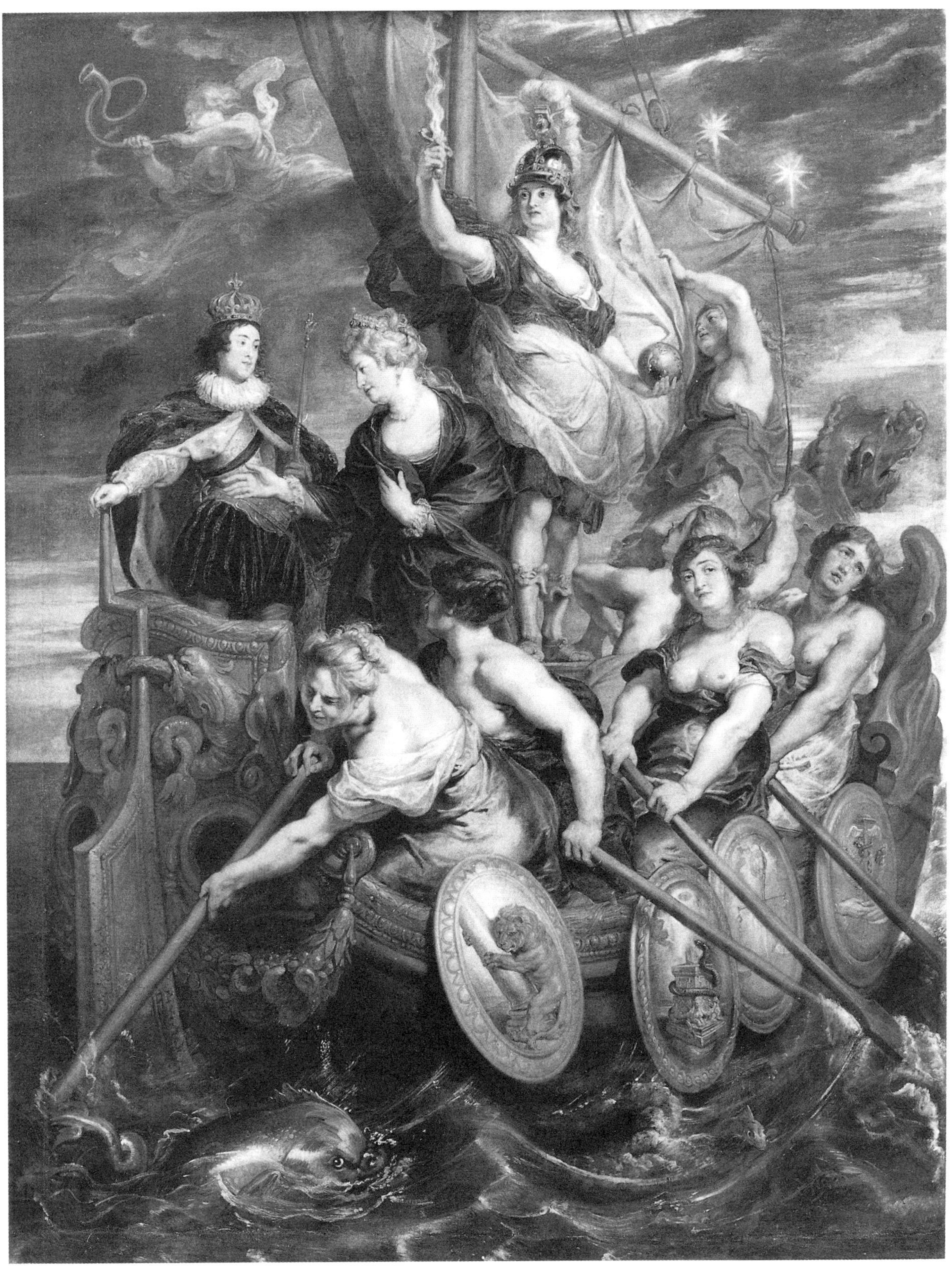

1. Peter Paul Rubens, *The Ship of State* or *The Coming of Age of Louis XIII*, Paris, Musée du Louvre

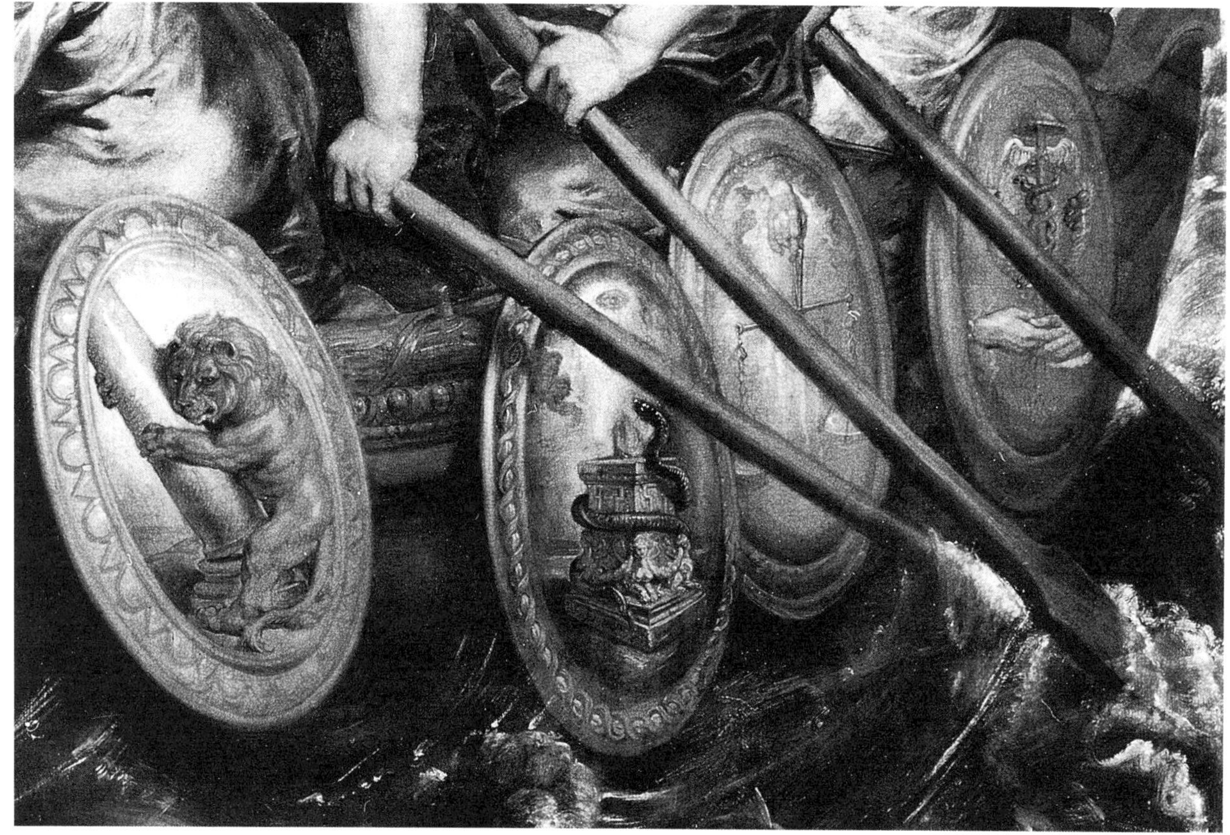

2. Detail of Fig. 1: shields along the side of the ship

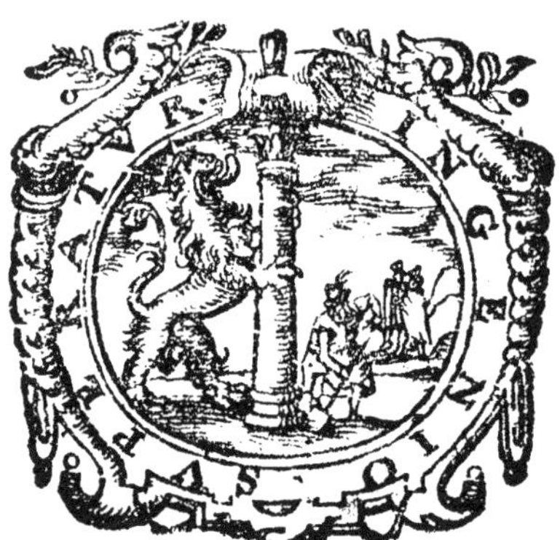

3. Printer's device of a lion holding a column, with the motto *Ingenio superatur*, in a book printed by Jan III van Waesberge

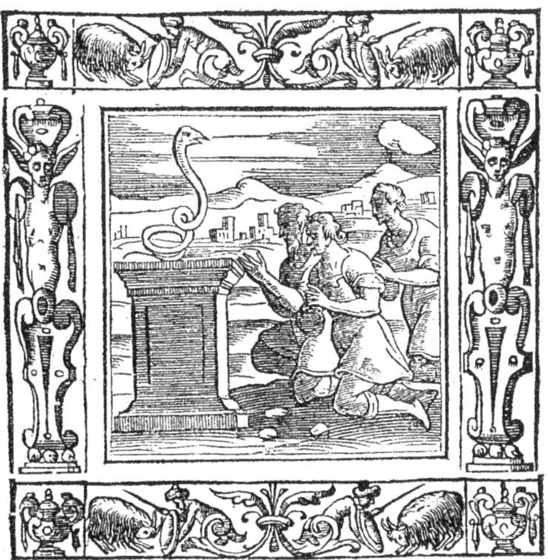

4. Emblem from Andrea Alciati's *Emblemata* (no. 150 in the Tozzi edition, Padua, 1621), with the motto *Salus publica*

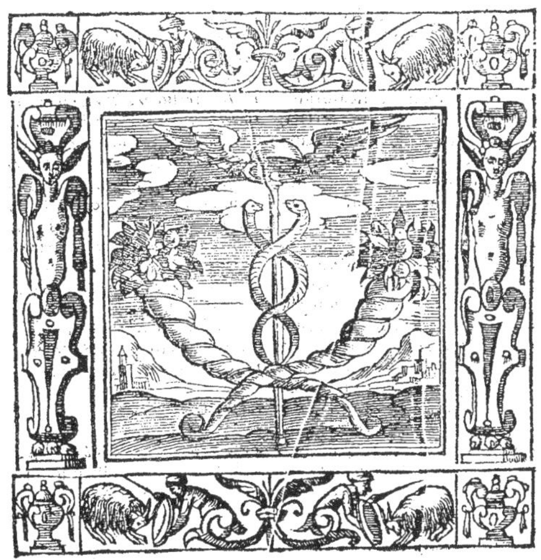

5. Emblem from Andrea Alciati's *Emblemata* (no. 119 in the Tozzi edition, Padua, 1621), with the motto *Virtuti fortuna comes*

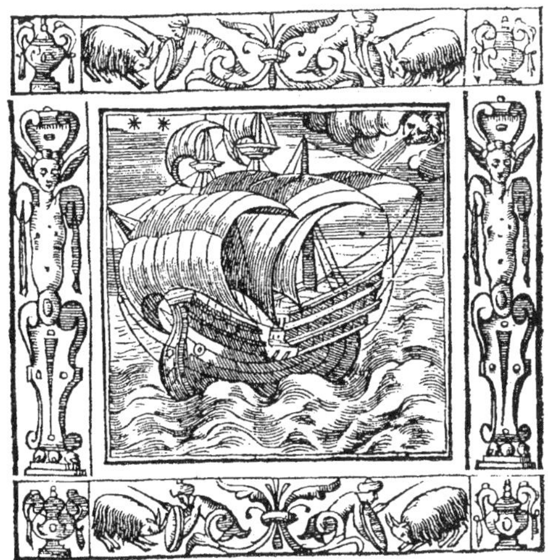

6. Emblem from Andrea Alciati's *Emblemata* (no. 43 in the Tozzi edition, Padua, 1621), with the motto *Spes proxima*

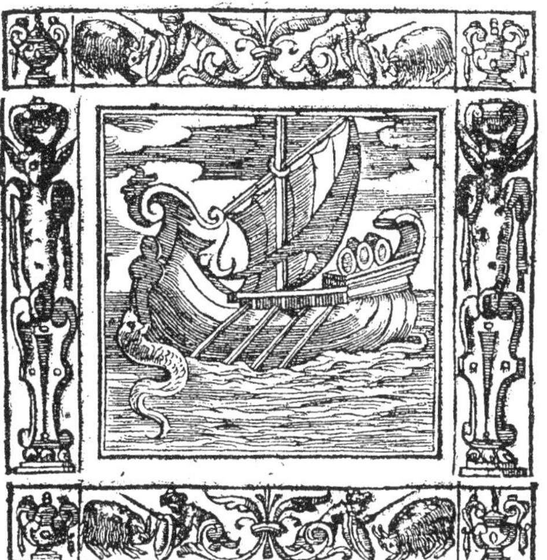

7. Emblem from Andrea Alciati's *Emblemata* (no. 83 in the Tozzi edition, Padua, 1621), with the motto *In facile à virtute desciscentes*

ICONCLASS and Its Application
to Primary Documents*

·

C A R O L   T O G N E R I

IN MAY 1664, Carlo Cesare Malvasia visited the Grimani Palace in Venice and was shown a small painting on copper depicting the Christ Child asleep on the cross in a landscape, and he wrote in his notes of the visit: "Del 1664 maggio in casa Grimani doppo aver veduto tante belle pitture portarono a basso a mostrarmi un rame di once dieci-otto in circa, stagnato, ove è il Signorino steso sopra la croce, di sua mano con poco di paesetto lontano; e mi dissero averne potuto avere cento doble, pare anche del Pesarese. Venezia 1664, perché non lo tenere fra l'altre pitture?"[1]

Fourteen years later, Malvasia included an abbreviated description of this picture when he wrote on the life of Guido Reni in his *Felsina pittrice*.[2] Countless copies of it have been referred to in the literature, and the archival documents that follow contain at least two more. The whereabouts of several versions are known, but only two of these are on copper: one, in Liverpool, at the Walker Art Gallery (Fig. 1), and another version once in the Orleans collection and now in The Art Museum, Princeton University (Fig. 2). This latter picture is in fact the only one of the two known works that is "tinned" or *stagnato* (as it is described above by Malvasia); the Liverpool picture is painted directly onto the copper.[3] The measurements of both of these pictures are very close to those indicated by Malvasia; the Princeton picture is slightly closer to the mark. Stephen Pepper has called the Princeton picture a copy after Reni's lost original,[4] and Richard Spear has suggested, based on documentary and technical evidence, that it "remains the only known 'original' of Reni's widely admired design."[5]

The ICONCLASS notation specifically assigned to the "Christ Child Sleeping on the Cross" is 11D238; when this is combined with the artist name "Reni," a search in the Getty Provenance

---

* The Inventories database of the Getty Provenance Index comprises a group of documents dedicated to unpublished seventeenth- and eighteenth-century inventories of collections in Italy, Spain, and The Netherlands. It serves as a complement to the department's other major project of indexing nineteenth-century auction catalogues. This paper refers to a variety of documents found in the Inventories database, which contains over 122,000 references to art objects, primarily paintings, and attempts to demonstrate how the project uses and manipulates the ICONCLASS (H. van de Waal et al., *ICONCLASS: An Iconographic Classification System* [Amsterdam, 1981]) system and structures to provide access to infor-

mation of this nature.

[1] *Le Carte di Carlo Cesare Malvasia* (Rapporto della Soprintendenza per i beni artistici e storici per le province di Bologna, Ferrara, Forlì e Ravenna 25), ed. L. Marzocchi (Bologna, 1980), 29.

[2] C. C. Malvasia, *Felsina pittrice*, vol. 2 (Bologna, 1678; rev. ed. Bologna, 1841), 65.

[3] R. E. Spear, "Notes on Two Copper Paintings by Domenichino and Guido Reni," *Record of The Art Museum, Princeton University* 48, no. 1 (1989), 32–36.

[4] D. S. Pepper, *Guido Reni* (New York, 1984), 296, Appendix I, no. B-8, A.

[5] Spear, "Two Copper Paintings" (as in note 3), 35.

Index Inventories database will render only one record, which describes a painting from a Balbi inventory taken in Genoa in 1658 that includes a reference to the Christ Child: "Nostro Signor Bambino che dorme sopra la croce di Guido."[6] A more encompassing search, using just the ICON-CLASS notation with no artist's name, will render a larger set of pictures from a variety of cities, by artists who depicted the same subject. In the majority of these cases there is no reference to the artist; a few, however, include not only attributions but also approximate sizes of the paintings and some indication of the support. In this latter search, in addition to the Balbi picture mentioned in the 1658 document, there is another citation of this subject which may add to the complicated process of trying to resolve an attribution for the Princeton picture. The reference, which cites a picture by Simone Cantarini, comes from a document discovered by Raffaella Morselli in the Archivio di Stato in Bologna: "Un quadretto p. traverso con un Puttino, che dorme su la Croce del Pesarese sul rame con Cornice dorata picolo."

This description comes from the inventory of Cesare Locatelli, a Bolognese nobleman who died in 1658, and who had at the time of his death a collection of pictures predominantly by Bolognese artists. These included thirteen pictures by Guido Reni, twenty-three pictures painted by other artists after compositions by Guido, and ten other paintings by Guido's student, Simone Cantarini, known as "Pesarese."[7] We know from Malvasia that Cantarini was in fact residing at the Palazzo Locatelli after he had left the bottega of Guido, and it would not have been unusual for a student to copy a work by his teacher or master, especially for a patron who so obviously admired Reni's work. Thus the picture we find in the Locatelli inventory may be a reference to yet another version of the painting by Reni, or it could possibly be a reference to the same picture Malvasia saw in Venice eight years later. Cesare Locatelli's son, Ercole, inherited the collection. Thirty-five years later, in 1693, when an inventory of his collection was taken, only a handful of the 400 pictures in the original inventory were found in Ercole's. It is tempting to explain the absence of the picture by Cantarini from the later collection by saying that it might have found its way into the Grimani Palace, but there is no evidence to suggest that it or any of the other pictures mentioned in the 1658 inventory entered that important Venetian collection.

The purpose of this paper is not to establish the authorship of the Princeton picture, but to use the story to illustrate how the standardized language of ICONCLASS can be used to search for a painting in the Getty Provenance Index's Inventories projects. The ICONCLASS system has continued to be an important issue for these databases of archival material. The Inventories projects from Italy, Spain, and The Netherlands can be merged together, as they are on the CD-ROM published by the Provenance Index, so that it is possible to search across the combined Dutch, Spanish, and Italian documents. The need for a controlled field for subjects is crucial for this project because of the mixture of languages (e.g., *croce, cruz, kruijs*). But it is also essential because of the nature of these documents, which are often in dialect and contain antiquated and idiosyncratic spelling, making searching in the modern-day form of each of these languages problematic.

---

[6] Not. Gio. Luca Rossi, Archivio di Stato, Genova, f. 6, anni 1657–59, 23 May 1658, published in P. Boccardo and L. Magnani, "La famiglia dei Balbi: La Committenza," in *Il Palazzo dell'Università di Genova: Il Collegio dei Gesuiti nella strada dei Balbi,* Università degli Studi di Genova (Genoa, 1987), 81.

[7] Raffaella Morselli in her *Collezionisti e quadrerie nella Bologna del Seicento,* published by The J. Paul Getty Trust, October 1998.

The manner in which these inventories were recorded, and by whom, also has an indirect effect on the understanding of the subject matter of the paintings contained in the documents. For example, while some noble families in the seventeenth and eighteenth centuries, for example, may have retained artists or experts to make valuations or identifications of their objects for the inventory process, a good number of middle-class collections were inventoried by local scribes who were often not specialists in the field of art. The Dutch documents in the database record many appraisers, often housewives, who were brought in to list and value household objects after the death of the owner of an estate, and in the course of doing so were entrusted with identifying paintings and art objects that were also found in the rooms of the deceased. This may explain why so many of the Dutch documents include paintings without an attribution to an artist and very little information about the subjects beyond simple descriptions such as "two landscapes" or "a saint" or "two badly painted pictures." In some cases there may have been legal reasons for intentionally obscuring the descriptions of the art objects. But for whatever reason, we in this century are often left with only very sketchy descriptions of the art objects in the majority of these documents, which makes subject identification a problem, and even more difficult when attempting to match these descriptions to the formal categories of ICONCLASS.

It is nevertheless possible to point to a number of exceptions, including two wonderful descriptions of a picture in two inventories of the Almirante de Castilla taken in Madrid in 1647: "ytten, Vio un Lienço de un respice finem con quatro cavezas de Muertes de Mano del españolo = Inventariado, a n,o 610 = Tasolo en quatro mill reales 4000"[8] and in 1691:

> Otra Pintura en lienzo que tiene de altto vara y media menos un dedo y de ancho dos varas
> y tercia menos un dedo que llaman el desengaño, en que sc ve una figura de un Angel con
> las alas tendidas y per broche del rropa de un joya, y en la mano Yzquierda una tarxetta con
> un Rettratto de medio cuerpo de un Emperador y la derecha arrimada a un glovo y sobre
> una messa un Relox de torezilla y tres retrattos de muxer una sarta de perlas una cadena de
> oro unas monedas de oro y platta y tres naypes de espadas, y al otro lado ay un Relox de
> Arena unas Armas libros y calaveras y un Candelero con una bela en dos mill Reales 2000.[9]

The larger entry (Fig. 3) is written with painstaking attention to the smallest detail: pearls, portrait miniatures of ladies, a tower clock, the spent candle, etc., are all included in the description. Jordan and Cherry[10] have connected these references to the *Vanitas* by Pereda (described in 1657 as *El desengaño del mundo*,[11] "The Disillusionment of the World"), which has been in the Kunsthistorisches Museum in Vienna since 1733 (Fig. 4).

---

[8] Not. Francisco Suárez de Rivera, Archivo Histórico de Protocolos, Madrid, Prot. 6233, ff. 258–452, inventory of Juan Alfonso Enríquez de Cabrera, Duque de Medina de Ríoseco y X Almirante de Castilla, 25 June 1647; transcribed in M. B. Burke, P. Cherry, et al., *Collections of Paintings in Madrid, 1601–1755* (Los Angeles, 1998), 423, no. 0368.

[9] Not. Juan de Medina, Archivo Histórico Nacional, Madrid, Sección Osuna, legajos 498-2, f.10-242 and f.498-3, f.3-168, inventory of Juan Gaspar Enríquez de Cabrera, Duque de Medina de Ríoseco y X Almirante de Castilla,

17 November 1691; ibid., 902, no. 0095.

[10] W. B. Jordan, *Spanish Still Life in the Golden Age 1600–1650*, exhib. cat., Fort Worth, Kimbell Art Museum (Fort Worth, 1985), 214–18; and W. B. Jordan and P. Cherry, *Spanish Still Life from Velázquez to Goya*, exhib. cat., London, National Gallery (London, 1995), 78ff.

[11] L. Díaz del Valle, "Epílogo y nomenclatura de algunos artífices: Apuntes varios, 1657–1659," in *Fuentes literarias para la historia del arte español*, ed. F. J. Sánchez Cantón, vol. 2 (Madrid, 1933), 372.

The ICONCLASS system was originally intended to aid in classifying the subject matter of *extant* works of art, with an emphasis on Dutch subjects. For projects such as the Inventories database, however, the Provenance Index is classifying titles and more often *descriptions*, and this difference has made our application of ICONCLASS a challenge when the original entry refers to no standard or recognizable subject. Pictures which are described simply as "figures," for example, especially if they are attributed to a painter who was traditionally known to do still lives, can cause problems. An entry with the description "a painting of Peter" may be intended to describe a solitary figure of St. Peter, but could also represent the story of Peter denying Christ, or either of the episodes of Peter in prison, or it could simply be a portrait of someone named Peter.

More problematic are those cases in which the scribe or the compiler of the document may have been mistaken about the subject. There is often confusion, for instance, between the two biblical subjects Judith with the head of Holofernes and Salome with the head of John the Baptist. These two episodes and their characters are often conflated in the documents, providing endless combinations and curious variations on the theme. One example is from an Aldobrandini-Pamphilj inventory of 1665, which shows that the compiler of the inventory was not certain which story was represented. He protects himself by saying that it could be either Herodias or Judith: "Un quadro in tavola d'una Erodiade ò Giuditta di Bernardino Lavino [sic], alto p. tre, e mezo, cornice lavorate dorata Segnato n. 169."[12] This entry has been connected with a picture in the Galleria Doria Pamphilj, now with an attribution to Andrea Solario and called *Salome with the Head of the Baptist.*

A second example, attributed to Correggio, from a Borghese inventory of 1693,[13] is "Una Giuditta che tiene la Testa di S. Gio. in mano," which is obviously a mistake, the compiler of the inventory having conflated the two episodes. A third record, from a Colonna inventory of 1667, reveals "Un quadro d'Oloferne, della testa di S. Gio Batta, che è pintada sopra una Tazza, con cornice azzurra . . .";[14] it is unclear what the scribe was trying to convey here. It seems probable that the work in question is a painting, "un quadro," and that it is framed, "con cornice azzurra." Beyond these two points one cannot be certain.

Several other examples of severed heads can be mentioned, such as that in Jan Agges's Amsterdam inventory of 1702,[15] where the reference is to "a chimneypiece, being Saul, David, and the head of Holifernes [sic], Italian." This same mistake is repeated in Italy: the Neapolitan inventory of Antonio Astuto of 1716 includes a painting which is described by Astuto, who was both the

---

[12] Inventory of Olimpia Aldobrandini-Pamphilj, 1665, Archivio Aldobrandini, Frascati, published by C. d'Onofrio, "Inventario dei dipinti del Cardinal Pietro Aldobrandini compilato da G. B. Agucchi nel 1603," *Palatino* 8, nos. 1–3 (March 1964), nos. 7–8 (August 1964), and nos. 9–12 (December 1964).

[13] Archivio Segreto Vaticano, Rome, Fondo Borghese, Busta N. 7504, transcribed in P. Della Pergola, "L'Inventario Borghese del 1693," *Arte antica e moderna*, no. 26 (April/June 1964), 219–30; no. 28 (October/December 1964), 451–67; and no. 30 (April/June 1965), 202–17.

[14] Inventory of Girolamo I Colonna, Rome, 1667,

Archivio Colonna, published in E. A. Šafarík et al., *Collezione dei dipinti Colonna, inventari 1611–1795* (Munich, 1996), 109, no. 134.

[15] Not. Johannes Commelin, Gemeentearchief Amsterdam, NAA 5624, ff. 213–275, postmortem inventory of Jan Agges, 27 February 1702: "Een schoorsteenstuk, zijnde Saul, David en 't hoofd van Holifernus, Italiaans." Six months after this inventory was taken, the picture was placed in a sale of Agges's collection, where it was still referred to as "David, met het Hoofd van Holifernus, van Paulo Veroneeze" in G. Hoet, *Catalogus of Naamlyst van Schilderyen* (The Hague, 1752), 64, no. 7.

owner and the artist, as "Un Davide con la testa d'Oloferne dipinto in tela di due palmi e mezzo e due, dipinto da me."[16] Also of note from another Neapolitan inventory is a painting by Andrea Vaccaro described as "Un altro quadro colla testa d'Oloferne, portata a Davide e molte donne dansanti seu festegianti con cornice dorata intagliata di pal. 8 e 6 di mano di Andrea Baccaro." This is found in the inventory of Donato Bianco in 1693.[17] This same error appears at least eight more times in other Italian documents from Naples, Rome, and Bologna.

And as evidence that mistaken iconography happens not only in the seventeenth and eighteenth centuries, a painting by Pieter Claesz. Soutman (Fig. 5), now in the Philadelphia Museum of Art, can be cited; this is published in a checklist of 1965 as being "Judith and Holofernes with the Head of John the Baptist" (by Jacob Jordaens).[18]

When we are fortunate enough to have a series of inventories from the same family spanning a wide range of dates, it is occasionally possible to track the same picture from one inventory to another, and if the description is different, or amplified, the identity of the subject or artist may be discovered. Such was the case with the Pereda *Vanitas* discussed above, and is also the case with the following three entries, all of which describe drawings that come from the family of the Conde de Monterrey. The first of these is dated April 1653 and describes a drawing by the Cavaliere d'Arpino: "Otro dibujo de dos Angeles de Josephe Arpin";[19] only a month later, in the valuation for the April document, the entry reads "Un dibujo de Josephe de Arpina de dos figuras de Ycaro Con su marco negro Le tasso en çiento y cinqta Reales 150."[20] Two years later, the subject reverts to the original description of "two angels."[21]

Another example shows that the inventories can sometimes be kind. A description of a picture called simply "Santa Mustiola," with an attribution to Cagnacci, is given in an inventory of the sculptor Giulio Cesare Conventi made in 1640; and, very importantly, it was the painter Cagnacci himself who did the description and evaluation of the paintings for this document, thus shedding some light on the picture which is nowhere else identified as this subject.[22] The picture described in this entry is very possibly the painting by Cagnacci today in the Musée Fabre in Montpellier (Fig. 6). The legend of St. Mustiola was most popular in Umbria, and particularly in Chiusi, where the noble patrician woman Mustiola visited St. Ireneus in jail and, because of their association, was subsequently brought before a tribunal. Upon seeing her, the prefect of the tribunal fell instantly in love, and proposed marriage to her. When she firmly refused, he sentenced her to death by scourg-

---

[16] Not. Giacomo Antonio Fontana, scheda 142, protocollo 14, ff. 81–120v, inventory of Antonio Astuto, 2 May 1716, reprinted in G. Labrot et al., *Documents for the History of Collecting: Italian Inventories*, vol. 1, *Collections of Paintings in Naples, 1600–1780* (Munich, 1992), 278–82.

[17] Not. Dionisio d'Alterio, Archivio di Stato, Naples, scheda 320, protocollo 9, inventory of Donato Bianco, 5 May 1693, discovered by Gerard Labrot.

[18] *Check List of Paintings in the Philadelphia Museum of Art* (Philadelphia, 1965), 36.

[19] Archivo Histórico de Protocolos, Madrid, Prot. 7.684, ff. 291v–302v, inventory of the estate of Manuel de Fonseca y Zúñiga, Conde de Fuentes y de Monterrey, 19 April 1653, published in Burke, Cherry, et al., *Paintings in Madrid* (as in note 8), 505, no. 0096.

[20] Archivo Histórico de Protocolos, Madrid, Prot. 7.684, ff. 332–351, valuation of the estate of Manuel de Fonseca y Zúñiga, Conde de Fuentes y de Monterrey, 5 May 1653, published in Burke, Cherry, et al., *Paintings in Madrid* (as in note 8), 514, no. 0099.

[21] Archivo Histórico de Protocolos, Madrid, Prot. 7.685, ff. 776–831, valuation of the estate of Manuel de Fonseca y Zúñiga, Conde de Fuentes y de Monterrey, 15 February 1655, published in Burke, Cherry, et al., *Paintings in Madrid* (as in note 8), 530, no. 0035.

[22] R. Morselli, *Guido Cagnacci*, exhib. cat., Rimini, Museo Civico, ed. D. Benati and M. Bona Castellotti (Milan, 1993), 92–95, no. 13; and Morselli, *Collezionisti e quadrerie* (as in note 7).

ing. A better vehicle could not be found for Cagnacci, whose repertoire is full of nude sainted martyrs and semiclothed women.

Entries which may refer to this same picture of St. Mustiola are also recorded in three sales in the nineteenth century. In databases developed by the Provenance Index which index nineteenth-century auction catalogues of paintings sold in England, France, and The Netherlands, three entries are listed which are attributed to Cagnacci. These are "A Female Martyr, the well known Picture from the Orleans Collection" (in a London sale),[23] and a "Magdelaine" in two Paris sales,[24] the identity of Mustiola having been lost in the two hundred years separating these sale catalogue references from the earlier archival documents.

The Provenance Index has been forced to make some decisions about all of these issues with regard to ICONCLASS which may in some ways be misleading. Where there is any element of doubt, as with St. John the Baptist and Holofernes, an ICONCLASS code for both episodes has been recorded, and it is left to researchers to disentangle all the possibilities and reach their own conclusions. The notation for "David and Goliath" has been the only code assigned to the works entitled "David with the Head of Holofernes," as it was felt that this could not refer to anything else. The example of a "figure of St. Peter" mentioned earlier would be classified under the first section in the ICONCLASS structure, which is religion, and indexed under an 11H category. This is distanced from the Bible and Division 7, which are used for specific biblical references. In other words, we make no assumptions in this case and rely on the literal description for classification. We have attempted to be consistent whenever we tread into these gray areas, but we have also adapted the ICONCLASS system to our own needs (for example, spaces in the notations have been deleted). We have also altered some rules in order to arrive at more precise classifications and to allow for more conventional sorting of subjects such as portraits.

There is no doubt that the ICONCLASS system itself is best adapted to computer databases, CD-ROM publications, and Web sites. The alpha-numeric coding eclipses most linguistic barriers, and the textual correlates (the text equivalent to the notation) allow one to search using a designated language with controlled vocabulary. For example, in the case of Salome, it is possible to use the notation 73C13341, or to search using the word "Salome" in the ICONCLASS text field. This latter search will retrieve a larger number of entries, which will also include references to Salome dancing, taking instruction from Herodias, etc. It is worth noting that the descriptions seen above in the documents did not contain the name "Salome," nor for that matter does the name appear in the Gospels, where she is always referred to as "the daughter of Herodias," or more often just "Herodias." The name "Salome" was apparently a third-century invention by a historian of Jewish literature, which does not exactly explain why it was not used by the time these documents were

---

[23] B. Fredericksen et al., *Index of Paintings Sold in the British Isles during the Nineteenth Century*, vol. 1, *1801–1805* (Santa Barbara, 1988), 152.

[24] B. Peronnet, B. Fredericksen, et al., *Répertoire des tableaux vendus en France au XIXe siècle*, vol. 1, *1801–1810* (Los Angeles, 1998): Lebrun sale, 10 August 1803, lot 17, p. 251: "La Magdelaine évanouie après s'être disciplinée. Figure d'une proportion de 3 quarts de nature. Ses cuisses sont couvertes d'une draperie bleue, & auprès d'elle se voient les instrumens de sa pénitence. Ce

Tableau faisoit partie de la précieuse collection du duc d'Orléans. Il était passé en Angleterre, d'où nous l'avons rapporté. Les amateurs savent combien les ouvrages de Cagnacci sont rares"; and Lebrun sale, 30 September 1806, lot 24: "La Magdelaine évanouie, après s'être mortifiée; proportion de trois quarts de nature en pied. Une draperie bleue couvre les cuisses de la sainte, & autour d'elle sont les instrumens de la pénitence. Ce rare Tableau provient de la collection du duc d'Orléans, & se trouve gravé dans le recueil d'estampes qu'on en a fait."

5 **Astrazioni e concetti**

51H42	Abbondanza, 'Abondanza'
54F12	Sorte, Fortuna
54F2	Vittoria
57	Moralità

6 **Storia**

61A	Eventi e situazioni storiche
61B	Personaggi storici maschili (ritratti ed episodi tratti dalla vita)
61BB	Personaggi storici femminili (ritratti ed episodi tratti dalla vita)
61D	Nomi geografici di paesi, regioni, montagne, fiumi ecc.
61E	Nomi di città e villaggi
61F	Nomi di edifici storici, siti, strade, ecc.
61I	Nomi di eventi e situazioni storiche

7 **La Bibbia**

71	L'Antico Testamento
71A	Dalla creazione alla cacciata, Caino e Abele
71B	Discendenti di Caino e Abele
71B3	Storia di Noè
71B4	La torre di Babele
71C	I patriarchi
71C1	Storia di Abramo
71C2	Storia di Isacco
71C3	Storia di Giacobbe
71D	Storia di Giuseppe
71E	L'età di Mosè e Giosuè
71F	L'età dei Giudici
71G	Storia di Saul
71H	Storia di David
71I	Storia di Salomone
71M	Storia di Elia
71N	Storia di Eliseo
71P	Storia di Daniele
71Q	Storia di Ester
71T	Libro di Tobit
71U	Libro di Giuditta
71V	Libro di Giona
71W	Libro di Giobbe
73	Il Nuovo Testamento
73A	San Giovanni Battista e Maria Vergine
73A1	Storia della nascita e giovinezza di San Giovanni Battista
73A2	Antenati e parenti di Cristo

5 **Abstract Ideas and Concepts**

51H42	Abundance, 'Abondanza'
54F12	Luck, Fortune
54F2	Victory
57	Morality

6 **History**

61A	Historical events and situations
61B	Male historical persons (portraits and scenes from the life)
61BB	Female historical persons (portraits and scenes from the life)
61D	Geographical names of countries, regions, mountains, rivers, etc.
61E	Names of cities and villages
61F	Names of historical buildings, sites, streets, etc.
61I	Names of historical events and situations

7 **Bible**

71	Old Testament
71A	Creation to expulsion, Cain and Abel
71B	Descendants of Cain and Seth
71B3	Story of Noah
71B4	Tower of Babel
71C	The patriarchs
71C1	Story of Abraham
71C2	Story of Isaac
71C3	Story of Jacob
71D	Story of Joseph
71E	The time of Moses and Joshua
71F	The time of the Judges
71G	Story of Saul
71H	Story of David
71I	Story of Solomon
71M	Story of Elijah
71N	Story of Elisha
71P	Story of Daniel
71Q	Story of Esther
71T	Book of Tobit
71U	Book of Judith
71V	Book of Jonah
71W	Book of Job
73	New Testament
73A	John the Baptist and Mary
73A1	Story of the birth and youth of John the Baptist
73A2	Ancestors and parents of Christ

Text Fig. 1. Page from the outline of the categories in the ICONCLASS system, as published by Eduard Šafařík in *Collezione dei dipinti Colonna, inventari 1611–1795* (Munich, 1996) being recorded. Only once does the name appear in almost 200 entries in the inventories with the subject, and that is from a document from Rome dated 1711. Fortunately, the ICONCLASS text that accompanies the notation is "Story of Salome," and as such will allow the user to search on "Salome," rather than on the more veiled descriptions "Herodias" or "Daughter of Herodias."

In printed form, the ICONCLASS system requires more work on the part of the reader, who has to be aware of the fact that there is a strict division between the first section (religion and magic) and the seventh division (the Bible) or that horses are considered a mode of transportation and are separated from the numbers for cows and sheep, which are classified as part of the cattle "industry." An ear of corn growing in a field is in the 47 I section under "agriculture," but an ear of corn by itself, or being eaten, would be in a different book under "nutrition and nourishment," which makes finding or classifying a description which simply says "corn" rather complicated. For the publications in the Inventories series, both artist and subject indexes have been used to allow access to the printed transcriptions of the documents, and for the book on the Colonna family inventories with Eduard Šafařík, which was completely in Italian, a translation of the outline (Text Fig. 1) was generously provided by the Istituto Centrale per il Catalogo e la Documentazione, so that non-English speakers would be given a key to the layout of the material.

After reading of the complications of using ICONCLASS to classify these archival inscriptions, one may wonder why the Getty Provenance Index chose to implement the systems in the first place, and the answer is simply that there was nothing better fifteen years ago when the project started, nor is there now. While those with more traditional tastes may argue that it is sacrilegious to place religion and magic in the same category, the fact is that the system has been embraced by a number of projects in many different cultures and languages. There is no question that the process of inputting archival documents is greatly slowed down by the time it takes to analyze a description and assign an appropriate notation. The ICONCLASS Browser has saved a considerable amount of time and has improved the ways to search the system for numbers and subjects. However, the overall efficiency and reliability of the Provenance Index's adaptation of the ICON-CLASS system is ultimately dependent upon the people responsible for assigning the notations. It requires a considerable amount of correlation, editing, and agreement for consistency. Nevertheless, the application of this system is a crucial step in terms of making this archival information even more accessible and retrievable, and as its use becomes more widespread, it will inevitably become a standard fixture in our field, a type of *Esperanto* for art historians.

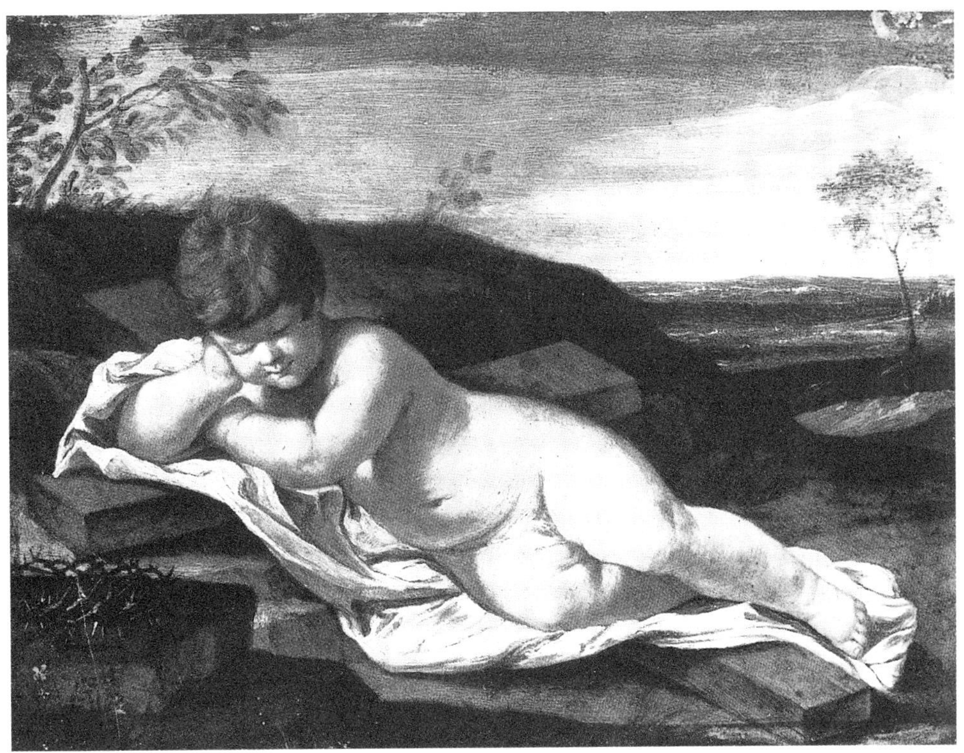

1. After Guido Reni, *The Christ Child Asleep on the Cross*, National Museums and Galleries on Merseyside, Walker Art Gallery, Liverpool

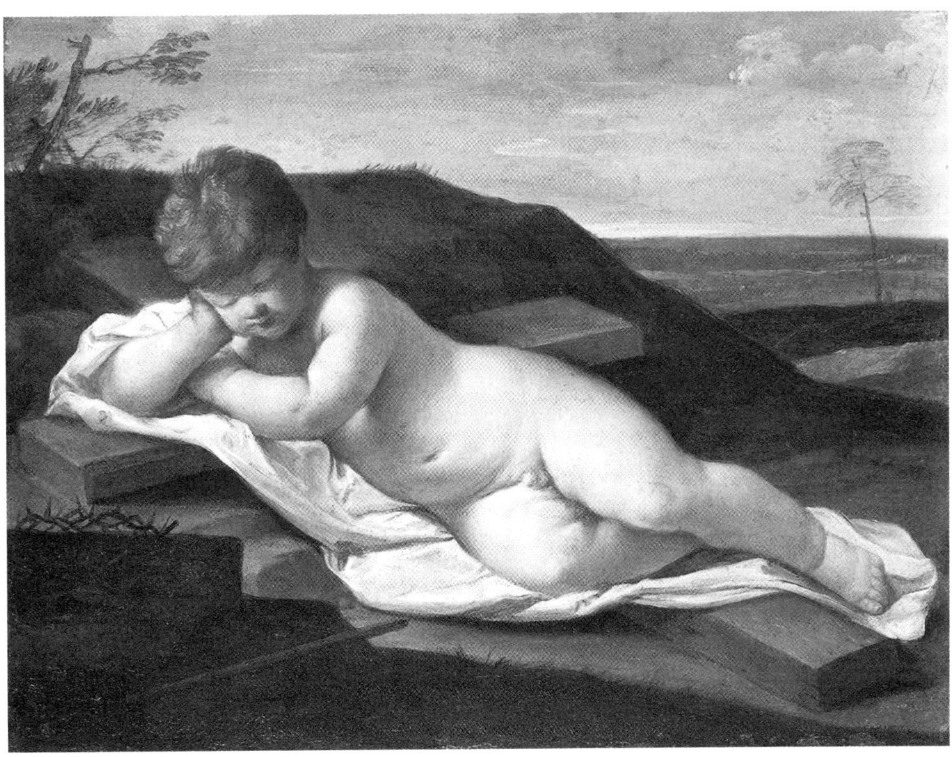

2. Guido Reni (studio?), *The Christ Child Asleep on the Cross*, The Art Museum, Princeton University, gift of J. Lionberger Davis, Class of 1900

Otra Pintura en lienzo que tiene
de alto Vara y media menos Vn
dedo y de ancho dos Varas y ten-
dra menos Vn dedo quellaman
el desengaño, en que se Ve Vna
figura de Vn Angel con las alas
tendidas y por broche del rostro
de Vna soja, y en la mano iz-
quierda Vna Varas...ca con

Vn retrato de medio cuerpo de
Vn Emperador y la deçicha
arrimada a Vn globo sobre
Vna messa Vn Relox de sobrecilla
tres retratos de muger Vna sarta
de perlas Vna cadena de oro Vnas
monedas de oro y plata y tres
naypes des pagas, y a lo te-
ado ay Vn Relox de Brena bria
armas libros calaueras en
Candelero con Vna bela en [...]
mill Reales ——————————— 20—

3. Entry for Antonio de Pereda's *Vanitas* from the inventory of the Almirante de
Castilla, 1691

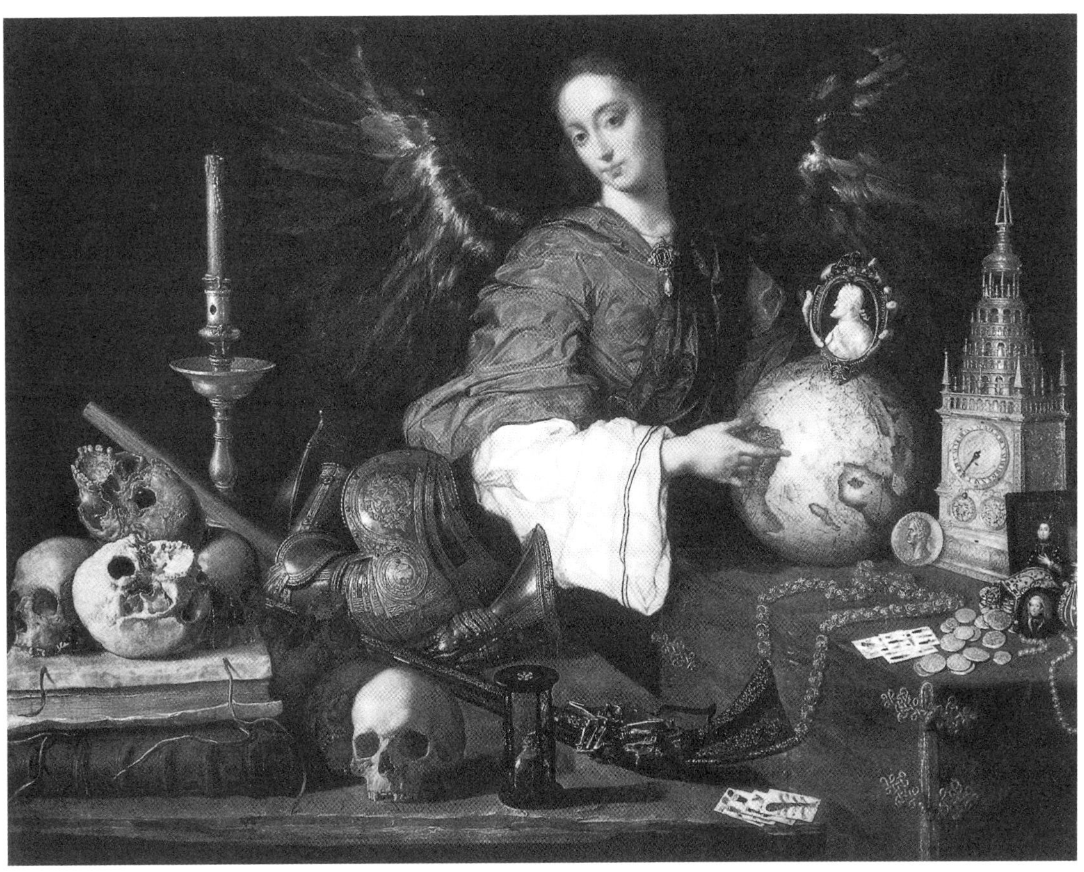

4. Antonio de Pereda, *Vanitas*, Kunsthistorisches Museum, Vienna

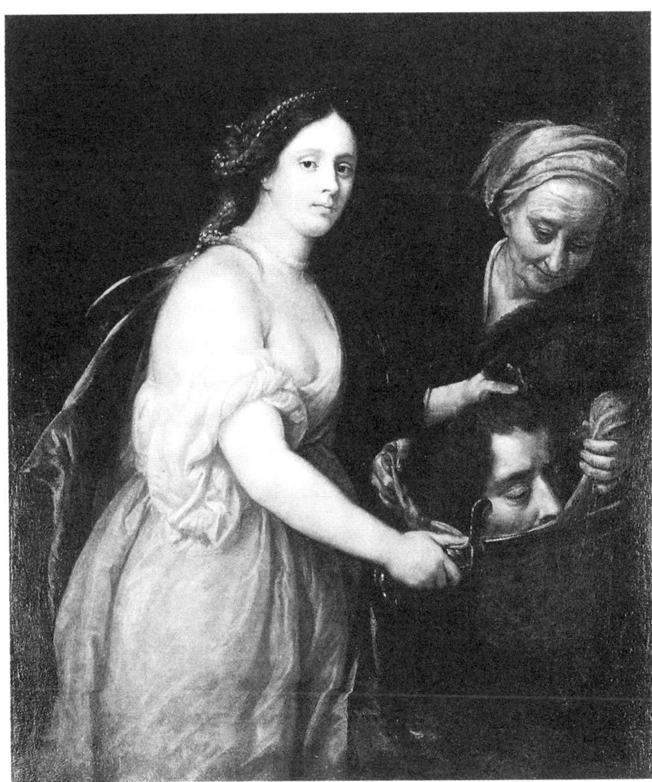

5. Attributed to Pieter Claesz.
Soutman, *Judith with the Head of
Holofernes*, Philadelphia Museum of
Art, Philadelphia, Pennsylvania, gift of
Mrs. George H. Frazier

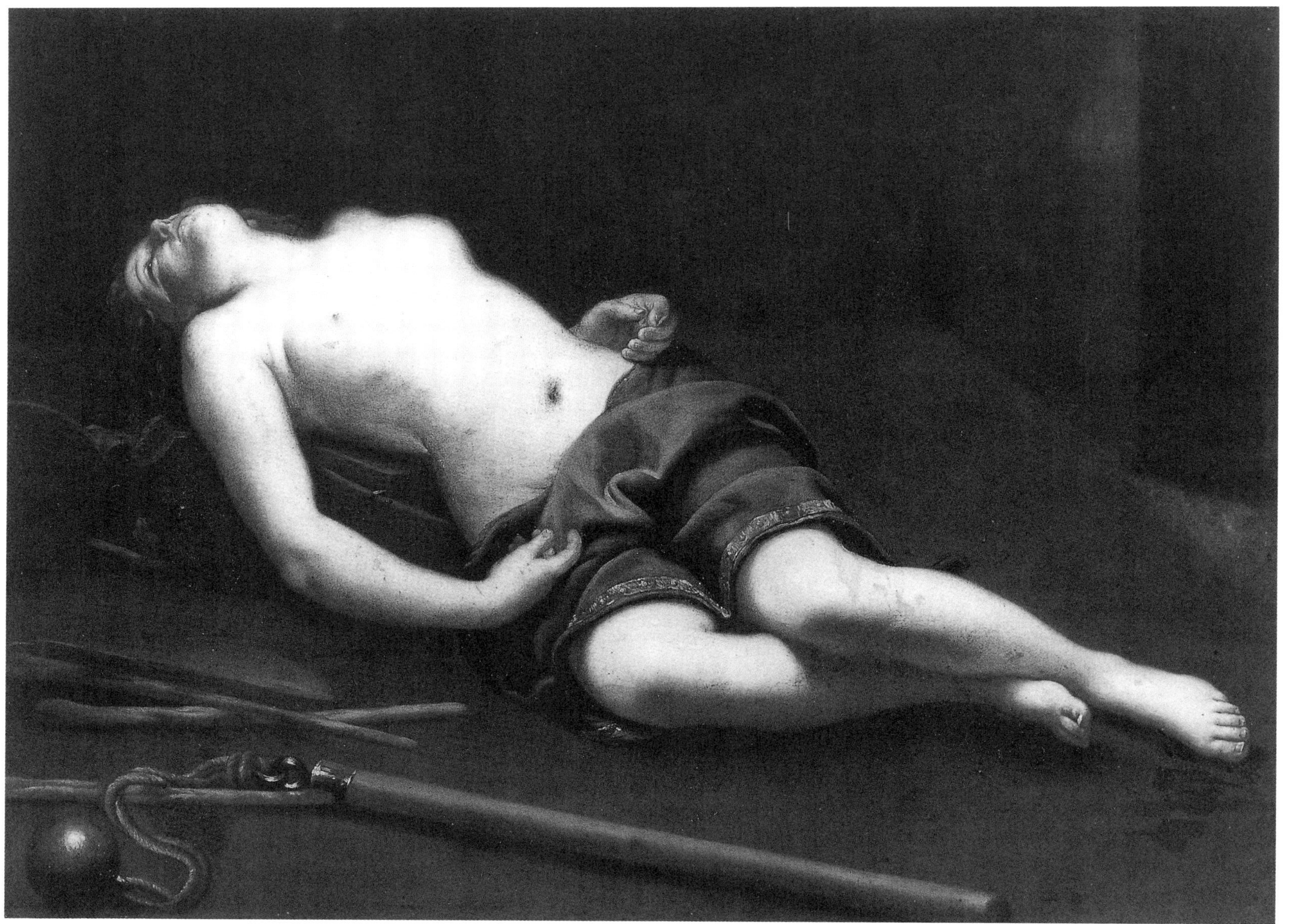

6. Guido Cagnacci, *A Dead Martyr (Saint Mustiola?)*, Musée Fabre, Montpellier

Ululas Athenas: Owls to Athens

·

HANS BRANDHORST

IN HIS FAMOUS storehouse of classical wisdom, the *Adagiorum Chiliades*, Erasmus discussed the proverb *Ululas Athenas*, "(carrying) owls to Athens."[1] This proverb, so he said, "will fit stupid traders who transport their wares to a place where they are more abundant anyway . . . ." If you want to make use of this metaphor in a speech, so Erasmus advises, it adds to its attractiveness if you transfer it to the things of the mind. The example is given whereby "so-and-so teaches a man wiser than himself, or gives advice to a man wise in counsel." When talking about the application of the proverb, Erasmus refers to Cicero, who used it to adorn his apologies for sending some of his verses to the famous poet Quintus.

This teaches that it is not only stupid to take owls to Athens, but also that people, even as clever as Cicero, have always persisted in doing so. Thus, by illustrating my remarks about iconographic description with samples of my own attempts at Christian iconography, I know I am being stupid. However, I also know that if I still pursue that goal I join the company of men far better than I.

Iconographic description is like different biotopes which may cause animals to develop different qualities and habits. Similarly, variations in the purpose of iconography or in the instruments with which it is practised can produce widely different breeds of description. This observation can be made at different levels. It is possible, for example, to describe the pictures in a book of hours as seen through the eyes of the postulated original owner, and try to apply a reconstruction of that person's terminology. This approach was chosen, with empathy and imagination, by Claire Donovan in her book on the De Brailes Hours.[2] There, the description of the illustrations of a book of hours is embedded in a reconstruction of the devotional routine in which it supposedly functioned. Although this reconstruction is hypothetical, the perspective chosen makes the reader acutely aware of the fact that all relevant characteristics of such a book are a consequence of human decisions.

It is also possible to describe the prefatory miniatures of a twelfth-century psalter as an aid to biblical instruction within the broader context of the education of a youthful owner. The psalter was known to be used in this manner, and occasionally surviving copies, such as the Leiden psalter of St. Louis, document this, or at least pretend to. Alternatively, a description of this type of miniature may depart from the viewpoint that they were used in a devotional or (semi-)liturgical context.

---

[1] Adage 1 ii 11.

[2] C. Donovan, *The De Brailes Hours: Shaping the Book of* *Hours in Thirteenth-Century Oxford* (London, 1991).

A completely different type of description would have to be made to serve a stylistic assessment of a manuscript, such as an attempt to date or localise it, or even perhaps to distinguish the "hands" that made it.

The purpose of this paper is not to undertake a survey of possible research goals, nor to discuss in a general manner how various goals may influence the translation of visual experience into language. Instead, the aim is to concentrate on what F. P. Pickering once called "the most frequently used tool of scholarly method," that is, the comparison, and in particular the iconographic comparison. The aim is to look at the application of this tool firstly and very briefly in the study of a series of pictures, in this case a prefatory miniature series in English psalters; and secondly and in more detail, at that of the comparison of individual miniatures.

The most efficient way to further limit the scope of this paper is with a small case study; that is, by analysing the type of iconographical arguments used in a few specific cases. These cases will, I hope, be seen as representative samples and will focus on the relationship between a few series of miniatures and on the iconographic sources of one such series.

The Comparison of Series

The first type of iconographic comparison, between a series of pictures, is derived from a group of English psalters, all dated to roughly the last quarter of the twelfth century.[3] Disagreement exists about the localisation of the manuscripts and this disagreement centers, at least partially, on different assessments of the extent to which their miniature cycles are related iconographically. One scholar refers to the miniature cycle of Copenhagen, Royal Library, Ms. Thott 143 2º, as being "almost identical" to that of Oxford, Bodleian Library, Ms. Gough lit. 2. Another scholar refutes this and says there are no arguments for such a pairing. A third expert sees close links, including iconographical ones, between the Gough cycle and two other cycles, that of Leiden, Bibliotheek der Universiteit, Ms. BPL 76 A, and that of a so-called New Testament picture book. A fifth and sixth psalter—Oxford, Bodleian Library, Ms. Douce 293, and Glasgow, University Library, Ms. Hunter 229—are also drawn into this complex comparison by several scholars.

The critical analysis of this discussion is complicated by differences in the level of detail in the analyses, which may be found in general manuscript surveys, exhibition catalogues, and articles, but also in monographs. In this case, for example, a general and isolated assertion such as "very rarely does the Copenhagen psalter diverge from the iconography of the Gough psalter" is to be found side-by-side with incidental observations of details supporting general conclusions such as "features like the frontal Christ blessing in the Betrayal scene [in the picture book] resemble those in the Leiden psalter . . . ." Furthermore, there are descriptions in monographs of individual scenes which comment on their overall composition, such as "the Thott composition [of the Betrayal scene] is as unusual as it is forceful . . . ." There are also a number of assertions based on smaller details like the similarity of postures, gestures, or particular attributes.

---

[3] Some of the more pertinent contributions to this discussion may be found in P. D. Stirnemann, "The Copenhagen Psalter" (Ph.D. diss., Columbia University, 1976); C. M. Kauffmann, *Romanesque Manuscripts 1066–1190* (A Survey of Manuscripts Illuminated in the British Isles, vol. 3) (London, 1975); and N. J. Morgan, *Early Gothic Manuscripts*, pt. 1, *1190–1250* (A Survey of Manuscripts Illuminated in the British Isles, vol. 4) (London, 1982).

However perceptive observations like these may be, their relevance is threatened if certain methodological points are not taken into account. It is necessary to include as many other series of images as is possible in the assessment if any thematic similarities are to be studied. Since we lack external criteria to measure thematic resemblance, one postulated similarity is relative only to other similarities. Statements about the similarity of series of miniatures are often founded on observations of individual miniatures; here, too, of course, similarities can only be established against the background of a sufficiently large corpus (Figs. 1–4).

Independent evidence about the contemporary assessment of iconographic particularities is often lacking. It is necessary, for example, to try to evaluate exactly how the contemporary observer perceived the presence of the Holy Ghost in the Annunciation to the Virgin; how the observer evaluated different attributes of the Virgin, such as an unfolded scroll with "Fiat michi secundum verbum tuum" or a closed book; how the presence of the Father at the Baptism of Christ affected the reading of this scene. It is necessary, insofar as it is possible, to see the effect that iconographic variations of a particular subject cause in the observer's mind, and how these variations affected its role in a cycle of miniatures. Our perception of thematic similarity and difference may well be at odds with that of a contemporary observer.

We have little insight into the "repertoire" of a particular miniaturist or workshop, which is a serious handicap when trying to infer historical relations between objects and the people responsible for their production. It is possible to illustrate this with an example taken from the psalters in Munich (Bayer. Staatsbibl., Ms. clm. 835) and in Cambridge (Trinity College Library, Ms. B.11.4) (Figs. 5 and 6). In both manuscripts the "formula" for a Flight into Egypt is incorporated in a representation of Jacob and his family on their way to Joseph in Egypt. Both manuscripts also contain a Flight into Egypt. In each case the actual Flight into Egypt is different from the "flight-formula" which is incorporated in the Jacob scene. Furthermore, the Flight into Egypt in the Munich psalter is formally different from that in the Trinity College psalter. The dangers of interpreting formal similarities or differences as confirming or refuting family relationships between objects is highlighted when several variations of the same scene are found in a single manuscript.

The Comparison of Individual Miniatures

Examples of the second type of comparison, namely, between individual pictures, are characteristic of monographic studies, where they frequently play a role in attempting to expose "iconographic roots." The art historian's second nature frequently attempts to establish iconographic "sources" and "models" for the object of study, and the problematic aspects of this procedure tend to be overlooked.

The scarcity of contemporary comments, for example, makes it difficult to estimate the relevance to medieval observers of morphological details that are usually highlighted in modern studies. In the initial phases of most studies, morphological similarities within the context of a particular subject are proposed. This is due to the fact that the sources of a particular iconographic detail are being searched for. The theme, rather than the morphological detail itself, is usually taken as the point of departure. This has to do with the way scholarly instruments are organized. Subject titles, such as the Annunciation to the Shepherds or the Baptism of Christ, for example, often are primary or only entry points when consulting iconographic indices. Yet this cannot be the entire reason, since the organization of scholarly instruments is also a response to the way research is done. Art historians tend to isolate the formal details that are being focused on from their formal context, while using that same context as a vehicle for the search of those particulars. Apparently it is difficult to consider pictorial elements as having distinct meaning, like words in a sentence. Assertions about morphological details often mix references to broad concepts and specific objects. We may read, for example, that the representation of the Visit of the Three Angels in the Ingeborg Psalter follows the Byzantine tradition that is best illustrated by the Cappella Palatina in Palermo, or that the St. Albans Psalter's Expulsion from Paradise has an important feature in common with an Early Christian prototype which is represented by the S. Marco mosaic of the Expulsion.

These points are illustrated by examples in a book on the Winchester Psalter (London, B.L., Ms. Cotton Nero C. IV).[4] In this study a series of individual observations leads to the conclusion that the miniaturist of the Winchester Psalter selected from Anglo-Saxon and Ottonian sources in a more liberal manner than, for instance, the artist who illuminated the St. Albans Psalter. In this instance the conclusion itself is not an issue. The issue, however, is the iconographic comparisons that lead up to that conclusion. The interest is in the iconographic arguments that support the belief that the Winchester Psalter's Annunciation to the Shepherds demonstrates the "self-consciously eclectic" attitude of the Winchester miniaturist.

According to the overall argument, the St. Albans, as well as the Winchester artist, in general followed Anglo-Saxon models, such as the Sacramentary of Robert of Jumièges. The choir of angels in an aureole is a feature which both psalters share with the Sacramentary. The St. Albans Psalter borrowed the messenger angel confronting the shepherds. The Winchester miniaturist, however "selected other elements like the startled shepherd closest to the messenger angel on the ground who draws back in surprise" (Fig. 7). These comparisons are often concerned with seemingly minute details. This poses serious problems for their critical evaluation, firstly, because remarks about details are made only incidentally; but even when descriptions are of the necessary level of detail, the flexibility of natural language often prevents us from finding every instance of a certain particularity.

It is useful at this point to consult a computerized survey of such manuscripts, undertaken by this writer, to check whether it pays off to invest so much time in describing details as systematically and consistently as is possible, and to do so with the help of the controlled vocabulary of ICON-CLASS. The Anglo-Saxon element of the "startled shepherd . . . who draws back in surprise" needs to be searched for first. Close reading of the text reveals that it must be the gesture with the hand in front of the face which suggests the borrowing or influence.

At least ten instances of someone holding a hand in front of his face in a "protective manner" can be found in the database. In approximately half of the examples retrieved this gesture is made by shepherds. In the other cases it is made by Moses in front of the burning bush; one of the Magi upon seeing the Star of Bethlehem; Nebuchadnezzar's executioner stirring up the furnace's fire with Shadrach, Meshach, and Abednego; a disciple at Christ's disappearance from Emmaus; one of the Magi looking up at the angel warning him and his companions not to return to Herod; and one of the disciples watching Christ's Ascension (Figs. 8 and 9).

---

[4] K. E. Haney, *The Winchester Psalter: An Iconographic Study* (Leicester, 1986).

The problem of whether a contemporary observer would associate this gesture with a distinctive meaning, and if so, with which one(s), underlies this set of records. Sources that could provide an unequivocal answer are lacking. All that can be done is to formulate and test a hypothesis stating that this gesture has a more or less autonomous meaning in the type of contexts in which it has been found. The fact that it is to be found in a number of different contexts at least suggests that its meaning is not exhaustively defined by the text of Luke 2:9: "et claritas Dei circumfusit illos et timuerunt timore magno." Instead it would seem to have the more general narrative function of detailing the presence of phenomena like (supernatural) light or heat, and emotions like awe or fear. The possibility that the gesture has a general meaning has another implication. Its frequency may also weaken the possibility of a relationship between the two objects. The strengthening of one case may weaken the other.

In the claim that Ottonian sources were used by the Winchester artist the general notion of a "tradition" is again blended with references to specific manuscripts. Some of these references relate to more general features. The absence of a standing angel, for example, is seen as a link between the Winchester Psalter and an Ottonian source such as the Codex Egberti in Trier (Fig. 10).[5] More detailed comparisons can be made with this codex, in particular with the postures and gestures of the shepherds. The second example to be studied in this paper is the shepherd who rests his elbow on his staff and supports his head with his hand in both the Codex Egberti and the Winchester Psalter.

While acknowledging the general parallels, it is important not to ignore the dissimilarities. These are closely related to general compositional differences. In the Ottonian codex the angels hover in the air as a group of busts to the right of the three shepherds, who turn left to face them. In the psalter, moving from left to right, the angels occupy the full width of the scene. The shepherd on the far right turns right to face them. While the orientation of the Winchester shepherd is the reverse of that of the Ottonian example, the position of his arms is not: he still rests his chin on his right hand, and holds his staff with his left. Further differences between the two figures include the stance of the legs, the grip on the staff, and the position of the hand under the chin. If these similarities and dissimilarities are taken into account, it cannot be stated that the two shepherds assume poses that are strikingly similar. If any element can be described as unusual, it is that in spite of the global differences in posture, they share conspicuous details.

It should be realised that by suggesting a genealogical model and copy type of relationship to explain a specific formal parallel, the researcher responds, to paraphrase Staale Sinding-Larsen, in a ritual rather than in an analytical way to the problem at hand.[6] But even if the issue is reduced to that of the transmission of form, it is impossible to escape the question of how the degree of kinship between these two representations of a shepherd can be determined. The central issue remains: how can it be determined that this similarity indicates or proves the existence of a specific relationship?

The proximity of the details which cannot be established on the basis of the two miniatures alone is crucial in resolving this problem. The extent of a formal similarity between (parts of) two

<hr>

[5] Trier, Stadtbibliothek, Ms. 24, f. 13v.

[6] S. Sinding-Larsen, *Iconography and Ritual: A Study of* *Analytical Perspectives* (Oslo, 1984), 124.

images can only be assessed if (parts of) other images are included in the comparison; one morphological similarity is relative only to other similarities. Those two forms may be considered to be the most similar in that they resemble each other more than they resemble other forms. When additional material is introduced into the comparison, it is easy to see that defining the boundaries of the form in question may be more complex than could be anticipated.

The first problem is that two forms in this analysis diverge in the respects just described. A second example of this pose, where the hand supports the head and the elbow rests on the staff, immediately adds to the complexities. If, for the present purpose, these are excluded, and the study concentrates on the formal comparison per se, it could be argued that the shepherd who faces the angel in the Annunciation to the Shepherds in Cambridge, Emmanuel College Library, Ms. 252, drives a wedge between the Winchester and Egberti examples. It shares with the first example the hood, the torso turning to its right, and the grip of the left hand on the staff. The legs, on the other hand, which are more or less frontal in the Winchester Psalter, are seen in profile, one in front of the other. Thus they almost mirror the stance of the legs of the Egberti shepherd. The head, which is in profile, rests on the open hand. This means that the position of the hand relative to the head is different in all three manuscripts.

If it is accepted that the comparison allows for this variation in the relationship between head and hand, a third scene from the catalogue may be introduced; this is the Anointment of David from the Winchester Psalter itself. Here Jesse assumes a pose that closely mirrors that of the Winchester shepherd. The main difference is in the position of the left hand, which Jesse holds as if he were pushing some kind of object against his cheek. Apart from thus adding to our group of hand-to-head variants, this scene also adds another context in which the pose may occur (Fig. 11).

Overstepping the boundaries of the Annunciation to the Shepherds, the formal comparisons may be continued by including material from outside the narrow circle of twelfth- and early thirteenth-century English psalters. Pointed in this direction by the Winchester Anointment of David, we can include the Pierpont Morgan Library Ms. M. 619 verso, a single leaf related to the Winchester Bible. Another example of the same subject is found in this folio. The orientation of the composition is the reverse of that of the Winchester Psalter's Anointment scene. The figure of Jesse on the Morgan leaf is positioned at the far right, instead of immediately behind David. His legs are crossed, his right hand is kept in front of his chest, but he rests his right elbow on his staff (Fig. 12). As a result, his posture as a whole appears less tense than that of the psalter's Jesse. The obvious question is whether the divergent posture of the arm moves this pose beyond the limit of what could still be called "similar" to that of the Winchester shepherd.

To extend the group even further, we can include the Cîteaux, or Harding Bible (Dijon, Bibliothèque Publique, Ms. 12-15). The figure of Jesse found in this manuscript is at the head of his *tribus*, as in the example from the Winchester Psalter. He is bent slightly forward and leans on his T-shaped staff, with its cross-bar held in his armpit (Fig. 12); this last detail recurs in representations of the Annunciations to the Shepherds in the database as well as in Ottonian manuscripts. From a purely formal point of view, a comparison of the Jesse in the Harding Bible with that of the Winchester shepherd could be rejected because his posture differs too much. In a broader perspective, the fact cannot be disregarded that in two representations of David's Anointment Jesse is depicted in a pose that is also assumed by shepherds. In addition to that, the verso of the Morgan leaf is thought by several scholars to be related to the David cycle in the Harding Bible.

It is not the purpose of this paper to undertake a survey of variants of this pose where the elbow rests on a (T-shaped) staff. A detour via more traditional subject titles, or an even longer detour of leafing through whatever (published) material may be relevant would have to be undertaken. However, we should include a few Nativity scenes and one last Annunciation to the Shepherds where variants of this posture are also to be found. Nativity scenes are included in this study because these often incorporate elements of, are conflated with, or else share the picture space with an Annunciation to the Shepherds.

The first example is from the Nativity scene of the Klosterneuburg altarpiece.[7] Joseph is seated at the feet of the Virgin, holds a T-shaped staff with his left hand, rests his right elbow on his left hand, and leans his head against the back of his hand. It is necessary at this stage to evaluate the importance of his seated pose, and to see if it detracts from the similarity between the Klosterneuburg Joseph and the Winchester shepherd. Variants of this posture of Joseph can be easily found, for example, in the Peterborough Psalter in Brussels.[8]

The final example of the Annunciation to the Shepherds scene to be mentioned is in the Hours of Jeanne d'Evreux.[9] In this example there is one shepherd who is seated, like Joseph, with his chin resting in his hands and his elbow on his shepherd's crook, while another one brings his left hand to his head, but does not quite reach it, and holds his staff against his lower left arm.

CONCLUSION

With little difficulty some additional examples of the pose with the elbow on the staff can be found in the database. These examples show that the pose was assumed by shepherds, by Joseph (seated), and by Jesse. When looking at examples in this last category the equivalent and related posture of leaning on the staff which is held in the armpit was discovered. After examining these images, the question still remains as to what extent the Egberti and Winchester shepherds are "strikingly similar." It is also necessary to see how they influence any evaluation of the hypothesis centered on the Winchester artist as "incorporating details from an Ottonian source." These are questions which will remain unanswered by this paper. These comparisons are referred to not for the sake of their content, but because they illustrate the interesting discrepancy between what could be called the myopic perspective on iconography, and the general lack of systematic documentation of precisely those details that are often so central to our argument. Data has been shown only to suggest that such tools can be used for the critical analysis of iconographic arguments. The reason why this writer may be considered to be breeding his own owls can now, I hope, be understood a little better.

[7] H. Buschhausen, "The Theological Sources of the Klosterneuburg Altarpiece," in *The Year 1200* (New York, 1975), 136, fig. 14.

[8] Brussels, B.R., Ms. 9961-62, f. 10v. The same miniature also has an Annunciation to the Shepherds with the shepherd closest to the messenger holding his hand over his head; see L. Freeman Sandler, *The Peterborough Psalter and Other Fenland Manuscripts* (London, 1974), 20, fig. 18.

[9] New York, The Cloisters, Ms. 54.1.2, f. 62: L. M. C. Randall, *Images in the Margins of Gothic Manuscripts* (Berkeley and Los Angeles, 1966), fig. 254.

APPENDIX

Two kinds of computer screendumps are included.[10] It would be impossible to include all of the screens and searches or to try to show the entire database on paper. The majority of the illustrations that were shown during the presentation of the paper are included here. The second part of the appendix contains a small selection of screens from my catalogue of the prefatory miniatures in English psalters surviving from the period circa 1045–1225. Being static screenshots, the illustrations included here can only give an incomplete impression of what is possible. I am therefore including some supplementary notes.

1. Notes on the Illustrations

Figs. 1 and 2: Twelve (of a total of seventeen) examples of the Baptism of Christ. The thematic comparison of a series of miniatures is a highly complex process. Yet even the most cursory study of this small group of manuscripts reveals that the general layout of their miniature cycles differs considerably. For example, the overall length of the cycles varies;[11] miniatures may be monoscenic as well as polyscenic; and they may face each other in regular alternation, or they may be painted only on rectos. Even if cycles share a series of scenes, it does not necessarily follow that these would appear in identical fashion to the observer. Variations in the arrangement of scenes will change the immediate context of a subject, and thus could be intended to stimulate different readings and associations in the contemporary observer.

The differences in the physical layout of miniature cycles make comparing them difficult, but the poverty of contextual information adds a great deal more to problems such as who commissioned these manuscripts, where exactly were they used and by whom, and how the miniature cycles functioned in the actual practice of liturgy or private prayer. The scarcity of information on issues such as these enhances the strength of the iconographic evidence. At the same time, it severely complicates the task of iconographic description. Changes in the context in which they were used, from biblical instruction to private devotion or liturgy, will have caused shifts in the interpretation of the images by contemporary observers.[12] The iconography itself, however, is the main evidence of such changes. This appears to create a methodological dilemma. The reconstruction of the contexts and use of the imagery needs to be undertaken irrespective of how hypothetical this may be. The subject matter in a corpus of images needs to be systematically identified and catalogued. The problem facing such a reconstruction is to determine what descriptive apparatus to apply, given that the factors that determine such an interpretation, description and context, are precisely what needs to be reconstructed.

The problem is lessened if the descriptions are appreciated for what they are: provisional statements about the contents of pictures made with the help of a modern vocabulary, which in cases like ICONCLASS or the Index of Christian Art subject headings, imparts a great deal of

---

[10] All of the photographs which appear in these screendumps were provided by the owners of the manuscripts and were digitized by the author for use in his database.

[11] For example: Thott has sixteen monoscenic miniatures, Gough has twenty-two, Douce has seventeen scenes in sixteen miniatures, the picture book has forty-eight scenes on fifty miniature pages, while Hunter has twenty-two scenes in thirteen miniatures that obviously alternate between mono- and polyscenic, and Leiden BPL has sixty scenes in twenty-three miniatures, as a rule, polyscenic.

[12] Cf. Sinding-Larsen, *Iconography and Ritual* (as in note 6), passim, but especially chap. 1, pt. C, "The Iconographical Subject as a Process and as a Flexible Entity."

iconographic expertise. Only after processing as much material as we can manage with this arbitrary, yet informed terminology can an attempt be made at historical interpretation.

Figs. 3 and 4: The Baptism scenes in Thott and Gough. Any comparison of cycles of miniatures must take into account iconographic detail beyond basic subject labels such as the Nativity or the Crucifixion. An attempt to systematically describe the iconographic details of pictures, however, has to deal with a variant of the methodological issue mentioned above: How to decide which details deserve to be included if their significance cannot be determined externally? The circle is broken if it is realised that iconographic descriptions can never claim more than a provisional status, and that their primary purpose is to bring our object of historical discourse into the field in the first place.

This means that descriptions should facilitate tracing iconographic elements across the whole corpus of images that are being surveyed. It should be easy to find out whether the Father or the Holy Ghost is represented in Baptism scenes, but that also holds for details of the postures of Christ or St. John the Baptist. These should be capable of being retrieved across the whole corpus, independent of the Baptism context. A query for an iconographic "statement" like "hands in front of the chest, palms frontal" links together subjects like the Anointment of Saul, the Coronation of David, Samuel presented to Eli by Hannah, and Pentecost, all of which have features of form and/or content in common with the Baptism.

2. Catalogue Sample

The electronic catalogue of psalter miniatures was designed solely for the presentation at the Index conference. It should be seen as one of many possible ways to gain access to the data. Its basic idea was to create four ways to approach the data by simply browsing: by manuscript, by subject, by iconographic detail, by titulus and inscription.

With the exception of the first option, where browsing is by manuscript and folio, the browsing process is regulated by the hierarchic structure of the ICONCLASS system. For example: when browsing by "Subject," a list of broad ICONCLASS categories is shown (Fig. 13). Upon selection, a thumbnail gallery is presented of all miniatures where the main subject falls within that category (Fig. 14).

Figs. 13, 14, and 15: From the photo gallery it is possible to move to the digital reproduction of a miniature with the accompanying iconographic description of its subject matter (Fig. 15). This description of an individual scene is the final step in every browse action. The number of intermediate steps in the browsing process depends on the number of individual descriptions that fall within a certain category. For example: it takes four steps in "Browse by Iconographic Detail" to reach the level shown in Figure 16. Here thirty-four references are grouped for the concept "31AA25161, arm or hand held in front of the chest –AA– both arms or hands."

Figs. 16 and 17: Even the texts of the tituli and the inscriptions, which are all present in transcription in the database, are arranged according to the subject to which they belong. They are reached in two steps of browsing. The intermediate step is represented in Figure 17.

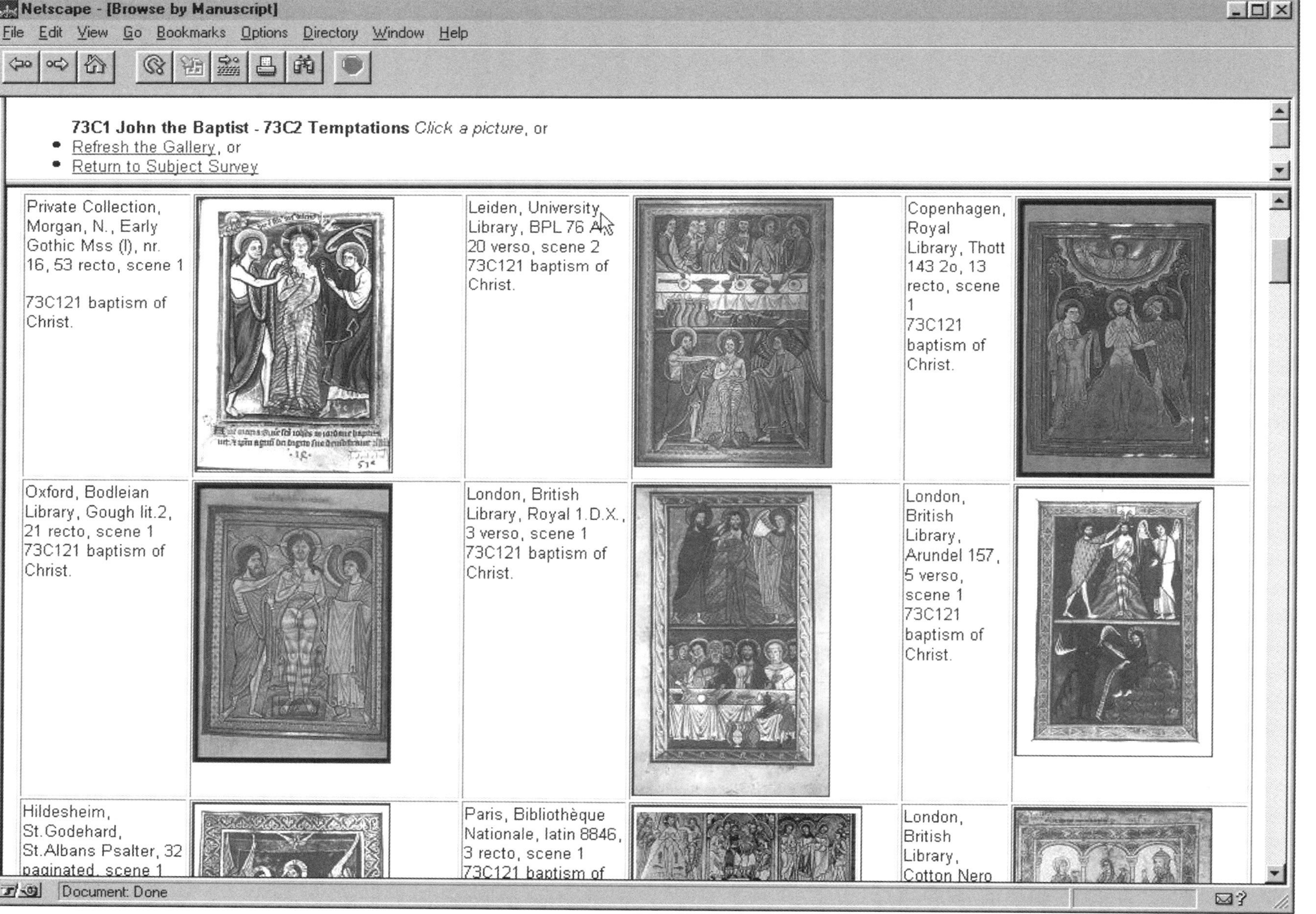

1. Six examples of the Baptism of Christ; see Appendix, part 1

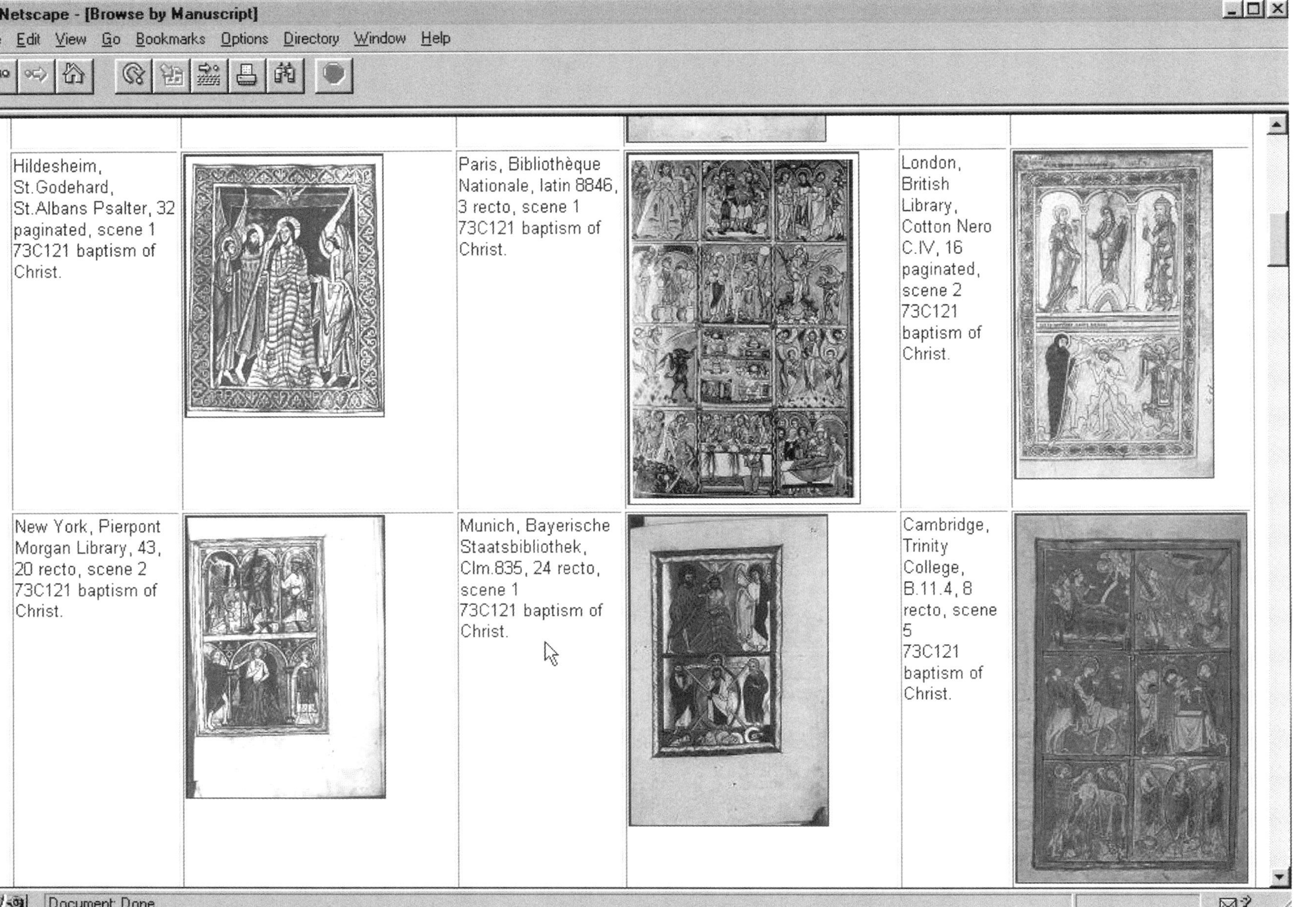

2. Six additional examples of the Baptism of Christ; see Appendix, part 1

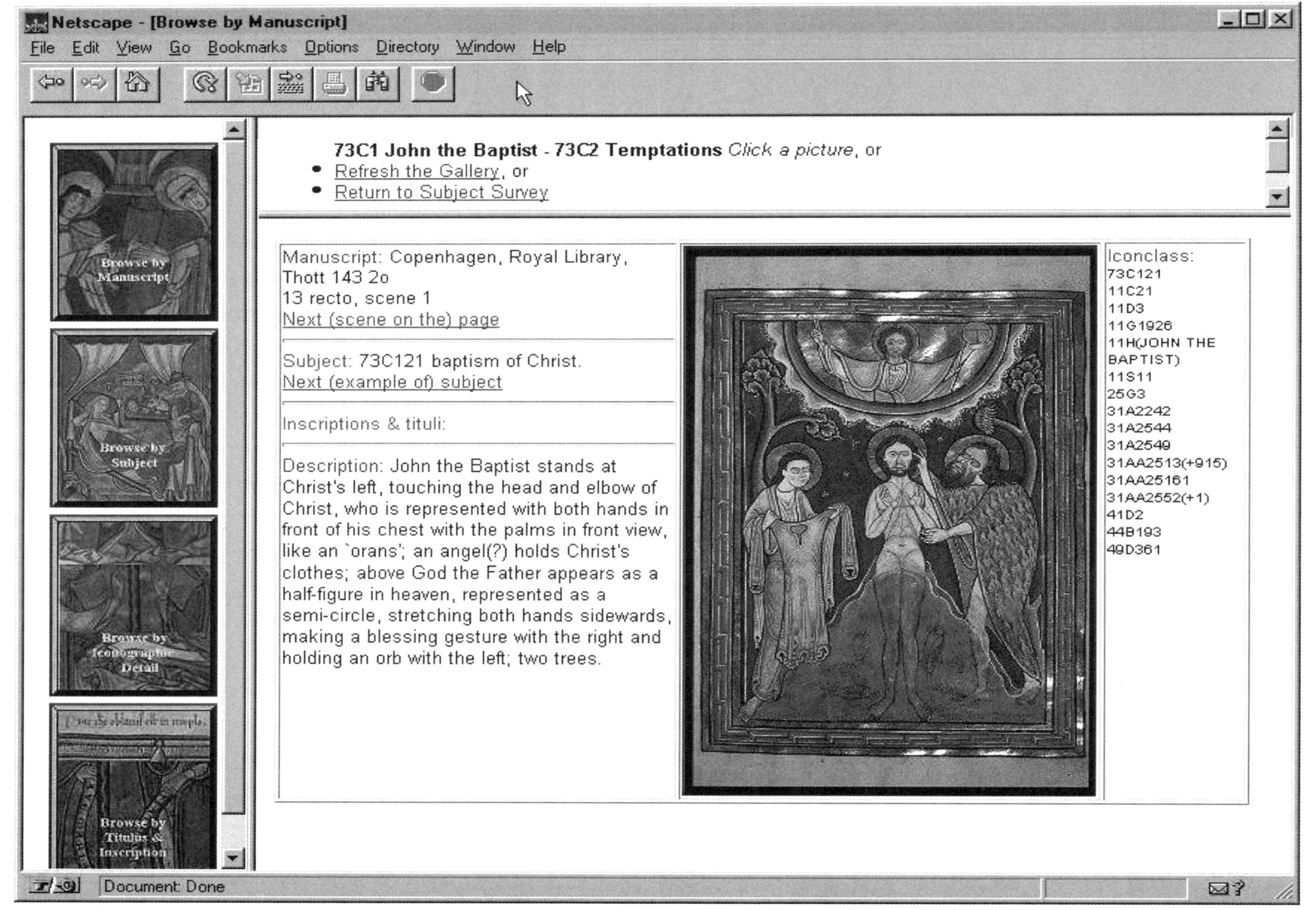

3. Baptism scene in Copenhagen, Royal Library, Ms. Thott 142 2º, f. 13r; see Appendix, part 1

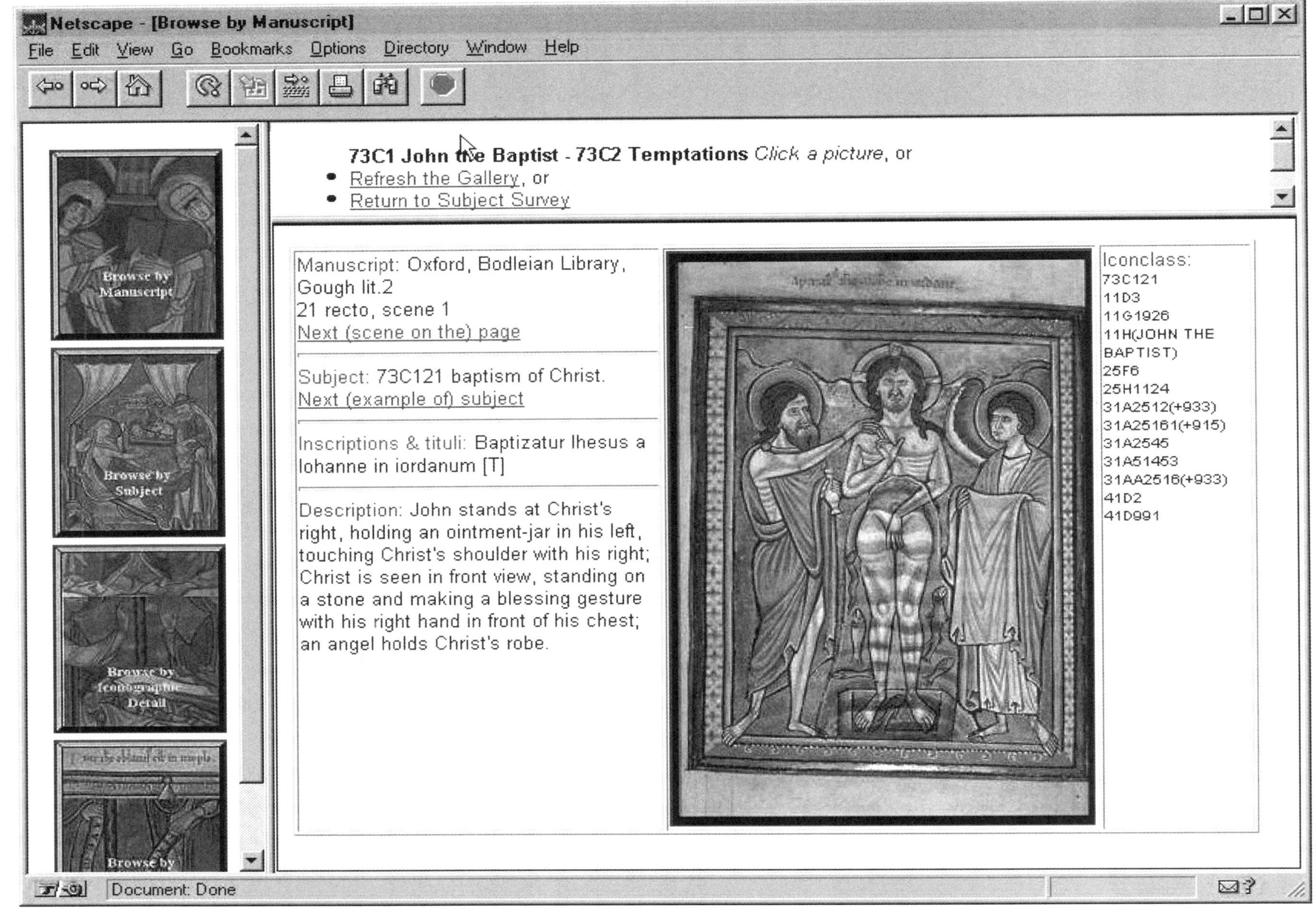

4. Baptism scene in Oxford, Bodleian Library, Ms. Gough lit. 2, f. 21r; see Appendix, part 1

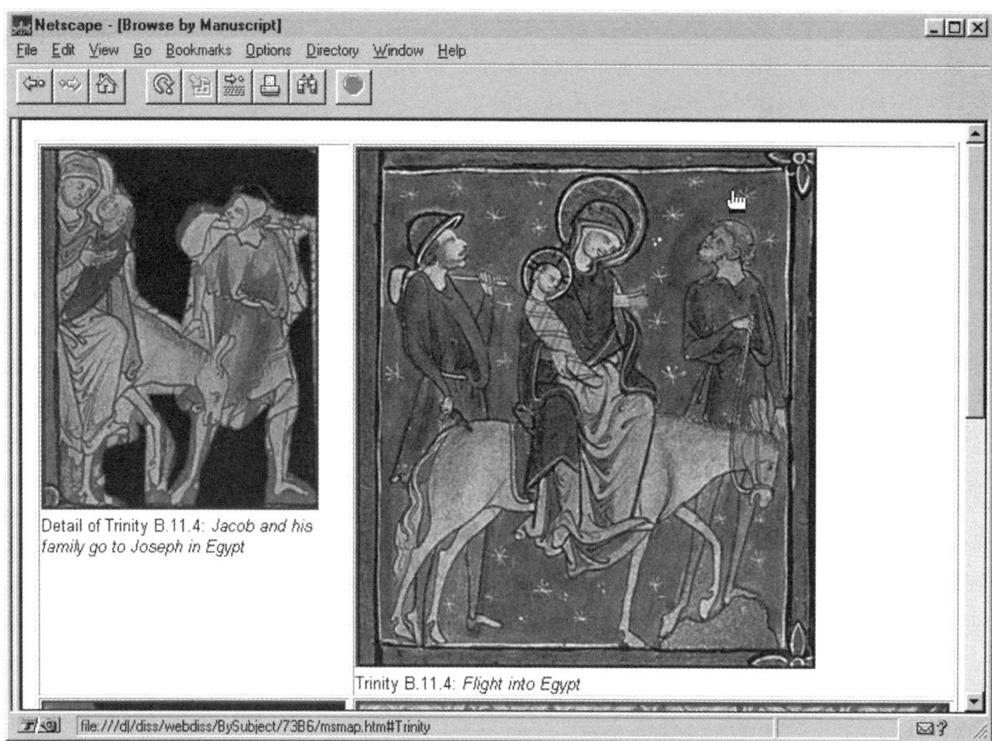

5. Models of the Flight: Jacob and his family on their way to Joseph in Egypt and the Flight into Egypt in Cambridge, Trinity College Library, Ms. B.11.4, ff. 1v and 8r; see Appendix, part 1

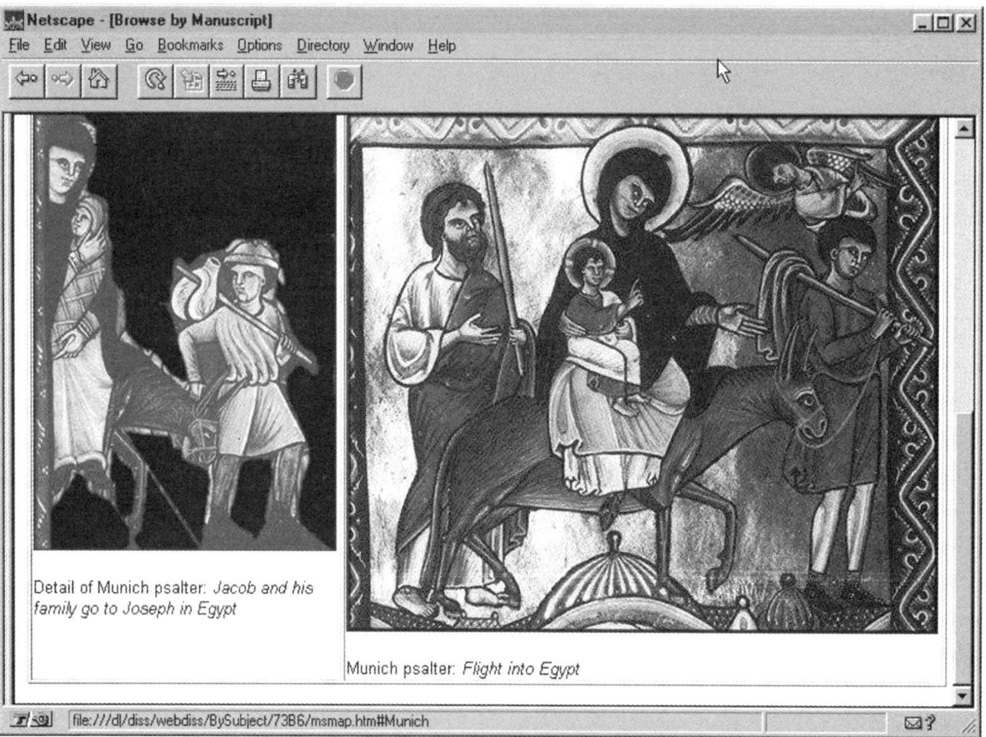

6. Models of the Flight: Jacob and his family on their way to Joseph in Egypt and the Flight into Egypt in Munich, Bayerische Staatsbibliothek, Ms. Clm. 835, ff. 16v and 23v; see Appendix, part 1

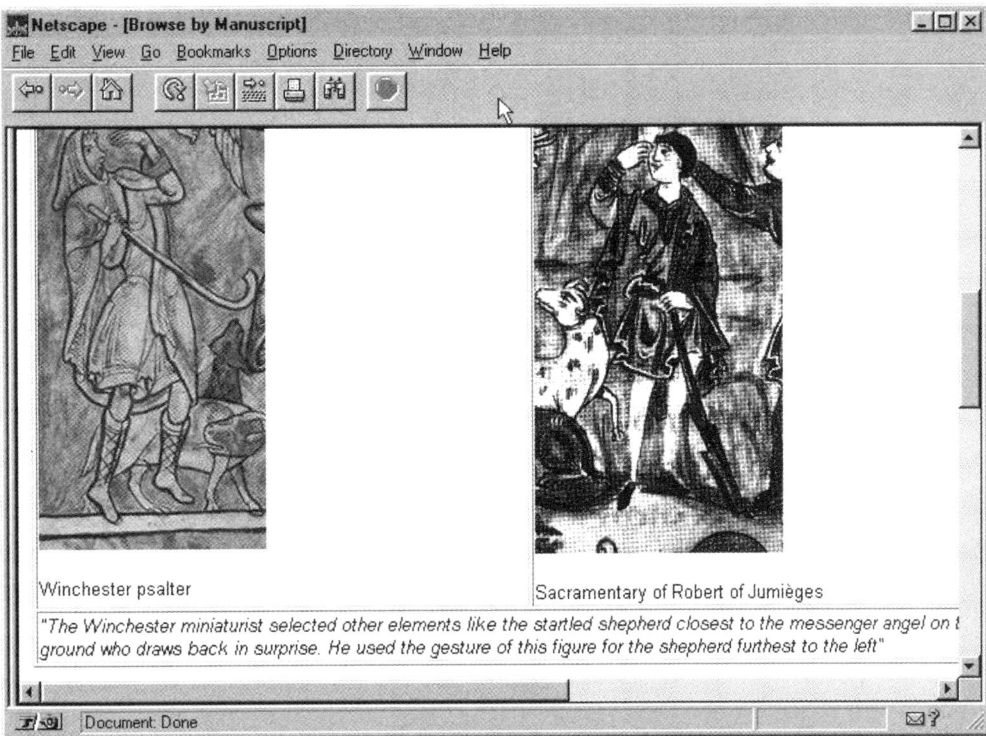

7. "Startled shepherds" in the Winchester Psalter (London, British Library, Ms. Cotton Nero C. IV, f. 11r) and the Sacramentary of Robert of Jumièges (Rouen, Bibiothèque Municipale, Ms. Y 6, f. 33r)

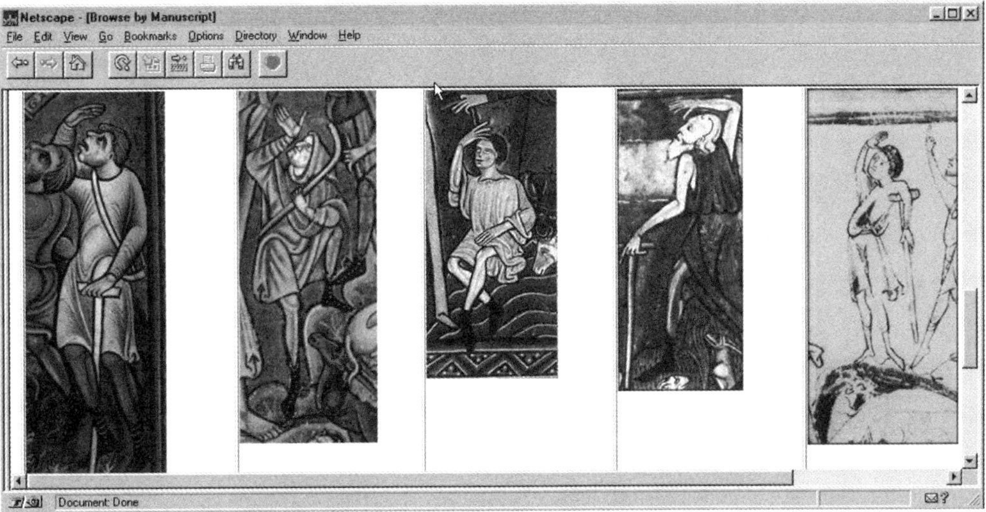

8. Results of a query in the database on the ICONCLASS concept 31A2531(+9161), "hand bent toward the head, protecting," but filtered for the Annunciation to the Shepherds

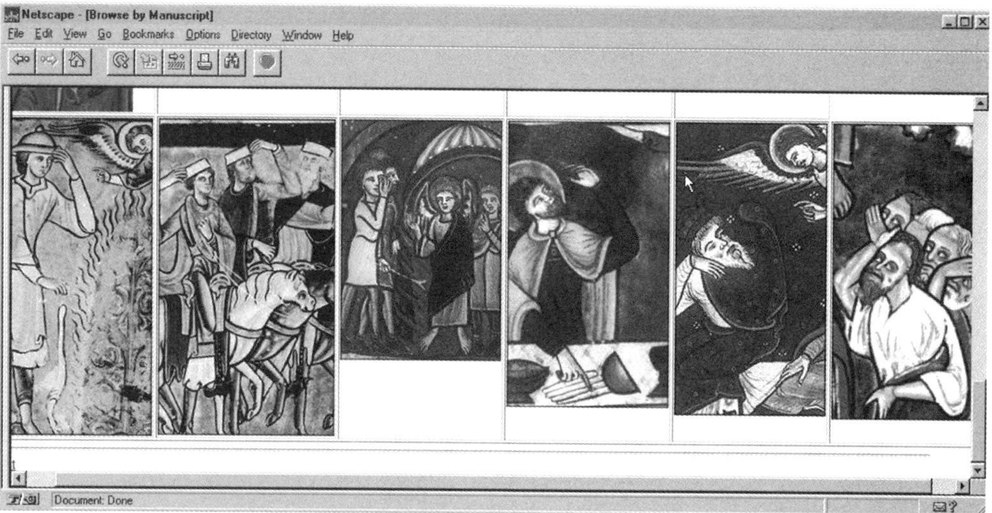

9. The rest of the search result for 31A2531(+9161), "hand bent toward the head, protecting"

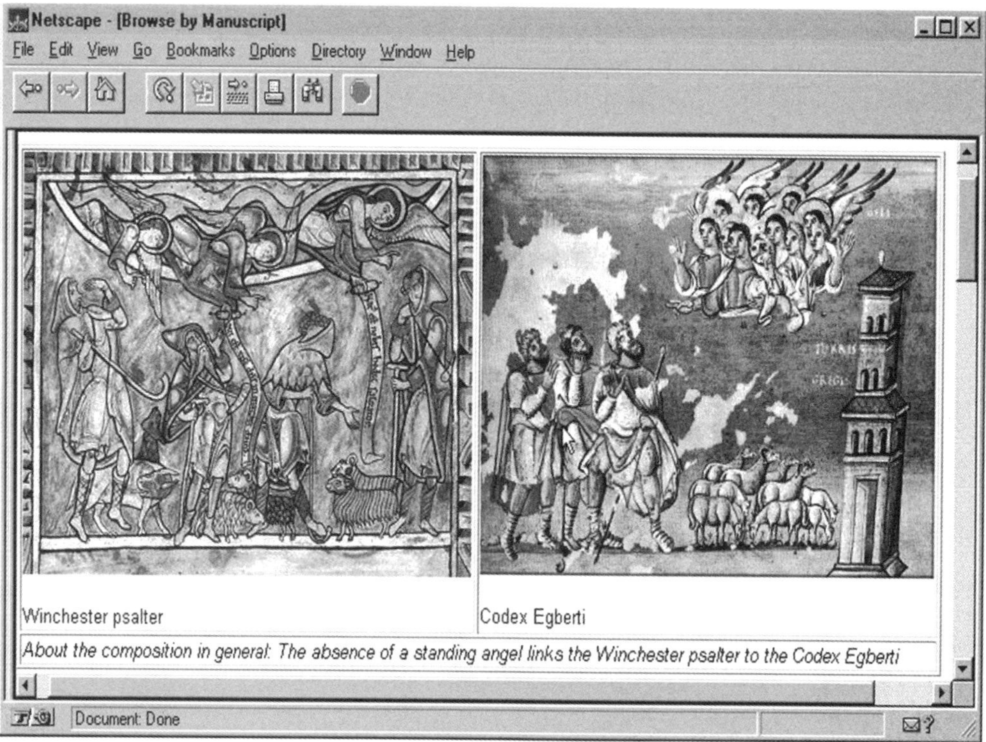

10. The Annunciation to the shepherds in the Winchester Psalter, f. 11r, and the Codex Egberti (Trier, Stadtbibliothek, Ms. 24, f. 13v)

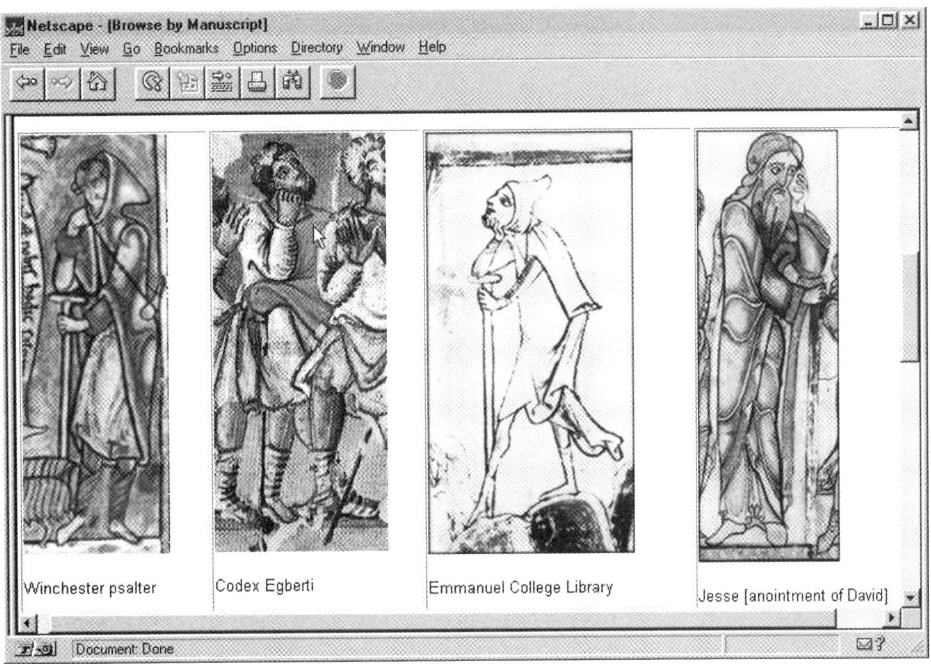

11. Shepherds from the Winchester Psalter, f. 11r, the Codex Egberti, f. 13v, and Cambridge, Emmanuel College Library, Ms. 252, f. 7v; and Jesse from the Winchester Psalter's Anointment of David, f. 7r

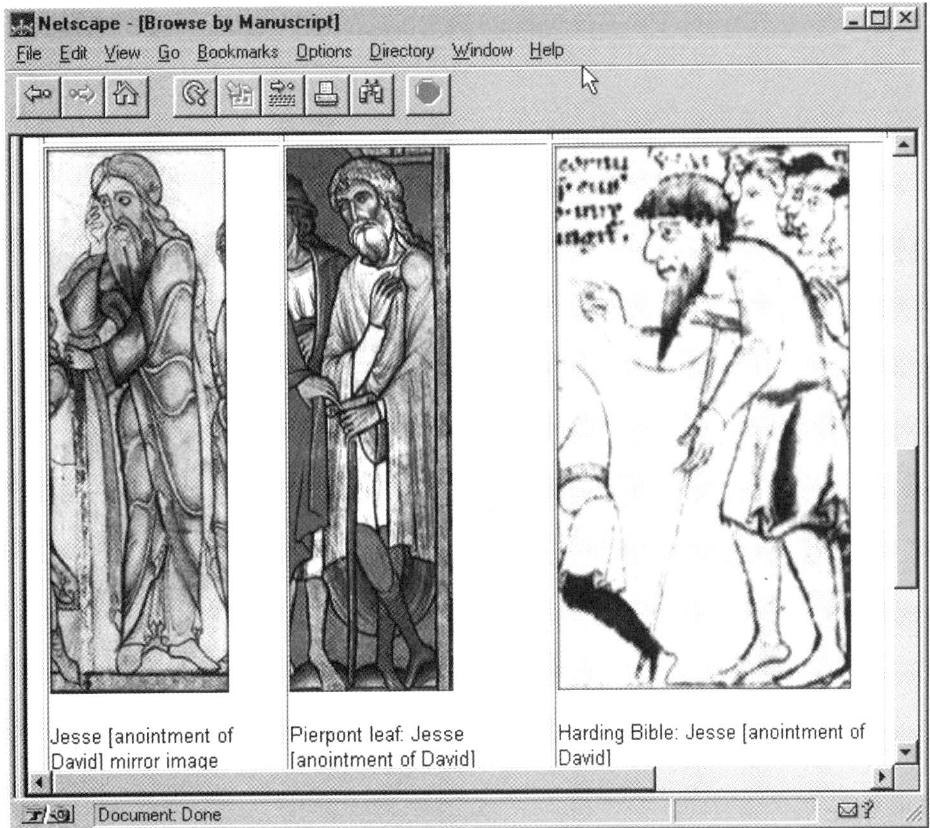

12. Jesse From the Winchester Psalter (mirror image of the last detail in Fig. 11), Pierpont Morgan Library, Ms. M 619, and the Harding Bible, f. 13r

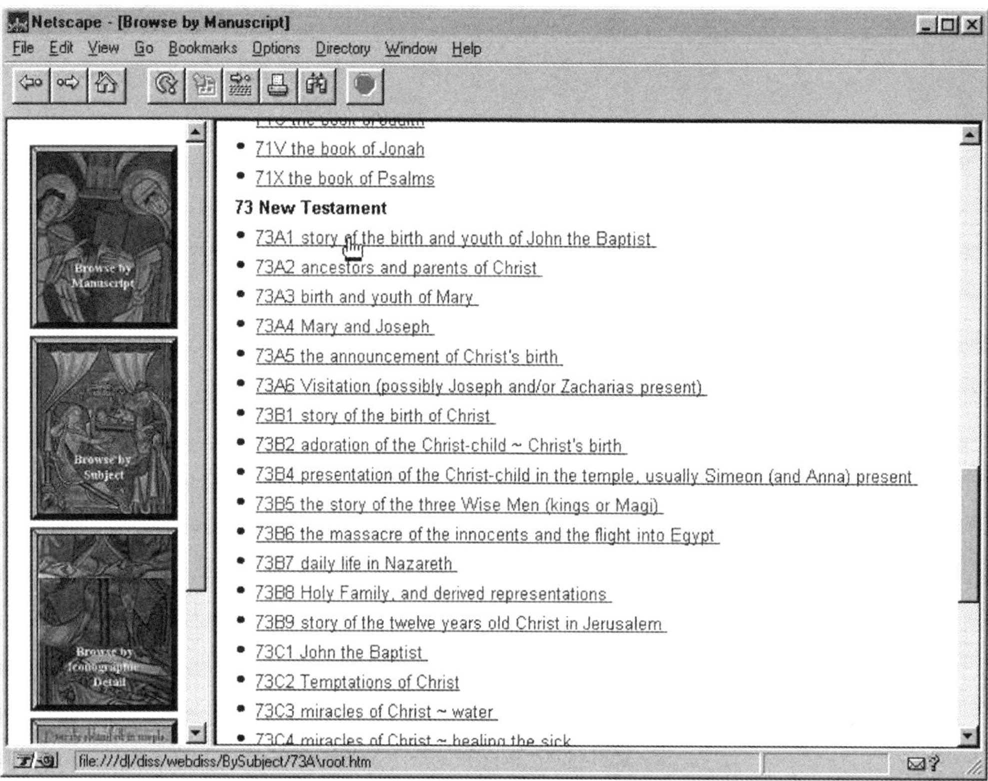

13. Results of browsing by "Subject," with a list of broad ICONCLASS categories; see Appendix, part 2

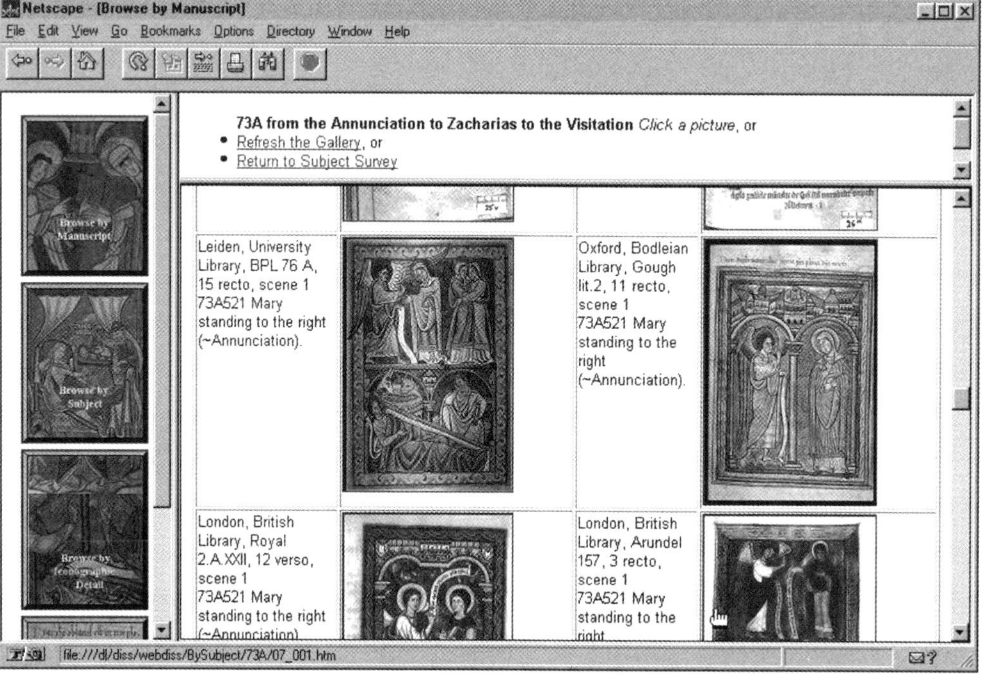

14. Results of selecting a broad ICONCLASS category: a thumbnail gallery with all miniatures where the main subject falls within the category; see Appendix, part 2

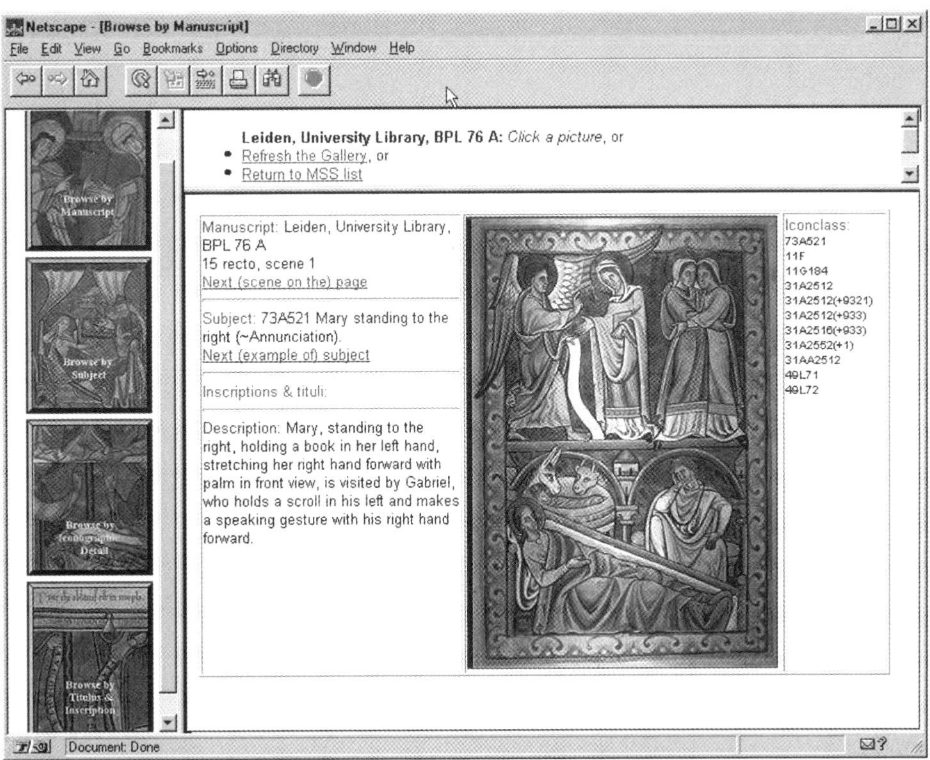

15. Digital reproduction of a miniature with the accompanying iconographic description of its subject matter; see Appendix, part 2

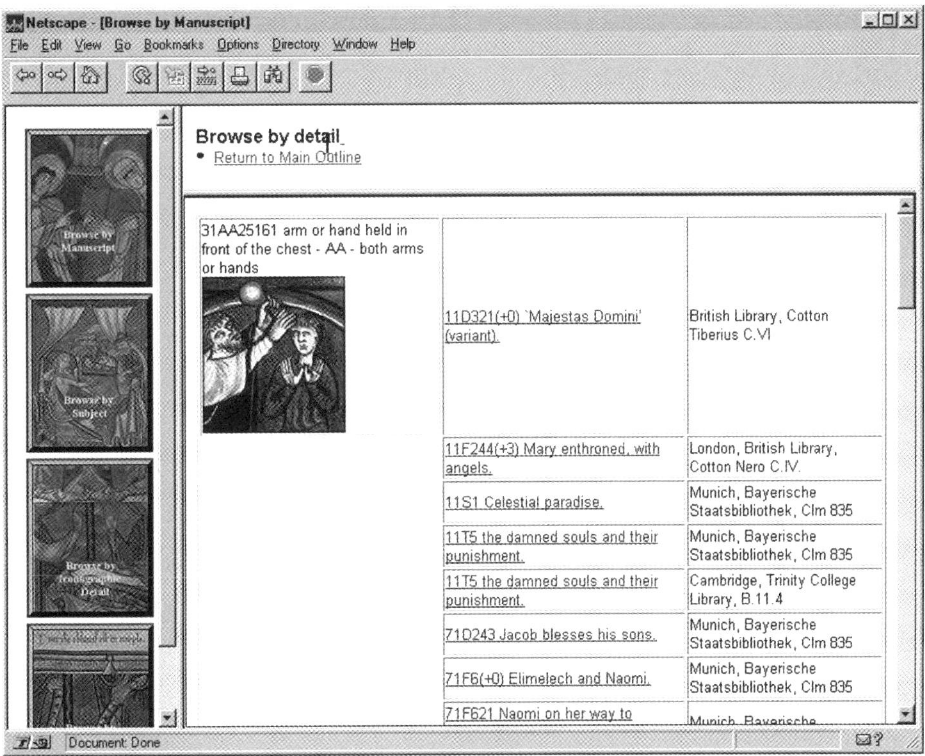

16. Results of browsing for the concept "31AA25161 arm or hand held in front of the chest –AA– both arms or hands"; see Appendix, part 2

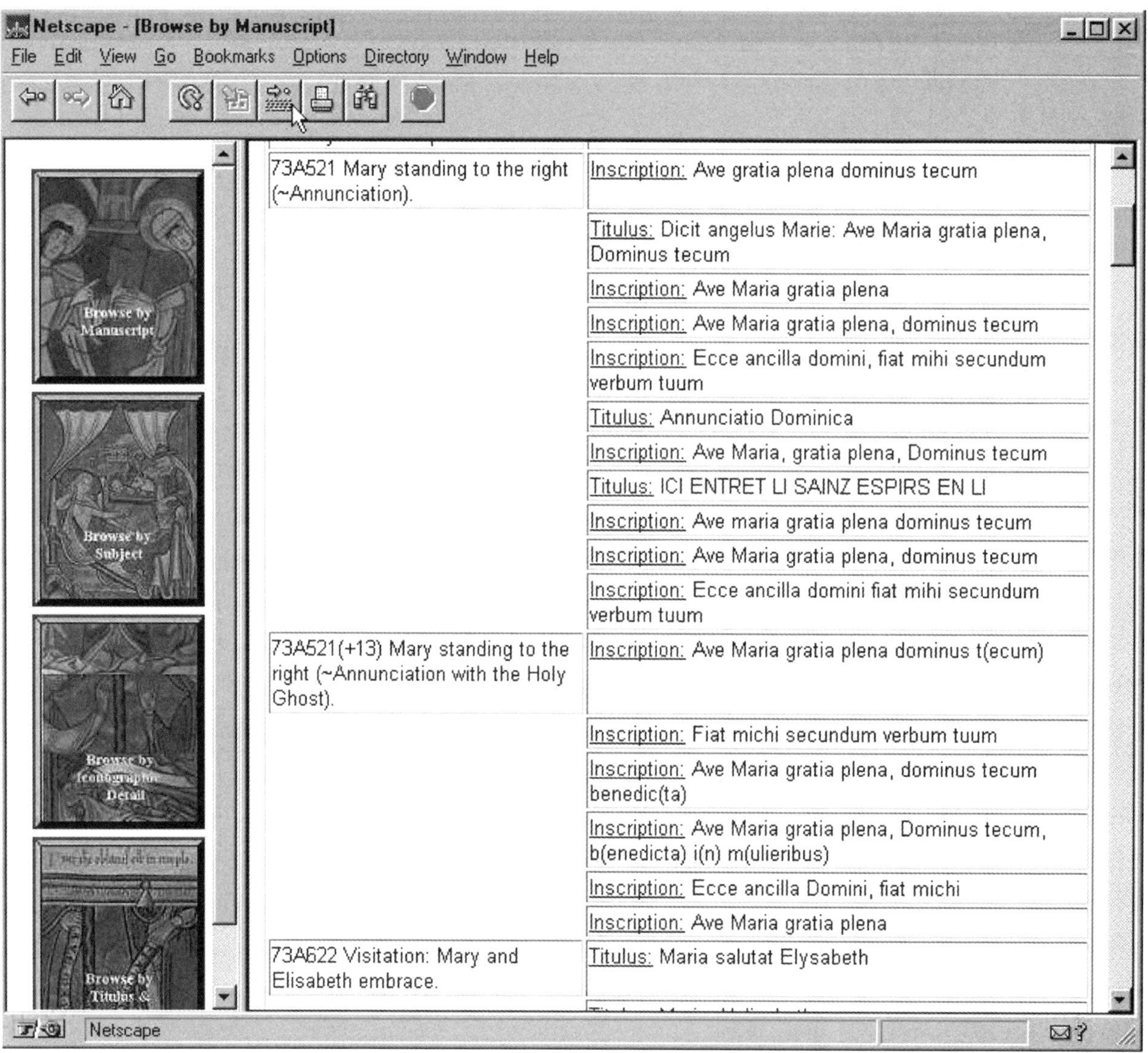

17. Intermediate step in browsing for tituli and inscriptions; see Appendix, part 2

Translating ICONCLASS and the Connectivity Concept of the Iconclass2000 Browser

·

JÖRGEN VAN DEN BERG AND

GERDA G. J. DUIJFJES-VELLEKOOP

THIS PAPER does not attempt to discuss the history or nature of the ICONCLASS system; numerous publications on the concept, structure, and development of the system have already been published. Instead, the purpose is to deal with the two most recent developments which concern the multilingual translations and release of the new browser.

TRANSLATING THE ICONCLASS SYSTEM

In 1996–97, the ICONCLASS Research and Development Group (IRDG) approached researchers in documentation centers in Germany, Finland, Italy, Hungary, and Chile to enquire about projects involved with the translation of ICONCLASS. These contacts have resulted in collaboration with translators, and are aimed at two main goals. Firstly, these contacts safeguard the integrity of ICONCLASS as a documentation standard and, secondly, they create data files that can be used with the ICONCLASS Browser. Software is being developed by Computer en Letteren of the Universiteit Utrecht to enable the creation of such data files. In addition to the above languages, the IRDG has also initiated projects to translate the system into French and Spanish. The modular, easy-connectivity concept of the ICONCLASS Browser is once more proving its worth, as it allows new translations to be used with all Browser editions, even those published on CD-ROM.

Van de Waal's decision to publish ICONCLASS in English (1972–85) made the system internationally accessible from the start. Major art-historical documentation centers, not only in Great Britain and the United States, but also in Germany, Italy, and Japan, have applied ICONCLASS as the preferred standard for iconographic description from the late 1970s onward. Van den Berg's decision to create an ICONCLASS Browser for a Windows platform (1989), which is the subject of the second part of this paper, enabled easy connectivity with other Windows applications and further stimulated its universal acceptance. Many years of experience in indexing with the system and new technology are now resulting in ICONCLASS applications on CD-ROM and on the Internet. With increased use and greater autonomy for various languages, the appearance of ICONCLASS in the vernacular of non-English-speaking countries is only a matter of time. Partial translations have existed in German and Italian since ca. 1986.[1]

TRANSLATION PROJECTS

The IRDG's present concern with translating ICONCLASS dates from August 1996, when the Istituto Centrale per il Catalogo e la Documentazione (ICCD, Rome) announced the forthcoming publication of an Italian translation of the system. When translations of ICONCLASS are going to be published officially, it is in the interest of the entire user group that they should contain all ICONCLASS concepts in their proper hierarchies. The IRDG would like to safeguard the integrity of the system in translated editions without infringing the translators' rights of intellectual authorship of translated text and keywords.

There are at present six translation projects:

LANGUAGE	ORGANIZATION
Italian	ICCD (Rome, Italy)
German	Bildarchiv Foto Marburg (Marburg, Germany)
French	IRDG (Utrecht, The Netherlands)
Spanish	IRDG (Utrecht); Inventario Patrimonio Cultural (Santiago, Chile)
Finnish	Finnish National Gallery, Central Archives (Helsinki, Finland)
Hungarian	Dr. Tamas Sajo (Central European University, Budapest, Hungary)

The projects for translations into French and Spanish were set up by the IRDG with a view to expediting the translations into these two important languages. All the translation projects now share information, which results in the exchange of data for the checking of notations, testing of procedures, and building data files.

TRANSLATING ICONCLASS: TEXTUAL CORRELATES AND KEYWORDS

When the ICONCLASS system is used for iconographic description of works of art, notations are attached to descriptions and reproductions of these works, for example, in the DIAL index (Fig. 1) or the Marburg database (Fig. 2). The notations are alphanumerical codes, which are in essence language-independent. In this system the *meaning* of notations is expressed in words or phrases in natural language which is the *textual correlate* of the notation.[2] In current editions of ICONCLASS

---

[1] The so-called ICO-Datei (MIDAS) knows fields for future translations of textual correlates and keywords into German, Spanish, Italian and French. See L. Heusinger, *Marburger Informations-, Dokumentations- und Administrations-System (MIDAS) Handbuch*, Bildarchiv Foto Marburg (Munich, 1994), 403–4.

[2] Also referred to as "definition," "description," "explanation," "subject," or "Erläuterung." In applications it is often displayed either as text or as a hyperlink from a notation to its "Path"—a feature of the ICONCLASS Browser—or as both.

the language of the textual correlates is English, as are the *keywords* that give access to the system.[3] Translations of the system are concerned with these textual correlates and keywords. The actual descriptors, the notations, remain untouched.[4] This makes translating ICONCLASS relatively easy compared to translating a thesaurus of terms.

Textual Correlates

The fact that notations do not change when the text denoting their meaning is translated gives the translator relative freedom in choosing the terms by which the concept is best defined. The textual correlate—the concept for which the notation stands—may be expressed by:

- a single word
- a shorter or longer phrase
- a full sentence
- a short story or a detailed iconographic description:

24 A 2	sunset
41 D 3	folk costume, regional costume
73 A 6	Visitation (possibly Joseph and/or Zacharias present) (Lk. 1:39–56)
71 C 13 13 11	when Abraham has his hand raised to kill Isaac, an angel restrains Abraham's hand
11 U 1	comprehensive representation of Last Judgment: Christ (with sword and lily), often surrounded by elders and sometimes accompanied by Mary and John the Baptist, appears in the sky with trumpeting angels (and sometimes angels holding the instruments of the Passion); after the resurrection of the dead, the blessed are led to heaven by angels, and the damned are dragged into hell by devils

The "duality" of ICONCLASS is reflected in the complexity of translating the textual correlates.[5] Whereas the narrative and enumerative parts of ICONCLASS (11 H [Saints], large parts of Division 7 [Bible] and Division 9 [Classical Mythology]) translate as a piece of text, the translation of other parts, such as Division 4 (Society, Civilization, Culture), is as demanding as translating a multilingual language thesaurus.

Keywords and Cross-References

Keywords in ICONCLASS give access to the subjects in the system, and are as varied as is possible, ranging from words denoting general human occupations, like eating, drinking, worshipping, and dying, to very specialized terms like biblical names, Madonna types, or names of Ripa per-

[3] H. van de Waal, *ICONCLASS: An Iconographic Classification System*, compiled and edited by L. D. Couprie, R. H. Fuchs, E. Tholen, G. Vellekoop, et al. (Amsterdam, 1973–85); computer version: ICONCLASS Browser®, comprising ICONCLASS System, Index, and Bibliography (Utrecht, 1992, 1994, 1997).

[4] There is one exception: at certain points ICONCLASS allows further specific subdivision by *name* in brackets. This very productive procedure is extremely language-dependent.

[5] On the "duality" of ICONCLASS, see J. P. J. Brandhorst, "Quantifyability in Iconography," *Knowledge Organization: International Journal Devoted to Concept Theory, Classification, Indexing, and Knowledge Representation* 20, no. 1 (1993), 13.

sonifications. In the early 1960s, Van de Waal and his collaborators compiled the first draft versions of the Alphabetical Index. Among their sources were the Rotulus[6] and the subject terms of the Index of Christian Art. The art historians Leendert Couprie and Rudi Fuchs devoted much time and intellectual effort to the construction of "semantic circles," showing semantic and visual relationships between subjects, which were to be expressed by cross-references between keyword entries (Figs. 3 and 4). Much of this expert knowledge has been preserved in the present ICONCLASS Browser, which contains almost 5,000 "see" and "see also" references between keywords.

Lists of Keywords Used to Generate Cross-References

An integral translation of the English keywords was made available to the team members at the start of the project of developing an Italian translation.[7] Not only does this *Parole* list (at right) enable us to create keywords for the data file, it also allows the creation of a complex network of cross-references. An experiment with the *Parole* list has shown that computer-generated cross-references between Italian and English keywords greatly improve keyword access.

PAROLE (ICCD)

abacus	abaco
abandoning	abbandonare
abbess	badessa
abbey	abbazia
abbot	abate
abdication	abdicazione
abducting	rapire
abhorrence	aborrimento
ability	abilitá
ablactatio	ablactatio
ablution	abluzione

DATA AND SOFTWARE FOR TRANSLATORS

ICONCLASS data have been provided to translators and programs have been developed to check translations and safeguard the integrity of the system. The principal aids to translators include:

- lists of ICONCLASS system data (notations and textual correlates)
- lists of keywords, in alphabetical order
- lists of keywords in systematic order, prearranged as they are organized in the ICONCLASS system[8]
- lists of "see" and "see also" references between keywords
- program to check translations for presence and absence of notations
- program to "merge" translated data into the IRDG's source files, while retaining built-in knowledge of the ICONCLASS system
- program to check lists of keywords, e.g., for one-too-many translations of English keywords
- program to build thousands of "see also" references in the target language
- program to build data files for the Browser

---

[6] The Rotulus is the list of index terms to W. S. Heckscher's *Index Iconologicus.*

[7] M. L. Polichetti and M. Lattanzi, "The ICCD Project for an Italian Version of ICONCLASS," trans. Baca, in *[Proceedings of the] International Terminology Working Group Meeting* (Amsterdam: Getty, 5 September 1996), unpaginated.

[8] Classified structure of keywords also proved of great use in a multilingual thesaurus project: S. G. D. Clarke, "The Construction of a Multilingual Thesaurus Based on a Classified Structure," paper presented at the International Terminology Working Group Meeting, Paris, 5 September 1997.

First Results: German, French, and Italian Files

The first foreign-language file to be converted into a data file for the ICONCLASS Browser contained some 3,000 ICONCLASS notations, textual correlates, and corresponding keywords in German. The file, which was manually created, contained only 12 percent of the ICONCLASS notations and none of its rules. Nevertheless, it was very useful in showing how to proceed. It showed convincingly that:

- the aim must always be to build a complete system, containing all hierarchical levels
- building a *mixed* file of partly target, partly source language would seem to be a commendable alternative if a substantial part of the system has been translated—for example, notations that are actually used in the database—but an integral translation is not expected in the near future
- translating keywords separately makes it possible to observe and retain the present lack of redundancy in assigned keywords, and enables the creation of extra cross-references

The merging program ICXMRG.EXE[9] that resulted from these observations was first tested on the translation of Division 7 (Bible) into French (Fig. 5). Merging the French file with the ICONCLASS source produced a new source file with the following characteristics:

- French textual correlates replace their English equivalents
- all built-in knowledge is kept
- omitted notations retain their English text

A "log" file created by the program checks on notations that are missing in the translation, and also lists "non-ICONCLASS" notations, which must be checked manually. Keyword access is in English in this first French data file, because integral translation of French keywords is not yet available. The file functions satisfactorily with all of the ICONCLASS Browsers.[10]

The Italian keyword list (*Parole*) was then used to test the "keywords switch" of ICXMRG. EXE. This produced a data file with all Italian keywords (textual correlates still mainly in English, only Division 71 [Old Testament] in Italian). Cross-references between Italian keywords were generated on the basis of existing cross-references with English keywords (Fig. 6).

Multilingual ICONCLASS

The new Iconclass2000 Browser for Windows has a menu option that allows the user to select the preferred language for the system file. The browser does not support the simultaneous display of several languages in different fields in one browser display. With the multi-user, multi-document capability of the new Iconclass2000 Browser, it is possible to start several browsers in a row and select a different language for each one of them, which brings us very close to a "multilingual" ICONCLASS (Figs. 7 and 8).

---

[9] Software developed by drs. Ronald Kunenborg, Computer en Letteren, Universiteit Utrecht.

[10] (1) ICONCLASS Browser for Windows 3.1 (standalone); (2) ICONCLASS Evaluation CD-ROM; (3) ICONCLASS Browser with special interface, attached to the CD-ROMs of the DISKUS series); (4) the Iconclass2000 Browser for Windows 95 and Windows NT; (5) the WWW Browsers (Java Applets).

The new auxiliary software checks translations for the use of correct notations. It merges translations and original files to build data files in the target language that can be used by ICONCLASS Browsers. By creating data files that can be used with all current versions of the ICONCLASS Browser, the software has immediate benefits for the target-language community, as it guarantees:

- standard method of using ICONCLASS
- easy connectivity with other programs
- sophisticated access to the data
- added value of ICONCLASS's built-in knowledge and application rules

Translations that can be used as data files in the new ICONCLASS Browsers, together with those on the Internet, will bring the possibility of searching for information in international databases closer.

THE CONNECTIVITY CONCEPT OF THE ICONCLASS2000 BROWSER, OLE, AND MACROS

Smooth connectivity of the new ICONCLASS Browser with other Windows programs was the first priority in designing the new Iconclass2000 Browser. The aim in this part of the paper is to highlight some of these features and to illustrate how users can fully exploit the connectivity elements in their own situations, if their work includes using ICONCLASS notations in text or database files. The user-friendly way in which the new browser connects to translations of ICONCLASS anticipates the results of current work on translations, which is described elsewhere in this paper. Every solution attempts to facilitate user needs, with the least possible programming, by the efficient application of new techniques.

When the ICONCLASS user upgrades to the new Iconclass2000 Browser for Windows 95 and Windows NT, the first thing to be noticed is the redesigned user interface. Buttons and menu options enable new and improved ways of browsing and searching the ICONCLASS system and querying the Bibliography. Although several publications could be written on these new features, they will not be dealt with in this study. Their design should provide intuitive operation, and, if this fails, the user can resort to on-line help options. Instead, this paper would like to draw attention to what has been the fundamental philosophy in redesigning the browser. Powerful, recently developed computer techniques like OLE (Object Linking and Embedding) have been employed to create a reliable tool that facilitates and promotes the use of the system as a standard for iconographic indexing and subject retrieval of images. This is a tool that can be easily accessed from within other programs, and the sole use of which greatly enriches translations of ICONCLASS.

There are several ways in which the Iconclass2000 Browser can be accessed from within standard Windows applications such as database management programs, text processors, multimedia presentation tools, or spreadsheet programs. It is important to realize that this can be accomplished without having to do any programming. Microsoft has developed a special enabling technique called Object Linking and Embedding (OLE). Thanks to this technique, any document can include not only straightforward text, but also well-defined OLE objects, such as image objects, graphical objects, word-art objects, speech objects, etc. The Iconclass2000 Browser is fully OLE compliant. It is a full OLE server and also allows OLE automation. The OLE methods for Windows have only become available to their full extent in recent versions of Windows 95 applications.

ICONCLASS can be inserted into a document by applying the following options from the Word menu: Insert ⇒ Object ⇒ select tab Create New ⇒ select from the list of objects one of the following:

ICONCLASS Browse   ICONCLASS Bibliography   ICONCLASS Search

Clicking on the OK button will insert the selected object into the required document. When this icon is double-clicked the browser will be activated. This appears with one of the three major functions it offers. The features of Object Linking and Embedding are available in many other (also non-Microsoft) OLE-compliant applications (Fig. 9). Although its use is limited, the functionality can be expanded to a more sophisticated level, as will be explained in the next section.

Using Macros to Access ICONCLASS Browser Functions

Macros can help the user manage the system browser in an even more sophisticated manner by embedding ICONCLASS objects in the document. After opening and reading a special file containing the macro source text, the ICONCLASS macros become instantly available on a convenient toolbar menu at the top right-hand side of the button bar.[11] A message may first appear in a dialog box concerning the use of macros in general; in that situation it can be assumed that the "Enable Macros" command has been activated. It is possible to build personalized macros and adjust the ICONCLASS menu in the Word toolbar to suit individual taste.

Some examples of macros that can be accessed from a simple menu selection have already been included (Fig. 10):

· Start the ICONCLASS Browser with a selected notation as argument

If a notation in the text is selected (by dragging the mouse over the characters) and the "Browse Open" option is chosen from the ICONCLASS macro menu, the browser will start and place its focus on the selected notation. By clicking aside the browser window on the Word window, the user is returned to the editor (Fig. 11).

· Start the ICONCLASS Browser with a selected keyword as argument

If a (key)word in the text document is selected (by double-clicking on the word) and the "Search Open" option is chosen from the ICONCLASS macro menu the browser will start the search screen with the selected word inserted in the edit box. It is then possible to search for any references in the system. Clicking on the browser window in the Word document window brings ICONCLASS to the background of the document view (Fig. 12).

· Give the full context of an ICONCLASS notation

---

[11] The macro source text is distributed with the Browser; for further details see the ICONCLASS website (http://iconclass.let.uu.nl/) or the Iconclass2000 distribution CD-ROM.

If the user wants to know the exact meaning of a notation in the text, it is possible to select the notation (by dragging the mouse over it) and choose "Show Path" from the macro menu. In a dialog box, the browser will display the full context and meaning of the notation (Fig. 13).

· Obtain the textual correlate of a notation and insert the text in the document

It is also possible to expand a notation in the document text with its meaning. When the user selects the notation and chooses "Obtain Correlate" from the macro menu, the browser will append the textual correlate in the text at cursor position. If the user had selected 23U22 when this menu option was activated, the text would have been appended to read "23U22 hourglass."

· Insert the most recently exported notation into the document

Another useful option allows the user to import the ICONCLASS notation last selected from the browser directly into the text. For example, when the "Browse Open" option is selected from the macro menu, the browser is started. A concept can be chosen by browsing the system's hierarchy. Once the concept has been found it is necessary to click on the "Export" button once. The Word window should then be selected to leave the browser while keeping it active in the background. If the "Obtain Last Exported Notation" is chosen from the macro menu, it will be inserted into the text.

· Insert the full context of a notation, including keywords

It is necessary to browse the system's hierarchy until the right concept has been found. Then select the "Keywords" button once, and the "Copy All" button of the Keywords dialog box. When the Word document window is selected, the browser is still kept active in the background. On selecting "Obtain Last Exported Keywords" from the ICONCLASS macro menu, the full context of the concept, including textual correlates and keywords, will be inserted into the text. If 23U22 was the selected notation, this is what the inserted text will look like:

2	Nature
	nature
23	time
	time
23U	chronology
	chronology
	time
23U2	(instruments for) measurement of time
	instrument
	chronometry
	measuring
23U22	hourglass
	hourglass

How to Visualize ICONCLASS Notations Assigned to Records in a Database

The new browser is capable of visualizing notations that were assigned in the database. These notations reside within the data structure of the users database and are usually only accessible from within the individual application. It is possible to enable the browser to make this data more *visible* and *meaningful*. By browsing the list of notations, the user would have a general idea of the concepts that are present, and those that are not; about what is abundantly there, and what is there only incidentally. This would give the user a clue as to what to search for, and long meaningless searches could be avoided.

The ICONCLASS Browser has no knowledge of the individual application. It is therefore, strictly speaking, virtually impossible to link the browser closely to the individual's application without a (major) programming effort by specialists. The design of the new Iconclass2000 Browser anticipates this principal drawback and offers a solution which requires a minor effort on the part of the client. To make the browser aware of the concepts recorded in the database, it needs to generate a straightforward list with all of the notations in the database. Most database management systems have a facility to export and store attribute data, in this case ICONCLASS notations, in a separate ASCII file. This means that the file should be readable with a simple editor like Notepad. The file does not need to be a sorted file. All it should contain is the list of all recorded notations. A sample of such a file (sorted for readability) is given here at the right. Notice the repetition of notations 11 C 2, and 11 C. This is not unusual, as they come from different records in the database.

A small program accompanying the new browser can read this file with collection-dependent data, and convert it to a table that is accessible to the browser. The program is simple to use. The "Choose" button of the program allows you to select the notations file; then the "Parse" function is activated, which creates a new table for access by the browser. The program parses the file, sorts it, and computes notation hierarchies. By clicking on the "Test" button, the new file is offered to the browser. The system can be browsed immediately to see the results. Every time a concept is selected the "assigned" field on the status line at the bottom of the window is updated. It tells how many times a certain concept occurs in records in the collection database. In this way a detailed insight is given into which concepts are used in the collection, and how frequently. The feature allows the user to visualize the semantic domain of the data (Fig. 14).

```
1
10
11 (+5)
11 B 12 1
11 B 23
11 B 32 21
11 B 32 22 (+31)
11 B 32 3
11 B 32 32 (+3)
11 B 32 32
11 B 33 1
11 C 12
11 C 15
11 C 2
11 C 2
11 C 21 1
11 C 21
11 C 23 (+31)
11 C 23 1
11 C 4 (+13)
11 C
11 C
```

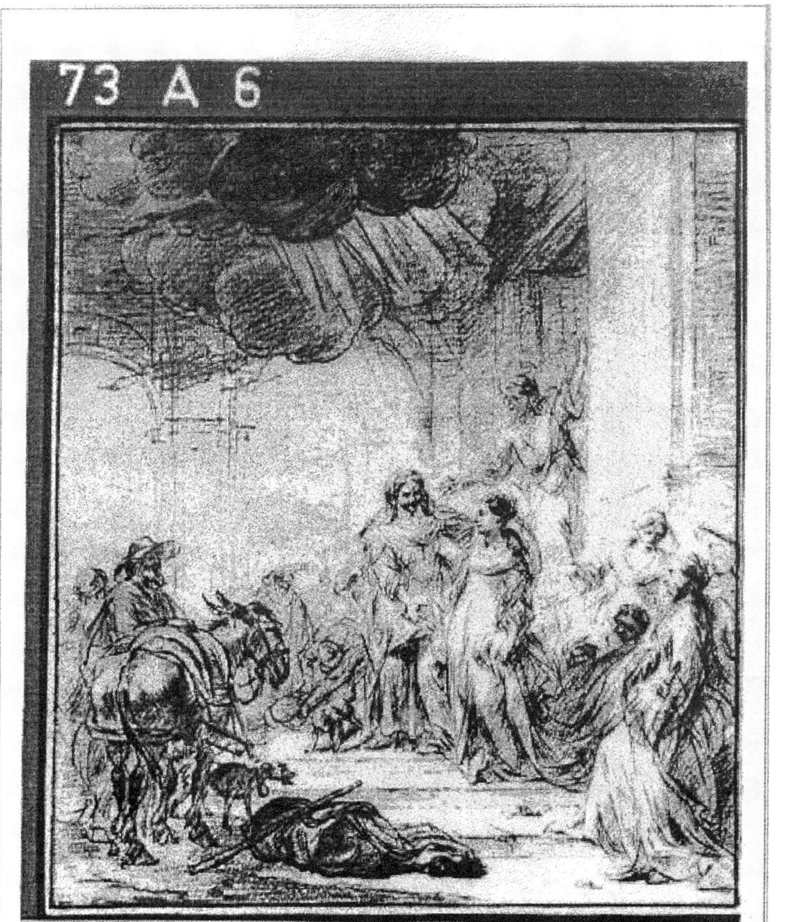

1. DIAL (Decimal Index of the Art of the Low Countries) photocard with ICONCLASS notation

	3100	Bantzer, Carl Ludwig Noah
unkt.	3475	Maler
	5060	Datierung
Dat.	5064	1897/1898
	5200	Schwälmer Tanz
	5220	Malerei
g	5222	Tafelmalerei
riff	5230	Bild
er.	5260	Öl
Mat	5280	Leinwand
reite	5360	95 × 165
n.	5500	43 C 94 2 [+6] & 41 D 3 & 61 D [SCHWALM]

2. Record in a HIDA (Marburg Classification Standard) database

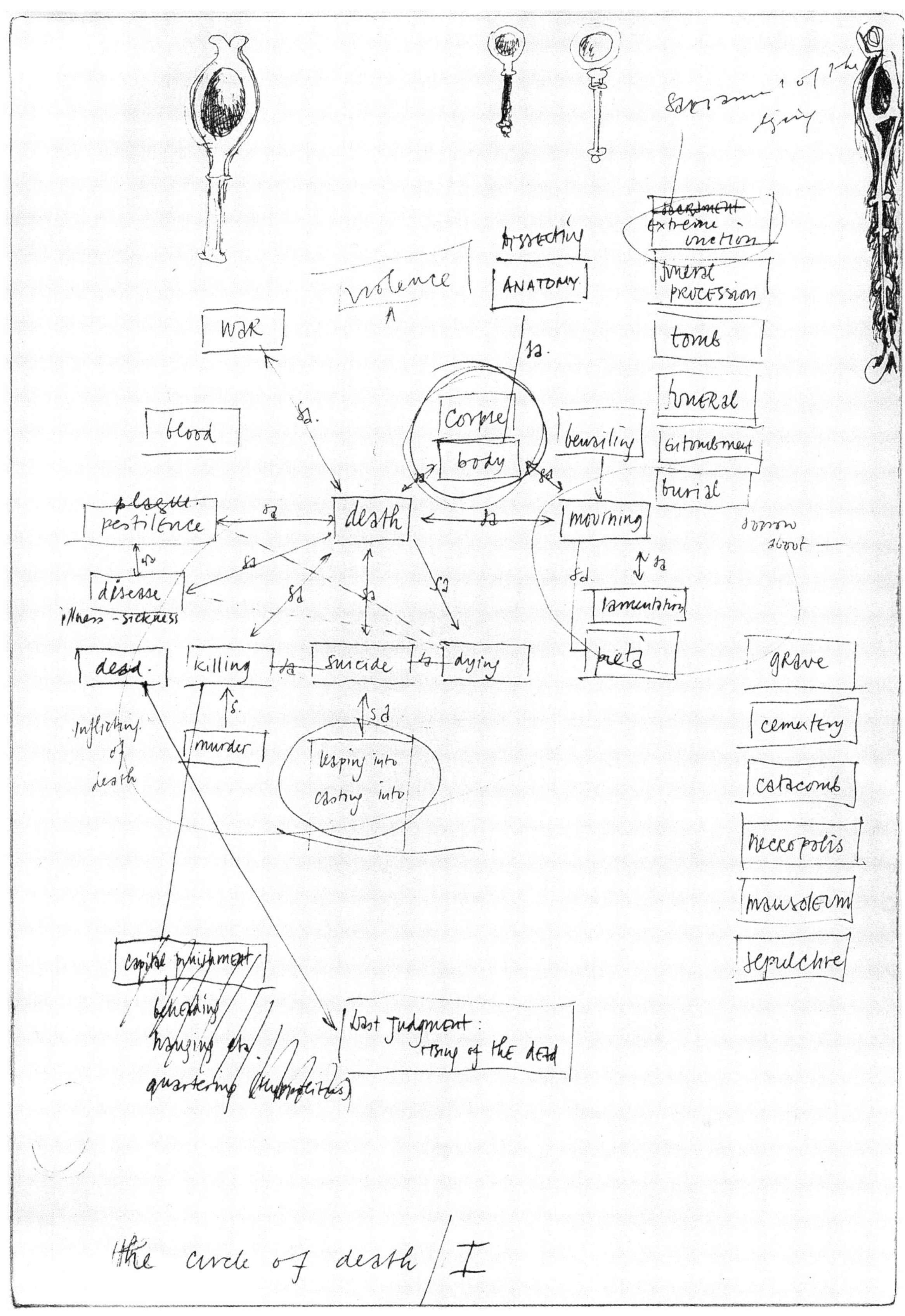

3. Document showing the evolution of "the circle of death / I" (Rudi H. Fuchs)

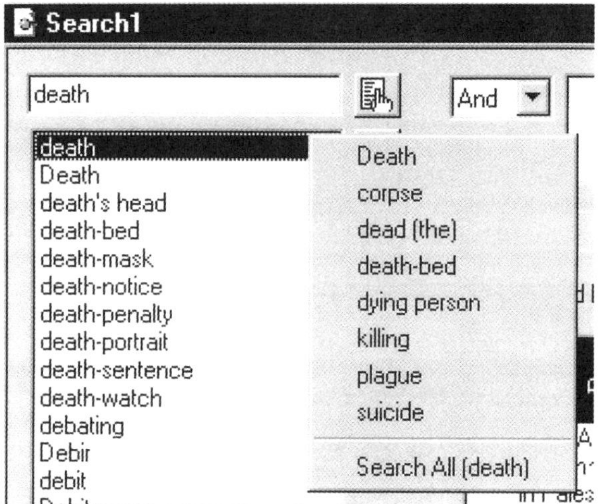

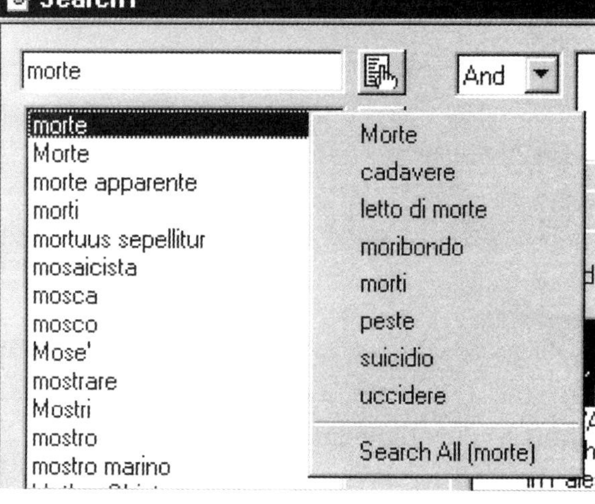

4. "See also" references from "death"

6. "See also" references from "morte"

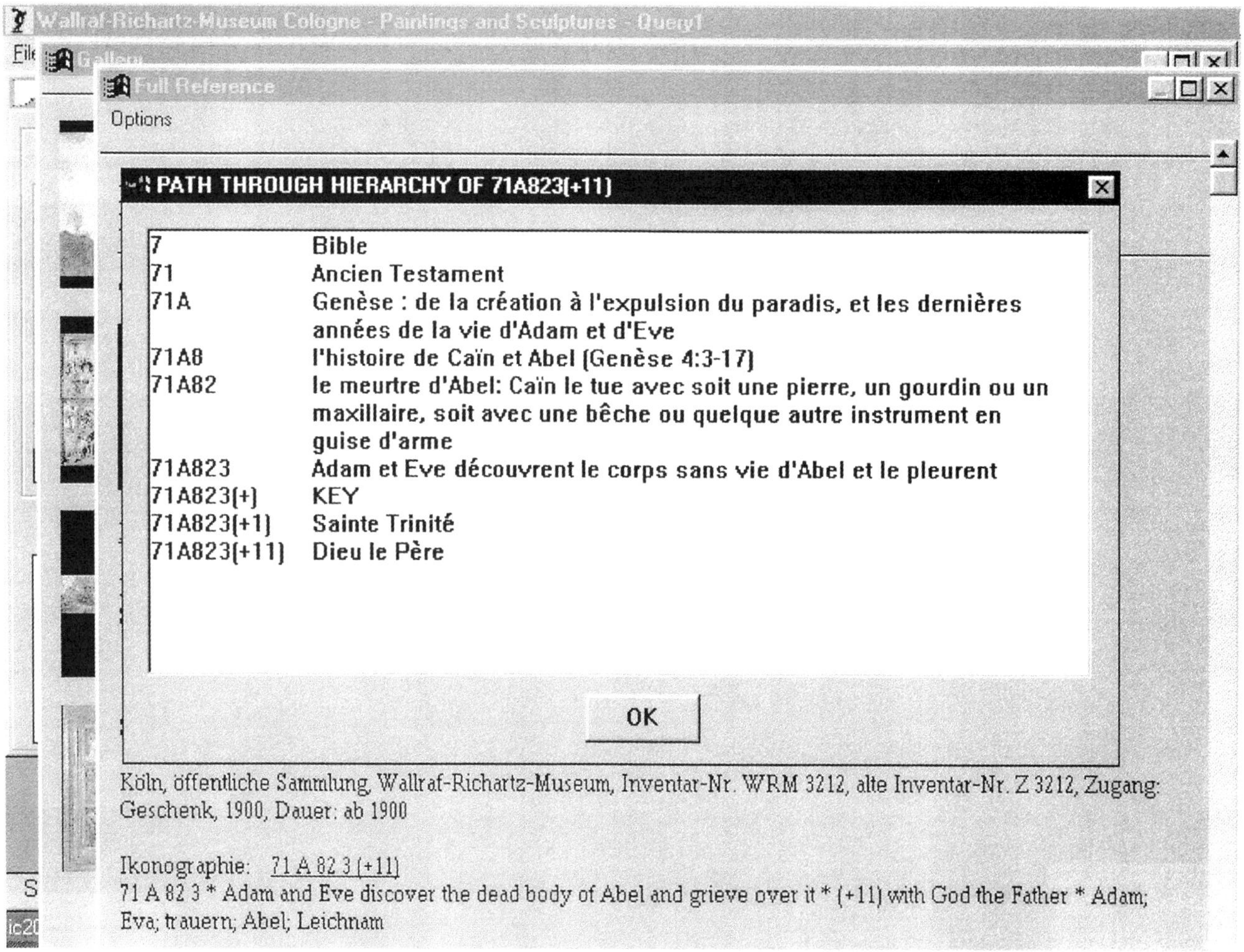

5. Biblical iconography displayed in French on an existing CD-ROM, *Wallraf-Richartz-Museum Cologne: Collection of Paintings and Sculptures* (DISKUS series 007; Munich, 1996)

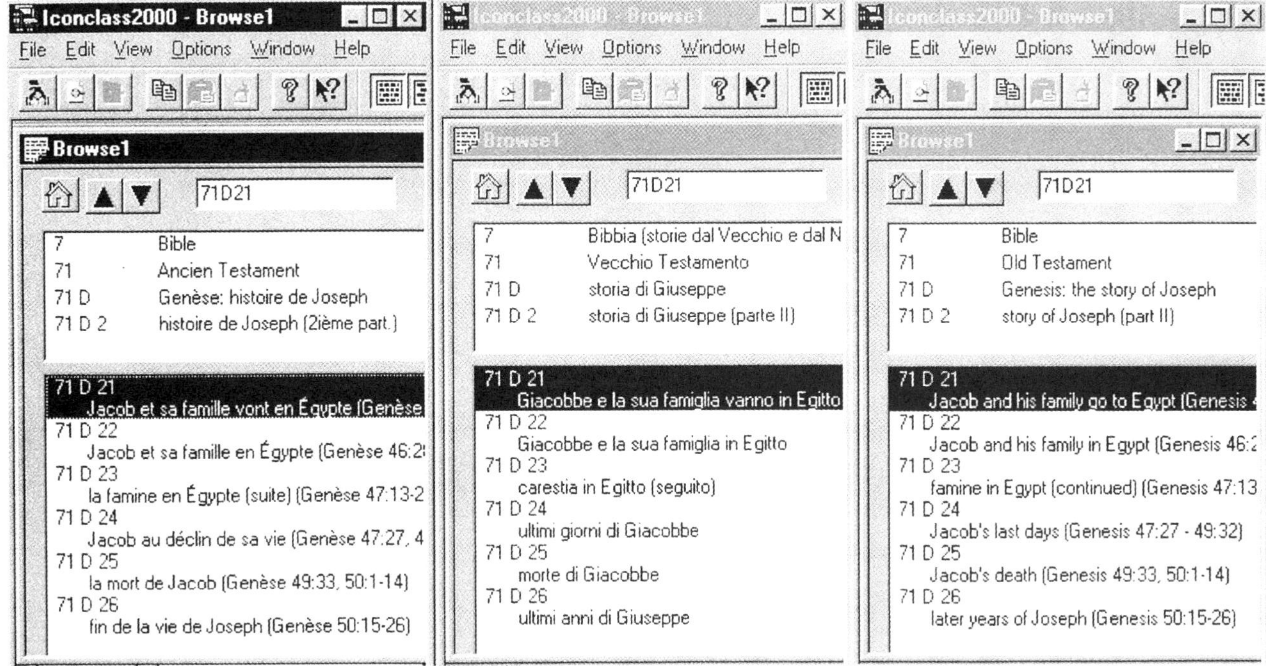

7. Multilingual ICONCLASS: three browsers running simultaneously, each accessing a different data file

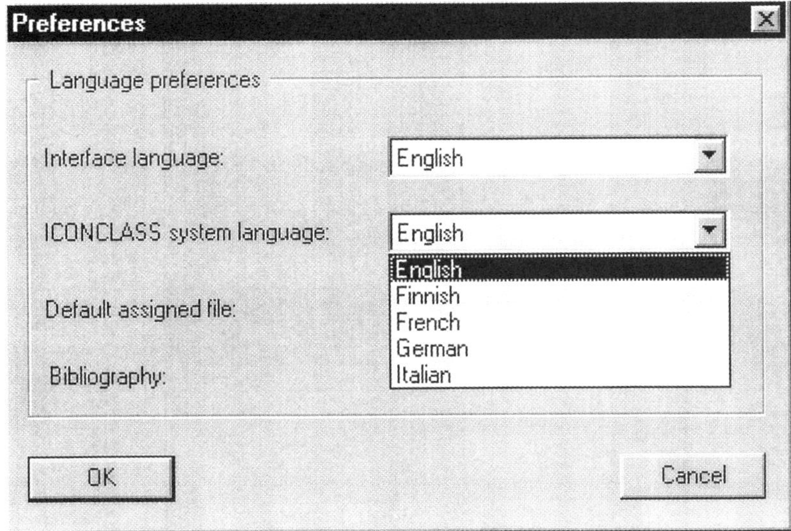

8. Option in "File Preferences": lets the user change the ICONCLASS System language.

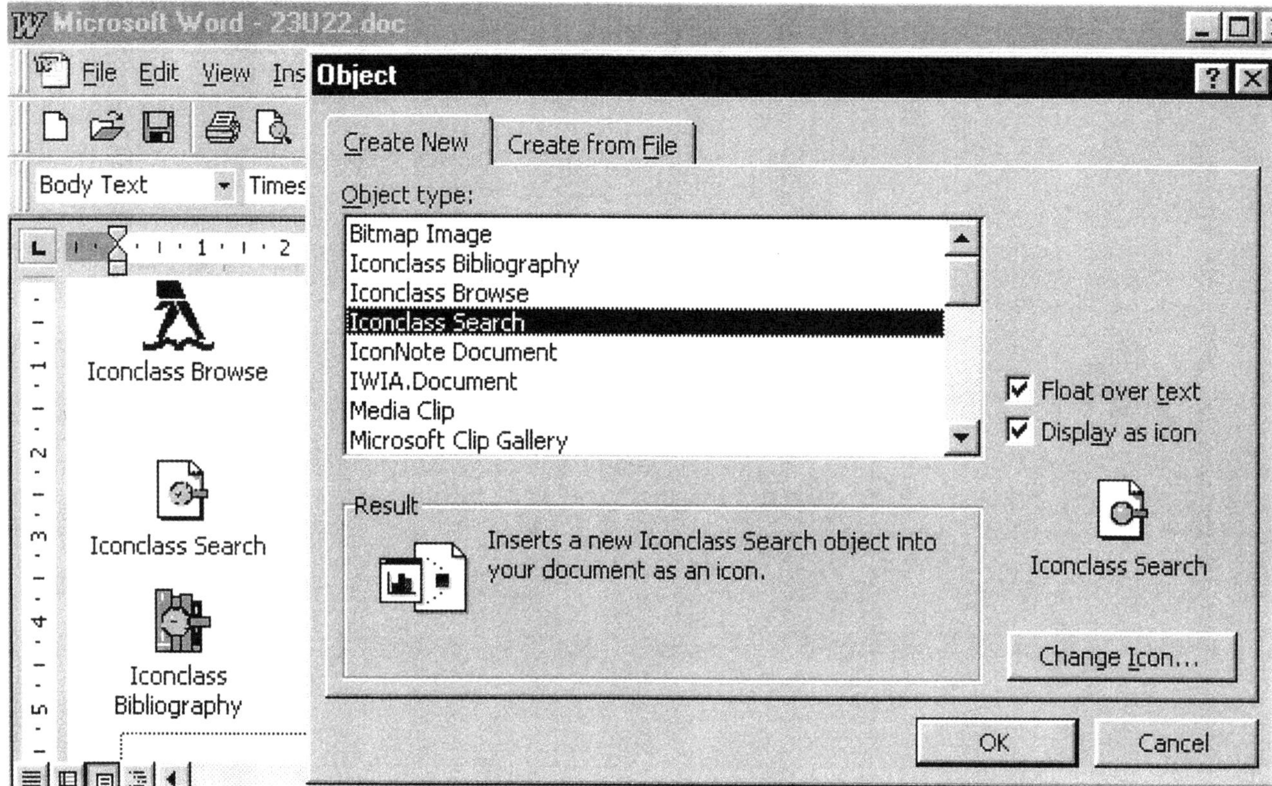

9. Inserting ICONCLASS Objects in a Word document

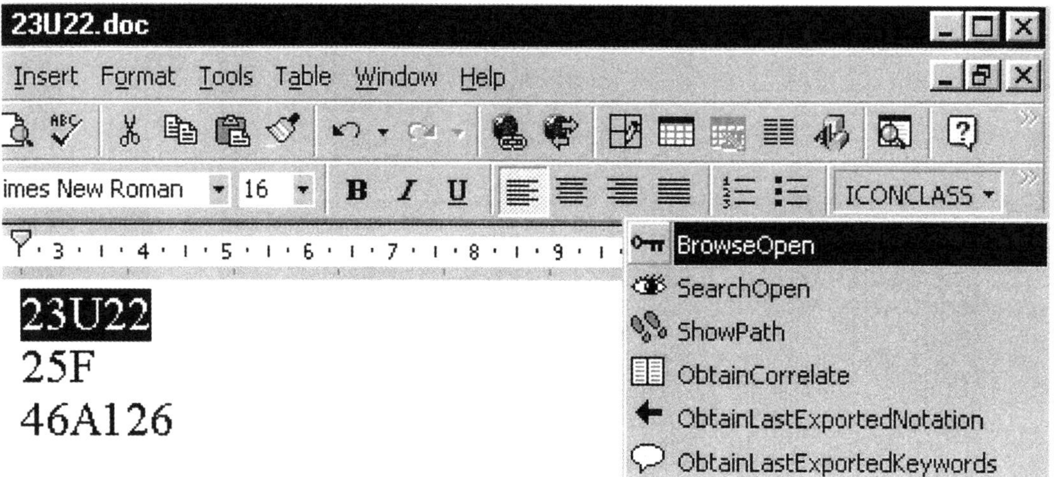

10. Using the ICONCLASS macro menu, several options (OLE automation services, in Microsoft language) that the ICONCLASS Browser exposes can be accessed from within the Word document. They can be helpful when working with ICONCLASS notations in text.

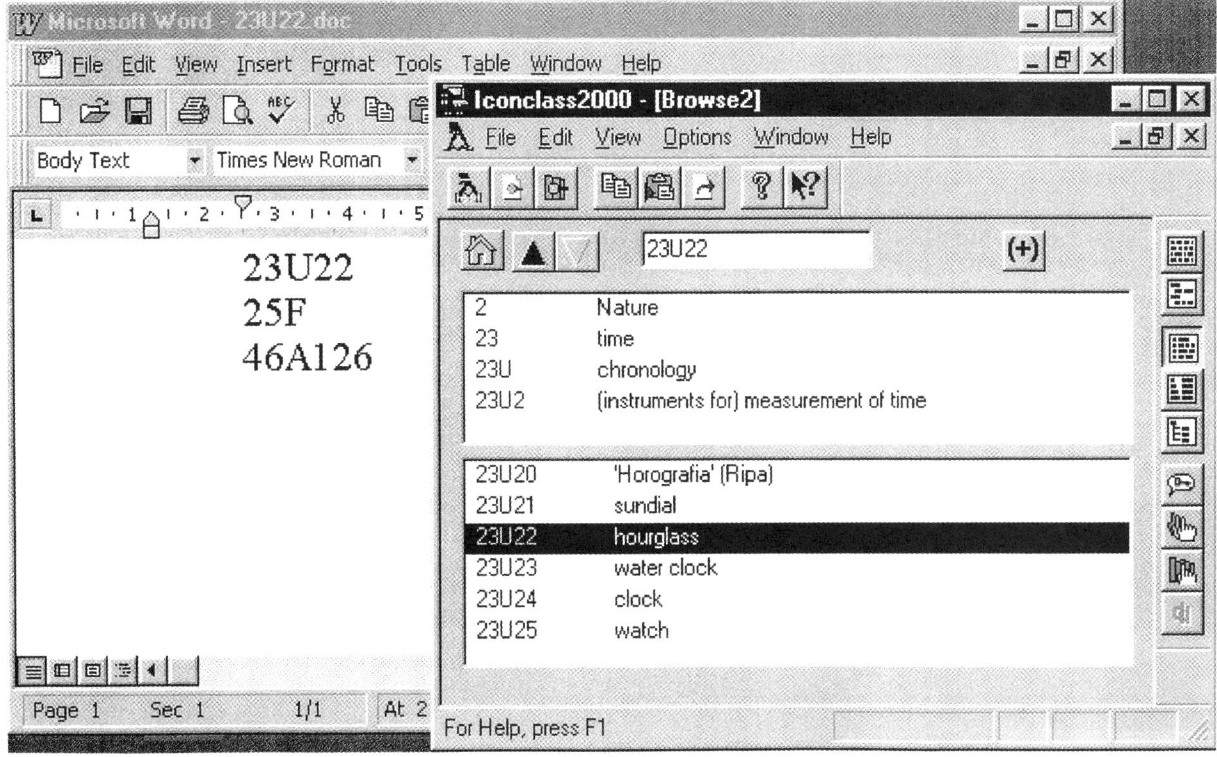

11. The ICONCLASS Browser window with focus on a notation

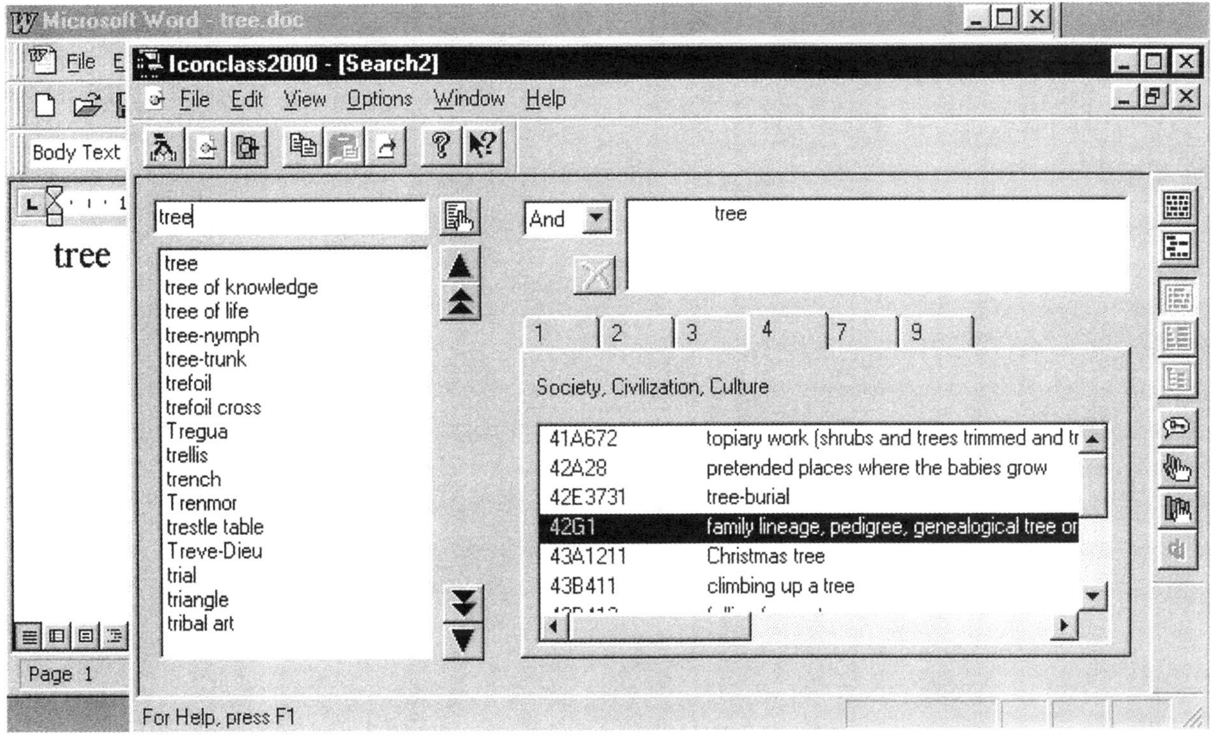

12. The ICONCLASS Browser "Search" window, with focus on a keyword ("tree") used to search the system. The results of the search are presented "behind" different tabs representing the main categories of ICONCLASS.

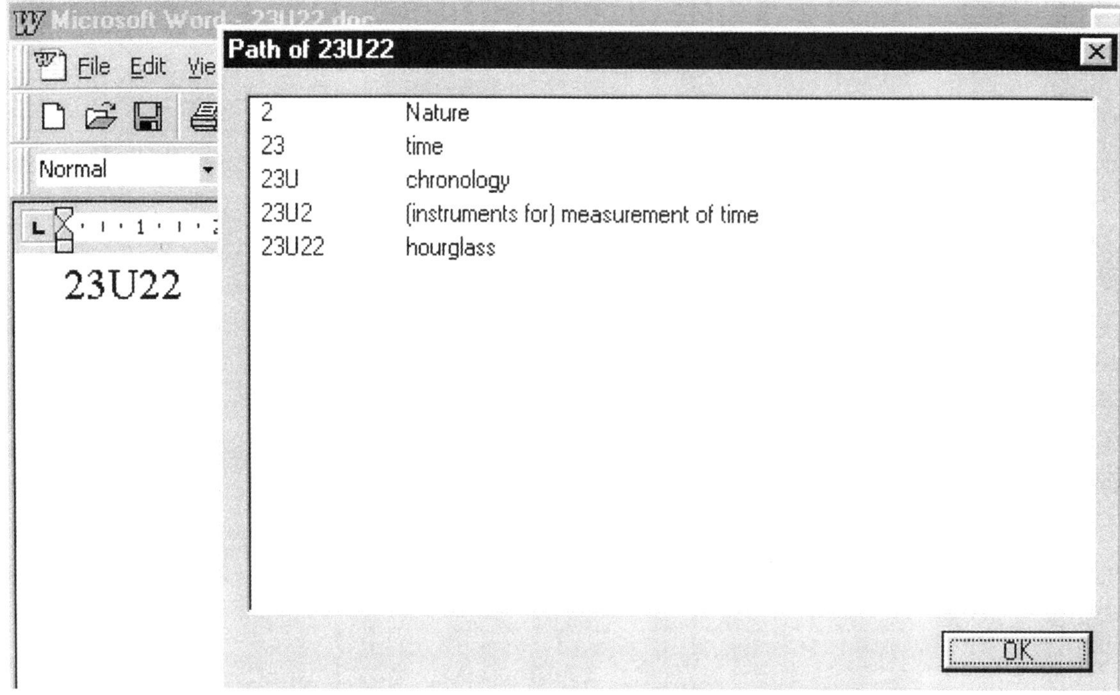

13. The full context of ICONCLASS notation 23U22

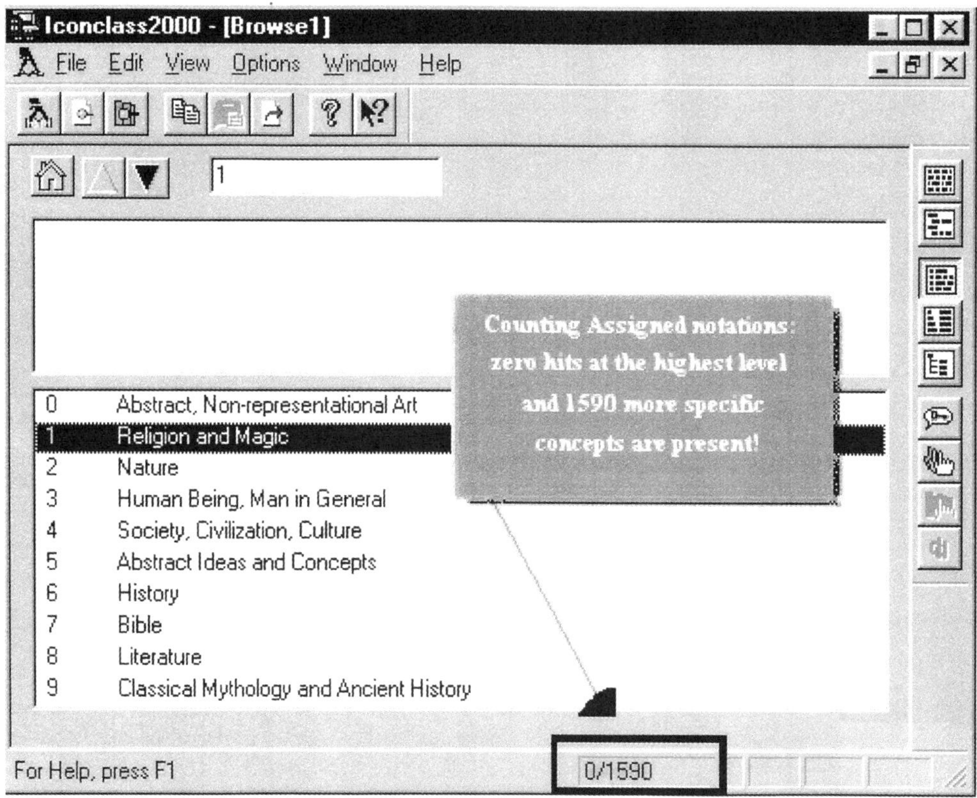

14. The Browse window with the counting of assigned notations on the status line at the bottom of the window; every time a concept is focused on, the notations counter is updated.

Index

•

Aaron, 77, 208, 209

abandonment, 233, 235

Abingdon Apocalypse (London, British Library, Ms. Add. 42555), 25, 34

Abraham: journey of, 175; sacrifice of, 78; tithes to Melchizedek, 172, 173

Adam, rebuked by God, 175, 183

Adam and Eve: 71; clothed by God, 183, 187; introduction of, 143; judgment of, 139, 140, 171; labor of, 173, 175, 178, 185, 187; nakedness of, 173. *See also* Expulsion

Ademar of Chabannes, 111, 116–18

adultery, 92, 100, 102

Aesculapius, 248

Aequitas (personification), 245, 247, 249

Africans, 29, 36

Agatha (saint), martyrdom of, 58

Agges, Jan, inventory, 262

Agostino, Giovanni d', 154, 157–59

Aix-en-Provence, Bibliothèque Méjanes, Ms. 15 (psalter), 51–52

Albenga, Biblioteca Capitolare, Ms. s.n., 93

Aldobrandini-Pamphilj family, inventory, 262

Alciati, Andrea, *Emblemata*, 248–54

Alfonso X El Sabio, *Cantigas*, 17

allegorical figures. *See names of personifications*

Amalthea, in Alciati emblem, 249

Ambrose (saint, bishop of Milan): 115; on Jews and Cain, 181; Amesbury Psalter (Oxford, All Souls College, Ms. 6), 178

Amicitia (personification), 253

Amiens, Bibliothèque Municipale, Ms. 108 (Pamplona Bible), 59

Anastasis, 12

Anderson, Sophie, 233

Andrew (abbot of St. Martial), 112

angels: 6, 29, 33, 80, 113, 114, 138, 152, 155, 159, 208, 209, 263, 274; addressing Adam, 173; fall of, 33, 175, 178; guardian, 90; of Satan, 35; sculpture of in Santa Maria del Fiore (Florence), 154, 157; visit to Lot, 144; warning Magi, 274. *See also* Gabriel

Anna and Joachim, meeting at Golden Gate, 50

Annals of Ghent, 54, 56

Anne (saint), 61

Annunciation: 50, 91, 152, 153, 157, 159, 160, 176, 180; in English psalters, 276; to shepherds, 273, 277

Antichrist, 33–35

Apocalypse, 172, 186. *See also specific Apocalypse manuscripts by name or location*

Aquinas, Thomas, climatic theories of, 26

Arezzo, Arca di San Donato, 153, 154

Arezzo, cathedral, 7, 151–61

Arezzo, Museo d'Arte Medievale e Moderna, 151, 159, 160

Arezzo, Pieve di Santa Maria, 158, 161

Ariadne, 230, 233–34

Aristotle, climatic theories of, 28

Arpino, Cavaliere d', 263

Arsenal Bible (Paris, Bibliothèque d'Arsenal, Ms. 5211), 12

Art and Architecture Thesaurus, 218

Ashburnham Pentateuch (Paris, Bibliothèque Nationale de France, nouv. acq. lat. 2334), 6, 71–74, 76, 77–81

Assumption, 179, 182

Astuto, Antonio, inventory, 262

Augsburg, Universitätsbibliothek, Cod. 1.2.4.15, 188

Augustine (saint): 6, 75–80, 111, 172, 181, 182, 205

Austriclinian (saint), 112, 116, 118–19

Autun, St. Lazarus, 29

avarice, 92, 93, 96, 99

Ave: Maria, 92, 102; prayers to Christ, 90

Balbi family, inventory, 260

Baldovino, Bertoldino di, 158

Balduccio, Giovanni di, 156

Baltimore, Walters Art Gallery, Ms. W. 40, 101

Baptism. *See* Christ, baptism of

Bartholomew (saint), martyrdom of, 55, 57–58

Basel, Bibliothek der Universität, Ms. D.II.11, 62

Beatitudes, 99, 212

Becket, Thomas à, 119

Bedford Hours (London, British Library, Ms. Add. 18550), 100

Bellerus, Petrus, 249

Berlin, Staatliche Museum, Kupferstichkabinett, Kdz. 3392, Sienese drawing, 158

Berlin, Staatsbibliothek, Ms. Theol. Lat. (Quedlinburg Itala), 74